Read This First

The information in this book is as up to date and accurate as we can make it. But it's important to realize that the law changes frequently, as do fees, forms, and procedures. If you handle your own legal matters, it's up to you to be sure that all information you use—including the information in this book—is accurate. Here are some suggestions to help you:

First, make sure you've got the most recent edition of this book. To learn whether a later edition is available, check the edition number on the book's spine and then go to Nolo's online Law Store at www.nolo.com or call Nolo's Customer Service Department at 800-728-3555.

Next, even if you have a current edition, you need to be sure it's fully up to date. The law can change overnight. At www.nolo.com, we post notices of major legal and practical changes that affect the latest edition of a book. To check for updates, find your book in the Law Store on Nolo's website (you can use the "A to Z Product List" and click the book's title). If you see an "Updates" link on the left side of the page, click it. If you don't see a link, that means we haven't posted any updates. (But check back regularly.)

Finally, we believe accurate and current legal information should help you solve many of your own legal problems on a cost-efficient basis. But this text is not a substitute for personalized advice from a knowledgeable lawyer. If you want the help of a trained professional, consult an attorney licensed to practice in your state.

10th edition

The California Landlord's Law Book:

Rights and Responsibilities

by Attorneys David Brown, Ralph Warner
& Janet Portman

TENTH EDITION	MARCH 2004
Editor	JANET PORTMAN
Book Design	STEPHANIE HAROLDE
	JACKIE MANCUSO
Cover Design	KEN ARMISTEAD
Production	MARGARET LIVINGSTON
Proofreading	SUSAN CARLSON GREENE
CD-ROM Preparation	ANDRÉ ZIVKOVICH
Printing	DELTA PRINTING SOLUTIONS, INC.

Brown, David Wayne, 1949-
    The California landlord's law book. Rights and responsibilties / by David Brown, Janet
Portman, & Ralph Warner ; edited by Janet Portman; illustrated by Linda Allison. -- 10th ed.
        p. cm.
    Includes index.
    ISBN 1-4133-0000-6 (alk. paper)
    1. Landlord and tenant--California--Popular works. I. Title: Landlord's law book.
II. Title: Rights and responsibilities. III. Warner, Ralph E. IV. Portman, Janet. V. Title.

KFC145.Z9B76 2004
346.79404'34--dc22

                                        2003066240

For information on bulk purchases or corporate premium sales, please contact the Special
Sales Department. For academic sales or textbook adoptions, ask for Academic Sales. Call
800-955-4775 or write to Nolo at 950 Parker Street, Berkeley, CA 94710.

thank you

This book could not have been published without the generous assistance of many people. A special thank you to Stephanie Harolde, who, in addition to word processing virtually the entire manuscript, made numerous helpful suggestions, nearly all of which were incorporated. Steve Elias, Carol Pladsen and Carol Marciel also made extremely helpful comments and suggestions. We would also like to acknowledge the generous help of Mike Mansel, a commercial insurance specialist in Walnut Creek; Joe Kelly, President of K&S Company, specialists in property management; D. J. Soviero, an attorney specializing in landlord/tenant law based in San Francisco; Jo Biel, a legal administrator with Eviction Assistance in San Francisco; Ira Serkes, a Berkeley Realtor with RE/MAX; and Bradley Booth, Assistant Chief Counsel, Department of Fair Employment and Housing. Thanks, too, to Darlene Hopper and Coral Swain for their assistance in typing the earlier and later manuscripts, respectively.

Special thanks to Marcia Stewart, Mary Randolph, Patricia Gima and Lisa Goldoftas. Thanks also to Terri Hearsh, Barbara Hodovan, Amy Ihara, Robin Leonard, Jackie Mancuso, Ely Newman, André Zivkovich, John O'Donnell, Kate Thill, Sayre Van Young, Erica Etelson and, especially, Ken Armistead, who was responsible for the wonderful front cover design.

about the authors

David Brown practices law in the Monterey, California, area, where he has represented both landlords and tenants in hundreds of court cases—most of which he felt could have been avoided if both sides were more fully informed about landlord/tenant law. Brown, a graduate of Stanford University (chemistry) and the University of Santa Clara Law School, and is the author of *Fight Your Ticket, Beat Your Ticket* and *The California Landlord's Law Book: Evictions* and the co-author of *The Guardianship Book.*

Ralph Warner is founder and publisher of Nolo, and an expert on landlord/tenant law. He is the coauthor of *The California Tenant's Handbook.* Ralph has been a landlord, a tenant, and, for several years, a property manager. Having become fed up with all these roles, he bought a single-family house.

Janet Portman, an attorney and Nolo's Book and Software Publisher, received undergraduate and graduate degrees from Stanford and a law degree from Santa Clara University. She is an expert on landlord-tenant law and the coauthor of *Every Tenant's Legal Guide, Renters' Rights, Leases & Rental Agreements* and *Leasing Space for Your Small Business.* As a practicing attorney, she specialized in criminal defense, conducting trials and preparing and arguing appeals before the Court of Appeal and the California Supreme Court. Janet is the editor of several Nolo books in other areas of law.

about the illustrator

Linda Allison was born before the invention of the computer and has been one step ahead of the game ever since. There is absolutely no truth to the rumor that she just sits around the house all day and makes little drawings.

contents

INTRODUCTION

1

RENTING YOUR PROPERTY: HOW TO CHOOSE TENANTS AND AVOID LEGAL PITFALLS

2

UNDERSTANDING LEASES AND RENTAL AGREEMENTS

3

BASIC RENT RULES

4

RENT CONTROL

5

SECURITY DEPOSITS

6

PROPERTY MANAGERS

7

GETTING THE TENANT MOVED IN

8

LAWYERS, LEGAL RESEARCH, EVICTION SERVICES AND MEDIATION

9

DISCRIMINATION

10

COTENANTS, SUBTENANTS, AND GUESTS

11

THE LANDLORD'S DUTY TO REPAIR AND MAINTAIN THE PROPERTY

12

THE LANDLORD'S LIABILITY FOR DANGEROUS CONDITIONS, CRIMINAL ACTS, AND ENVIRONMENTAL HEALTH HAZARDS

13

LANDLORD'S RIGHT OF ENTRY AND TENANT'S PRIVACY

14

RAISING RENTS AND CHANGING OTHER TERMS OF TENANCY

15

RETALIATORY RENT INCREASES AND EVICTIONS

16

THE THREE-DAY NOTICE TO PAY RENT OR QUIT

17

SELF-HELP EVICTIONS, UTILITY TERMINATIONS, AND TAKING TENANTS' PROPERTY

18

TERMINATING TENANCIES

19

WHEN A TENANT LEAVES: MONTH-TO-MONTH TENANCIES, FIXED-TERM LEASES, ABANDONMENT, AND DEATH OF TENANT

20

RETURNING SECURITY DEPOSITS

21

PROPERTY ABANDONED BY A TENANT

APPENDIX A

HOW TO USE THE CD-ROM

APPENDIX B

TEAR-OUT FORMS

APPENDIX C

RENT CONTROL CHART

INTRODUCTION

Here is a concise legal guide for people who own or manage residential rental property in California. It has two main goals: to explain California landlord/tenant law in as straightforward a manner as possible, and to help you use this legal knowledge to anticipate and, where possible, avoid legal problems.

This book, *The California Landlord's Law Book: Rights and Responsibilities,* is the first of a two-volume set. Here we concentrate on the legal rules associated with most aspects of renting and managing residential real property. For example, we include information on leases, rental agreements, managers, credit checks, security deposits, discrimination, invasion of privacy, the landlord's duty to maintain the premises, and much more. We provide practical, easy-to-use checklists and forms throughout this book. *The California Landlord's Law Book: Evictions* contains all the forms and instructions necessary to end a tenancy, including a step-by-step guide to doing your own evictions.

In this book, we've written a roughly chronological treatment of subjects important to landlords—beginning with taking rental applications and ending with returning security deposits when a tenant moves out. But you shouldn't wait until a problem happens to educate yourself about the law.

With sensible planning, the majority of serious legal problems encountered by landlords can be either minimized or avoided. For example, in Chapter 11 we show you how to plan ahead to deal with those few tenants who will inevitably try to invent bogus reasons why they were legally entitled to withhold rent. Similarly, in Chapter 9 we discuss ways to be sure that you, your managers, and other employees know and follow antidiscrimination laws and, at least as important, make it clear that you are doing so.

We believe that in the long run a landlord is best served by establishing a positive relationship with tenants. Why? First, because it's our personal view that adherence to the law and principles of fairness is a good way to live. Second, your tenants are your most important economic asset and should be treated as such. Think of it this way: From a long-term perspective, the business of renting

residential properties is often less profitable than is cashing in on the appreciation of that property. Your tenants are crucial to this process, since it is their rent payments that allow you to carry the cost of the real property while you wait for it to go up in value. And just as other businesses place great importance on conserving natural resources, it makes sense for you to adopt legal and practical strategies designed to establish and maintain a good relationship with your tenants.

A special word is appropriate for those of you who live in areas covered by rent control ordinances. These laws not only establish how much you can charge for most residential living spaces, they also override state law in a number of other ways. For example, many rent control ordinances restrict a landlord's ability to terminate month-to-month tenancies by requiring "just cause for eviction." We handle rent control in two ways: First, as we explain your rights and responsibilities under state law in the bulk of this book, we indicate those areas in which rent control laws are likely to modify or change these rules. Second, we provide a detailed discussion of rent control in Chapter 4. This chapter is designed to be used along with a careful reading of your local rent control ordinance.

We make frequent references to the California Civil Code (CC) and the California Code of Civil Procedure (CCP), important statutes that set out landlords' rights and responsibilities. A table of common abbreviations used throughout this book is included below. There are many times when you will surely want to refer to the complete statute or case. (See Recommended Reading, below.) Chapter 8 shows you how to do legal research.

Finally, may we wish you nothing but good managers, good tenants, and, above all else, good luck.

If you are renting out your condominium or townhouse, use this book in conjunction with your homeowners' association's CC&Rs (covenants, conditions and restrictions). These rules may affect how you structure the terms and conditions of the rental and how your tenants may use the unit. For example, many homeowners' associations control the number of vehicles that can be parked on the street. If your association has a rule like this, your renters will need to comply with it, and you cannot rent to tenants with too many vehicles without running afoul of the rules.

You need to be aware that an association rule may be contrary to federal, state or local law. For instance, an association rule that banned all persons of a certain race or religion from the property would not be upheld in court. And owners of condominium units in rent-controlled areas must comply with the ordinance, regardless of association rules to the contrary. Unfortunately, it's not always easy to know whether an association rule will pass legal muster. To know whether a particular rule is legally permissible is an inquiry that, in some cases, is beyond the scope of this book.

Finally, do not use this book if you are renting commercial property for your business or a space or unit in a mobile home park or marina. These situations are governed by entirely different sets of laws. If you are renting out a live/work unit (such as a loft), you will be subject to state laws governing residential units, and you may have additional requirements (imposed by building codes) that pertain to commercial property as well. Check with your local building inspector's office for the rules governing live/work units.

Abbreviations Used in This Book

We use these standard abbreviations throughout this book for important statutes and court cases covering landlord rights and responsibilities.

CALIFORNIA CODES

CC	Civil
CCP	Civil Procedure
UHC	Uniform Housing
B&P	Business and Professions
H&S	Health and Safety
CCR	Code of Regulations

FEDERAL LAWS

U.S.C.	United States Code

CASES

Cal. App.	California Court of Appeal
Cal. Rptr.	California Court of Appeal and California Supreme Court
Cal.	California Supreme Court
F. Supp.	United States District Court
F.2d, F.3d	United States Court of Appeal
U.S.	United States Supreme Court

OPINIONS

Ops. Cal. Atty. Gen.	California Attorney General Opinions

GUIDE TO ICONS USED IN THIS BOOK

 = Warning

 = Related Topics in Other Chapters

 = Related Resources

 = Rent Control

 = Tip

 = Professional Advice Recommended

 = Forms CD-ROM and Tear-Out Forms

Recommended Reading

Here are essential additions to every landlord's (tax-deductible) library.

California Civil Code (CC) and *California Code of Civil Procedure* (CCP). The basic state laws that regulate the landlording business. These books can be ordered from Nolo (800-992-6656) and are also available at most public libraries. To read California statutes online, go to the Nolo website (www.nolo .com) and choose State Laws under the Legal Research Center heading.

Rent Control Ordinances. If you own rental property in a rent control city, it's crucial that you have a current copy of the local ordinance. You can get a copy from your city rent control board or online. (See Appendix C.) ■

1

RENTING YOUR PROPERTY: HOW TO CHOOSE TENANTS AND AVOID LEGAL PITFALLS

All landlords typically follow the same process when renting property. We recognize that a landlord with 40 (or 400) units has different business challenges than a person with an in-law cottage in the backyard or a duplex around the corner. Still, the basic process of filling rentals remains the same:

1. Decide the terms of your rental, including rent, deposits, and the length of the tenancy.

2. Advertise your property.

3. Accept applications.

4. Screen potential tenants.

5. Choose someone to rent your property.

In this chapter, we examine the practical and legal aspects of each of these steps, with an eye to avoiding several common legal problems. Because the topic of discrimination is so important we devote a whole chapter to it later in the book (Chapter 9), including advice on how to avoid discrimination in your tenant selection process.

A. Adopt a Rental Plan and Stick to It

Before you advertise your property for rent, you'll want to make some basic decisions, which will form the backbone of your lease or rental agreement—how much rent to charge, when it is payable, whether to offer a fixed-term lease or a month-to-month tenancy, and how much of a security deposit to require. You'll also need to decide the responsibilities of a manager (if any) in renting out your property.

If you haven't made these important decisions, the details you need are in Chapters 2, 3, 5 and 6.

In renting residential property, be consistent when dealing with prospective tenants. The reason for this is simple: If you don't treat all tenants more or less equally—for example, if you arbitrarily set tougher standards for renting to a racial minority—

you are violating federal laws and opening yourself up to lawsuits.

Of course, there will be times when you will want to bargain a little with a prospective tenant—for example, you may let a tenant have a cat in exchange for paying a higher security deposit (as long as it doesn't exceed the legal limits set by law). As a general rule, however, you're better off figuring out your rental plan in advance and sticking to it.

B. Advertising Rental Property

In some areas, landlords are lucky enough to fill all vacancies by word of mouth. If you fit this category, skip to the next section.

There is one crucial point you should remember about advertising: Where you advertise is more important than how you advertise. For example, if you rent primarily to college students, your best bet is the campus newspaper or housing office. Whether you simply put a sign in front of your apartment building or work with a rental service or property management company, be sure the way you advertise reaches a sufficient number of the sort of people who are likely to meet your rental criteria.

Legally, you should have no trouble if you follow these simple rules:

Make sure the price in your ad is an honest one. If a tenant shows up promptly and agrees to all the terms set out in your ad, you may run afoul of the law if you arbitrarily raise the price. This doesn't mean you are always legally required to rent at your advertised price, however. If a tenant asks for more services or different lease terms, which you feel require more rent, it's fine to bargain and raise your price. And if competing tenants begin a bidding war, there's nothing illegal about accepting more rent—as long as it is truly freely offered. However, be sure to abide by any applicable rent limits in local rent control areas.

Don't advertise something you don't have. Some large landlords, management companies, and rental services have advertised units that weren't really available in order to produce a large number of prospective tenants who could then be "switched" to higher-priced or inferior units. This type of advertising is illegal, and many property owners have been prosecuted for bait-and-switch practices.

Be sure your ad can't be construed as discriminatory. Ads should not mention age, sex, race, religion, disability, or adults-only—unless yours is senior citizens' housing. (Senior citizens' housing must comply with CC § 51.3. Namely, it must be reserved for persons over age 62, or be a complex of 150 or more units [35 in nonmetropolitan areas] for persons over age 55.) Neither should ads imply through words, photographs, illustrations, or language that you prefer or discriminate against renters because of their age, sex, race, and so on. For example, if your property is in a mixed Chinese and Hispanic neighborhood and if you advertise only in Spanish, you may be courting a fair housing complaint. In addition, any discrimination against any group that is unrelated to a legitimate landlord concern is illegal. For example, it's discriminatory to refuse to rent to unmarried couples, because the legal status of their relationship has nothing to do with whether they will be good, stable tenants.

EXAMPLE

An ad for an apartment that says "Young, female student preferred" is illegal, since sex and age discrimination are forbidden by both state and federal law. Under California law, discrimination based on the prospective tenant's occupation also is illegal, since there is no legitimate business reason to prefer tenants with certain occupations over others.

If you have any legal and nondiscriminatory rules on important issues, such as no pets, it's a good idea to put them in your ad. This will weed out those applicants who don't like your terms. But even if you don't include a "no pets" clause, you won't be obligated to rent to applicants with pets. You can still announce the policy at the time you interview a prospective tenant—and you can use your discretion when deciding whether their pets are acceptable.

C. Dealing With Prospective Tenants

It's good business, as well as a sound legal protection strategy, to develop a system for screening prospective tenants. Whether you handle reference checking and other tasks yourself or hire a manager or property management company, your goal is the same—to select tenants who will pay their rent on time, keep their rental in good condition, and not cause you any legal or practical hassles later.

Never, never let anyone stay in your property on a temporary basis. Even if you haven't signed a rental agreement or accepted rent, giving a person a key or allowing him or her to move in as much as a toothbrush can give that person the legally protected status of a tenant. Then, if the person won't leave voluntarily, you will have to file a lawsuit to evict him or her.

1. The Rental Application

Each prospective tenant—everyone age 18 or older who wants to live in your rental property—should fill out a written application. This is true whether you're renting to a married couple sharing an apartment or to a number of unrelated roommates.

You'll find a tear-out version of the Rental Application in Appendix B. The CD-ROM that accompanies this book also includes this form.

Complete the box at the top of the Rental Application, listing the property address and amounts due before the tenants may move in.

Ask all applicants to fill out a Rental Application form, and accept applications from everyone who's interested in your rental property. Refusing to take an application may unnecessarily anger a prospective tenant, and will make him or her more likely to look into the possibility of filing a discrimination complaint. Make decisions about who will rent the property later.

Rental Application

Separate application required from each applicant age 18 or older.

THIS SECTION TO BE COMPLETED BY LANDLORD

Address of Property to Be Rented: __178 West 8th St., Apt. 6, Oakland, CA__

Rental Term: ☐ month to month ☒ lease from __March 1, 200x__ to __February 29, 200x__

Amounts Due Prior to Occupancy

First month's rent .... $ __1,200__

Security deposit .... $ __1,800__

Credit-check fee .... $ __30__

Other (specify): _____ $ _____

TOTAL .... $ __3,030__

Applicant

Full Name—include all names you use(d): __Hannah Silver__

Home Phone: (__510__) __555-3789__   Work Phone: (__510__) __555-4567__

Social Security Number: __123-000-4567__   Driver's License Number/State: __CA V123456__

Other Identifying Information: _____

Vehicle Make: __Toyota__   Model: __Tercel__   Color: __White__   Year: __1994__

License Plate Number/State: __CA 123456__

Additional Occupants

List everyone, including children, who will live with you:

Full Name	Relationship to Applicant
Dennis Olson	Husband

Rental History

Current Address: __39 Maple St., Oakland, CA__

Dates Lived at Address: __May 1990 - date__   Reason for Leaving: __Wanted bigger place__

Landlord/Manager: __Jane Tucker__   Landlord/Manager's Phone: (__510__) __555-7523__

Previous Address: __1215 Middlebrook Rd., Palo Alto, CA__

Dates Lived at Address: __June 1987 - May 1990__   Reason for Leaving: __New job in East Bay__

Landlord/Manager: __Ed Palermo__   Landlord/Manager's Phone: (__650__) __555-3711__

Previous Address: 152 Highland Dr., Santa Cruz, CA

Dates Lived at Address: Jan. 1986 - June 1987   Reason for Leaving: Wanted to live closer to work

Landlord/Manager: Millie & Joe Lewis   Landlord/Manager's Phone: (831) 555-9999

Employment History

Name and Address of Current Employer: Argon Works, 54 Nassau Rd., Berkeley, CA

Phone: (510)   555-2333

Name of Supervisor: Tom Schmidt   Supervisor's Phone: (510) 555-2333

Dates Employed at This Job: 1990 - date   Position or Title: Marketing Director

Name and Address of Previous Employer: Palo Alto Tribune

13 Junction Rd., Palo Alto   Phone: (650)   555-2366

Name of Supervisor: Dory Krossber   Supervisor's Phone: (650)   555-1111

Dates Employed at This Job: 1986 - 1990   Position or Title: Marketing Assistant

Income

1. Your gross monthly employment income (before deductions): $ 4,000

2. Average monthly amounts of other income (specify sources): $

 husband's salary $ 3,000

TOTAL: $ 7,000

Credit and Financial Information

Bank/Financial Accounts	Account Number	Bank/Institution	Branch
Savings Account:	1222345	Cal West	Berkeley, CA
Checking Account:	789101	Cal West	Berkeley, CA
Money Market or Similar Account:	234789	City Bank	San Francisco, CA

Credit Accounts & Loans	Type of Account (Auto loan, Visa, etc.)	Account Number	Name of Creditor	Amount Owed	Monthly Payment
Major Credit Card:	Visa	123456	City Bank	$1,000	$500
Major Credit Card:	Dept. Store	45789	Macy's	$500	$500
Loan (mortgage, car, student loan, etc.):					
Other Major Obligation:					

Miscellaneous

Describe the number and type of pets you want to have in the rental property:

No pets

Describe water-filled furniture you want to have in the rental property: ————————————

Do you smoke?   ☐ yes   ☒ no

Have you ever: Filed for bankruptcy? ☐ yes   ☒ no   Been sued? ☐ yes   ☒ no

Been evicted? ☐ yes   ☒ no   Been convicted of a crime? ☐ yes   ☒ no

Explain any "yes" listed above:

References and Emergency Contact

Personal Reference: Joan Stanley   Relationship: friend, co-worker

Address: 785 Spruce St., Berkeley

Phone: (510) 555-4578

Personal Reference: Marnie Swatt   Relationship: friend

Address: 785 Pierce Ave., San Francisco

Phone: (415) 555-7878

Contact in Emergency: Connie and Martin Silver   Relationship: Parents

Address: 123 Gorham St., Princeton, N.J.

Phone: (609) 555-8765

I certify that all the information given above is true and correct and understand that my lease or rental agreement may be terminated if I have made any material false or incomplete statements in this application. I authorize verification of the information provided in this application from my credit sources, credit bureaus, current and previous landlords and employers, and personal references. I understand that if I have initiated a "security freeze" on my credit information with any of the credit reporting agencies, I will promptly lift the freeze for a reasonable time so that my credit report may be accessed by the Landlord/Manager; and I understand that if I fail to do so, the Landlord/Manager may consider this an incomplete application. (CC § 1785.11.2.) This permission will survive the expiration of my tenancy.

Feb. 15, 200x   _Hannah Silver_

Date   Applicant

Notes (Landlord/Manager):

The Rental Application form includes a section for you to note the amount and purpose of any credit check fee. (Section 2, below, discusses credit check fees.) If you do not charge credit check fees, simply fill in "none" or "N/A".

Be sure all potential tenants sign the Rental Application, authorizing you to verify the information and references. (Some employers and others require written authorization before they will talk to you.) You may also want to prepare a separate authorization, so that you don't need to copy the entire application and send it off every time a bank or employer wants proof that the tenant authorized you to verify the information. See the sample Consent to Background and Reference Check, below.

You'll find a tear-out version of the Consent to Background and Reference Check in Appendix B. The CD-ROM that accompanies this book also includes the form.

Don't take incomplete rental applications. Landlords are often faced with anxious, sometimes desperate people who need a place to live immediately. Some people tell terrific hard-luck stories as to why normal credit- and reference-checking rules should be ignored in their case and why they should be allowed to move right in. Don't believe any of it. People who have planned so poorly that they will literally have to sleep in the street if they don't rent your place that day are likely to come up with similar emergencies when it comes time to pay the rent. Always make sure that prospective tenants complete the entire Rental Application, including Social Security number, driver's license number or other identifying information (such as a passport number), current employment, and emergency contacts. You may need this information later to track down a tenant who skips town leaving unpaid rent or abandoned property. (See Chapters 19 and 21.)

Consent to Background and Reference Check

I authorize _Jan Gold_

to obtain information about me from my credit sources, current and previous landlords and employers, and

personal references, to enable _Jan Gold_ to evaluate my rental application. I authorize my credit

sources, credit bureaus, current and previous landlords and employers, and personal references to disclose to

Jan Gold information about me that is relevant to

Jan Gold 's decisions

regarding my application and tenancy. This permission will survive the expiration of my tenancy.

Sandy Meyer
Name

4 Elm Rd., Sacramento, CA
Address

_916-555-9876_
Phone Number

May 2, 200x   _Sandy Meyer_
Date   Applicant

2. Credit Check and Screening Fees

State law limits credit check or application fees you can charge prospective tenants, and specifies what you must do when accepting these types of screening fees. (CC § 1950.6.) You can charge only "actual out-of-pocket costs" of obtaining a credit or similar tenant "screening" report, plus "the reasonable value of time spent" by you or your manager in obtaining a credit report or checking personal references and background information on a prospective tenant. Section D, below, covers credit reports and other screening efforts.

The maximum screening fee you can charge each applicant is $30, but you can adjust for inflation by consulting the Consumer Price Index for the nearest metropolitan area (for example, in 2002, Sacramento residents could charge $33). To determine the allowable charge, go to the Consumer Price Index website at www.bls.gov/cpi and search for the article, "How to Use the Consumer Price Index for Escalation."

Upon an applicant's request, you must provide a copy of any consumer credit report you obtained on the individual. You must also give or mail the applicant a receipt itemizing your credit check and screening fees. If you end up spending less (for the credit report and your time) than the fee you charged the applicant, you must refund the difference. (This may be the entire screening fee if you never get a credit report or check references on an applicant.)

Finally, you cannot charge any screening or credit check fee if you don't have a vacancy and are simply putting someone on a waiting list (unless the applicant agrees to this in writing).

In light of state limits on credit check fees, we recommend that you:

- charge a credit check fee only if you intend to actually obtain a credit report

- charge only your actual cost of obtaining the report, plus $10, at most, for your time and trouble

- charge no more than $30 per applicant in any case (unless you include an adjustment based on the CPI)

- provide an itemized receipt at the same time you take an individual's rental application (a sample receipt is shown below), and

- mail each applicant a copy of his or her credit report as a matter of practice.

Application Screening Fee Receipt

This will acknowledge receipt of the sum of $ _____ by _____ [Property Owner/ Manager] from _____ [Applicant] as part of his/her application for the rental property at _____[Rental Property Address].

As provided under California Civil Code Section 1950.6, here is an itemization of how this $ _____ screening fee will be used:

Actual costs of obtaining Applicant's credit/screening report $ _____

Administrative costs of obtaining credit/screening report and checking Applicant's references and background information $ _____

Total screening fee charged $ _____

_____   _____
Date   Applicant

_____   _____
Date   Owner/Manager

You'll find a tear-out version of the Application Screening Fee Receipt in Appendix B. The CD-ROM that accompanies this book also includes the form.

Nonrefundable move-in fees are illegal. Any "payment, fee, deposit, or charge" that is intended to be used to cover unpaid rent or damage or that is intended to compensate a landlord for costs associated with move-in, is legally considered a security deposit and is covered by state deposit laws. (Chapter 5 covers security deposits.)

3. Terms of the Rental

Be sure your prospective tenant knows all your general requirements and any special rules and regulations before you get too far in the process. This will help avoid situations where your tenant backs out at the last minute (he thought he could bring his three dogs and your lease prohibits pets) and help minimize future misunderstandings.

To put together a rental agreement or lease, see Chapter 2. Once you've signed up a tenant and want to clearly communicate your rules and regulations, see Chapter 7.

4. Landlord Disclosures

California landlords are legally obligated to make several disclosures to prospective tenants. You can add the military, utility, and environmental disclosures to the rental application or put them on a separate sheet of paper attached to the rental application. Or, you can decide to make disclosures part of your lease or rental agreement. The Megan's Law disclosure must be on the lease or rental agreement. (See Clause 24, Additional Provisions, in Chapter 2.)

a. Megan's Law Database.

Every written lease or rental agreement must inform the tenant of the existence of a statewide database of the names of registered sexual offenders. Members of the public may contact the state's Department of Justice or local law enforcement and inquire as to whether a certain individual is on the list. You must use the following legally required language for this disclosure:

"Notice: The California Department of Justice, sheriff's departments, police departments serving jurisdictions of 200,000 or more, and many other local law enforcement authorities maintain for public access a database of the locations of persons required to register pursuant to paragraph (1) of subdivision (a) of Section 290.4 of the Penal Code. The database is updated on a quarterly basis and is a source of information about the presence of these individuals in any neighborhood. The Department of Justice also maintains a Sex Offender Identification Line through which inquiries about individuals may be made. This is a "900" telephone service. Callers must have specific information about individuals they are checking. Information regarding neighborhoods is not available through the "900" telephone service. (Civil Code Sec. 2079.10a.)" Chapter 12, Section A explains your duties under this law in more detail. The rental agreement and lease in Appendix B include this mandatory disclosure.

b. Location Near Former Military Base

If your property is within a mile of a "former ordnance location"—an abandoned or closed military base in which ammunition or military explosives were used—you must notify all prospective tenants in writing. (CC § 1940.7.) A sample Disclosures by Property Owner form is shown below.

It is not necessary to warn prospective tenants of the existence of current ordnance locations, such as presently existing army or navy bases.

Although there are no penalties stated in the law for failure to warn, and although the law applies only

Disclosures by Property Owner(s)

The owner(s) of property located at ___1234 State Avenue, Apartment 5, Los Angeles, California___

_____

_____

make(s) the following disclosure(s) to prospective tenant(s) and/or employee(s):

Location near former military base. State law requires property owners to disclose to all prospective

tenants, before they sign any rental agreement or lease, if the property they are seeking to rent is within

one mile of a former ordnance area (military base) as defined by California Civil Code Section 1940.7.

Details regarding the former military base near the property listed above are as follows:

Between 1942-1945, the U.S. Army used the nearby area bounded by 6th and 7th Streets and 1st and

3rd Avenues in the City of Los Angeles as a reserve training area. Unexploded rifle ammunition has been

found there.

_____

_____

_____

_____

_____

_____

_____

_____

_____

Daryl White	_9/19/200x_
Owner's Signature	Date

I have read and received a copy of the above Disclosures by Property Owner(s).

Susan Johnson	_9/19/200x_
Signature	Date
Thomas Johnson	_9/19/200x_
Signature	Date

to former ordnance locations actually known by the owner, it's only a matter of time before someone sues their landlord for negligently failing to warn of a former military base the landlord "should have known about." Therefore, if you have the slightest idea your property is within a mile of a former military base or training area, check it out. You might start by asking the reference librarian at a nearby public library or by writing a letter to your local Congressional representative. If you have a particular location in mind, you can also check with the County Recorder, who will show you how to trace the ownership all the way back to the turn of the century for any indication the property was at one time owned or leased by the government.

c. Periodic Pest Control

Registered structural pest control companies have long been required to deliver warning notices to owners and tenants of properties that were about to be treated as part of an ongoing service contract—but the warning notice had to be issued only once, at the time of the initial treatment. This meant that subsequent tenants would not receive the warning. Now, as of January 1, 2001, the landlord must give a copy of this notice to every new tenant who occupies a rental unit that is serviced periodically. The notice must contain information about the frequency of treatment. (B&P § 8538; CC § 1940.8.)

d. Shared Utility Arrangements

State law requires property owners to disclose to all prospective tenants, before they move in, any arrangements where a tenant might wind up paying for someone else's gas or electricity use. (CC § 1940.9.) This would occur, for example, where a single gas or electric meter serves more than one unit, or where a tenant's gas or electric meter also measures gas or electricity that serves a common area—such as a washing machine in a laundry room or even a hallway light not under the tenant's control. We address this issue in detail in Chapter 2. While you may use the Disclosures by Property Owner form, your lease or

rental agreement is the more appropriate place to disclose shared utility arrangements. (See Clause 9 of our sample lease and rental agreement.)

e. Intentions to Demolish the Rental

If you plan on demolishing your rental property, you or your agent must give written notice to applicants, new tenants, and current tenants. (CC § 1940.6.) The steps you must follow depend on whether you're notifying applicants, new tenants, or current tenants.

• **Applicants and new tenants.** If you have applied for a permit to demolish their unit, you must disclose this before entering into a rental agreement or even before accepting a credit check fee or negotiating "any writings that would initiate a tenancy," such as a holding deposit. (CC § 1940.6(a)(1)(D).)

• **Existing tenants (including tenants who have signed a lease or rental agreement but haven't yet moved in).** These tenants are entitled to notice *before* you apply for a demolition permit (but the law doesn't specify how much advance warning you must give the tenant). The notice must include the earliest approximate date that you expect the demolition to occur, and the earliest possible date that you expect the tenancy will terminate (you cannot demolish prior to the estimated termination date).

This disclosure requirement packs a punch—if you fail to give written notification as explained above, a tenant or prospective tenant can sue you for damages (and attorney's fees, which makes such a suit attractive to a lawyer). You can be ordered to pay the tenant's actual damages (such as the cost of living in a motel while looking for a new residence) and moving expenses, as well as a civil penalty (payable to the tenant) of up to $2,500.

f. Environmental Hazards

Federal law requires landlords to warn tenants about the presence of asbestos and lead paint hazards in the rental property. The subject of landlord liability for environmental hazards is discussed in detail in Chapter 12. Appendix B includes a copy of the required lead-based paint disclosure form.

California landlords must also disclose the presence of dangerous mold. As of January 2002, if you know that a rental unit has toxic mold levels exceeding state Department of Health Services (DHS) guidelines, you must disclose that fact to current and prospective tenants. (H&S § 26147.) As of this writing, however, the DHS has not yet adopted these guidelines. When they do, they will post them on their website at www.dhs.ca.gov. Chapter 12, Section F discusses mold in detail.

You'll find a tear-out version of the required lead-based paint disclosure form in Appendix B. The CD-ROM that accompanies this book also includes this form.

g. Smoking

Landlords are free to specify that some parts (or all of) their property will be smoke free. For example, you may want to prohibit smoking in individual units, but permit it in common areas or certain common areas. In Chapter 2, we explain how to use Clause 23 to describe your policy.

Before you get to the point of negotiating a lease or rental application with applicants, however, you may want to tell them about your policy. You don't want complaints later from a nonsmoker who didn't realize that you permitted smoking in the common areas. Nor do you want the complaint of a smoker who assumed that smoking in an individual unit would be okay.

f. Controlled Substance Releases

Landlords must tell applicants and tenants about any "controlled substance" releases on or under the residential property. (CC § 1940.7.5, set to expire on January 1, 2006 unless extended by the legislature and governor.) The disclosure is intended to encourage property owners to clean up waste and seepage from illegal drug labs, particularly methamphetamine labs, and to warn prospective tenants of the potential hazards. Marijuana is not covered by the term "controlled substance."

Landlords must also give applicants and tenants copies of any notices from law enforcement or health departments that concern the presence of such substances. Failure to abide by the terms of this disclosure law can result in civil penalties of up to $5,000, plus actual damages suffered by any applicant or tenant.

D. Checking Background, References, and Credit History of Potential Tenants

If an application looks good, the next step is to follow up thoroughly. The time and money you spend are the most cost-effective expenditures you'll ever make.

Be consistent in your screening. You risk a charge of illegal discrimination if you screen certain categories of applicants more stringently than others. Make it your policy, for example, to always require credit reports; don't just get a credit report for a single parent applicant.

Here are six steps of a very thorough screening process. You should always go through at least the first three to check out the applicant's previous landlords, income and employment, and run a credit check.

1. Check With Previous Landlords and Other References

Always call previous landlords or managers for references—even if you have a written letter of reference from a previous landlord. Also, call previous employers and personal references listed on the rental application.

To organize the information you gather from these calls, use the Tenant References form, which lists key questions to ask previous landlords, managers and other references.

You'll find a tear-out version of the Tenant References form in Appendix B. The CD-ROM that accompanies this book also includes this form.

Be sure to take notes of all your conversations and keep them on file. This information will come in handy should a rejected tenant ever ask why he wasn't chosen or file a discrimination charge against you. (These issues are covered in the discussion of recordkeeping in Section E, below.)

Bad tenants often provide phony references. Make sure you speak to a legitimate landlord or manager, not a friend of the prospective tenant posing as one. One suggestion is to call the number given for the previous landlord or manager and simply ask for the landlord or manager by name, rather than begin by saying that you are checking references. If the prospective tenant has really given you a friend's name, the friend will probably say something that gives away the scam.

If you still have questions, consider driving to the former address and checking things out in person. Finally, if you have any doubts, ask the previous landlord or manager to pull out the tenant's rental application so you can verify certain facts, such as the tenant's Social Security number. If the so-called landlord can't do this, you are perhaps being conned.

2. Verify a Potential Tenant's Income and Employment

You want to make sure that all tenants have the income to pay the rent each month. Call the prospective tenant's employer to verify income and length of employment. Again, make notes of your conversations on the Tenant References form, discussed above.

Some employers require written authorization from the employee. You will need to mail or fax them a copy of the release included at the bottom of the Rental Application form, or the separate Consent to Background and Reference Check form.

If you feel that verifying an individual's income by telephone or accepting a note from her boss is not reliable enough, you may require applicants to provide copies of recent paycheck stubs. It's also reasonable to require documentation of other sources of income (such as disability or other benefits checks). Where a large portion of an applicant's income is from child support or alimony payments, you might want to ask for a copy of the court decree for the support payments. However, don't go overboard by asking for copies of tax returns or bank statements, except possibly from self-employed persons.

How much income is enough? Think twice before renting to someone if the rent will take more than one-third of their income, especially if they have a lot of debts. Be careful, however, if you're dealing with an applicant who is disabled and who cannot meet the "one-third" standard. If that applicant is otherwise qualified and presents you with a cosigner, you will need to evaluate the cosigner's financial ability and trustworthiness, despite any rules you may have against dealing with cosigners. (*Giebeler v. M & B Associates*, 2003 WL 22119329, ____ F.3d ____, (2003).) Cosigners are discussed in detail in Chapter 2, Section E; your duty to provide accommodations for disabled renters is covered in Chapter 5, Section C7.

Be careful if you ask to see proof of an applicant's citizenship or immigration status.
Under federal law, you're probably on solid ground if you ask all applicants for proof of immigration status. See Chapter 9, Section A5 for more details.

Tenant References

Name of Applicant: _Will Berford_

Address of Rental Unit: _123 State Street, Los Angeles, CA_

Previous Landlord or Manager

Contact (name, property owner or manager, address of rental unit): _____

Kate Steiner, 345 Mercer St., Los Angeles, 310-555-5432

Date: _February 4, 200x_

Questions

When did tenant rent from you (move-in and move-out dates)? _December 1994 to date_

What was the monthly rent? _$750_

Did tenant pay rent on time? _A week late a few times_

Was tenant considerate of neighbors—that is, no loud parties and fair, careful use of common areas? _____
Yes, considerate

Did tenant have any pets? If so, were there any problems? _Yes, he had a cat, contrary to rental_
agreement

Did tenant make any unreasonable demands or complaints? _No_

Why did tenant leave? _He wants to live someplace that allows pets_

Did tenant give the proper amount of notice before leaving? _Yes_

Did tenant leave the place in good condition? Did you need to use the security deposit to cover damage?
No problems

Any particular problems you'd like to mention? _No_

Would you rent to this person again? _Yes, but without pets_

Other Comments: _____

Employment Verification

Contact (name, company, position): _Brett Field, Manager, Chicago Car Company_

Date: _February 5, 200x_

Salary: _$30,000_ Dates of Employment: _March 1993 to date_

Comments: _No problems. Fine employee. Will is responsible and hardworking._

Personal Reference

Contact (name and relationship to applicant): _Sandy Cameron, friend_

Date: _February 5, 200x_ How long have you known the applicant? _five years_

Would you recommend this person as a prospective tenant? _Yes_

Comments: _Will is very neat and responsible. He's reliable and will be a great tenant._

Credit and Financial Information

Mostly fine—see attached credit report

Notes, Including Reasons for Rejecting Applicant

Applicant had a history of late rent payments and kept a cat, contrary to the rental agreement.

3. Obtain a Credit Report From a Credit Reporting Agency

Many landlords find it essential to check a tenant's credit history with at least one credit reporting agency. These agencies collect and sell credit and other information about consumers—for example, whether they pay their bills on time or, if reported by prior landlords, whether they've failed to pay the rent. As long as you use the information only to help you decide whether to rent to that person, or on what terms, you do not need the applicant's consent.

However, many people *think* that you must have their written consent before pulling a credit report to evaluate them as prospective tenants. For that reason, we have explicitly called for applicants' consent in our application (and on a separate form). But there's another reason for our caution: This written consent should help you if later, when the applicant is a tenant (or an ex-tenant), you decide that you need an updated credit report. For example, you may want to consult a current report in order to help you decide whether to sue a tenant who has skipped out and owes rent. Without a broadly written consent, your use of a report at that time might be illegal. (FTC "Long" Opinion Letter, July 7, 2000.)

Never order a credit report unless you are doing so in order to evaluate a potential (or current or ex-) tenant. If you ask for a report for any other reason (such as a wish to check out the solvency of your future son-in-law or the resources of your ex-business partner whom you're considering suing), you could face a lawsuit and penalties of thousands of dollars.

Information covers the past seven to ten years. To run a credit check, you'll need a prospective tenant's name, address and Social Security number (or other identifying information, such as a driver's license number or passport number).

Some credit reporting companies also gather and sell "investigative reports" or background checks about a person's character, general reputation, personal characteristics or mode of living. If you order one of these background checks, federal law requires that you disclose certain information to the prospective tenant. (See "Background Checks Trigger Disclosures Under the Fair Credit Reporting Act," below.)

If you own many rental properties and need credit reports frequently, consider joining one of the three largest credit reporting agencies—Equifax, Trans Union or Experian (formerly TRW)—which charge about $20–30 in annual fees plus $10–$15 per report. You can find their numbers and those of other tenant-screening companies in the Yellow Pages of the phone book under "Credit Reporting Agencies." Or, if you only rent a few units each year, see if your local apartment association (there are about two dozen in California) offers credit reporting services. With some credit reporting agencies, you can obtain an oral credit report the same day it's requested, and a written one within a day or two.

Landlords who have accounts or other ongoing business relations with the credit reporting agencies need not supply an applicant's date of birth (DOB) in order to get a report—a name and Social Security number will suffice. However, consumers ordering their own credit report must supply their DOB; and, presumably, small-scale landlords, who have no reason to set up an account with a credit reporting agency, could order reports as if they were the applicant, after asking the applicant for their DOB. We urge you not to try this route, because once you have a DOB, you open the door to a discrimination claim if you reject an older applicant who decides to impute age discrimination motives to your decision. Instead, investigate setting up an account or join an apartment association.

TENANTS WITH "SECURITY FREEZES" ON THEIR CREDIT REPORTS

Consumers in California may place a "freeze" on their credit reports, preventing anyone but specified parties (such as law enforcement) from getting their credit report. (CC § 1785.11.2 and following.) Credit reporting agencies must implement the freeze within five days of receiving the request. However, the consumer can arrange for specified persons—such as a landlord or management company—to have access to their report; or the freeze itself can be suspended for a specified period of time. When a consumer arranges for a freeze, the agency must give the consumer information on how to arrange for selective access or how to lift the freeze. (CC § 1785.15(f).)

If an applicant has placed a freeze on his or her credit report, you'll need access. Our Rental Application advises applicants that they are responsible for lifting the freeze so that you can receive a copy of their report. If they fail to do so, the application will be incomplete, which is grounds for rejecting that application. (CC § 1785.11.2(h).)

4. See If Any "Tenant-Reporting Services" Operate in Your Area

Just as regular credit reporting agencies keep tabs on retail purchasers' creditworthiness, businesses such as UD Registry of Van Nuys keep tabs on eviction suits (called unlawful detainer, hence the "UD") filed against tenants. The fact that a tenant has been involved in an eviction lawsuit, regardless of the outcome, can be reported by the tenant-reporting services. (These agencies will have a difficult time, however, learning of eviction lawsuits that the tenant won, as explained below in Subsection 6.) Your local apartment association may recommend other services of this type. Tenant-reporting services charge from $20 to $50. As with credit reporting agencies, if you don't rent to an applicant because of information

from a tenant-reporting service, you must notify the applicant of the nature of the report and give her the name and address of the company.

5. Check With the Tenant's Bank to Verify Account Information

If an individual's credit history raises questions about his financial stability, you may want to take this additional step. If so, you'll probably need an authorization form such as the one included at the bottom of the Rental Application, or the separate Consent to Background and Reference Check form. Banks differ as to the type of information they will provide over the phone. Generally, banks will at most only confirm that an individual has an account and that it is in good standing.

Be wary of an applicant who has no checking or savings account. It could be because the individual bounced so many checks her bank dropped her.

6. Review Court Records

If your prospective tenant has lived in the area, you may want to review local court records to see if she has been sued in a collection or eviction lawsuit. Checking court records may seem like overkill, but now and then it's an invaluable tool if you suspect a prospective tenant may be a potential troublemaker. Since court records are kept for several years, this kind of information can supplement references from recent landlords. You can get this information from the superior court for the county in which the applicant lived.

Recent legislation narrows somewhat your ability to learn whether an applicant has been involved in an eviction lawsuit. As of January 1, 2004, courts are required to keep records on eviction lawsuits secret and sealed for 60 days from the date the landlord filed the unlawful detainer complaint. If the tenant wins the case within that 60 days, the court must keep the records sealed indefinitely. The sealing requirement does not affect eviction lawsuits that were filed before January 1, 2004. (CCP Sec. 1161.2.)

You'll need to go in person and ask the civil clerk to show you the Defendants' Index, usually kept in microfiche form. If a prospective tenant's name is listed, jot down the case number so you can check the actual case file for details on the lawsuit and its resolution. You can often determine if a prospective tenant asserted a reasonable defense and if any judgment against her was paid off.

E. CHOOSING—AND REJECTING— AN APPLICANT

After you've collected applications and done some screening, you can start sifting through the applicants. Start by eliminating the worst risks: people with negative references from previous landlords or a history of nonpayment of rent, poor credit, or previous evictions. Then make your selection.

Assuming you choose the candidate with the best qualifications (credit history, references, income), you should have no legal problem. But what if you have several more or less equally qualified applicants? The best response is to use an objective tie-breaker. Give the nod to the person who applied first. But be extra careful not to always select a person of the same age, sex, or ethnicity among applicants who are equally qualified. For example, if you are a large landlord who frequently faces tough choices and who always avoids an equally qualified minority or disabled applicant, you are exposing yourself to charges of discrimination.

See Chapter 9 for a detailed discussion on how to avoid illegal discrimination when choosing an applicant.

1. Recordkeeping

A crucial reason for any tenant-screening system is to document how and why you chose a particular tenant. Be sure to note your reasons for rejection— such as poor credit history, pets (if you don't accept

pets), insufficient income relative to the rent, a negative reference from a previous landlord, or your inability to verify information—on the Tenant References form or separate paper. Keep organized files of applications, credit reports, and other materials and notes on prospective tenants for at least three years after you rent a particular unit.

These Tenant References forms may become essential evidence in your defense if a disappointed applicant complains to a fair housing agency or sues you for discrimination. With your file cabinet full of successful and unsuccessful applications, you can:

- find the applicant's form and point to the stated, nondiscriminatory reason you had for denying the rental. Of course, the rejection must be supported by the facts—you can't reject on the basis of a negative employer reference if you never called the employer, and

- pull out other applications that show that you consistently rejected applicants with the same flaw (such as insufficient income), regardless of color, religion and so on. This kind of documentation will make it difficult for someone to claim there was a discriminatory motive at work.

Another reason to back up your decisions and keep applications on file is that a rejected applicant may want you to explain your reasons, apart from any claim of discrimination, as explained below.

Make sure you organize and update your records after a tenant moves in. Set up an individual file for each new tenant, including the tenant's rental application, references, credit report, signed lease or rental agreement, and the Landlord/Tenant Checklist (discussed in Chapter 7). After a tenant moves in, keep copies of your written requests for entry, rent increase notices, records of repair requests and how and when they were handled, and any other correspondence or relevant information. A good system to record all significant tenant complaints and repair requests will provide a valuable paper trail should disputes develop later—for example, over your right to enter a tenant's unit or the time it took for you to fix a problem. Be sure to keep up to date on the tenant's phone number, place of work, and emergency contacts. You should also note the tenant's bank. (You can get this information from the monthly rent check.) If a tenant leaves owing you money above the security deposit amount and you sue and receive a court judgment, you may be able to collect that money from his wages or bank account.

2. Information You Must Provide Rejected Applicants

The Fair Credit Reporting Act, as amended by the Fair and Accurate Credit Transactions Act of 2003, requires you to give certain information to applicants whom you reject (or take other negative action towards) as the result of a report from a credit reporting agency (credit bureau) or from a tenant-screening or reference service. (15 U.S.C. §§ 1681 et. seq.) Known as "adverse action reports," these notices must be given not only to applicants who are rejected, but also to those whom you accept with qualifications, such as requiring a cosigner on the lease, a higher deposit, or more rent than others pay based on the report. The federal requirements do not apply if your decision is based on information that you (or your employee) gathered on your own.

If you do not rent to someone (or you impose qualifications) because of negative information (even if other factors also played a part in your decision) or due to an insufficient credit report, you must give the applicant the name and address of the agency that provided the credit report. You must tell the applicant that he or she has a right to obtain a copy of the file from the agency that reported the negative information, by requesting it within the next 60 days. You

must also tell the rejected applicant that the credit reporting agency did not make the decision to reject them as a tenant and cannot explain the reason for the rejection. Finally, you must tell applicants that they can dispute the accuracy of their credit report and add their own consumer statement to their report.

Use the Notice of Denial Based on Credit Report Information form, shown below, to comply with the federal Fair Credit Reporting Act when you reject an applicant because of an insufficient credit report or negative information in the report.

Appendix B includes a blank, tear-out copy of the Notice of Denial Based on Credit Report Information form. The CD-ROM that accompanies this book also includes this form.

Notice of Denial Based on Credit Report Information

To: _____

Applicant

_____

Street Address

_____

City, State, and Zip Code

THIS NOTICE is to inform you that your application to rent the property at _____ [rental property address] has been denied because of [check all that apply]:

☐ Insufficient information in the credit report provided by _____ [name, address, and telephone number of consumer credit reporting agency providing credit report; include toll-free telephone number if this is a national credit reporting agency]

☐ Negative information in the credit report provided by _____ [name, address, and telephone number of consumer credit reporting agency providing credit report; include toll-free telephone number if this is a national credit reporting agency]

The consumer credit reporting agency noted above did not make the decision not to rent to you and cannot explain why your application was rejected. It only provided information about your credit history.

Providing this notice meets the requirements of the federal Fair Credit Reporting Act as amended by the Fair and Accurate Credit Transactions (FACT) Act of 2003 (15 U.S.C. §§ 1681 and following). You have the right under this Act to obtain a free copy of your credit report from the consumer credit reporting agency named above, if your request is made within 60 days of this notice or if you have not requested a free copy within the past year. (15 U.S.C. § 1681(j)). You also have the right to dispute the accuracy or completeness of your credit report and add your own "consumer statement" (up to 100 words) to the report (15 U.S.C. § 1681(i)). For more information, contact the above-named consumer credit reporting agency.

_____   _____

Date   Owner/Manager

F. HOLDING DEPOSITS

Accepting a holding deposit is legal, but we don't advise it. This type of deposit is usually offered by a tenant who wants to hold a rental unit pending the result of a credit check, or until she can come up with enough money for the rent and a formal deposit. Why not take a holding deposit? Simply because it does you little or no good from a business point of view, and all too often results in misunderstandings or even legal fights.

EXAMPLE

A landlord, Jim, takes a deposit of several hundred dollars from a prospective tenant, Michael. What exactly is Jim promising Michael in return? To rent him the apartment? To rent Michael the apartment only if his credit checks out to Jim's satisfaction? To rent to Michael only if he comes up with the rest of the money before Jim rents to someone who comes up with the first month's rent and deposit? If Jim and Michael disagree about the answers to any of these questions, it can lead to needless anger and bitterness. This can sometimes even spill over into a small claims csourt lawsuit alleging breach of contract.

Another prime reason to avoid holding deposits is that the law is very unclear as to what portion of a holding deposit a landlord can keep if a would-be tenant changes his mind about renting the property or doesn't come up with the remaining rent and deposit money. The basic rule is that a landlord can keep an amount that bears a "reasonable" relation to the landlord's costs, for example, for more advertising and for prorated rent during the time the property was held vacant. Keeping a larger amount will amount to an unlawful "penalty."

If, contrary to our advice, you decide to take a holding deposit, it is essential that both you and your prospective tenant have a clear understanding. The only way to accomplish this is to write your agreement down, preferably on the holding deposit receipt, including the amount of the deposit, the dates you will hold the rental property vacant, the term of the rental agreement or lease, and conditions for returning the deposit.

We've provided you with a sample Receipt and Holding Deposit Agreement that you can adapt to your situation—it will work for a lease or a month-to-month agreement. If your agreement to rent property to a particular individual is not contingent upon your receiving a credit report and satisfactory references, simply delete this sentence from the last paragraph of the form.

You'll find a tear-out version of the Receipt and Holding Deposit Agreement in Appendix B. The CD-ROM that accompanies this book also includes this form.

Receipt and Holding Deposit Agreement

This will acknowledge receipt of the sum of $_____200.00_____ by _____Jim Chow_____

_____ ("Landlord") from _____

_____Michael Blake_____ ("Applicant") as a holding deposit to hold vacant the

rental property at _____123 State Street, City of Los Angeles, California_____

_____, until

_____February 5, 200x_____ at _____5 P.M_____. The property will be rented to Applicant on a

_____month-to-month_____ basis at a rent of $_____400_____ per month, if Applicant signs Landlord's written

_____rental agreement_____ and pays Landlord the first month's rent and a $_____1,200_____

security deposit on or before that date, in which event the holding deposit will be applied to the first month's

rent.

This Agreement depends upon Landlord receiving a satisfactory report of Applicant's references and credit

history. Landlord and Applicant agree that if Landlord offers the rental but Applicant fails to sign the Agreement

and pay the remaining rent and security deposit, Landlord may retain from this holding deposit a sum equal to

the prorated daily rent of $_____30_____ per day until the unit is rerented, plus a $_____50_____ charge to

compensate Landlord for lost rents and the time and expense incurred by the need to rerent.

Michael Blake   February 2, 200x
_____   _____
Applicant   Date
Jim Chow   February 2, 200x
_____   _____
Landlord   Date

2

UNDERSTANDING LEASES AND RENTAL AGREEMENTS

It is essential that every landlord understand California law as it applies to rental agreements and leases. Let's begin with the basics. There are three legal ways to create residential tenancies:

- oral rental agreements
- written leases, and
- written month-to-month rental agreements.

We'll look at each of these types of agreements in detail and provide sample lease and rental agreement forms with a description of each specific clause. We'll also point out illegal lease and rental agreement provisions.

A. ORAL AGREEMENTS ARE NOT RECOMMENDED

Oral (spoken) leases or rental agreements are perfectly legal for month-to-month tenancies and for leases for a year or less (although there's some information you must write down, as explained below). (CC § 1624.) Typically, you agree to let the tenant move in, and the tenant agrees to pay a set amount of rent, once or twice a month or even weekly. Years ago, the amount o2 notice that you needed to give a tenant to raise the rent or terminate the tenancy was pretty simple—it corresponded to the frequency of the rent payment. Now, however, the notice periods vary considerably, depending on the size of the rent raise and, for terminations, the duration of the tenancy and the identity of who's doing the terminating (landlord or tenant). These complications (explained in Chapters 14 and 18) are powerful reasons to use our written rental agreement, in which the rules are specified.

While oral agreements are easy and informal, it is rarely wise to use one. As time passes and circumstances change, people's memories (including yours) have a funny habit of becoming unreliable. You can almost count on tenants claiming that certain oral promises weren't kept or "forgetting" key agreements.

Most landlords choose to impose conditions on the tenancy, such as regulating or prohibiting pets and subletting. In addition, landlords often include a clause providing the landlord with the right to recover attorney fees if it is necessary to evict a tenant.

Oral leases, while legally enforceable (for up to one year), are even more dangerous than oral rental agreements, because they require that one important term—the length of the lease—be accurately remembered by both parties over a considerable time. If something goes wrong with an oral agreement, the parties are all too likely to end up in court, arguing over who said what to whom, when, and in what context.

This book is based on the assumption that you will always use either a written rental agreement or a lease.

INFORMATION YOU MUST WRITE DOWN

Even if every other aspect of your rental agreement or lease is reflected in an oral agreement, you must write down certain information and give it to the tenant:

- the name, phone number, and address of the manager, if any

- the name, phone number, and address of the owner or someone authorized to accept service of process and all notices and demands from you

- the name, phone number, and address of the person authorized to receive rent (if rent may be paid personally, include the days and hours that the person will be available to receive payments), and

- the form in which rent may be paid, such as check, money order, or cash.

The law also specifies how to deliver this information. You can include it in a written document that you give to the tenant (such as a lease, rental agreement, or other writing), post it in an elevator and one additional conspicuous place on the property, or post it in two conspicuous places. This information must be supplied within 15 days of entering into an oral agreement and once a year, on 15 days' notice, if requested by the tenant. You must keep the information up to date. (Civil Code §§ 1962 and 1962.5.)

After you've gone to the trouble of supplying this written information (you could model your form on Clauses 5 and 23 of our written agreements), you'll realize that you may as well use our written rental agreement or lease, which provides places for you to convey the details.

B. WRITTEN AGREEMENTS: WHICH IS BETTER, A LEASE OR A RENTAL AGREEMENT?

There are two kinds of written landlord/tenant arrangements:

- rental agreements, and
- leases.

Written rental agreements provide for a tenancy for an indefinite period of time, and can be terminated by either party by the giving of a written notice, very commonly 30 days. Where the rent is paid monthly, these are called "month-to-month" tenancies. They automatically renew each month (or other time period agreed to in writing) unless one of the parties gives the other the proper amount of written notice to teminate the agreement. The notice period is 30 days for a month-to-month tenancy that has lasted less than a year, 60 days if the tenant has rented for a year or more and 90 days if the tenant's rent is government-subsidized under a contract between the landlord and a housing agency. (CC § 1954.535.) The rental agreements in this book are month to month.

With a written lease, you fix the term of the tenancy—most often for six months or a year, but sometimes longer. At the end of the lease term, you have a few options. You can:

- decline to renew the lease
- sign a new lease for a set period, or
- do nothing—which means your lease will convert to a month-to-month tenancy if you continue to accept monthly rent from the tenant.

There isn't much legal difference between a lease and a rental agreement—with the exception, of course, of the period of occupancy. To decide whether a lease or rental agreement is better for you, read what follows and carefully think about your own situation.

1. Month-to-Month Rental Agreement

When you rent property under a month-to-month rental agreement, these rules apply:

- **On 30 or 60 days' written notice, you may change the amount of rent (subject to any rent control ordinances).** You may increase (or decrease) the amount of rent in all areas that don't have rent control ordinances on 30 days' notice. For increases over 10%, 60 days' notice is required. (See Chapter 14 for guidance on understanding the 60-day situation.) Cities with rent control ordinances may restrict the amount of rent you may charge or add requirements for notifying the tenant of a rent increase. (See Chapter 4 for more on rent control.)

- **On 30 days' written notice, you may change other terms of the tenancy.** You may make other changes in the terms of the tenancy on 30 days' notice, such as increasing the deposit amount (if you're not charging the maximum allowed by law), adding or modifying a no-pets clause, or making any other reasonable change. Again, however, cities with rent control ordinances may restrict your right to do this.

- **You may end the tenancy with 30 (or 60 or 90) days' written notice.** You may end a tenancy at any time on 30 days' notice if the tenant has stayed less than a year, and on 60 days' notice if the tenancy has lasted a year or more. However, there are some widespread exceptions: Rent control ordinances in some cities do not allow this type of termination; and some government-subsidized tenancies require 90 days' notice. (See Chapter 18, Section A for more information on the 60-day requirements.)

Under just-cause eviction provisions of rent control ordinances in cities such as Los Angeles and San Francisco, you must have a good reason—one of those listed in the ordinance—to evict a tenant. We discuss rent control in detail in Chapter 4.

- **A tenant who wants to leave needs to give you only 30 days' notice.** A month-to-month tenancy might mean more tenant turnover. Tenants who know they may legally move out with only 30 days' notice may be more inclined to do so than tenants who make a longer commitment. If you live in an area where it's difficult to find tenants, you may wisely want tenants to commit for a longer time period, such as a year. But as discussed below, a fixed-term lease can't guarantee against turnover, either.

2.   Fixed-Term Lease

With a fixed-term lease, these rules apply:

- **You can't raise the rent until the lease runs out.** The only exception is where the lease specifies a specific increase in rent (and local rent control laws don't limit rent increases). It's important that the rent increase date and amount be stated and certain (such as, "on June 1, 200X, rent will increase by $50"). A court will not enforce a vague statement that the landlord has the right to increase the rent.

- **You can't change other terms of the tenancy.** A lease is a contract whose terms are fixed for the lease period. Changes are allowed only where the lease says they're allowed, or where the tenant agrees in writing to a modification of the terms.

- **You usually can't evict before the lease term expires.** Unless the tenant fails to pay the rent or violates another significant term of the lease, such as repeatedly making too much noise or damaging the property, you're stuck with the tenant until the lease term runs out. (The eviction process and rules are described in Chapter 18.)

- **You may reduce your turnover rate.** Many people make a serious personal commitment when they enter into a long-term lease, in part because they think they'll be liable for quite a few months' rent if they up and leave.

This last reason merits some explaining. It used to be that the major advantage of leasing for fixed terms, such as a year or more, was that a landlord obtained a fair degree of security. The tenant was on the hook to pay for a greater length of time than provided by month-to-month agreements. A tenant who broke the lease and left before it expired was still legally responsible for the rent for the entire lease term. And, if the tenant could be located, the landlord could sue and obtain a court judgment for the balance of the rent.

This is no longer true in most circumstances. Nowadays, landlords who sue the departing (lease-breaking) tenant for the rent due for the rest of the lease term are required to "mitigate" (or minimize) the financial consequences the tenant would suffer as a result of the broken lease. That means the landlord must use reasonable efforts to rent the unit to another suitable tenant at the same or a greater rent. If the landlord rerents the unit (or if a judge believes it could have been rerented with a reasonable amount of effort), the lease-breaking tenant is off the hook except for the months that the unit was vacant while the landlord searched.

This all adds up to a simple truth: A lease no longer provides much income security to a landlord. Indeed, a lease is now something of a one-way street running in the tenant's direction. This is because, especially in a tight market, the mitigation-of-damages rule allows a tenant to break a lease with little or no financial risk. And, even if the tenant does end up owing the landlord some money for the time the unit was empty, collecting the money can be more trouble than it is worth. (We discuss tenants' moving out and breaking leases in detail in Chapter 19.) Not surprisingly, many landlords prefer to rent from month to month, particularly in urban areas where new tenants can often be found in a few days.

There can still be, however, practical advantages to leasing for a fixed period, despite these legal rules. You'll probably prefer to use leases in areas where there is a high vacancy rate or it is difficult to find tenants. Remember, if you can't find another suitable tenant to move in, the former tenant whose lease hasn't expired is still liable for the rent. So, if you are renting near a college that is in session only for eight months a year, or in a vacation area that is deserted for months, you are far better off with a year's lease. Remember, though, that a seasonal tenant is almost sure to try to get someone to take over the tenancy, and unless you have sound business reasons for rejecting the substitute, you'll be stuck with him—or you'll lose your legal right to ask for more damages from the departing tenant.

TENANTS WHO ENLIST MAY BREAK A LEASE OR RENTAL AGREEMENT

The Servicemembers' Civil Relief Act helps active duty military personnel handle legal affairs. (50 App. U.S.C.A §§ 501 and following.) Among its provisions, it allows tenants who enter active military service (or are called up to the National Guard for more than one month at a time) *after* signing a lease or rental agreement to break the lease or agreement. Chapter 19, Section B explains the procedures.

---

3. Variations on the Standard One-Year Lease

If you're planning to use a lease, chances are you'll select a standard one-year lease. But there are other options available. Here are a few.

a. Long-Term Leases

Most leases run for one year. This makes sense, as it allows you to raise the rent at reasonably frequent intervals if market conditions allow. Leasing an apartment or house for a longer period—two, three, or even five years—can be appropriate, for example, if you're renting out your own house because you're taking a two-year sabbatical, or if the tenant plans to make major repairs or remodel your property.

One danger with a long-term lease is that inflation can eat away at the real value of the rent amount. A good way to hedge against this danger in all leases of more than a year is to provide for annual rent

increases that are tied to Consumer Price Index (CPI) increases during the previous year.

Here is a sample clause:

"Landlord and Tenant agree that the rent will increase on the ___ day of the _____ month of each year by the same percentage as the regional and most local Consumer Price Index has increased during the previous twelve months."

The Consumer Price Index most commonly used is the "All-Urban Consumers" for the nearby large metropolitan area. The U.S. Department of Labor publishes figures for the Los Angeles/Long Beach/Anaheim/Santa Monica/Santa Ana area and the San Francisco/Oakland/San Jose area each May. In Los Angeles, the figure is published each May 30 by the Community Development Department. Other cities' rent control boards keep records of the applicable figure, even where the rent increase allowed each year isn't directly tied to the CPI. (See Chapter 4 on rent control.)

STAY ON TOP OF THE CPI

If you factor in a rent increase by tying it to the CPI, you'll need to get accurate information on the yearly increase. Go to the Department of Labor website at http://stats.bls.gov/news.release/cpi.toc.htm.

For this sort of rent increase, no formal notice is required. Simply send the tenant a letter reminding him of the lease term calling for the increase and demonstrating how you calculated the amount.

b. Options to Renew a Lease

Commercial leases often contain a renewal option. An option to renew is essentially a standing offer by the landlord to the tenant, which the tenant can accept or not in the manner and time frame set forth in the option. The option to renew concept is not commonly used in residential rentals, but a tenant occasionally requests one.

We usually advise against using option clauses, for several reasons. First, an option to renew a lease leaves it entirely up to the tenant as to whether to continue the tenancy. Without such an option, both the tenant and the landlord must agree on a renewal. Remember, by the time the lease is about to expire, you might not want to continue the tenancy. Unless you receive a very high guaranteed rent for the initial term, or a lump-sum payment in consideration for including the option clause, you have very little to gain and a lot to lose by giving an option to renew.

Second, when the tenant exercises the option, the new tenancy often continues on the same terms as before, which may not be to your advantage. Here's what happens: To be legal, option clauses must clearly set forth the terms of the renewed tenancy, including the new term, the rent (which can be different from the rent for the first term if the option clause clearly says so) and so forth. Most clauses do this by simply referring to the initial lease terms. (An option clause which leaves any significant term, such as rent or length of term, to further negotiation, or words to that effect, is of no effect and is not legally binding.) Since you may be able to obtain a higher rent after the initial term of six or twelve months, it's obviously not in your best interest to include an option that allows the tenant to remain at the same rent. But since you don't know at the outset what a fair market rent would be—or whether you will become fed up with dogs and decide to ban pets— you can't provide for these new terms.

Finally, drafting option clauses can be very tricky. Even the slightest mistake may do you a great deal of harm or, at the very least, render the option clause of no effect and add uncertainty to the entire situation. If you want to include a renewal or other option in a lease, contact an attorney.

c. Options to Purchase

An "option to purchase" or "lease option" is a contract where an owner leases a house (usually from one to five years) to a tenant for a specific monthly rent (which may increase during the contract term) and gives the tenant the right to buy the house for a price established in advance. Depending on the contract, the tenant can exercise the option to purchase at any time during the lease period, or at a date specified, or for a price offered by another person who makes a purchase offer, subject to the tenant's "right of first refusal" to match the offered price.

If your property should be easy to sell, why share your chance at future appreciation with a tenant? This, in addition to the fact that drafting option clauses is pretty difficult, should give you pause.

Here are some situations when you might consider a tenant's request for a lease option:

- you have a negative cash flow and think the short-run return (initial option fee, higher-than-normal rent, tax advantages) is worth it

- you plan to sell your property soon and think that it might be difficult to sell, or

- you think your tenant will take better care of your house, and perhaps even improve it.

Needless to say, never sign an option, whether included in a lease or not, without consulting a lawyer. If you're thinking of selling, and a tenant or prospective tenant asks for an option to purchase, you might simply reply that you'll consider selling at the expiration of the lease. For a sample lease option contract, see *For Sale by Owner in California,* by George Devine (Nolo).

C. COMMON LEGAL PROVISIONS IN LEASE AND RENTAL AGREEMENT FORMS

This section discusses each clause in the lease and rental agreement forms provided in this book.

Except for the important difference in how long they run (see Clause 4 in our forms), leases and written rental agreements are so similar that they are sometimes hard to tell apart. Both cover the basic terms of the tenancy (such as amount of rent and date due). Except where indicated below, the clauses are identical for the lease and rental agreements included here.

In Appendix B and on the CD-ROM, we provide you with two clearly labeled tear-out forms: a Month-to-Month Residential Rental Agreement and a Fixed-

Term Residential Lease. You should copy and use the one more appropriate to your rental needs. We include a sample filled-in Fixed-Term Residential Lease in this chapter.

HOW TO PREPARE ATTACHMENT PAGES

If you are using the CD-ROM when you first prepare the lease or rental agreement, you won't have to prepare a separate Attachment if you want to add something to a clause or add a new clause—your word processor will allow you to insert material into the original. However, if you later want to change the terms, or if you are using the tear-out and run out of room, you'll have to use a separate document—an Attachment—as described below, and attach it to the original. (If your additions or modifications are very slight and can be done in the margins of the lease or rental agreement, you may want instead to enter them there. Be sure that all tenants and the landlord initial and date the insertions.)

1. At the first place that you run out of room, or want to add a clause or change a clause, begin your entry and then write "Continued on Attachment 1." Similarly, if there is another place where you run out of room, add as much material as you can and then write "Continued on Attachment 2," and so on.

2. Using the tear-out Attachment to Lease/Rental Agreement form in Appendix B, or the electronic file on the CD-ROM that accompanies this book, number the attachment "1," "2," and so on, in the form's title. You'll need a separate attachment page every time you continue a clause, modify a clause, or add a new clause.

3. The Attachment form gives you spaces to continue a clause, modify a clause, or add a new clause. Check the appropriate box and fill in the information. Computer users can simply delete the sections that don't apply.

4. Be sure to have everyone who signs the original lease or rental agreement sign and date the attachment.

5. Staple the Attachment page to the lease or rental agreement.

You'll find a tear-out version of the Attachment Page in Appendix B at the back of the book. The CD-ROM also contains this file. You can word process this file to add its title ("Attachment A") and the information you want to add.

Foreign language note. If you and your tenant discuss your lease or written month-to-month rental agreement primarily in Spanish, Chinese, Tagalog, Vietnamese, or Korean, you must give the tenant an unsigned version of the rental document in that language before asking him to sign. This rule does not apply (that is, you may present your English version only) if the tenant has supplied his own translator who is not a minor and who can speak *and read* the particular language and English fluently. If the translator is supplied by the tenant but does not meet these two requirements, or if the translator is you or someone in your employ or otherwise supplied by you (for example, your fluent daughter), you will have to present a foreign language version of your rental document. (CC § 1632.) Appendix B and the CD-ROM include Spanish versions only of our lease and rental agreement. Remember that you will have to provide your own foreign language versions of the information you add to the blanks.

Choose your lease or rental agreement carefully! In addition to the forms in this book, there are dozens of different printed forms in use in California, and provisions designed to accomplish the same result are worded differently. Unfortunately, some of these agreements are written so obtusely that it is hard to understand what they mean. Ambiguous terms, fine print, and legalese will only lead to confusion and misunderstanding with your tenants. Contrary to what many form writers seem to believe, it is not illegal to use plain English on lease and rental agreement forms. We have done our best to provide clearly written agreements. If you use a different form, be sure to avoid leases or rental agreements with illegal or unenforceable clauses. (See Section F, below.) You may need to use a special government lease if you rent subsidized housing. (See Chapter 9, Section C.)

CLAUSE 1.   IDENTIFICATION OF LANDLORD AND TENANTS

This Agreement is made and entered into on
_____, 20____, between
_____ ("Tenants") and
_____ ("Landlord"). Each Tenant
is jointly and severally liable for the payment of rent and
performance of all other terms of this Agreement.

Every lease or rental agreement must identify the landlord and the tenant(s)—usually called the "parties" to the agreement. Any competent adult—at least 18 years of age—may be a party to a lease or rental agreement. (A teenager under age 18 may also be a party to a lease if he or she has achieved legal adult status through a court order, military service, or marriage.)

Fill in the date you'll be signing. Next, fill in the names of all adults who will live in the premises, including both members of a married couple or registered domestic partners. If anyone else will be financially responsible for paying the rent (even if they won't be living in the premises), list their names. See the discussion of cosigners in Section E, below.

In the last blank, list the names of all owners.

The last sentence states that all tenants are jointly and severally liable for paying rent and adhering to the terms of the agreement. This means that each tenant is legally responsible for the whole agreement and rent. (How cotenants divide that rent among themselves is up to them, not the landlord.) This protects the landlord, who can legally seek full compensation from any of the tenants (or terminate as to all for the misdeeds of one) should a problem arise. Chapter 10 discusses the legal obligations of cotenants.

FAMILY DAY CARE HOMES

Under state law (H&S § 1597.40), a landlord may not prevent a tenant from using rental premises as a licensed family day care home. A tenant who obtains a state license to run a family day care home may do so legally—even if your lease or rental agreement prohibits the operation of a business on the premises, or limits the number of occupants. Local zoning and occupancy limits don't apply to a state-licensed family day care home, though building codes do, as explained further below.

A tenant who wants to run a child care operation must obtain a state license to run a family day care home. Before the county's social services department will issue a license, it will send a fire inspector or other official to examine the space and determine whether the planned operation is consistent with state law, as set out in the Uniform Building Code (counties adopt this code, which is amended every three years). The rules are as follows (2001 California Building Code, California Code of Regulations Title 24, Part 2, Volume 1):

Small Family Day Care. These are for eight or fewer children (any children under ten who live in the rental count towards the total). These day cares are exempt from state fire and life safety regulations. This means that you must allow them, but state law does not regulate their placement in the building, as is true for larger day cares.

Large Family Day Care. These are for 9 to 14 children (again, children of the tenant under the age of ten count toward the total). These operations are regulated depending on the nature of the rental property:

- **Single-family homes, duplexes and townhouses.** Tenants may operate large daycares, but cannot have children above the first floor unless the building has fire sprinklers and a direct exit from the upstairs to the outside. Large Family Day Cares must have two exits remotely located from each other. The exits also can't pass through a garage. Only one exit may be a sliding door. Typically, people use their front door and a sliding patio door. Inspectors have denied a permit to tenants in a townhouse whose second exit went to an enclosed back patio area with no way out.

- **Apartments and condominiums.** Tenants cannot operate a Large Family Day Care in rental units in these buildings, but can operate a Small Family Day Care, and can do so in upstairs units.

In addition to meeting the requirements explained above, you may condition the operation of a day care center on the following reasonable and legal rules:

- The tenant must notify you in writing of his intent to operate a family day care home—after having first obtained a state license—30 days before starting the child care operation.

- You may charge a tenant who opcqÅÑes a family day care home a higher security deposit than you charge tenants with similar units, without being liable for illegal discrimination. The maximum dollar limits on deposits—two months' rent for unfurnished units and three months' rent for furnished units—still apply. (See Chapter 5, Section C.)

If a tenant operates a day care facility, consider the impact this may have on your property insurance. If you have a commercial policy (you'll have one if landlording is your business), chances are that there is no problem (confirm this with your broker). But if you are renting out a home that is insured under a homeowners' policy, your policy may not cover damage or claims that result from the tenant's business. Check with your agent or broker to find out.

CLAUSE 2.   IDENTIFICATION OF PREMISES AND OCCUPANTS

Subject to the terms and conditions set forth in this Agreement, Landlord rents to Tenants, and Tenants rent from Landlord, for residential purposes only, the premises located at _____, California ("the premises"). The premises will be occupied by the undersigned Tenants and the following minor children: _____
_____.

In this clause, you identify the property being rented and who will live in it. The words "for residential purposes only" are to prevent a tenant from using the property for conducting a business that might affect your insurance or violate zoning laws.

In the first blank, fill in the address of the unit or house you are renting. If there is an apartment number, specify that as well.

In shared housing situations, you'll need to clearly state, in your own words, what the rental includes.

EXAMPLE

You are renting a small cottage in your backyard that comes with kitchen privileges in your house. You might fill in, "Back cottage at 1212 Parker St., Visalia, California, with kitchen privileges in main house."

If you need more room, perhaps to explain exactly what the kitchen privileges or other rental conditions include, start by filling in the address of the property. Then add the words "as more fully described in Attachment 1 to this Agreement." Next, prepare a separate "Attachment 1" and define the

---

INVESTIGATE BEFORE LETTING A TENANT RUN A HOME BUSINESS

Millions of Californians run a business from their house or apartment. If a tenant asks you to modify Clause 2 to allow him to operate a business, you have some checking to do—even if you are inclined to say yes.

For one, you'll need to check local zoning laws for restrictions on home-based businesses, including the type of businesses allowed (if any), the amount of car and truck traffic the business can generate, outside signs, on-street parking, the number of employees, and the percentage of floor space devoted to the business. In Los Angeles, for example, dentists, physicians (except for psychiatrists), and unlicensed massage therapists may not operate home offices. In addition, photo labs and recording studios are banned.

You'll also want to consult your insurance company as to whether you'll need a more expensive policy to cover potential liability of employees or guests. In many places, a home office for occasional use will not be a problem. But if the tenant wants to operate a business, especially one with people and deliveries coming and going, such as a therapy practice,

jewelry importer, or small business consulting firm, your insurance coverage may become an issue. Also, you should seriously consider whether neighboring tenants will be inconvenienced. (Where will visitors park, for example?)

You may also want to require that the tenant maintain certain types of liability insurance, so that you won't wind up paying if someone gets hurt on the rental property—for example, a business customer who trips and falls on the front steps. And you may want to insist that you be added as "additional insured" on the tenant's policy, which will protect you if you are sued because your tenant acted carelessly towards his customer or client.

Finally, be aware that if you allow a residence to be used as a commercial site, your property may need to meet the accessibility requirements of the federal Americans With Disabilities Act (ADA). For more information on the ADA, contact the Department of Justice, Office on the Americans With Disabilities Act, Civil Rights Division, in Washington, DC at 800-514-0301 (800-514-0383 TDD), or check the ADA website at www.usdoj.gov/crt/ada/adahom1.htm.

Fixed-Term Residential Lease

1. **Identification of Landlord and Tenants.** This Agreement is made and entered into on ___November 14___, 20_0x_, between _____Sharon and Hank Donaldson_____ ("Tenants") and _____Lionel Jones_____ ("Landlord"). Each Tenant is jointly and severally liable for the payment of rent and performance of all other terms of this Agreement.

2. **Identification of Premises and Occupants.** Subject to the terms and conditions set forth in this Agreement, Landlord rents to Tenants, and Tenants rent from Landlord, for residential purposes only, the premises located at _____123 Sendaro Street, Fresno_____, California ("the premises"). The premises will be occupied by the undersigned Tenants and the following minor children: _____Jan Donaldson_____.

3. **Limits on Use and Occupancy.** The premises are to be used only as a private residence for Tenants and any minors listed in Clause 2 of this Agreement, and for no other purpose without Landlord's prior written consent. Occupancy by guests for more than ten days in any six-month period is prohibited without Landlord's written consent and will be considered a breach of this Agreement.

4. **Defining the Term of the Tenancy.** The term of the rental will begin on _____December 1_____, 20_0x_ and shall expire on _____November 30_____, 20_0x_ Should Tenants vacate before expiration of the term, Tenants shall be liable for the balance of the rent for the remainder of the term, less any rent Landlord collects or could have collected from a replacement tenant by reasonably attempting to rerent. Tenants who vacate before expiration of the term are also responsible for Landlord's costs of advertising for a replacement tenant.

5. **Amount and Schedule for the Payment of Rent.** Tenants will pay to Landlord a monthly rent of $ _____775_____, payable in advance on the _____1st_____ day of each month, except when that day falls on a weekend or legal holiday, in which case rent is due on the next business day. Rent will be paid to _____Lionel Jones_____ at _____125 Sendaro Street, Fresno, California 93656_____, or at such other place as Landlord may designate.

   a.   The form of payment will be ❏ cash ☒ personal check ❏ certified funds or money order ❏ credit card ❏ automatic credit card debit ❏ bank debit

   ❏   b. [Check if rent will be accepted personally, not by mail.] Rent is accepted during the following days and hours: _____

   ❏   c. [Check if rent will be paid by electronic funds transfer.] Rent may be paid by electronic funds transfer to account number _____ in the name of _____

          Account Number   Account Holder

   at _____, _____branch, a financial institution located at _____,

       Branch   Bank Address

   telephone ( ) - _____ .

          Telephone

   ❏   d. On signing this agreement, Tenants will pay to Landlord for the period of ___December___, 20_0x_ through ___November___, 20_0x_ the sum of $ _775.00_ as rent, payable in advance as specified.

6. **Late Charges.** Tenants will pay Landlord a late charge if Tenants fail to pay the rent in full within _five_ days after the date it is due. The late charge will be $_____5.00_____, plus $_____5.00_____ for each additional day that the rent continues to be unpaid. The total late charge for any one month will not exceed $_____35.00_____. Landlord does not waive the right to insist on payment of the rent in full on the date it is due.

particulars of what you are renting. Staple the attachment to the lease or rental agreement.

Note on garages and outbuildings. If any particular part of the property is not being rented, such as a garage or shed you wish to use yourself or rent to someone else, make this clear by specifically excluding it from your description of the premises. If you don't, the tenant has rented it.

EXAMPLE

"Single-family house at 1210 Parker St., Visalia, California, except for the two-car garage."

In the last blank, list the names of any minor children who will be living in the rental property, or put "None," as appropriate. If, however, you are worried about the possibility of overcrowding if the family has more children, you should state the number of minor children—"Two children, Adam and Amy." But avoid language that might be considered discriminatory against children (for example, never write "…and no children," or "…and only one child").

You can legally establish reasonable space-to-people ratios, but you cannot use overcrowding as an excuse for refusing to rent to tenants with children. Discrimination against families with children is illegal, except in housing reserved for senior citizens only.

To avoid discriminating against families with children, your safest bet is to adopt an across-the-board "two-plus-one" policy: You allow two persons per bedroom plus one additional occupant. Thus, a landlord who draws the line at three people to a one-bedroom, five to a two-bedroom and seven to a three-bedroom unit will be on safe ground in this regard. (For a detailed discussion of occupancy limits and discrimination, see Chapter 9, Section D.)

CLAUSE 3.   LIMITS ON USE AND OCCUPANCY

> The premises are to be used only as a private residence for Tenants and any minors listed in Clause 2 of this Agreement, and for no other purpose without Landlord's prior written consent. Occupancy by guests for more than ten days in any six-month period is prohibited without Landlord's written consent and will be considered a breach of this Agreement.

This clause lets the tenants know they may not move anyone else in as a permanent resident without your consent.

When it comes to restricting how long guests may stay, it usually makes sense to include a reasonable time limit in your lease or rental agreement. The agreements in this book allow up to ten days in any six-month period. Even if you do not plan to strictly enforce restrictions on guests, this provision will be very handy if a tenant tries to move in a friend or relative for a month or two, calling her a guest. It will give you leverage either to ask the guest to leave or to request that the guest apply to become a tenant, with an appropriate increase in rent (unless any rent control ordinance forbids an increase). Restrictions on guests may not be based on the age or sex of the occupant or guest.

CLAUSE 4.   DEFINING THE TERM OF THE TENANCY

a.   Lease Provision

The lease form contains the following provision, setting a definite date for the beginning and expiration of the lease:

> The term of the rental will begin on _____, 20_____, and will expire on _____, 20_____. Should Tenants vacate before expiration of the term, Tenants will be liable for the balance of the rent for the remainder of the term, less any rent Landlord collects or could have collected from a replacement tenant by reasonably attempting to rerent. Tenants who vacate before expiration of the term are also responsible for Landlord's costs of advertising for a replacement tenant.

The above lease provision obligates both the landlord and the tenants for a specific term. It also includes a warning that explains the tenants' liability for breaking the lease. (See Chapter 19 for more details on tenant's liability for breaking a lease.)

In the blanks, fill in the starting date and the expiration date. Leases usually last six, 12 or 24 months, but of course this is up to you and the tenants.

b. Rental Agreement Provision

The rental agreement form contains the following provision for a month-to-month tenancy:

> The rental will begin on _____, 20__, and will continue on a month-to-month basis. This tenancy may be terminated by Landlord or Tenants and may be modified by Landlord, by giving 30 days' written notice to the other, or 60 days' notice by Landlord to Tenants, in accordance with Civil Code § 827 or 1946.1 (subject to any local rent control ordinances that may apply).

In the blank, fill in the date the tenancy will begin. With this clause, you'll normally need to give tenants 30 days' written notice before changing or terminating their tenancy. (You'll need to give 60 days' notice for a rent increase of more than 10% or to terminate a tenancy that's lasted a year or more, and 90 days to terminate a government-subsidized tenancy.) (See Chapters 14 and 18.) (CC §§ 827(b), 1946.1, 1954.535.)

While 30 or 60 days is the most common notice period, you may want to agree that the tenants get a longer notice period—say 75 or 90 days. Cross out (or delete) the printed times and write in your own. Interestingly, when a tenant has stayed for a year or more, he need give only 30 days' notice to terminate the tenancy—but the landlord must give 60 days'. Some landlords report that they file fewer eviction lawsuits when they give tenants a generous amount of time in which to find another place.

Don't reduce the tenant's notice period. Agreements reducing the notice period for terminating the tenancy to as few as seven days used to be legal under Civil Code § 1946. We think such provisions are illegal as of January 1, 2003, when Section 1946.1 became effective. Section 1946.1 does not refer to the possibility of a shortened notice period.

A landlord's right to terminate or change the terms of a tenancy, even one from month to month, is limited by local rent control ordinances. Such ordinances not only limit rent and other terms of tenancies, but usually also require the landlord to have a good reason to terminate a tenancy. (We discuss rent control in Chapter 4.)

CLAUSE 5. AMOUNT AND SCHEDULE FOR THE PAYMENT OF RENT

> Tenants will pay to Landlord a monthly rent of $_____, payable in advance on the _____ day of each month, except when that day falls on a weekend or legal holiday, in which case rent is due on the next business day. Rent will be paid to _____ at _____ or at such other place as Landlord will designate from time to time.
>
> a. The form of the payment will be: ❏ cash ❏ credit card ❏ automatic credit card debit ❏ bank debit
>
> ❏ b. [Check if rent will be accepted personally, not by mail.] Rent is accepted during the following days and hours:
>
> _____
>
> ❏ c. On signing this Agreement, Tenants will pay to Landlord for the period of _____, 20__, through _____, 20__, the sum of $_____ as rent, payable in advance.

In this provision, specify the amount of the monthly rent and when, where and to whom the rent is paid.

We discuss how to set a legal rent and where and how rent is due in Chapter 3. Before you fill in the blanks, please read that discussion.

Specify the amount of monthly rent in the first blank. Then indicate when the monthly rent is to be paid—usually on the first of the month, but you can set another time frame. Next, specify to whom and where the rent is to be paid.

5a. You need to specify what form of payment you'll accept, such as cash, cashier's check, money order, or personal check. Be sure to check all boxes that apply.

5b. Check this box if the tenant will pay the rent in person at the address stated earlier in this clause. Under state law, you must indicate the days and hours when rent can be paid at this address—for example, "Monday through Friday, 9:00 AM to noon; 1:00 PM to 5:00 PM."

5c. If the tenants move in before the regular rental period—let's say on June 19th—and you want rent due on the first of every month, you can specify the prorated amount due for the first month. That will avoid any question or confusion about what you expect to be paid. Specify the move-in date and the ending date of that rental period, such as "June 19, 200x through June 30, 200x." Divide the monthly rent by 30 (even for 31-day months or February—it's easier) and multiply by the number of days in the first rental period. For example, $900/30 = $30. $30 x 12 days = $360. Finally, fill in the prorated amount due.

There are several ways to collect rent from tenants who move in midmonth. Especially if the tenant moves in at the end of the month, you may want to collect for that period plus another full month. Read the discussion in Chapter 7, Section C.

5d. This subclause appears only in the lease. It asks you to figure the total rent due for the length of the lease. To figure the sum, multiply the monthly rent times the number of months in the lease (add any prorated rent for the initial month if the tenant moves in midmonth). The value of this clause is that it reminds tenants that they are responsible for rent for the entire term (perhaps they'll think twice before

cavalierly breaking the lease). Of course, if tenants do break the lease, in most situations you are required to use reasonable efforts to rerent, and once you do, the original tenants' responsibility for the balance of rent due under the lease ends. (See Chapter 19, Section B.)

CLAUSE 6. LATE CHARGES

Tenants will pay Landlord a late charge if Tenants fail to pay the rent in full within ___ days after the date it is due. The late charge will be $_____, plus $_____ for each additional day that the rent continues to be unpaid. The total late charge for any one month will not exceed $_____. Landlord does not waive the right to insist on payment of the rent in full on the date it is due.

Late charges provide an incentive for tenants to pay rent on time and make sense when used with discretion. Unfortunately, landlords sometimes try to charge excessive late fees and, by so doing, get themselves into legal hot water and incur tenant hostility. Your late fee must correspond as closely as possible to the real monetary consequences you suffer (called "actual damages") when the rent is late. See Chapter 3, Section D for help in setting legal late fees.

Some cities with rent control ordinances regulate the amount of late fees. Check any rent control ordinances or regulations applicable to your property before establishing a late fee.

In the first blank, specify when you will start charging a late fee. You can charge a late fee the first day rent is late, but many landlords don't charge a late fee until the rent is two or three days late. Next, fill in the late charge for the first day rent is late, followed by the amount for each additional day. Finally, fill in the maximum late charge.

For advice on setting a late charge policy, see Chapter 3.

CLAUSE 7. RETURNED CHECK AND OTHER BANK CHARGES

In the event any check offered by Tenants to Landlord in payment of rent or any other amount due under this Agreement is returned for lack of sufficient funds, a "stop payment" or any other reason, Tenants will pay Landlord a returned check charge in the amount of $_____.

It's legal to charge the tenant an extra fee if a rent check bounces—assuming you agree to accept checks. (If you're having a lot of trouble with bounced checks, you may decide to change your agreement to accept only cash or money order

payments for rent.) As with late charges, bounced check charges must be reasonable. You should charge no more than the amount your bank charges you for a returned check (such as $10 to $15 per returned item; check with your bank), plus a few dollars for your trouble.

In the blank, fill in the amount of the returned check charge. If you won't accept checks, fill in "N/A" or "Not Applicable."

For more detail on returned check charges, see Chapter 3.

CLAUSE 8. AMOUNT AND PAYMENT OF DEPOSITS

On signing this Agreement, Tenants will pay to Landlord the sum of $_____ as a security deposit. Tenants may not, without Landlord's prior written consent, apply this security deposit to the last month's rent or to any other sum due under this Agreement. Within three weeks after Tenants have vacated the premises, Landlord will furnish Tenants with an itemized written statement of the reasons for, and the dollar amount of, any of the security deposit retained by the Landlord, receipts for work done or items purchased, if available, along with a check for any deposit balance. Under Section 1950.5 of the California Civil Code, Landlord may withhold only that portion of Tenants' security deposit necessary to: (1) remedy any default by Tenants in the payment of rent; (2) repair damages to the premises exclusive of ordinary wear and tear; (3) clean the premises if necessary to restore it to the same level of cleanliness it was in at the beginning of the tenancy; and (4) remedy any default by tenants, under this agreement, to restore, replace or return any of landlord's personal property mentioned in this agreement, including but not limited to the property referred to in Clause 11.

Landlord will pay Tenants interest on all security deposits as follows:

❑ a. Per state law, no interest payments are required.

❑ b. Local law requires that interest be paid or credited, or landlord has voluntarily decided to do so, which shall occur as follows:

_____

_____.

By law, as of January 1, 2003, any payment, fee, deposit, or charge that is paid by the tenant "at the beginning of the tenancy" (other than credit check fees; see Chapter 1, Section C2) is a security deposit, as long as the landlord intends to use it for any of the purposes mentioned in paragraphs (1) through (4) of Clause 8 above. A fee that is intended to "reimburse the landlord for costs associated with processing a new tenant" also comes within this definition of a security deposit. We think that this means that so-called "tenant initiation expense reimbursement" fees ("TIER" fees), which are upfront fees that cover the time spent moving the tenant in and processing the paperwork, are no longer legal.

In short, any "cleaning deposit," "cleaning fee," "security deposit," or "last month's rent," or anything paid by the tenant upfront other than the first month's rent or a legitimate credit check fee, is a security deposit (CC § 1950.5(b)), and subject to the laws that control the amount and uses of security deposits.

The use and return of security deposits is a frequent source of disputes between landlords and tenants. For example, a tenant may assume that the deposit, if it is equal to one month's rent, is the same as "last month's rent" and try to apply it this way a month before moving out. To avoid confusion, our lease and rental agreements are clear on the subject. You should make the point again in a move-in letter. (See Chapter 7.)

The amount and use of security deposits are limited by state law. To determine the maximum amount of security deposit you can charge, read Chapter 5 before completing this section. Chapter 20 provides details on returning deposits, including requirements that a tenant be offered the option of an initial, pre-move-out inspection and the opportunity to correct problems before moving out, penalties for failing to return deposits within the three weeks required by state law, and a requirement that you provide receipts for cleaning and repairs.

Once you've decided how much security deposit you can charge, fill in that amount in the blank. Then check either "a" or "b." Check "a" if your property is not located in a city that requires payment of interest. Check "b" if interest payments must be made or credited, and summarize the requirement. You may copy the explanation from the chart of Cities Requiring Interest or Separate Accounts for Security Deposits, found in Chapter 5, Section F.

Consider offering interest even if you aren't legally required to do so. Tenants will appreciate your willingness to give them the interest their money has earned. Since state law doesn't regulate the manner in which you should handle interest, you can choose any convenient and fair method. For example, you might use the same rate as offered by a major bank on savings accounts, and you could give a rent credit at the end of six months' residence.

CLAUSE 9.   UTILITIES

Tenants will be responsible for payment of all utility charges, except for the following, which will be paid by Landlord:

_____

_____.

❑ Tenants' gas or electric meter serves area(s) outside of their premises, and there are not separate gas and electric meters for Tenants' unit and the area(s) outside their unit. Tenants and Landlord agree as follows:

_____

_____.

This clause helps prevent misunderstandings. Normally, landlords pay for garbage (and sometimes water, if there is a yard) to help make sure that the premises are well maintained. Tenants usually pay for other services, such as phone, gas and electricity. In the blank, fill in the utilities you—not the tenants—will be responsible for paying. If you'll pay a portion of the utilities, indicate that—for example, "all utilities except phone" or "half of the electricity and half of the gas." If the tenant will pay all utilities, fill in "N/A" or "Not Applicable."

As mentioned in Chapter 1, state law requires landlords to notify all prospective tenants, before they move in, if their gas or electric meter serves any areas outside their dwelling. (CC § 1940.9.) This law specifically applies where:

7. **Returned Check and Other Bank Charges.** In the event any check offered by Tenants to Landlord in payment of rent or any other amount due under this Agreement is returned for lack of sufficient funds, a "stop payment" or any other reason, Tenants will pay Landlord a returned check charge in the amount of $_____20.00_____.

8. **Amount and Payment of Deposits.** On signing this Agreement, Tenants will pay to Landlord the sum of $___1,000.00___ as a security deposit. Tenants may not, without Landlord's prior written consent, apply this security deposit to the last month's rent or to any other sum due under this Agreement. Within three weeks after Tenants have vacated the premises, Landlord will furnish Tenants with an itemized written statement of the reasons for, and the dollar amount of, any of the security deposit retained by the Landlord, receipts for work done or items purchased, if available, along with a check for any deposit balance. Under Section 1950.5 of the California Civil Code, Landlord may withhold only that portion of Tenants' security deposit necessary to: (1) remedy any default by Tenants in the payment of rent; (2) repair damages to the premises exclusive of ordinary wear and tear; (3) clean the premises if necessary to restore it to the same level of cleanliness it was in at the beginning of the tenancy; and (4) remedy any default by tenants, under this agreement, to restore, replace, or return any of Landlord's personal property mentioned in this agreement, including but not limited to the property referred to in Clause 11.

Landlord will pay Tenants interest on all security deposits as follows:

☒ a. Per state law, no interest payments are required.

☐ b. Local law requires that interest be paid or credited, or landlord has decided voluntarily to do so, which will occur as follows:

_____

_____

9. **Utilities.** Tenants will be responsible for payment of all utility charges, except for the following, which will be paid by Landlord:

garbage and water

_____

☐ Tenants' gas or electric meter serves area(s) outside of their premises, and there are not separate gas and electric meters for Tenants' unit and the area(s) outside their unit. Tenants and Landlord agree as follows:

_____

_____

10. **Prohibition of Assignment and Subletting.** Tenants will not sublet any part of the premises or assign this Agreement without the prior written consent of Landlord.

11. **Condition of the Premises.** Tenants agree to: (1) keep the premises clean and sanitary and in good repair and, upon termination of the tenancy, to return the premises to Landlord in a condition identical to that which existed when Tenants took occupancy, except for ordinary wear and tear; (2) immediately notify Landlord of any defects or dangerous conditions in and about the premises of which they become aware; and (3) reimburse Landlord, on demand by Landlord, for the cost of any repairs to the premises, including Landlord's personal property therein, damaged by Tenants or their guests or invitees through misuse or neglect.

Tenants acknowledge that they have examined the premises, including appliances, fixtures, carpets, drapes and paint, and have found them to be in good, safe, and clean condition and repair, except as noted here:

See Landlord/Tenant Checklist attached.

_____

_____

12. **Possession of the Premises.** If, after signing this Agreement, Tenants fail to take possession of the premises, they will still be responsible for paying rent and complying with all other terms of this Agreement. In the event Landlord is unable to deliver possession of the premises to Tenants for any reason not within Landlord's control, including, but not limited to, failure of prior occupants to vacate or partial or complete destruction of the premises, Tenants will have the right to terminate this Agreement. In such event, Landlord's liability to Tenants shall be limited to the return of all sums previously paid by Tenants to Landlord.

- there are not separate gas and electric meters for each unit, and

- a tenant's meter serves any areas outside his unit (even a light bulb not under the tenant's control in a common area).

If both these conditions apply, you are required to do one of the following:

- pay for the utilities for the tenant's meter yourself, by placing that utility in your own name

- correct the situation by separately metering the area outside the tenant's unit, or

- enter into a separate written agreement with the tenant, under which the tenant specifically agrees to pay utilities on his own meter, knowing he's paying for others' utilities, too.

We prefer the first and second methods above. Regardless of how few dollars a month a tenant may be paying for another tenant's or the common area utilities, a tenant faced with this sort of uncertainty will usually demand a concession on rent; this will probably cost you more in the long run than if you either added a new meter or simply paid for the utilities yourself.

Here are some examples of ways to handle shared utility arrangements.

EXAMPLE 1

"Landlord will pay for the utilities for the Tenants' meter, and will place that utility in Landlord's own name."

EXAMPLE 2

"Tenants will pay for gas and electricity charged to their meter, with the understanding that they may be paying for others' utility charges."

In a situation where you share housing with the tenant, or where there is only one meter for several units, define who is responsible for what portion of the utilities in more detail. If you do, replace Clause 9 of our form with these words: "Tenants shall pay for utility charges as follows: *[fill in the charges]*."

CONSIDER WATER SUBMETERING

For many years, the Environmental Protection Agency (EPA) classified landlords who billed tenants separately for water as sellers of public water. Landlords had to comply with the Safe Drinking Water Act, which requires water testing and treatment. Since residential landlords have no ability to store or treat drinking water destined for their tenants, they were discouraged from installing submeters.

In December 2003, the EPA changed its rather illogical stance somewhat. Landlords who bill separately by using submeters are no longer considered water sellers, but only if they use submeters. If you divide your property's water bill among residents based on a ratio of floor space, number of occupants, or some other quantitative measure, you will still be considered a seller. The EPA justifies this stubbornness not on the grounds that ratio billing makes you capable of storing, testing, and treating the water, but on the theory that ratio billing does not encourage water conservation to the same extent as submetering. (Applicability of the Safe Drinking Water Act to Submetered Properties, 68 Fed. Reg. 74,233 (2003).)

Evidence suggests that submetering may well be worth your time and trouble. A 1999 study of apartments that were charged for only their own water resulted in a usage drop of between 18% to 39%. (Ray Smith, *Brace Yourself for Another Monthly Bill*, Wall St. J., Oct. 23, 2003.) First, however, check your local ordinances for any restrictions on selling water. The California Public Utilities Commission has historically not regulated owners who bill residents separately for water, but some cities, including Petaluma, Santa Clara, San Bruno, and Vacaville prohibit reselling. (Source: *Overview of Retrofit Strategies*, prepared for the U.S. Department of Housing and Urban Development by Water Resources Engineering, Inc., 2002.)

CLAUSE 10. PROHIBITION OF ASSIGNMENT AND SUBLETTING

Tenants will not sublet any part of the premises or assign this Agreement without the prior written consent of Landlord.

Clauses 1–3 spell out the total number of adult occupants, and let tenants know that they may not move anyone else in as a permanent resident. Clause 10 enforces this with an antisubletting clause, breach of which is grounds for eviction.

Clause 10 won't stop a tenant from bringing in a spouse or child later; in fact, if you tried to do so, you could be sued for illegal discrimination as discussed in Chapter 9. You may not want to strictly enforce Clause 3's restriction on guests, but it will be very handy to have if a tenant tries to move in a friend or relative for a month or two, calling her a guest. Restrictions on guests may not be based on the age or sex of the occupant or guest, as discussed in Chapter 10.

Clause 10 is designed to prevent your tenant from leaving in the middle of the month or of a lease term and finding a replacement—maybe someone you wouldn't choose to rent to—without your consent. It also prevents a tenant from subleasing during a vacation or renting out a room to someone unless you specifically agree.

By including Clause 10 in your lease, you have the option not to accept a sublet or assignment if you don't like or trust the person your tenant proposes to take over the lease. If, however, the tenant wishes to leave early and provides you with another suitable tenant, you can't both hold the tenant financially liable for breaking the lease and unreasonably refuse to rent to another tenant who is in every way suitable. (We discuss lease-breaking tenants in detail in Chapter 19.)

The issue of who is and who is not a tenant, and legal liability for paying the rent and meeting all the conditions of the lease or rental agreement, can be very confusing and cause all kinds of problems. See Chapter 10 for a discussion of this topic and how using California's "lock-in" option may limit your financial losses when a tenant leaves early.

CLAUSE 11. CONDITION OF THE PREMISES

Tenants agree to: (1) keep the premises clean and sanitary and in good repair and, upon termination of the tenancy, to return the premises to Landlord in a condition identical to that which existed when Tenants took occupancy, except for ordinary wear and tear; (2) immediately notify Landlord of any defects or dangerous conditions in and about the premises of which they become aware; and (3) reimburse Landlord, on demand by Landlord, for the cost of any repairs to the premises, including Landlord's pesonal property therein, damaged by Tenants or their guests or invitees through misuse or neglect.

Tenants acknowledge that they have examined the premises, including appliances, fixtures, carpets, drapes and paint, and have found them to be in good, safe and clean condition and repair, except as noted here:

_____

_____

_____

_____.

Clause 11 makes it clear that if a tenant damages the premises (for example, breaks a window or scratches hardwood floors), it's his responsibility to pay for fixing the problem.

In the blanks after the words "except as noted here," clearly describe any defects or damages to the premises. If there are none, state that. You and your tenants may find it easiest to go through the rental unit before the tenants move in and fill out a Landlord/Tenant Checklist, describing what is in the rental unit and noting any problems.

Chapter 7 provides details on the Landlord/Tenant Checklist and other means to minimize disputes about who's responsible for damage or repairs. If you decide to use the checklist, fill in the words "See Landlord/Tenant Checklist, attached."

You'll find a tear-out version of the Landlord/Tenant Checklist in Appendix B. The CD-ROM that accompanies this book also includes this form.

Clause 11 requires tenants to alert you to defective or dangerous conditions. We can't emphasize enough the importance of establishing a system for tenants to regularly report on the condition of the premises and defective or dangerous conditions. This is covered in detail in Chapter 11.

Don't fail to maintain the property. If your tenants or their guests suffer injury or property damage as a result of poorly maintained property, you may be held responsible for paying for the loss. Chapter 12 covers liability-related issues.

CLAUSE 12. POSSESSION OF THE PREMISES

> If, after signing this Agreement, Tenants fail to take posses-sion of the premises, they will still be responsible for paying rent and complying with all other terms of this Agreement. In the event Landlord is unable to deliver possession of the pre-mises to Tenants for any reason not within Landlord's con-trol, including, but not limited to, failure of prior occupants to vacate or partial or complete destruction of the premises, Tenants will have the right to terminate this Agreement. In such event, Landlord's liability to Tenants will be limited to the return of all sums previously paid by Tenants to Landlord.

This clause explains that if the tenants choose not to move in after they have signed a lease or rental agreement, they will still be required to pay rent and satisfy other conditions of the lease or rental agree-ment. Of course, you would be legally required to begin reasonable efforts to rerent the unit, and would be able to collect rent from the original, would-be occupants only until you rented the unit to someone else. (See Chapter 19, Section B for an explanation of the "mitigation of damages" rule.)

This clause also protects you if you're unable, for reasons beyond your control, to turn over possession after having signed the agreement—for example, if a fire spreads from next door and destroys the premises, or if you can't turn over possession because the current tenant refuses to leave (and becomes a "holdover tenant"). It limits your financial liability to new tenants to the return of any prepaid rent and security deposits (the "sums previously paid" in the language of the

clause). A disappointed tenant would not be able to sue you for the cost of temporary housing while he waited for you to evict a holdover tenant. And if the only substitute rental the waiting tenant could find was more expensive than the rent he would have paid you, he could not sue you for the difference. You don't need to add anything to this clause.

CLAUSE 13. PETS

> No animal, bird or other pet shall be kept on the premises without Landlord's prior written consent, except properly trained dogs needed by blind, deaf, or disabled persons and:
>
> ❑ a. None.
>
> ❑ b. _____
> _____,
> under the following conditions:
> _____
> _____.

This clause is designed to prevent tenants and their guests from keeping pets without your written permission. This is not to say that you will want to apply a flat "no-pets" rule. It does provide you with a legal mechanism to keep your premises from being knee-deep in Irish wolfhounds. Without this sort of provision, particularly in a fixed-term lease that can't be terminated on 30 days' notice, there's little to prevent your tenant from keeping dangerous or nonhousebroken pets on your property (except for city ordinances prohibiting tigers and the like).

Check "a" if you want to forbid pets. You have the right to prohibit all pets, with the exception of trained dogs used by blind, deaf, or physically or mentally disabled people. You may not charge an extra pet deposit on account of any trained dog. (CC §§ 54.1, 54.2.)

To allow pets, check "b" and identify the type and number of pets—for example, "one cat." If you allow pets, you're wise to spell out your pet rules —for example, you may want to specify that the tenants will keep the yard free of all animal waste. You may also want to charge a higher security deposit, if you aren't already requiring the maximum allowed by law.

It is important to educate tenants from the start that you will not tolerate dangerous or even apparently dangerous pets, and that as soon as you learn of a worrisome situation, you have the option of insisting that the tenant get rid of the pet (or move). You may want to use the space under part "b" to advise tenants that their pets must be well trained and non-threatening; or you could set out your policy in your Rules and Regulations, if you have them. As long as you or your management follow through with your policy—by keeping an eye on what goes on and listening to and acting on any complaints from other tenants or neighbors—such a clause will help you avoid liability if a tenant's pet injures someone on or even near your property. Your policy might look something like this:

"Tenant's pet(s) will be well behaved, will be under Tenant's control at all times and will not pose a threat or apparent threat to the safety of other tenants, their guests, or other people on or near the rental premises. If, in the opinion of Landlord, tenant's pet(s) pose such a threat, Landlord will serve Tenant with a Three-Day Notice to Cure (remove pet from the premises) or Quit (move out)."

Enforce no-pets clauses. When faced with tenants who violate no-pets clauses, landlords often ignore the situation for a long time, then try to enforce it later when friction develops over some other matter. This could backfire. In general, if you know a tenant has breached the lease or rental agreement (for example, by keeping a pet) and do nothing about it for a long time, you risk having legally waived your right to object. You can preserve your right to object by promptly giving the tenant an informal written notice as soon as the pet appears, then following through with a Three-Day Notice to Perform Covenant or Quit. See Chapter 4 for details on rent control and Chapter 18 for a discussion of three-day and 30-day notices.

RENTING TO PET OWNERS

Project Open Door, an ambitious program of the San Francisco Society for the Prevention of Cruelty to Animals (SPCA), seeks to show landlords how to make renting to pet-owning tenants a satisfying and profitable experience. The SPCA offers landlords:

- checklists to help screen pet-owning tenants

- pet policy agreements to add to standard leases and rental agreements, and

- free mediation if landlords and tenants have problems after moving in, such as neighbor complaints.

For more information, contact the San Francisco SPCA at 2500 16th St., San Francisco, CA 94103, 415-554-3000, or check their website at www.sfspca.org/opendoor.

SHOULD YOU REQUIRE A SEPARATE SECURITY DEPOSIT FOR PETS?

Some landlords allow pets but require the tenant to pay a separate deposit to cover any damages caused by the pet. This is legal only if the deposit charged for the pet, when added to the amount charged for the security deposit, does not exceed the maximum amount that can be charged for a deposit. (See Chapter 5.)

Separate pet deposits are usually a bad idea because they limit how you can use that part of the security deposit. For example, if the pet is well behaved but the tenant trashes your unit, you can't use the pet portion of the deposit to clean up after the human. If you want to protect your property from damage done by a pet, you are probably better off charging a slightly higher rent or security deposit to start with (assuming you are not restricted by rent control or the upper security deposit limits). It is also illegal to charge an extra pet deposit for people with trained guide dogs, signal dogs, or service dogs.

13. Pets. No animal, bird or other pet shall be kept on the premises without Landlord's prior written consent, except properly trained dogs needed by blind, deaf, or disabled persons and:

☐ a. None.

☒ b. _one cat_____, under the following conditions:

_____

14. Landlord's Access for Inspection and Emergency. Landlord or Landlord's agents may enter the premises in the event of an emergency or to make repairs or improvements, supply agreed services, show the premises to prospective buyers or tenants, and conduct an initial move-out inspection requested by tenants. Except in cases of emergency, Tenants' abandonment of the premises, or court order, Landlord will give Tenants reasonable notice of intent to enter and shall enter only during regular business hours of Monday through Friday from 9:00 a.m. to 6:00 p.m. and Saturday from 10:00 a.m. to 1:00 p.m. The notice will include the purpose, date, and approximate time of entry

15. Extended Absences by Tenants. Tenants agree to notify Landlord in the event that they will be away from the premises for _____10_____ consecutive days or more. During such absence, Landlord may enter the premises at times reasonably necessary to maintain the property and inspect for damage and needed repairs.

16. Prohibitions Against Violating Laws and Causing Disturbances. Tenants are entitled to quiet enjoyment of the premises. Tenants and their guests or invitees will not use the premises or adjacent areas in such a way as to: (1) violate any law or ordinance, including laws prohibiting the use, possession, or sale of illegal drugs; (2) commit waste or nuisance; or (3) annoy, disturb, inconvenience, or interfere with the quiet enjoyment and peace and quiet of any other tenant or nearby resident.

17. Repairs and Alterations

a.   Tenants will not, without Landlord's prior written consent, alter, rekey, or install any locks to the premises or install or alter any burglar alarm system. Tenants will provide Landlord with a key or keys capable of unlocking all such rekeyed or new locks as well as instructions on how to disarm any altered or new burglar alarm system.

b.   Except as provided by law or as authorized by the prior written consent of Landlord, Tenants will not make any repairs or alterations to the premises. Landlord will not unreasonably withhold consent for such repairs, but will not authorize repairs that require advanced skill or workmanship or that would be dangerous to undertake. Landlord will not authorize repairs unless such repairs are likely to return the item or element of the rental to its predamaged state of usefulness and attractiveness.

18. Damage to the Premises. In the event the premises are partially or totally damaged or destroyed by fire or other cause, the following will apply:

a.   If the premises are totally damaged and destroyed, Landlord will have the option to: (1) repair such damage and restore the premises, with this Agreement continuing in full force and effect, except that Tenants' rent will be abated while repairs are being made; or (2) give written notice to Tenants terminating this Agreement at any time within thirty (30) days after such damage, and specifying the termination date; in the event that Landlord gives such notice, this Agreement shall expire and all of Tenants' rights pursuant to this Agreement will cease.

b.   Landlord will have the option to determine that the premises are only partially damaged by fire or other cause. In that event, Landlord will attempt to repair such damage and restore the premises within thirty (30) days after such damage. If only part of the premises cannot be used, Tenants must pay rent only for the usable part, to be determined solely by Landlord. If Landlord is unable to complete repairs within thirty (30) days, this Agreement will expire and all of Tenants' rights pursuant to this Agreement will terminate at the option of either party.

c.   In the event that Tenants, or their guests or invitees, in any way caused or contributed to the damage of the premises, Landlord will have the right to terminate this Agreement at any time, and Tenants will be responsible for all losses, including, but not limited to, damage and repair costs as well as loss of rental income.

d.   Landlord will not be required to repair or replace any property brought onto the premises by Tenants.

CLAUSE 14. LANDLORD'S ACCESS FOR INSPECTION AND EMERGENCY

Landlord or Landlord's agents may enter the premises in the event of an emergency or to make repairs or improvements, supply agreed services or show the premises to prospective buyers or tenants and conduct an initial move-out inspection requested by Tenants. Except in cases of emergency, Tenants' abandonment of the premises, or court order, Landlord will give Tenants reasonable notice of intent to enter and will enter only during regular business hours of Monday through Friday from 9:00 a.m. to 6:00 p.m. and Saturday from 10:00 a.m. to 1:00 p.m. The notice will include the purpose, date, and approximate time of the entry.

The law limits your right to enter property in the tenant's absence or without her permission. Although these limits apply regardless of what an agreement or lease says, it's best to put the limits in writing to avoid problems later on.

This clause makes it clear to the tenant that you have a legal right of access to the property to make repairs or show the premises for sale or rental, provided you give the tenant reasonable notice, which is presumed to be 24 hours. However, the notice period is 48 hours if the purpose of the entry is a move-out inspection requested by the tenant regarding possible security deposit deductions. (See Chapters 5 and 20 for information on collecting and returning deposits.) Chapter 13 provides details on a landlord's right to enter rental property and notice requirements.

This clause defines regular business hours to include weekdays and part of Saturday. The law does not, however, specify exactly what are "normal business hours." A tenant could, for example, object to your entering the premises on a Saturday morning. Common sense suggests that you be considerate of your tenants and do your best to accommodate their schedules.

CLAUSE 15. EXTENDED ABSENCES BY TENANTS

Tenants agree to notify Landlord in the event that they will be away from the premises for _____ consecutive days or more. During such absence, Landlord may enter the premises at times reasonably necessary to maintain the property and inspect for damage and needed repairs.

This clause requires that the tenants notify you when leaving your property for an extended time.

In the blank, fill in the time frame that you'd like to be notified of. Fourteen days is common, but you may opt for an altogether different period of time. For example, if you live in Truckee or anywhere else where it snows, checking your property on a daily basis during the winter may be prudent, to make sure the pipes haven't burst.

WASTE AND NUISANCE: WHAT ARE THEY?

In legalese, **waste** is the causing of severe property damage to real estate, including a house or apartment unit, which goes way beyond ordinary wear and tear. Punching holes in walls, pulling out sinks and fixtures, and knocking down doors are examples of "committing waste."

Nuisance means behavior that prevents neighbors from fully enjoying the use of their own homes. Continuous loud noise and foul odors are examples of legal nuisances that may disturb nearby neighbors.

CLAUSE 16. PROHIBITIONS AGAINST VIOLATING LAWS AND CAUSING DISTURBANCES

Tenants are entitled to quiet enjoyment of the premises. Tenants and their guests or invitees will not use the premises or adjacent areas in such a way as to: (1) violate any law or ordinance, including laws prohibiting the use, possession, or sale of illegal drugs; (2) commit waste or nuisance; or (3) annoy, disturb, inconvenience, or interfere with the quiet enjoyment and peace and quiet of any other tenant or nearby resident.

This type of clause is found in most form leases and rental agreements. Although it's full of legal gobbledygook, it's probably best to leave it as is, since courts have much experience in working with these terms. If the tenant causes a nuisance, seriously damages the property, or violates the law—for example, deals drugs—you may be able to evict even without such a provision in the agreement. It will, however, be easier to evict if you can point to an explicit lease provision.

If you want to add specific rules—for example, no loud music played after midnight—add them to Clause 24: Additional Provisions.

Take a moment to look again at the first sentence in this clause, which states that tenants are entitled to "quiet enjoyment." As just explained, this means that neighboring tenants are entitled to peace and quiet—and if the tenant who's signing this document seriously interferes with this right, you have the power to terminate his tenancy. It also means that you are promising to maintain an atmosphere of peace and quiet. So, if the tenant who signs this lease comes to you with credible proof that a neighboring tenant is making it impossible to reasonably enjoy his rented home, you must, according to your promise in the lease or rental agreement, takes steps to calm things down (or clean them up). If you don't, your aggrieved tenant can point to your violation of this clause as grounds for breaking the lease (with no liability for future rent).

CLAUSE 17. REPAIRS AND ALTERATIONS

a. Tenants will not, without Landlord's prior written consent, alter, rekey, or install any locks to the premises or install or alter any burglar alarm system. Tenants will provide Landlord with a key or keys capable of unlocking all such rekeyed or new locks as well as instructions on how to disarm any altered or new burglar alarm system.

b. Except as provided by law or as authorized by the prior written consent of Landlord, Tenants will not make any repairs or alterations to the premises. Landlord will not unreasonably withhold consent for such repairs, but will not authorize repairs that require advanced skill or workmanship or that would be dangerous to undertake. Landlord will not authorize repairs unless such repairs are likely to return the item or element of the rental to its predamaged state of usefulness and attractiveness.

The first part of this clause forbids the tenant from rekeying the locks or installing a burglar alarm system without your consent, and provides that you are entitled to duplicate keys and instructions on how to disarm the alarm system. See Chapter 12 for more

information on your responsibility to provide secure premises, and Chapter 13 for information on your right to enter rental property in an emergency.

The second part of Clause 17 makes it clear that alterations and repairs without the landlord's consent aren't allowed. The "except as provided by law" language is a reference to the "repair-and-deduct" remedy the tenants may use to repair health- or safety-threatening defects. By law, landlords must maintain and repair their rental property in accordance with certain minimum standards. (CC § 1941.1.) If a landlord refuses to do so, after reasonable notification by the tenant, a tenant may arrange for certain repairs and deduct the cost from the next month's rent. (CC § 1942.) The tenant always has the right to use this statutory procedure, no matter what a lease says. (See Section F3, below.) If you don't keep the property in habitable condition, tenants may also have the right to withhold rent and even sue. (See Chapter 11.)

If mutually agreeable to you and the tenants, the tenants may agree in writing to perform necessary repairs or maintenance such as mowing the lawn in exchange for a rent reduction. Section F3 provides more details on this type of arrangement.

Section b in this clause makes it clear that alterations and repairs without your written consent aren't allowed. If you wish, you may authorize a tenant improvement or alteration, such as the installation of a bookshelf or plantings in the backyard. Use the Tenant Alterations to Rental Unit form, which is fully explained in Chapter 11, Section L.

CLAUSE 18. DAMAGE TO THE PREMISES

In the event the premises are partially or totally damaged or destroyed by fire or other cause, the following shall apply:

a. If the premises are totally damaged and destroyed, Landlord will have the option to:

(1) repair such damage and restore the premises, with this Agreement continuing in full force and effect, except that Tenants' rent will be abated while repairs are being made; or

(2) give written notice to Tenants terminating this Agreement at any time within thirty (30) days after

such damage, and specifying the termination date; in the event that Landlord gives such notice, this Agreement will expire and all of Tenants' rights pursuant to this Agreement will cease.

b. Landlord will have the option to determine that the premises are only partially damaged by fire or other cause. In that event, Landlord will attempt to repair such damage and restore the premises within thirty (30) days after such damage. If only part of the premises cannot be used, Tenants must pay rent only for the usable part, to be determined solely by Landlord. If Landlord is unable to complete repairs within thirty (30) days, this Agreement will expire and all of Tenants' rights pursuant to this Agreement will terminate at the option of either party.

c. In the event that Tenants, or their guests or invitees, in any way caused or contributed to the damage of the premises, Landlord will have the right to terminate this Agreement at any time, and Tenants will be responsible for all losses, including, but not limited to, damage and repair costs as well as loss of rental income.

d. Landlord will not be required to repair or replace any property brought onto the premises by Tenants.

This clause addresses what will happen if the premises are seriously damaged by fire or other calamity. This provision places responsibility on tenants for damage caused by their acts or by people they've allowed in the premises. Basically, it seeks to limit your risk to 30 days' rental value, even if the damage was your responsibility. You don't need to add anything to this clause. (See Chapter 11, Section H for a discussion of liability for rent if the premises are partially or totally destroyed.)

CLAUSE 19. TENANTS' FINANCIAL RESPONSIBILITY AND RENTERS' INSURANCE

Tenants agree to accept financial responsibility for any loss or damage to personal property belonging to Tenants and their guests and invitees caused by theft, fire, or any other cause. Landlord assumes no liability for any such loss. Landlord recommends that Tenants obtain a renters' insurance policy from a recognized insurance firm to cover Tenants' liability, personal property damage and damage to the premises.

This clause forces the tenants to assume responsibility for damage to their own belongings. It also suggests that tenants obtain renters' insurance.

One change you may wish to make in this clause involves requiring renters' insurance. If you absolutely wish to require insurance, substitute the following paragraph for the last sentence of Clause 19:

Landlord assumes no liability for such loss and requires Tenants, within 10 days of the signing of this Agreement, to obtain insurance which will:

a. reimburse Landlord for cost of fire or water damage and vandalism to the premises

b. indemnify Landlord against liability to third parties for any negligence on the part of Tenants or their guests or invitees and

c. cover damage to Tenants' personal possessions to a minimum of $_____. Tenants shall provide Landlord with proof of such insurance.

Your move-in letter (see Chapter 7) is the place to highlight your policy on renters' insurance.

CLAUSE 20. WATERBEDS

No waterbed or other item of water-filled furniture may be kept on the premises without Landlord's written consent.

❑ Landlord grants Tenants permission to keep water-filled furniture on the premises. Attachment _____: Agreement Regarding Use of Waterbed is attached to and incorporated into this Agreement by reference.

Whether you can refuse to rent to a tenant with a waterbed depends on when the property was built. Here are the rules.

Property built before January 1, 1973. If your property's "certificate of occupancy" (final approval of initial construction by local building department) was issued before January 1, 1973, you may legally refuse to rent to a tenant who has a waterbed. This isn't to say that you should ban waterbeds if your property was built before 1973. Wooden floors built to current standards, or even the standards 20 or 30 years ago, can withstand pressures of at least 60 pounds per square foot, and a typical queen-sized waterbed exerts about 50 pounds per square foot. (Poured concrete floors, of course, pose no problem.)

19. Tenants' Financial Responsibility and Renters' Insurance. Tenants agree to accept financial responsibility for any loss or damage to personal property belonging to Tenants and their guests and invitees caused by theft, fire, or any other cause. Landlord assumes no liability for any such loss. Landlord recommends that Tenants obtain a renters' insurance policy from a recognized insurance firm to cover Tenants' liability, personal property damage, and damage to the premises.

20. Waterbeds. No waterbed or other item of water-filled furniture may be kept on the premises without Landlord's written consent.

☐ Landlord grants Tenants permission to keep water-filled furniture on the premises. Attachment _____: Agreement Regarding Use of Waterbed is attached to and incorporated into this Agreement by reference.

21. Tenant Rules and Regulations

☐ Tenants acknowledge receipt of, and have read a copy of, tenant rules and regulations, which are labeled Attachment _____ and attached to and incorporated into this Agreement by reference. Landlord may change the rules and regulations without notice.

22. Payment of Attorney Fees in a Lawsuit. In any action or legal proceeding to enforce any part of this Agreement, the prevailing party ☐ will not/ ☒ will recover reasonable attorney fees and court costs.

23. Authority to Receive Legal Papers. Any person managing the premises, the Landlord and anyone designated by the Landlord are authorized to accept service of process and receive other notices and demands, which may be delivered to:

☐ a. the manager, at the following address and telephone number: _____

_____

_____

☐ b. the Landlord, at the following address and telephone number: _____

_____

_____

☐ c. the following:

_____

_____

_____

_____

24. Additional Provisions

☐ a. None

☐ b. Additional provisions are as follows:

_____

_____

25. State Database Disclosure. Notice: The California Department of Justice, sheriff's departments, police departments serving jurisdictions of 200,000 or more and many other local law enforcement authorities maintain for public access a database of the locations of persons required to register pursuant to paragraph (1) of subdivision (a) of Section 290.4 of the Penal Code. The database is updated on a quarterly basis and is a source of information about the presence of these individuals in any neighborhood. The Department of Justice also maintains a Sex Offender Identification Line through which inquiries about individuals may be made. This is a "900" telephone service. Callers must have specific information about individuals they are checking. Information regarding neighborhoods is not available through the "900" telephone service. (Civil Code § 2079.10a)

Property built on or after January 1, 1973. If your property was built after 1973, you may have no choice. State law prohibits landlords of such property from refusing to rent to (or renew leases with) tenants because they have waterbeds, or refusing to allow tenants to use waterbeds, if:

- the tenant obtains a replacement-value $100,000 waterbed insurance policy

- the pressure the waterbed puts on the floor does not exceed the floor's pounds-per-square-foot weight limitation (as stated above, this should be no problem for dwellings constructed after 1973)

- the waterbed is held together by a pedestal or frame

- the tenant installs, maintains and moves the waterbed in accordance with the standards of the manufacturer's retailer or state, whichever are more stringent

- the tenant gives the landlord at least 24 hours' written notice of his intention to install, move, or remove the waterbed, and allows the landlord to be present when this occurs

- the waterbed conforms to construction standards imposed by the State Bureau of Home Furnishings and displays a label to that effect, and

- the waterbed was constructed after January 1, 1973. (CC § 1940.5.)

If your property was built before 1973 and you wish to ban waterbeds, you may cross off the words "without Landlord's written consent."

If you choose to allow waterbeds, or your property was built in 1973 or later and your tenant plans to have a waterbed, check the box and complete the self-explanatory fill-in-the-blanks Attachment: Agreement Regarding Use of Waterbed, which is provided in Appendix B. Remember to fill in the number of the attachment.

Security deposits may be increased. You can charge a higher security deposit for tenants with waterbeds, equal to an additional one-half month's rent. (See Chapter 5.)

CLAUSE 21. TENANT RULES AND REGULATIONS

❑ Tenants acknowledge receipt of, and have read a copy of, tenant rules and regulations, which are labeled Attachment _____ and attached to and incorporated into this Agreement by reference. Landlord may change the rules and regulations without notice.

Many landlords don't worry about detailed rules and regulations ("R and Rs"), especially when they rent single-family homes or duplexes. However, in large buildings, rules are usually important to control the use of common areas and equipment.

Check the box if you plan to use tenant rules, and fill in the attachment number. Remember to also label the rules and regulations with the attachment number. This clause gives you the authority to evict a tenant who persists in seriously violating your code of tenant rules and regulations.

The final sentence in Clause 21 gives you the right to vary your rules and regulations, and to do so without needing to give notice. A word of caution here: Don't be tempted to push key provisions of the rental into your R and Rs, thinking that doing so enables you to change them at will (which you can't do when the provision is in a lease or rental agreement attachment). A judge will see this ruse for what it is and will side with a tenant who protests when, for example, you ban pets in your R and Rs (but the tenant's lease says nothing about pets). Instead, use your R & Rs to spell out day-to-day details of how your building works, as explained below in "What's Covered in Tenant Rules and Regulations."

WHAT'S COVERED IN TENANT RULES AND REGULATIONS

Tenant rules and regulations typically cover issues such as:

- elevator safety and use
- pool rules
- garbage disposal and recycling times and places
- parking garage regulations
- lockout and lost key charges
- security system use
- excessive noise
- pet behaviaor
- use of grounds
- maintenance of balconies and decks (for instance, no drying clothes on balconies)
- display of signs in windows, and
- laundry room rules.

CLAUSE 22. PAYMENT OF ATTORNEY FEES IN A LAWSUIT

In any action or legal proceeding to enforce any part of this Agreement, the prevailing party ❑ will not/ ❑ will recover reasonable attorney fees and court costs.

Many landlords assume that whenever they sue a tenant over the interpretation of the lease (or to enforce it) and win, the court will order the losing tenant to pay the landlord's attorney fees and court costs, such as filing fees and deposition costs. However, this is true only if a written agreement specifically provides for it. This is why it can be important to have an "attorney fees" clause in your lease. That way, if you hire a lawyer to bring an eviction suit and win, the judge will order your tenant to pay your attorney fees.

By law, an attorney fees clause in a lease or rental agreement works both ways. (CC § 1717.) That is, if your tenants prevail in a lawsuit, and the lease or written rental agreement contains such a clause, you must pay their "reasonable attorney fees" in an amount determined by the judge. This is true even if the clause is worded so that it requires payment of attorney fees only by the tenant if you win and not vice-versa.

Maybe you don't want to provide for attorney fees. Some landlords choose not to allow for attorney fees because of their experience that money judgments against evicted tenants are very often uncollectible. So, in practice, the clause does not help the landlord. And such a clause may hurt him, because it works both ways: If the landlord loses a lawsuit, the landlord pays the tenant's attorney fees, and that judgment *will* be collectible. Also, attorney fees clauses don't cover all legal disputes. They cover fees only for lawsuits that concern the meaning or implementation of a rental agreement or lease—for example, a dispute about rent, security deposits, or your right to access (assuming that the rental document includes these subjects). An attorney fees clause would not apply in a personal injury lawsuit.

If you intend to do your own legal work in any potential eviction or other lawsuit, even if the tenant hires a lawyer, you will almost surely conclude that it is wiser not to allow for attorney fees. You don't want to be in a situation where you'd have to pay the tenant's attorney fees if the tenant wins, but the tenant wouldn't have to pay yours if you won because you didn't hire a lawyer.

If you don't want to allow for attorney fees, check the first box before the words "will not" and cross out the word "will."

If you want to be entitled to attorney fees if you win—and you're willing to pay attorney fees if you lose—check the second box before the words "will recover" and cross out the words "will not."

CLAUSE 23. AUTHORITY TO RECEIVE LEGAL PAPERS

Any person managing the premises, the Landlord, and anyone designated by the Landlord are authorized to accept service of process and receive other notices and demands, which may be delivered to:

❑ a. the manager, at the following address and telephone number:

_____

_____

❑ b. the Landlord, at the following address and telephone number:

_____

_____

❑ c. the following:

_____

_____

_____

By law, you must give your tenants information about everyone who is authorized to receive rent and notices and legal papers, such as lawsuits from the tenants. (CC §§ 1961-1962.7.) For this purpose, you must provide the name, phone number, and street address of:

• the manager, if any, or any other person who receives rent payments, and

• you or someone else you authorize to receive notices and legal papers on your behalf.

These written disclosures, as well as ones regarding where and how rent must be paid (Clause 5, above) are required even if the agreement is oral. You must provide this information to the tenant within 15 days of entering into an oral rental agreement, and once each year (if asked) on 15 days' notice. Since you must use a written document to convey this

information, you may as well use the written rental agreement we provide. In the meantime, if your agreement with your tenant is oral, use the language above and in Clause 5 to draft the required written disclosure.

Do you trust your manager? It's unwise to have a manager you don't trust receive legal papers on your behalf. You don't, for example, want a careless apartment manager to throw away a notice of a lawsuit against you without informing you. That could result in a judgment against you and a lien against your property in a lawsuit you didn't even know about. (For more information on using property managers, see Chapter 6.)

CLAUSE 24. ADDITIONAL PROVISIONS

❑ a. None

❑ b. Additional provisions are as follows: _____

_____

_____

_____

_____.

In this clause, you may list any additional provisions you want to address in the lease or rental agreement. If there are no additional provisions, check "a."

If you want to include additional clauses in your lease or rental agreement, check "b." For example, if you agree that the unit will be repainted before the tenant moves in, with you supplying the paint and painting supplies and the tenant contributing labor, you could add a clause to the rental agreement like the one shown below.

EXAMPLE

Landlord will pay for up to $150 worth of paint and painting supplies. Tenant will paint the living room, hall and two bedrooms, using off-white latex paint on the walls, and water-based enamel on all wood surfaces (doors and trim). Paint and supplies will be picked up by Tenant from ABC Hardware and billed to Landlord.

ADDITIONAL PROVISIONS YOU MAY WANT TO ADD

Some landlords find it helpful to spell out exactly how they expect their tenants to take care of the premises. Here are some key areas:

- **smoke detectors (frequency for checking and replacing batteries):** "Tenants agree to test all smoke detectors at least once a month and to report any problems to Landlord in writing. Tenants agree to replace all smoke detector batteries as necessary."

- **yard work and other maintenance:** "Tenants agree to regularly water and maintain the grounds, including lawn, shrubbery, and flowers."

- **rules for taking care of furniture or other items on the premises:** "Tenants will keep the hot tub covered when not in use. Tenants will use and clean the hot tub regularly, according to the manufacturer's instructions attached to this Agreement as Attachment 1."

- **smoking:** Landlords are increasingly specifying where, if at all, tenants and guests may smoke. You may want to prohibit smoking in all common areas ("Tenants and their business and social guests will not smoke in common areas, including the hallways, lobbies, garage, parking lot, pool area, or walkways") and even in individual units ("Tenants and their business and social guests will not smoke in Tenant's rented premises"). If your property offers a children's play area or a "tot lot" sandbox area, you must prohibit smoking within 25 feet. (H&S § 104495.)

CLAUSE 25. STATE DATABASE DISCLOSURE

Notice: The California Department of Justice, sheriff's departments, police departments serving jurisdictions of 200,000 or more, and many other local law enforcement authorities maintain for public access a database of the locations of persons required to register pursuant to paragraph (1) of subdivision (a) of Section 290.4 of the Penal Code. The database is updated on a quarterly basis and is a source of information about the presence of these individuals in any neighborhood. The Department of Justice also maintains a Sex Offender Identification Line through which inquiries about individuals may be made. This is a "900" telephone service. Callers must have specific information about individuals they are checking. Information regarding neighborhoods is not available through the "900" telephone service." (Civil Code Sec. 2079.10a)

Every lease or rental agreement must include this disclosure. You need not add anything here.

CLAUSE 26. GROUNDS FOR TERMINATION

The failure of Tenants or Tenants' guests or invitees to comply with any term of this Agreement, or the misrepresentation of any material fact on Tenants' Rental Application, is grounds for termination of the tenancy, with appropriate notice to Tenants and procedures as required by law.

This clause states that any violation of the lease or rental agreement by the tenants, or by the tenants' business or social guests, is grounds for terminating the tenancy, according to the procedures established by state or local laws. Making the tenants responsible for the actions of their guests can be extremely important—for example, you'll want to be able to take action if you discover that the tenant's family or friends are dealing illegal drugs on the premises or have damaged the property. Chapter 12 discusses terminations and evictions for tenant violations of a lease or rental agreement.

This clause also tells the tenant that if he has made false statements on the rental application concerning an important fact—such as his prior criminal history—you may terminate the tenancy. You don't need to add any language to this clause.

26. Grounds for Termination of Tenancy. The failure of Tenants or Tenants' guests or invitees to comply with any term of this Agreement, or the misrepresentation of any material fact on Tenants' Rental Application, is grounds for termination of the tenancy, with appropriate notice to Tenants and procedures as required by law.

27. Entire Agreement. This document constitutes the entire Agreement between the parties, and no promises or representations, other than those contained here and those implied by law have been made by Landlord or Tenants. Any modifications to this Agreement must be in writing signed by Landlord and Tenants.

_____   _____
Landlord/Manager   Date

_____
Landlord/Manager's Street Address, City, State & Zip

_____   _____
Tenant   Date

_____   _____
Tenant   Date

_____   _____
Tenant   Date

CLAUSE 27. ENTIRE AGREEMENT

This document constitutes the entire Agreement between the parties, and no promises or representations, other than those contained here and those implied by law, have been made by Landlord or Tenants. Any modifications to this Agreement must be in writing signed by Landlord and Tenants.

_____
Landlord/Manager   Date

_____
Landlord/Manager's Street Address, City, State & Zip

_____
Tenant   Date

_____
Tenant   Date

_____
Tenant   Date

This clause states that all important aspects of the rental deal between you and the tenant have been addressed in the lease or rental agreement. It protects you against any claim by the tenant that there were additional oral understandings that you must comply with. Similarly, you will not be able to claim that the tenant orally agreed to an important provision that's not reflected in the document. Finally, it establishes that any changes must be in writing.

D. HOW TO MODIFY AND SIGN FORM AGREEMENTS

Our lease and rental agreement forms have been designed to protect your broad legal interests, but they may not fit your exact situation. For example, if your building has a garage, you may want to incorporate rules in the lease or rental agreement regarding specific parking requirements.

1. Before the Agreement Is Signed

The easiest way to change a preprinted form agreement is to cross out unwanted portions and write in desired changes on the standard forms. With major alterations, you may retype one of our forms and add your own provisions. If you make fundamental changes, however, you may wish to have your work reviewed by an experienced landlords' lawyer. (See Chapter 8.)

If the changes are lengthy, use a separate sheet of paper. Type the same heading as used on the original document, identify the parties and make it clear that you are adding provisions to the lease or rental agreement. See "How to Prepare Attachment Pages," earlier in this chapter.

For example, if you agree that the unit will be repainted before the tenant moves in, with you supplying the paint and painting supplies and the tenant contributing labor, you could add a clause to the rental agreement like the one shown earlier (Clause 24).

2. Signing the Lease or Rental Agreement

At the end of the lease or rental agreement, there's space to include the signature and street address at which the landlord and anyone authorized to manage the premises may be personally served with legal papers. There's also space for the tenants' signatures.

Be sure your tenants review the lease or rental agreement before signing and are clear about all your terms and rules and regulations. Chapter 7 discusses how to get your new tenancy off to the right start.

If you've altered a standard form by writing or typing in changes, be sure that you and all tenants initial the changes when you sign the document.

Give each tenant a copy of the signed lease or rental agreement.

3. After the Agreement Is Signed

All amendments to your lease or rental agreement must be in writing to be legally binding.

If you want to change one or more clauses in a month-to-month rental agreement, there is no legal requirement that you get the tenant's consent (although it's always a good idea to do so). You can simply send the tenant a 30-day notice of the change, unless a local rent control ordinance requires more notice or prohibits the change you want to make. (However, if the change is a rent increase of more than 10%, you must give 60 days' notice, as explained in Chapter 14.) However, if you use

Amendment to Lease or Rental Agreement

This is an Amendment to the lease or rental agreement dated ___March 18___, 20_OX_ (the "Agreement")

between ___Olivia Matthews___ ("Landlord")

and ___Steve Phillips___ ("Tenants")

regarding property located at ___123 Flower Lane, San Diego, California___

_____ ("the premises").

Landlord and Tenants agree to the following changes and/or additions to the Agreement:

1. Beginning on June 1, 200X Tenant shall rent a one-car garage, adjacent to the main premises, from Landlord for the sum of $75 per month.

2. Tenant may keep one German Shepherd dog on the premises. The dog shall be kept on a leash in the yard unless Tenant is present. Tenant shall clean up all animal waste from the yard on a daily basis.

Tenant agrees to repair any damages to the yard or premises caused by his dog, at Tenant's expense.

In all other respects, the terms of the Agreement shall remain in effect.

Olivia Matthews
_____
Landlord/Manager

May 20, 200X
_____
Date

Steve Phillips
_____
Tenant

May 20, 200X
_____
Date

_____
Tenant

_____
Date

_____
Tenant

_____
Date

a lease, you cannot unilaterally change the terms of the tenancy. We discuss the mechanics of changing terms of a rental agreement by use of such notice in Chapter 14.

If you wish to make mutually agreed upon changes to a written rental agreement or lease after it is signed, there are two good ways to accomplish it. The first is to agree to substitute a whole new agreement for the old one. The second is to add the new provision as an amendment to the original agreement. An amendment need not have any special form, so long as it clearly refers to the agreement it's changing and is signed by the same people who signed the original agreement.

You'll find a tear-out version of the Amendment to Lease or Rental Agreement in Appendix B. The CD-ROM that accompanies this book also includes this form. A sample is shown above.

E. COSIGNERS

Some landlords require cosigners on rental agreements and leases, especially when renting to students who depend on parents for much of their income. The cosigner signs a separate agreement or the rental agreement or lease, under which she agrees to pay any rent or damage-repair costs the tenant fails to pay.

1. The Practical Value of a Cosigner

In practice, a cosigner's promise to guarantee the tenant's rent obligation often has little value, because the threat of eviction is the primary factor that motivates a tenant otherwise reluctant to pay the rent. The problem is, you cannot sue a cosigner along with the tenant in an eviction suit. The cosigner must be sued separately either in a regular civil lawsuit or in small claims court. So as far as going after the cosigner on the tenant's rent obligation is concerned,

your best weapon—the possibility of an eviction lawsuit—is unavailable.

Another legal obstacle to enforcing of a cosigner's promise is that the promise is not enforceable if the lease or rental agreement has been changed without the cosigner's written approval. See *Wexler v. McLucas,* 48 Cal. App. 3d Supp. 9 (1975). Even the simple renewal of a lease involving the signing of a new document by the landlord and the tenant (but not by the cosigner) will eliminate the cosigner's liability—so may a rent increase or other change in the terms of tenancy. Taking this one step further, a court might refuse to hold a cosigner liable for any period beyond that of the original lease term, where the tenancy has since become a month-to-month agreement. Since lease expirations, renewals, and rent increases usually occur over the life of a residential tenancy, a landlord who foregoes the nuisance of getting the cosigner's signature every time an element of the tenancy changes may wind up with a worthless promise.

In sum, the benefits of having a lease or rental agreement cosigned by someone who won't be living on the property are almost entirely psychological. A tenant who thinks you can look to the cosigner—usually a relative or close friend of the tenant—may be less likely to default on the rent. Similarly, a cosigner asked to pay the tenant's debts may persuade the tenant to pay.

2. Cosigners and Disabled Applicants

Because of the practical difficulties associated with cosigners, many landlords refuse to consider them, which is legal in every situation but one: If a disabled tenant with insufficient income (but otherwise suitable) asks you to accept a cosigner who will cover the rent if needed, you must relax your blanket rule at least as far as investigating the suitability of the proposed cosigner. If the proposed cosigner is solvent and stable, federal law requires you to accommodate that applicant by allowing the cosigner, despite your general policy. (See Chapter 9, Section C for more on accommodating disabled applicants and tenants.)

3. Accepting Cosigners

If you decide to accept a cosigner, you may want to have that person fill out a separate rental application and agree to a credit check—after all, a cosigner who has no resources or connection to the tenant will be completely useless. Should the tenant and the prospective cosigner object to these inquiries and costs, you may wonder how serious they are about the guarantor's willingness to stand behind the tenant. Once you are satisfied that the cosigner can genuinely back up the tenant, add a line at the end of the lease for the dated signature, phone, and address of the cosigner.

F. ILLEGAL LEASE AND RENTAL AGREEMENT PROVISIONS

Because some landlords have drafted leases and rental agreements that contained provisions that attempted to take away various tenant protections of California law, the Civil Code now expressly forbids the use of many types of illegal provisions. (CC § 1953.)

Unfortunately, a few landlords still intentionally include illegal provisions to try to intimidate tenants. Doing this is counterproductive, because a lease or rental agreement containing too many illegal clauses may be disregarded in its entirety should you ever end up in court. In addition, several district attorneys have sued landlords who routinely and flagrantly use leases with illegal clauses. As a result, several landlords have been fined.

1. Waiver of Rent Control Laws

Cities that have rent control ordinances specifically forbid lease or rental agreement provisions by which a tenant gives up (or waives) any rights granted by the rent control ordinance. California's statewide rent control law, which limits the ability of cities to impose certain aspects of rent control (such as vacancy control), does nothing to change this rule. Thus, any rental agreement provision excusing the landlord from complying with rent ceilings or just-cause-for-eviction requirements would be of no legal effect. Moreover, attempting to do so may result in fines and even criminal prosecution.

See Chapter 4 for a detailed discussion of rent control.

2. Liquidated Damages Clauses

If your tenant breaks an important lease provision or house rule, such as the promise to use only a certain parking space, and you suffer economic damages as a result of the tenant's lease violation, you can sue the tenant to recoup those losses. For example, a tenant who deliberately uses the parking spot reserved for delivery trucks, making it impossible for supplies to be delivered, could reasonably be asked to cover your cost of sending your manager to pick up the supplies offsite.

Landlords sometimes attempt to deter tenant rule breaking, and save themselves a trip to court, by announcing in the lease or rental agreement—in advance of any misbehavior by the tenant—that violations of lease clauses or rules and regulations will result in a predetermined monetary penalty. The effect of a clause like this is to put a definite money value on the violation, regardless of the *actual* monetary damages suffered by the landlord. In legalese, these clauses are called "liquidated damages" clauses, and they are generally illegal in residential rental contracts in California. (CC § 1671.) You may use them only if it would be extremely difficult to measure the actual damages—if and when they occur. But landlords are rarely in this position—if your tenant violates a lease provision that ends up costing you money, you can usually calculate the amount after the dust has settled—which means that a liquidated damages clause is rarely legal in your business.

This said, the fact is that many California landlords routinely use liquidated damages clauses in their leases and rental agreements—and get away with it. Practically speaking, if the amount you charge is reasonably close to your actual losses, a tenant gains little by challenging it. The reason: A judge might throw out the clause, but you can still sue for your actual damages—which means that, in the end, the tenant will end up paying your actual losses if you can prove your case. The lesson here is that if you choose to use a liquidated damages clause, be fair and reasonable when setting the amount.

EXAMPLE

Martin allowed his tenants to keep dogs, but because he was concerned about his landscaping, he wanted to make sure the dogs were on leash at all times. The pet clause in Martin's lease specified a $100 fee if a tenant's dog was observed off leash, and a $150 fee for subsequent incidents.

Sonya's terrier Moka got loose one day and tore up a tulip bed near the rental office. When Martin attempted to collect, Sonya protested, arguing that there was much less than $100 worth of damage. Martin sued in small claims court, but the judge agreed with Sonya and awarded Martin only $50, representing the actual cost of replacing the bulbs and one hour of the gardener's time for replanting.

The next time Martin spied Moka on the loose, he got smart. Since his lease provided that repeated and serious violations of the lease were grounds for termination, Martin terminated Sonya's lease.

3. Waiver of Repair-and-Deduct Rights

Landlords must maintain and repair their rental property in accordance with certain minimum standards. (CC § 1941.) If a landlord refuses to do so, a tenant may arrange for certain repairs and deduct the cost from the next month's rent. (CC § 1942.) Further, a tenant cannot give up or modify those rights in a lease or rental agreement. (CC § 1942.1.)

There is one exception to this rule, however: If the tenant specifically agrees to repair and maintain all or part of the property in exchange for lower rent, the repair-and-deduct rule can be waived. Although in principle this would seem to be a broad exception, it is not broad in practice. Judges look to see if the tenant's promise to keep the premises in repair was really in exchange for lower rent and was not just a way for the landlord to avoid legal responsibilities. Chances are the tenant's waiver will be upheld if, in the written lease, a tenant handy with tools agrees to repair or maintain the property in exchange for rent that's considerably lower than fair market rent, but not otherwise.

Following is an example of a valid clause that could be included in your lease or rental agreement.

EXAMPLE

Tenants agree to be responsible for all routine repairs and maintenance to the premises covered by this lease in exchange for a monthly rent of $900. This amount is approximately $200 less than the fair market rent for the premises, which is agreed to be $1,100.

All said and done, we advise against this sort of arrangement. For one thing, even if you include this provision, it doesn't relieve you of your obligation to the city or county to comply with local housing codes. You retain this obligation even if tenants breach a rental agreement or lease provision requiring them to maintain the premises in compliance with city and county regulations. In other words, the city and county have no interest in what you and the tenant agree to, but will hold you responsible if there is a code violation problem.

A better approach is this: If you want your tenant to fix up the property, fine, but pay the tenant by the hour or the job for work agreed on in advance. It's better to pay the tenant separately and collect the regular market rent. That way, if you're unhappy with the tenant's work, you can simply fire the tenant and still be entitled to the full rent. If, on the other hand, you agree to reduce the rent in exchange for work, you may be stuck for a long time with reduced rent in exchange for the tenant's poor-quality work. (Chapter 11 discusses landlords' liability and tenants' repair-and-deduct rights in detail.)

4. Right of Inspection

A landlord can't just walk in any time to inspect or repair the property or to show it to prospective renters or buyers. Except in an emergency, the law requires a landlord to give a tenant reasonable notice, which is generally 24 hours (though you must give 48 hours' notice when scheduling an initial move-out inspection). Nevertheless, some leases and rental agreements have provisions that purport to allow a landlord to enter with little or no notice. This type of provision is illegal. (CC § 1953.) (Chapter 13 covers landlords' right of entry and tenants' privacy.)

5. Provision That the Landlord Is Not Responsible for Tenant Injuries or Injuries to a Tenant's Guests

Often called an "exculpatory clause," this provision says that if the landlord fails to maintain the property and the tenant or her guests suffer injury or property damage as a result, the landlord can't be held responsible for paying for the loss. This provision is void and of absolutely no use to a landlord, and will not be upheld in court if a tenant or a guest suffers personal injury or property damage that results from the landlord's negligence. (For more on landlords' liability, see Chapter 12.)

6. Provision Giving Landlord Self-Help Eviction Rights

Some leases and rental agreements contain a clause that appears to allow the landlord to come in and throw the tenant out, or at least change the locks and remove her property, if she doesn't pay the rent. This clause is void. (CC § 1953.) If you do resort to illegal

means to evict a tenant, this type of clause won't protect you in a tenant's lawsuit for unlawful eviction. No matter what the lease says, you have to sue and get a court order to remove an unwilling tenant legally. (See Chapters 17 and 18 and *The California Landlord's Law Book: Evictions* for details on evictions.)

7. Waiver of Right to Legal Notice, Trial, Jury, or Appeal

A lease or rental agreement clause under which a tenant gives up any procedural right in a lawsuit you or the tenant might bring to enforce the lease or rental agreement is also void. This protects the tenant's right to proper service of a Three-Day Notice to Pay Rent or Quit (three-day notice periods cannot be reduced by agreement) or other termination notice, and the right to present a defense in a lawsuit, trial by jury, appeal, and so on. (CC § 1953.) You also cannot include a clause forcing the tenant to submit personal injury claims to binding arbitration (though if a dispute or a lawsuit were to develop over such an issue, you and the tenant could always agree later to abide by binding arbitration). (*Jaramillo v. JH Real Estate Partners, Inc.*, 3 Cal.Rptr.3d 525 (2003).) The *Jaramillo* case leaves you free to require in the lease or rental agreement that tenantability claims (habitability claims raised under Civil Code § 1941.2) be handled through binding arbitration, but we strongly recommend against doing so. By the time you're done with arbitration (including, if you win, a trip to court to record the arbitrator's decision), you may as well have initiated an eviction lawsuit.

8. Waiver of Right to Deposit Refund

A landlord must, within three weeks after the tenant vacates the property, mail the tenant a refund of his deposit or, if the deposit is not completely refunded, a written itemization as to how it was applied to back rent, costs of cleaning, repairs, and the like. (See Chapter 20 for details on returning security deposits.) Any provision waiving or modifying the tenant's rights in this respect is void and of no effect. (CC § 1953.)

9. Restricting Tenants' Access to Other Tenants' Units for Distributing Literature

A clause in a lease or rental agreement that attempts to prevent or restrict a tenant from communicating with other tenants (for the purpose of organizing a tenants' association, for example) is illegal. However, under very limited circumstances, you may be able to legally limit the posting or dropping of flyers or other advertisements, political in nature or not, on, near, or under tenants' doors. Proceed with extreme caution, however. The California Supreme Court has ruled that a landlord may properly forbid the posting and delivery of flyers only where access to common hallways is forbidden to all solicitors, where locked doors secure common hallways from visitors, and only if the lease, rental agreement, or properly distributed house rules or regulations clearly state the prohibition. (*Golden Gateway Center v. Gateway Tenants' Assn.*, 26 Cal.4th 1013 (2001).) Because this exception is so limited and this area is fraught with serious potential liability, we recommend that you contact a lawyer before attempting to limit access in this manner. Better still, especially if tenants are organizing in opposition to you, meet with them (and use a mediator if necessary) and deal with their concerns directly.

10. Shortening the Termination Notice Period

As we saw earlier in Section C, above, regarding Clause 4 of our form Agreement, your ability to shorten the notice periods when terminating a month-to-month tenant has been curtailed. If the tenant has resided in the unit for a year or more, you must give 60 days'; and for all others, you must give 30 days' notice. A court will not enforce any shorter periods—in other words, if you file an eviction lawsuit based on the tenant's refusal to move following your too-short notice period, your case will be tossed out of court by the judge and you'll have to start over, with the correct notice period.

11. Other Illegal Provisions

Just because a particular type of lease clause isn't listed above doesn't mean it's legally enforceable. Courts can and do exercise the power to refuse to enforce what they consider to be illegal or outrageous clauses in leases and rental agreements. Some examples: provisions for excessive late charges (discussed in Chapter 3), and shortcuts the landlord can use to recover possession if he believes the property to be abandoned (covered in Chapter 21). Also, the legality of certain provisions may depend on such factors as the date your property was built (see, for example, Clause 20 of our lease or rental agreement regarding waterbeds). ■

3

BASIC RENT RULES

To state the obvious, one of your foremost concerns as a landlord is receiving your rent—on time and without hassle. It follows that you need a good grasp of the legal rules governing rent.

In this chapter, we review California's basic rent laws. However, several topics we discuss in other chapters can affect your rights under these laws, including:

Condition of the premises. If a landlord fails to fulfill his obligation to keep up the premises, the tenant's duty to pay rent is affected correspondingly. Under state law, a tenant may claim that the landlord's failure to repair and maintain the property justifies withholding rent. The validity of such claims, and the amount of rent, if any, that can legally be withheld may ultimately be determined by a judge in an eviction lawsuit. We discuss this process in detail in Chapter 11.

How and when you notify tenants of rent increases. Chapter 14 describes the legal process for raising rents.

How you enforce rent payments. You can give tenants who don't pay their rent on time a Three-Day Notice to Pay Rent or Quit. We show you how in Chapter 16.

Local rent control laws. Fifteen California cities have rent control ordinances that dictate how much rent you can charge (and cover many other aspects of your business). These ordinances are in turn affected by a statewide law, the Costa-Hawkins Rental Housing Act. We discuss rent control in Chapter 4.

Cities With Rent Control Ordinances

Berkeley	Oakland
Beverly Hills	Palm Springs
Campbell (mediation only)	San Francisco
East Palo Alto	San Jose
Fremont (mediation only)	Santa Monica
Hayward	Thousand Oaks
Los Angeles	West Hollywood
Los Gatos	

A. HOW MUCH CAN YOU CHARGE?

There is no state or federal law that dictates how much rent landlords can charge. In other words, you can legally charge as much rent as you want (and a tenant will pay) unless your premises are subject to a local rent control ordinance. You may wish to check newspaper want ads for comparable rents in your area, or contact local real estate and property management companies.

Many wise landlords choose to charge slightly less than the going rate as part of a policy designed to find and keep excellent tenants.

As with any business arrangement, it usually pays in the long run to have your tenants feel they are getting a good deal. In exchange, you hope the tenants will be responsive to your needs as a landlord. This doesn't always work, of course, but it's our experience that tenants who feel their rent is fair are less likely to complain over trifling matters. Certainly, it's obvious that tenants who think you are trying to squeeze every last nickel out of them are unlikely to think twice before calling you about a clogged toilet at 11 p.m.

B. WHEN RENT IS DUE

Most lease and rental agreements, including the ones in this book, call for rent to be paid monthly, in advance, on the first day of the month. The first of the month is customary and convenient because many people get their paychecks on the last workday of the month, just in time to pay rent on the first of the following month. Also, beginning a new month itself reminds people to pay monthly bills that are due on the first. (Hopefully, your tenant will learn to associate flipping the calendar page with paying the rent on time.)

It is perfectly legal to require rent to be paid on a different day of the month, which may make sense if the tenant is paid at odd times. Some landlords make the rent payable each month on the date the tenant first moved in. We think it's easier to prorate rent for a short first month and then require that it be paid on the first of the next month. (See Chapter 7, Section C.) But if you only have a few tenants, and don't mind having different tenants paying you on different days of the month, it makes no legal difference.

You are not legally required to have your tenant pay rent on a monthly basis. If you wish, you and the tenant can agree that the rent be paid twice a month, each week or on whatever schedule suits you. The most common variation on the monthly payment arrangement is having rent paid twice a month. This is a particularly good idea if you have tenants who receive government benefits or who have relatively low-paying jobs and get paid twice a month. Such tenants may have difficulty saving the needed portion of their mid-month check until the first of the month.

If your rental agreement (whether written or oral) is for an unspecified term (as opposed to a lease for a specific period), you should be aware that the length of time between rent payments affects other important rights. Specifically, the notice period you must give your tenant in order to change the terms of the tenancy or terminate it (and the notice the tenant must give you) is normally the same number of days as the period between rent payments—typically 30 days. (CC §§ 827(a), 1946, 1946.1.) This is true un-

less your rental agreement specifically establishes a different notice period, or a local rent control ordinance changes the rules on termination (a topic covered in Chapter 4). This general rule also applies to the notice period you must give your tenants to raise the rent, subject, of course, to any rent increase limitations of local rent control ordinances. In addition, you must give 60 days' notice of a rent increase of more than 10%, as explained in Chapter 14. (CC § 827(b).)

EXAMPLE 1

On March 10, landlord Marion Carty signs a month-to-month rental agreement with Carol Tomson. Carol rents an apartment for $550, payable on the tenth day of each month. Because the interval between rent payments is a month, Marion must give Carol at least 30 days' written notice if she wants to raise the rent, change any other term of the rental agreement or terminate the tenancy. (However, Carol is entitled to 60 days' notice of termination if she stays for a year or more, as explained in Chapter 18, Section A.) If Carol wants to leave, she too must give 30 days' notice to Marion.

EXAMPLE 2

Ken Tanaka rents out rooms on a weekly basis, with the rent payable every Friday. Because the interval between rent payments is one week, Ken must give his tenants one full week's notice if he wishes to raise the rent or have them move out. So for a rent increase or termination of tenancy to take effect the following Friday, Ken must give his tenants written notice to that effect no later than the Friday before.

Once you have established the rental amount and the day of payment, you should insist that rent be paid in advance to cover the following month or other period. For example, rent should be due on the first day of the month for that month, and it should be paid on or before that day. It may seem obvious to require tenants to pay rent in advance. You would probably never consider allowing a tenant who moved in on the first day of the month to wait to pay rent until the 31st. We belabor this point because California law, following an ancient rule traceable to feudal times, states that in the absence of an agreement to the contrary, rent is due at the end of the rental term. (CC § 1947.) In other words, unless the agreement states that rent is due in advance, you may have trouble getting the tenant to pay at the beginning of the rental period.

1. Weekends and Holidays

If the rent due date specified in a lease or rental agreement falls on a weekend or holiday, the rule is that the tenant must still pay on the due date specified in the agreement. For example, if the lease says that rent is due on the first day of each month, it is due on January 1st, even though that day is a holiday, New Year's Day. As another example, if the rent is due on the 15th day of the month, but one month that day falls on a Saturday or Sunday, the rent is still legally due on the 15th. Although some laws might be read to give the tenant an extension of time to pay the rent if the due date falls on a weekend or holiday (CC §§ 7,11, CCP Sec. 12a), the courts have ruled that these laws do not extend rent deadlines under a lease or rental agreement. (*Gans v. Smull* (2003) 111 Cal.App.4th 985 (2003).)

Of course, if the lease or rental agreement specifically gives the tenant the option of paying rent on the next business day—as do the lease and rental agreements in this book—then the due date will be extended as provided in the rental document. (Returning to the example in the paragraph above, under the Nolo lease and rental agreement, for example, rent would be due on January 2, as long as that day is a weekday. If January 1 is a Friday, however, rent isn't due until the following Monday.) In the absence of a "next business day" provision, the lease means what it says as far as the date on which the rent is due.

Figuring the exact due date isn't really all that important unless you have to file an eviction lawsuit based on the tenant's nonpayment of the rent, where counting days correctly can be crucial. Chapter 16 covers starting the eviction process with a Three-Day Notice to Pay Rent or Quit; evictions are covered in detail in *The California Landlord's Law Book: Evictions*.

2. Grace Periods

Now let's clear up a giant myth. Lots of tenants are absolutely convinced that if they pay by the 5th (or sometimes the 7th or even the 10th) of the month, they have legally paid their rent on time and should suffer no penalty because they are within a legal grace period. Some states give tenants a grace period, but not California. Quite simply, there is no law in California that gives tenants a five-day or any other grace period when it comes to paying the rent. As we'll discuss more thoroughly in Chapter 16, a landlord can legally proceed with the first step necessary to evict a tenant—serving a Three-Day Notice to Pay Rent or Quit—the day after the rent is legally due but unpaid.

In practice, most tenants get a grace period, because landlords usually don't get upset about late rent until it's more than a few days late, and many rental agreements and leases do not begin assessing the tenant late charges until at least five days after the due date. But you are definitely within your legal rights to insist that the rent be paid on the day it is due. In our opinion, if you wait more than five days to collect your rent, you are running your business unwisely, unless your particular circumstances warrant a longer period.

C. WHERE AND HOW RENT IS DUE

You should specify in your lease or rental agreement where and how the tenant should pay the rent. (See Clause 5 in Chapter 2, Section C.) Some form rental agreements require the rent to be paid personally at the landlord's place of business. This makes the tenant responsible for getting the rent to the landlord or manager at a certain time or place, and avoids issues such as whether or not a rent check was lost or delayed in the mail.

You should also specify whether rent should be paid by cash, check, or money order. Some landlords, concerned with security and the need to write receipts, accept checks only. Others are more concerned about bounced checks and will accept only cash, certified checks, or money orders.

Some landlords require tenants to deposit the rent into the landlord's bank account. Because of the difficulty of tracking deposits—and stopping them if necessary after terminating a tenancy—we urge you not to accept rent this way. If you must do this, your lease or rental agreement should specify the name and street address of the bank or other financial institution where rent deposits are to be made. The place of deposit must be within five miles of the property. (CC § 1962, CCP § 1161(2).)

Once in a while, when relations between a landlord and a tenant are beginning to break down for other reasons, there will be misunderstandings about where and how the rent must be paid. Sometimes a landlord who's been burned by bounced checks from a particular tenant will suddenly demand nothing less than cash or a certified check or money order, and that rent may be paid only during certain hours at the manager's office.

Be careful. It may be illegal to suddenly change your terms for payment of rent—unless you are simply enforcing an existing term. For example, if your agreement states that you only accept cash or a money order, you are on solid ground when you tell a check-bouncing tenant that you'll no longer accept checks, and that your previous practice of doing so was merely an accommodation not required of you under the rental agreement.

If, however, your lease or rental agreement doesn't say where and how rent is to be paid, the law states that past practice generally controls how rent is paid until you properly notify the tenant of a change.

It's not a good practice to accept rent by mail, except as an accommodation where the lease or rental agreement requires rent to be paid personally to the landlord or manager. In the absence of a provision requiring tenants to pay rent in person, a landlord's practice of accepting rent by mail may enable the tenant to continue paying by mail, and to claim "the check's in the mail" in response to a Three-Day Notice to Pay Rent or Quit. If you want to require tenants to pay rent at your office, home, or other place, you should specify that in the lease or rental agreement, along with the days and hours someone will be present to accept the rent. If you want to change your practice and the tenancy is month to month, you must formally change the agreement with a written 30-day notice.

If you rent under a lease, you will have to wait until the lease runs out and change your terms for payment of rent in the new lease.

Now suppose you wish to make a change with regard to whether the rent must be paid by cash or check. The past-practice rule stated above doesn't apply in this case. The law presumes that a lease that doesn't specify how rent is to be paid requires the rent to be paid in cash. (Strom v. Union Oil Co., 88 Cal. App. 2d 78, 84, 198 P.2d 357 (1948).) So, if you don't want to continue accepting a tenant's checks, simply notify her of this fact, in writing. This kind of notice is effective immediately.

You should not accept postdated checks under any circumstances. A postdated check is legally a note promising to pay on a certain date. If you accept a postdated check, you have accepted a note, rather than cash, for the rent, and a tenant facing eviction could argue that you accepted the "note" in lieu of cash.

RENT "ALLOTMENTS" FROM SERVICEMEMBERS

If your tenant is a member of the United States military, you may be asked to accept a direct deposit, called an allotment, from the tenant's military pay. The procedure is explained in the Military Pay Manual, Chapter 42, Sections 4201 and following. Servicemembers can use an online tool, called "My Pay," to set up and change allotments.

Keep in mind that this rent payment method is not much different than agreeing that rent will be transferred directly from the tenant's bank account to yours, described earlier in this section. We cautioned against this rent payment method, since it's difficult to track (and stop) such payments. On the other hand, it is convenient for servicemembers who are overseas to pay the rent this way (and the allotment is taken out before the balance of the paycheck is available to the servicemember). Should you decide to accept allotments, be sure you understand how they work and whether the transfer can be timed to coincide with the rent due date.

D. LATE CHARGES

A common and effective way to encourage tenants to pay the rent on time is to impose a late charge or fee. You may be wondering how a preset late fee can withstand the ban on liquidated damages explained in Chapter 2, Section F. After all, it's often simple enough to calculate the interest you've lost on that late rent and the time you spent reminding the tenant to pay up. Since you can measure those actual damages when they occur, you should charge the tenant for them only after they occur.

Well, that's what we think, and an ancient but still valid case actually says so. (*Jack v. Sinsheimer*, 125 C 563 (1899).) But this hasn't stopped legions of landlords from imposing *reasonable* late fees and getting away with it. If your preset late fee in fact

corresponds to what your actual damages are likely to be, a tenant has little incentive to challenge it, since the tenant would be liable for the actual damages anyway. How you label the consequence of being late with the rent makes little difference to your tenant, as long as it's fair.

Some cities with rent control ordinances explicitly regulate the amount of late fees. Check any rent control ordinances that affect your properties.

For these reasons, you must be very careful how you structure your late fee policy. Your fee should correspond as closely as possible to the real monetary consequences of getting the rent late. You should be on safe footing as long as you follow these principles:

- The late charge should not begin until after a reasonable grace period of three to five days. Imposing a stiff late charge if the rent is only one or two days late may not be upheld in court.

- If you use a flat fee, it should not exceed 4–6% of the rent ($30 to $45 on a $750-per-month rental). A late charge much higher than this (say, a 10% charge of $75 for being one day late with rent on a $750-per-month apartment) would probably not be upheld in court.

- If you adopt a late charge that increases with each additional day of lateness, it should be moderate and have an upper limit. A late charge that increases without limit each day could be considered interest charged at a usurious rate. (Ten dollars a day on a $1,000 per month rent is 3650% annual interest.) A more acceptable late charge would be $10 for the first day rent is late, plus $5 for each additional day, with a maximum late charge of 4%–6% of the rental amount.

- Don't try to disguise excessive late charges by giving a "discount" for early payment of rent. One landlord we know concluded he couldn't get away with charging a $50 late charge on a late $425 rent payment, so, instead, he designed a rental agreement calling for a rent of $475 with a $50 discount if the rent was not more than three days late. Ingenious as this ploy sounds, it is unlikely to stand up in court, unless the discount for timely payment is very modest. Giving a relatively large discount is in effect the same as charging an excessive late fee, and a judge is likely to see it as such and throw it out.

Anyway, we think all this fooling around with late charges is wasted energy. If you want more rent for your unit, raise the rent (unless you live in a rent control area). If you are concerned about tenants paying on time—and who isn't—put your energy into choosing responsible tenants. Be consistent about enforcing rent due dates, following through with a Three-Day Notice to Pay Rent or Quit—the first legal step in a possible eviction—no later than six or seven days after the rent is due.

If you have a tenant with a month-to-month tenancy who drives you nuts with late rent payments, and a reasonable late charge doesn't resolve the situation, terminate the tenancy with a 30-, 60-, or 90-day notice, as described in Chapter 18.

Local rent control ordinances may regulate the way you handle a termination. If you can't use a 30-, 60-, or 90-day notice, either because the tenant has a lease or because rent control laws are too restrictive, serve the tenant with a Three-Day Notice to Pay Rent or Quit the day after the rent is due, and follow through with an eviction if the rent isn't paid in full within the three-day period.

E. RETURNED CHECK CHARGES

In Chapter 2, we suggest a rental agreement provision requiring the tenant to pay bad check charges equal to what the bank charges you, plus a few dollars for your trouble (Clause 7 in Chapter 2, Section C). State law sets a limit of $25 for the first bounced check and

$35 for subsequent checks. (CC § 1719.) State law also provides that anyone who fails to pay a bounced check is liable for a penalty equal to three times the amount of the check up to $1,500, plus the amount of the check, plus service charge. However, this penalty can be collected only by waiting 30 days after sending the person who wrote the check a demand letter, then filing a regular civil lawsuit in superior court or small claims court. This law is of little use to landlords for two reasons:

- First, a landlord faced with a check-bouncing tenant should never wait 30 days, but should give the tenant a Three-Day Notice to Pay Rent or Quit right away, then sue for eviction if the tenant doesn't make the check good within three days.

- Second, even if a landlord served both a Three-Day Notice to Pay Rent or Quit on the tenant, plus a 30-day bad check demand letter, he would have to file two separate lawsuits: a fast-moving unlawful detainer lawsuit for eviction, and a regular civil lawsuit for the bounced check penalty. Two lawsuits are necessary because the law doesn't allow landlords to ask for any money other than rent in eviction lawsuits.

Don't call bounced check fees "additional rent," thinking you can collect them with the rent. This ploy might work for commercial leases, but it won't get you very far with a residential tenancy.

It's better to serve the tenant a three-day notice demanding the rent (but not a late charge or bad check charge) as soon as you find out a tenant's check bounces. Then follow through with an eviction lawsuit—well before 30 days has passed—and forget about penalties you may ultimately be unable to collect anyway.

Don't redeposit rent checks that bounce. It is a poor idea to let your bank redeposit rent checks that bounce, something they will normally do unless you request that bad checks be returned to you immediately instead. Why should you prevent resubmissions? For two excellent reasons. The first is that it alerts you to the fact that the rent is unpaid much sooner than if the check is resubmitted and returned for nonpayment a second time. You can use this time to contact the tenant to ask that the check be made good immediately. If it is not, you can promptly serve a three-day termination notice. (See Chapter 18.)

The second reason that you want to get the check back quickly is that, if it is resubmitted and again there are insufficient funds to cover it, the normal bank procedure is to punch holes in it. If this is done, the check can never again be presented for payment. If it's returned to you before it is punched, however, you can hold on to it. Even after you succeed in evicting the tenant for nonpayment, or after the tenant has just voluntarily left, you can periodically call the tenant's bank over the next few months to see if enough funds have been deposited to cover it. In a surprising number of instances, a tenant will eventually put more money in the account, often giving you the chance of collecting your money by cashing the check.

Eviction warning! Do not demand late charges or bad check charges when you give a tenant a Three-Day Notice to Pay Rent or Quit. We discuss the proper procedures for giving a written three-day notice preceding an eviction lawsuit in Chapter 16.

F. PARTIAL RENT PAYMENTS

On occasion, a tenant suffering a temporary financial setback will offer something less than the full month's rent, with a promise to catch up in partial payments as the month proceeds, or full payment at the first of the next month. Although generally it isn't good business practice to allow this, you may wish to make an exception where the tenant's financial problems truly appear to be temporary and you have a high regard for the person. But we recommend that you verify a tenant's hard-luck story by asking questions and then checking the story out by

calling the hospital, the employer, or anyone else the tenant says can back her up.

1. Routinely Accepting Partial Payment

There is generally no legal problem if you accept partial rent payments. If you accept less than a full month's rent from a tenant, you certainly do not give up the right to the balance. Indeed, you can normally accept a partial payment one day and demand full payment the next. Even the words "paid in full" on a tenant's check can be ignored if you're careful: You will not lose your right to more money owed you by cashing the tenant's check if you cross out the offending language before you cash the check. (CC § 1526.)

If you regularly accept rent in installment payments (despite a written agreement that rent is due in one payment in advance), you may have legally changed the terms of your rental agreement.

EXAMPLE

You routinely allow your tenant Larry, whose $800 rent is due on the first of the month, to pay $400 on the first and the other $400 on the 15th. Nine months later, you get tired of this arrangement. After receiving $400 on the first day of the month, you give Larry a three-day notice on the second of the month to pay the rest of the rent or quit. This may not work. You may be stuck with getting $400 on the first and $400 on the 15th for the balance of the term of the lease or, in the case of a written or oral rental agreement, until you give him a written notice of change in the terms of tenancy. (See Chapter 14.) Why? Because a judge in an eviction lawsuit may rule that, by giving Larry this break every month for almost a year, coupled with his reliance on your practice, you in effect changed the terms of the lease or rental agreement. Viewed this way, your three-day notice to pay the full rent or leave would be premature, because the second $400 isn't due until the 15th.

If the tenancy is from month to month, you can reinstate the original payment terms by "changing" the terms back to what the rental agreement says they are,

---

Notice of Reinstatement of Terms of Tenancy

To: __Sam Jones__ ,
          Name

Tenant(s) in possession of the premises at __123 Fourth Street__ ,
                                          Street Address

City of __Los Angeles__ , County of __Los Angeles__ ,
California.

When you rented the premises described above, the rental agreement specified that your rent would be due and payable on the first day of each month. Although the undersigned has allowed you to vary this payment arrangement, your late rental payments can no longer be tolerated.

Therefore, please be advised that effective 30 days from the date of service on you of this notice, your monthly rent will be due and payable on the first day of the month, for that month.

Roy Jefferson   _August 12, 200X_
Landlord/Manager   Date

---

with a 30-day written notice. A sample form is shown above. You don't have to worry about this problem if you accept partial payments only a few times on an irregular basis. And accepting partial payments more often than this really isn't good landlording anyway, unless you truly are willing to change the terms of the lease or rental agreement. If you are, do it in writing.

You'll find a tear-out version of the Notice of Reinstatement of Terms of Tenancy in Appendix B. The CD-ROM that accompanies this book also includes this form.

2. Accepting Partial Payment After a Three-Day Notice

It's a trickier situation if you accept partial rent payments after giving the tenant a three-day notice to pay the rent in full or quit. The basic legal rule is this: If your tenant responds to a three-day notice with less than the amount stated in the notice, you can either refuse to accept it or accept the lesser amount and serve a new three-day notice demanding the balance. You probably cannot accept the partial payment and base an eviction lawsuit on the original three-day notice. This is simply because the law requires that in any eviction lawsuit you file, the rent that's past due as of the date of filing must be the same as the rent demanded in the three-day notice.

For example, if you served a notice demanding the rent of $600, and the tenant paid $500, you would be filing a defective eviction suit based on a $600 three-day notice when only $100 was due. Also, any acceptance of rent by the landlord after serving the tenant a three-day notice is considered a waiver of the breach complained of in the notice, so that a new notice, demanding only the balance, would have to be given. This is more fully explained in _The California Landlord's Law Book: Evictions_, which provides step-by-step advice on how to do your own evictions.

3. Written Agreements to Accept Late Rent

If you do give a tenant a little more time to pay, monitor the situation carefully. You don't want to provide extension after extension, until the tenant is three months in arrears with no chance to bring the account current. One way to prevent this is to put a payment schedule in writing. This binds you—you can't get mad at the tenant and demand the rent or initiate an eviction lawsuit sooner. But more important, it also gives both you and the tenant a benchmark against which to measure the tenant's efforts to catch up on the rent. If you give the tenant two weeks to catch up but the rent remains unpaid, the written agreement precludes any argument that you had really said "two to three weeks."

If the tenant does not pay the rest of the rent when promised, you can, and should, follow through with a Three-Day Notice to Pay Rent or Quit (covered in Chapter 16) and, if need be, initiate an eviction lawsuit if payment is still not forthcoming.

4. Oral Agreements to Accept Late Rent

Don't rely on an oral agreement with a tenant who promises to catch up on back rent. To be legally binding, an oral agreement must include a promise by the tenant to give you something over and above a promise to pay rent already due. For example, the tenant could agree to pay a late fee.

EXAMPLE 1

Nancy approaches her landlord Robin with a sad story about needing to send money to her ailing mother. Nancy asks if she can pay half the rent on the first of the month (the day it is due) and the remaining half two weeks late. Robin agrees, but nothing is written and Nancy does not promise to provide any extra payment or other advantage in exchange for Robin's forbearance. The next day, Robin finds out Nancy has lost her job and been arrested for possession of cocaine. He asks her to pay the full rent immediately. This is legal. Nancy's original promise was not legally binding because Robin made no promise in exchange for it.

EXAMPLE 2

Now let's change this example slightly and assume that in exchange for the right to pay half of the rent late, Nancy promised to sweep the parking lot twice a week and turn on the pool filter every morning. Now, Nancy and Robin have entered into a valid contract, and Robin has a legal obligation to stick to his end of the bargain as long as Nancy honors her agreement.

Agreement for Partial Rent Payments

This Agreement is made between _____ Betty Wong _____,

hereinafter "Tenant(s)," and _____ John Lewis _____,

hereinafter "Landlord/Manager," who agree as follows:

1. That _____ Betty Wong _____

    Tenant(s)

    has/have paid __ one-half of her $500 rent for Apartment #2 at 111 Billy St., Fair Oaks, CA __

    _____

    on ___ March 1 _____, 20 OX , which was due _____ March 1 _____, 20 OX .

2. That _____ John Lewis _____

    Landlord/Manager

    agrees to accept all the remainder of the rent on or before ___ March 15 _____, 20 OX and to hold off

    on any legal proceeding to evict ___ Betty Wong _____

    Tenant(s)

    until that date.

_John Lewis_____   _March 2, 200X_____
Landlord/Manager   Date

_Betty Wong_____   _March 2, 200X_____
Tenant   Date

_____   _____
Tenant   Date

_____   _____
Tenant   Date

4

RENT CONTROL

California has no statewide law establishing rent control, nor does it have a state law preventing rent control. Consequently, cities may (and have) establish rent control on a local basis, either through the initiative process or by the act of a city council. However, California does have a state law that restricts the ability of local governments if they wish to enact rent control for their localities. This law, called the Costa-Hawkins Rental Housing Act, forbids the imposition of any rent control on new tenancies in single-family homes and condos (applies to tenancies that began after January 1, 1996) and requires that controls on rent be lifted when there is a voluntary vacancy or a vacancy following an eviction for a good reason (such as nonpayment of rent). (CC §§ 1954.50 to 1954.53.)

Some form of rent regulation now exists in 15 California cities. You'll need to read this chapter if your property is located in a city with rent control ordinances; see the list below.

Cities With Rent Control Ordinances

Berkeley	Oakland
Beverly Hills	Palm Springs
Campbell (mediation only)	San Francisco
East Palo Alto	San Jose
Fremont (mediation only)	Santa Monica
Hayward	Thousand Oaks
Los Angeles	West Hollywood
Los Gatos	

Rent control ordinances generally control more than how much rent a landlord may charge. For example:

- Many cities' ordinances also govern how—and under what circumstances—a landlord may terminate a tenancy, even one from month to month, by requiring the landlord to have just cause to evict.

- Several cities, most notably Los Angeles, require landlords to register their properties with a local rent control agency.

- Finally, several cities regulate security deposits (by requiring interest) and impose notice requirements for rent increases and termination of tenancies that are different from the state law requirements we discuss in Chapters 5, 14, 16, and 18.

No two rent control ordinances are identical, even as to how rents may be increased. For example, some cities have elected or appointed boards that have the power to adjust rents; others automatically allow a certain percentage rent increase each year as part of their ordinances. We review basic rent control provisions in this chapter and how they compare among cities. We summarize each city's ordinance in a Rent Control Chart in Appendix C.

Get up-to-date information. Cities change their rent control laws frequently, and court decisions also affect them. In short, you should read the material here to get a broad idea of rent control. If the property you rent is in a city that has rent control, it is imperative that you also contact your city or county to get an up-to-date copy of the ordinance and any regulations interpreting it. Your city's website will likely also have useful information. (See the website information in Appendix C.)

A. PROPERTY EXEMPT FROM RENT CONTROL

Not all rental housing within a rent-controlled city is subject to rent control. Under state law, property that was issued a certificate of occupancy after February 1995 is exempt from rent control. (CC § 1954.52.) Furthermore, almost all cities have exempted from rent control any "new construction" built after the effective date of the ordinance. Most cities also exempt owner-occupied buildings with four (or sometimes three or two) units. A few cities also exempt "luxury units" that rent for more than a certain amount. And as of January 1, 1999, all tenancies for single-family homes and most condos are exempt under state law if the tenancy began after January 1, 1996.

Unfortunately, an ordinance can sometimes be ambiguous, leaving the landlord and tenant to wonder whether or not the property is covered. If the local rent board can't give you a straight answer—or you're reluctant to contact them—you may need to consult an attorney who's familiar with your community's rent control ordinance.

B. LOCAL RENT CONTROL ADMINISTRATION

Most rent control ordinances are administered by a rent control board whose members are appointed (elected in Santa Monica and Berkeley) by the mayor or city council (board of supervisors in San Francisco). In some cities, these boards determine the amount of an allowable across-the-board rent increase each year, applicable to all properties covered by the ordinance. They also conduct individual hearings where landlords seek an additional increase over and above that amount. As a general rule, appointed boards are more evenhanded than elected ones. The name, address and phone number of each board is given in the Rent Control Chart in Appendix C.

C. REGISTRATION OF RENTAL PROPERTIES

The cities of Berkeley, East Palo Alto, Los Angeles, Palm Springs, Santa Monica, Thousand Oaks and West Hollywood all require the owners of rent-controlled property to register the property with the agency that administers the rent control ordinance. This allows the rent board to keep track of the city's rental units, as well as to obtain operating funds from the registration fees.

These cities forbid landlords who fail to register their properties from raising rent. In fact, cities may require a landlord to refund past rent increases if the increases were made during a period in which the landlord failed to register property. The courts have ruled that it is unconstitutional for rent control ordinances requiring registration to allow tenants to withhold rents just because the property isn't registered. (*Floystrup v. Berkeley Rent Stabilization Board,* 219 Cal. App. 3d 1309 (1990).)

Some cities, including Berkeley and Santa Monica, impose fines on landlords who fail to register property. However, both of these types of penalties are now limited by a state law (CC § 1947.7) in cases where the landlord's failure to register was not in bad faith and was quickly corrected (that is, the landlord registered the property) in response to a notice from the city. To make things easier for landlords who make honest mistakes, state law now requires cities to allow landlords to phase in, over future years, any rent increases that would have been allowed had the property been registered, if the following conditions are met:

- the landlord's original failure to register the property was unintentional and not in bad faith

- the landlord has since registered the property as required by the city and paid all back registration fees, and

- the landlord has paid back to the tenant any rents collected in excess of the lawful rate during the time the property wasn't properly registered.

EXAMPLE

Three years ago, Carla bought a triplex in a rent control city. She planned to live in one of the units three months out of the year, and rent it out the other nine months. Carla had been advised by her family lawyer that her property was "owner occupied," and thus not subject to registration or rent controls, even though she only lived there three months out of the year. Each time Carla rented her property to a new tenant for nine months, she increased the rent by 10%. She also increased the rent for the other units each year. A tenant complained to the rent board, which determined the property should have been registered. Since it hadn't been registered, Carla's three years of rent increases were illegal, and the proper rent was what she charged three years before. If Carla registers the property and refunds the excess rent she collected to all her tenants, she can phase in the increases the city would have allowed during her three years, had the prop-

erty been registered. The city can't fine Carla for failure to register her property because she had acted in good faith on the poor advice of a lawyer.

This law is fairly complicated, as are the typical local ordinances and regulations in cities that require registration of units. Should you run afoul of your city's rent control board and be faced with having to refund back rent increases for a substantial period or pay other substantial penalties, you should probably see a lawyer familiar with the local rent control ordinance and regulations.

D. RENT FORMULA AND INDIVIDUAL ADJUSTMENTS

Each city has a slightly different mechanism for allowing rent increases. All cities allow periodic (usually yearly) across-the-board increases for existing tenants. The amount of the increase may be set by the rent control board, or the ordinance may allow periodic increases of either a fixed percentage or a percentage tied to a local or national consumer price index.

1. Mild Rent Control

Rent control is considered mild in the Bay Area cities of San Jose, Hayward, and Los Gatos. To begin with, none of these cities' ordinances require landlords to register units with the board.

Although the rent control ordinances of these areas set forth a certain formula (usually fairly generous, in the 5%–8% range) by which rents can be increased each year, it is possible for landlords to raise the rent above this figure and still stay within the law. Each of these cities' ordinances requires a tenant whose rent is increased above the formula level to petition the board within a certain period (usually 30 days) and protest the increase. If no tenants protest the increase within the time allowed, the increased rent is legally effective, even though it is higher than the formula increase. If a tenant protests the increase, then the board schedules a hearing to decide if the entire increase should be allowed.

RENT MEDIATION

Some cities, most notably the Bay Area cities of Campbell and Fremont, have adopted voluntary rent guidelines or landlord/tenant mediation services. Voluntary guidelines, of course, do not have the force of law. However, it's often an excellent idea for you to comply with voluntary rent guidelines or to handle a dispute by mediation. The alternative may be hiring a lawyer to sue a tenant who refuses to pay a rent increase and going to court to obtain a money judgment you may never collect.

Keep in mind that several cities have rent control at least in part because some landlords completely ignored voluntary guidelines and mediation services, causing tenants to show up at polls and support rent control in record numbers.

We discuss mediation in more detail in Chapter 8.

---

2. Moderate-to-Strict Rent Control

Unlike the practice in cities with mild rent control, landlords in cities with moderate-to-strict rent control bear the burden of petitioning the rent board for an above-formula rent increase and of justifying the need for such an increase based on certain cost factors listed in the ordinance, such as increased taxes or capital improvements. These cities also require the landlord to show a good reason (called "just cause"—see Section H) to evict a tenant.

The rent control laws of Los Angeles, San Francisco, Beverly Hills, Oakland, Palm Springs, and Thousand Oaks have traditionally been considered "moderate," while the rent control laws of Berkeley, East Palo Alto, Santa Monica, and West Hollywood have been considered "strict."

Until 1996, the main difference between moderate and strict rent control was that cities with the moderate approach allowed a landlord to raise the rent when a tenant vacated the property voluntarily or was evicted for just cause. This was known as "vacancy decontrol." Strict rent control cities did not allow for such increases (these cities practiced "vacancy control"). But, as of January 1, 1996, state law requires all cities to allow vacancy decontrol. (CC § 1954.53.) (We discuss vacancy decontrol in more detail in Section G, below.) This means there is now little difference between rent control in moderate cities and rent control in strict cities. (One of the remaining differences is that landlords in strict rent control cities must register their properties with the rent control board. Berkeley and Santa Monica also allow tenants to petition for lower rents based on a landlord's failure to maintain or repair rental property.)

Landlords may not, however, raise rents (even after a voluntary vacancy or eviction for cause) where the landlord has been cited for serious health, safety, fire or building code violations that the landlord has failed to remedy for six months preceding the vacancy. (CC § 1954.53(f).)

3. Hearings and Rent Adjustments

Almost all cities with rent control have a hearing procedure to handle certain types of complaints and requests for rent adjustments. The hearing procedures are described in detail in Section I, below.

4. Rent Agreed to by the Tenant

In cities with moderate and strict rent control, which require the landlord to petition the board before increasing the rent over a certain amount, a landlord can't circumvent the ordinance by having the tenant agree to an illegal rent. Even if a tenant agrees in writing to pay a higher rent and pays it, he can sue to get the illegal rent back. (*Nettles v. Van de Lande*, 207 Cal. App. 3d Supp. 6 (1988).) This cannot happen, however, in cities with mild rent control that require the tenant to object to a rent increase or have it go into effect.

E. SECURITY DEPOSITS

Several local rent control ordinances require landlords to keep security deposits (including "last month's rent") in interest-bearing accounts and to pay interest on them. See "Other Features" in the Rent Control Chart in Appendix C for details on various cities' deposit laws.

F. CERTIFICATION OF CORRECT RENT LEVELS BY BOARD

Cities that require registration must certify in writing, on request of the landlord or tenant, the correct rent level for the property under state law. (CC § 1947.8.) When the landlord or tenant requests such a certificate from the board, the board must send copies to both the landlord and tenant. Each of them then has 15 days to file an appeal with the board challenging the rent level, by filing a written notice on a form available from the board. The board must then decide the appeal within 60 days. If the certificate rent level is not appealed by the landlord or tenant within 15 days, it cannot be challenged later, except by the tenant if the landlord was guilty of intentional misrepresentation or fraud with regard to information supplied to the city in the request for the certificate.

G. VACANCY DECONTROL

Landlords now have free rein to raise the rent when a unit is vacated. This feature, called vacancy decontrol, is required by state law as of January, 1999. In practice, it means that rent control applies to a particular rental unit only as long as a particular tenant (or tenants) lives there. If that tenant voluntarily leaves or is evicted for nonpayment of rent, the property will be subject to rent control again after the new (and presumably higher) rent is established. But in Hayward, Palm Springs, and Thousand Oaks, the property is no longer subject to rent control following a voluntary vacancy.

The effect of this state law is unclear where the tenant is evicted for a reason other than nonpayment of rent (such as a violation of a lease clause). City ordinances with their own vacancy decontrol provisions generally allow increases, but state law doesn't seem to do so. So if your property is subject to rent control (and is not in Hayward, Palm Springs, or Thousand Oaks), check with your rent board before increasing rents following a vacancy for a lease violation (or illegal act) other than nonpayment of rent.

Tenants may try to get around vacancy decontrol. Some tenants try to keep the rent low by unofficially subletting part or all of the premises to a new tenant, who may in turn sublet to someone else, and so forth. Under some rent control ordinances, a landlord cannot raise the rent, and cannot evict the tenant, unless the lease or rental agreement forbids subleasing or assignment without your permission (as ours does). (See Clause 10 of our form agreements in Chapter 2.) As long as subletting is a breach of the lease or rental agreement, you can legally evict tenants who sublet, or, under the Costa-Hawkins law, you can legally raise the rent in accordance with the formula. A landlord's consent to a sublease cannot be unreasonably withheld. However, if the tenant's subleasing of the property is designed to circumvent the rent control ordinance's provision for higher rent when occupancy changes, the landlord's refusal to consent to the sublease isn't unreasonable. (For details on subtenants and subleasing, see Chapter 10.)

If, however, the tenant acquires a roommate, and you treat the new occupant as a tenant (by accepting rent from him or her, for example), you may not be able to raise the rent when the original tenant leaves. (CC § 1954.53(d).)

H. TENANT PROTECTIONS: JUST CAUSE EVICTIONS

Unfortunately, some unscrupulous landlords have sought to evict tenants solely in order to take advantage of vacancy decontrol. In other words, in order to charge more rent, which could only be done with a new tenancy, the landlord would evict the current tenant, often for little or no reason beyond the desire for more rent. To guard against such abuse, most rent control ordinances require the landlord to show "just cause" for eviction. Cities that require landlords to show just cause to evict require the landlord, for example, to give a reason for eviction in a notice terminating a month-to-month tenancy, even though state law does not require it. Under such just cause eviction provisions, the landlord must also prove the reason in a court proceeding.

Under CC § 1954.53(c), landlords whose property is subject to rent control may raise rents pursuant to state law only where the tenant left voluntarily or was evicted for nonpayment of rent. So, state law gives no advantage to landlords who evict for any reason other than nonpayment of rent.

Cities That Require Just Cause for Eviction

Berkeley	Palm Springs
Beverly Hills	San Francisco
East Palo Alto	Santa Monica
Hayward	Thousand Oaks
Los Angeles	West Hollywood
Oakland	

Note: San Jose and Los Gatos, two of the mild rent control cities, do not have just cause eviction. The ordinances, however, penalize a landlord who tries to evict a tenant in retaliation for asserting a tenant right. The tenant has the burden of proving that the landlord's motive was retaliatory. (See Chapter 15 for details on retaliatory evictions.)

Rent control ordinances that require just cause for eviction list acceptable reasons for eviction. The common reasons are discussed below.

See Chapter 18, Section C for more details and procedures on evicting tenants in rent control cities requiring just cause for eviction.

1. Tenant Violates Lease or Rental Agreement

If a tenant violates the lease or rental agreement, the landlord has just cause for eviction. The landlord must first serve the tenant with a three-day notice. (The particular type of notice depends on the violation—see Chapters 16 and 18.) City ordinances list violations that are just cause for eviction. Typical reasons are:

- Tenant has not paid rent after being served with a Three-Day Notice to Pay Rent or Quit. This is the most common way tenants violate their lease or rental agreement.

- Tenant continues to violate a lease or rental agreement provision, such as keeping a dog on the property in violation of a no-pets clause, after being served with a three-day notice to correct the violation or leave.

- Tenant has caused substantial damage to the premises and has been served with an unconditional three-day notice specifying the damage done and telling her to vacate. Some cities require the landlord to give the tenant the option of repairing the damage.

- Tenant is seriously disturbing other tenants or neighbors, and has been given a three-day notice specifically stating when and how this occurred.

Some cities require that the notice give the tenant the option of stopping the offending conduct.

- Tenant has committed an illegal activity on the premises and has been given a three-day notice setting forth the specifics. Minor illegal activity, such as smoking marijuana, is not sufficient cause, although dealing drugs is. In fact, landlords who fail to evict drug dealers can face serious liability. (See Chapter 12.)

Other activities which constitute cause for eviction include engaging in an illegal business (such as prostitution) or even an otherwise legal business that's in violation of local zoning laws, or overcrowding the unit in violation of local health codes.

Some just cause eviction provisions are more stringent than others. In Berkeley and Santa Monica, a tenant who violates a lease or rental agreement—for example, moves in too many people, damages the premises, makes too much noise—must first be notified of the problem in a written notice (often called a cease-and-desist notice) and given a "reasonable" time to correct it (even though state law does not always require this). What is reasonable depends on the circumstances. A tenant who makes too much noise should be able to stop doing so in a day at most, whereas a tenant who damages the premises by breaking a window might reasonably be given a week to fix the window. Only after such a notice is given, and the tenant still fails to correct the problem, can you evict the tenant for the lease or rental agreement violation, starting with a three-day notice.

2. Landlord or Immediate Family Member Wants to Move Into Rent-Controlled Property

All rent control cities that require just cause to evict allow a landlord to terminate a month-to-month or other periodic tenancy if the landlord wants to reside in the unit, or wants to provide it to a member of his immediate family. These cities generally require that no similar unit be available for the landlord or family member in the same or in another building the landlord owns, and that the landlord give the tenant a 30-day termination notice setting this out as the basis for eviction. San Francisco has a permanent moratorium on certain owner move-in evictions. For details, see the Rent Control Chart in Appendix C.

"Family member" is defined differently in different cities. In Berkeley and Santa Monica, family members include only parents and children. In cities with more inclusive definitions, such as San Francisco and Los Angeles, family members also include brothers, sisters, grandparents, and grandchildren. When property is owned by several people, either as co-tenants or through a joint venture, small corporation or partnership, cities have different ways of defining who qualifies for the status of a landlord for purposes of claiming priority over an existing tenant if they, or a family member, wish to live in the property.

There has been some abuse of this provision by landlords who evict a tenant claiming they or a family member wants to rent the premises, but then, after the tenant has moved out, simply move in a nonfamily member—at a higher rent. Under the Costa-Hawkins law, no rent increase is allowed unless the tenant leaves voluntarily or is evicted for nonpayment of rent. In response, cities have amended their ordinances, and the Legislature has passed a law, to impose fines on landlords who do this. State law requires that in rent-controlled cities that mandate registration, landlords who evict tenants on the basis of wanting to move a relative (or the landlord) into the property must have the relative actually live there for six continuous months. (CC § 1947.10.) Some cities impose a longer residence period (notably San Francisco, which requires three years). If the relative stays a shorter time, the tenant can sue the landlord in court for actual and punitive damages.

If a court determines that the landlord or relative never intended to stay in the unit, the tenant can move back in. The court can also award the tenant three times the increase in rent she paid while living somewhere else and three times the cost of moving back in. If the tenant decides not to move back into the old unit, the court can award her three times the amount of one month's rent of the old unit and three times the costs she incurred moving out of it. The tenant can also recover attorney fees and costs. (CC § 1947.10. See also *Zimmerman v. Stotter,* 160 Cal. App. 3d 1067, 207 Cal. Rptr. 108 (1984). In this case, the landlord had earlier won an eviction lawsuit, on the basis that he didn't use the phony relative ploy. Despite the landlord's win, the tenant was allowed to bring suit for damages, claiming that the landlord did use the phony relative ploy, although it didn't become obvious until after the tenant was evicted and the property rerented. The tenant won the case.) In another case, the court awarded a San Francisco tenant $200,000 for a wrongful eviction based on a phony relative ploy. *(Beeman v. Burling,* 216 Cal. App. 3d 1586, 265 Cal.Rptr. 719 (1990).)

3. Other Reasons for Just Cause Evictions

In cities that require landlords to show just cause for eviction, landlords can also terminate a month-to-month or other periodic tenancy for any of the following reasons. The landlord must, however, give the tenant a 30-day termination notice if the tenant has occupied the property for less than a year, 60 days' if the tenant has stayed a year or more and 90 days' for certain government-subsidized tenancies. The notice must specifically set forth the basis for the eviction.

- The tenant refuses to enter into a new lease containing the same terms as a previous expired one.

- The tenant refuses, following a written request, to allow the landlord to enter the premises when he has a right to do so. For example, the tenant refuses to allow the landlord access to fix a hazardous condition on the property, a reason for which the landlord has a legal right to enter. (See Chapter 13.)

- The landlord seeks to substantially remodel the property, after having obtained the necessary building permits. However, the current tenant must be allowed the right of first refusal to move back in after the remodeling is completed—at the original rent plus any extra "pass-through" increases allowed by the particular rent control ordinance. This provision is designed to allow the landlord to recoup part of the cost of capital improvements.

- The landlord, after having complied with any local condominium conversion ordinance and having applied for and received the necessary permits, seeks to convert an apartment complex to a condominium complex.

- The landlord seeks to permanently remove the property from the rental market under the "Ellis Act." For this type of termination, 120 days' notice is required, and if the tenant is disabled or a senior citizen, one year's notice is needed. (Government Code §§ 7060-7060.7.)

I. RENT CONTROL BOARD HEARINGS

Disputes over rent usually get hammered out in a hearing before the local rent board. The hearing may be initiated by a tenant who protests a rent increase over the formula amount in a mild rent control city, or by a landlord in a city that requires landlords to first obtain permission before exceeding the formula increase.

In either case, the landlord must demonstrate the need for a rent increase higher than that normally allowed. This most often means establishing that business expenses (such as taxes, maintenance, and upkeep costs or applicable utility charges), as well as the amortized cost of any capital improvements, make it difficult to obtain a fair return on the landlord's investment given the current rent.

1. Initiating the Hearing

A hearing is normally initiated by the filing of a petition or application with the rent board. In describing this process, let's assume that a landlord is filing a petition in a strict or moderate rent control city that requires landlords to obtain permission before raising rents above the formula increase allowed. This process is approximately reversed in mild rent control cities that require the tenant to protest such an increase.

In some cities, including Los Angeles and San Francisco, there are two types of petitions a landlord seeking an above-formula rent increase can file. If an increase is sought because of recent capital improvements, the landlord files a "petition for certification" of such improvements. If a rent increase is sought on other grounds, a "petition for arbitration" is filed. The rent board can tell you which document you need to file.

The application form will ask for your name and mailing address; the address of the property or properties for which you're seeking the increase, including the numbers of any apartments involved; the affected tenants' names and mailing addresses; the dollar amounts of the proposed increases; and the reason for the requested increase, such as higher repair, maintenance, or utility charges or pass-through of recent capital improvements. Make sure that your justification for an increase is specifically allowed by your local ordinance.

Usually, you must pay a nominal filing fee, often based on the number of units or properties for which an increase is being sought. After your application is filed and your fees paid, you and the tenant (who in some cities may file a written reply to your request) are notified by mail of the date and place of the hearing, usually within a few weeks. In Los Angeles, San Francisco, and some other cities, city employees may inspect your property before the hearing. You are, of course, well advised to cooperate as fully as possible with such inspections.

2. Preparing for the Hearing

As a general rule, you will greatly increase your chances of winning your rent increase if you appear at the hearing fully prepared and thoroughly familiar with the issues, and make your presentation in an organized way.

Here's how to prepare:

a. Obtain a copy of the ordinance and any applicable regulations for the area in which your property is located. Then determine which factors the hearing officer must weigh in considering whether to grant your request. For example, in San Francisco, the hearing board will consider the cost of capital improvements, energy conservation measures, utilities, taxes, and janitorial, security, and maintenance services. Your job is to show that the increase you are requesting is allowed by the rent control ordinance. Sometimes an outline on a 3" x 5" index card will help you focus.

b. Gather all records, including tax statements, employee pay statements, and bills for repairs, maintenance, and any other costs (remodeling, repairs, or other capital improvements) having to do with the property.

c. Be prepared to testify how each item of documentation relates to your monthly operating costs. Also be prepared to produce witnesses who are familiar with any items you think might be contested. For example, if you know tenants are likely to argue that you didn't make major improvements to the building when in fact you did, arrange for the contractor who did the work to appear at the hearing.

If for some reason your witness cannot appear in person, you may still present a sworn written statement or declaration from that person. The declaration should be as specific as possible, including a description of the work done, dates, costs and any other relevant information. At the end of the declaration, the contractor or other person should write, "I declare under penalty of perjury under the laws of the State of California that the foregoing is true and correct," putting the date and her signature afterward. A sample Declaration follows.

d. Before your hearing, go and watch someone else's hearing. (If your city's hearings are not open to the public, you can almost always arrange to attend as an observer if you call ahead.) Seeing another hearing may make the difference between winning and losing at yours. This is because both your confidence and your capabilities will grow as you understand what interests the hearing officers who conduct the hearing. By watching a hearing, you will learn that while they are relatively informal, all follow some procedural rules. It is a great help to know what the common practices are so you can swim with the current, not against it.

e. If you feel it's necessary, consult an attorney or someone else thoroughly familiar with rent board hearings to discuss strategy. You are permitted to have an attorney represent you at a rent adjustment hearing, but this is probably not a good idea. You might prefer to be represented by your apartment manager or management company. If you do a careful job in preparing your case, you will probably do as well alone as with a lawyer or other representative. And remember, hearing officers (and rent boards) are local citizens who may well react negatively to a landlord who pleads poverty at the same time he is obviously able to pay a lawyer to argue his case.

3. The Actual Hearing

Once you've prepared for the hearing, it's time to make your case. Here's how to be most effective.

a. Before the Hearing Begins

Arrive at the hearing room at least a few minutes before it is set to begin. Check in with the clerk or other official. Ask to see the file that contains the papers pertaining to your application. Review this material to see if there are any comments by office workers, rent board investigators, or your tenants. Read the tenants' comments very closely and prepare to answer questions from the hearing officer on any of the points they raise.

DECLARATION OF TERRY JARMAN, CONTRACTOR

I, Terry Jarman, Licensed Contractor, declare:

I am a general construction contractor, licensed by the California State Contractor's Licensing Board. My contractor's license number is A-1234567.

Between January 1 and February 1, 200X, I contracted with Maria Navarro, the owner of the apartment complex at 1234 Fell Street, San Francisco, to replace plumbing, heating, and electrical systems installed in the 1930s and to repair a roof that had developed numerous leaks over six of the apartment units. The total cost was $75,000, which Ms. Navarro paid me in full.

Pursuant to the contract, I engaged the necessary plumbing, heating, electrical, and roofing subcontractors to perform the necessary work, which was completed on February 1, 200X.

I declare under penalty of perjury under the laws of the State of California that the foregoing is true and correct.

_____   _____
Terry Jarman, Licensed Contractor   Date

As you sit in the hearing room, you will probably see a long table, with the hearing officer seated at the head. In a few cities, the hearing is held before several members of the rent board, and they may sit more formally on a dais or raised platform used by the city council or planning commission. In any event, you, any tenants who appear, your representative, and any witnesses will be asked to sit at a table or come to the front of the room.

A clerk or other employee may make summary notes of testimony given at the hearing. In some cities, hearings are taped. If under the procedure followed in your city no record is kept, you have the right to have the proceedings transcribed or tape recorded at your own expense.

b. The Hearing Officer's Role

Rent board hearings are usually heard by a "hearing officer" who is a city employee or volunteer mediator or arbitrator. In a few cities, hearings are conducted by the rent board itself, with the chairperson presiding over the hearing. The hearing officer or rent board chairperson will introduce himself or herself and any other people in the room. If you have witnesses, tell the hearing officer. The hearing officer, or sometimes an employee of the rent board, will usually summarize your application, taking the information from your file. At some point, you will be sworn to tell the truth; it is perjury to lie at the hearing. When these preliminaries are complete, you or your tenant, depending on who initiated the proceeding, will have an opportunity to speak. A rent adjustment hearing is not like court. There are no formal rules of evidence. Hearing officers will usually allow you to bring in any information that may be important, though it might not be admissible in a court of law. Relax and just be yourself.

c. Making Your Case

Present your points clearly, in a nonargumentative way. You'll normally have plenty of time to make your case, so don't rush. At the same time, don't get carried away in unnecessary details. The hearing officer may well ask you questions to help you explain your position. Make sure you present all documentary evidence and witnesses necessary to back up your case.

Later, the hearing officer will allow the tenant or the tenant's representative to present his case and to ask you questions. Answer the questions quietly. It is almost always counterproductive to get into an argument. Even if you feel the tenant is lying or misleading, don't interrupt. You will be given time later to rebut the testimony. Direct all your argument to the hearing officer, not to the tenant or his representative.

When your witnesses are given the opportunity to testify, the normal procedure is simply to let them have their say. You may ask questions if the witness forgets something important, but remember, this is not a court, and you don't want to come on like a lawyer. Very likely, the hearing officer will also ask your witnesses questions. The tenant has the right to ask the witnesses questions as well. Similarly, you have the right to ask questions of the tenant and any witnesses.

In rare instances, you may get a hearing officer or rent board chairperson who dominates the hearing or seems to be hostile to you or to landlords in general. If so, you will want to stand up for your rights without needlessly confronting the hearing officer. Obviously, this can be tricky, but if you know your legal rights and put them forth in a polite but direct way, you should do fine. If you feel that the hearing officer is simply not listening to you, politely insist on your right to complete your statement and question your witnesses.

Just before the hearing ends, the hearing officer should ask if you have any final comments to make. Don't repeat what you have already said, but make sure all your points have been covered and heard.

At the end of the hearing, the hearing officer will usually tell you when you can expect the decision. A written decision will usually be mailed to you within a few days or weeks of the hearing. Some cities, however, do not issue written decisions; the hearing officer just announces the decision at the end of the hearing.

Be assured that it is illegal for hearing officers and rent boards to unfairly penalize landlords who made innocent mistakes filing or serving legal notices. (CC § 1947.7.) A landlord's good faith ("substantial compliance") in attempting to obey an ordinance prevents a rent board from imposing penalties.

4. Appealing the Decision

In most cities in which applications for increases are heard by a hearing officer, you have the right to appeal to the full rent board if you are turned down. Your tenants have this same right if you prevail. A form for making an appeal will be available from the rent board.

If you make an appeal, you must file it within a certain time. You may or may not have the opportunity to appear in person before the rent board.

The rent board will probably take as truth the facts as found by the hearing officer and limit its role to deciding whether the hearing officer applied the law to these facts correctly. (There is an exception to this general rule in some cities. If you arranged for a typed transcript of the original hearing at your expense or have paid to have the tape recording of the hearing made by the hearing officer typed, the rent board may review it.) On the other hand, the rent boards of some cities (including Los Angeles) will allow the entire hearing to be held all over again. (This is sometimes called a "de novo" hearing.) In addition, the board will not usually consider any facts you raise in your statement that you could have brought up at the hearing but didn't. If you've discovered a new piece of information since the time of the first hearing, however, the board may consider the new information.

If your tenants are appealing and you are satisfied with the earlier decision, you will want to emphasize the thoroughness and integrity of the earlier procedure and be ready to present detailed information only if it seems necessary.

The entire rent board will generally have more discretion to make a decision than does a single hearing officer. If your case is unique, the entire board may consider the implications of establishing a new legal rule or interpretation.

If you again lose before the entire board, or if your city only permits one hearing in the first place, you may be able to take your case to court if you are convinced the rent board or hearing board failed to follow the law or their own procedures. However, if yours is a situation where the hearing officer or board has broad discretion to decide issues such as the one you presented, you are unlikely to get the decision overturned in court. Speak to an attorney about this as soon as possible, as there is a time limit (usually 30 days) on how long you can take to file an appeal in court.

J. Legal Sanctions for Violating Rent Control

When rent control laws were first adopted in the 1970s, many landlords came up with imaginative ways to circumvent them. In cities with vacancy decontrol, landlords began terminating month-to-month tenancies so that they could raise rents. As noted above, this caused localities to enact just-cause-for-eviction protections. Similarly, where ordinances allowed landlords to evict tenants in order to make major repairs to the property or move in themselves or move in relatives, some landlords used these reasons to evict, but didn't follow through. That is, after evicting their tenants, they made few, if any, repairs, or failed to move themselves or a relative in for any length of time.

EXAMPLE

After purchasing a duplex, a Los Angeles landlord immediately served a 30-day notice on the tenant, on the grounds that she (the landlord) wanted to move her mother into the unit. The landlord evicted the tenant, but did not move her mother into the vacant unit. Instead, the landlord put the duplex back on the market for a much higher price. The tenant who had been evicted sued the landlord for many thousands of dollars and ultimately received a substantial settlement.

Other landlords deliberately reduced services or adopted obnoxious behavior to encourage their tenants to leave "voluntarily." This, in turn, was followed by more amendments to close such loopholes, with landlords devising more refined ways to avoid the new rules, and so forth.

Many landlords did get rid of low-paying tenants and raised rents. However, newer rent control ordinances, as well as recent changes in state law, have closed many of the original loopholes and now assess heavy financial penalties against landlords who try to circumvent a rent control or just-cause-eviction ordinance, such as by evicting tenants on false grounds of moving in relatives. A court case in Los Angeles gives an example of how much these loopholes have been tightened. A group of tenants obtained a $1.7 million settlement against the new owner of a residential hotel. The tenants alleged that the owner tried to drive out low-income residents, in violation of Los Angeles' just cause eviction laws, to make way for higher-paying tenants. (*Clark Hotel Tenants' Assn. v. May Wah International Enterprises, Inc.*, Los Angeles County Superior Court No. C-725383 (L.A. Daily Journal, August 1, 1991).)

Here are other penalties landlords may face for violating rent control ordinances:

- The law allows a tenant to sue a landlord for having made her life miserable, under the legal theory of "intentional infliction of emotional distress." The landlord's repeated refusals to repair (see Chapter 11), privacy violations (see Chapter 13), or threats can be the basis for such a lawsuit. (*Newby v. Alto Rivera Apartments,* 60 Cal. App. 3d 288, 131 Cal. Rptr. 547 (1976).)

- All rent control ordinances (except Palm Springs's) forbid lease or rental agreement clauses where the tenant supposedly gives up or waives her rights under the law. Thus, lease clauses that say "tenant knowingly gives up all his rights under any applicable rent stabilization ordinance" are of no legal effect. (See Section D4 of this chapter, above.)

- State law provides that in rent-controlled cities that require registration, a landlord who charges illegally high rent can be sued by the tenant in court for up to three times the rent collected in excess of the certified level, plus attorney fees and costs. (CC § 1947.11.)

Don't count on your insurance company to defend you if you break rent control laws and are sued by your tenants. Berkeley landlords who evicted tenants under the pretense that they intended to move family members into the house were successfully sued by the former tenants after the landlords rented the unit to someone else. The landlords' attempts to get their insurance carrier to foot the bill (for lawyers' fees and the eventual settlement) were unavailing. The court ruled that the illegal eviction was not covered under the landlords' homeowners' insurance policy. (*Swain v. California Casualty Insurance Co.,* 99 Cal.App.4th 1 (2002).)

The best way to avoid the possibility of legal hassles is to forget about trying to circumvent the intent behind a rent control law, if indeed you ever thought about it. Be aware that tenants and rent boards have become more sophisticated in spotting and countering landlord maneuvers.

Be extra careful to avoid a "retaliatory eviction." The few cities that don't require just cause for evicting a tenant (see Section H, above) do forbid evictions intended to retaliate against a tenant who exercised rights under the rent control law—by objecting to an illegal rent increase, for example. State law forbids this, too. The tenant has to prove in court that the landlord's reason for eviction was retaliation. (See Chapter 15 and *The California Landlord's Law Book: Evictions*, which covers evictions in detail, including all the causes allowed for eviction in rent control cities.)

Save your energies for working toward a repeal or amendment of any rent control law you think is unfair. If you live in a strict rent control city, you may want to consider selling your properties and buying others in areas that make it easier for you to operate. This may not be as difficult to do as you might imagine, given the number of groups of unrelated adults who are purchasing housing together as tenants-in-common. ■

5

SECURITY DEPOSITS

Most landlords quite sensibly ask for a security deposit before entrusting hundreds of thousands of dollars worth of real estate to a tenant. But it's easy to get into legal trouble over deposits, because they are strictly regulated by state law, and sometimes also by city ordinance. State law dictates how large a deposit you can require, how you can use it, when you must return it, and more. Some cities also require landlords to pay interest on deposits, and a few require landlords to put deposits in a separate account. What's more, you cannot modify these terms—regardless of what you put in a lease or rental agreement. It goes almost without saying that it is absolutely essential that you know the laws on security deposits and that you follow them carefully.

Exception for short-term rentals. The rules on deposits discussed in this chapter do not apply to short-term rentals where the occupancy is for 30 days or less. Someone who frequently rents out a vacation house, for example, for short periods need not worry about the laws discussed in this chapter.

Related Topics

- Lease and rental agreement provisions on security deposits: Chapter 2

- Highlighting security deposit rules in a move-in letter to the tenant: Chapter 7

- Importance of insurance as a back-up to security deposits: Chapter 12

- Using 30-day notices to raise the security deposit: Chapter 14

- Procedures on returning tenants' deposits and how to deduct for cleaning, damages, and unpaid rent: Chapter 20.

A. SECURITY DEPOSITS MUST BE REFUNDABLE

In the eyes of the law, a security deposit is money that a landlord collects from a tenant and holds in case the tenant fails to pay the rent or does not pay for damage he's caused to the rental unit. It doesn't matter what the landlord calls this money—a "cleaning deposit," "pet fee," or "last month's rent"—it's legally a security deposit as long as it's held for that purpose *and* used for that purpose. In legal shorthand, failing to pay the rent and not paying for damage are known as "tenant defaults."

Landlords typically collect a security deposit when the tenant moves in, along with the first month's rent. But the first month's rent is not considered part of the security deposit—for the simple reason that this rent money is being paid on time. On the other hand, money collected in advance can cover the tenant's *last* month's rent, because the landlord holds it as a kind of insurance in case the tenant leaves without paying for the last month.

Just about any money the tenant pays up front is considered a security deposit, except the initial (usually first month's) rent payment and a legitimate credit check fee of up to $30.00. (See Chapter 1, Section C2, for more on credit check or other screening fees.) Any other money you collect up front for administrative costs associated with choosing tenants or moving them into a rental unit, whatever you call such fees (cleaning deposits, cleaning fees, administrative charges, or "tenant initiation expense reimbursement" (TIER) fees) is also a security deposit, which means it must be returned to the tenant. To put it another way, it is no longer legal to ask the tenant to pay administrative costs.

It's also illegal to charge a hidden nonrefundable deposit by charging considerably more rent for the first month than for later months. (*Granberry v. Islay Investments*, 9 Cal. 4th 738 (1995). Also see *People v. Parkmerced Co.*, 198 Cal. App. 3d 683, 244 Cal. Rptr. 22 (1988).) It is illegal to charge a fixed fee for cleaning drapes or carpets or for painting, or to charge administrative "move-in" fees. All such fees are legally considered security deposits and must be refundable.

Recoup your administrative costs in your rent, not through move-in fees. It is no longer legal to charge your tenants for your administrative costs. To cover these overhead expenses, set the rent high enough.

B. How Landlords May Use Deposits

State law controls how landlords may use security deposits. (CC § 1950.5.) You can withhold all or part of the deposit if the tenant skips out owing rent or leaving his apartment filthy or damaged. The deposit may be used by the landlord "in only those amounts as may be reasonably necessary" to do the following four things only:

1. To remedy defaults in payment of rent

2. To repair damage to the premises caused by the tenant (except for "ordinary wear and tear")

3. To clean the premises, if necessary, when the tenant leaves. For tenancies that began on or after January 1, 2003, the amount of cleaning you may require cannot be more than will "return the unit to the same level of cleanliness it was in at the inception of the tenancy." (CC § 1950.5(a)(3).) In other words, if you delivered a merely broom-clean unit, you can't require your tenant to return it antiseptically spotless.

4. If the rental agreement allows it, to pay for the tenant's failure to restore or replace personal property

When a tenant moves out, you have three weeks to either return the tenant's entire deposit or provide an itemized statement of deposit deductions (along with invoices and receipts for work done or items purchased) and refund the deposit balance, if any. Chapter 20 provides detailed procedures for handling security deposits when the tenant leaves, including inspecting the premises, making proper deductions, notifying the tenant, supplying receipts, and dealing with small claims lawsuits.

C. Dollar Limits on Deposits

State law limits the amount you can collect as a deposit. (CC § 1950.5 (c).)

Unfurnished property. The deposit (including last month's rent) can't exceed two months' rent.

Furnished property. The deposit (including last month's rent) can't exceed three months' rent. Property is considered "furnished" if it contains at least essential furniture, such as a bed in each bedroom, a couch or chairs for the living area, an eating table with chairs and a refrigerator and stove.

There are two situations where other deposit limits apply.

Cities with rent control or deposit restrictions. Many cities with rent control ordinances, as well as Santa Cruz and Watsonville (which aren't rent-controlled), place further restrictions on deposit amounts and increases. (See Section F of this chapter, below.) Before attempting to set or raise a deposit in a rent-controlled city, be sure to obtain a copy of the rent control ordinance.

Waterbeds. If the tenant has a waterbed, the maximum allowed deposit increases by half a month's rent. So, if a tenant has a waterbed, you can charge a total deposit (including last month's rent) of up to 2.5 times the monthly rent for unfurnished property and 3.5 times the monthly rent for furnished property. (CC § 1940.5(h).)

EXAMPLE 1

Mario charges $500 per month rent for a two-bedroom apartment. Since Mario's apartment is unfurnished, the most he can charge is two months' rent, or $1,000 total deposit. It makes no difference whether or not the deposit is divided into last month's rent, cleaning fee, and so forth. In other words, if Mario charges a $200 cleaning deposit, a $300 security deposit, and $500 last month's rent (total $1,000), he is just within the law. Remember, the rent Mario collects for the first month doesn't count for this purpose.

EXAMPLE 2

Lenora rents out a three-bedroom furnished house for $1,000 a month. Since total deposits on furnished property can legally be three times the monthly rent, Lenora can charge up to $3,000 for last month's rent and deposits. This is in addition to the first month's rent of $1,000 that Lenora can (and should) insist on before turning the property over to a tenant. Realistically, Lenora might not find any takers if she insists on receiving $3,000 in deposits plus the first month's rent, for a total of $4,000. In the case of furnished property, the market often keeps the practical limit on deposits lower than the maximum allowed by law.

D. How to Increase Deposit Amounts

Since the amount of a deposit is tied to the rent, an increase in rent affects the amount of the deposit. You can normally change the amount of rent for a month-to-month tenancy, as well as other terms of the agreement, by giving the tenant a written 30-Day Notice of Change of Terms of Tenancy. (See Chapter 14.) If you increase the rent with a 30-day notice (or a 60-day notice for rent increases above 10% in one year—see Chapter 14, Section B), you can also legally increase the amount of the deposit.

EXAMPLE

A landlord who rents an unfurnished house or apartment to a tenant for $750 a month can charge total deposits (including anything called last month's rent) of two times that amount, or $1,500. If the deposit is for this amount, and the landlord raises the rent to $1,000, the maximum deposit the landlord is allowed to charge goes up to $2,000. The required deposit does not go up automatically. To raise the deposit amount, the landlord must use a 30-day notice.

If you have a fixed-term lease, you may not raise the security deposit during the term of the lease, unless the lease allows it and specifies the increase.

The ordinances of cities with rent control typically define controlled rent so broadly as to include all security deposits and last month's rent paid by the tenant. This means that if the city restricts your freedom to raise rents, it probably restricts your right to raise deposits as well. Also, since most cities that have special security deposit laws have them as part of a rent control ordinance, any property that is subject to that city's rent control laws is also subject to the city's deposit law. In such cities, the ordinance may therefore restrict the amount and manner in which you can raise a tenant's security deposit.

E. Last Month's Rent

Don't use the term "last month's rent" unless you want to be stuck with its literal meaning. If you accept an up-front payment from a tenant and call it last month's rent, you are legally bound to use it for that purpose only. There's no advantage to using this term, as the total deposit you can collect (two or three times the monthly rent, depending on whether the property is furnished), does not increase.

Here are two examples:

- You give your tenant a year's lease, from January 1 to December 31, and require an up-front payment of last month's rent. In this case, the tenant has paid the rent for December in advance.

- If you rent to your tenant from month to month, the tenant's last month's rent will take care of the rent for the last month, after the tenant gives a 30-day notice or you give the tenant a 30- or 60-day notice.

In either case, you can't use last month's rent as a security deposit for damage or cleaning charges.

If, instead, you require a security deposit and do not mention last month's rent, the tenant will have to pay the last month's rent when it comes due and then wait until after moving out to get the security deposit back. If the tenant damages the premises or fails to pay rent, you can hold on to the appropriate amount of the entire deposit.

EXAMPLE 1

Fernando's last tenant left his $600 per month apartment a mess when he moved out. Fernando wanted to charge his next tenant a nonrefundable cleaning fee, but couldn't because this is illegal. Instead, Fernando decided to collect a total of $1,200, calling $600 a security deposit and $600 last month's rent. His next tenant, Liz, applied this last month's rent when she gave her 30-day notice to Fernando. This left Fernando with the $600 security deposit. Unfortunately, when Liz moved out, she left $700 worth of damages, sticking Fernando with a $100 loss.

EXAMPLE 2

Learning something from this unhappy experience, Fernando charged his next tenant a simple $1,200 security deposit, not limiting any part of it to last month's rent. This time, when the tenant moved out, after paying his last month's rent as legally required, the whole $1,200 was available to cover the cost of any repairs or cleaning.

Avoiding the term "last month's rent" also keeps things simpler if the rent, but not the deposit, is raised before the tenant's last month of occupancy. The problem arises when rent for the tenant's last month becomes due. Has the tenant already paid in full, or does he owe more because the monthly rent is now higher? Legally, there is no clear answer. In practice, it's a hassle you can easily avoid by not labeling any part of the security deposit last month's rent.

EXAMPLE

Artie has been renting to Rose for three years. When Rose moved in, the rent was $800 a month, and Artie collected this amount as last month's rent. Over the years he's raised the rent to $1,000, without collecting any more also for last month's rent. During the last month of her tenancy, Rose applies the $800 last month's rent to the current $1,000 rent. Artie thinks that Rose should have to pay the $200 difference. Rose, however, thinks that, by having previously accepted the $800 as last month's rent, Artie had implicitly agreed to accept the $800 as full payment for that month. They end up in court fighting over something that could have been avoided.

F. INTEREST, ACCOUNTS, AND RECORDKEEPING ON DEPOSITS

No state law requires landlords to pay interest on security deposits. In most localities, you don't have to pay tenants interest on deposits, or put them in a separate bank account—unless you require this in your lease or rental agreement. (*Korens v. R.W. Zukin Corp.*, 212 Cal. App. 3d 1054, 261 Cal. Rptr. 137 (1989).) In other words, you can simply put the money in your pocket or bank account and use it, as long as you have it available when the tenant moves out.

However, several cities require landlords to pay or credit tenants with interest on security deposits. A few cities require that the funds be kept in separate interest-bearing accounts.

Here are a few things you should keep in mind about local requirements for interest payments on security deposits:

- All cities that require landlords to pay interest on security deposits have rent control, except Santa Cruz and Watsonville.

- All cities that require landlords to pay tenants interest during the tenancy allow the landlord to either pay it directly to the tenant or credit it against the rent.

- For those cities that require landlords to put deposits in separate accounts:

    - Only one account is required for all the landlord's deposits. You don't have to open one for each tenant's deposit.

    - All security deposits, including last month's rent, if collected, must be placed in the separate account.

- You do not have to pay interest to the tenant at a higher rate than the bank will pay, even if the city's ordinance says you have to pay more. For example, if the ordinance specifies 3% annual interest, but the bank pays only 1.5%, you need pay only 1.5% to the tenant. (*Action Apartment Assn. v. Santa Monica Rent Control Board*, 94 Cal.App.4th 587 (2002).)

The chart below summarizes the features of all California cities' deposit laws. If you own property in a rent control city and your property is exempt from rent control, these provisions obviously do not apply. (See "Exceptions" for each city in the Rent Control Chart in Appendix C.)

Some landlords have found that it is good public relations to pay tenants interest on their deposits, even if there is no local law requiring it. This, of course, is up to you.

G. INSURANCE AS A BACK-UP TO DEPOSITS

This isn't a book on how to buy landlord's insurance, but because insurance can compensate you for some damages caused by tenants, it is appropriate to mention insurance here. After all, the legal limits as to how much you can charge for deposits are so strict (and tenants' abilities to pay a judgment may be so limited) that you may want to get all the additional protection possible.

There are basically two broad types of policies to protect yourself from damage caused by your tenant:

- Landlord's insurance, which protects you from:

    - losses from fire and water damage, including lost rents while the property is being rebuilt or repaired, and

    - personal liability for injury to a tenant or someone else and illegal acts by you and your employees.

You will need landlord's insurance for many reasons (discussed in Chapter 12). You may also wish to include earthquake coverage in such a policy.

CITIES REQUIRING INTEREST OR SEPARATE ACCOUNTS FOR SECURITY DEPOSITS

CITY	ORDINANCE	INTEREST-BEARING ACCT	PAYMENTS DURING TENANCY	NOTES
BERKELEY	Rent Stabilization and Eviction for Good Cause Ordinance, § 13.76.070	Required. Account must be in a savings and loan insured by FSLIC (Federal Savings & Loan Insurance Corp.), or landlord must pay 10% annual interest.	All interest produced must be paid or credited in December of each year and when deposit refunded at end of tenancy. If interest not credited by January 10, tenant may, after notice to the landlord, compute the interest at 10% and deduct this from the next rent payment.	www.ci.berkeley.ca/rent/
EAST PALO ALTO	Ordinance 17-83, § 7	Required. Account must be insured by FSLIC, if account at savings and loan, or FDIC (Federal Deposit Insurance Corp.), if account at bank.	All interest produced must be paid in December of each year and when deposit refunded at end of tenancy.	
HAYWARD	Ordinance 83-023, § 13	Not required.	Landlord must pay interest on deposits held over a year, with payments made within 20 days of tenant's move-in "anniversary date" each year, and when deposit refunded at end of tenancy. Rate is set annually by city.	Violation can subject landlord to liability for three times the amount of unpaid interest owed.
LOS ANGELES	Municipal Code § 151.06.02	Not required.	Landlord must pay interest on deposits once a year and when deposit is refunded at end of tenancy, either directly or through rent credit. Rate is set annually by Rent Adjustment Commission.	
SAN FRANCISCO	Administrative Code, §§ 49.1-49.5 (Not part of city's rent control law.)	Not required.	Landlord must pay interest on deposits held over a year, with payments made on tenant's move-in "anniversary date" each year, and when deposit refunded at end of tenancy. Rate is set annually by Rent Board.	Ordinance does not apply to government-subsidized housing but may apply in other situations, even though property not subject to rent control.
SANTA CRUZ	Municipal Code §§ 21.02.010-21.02.100	Not required.	Landlord must pay interest as set by resolution of the city council on deposits held over a year, with payments made on tenant's move-in "anniversary date" each year, and when deposit refunded at end of tenancy.	Santa Cruz has no rent control law.
SANTA MONICA	City Charter § 5.40.09	Required. Account must be insured by FSLIC or FDIC.	Landlord must pay interest produced on deposits held for one year or more, each year by October 1, either directly or through rent credit.	Landlord cannot raise deposit during tenancy, even if rent is raised, unless tenant agrees.
WATSONVILLE	Municipal Code §§ 5.40.01-5.40.08	Not required	On deposits held over six months, landlord must pay interest or credit against rent. Payment or rent credit is due on January 1 and when deposit refunded at end of tenancy. Rate is set annually by city.	Watsonville has no rent control law.
WEST HOLLYWOOD	Municipal Code § 17.32.020	Not required.	Landlord must pay interest on deposits, with payments made or credited against rent in January or February of each year, and when deposit refunded at end of tenancy. Rate is set annually by city.	

• Renters' insurance, often called a "Tenant's Package Policy," which covers:

  - the tenant's liability to third parties— for example, injuries to guests that result from the tenant's neglect, such as a wet and slippery floor in the tenant's kitchen

  - damage to the tenant's own property caused by fire and water damage, and

  - certain types of damage to your building caused by the tenant's acts.

Our lease and rental agreements (see Clause 19 in Chapter 2, Section C) recommend that the tenant purchase renters' insurance. Our move-in letter (Chapter 7) highlights some of the risks tenants face unless they purchase insurance.

One advantage of requiring insurance is that if there is a problem caused by a tenant that is covered by the tenant's policy, your premium rate won't be affected even though your landlord's policy also covers the damage.

How does a tenant's policy help you if the place is damaged? Well, if damage is caused by fire or water (for example, the tenant leaves something burning on the stove, causing a kitchen fire), the tenant's policy, not yours, will be responsible. But what if a tenant simply moves out and destroys your property? In that case, a tenant's policy will not pay if it's clear the tenant committed the vandalism. Since it often isn't clear as to whether the tenant's conduct was due to deliberate vandalism, as opposed to carelessness and neglect, tenant's insurance companies often will pay at least part of a claim disputed in this respect. It may be difficult to determine whether a stranger, as opposed to the tenant, entered and caused the damage.

H. When Rental Property Is Sold

When rental property is sold, what should the landlord do with the deposits already collected? After all, when tenants move out, they want their deposit back. Who owes them the money? The responsibility can be shifted to the new owner, if the seller either:

• refunds the deposits to the tenants, which will enable the new owner to collect them himself, or

• transfers the deposits to the new owner. (CC § 1950.5(h).)

1. Seller Refunds the Deposit to Tenants

The first option is for the seller to refund the deposits (including last month's rent), less proper deductions, to each tenant, with a detailed itemization of the reason for and amount of each deduction as you would with any security deposit. We don't recommend this, because you're refunding the deposit before the tenant moves out—and thus before you're aware of any necessary deductions for cleaning and damages. This makes little sense, and requires the new owner to ask tenants for new deposits in the middle of their tenancy. (You could, of course, inspect the premises before refunding the deposit, but this would be inconvenient for both landlord and tenant.)

2. Seller Transfers Deposit to New Owner

We recommend this second option, which requires the seller to:

• Transfer the deposit to the new owner (less any lawful deductions for back rent owed and for any necessary cleaning and damages in excess of ordinary wear and tear that you know about at the time of transfer), plus any interest in cities that require payment of interest on deposits (see Section F, above), and

• Give the tenant a written notice of the change of ownership, itemizing all deductions and giving the new owner's name, address and phone number. The notice should be sent by first-class mail (preferably certified, return-receipt requested) or personally delivered.

The procedure for transferring the money to the new owner depends on whether you have established a separate account for tenants' deposits. If you have a separate account, you can simply make the change at the bank by transferring the account to the new buyer. If you have mixed the deposit money with your own, be sure to include a provision in the real property sales contract that itemizes the deposits for all the units and says the buyer acknowledges receipt of them (perhaps through a credit against the sale price) and that the buyer specifically agrees to take responsibility for the repayment of all deposits.

You'll find a tear-out version of the Notice of Sale of Real Property and of Transer of Security Deposit Balance in Appendix B. The CD-ROM that accompanies this book also includes this form. A sample notice is shown below.

As we stated earlier, you'll probably have no idea whether cleaning or damage deductions should be made. However, this type of notice can be used to deduct any back rent the tenant owes at the time of transfer. (Chapter 20 provides detailed instructions on how to itemize deductions and figure out rent due.)

If you don't properly transfer the deposit to the new owner and notify the tenants as required, the new owner will still be liable (along with you) to the tenants for any untransferred portion of the deposit. (One exception to this rule applies if the new owner can convince a judge that after making reasonable inquiry when buying the property, she erroneously concluded that the deposits were in fact transferred, or that the seller refunded them to the tenants before selling.) Also, the new owner can't increase the tenants' deposits to make up for your failure to transfer the money. The new owner, if stuck with this situation, will be able to sue you for any funds he's out by virtue of your failure to transfer and notify. (CC § 1950.5(j).) It's wise to make sure that the security deposit arrangement you and the buyer have

chosen is made part of the sales contract. At the end of this section, we suggest two clauses that you can use, depending on the timing of the transfer. Use the first clause if you and the buyer have not yet transferred the funds; use the second clause if the transfer has already occurred or is taking place at the same time as the property sale itself.

I. IF YOU'RE PURCHASING RENTAL PROPERTY

When buying rental property, make sure the seller follows one of the two legal options outlined above, and that all tenants have been notified of the transfer. (To double check, you might want to ask the seller to use the transfer forms and provide you with copies of each proposed notice.)

It's a good idea to make sure that the security deposit transfer is made a part of the sales contract. Below are two contract provisions you can use to suit the method you and the seller have chosen. Use the first clause if you and the seller have not yet transferred the funds; use the second clause if the transfer has already occurred or is taking place at the same time as the property sale itself.

Some other key points when you're buying rental property:

- Make sure you know the total dollar amount of security deposits. For a multiunit building, it could be tens of thousands of dollars. If it is substantial, and the seller is not transferring security deposit funds to you, you may want to negotiate an appropriate reduction in the sales price.

- You may not require the tenant to pay you an additional security deposit to replace any amount the seller failed to transfer, except for a legitimate deduction the seller made and of which the tenant has been notified. For example, if the seller deducted $125 for unpaid back rent, you can require the tenant to pay you an additional deposit of this amount.

Notice of Sale of Real Property and of Transfer of Security Deposit Balance
Civil Code Section 1950.5(h)(1)

To: _____Robert Fisher_____,
                                      Name

Tenant(s) in possession of the premises at _____123 Main Street_____,
                                                                    Street Address

City of ____Placerville_____, County of _____El Dorado_____, California.

The real property described above was sold on _____June 1,_____, 20 _OX_

to ___Jake Brummer_____,
                        Name of New Landlord

____456 Gold Street, Placerville, California_____,
                                      Street Address

whose telephone number is _____(916) 555-1234_____.
                                              Phone Number

Your security deposit, less any deductions shown below, has been transferred to the new landlord, who is now solely responsible to you for it.

Deposit Amount: $____500.00____

Deductions:

    Unpaid Back Rent: $____125.00____

    Other Deductions: $_____-0-_____

    Total Deductions: $____125.00____

Net Deposit Transferred to New Landlord: $____375.00____

Explanation of Deductions:

_____

_____

_____

_____

back rent due for month of June 200X $____125.00____

Please contact the new landlord, whose address and phone number are listed above, if you have any questions.

_Laurel Meyer_____   _June 15, 200X_____
Landlord/Manager   Date

- If you want to change the rental agreement or lease, you must use a 30- or 60-day notice (for month-to-month rental agreements, 60 days' for all rent increases over 10%) or wait until the end of the lease term. (See Chapter 14 for raising rents and changing other terms of tenancy.)

SAMPLE CONTRACT PROVISION TRANSFERRING TENANTS' DEPOSITS

1. Where Tenants' Deposits to Be Transferred to Buyer at Later Date

As part of the consideration for the sale of the property described herein, Seller shall transfer to Buyer all security, as that term is defined by Section 1950.5 of the Civil Code, deposited with Seller by tenants of the premises, after making any lawful deductions from each tenant's deposit, in accordance with Subdivision (h) of Section 1950.5. Seller shall notify Buyer and each tenant of the amount of deposit remaining on account for each tenant, and shall notify each tenant of the transfer to Buyer. Thereafter, Buyer shall assume liability to each tenant for the amount transferred after such lawful deductions.

2. Where Tenants' Deposits Already Transferred to Buyer

As part of the consideration for the sale of the property described herein, Buyer acknowledges transfer from Seller of all security, as that term is defined by Section 1950.5 of the Civil Code, deposited with Seller by tenants of the premises, after making any lawful deductions from each tenant's deposit, in accordance with Subdivision (h) of Section 1950.5. Seller shall notify Buyer and each tenant of the amount of deposit remaining on account for each tenant, and shall notify each tenant of the transfer to Buyer. Thereafter, Buyer shall assume liability to each tenant for the amount transferred after such lawful deductions.

■

6

PROPERTY MANAGERS

I f you've had enough of fielding tenants' repair requests, collecting rent, and looking after all the other day-to-day details of running a rental property business, you've probably thought about hiring a property manager.

You may not have a choice: State law requires that a manager reside on the premises of any apartment complex with 16 or more units. (Cal. Code of Regulations, Title 25, § 42.) But you may want to hire a resident manager even if you have a smaller number of units. If you own several apartment complexes (large or small), you may want to use a property management firm.

This chapter reviews the nuts and bolts of hiring and working with a manager or property management firm, including:

• how to select a manager or management company and delegate responsibilities

• whether your manager needs to be licensed

• contracts with managers

• your legal obligations as an employer

• how to protect yourself from liability for a manager's illegal acts, and

• how to fire or evict a manager.

For more information on hiring a property manager as an employee, see *Everyday Employment Law: The Basics,* by Lisa Guerin & Amy DelPo (Nolo).

A. HIRING YOUR OWN MANAGER

Many owners of small (less than 16-unit) apartment complexes do much of the management work themselves, hiring their own resident managers as needed. When a small landlord does hire a manager, it's typically a tenant who lives in a multiunit building. The tenant-manager collects rents, relays complaints, and keeps the building and yard clean. Or, the landlord collects the rent directly, leaving the manager mostly in charge of low-level maintenance and overall supervision of the tenants and premises.

The tenant-manager may get a reduced rent in exchange for performing these duties. Or, the tenant-manager may pay full rent and receive a separate salary.

1. Selecting the Right Manager

The person you hire to manage your property should be honest and responsible and have a good credit history. Careful screening is crucial. Follow the system we recommend for choosing tenants in Chapter 1. Look for a manager who communicates well—both with you and other tenants. The manager will receive legal documents and papers on your behalf, so make sure you can trust that person to notify you immediately.

If you select a manager from current tenants, pick one who pays rent on time and who you think will be meticulous about keeping records, particularly if collecting rent will be part of the job.

Avoid anyone who harbors biases based on race, national origin, religion, sex, sexual preference, or other group characteristics. This is especially important if the manager will be showing apartments, taking rental applications, or selecting tenants. And you'll need someone with a backbone—a manager who will be collecting overdue rents and serving three-day notices to pay rent or quit should not be fearful of minor confrontations with tenants.

Finally, if you want to delegate routine maintenance, make sure the person you choose knows how to do minor repairs, such as unclogging toilets, unsticking garbage disposals, and replacing light switches.

2. Setting the Manager's Duties

The manager's duties will depend largely on the number of units to be managed, your own needs, and the manager's abilities. Delegate more responsibilities if you live far away from the property or don't want to be involved in day-to-day details such as showing vacant units, collecting rents, and keeping the premises clean. The Residential Rental Property Management Memorandum (see Section B, below) includes a list of duties you may want to delegate.

3. Licensing Requirements

Owners of rental property can perform all leasing activities for their property without needing a real estate broker's license. Similarly, if you hire a manager who lives on the property, that person need not be licensed. (B&P §§ 10131, 10131.01.) Your tenant-manager can manage only the property the manager lives on. If you want this person's services at your complex across town, the manager will need to take and pass the licensing exam administered by the California Department of Real Estate (or be supervised by a broker, as explained below).

The rules are somewhat tricky for managers who do not live on the property. For example, suppose you want to pay a resident manager to also manage your second property, or you want to hire your retired brother-in-law, who lives in his own home, to manage your apartment complex. Unless each obtains a real estate license, they cannot take the job unless they will be supervised by a licensed broker or real estate sales person. Even then, they will be able to assume only the following duties, and only at a single location:

* show rental units to prospective tenants
* provide preprinted rental applications and respond to applicants' inquiries about the application
* accept deposits, fees for credit checks and other administrative duties, security deposits, and rent
* provide information about rental rates and other terms and conditions of the rental, as set out in a schedule provided by the owner, and
* accept signed leases and rental agreements.

As you can see, a nonlicensed, nonresident manager is limited to performing rather routine tasks that don't call for initiative or decision making. For instance, this manager would not be qualified to

negotiate a lease, deal with late rents or other violations of the rental agreement or lease, or appear in court on your behalf.

The rules boil down to this: Unless you manage your property yourself, or hire someone who will also live on each property, you'll have to deal with a licensed broker. You can hire one to manage the whole show or, if you want to use a nonlicensed manager at each property, you can look for a broker to supervise each nonlicensed manager. You may have a hard time finding a broker willing to take on supervisory duties—most brokers with property management experience will prefer to do the job themselves.

B. Avoiding Legal Problems

To avoid legal trouble down the road, follow the guidelines in this section when you hire a resident manager.

MOST TENANT-MANAGERS ARE EMPLOYEES, NOT INDEPENDENT CONTRACTORS

If you hire a tenant-manager, that person will usually be considered an employee by the IRS and other government agencies, even if *you* call them independent contractors. Employees are guaranteed a number of workplace rights that are not guaranteed to people who work as independent contractors. To be considered an independent contractor, a person must offer services to the public at large and work under an arrangement in which he or she controls both the outcome of the project and the means and method of accomplishing it. Most tenant-managers are legally considered to be employees because the property owner who hires them sets the hours and responsibilities and determines the particulars of the job.

Section B discusses employee rights and employer responsibilities.

---

1. Separate Employment From the Manager's Rental Agreement

When you decide to hire a tenant as a manager, you and the manager should sign two separate documents:

- a memorandum explaining the job and that the job can be terminated at any time for any reason by either party, and

- a month-to-month rental agreement that can be terminated by either party on 30 days' written notice (60 days' if the tenant occupies the premises for a year or more).

A single agreement covering employment and the tenancy is appropriate when you have a special manager's unit set up as both an office and residence. (See Section G, Evicting a Manager, below.)

If you have separate employment and rental agreements with a tenant-manager, the manager will pay the full rent and receive a separate salary. And if you fire a tenant-manager, there will be no question that he is still obligated to pay the full rent, as he has done all along. Because your obligations as an employer are the same whether you compensate the manager with reduced rent or a paycheck (you must still pay Social Security and payroll taxes, for example), the paperwork is no more difficult than using the rent-reduction method.

EXAMPLE

Louise uses two agreements with her new tenant-manager Sydney: a month-to-month rental agreement under which Sydney pays $600 rent each month, and a management agreement under which Louise pays Sydney $100 each week and which can be terminated without reason at any time by either party.

On January 1, Sydney pays his $600 rent to Louise. On January 7, Louise pays Sydney his weekly $100 and gives him a written notice saying his services as a manager are no longer required, but that he may stay on as a tenant. Louise no longer pays Sydney his weekly $100, and Sydney knows that in February he'll have to pay the regular rent of $600.

WHY NOT USE AN ORAL AGREEMENT?

Landlords and resident managers often agree orally on the manager's responsibilities and compensation, never signing a written agreement.

Even though oral agreements are usually legal and binding, they are not advisable. Memories fade, and the parties may have different recollections of what they agreed to. If a dispute arises between you and the manager, the exact terms of an oral agreement are difficult or impossible to prove if you end up arguing about them in court. It is a far better business practice to put your understanding in writing.

Giving a resident manager reduced rent in exchange for management services, on the other hand, isn't a good idea. If the manager doesn't properly perform his duties and you terminate the employment, you may run into problems when you insist that the ex-manager go back to paying the full rent.

If the ex-manager refuses to pay the full rent, your only alternative is to initiate an eviction lawsuit. (See Section G, below.) The lawsuit is almost sure to be complicated by the fact that the amount of rent due depends on whether the manager's employment was properly terminated and whether he owes any extra rent as a result of not performing his duties.

EXAMPLE

Boris and Thomas sign an agreement under which Thomas collects rents and handles routine repairs in exchange for $200 off the monthly rent of $600. When Thomas turns out to be an incompetent repairperson, Boris fires him as of the end of the month, and the next month demands the full $600 rent. Thomas refuses to pay more than $400, claiming he was fired unjustly. Although Boris is willing to keep Thomas as a regular tenant, he wants him to pay the rent. When Thomas won't pay it all, Boris serves him with a three-day notice demanding the $200. Thomas still refuses to pay, so Boris files an eviction lawsuit.

Boris could have avoided all this by having a separate employment agreement with Thomas covering management responsibilities (collecting rent and handling routine repairs), compensation ($200 per month), and termination policy (termination of management duties at any time with or without cause).

Below is an example of a sound written agreement that spells out the manager's responsibilities, hourly wage or salary, hours, and payment schedule.

You'll find a tear-out version of the Residential Rental Property Manager Memorandum in Appendix B. The CD-ROM that accompanies this book also includes this form.

To protect yourself from liability for your manager's illegal activities in carrying out his responsibilities, also prepare a more detailed set of instructions clarifying duties and basic legal guidelines. We show you how in Section D, below.

## 2.	Meet Your Obligations as an Employer

Whether you compensate a tenant-manager with reduced rent or a regular salary, you have specific legal obligations as an employer. You are also responsible for a certain amount of paperwork and recordkeeping. If you don't pay Social Security and meet your other legal obligations as an employer, you may face substantial financial penalties.

Especially if you're figuring out taxes for your employee (rather than having the work done by an accountant or tax preparer), you must keep good records. IRS Publication 334 (*Tax Guide for Small Businesses*) provides details about the records you must keep. Contact the IRS at 800-TAX-FORM to obtain a free copy of the publication. Or, go online to www.irs.gov/forms_pubs/pubs/index.htm and choose Form 334.

HELP WITH PAPERWORK

If you hate paperwork, your accountant can probably handle it for you. Or, payroll services can handle virtually all the details of employing a manager—for example, withholding Social Security and unemployment taxes—for a relatively small fee. To get cost quotes, check the Yellow Pages under Payroll Service or Bookkeeping Service.

Income taxes. The IRS considers the manager's compensation—whether in the form of payments or reduced rent—as taxable income to the manager. For that reason, your manager must fill out a federal W-4 form (Employee Withholding Allowance Certificate) when hired. You must deduct state and federal taxes from each paycheck, turn over withheld funds each quarter to the IRS and the California Franchise Tax Board, and give the manager a W-2 form (Wage and Tax Statement) at the end of the year.

For details on reporting and deduction requirements, contact the IRS (800-TAX-FORM), or browse their website at www.irs.gov. You can reach the California Franchise Tax Board at 800-852-5711, or look for information on their website at www.ftb.ca.gov.

Employer Identification Number. As an employer, you need a federal identification number that distinguishes you from other employers. If you are a sole proprietor, you can use your Social Security number. Otherwise, you can get an Employer Identification Number by completing Form SS-4 (Application for Employer Identification Number). Form SS-4 is available for free by calling the IRS at 800-TAX-FORM, or you can download the form from the IRS website at www.irs.gov/forms (type SS-4 into the search box).

Social Security and Medicare. Every employer must pay to the IRS a "payroll tax," currently equal to 7.65% of the employee's gross paycheck amount (before deductions) compensation. You must also deduct an additional 7.65% from the employee's

Residential Rental Property Manager Memorandum

1. Parties

This Agreement is between ___Jacqueline La Mancusa___,

Landlord of residential real property at ___1704 Donner Ave., Bakersfield, California___,

_____, and

___Bradley Marsh___,

Manager of the property. Manager will be renting unit ___5___ of the property under a separate written rental agreement that is in no way contingent upon or related to this agreement.

2. Beginning Date

Manager will begin work on ___April 10, 200X___.

3. Responsibilities

Manager's duties are set forth below:

Renting Units

☐ answer phone inquiries about vacancies

☒ show vacant units

☒ accept rental applications

☐ select tenants

☒ accept initial rents and deposits

☐ other (specify) _____

☐ _____

Vacant Apartments

☒ inspect unit when tenant moves in

☒ inspect unit when tenant moves out

☐ clean unit after tenant moves out, including:

    ☐ floors, carpets, and rugs

    ☐ walls, baseboards, ceilings, lights, and built-in shelves

    ☐ kitchen cabinets, countertops, sinks, stove, oven, and refrigerator

    ☐ bathtubs, showers, toilets, and plumbing fixtures

    ☐ doors, windows, window coverings, and mini-blinds

    ☐ other (specify) _____

    ☐ _____

Rent Collection

☒ collect rents when due

☒ sign rent receipts

☒ maintain rent collection records

☒ collect late rents and charges

☒ inform Landlord of late rents

☒ prepare late rent notices

☒ serve late rent notices on tenants

☒ serve rent increase and tenancy termination notices

☒ deposit rent collections in bank

☐ other (specify) _____

☐ _____

Maintenance

☐ vacuum and clean hallways and entryways

☒ replace lightbulbs in common areas

☐ drain water heaters

☒ clean stairs, decks, patios, facade and sidewalks

☒ clean garage oils on pavement

☒ mow lawns

☒ rake leaves

☒ trim bushes

☐ clean up garbage and debris on grounds

☐ other (specify) _____

☐ _____

Repairs

☒ accept tenant complaints and repair requests

☒ inform Landlord of maintenance and repair needs

☒ maintain written log of tenant complaints

☒ handle routine maintenance and repairs, including:

    ☒ plumbing stoppages

    ☒ garbage disposal stoppages/repairs

    ☒ faucet leaks/washer replacement

    ☒ toilet tank repairs

    ☒ toilet seat replacement

    ☒ stove burner repair/replacement

[X] stove hinges/knobs replacement

[X] dishwasher repair

[X] light switch and outlet repair/replacement

[X] heater thermostat repair

[ ] window repair/replacement

[ ] painting (interior)

[ ] painting (exterior)

[ ] replacement of keys

[ ] other (specify)

[ ] _____

Other Responsibilities

_____

_____

_____

_____

_____

4. Hours and Schedule

Manager will be available to tenants during the following days and times: ___Monday through Friday___
___3 p.m. - 6 p.m._____. If the hours required to carry out
any duties may reasonably be expected to exceed _____12_____ hours in any week, Manager shall notify
Landlord and obtain Landlord's consent before working such extra hours, except in the event of an
emergency. Extra hours worked due to an emergency must be reported to Landlord within 24 hours.

5. Payment Terms

a. Manager will be paid:

[ ] $ _____ per hour

[ ] $ _____ per week

[X] $ ___300_____ per month

[ ] Other: _____

b. Manager will be paid on the specified intervals and dates:

[ ] Once a week on every _____

[ ] Twice a month on _____

[X] Once a month on ___the first of the month_____

[ ] Other: _____

6. Ending the Manager's Employment

Landlord may terminate Manager's employment at any time, for any reason that is not unlawful, with or without notice. Manager may quit at any time, for any reason, with or without notice.

7. Additional Agreements and Amendments

a. Landlord and Manager additionally agree that: _____

_____

_____

_____

_____

_____

_____

_____

_____

_____

_____

_____

_____ .

b. All agreements between Landlord and Manager relating to the work specified in this Agreement are incorporated in this Agreement. Any modification to the Agreement must be in writing and signed by both parties.

8. Place of Execution

Signed at ___Fresno_____ , ___California_____
         City   State

___April 3, 200X_____   ___Jacqueline La Mancusa_____
Date   Landlord

___April 3, 200X_____   ___Bradley Marsh_____
Date   Manager

wages and turn it over (with the payroll tax) to the IRS quarterly. These FICA (Federal Insurance Contributions Act) taxes go toward the employee's future Social Security and Medicare benefits.

If you compensate your manager with reduced rent, you must still pay the FICA payroll tax. For example, an apartment owner who compensates a manager with a rent-free $500/month apartment must pay 7.65% of $500, or $38.25, in payroll taxes each month. The manager is responsible for paying another 7.65% ($38.25) to the IRS.

Contact the IRS at 800-TAX-FORM or their website noted above for deduction and reporting requirements and forms.

Minimum wage and overtime. However you pay your manager—by the hour or with a regular salary—you should monitor the number of hours worked to make sure you're complying with state and federal minimum wage laws. Overtime is calculated by the day, not by the week. If your manager works more than eight hours in any one day, that extra time is overtime, which you must compensate at one-and-one-half the rate of pay (on the other hand, if the manager works a few hours on a nonwork day, those hours are compensated at the regular rate of pay).

If the total number of hours a manager works, multiplied by the minimum hourly wage, exceeds the rent reduction or other fixed rate of pay, you are in violation of minimum wage laws. For example, a manager who works four 20-hour weeks during the month must receive at least $6.75/hour (as of January 1, 2002), or $540. A landlord who pays less—even if it's in the form of a rent reduction—will run afoul of the minimum wage laws. California minimum wage laws also require employers to pay time-and-a-half if an employee works more than eight hours a day.

Rent reductions. If you compensate your manager by a rent reduction, you can count only up to two-thirds of the "fair market rental value" of the apartment for the purpose of complying with minimum wage laws, and in no event more than $381.20

for a single employee or $563.90 for a couple. (Labor Code § 1182.8 and Industrial Welfare Commission Minimum Wage Order at Calif. Code of Regulations § 11000.) For example, if the rent is normally $500, and you charge the tenant-manager only $100/month, only $333 of the $400 rent reduction may be counted for minimum wage purposes. This is another reason why compensation by rent reduction is not a good idea.

You and the employee may agree that the employee will take compensatory time (comp time) off instead of overtime pay. Legally, that's permitted, as long as the agreement is in writing, the comp time is awarded at the rate of one-and-one-half times the overtime hours worked, and it is made available during the same pay period that the overtime hours were worked.

To make sure you comply with minimum wage laws, the agreement with your manager should limit the total number of hours worked each month, or provide for additional payment if the manager works more hours than anticipated.

For information on minimum wage laws, contact a local office of the State Department of Industrial Relations, Department of the State Labor Commissioner. You'll find this information and more at the Department's website at www.dir.ca.gov.

Disability and workers' compensation insurance. As an employer, you must provide disability and workers' compensation insurance. This coverage provides replacement income and pays medical expenses for employees who are injured or become ill as a result of their job. It's a no-fault system—an injured employee is entitled to receive benefits whether or not you provided a safe workplace, and whether or not the manager's own carelessness contributed to the injury. (You are, of course, required by federal and state laws to provide a reasonably safe workplace.) You, too, receive some protection, because the manager, in most cases, cannot sue you for damages over the injury.

If you don't provide workers' comp and disability and a manager is injured on the job—for example, by falling down the stairs while performing maintenance, or even by a violent tenant—you could face serious legal problems. You could be sued by the State Department of Industrial Relations and possibly by the injured manager. If you lose such a lawsuit, the court judgment will not be covered by any other kind of landlord's insurance.

Contact the local office of the State Employment Development Department for information about disability insurance payments, or visit their website at www.edd.ca.gov, where you'll find lots of information. Call your insurance agent regarding workers' compensation insurance.

Unemployment taxes. A manager who is laid off, quits for good reason, or is fired for anything less than gross incompetence or dishonesty is entitled to unemployment benefits. These benefits are financed by state payroll taxes paid by employers. The California Employment Development Department (EDD) may impose tax and penalty assessments (without first filing a lawsuit) against employers who don't pay required payroll taxes. Contact the local office of the EDD for the appropriate instructions and forms.

Annual W-2 form. You must provide employees with a W-2 form (Wage and Tax Statement) for the previous year's earnings by January 31. The W-2 form lists the employee's gross wages and provides a breakdown of any taxes that you withheld.

New Hire Reporting Form. Within a short time after you hire someone—20 days or less—you must file a New Hire Reporting Form with a designated state agency. The information on the form becomes part of the National Directory of New Hires, used primarily to locate parents so that child support orders can be enforced. Government agencies also use the data to prevent improper payment of workers' compensation and unemployment benefits or public assistance benefits. The State Department of Industrial Relations should be able to tell you how to get the forms and where to send them.

IMMIGRATION LAW

The Immigration and Nationality Act (INA), Title 8 of the U.S. Code, is a federal law that restricts the flow of foreign workers into American workplaces. The INA covers almost all employees hired since November 6, 1986.

Under the INA, it is illegal for an employer to:

- hire a worker whom the employer knows has not been granted permission by the U.S. Citizenship and Immigration Service (or USCIS, formerly the INS) to be employed in the United States (through a green card, visa, or Employment Authorization Document)

- hire any worker who has not completed INS Form I-9, the Employment Eligibility Verification Form, or

- continue to employ an unauthorized worker— often called an illegal or undocumented worker—hired after November 6, 1986.

For more information, contact the U.S. Citizenship and Immigration Service at 1-800-375-5283, listed in the telephone book under U.S. Department of Justice. For forms, call 800-375-5283. The USCIS website is www.uscis.gov.

C. MANAGEMENT COMPANIES

Property management companies generally take care of renting units, collecting rent, taking tenant complaints, arranging repairs and maintenance, and evicting troublesome tenants. Property management companies are often used by owners of large apartment complexes and by absentee owners too far away from the property to be directly involved in everyday details.

A management company acts as an independent contractor, not an employee. Typically, you sign a contract spelling out the management company's duties and fees. Most companies charge a fixed percentage—typically 5 to 10%—of the total rent collected. This gives the company a good incentive to keep the building filled with rent-paying tenants. (Think twice about companies that charge a fixed percentage of the rental value of your property, regardless of whether you have a lot of vacancies or turnover.)

QUESTIONS TO ASK WHEN YOU HIRE A MANAGEMENT COMPANY

- Who are its clients: owners of single-family houses, small apartments, or large apartment complexes? Look for a company with experience handling property like yours. Also ask for client references, so you can see if they are satisfied with the management company.

- What services are provided?

- What are the costs?

- Will the management company take tenant calls 24 hours a day, seven days a week?

- Is the company located fairly close to your property?

- Are employees trained in landlord/tenant law? Can they consult an attorney qualified in landlord/tenant matters?

- If your property is under rent control, are company personnel familiar with the rent control law?

- Can you terminate the management agreement without cause on reasonable notice?

Hiring a management company has a number of advantages. Compared to a tenant-manager, management company personnel generally develop a more professional, less emotional relationship with tenants, and are also usually better informed about the law. Another advantage is that you eliminate much of the paperwork associated with being an employer. Because you contract with a property management firm as an independent contractor, and it hires the people who actually do the work, you

don't have to worry about Social Security, unemployment, or workers' compensation.

The primary disadvantage of hiring a management company is the expense. For example, 10% of the $700 rents collected each month from tenants in a 20-unit complex amounts to $1,400 a month, or $16,800 per year.

If you hire a management company to manage your property, you still must have an onsite manager if your building has more than 16 units. If your rental property has only a few units, or you own a number of small buildings spread over a good-sized geographical area, the management company probably won't hire resident managers, but will simply respond to tenant requests and complaints from its central office.

Management companies have their own contracts, which you should read thoroughly and understand before signing. Be sure you understand how the company is paid and its specific responsibilities.

D. AN OWNER'S LIABILITY FOR A MANAGER'S ACTS

A landlord is legally responsible for the acts of a manager or management company, who is considered the landlord's "agent." For example, you could be sued and found liable if your manager:

- refuses to rent to a qualified tenant who is a member of a minority group or has children, or otherwise violates antidiscrimination laws (see Chapter 9)

- makes illegal deductions from the security deposit of a tenant who has moved out, or does not return the departing tenant's deposit within the three weeks allowed by law (see Chapters 5 and 20)

- ignores a dangerous condition, such as substandard wiring which results in an electrical fire causing injury or damage to a tenant, or a security problem that results in a criminal assault on a tenant (see Chapter 12)

- steals from or assaults a tenant (see Chapter 12)

- invades a tenant's privacy by flagrant and damaging gossip, trespass, or harassment (see Chapter 13).

SAMPLE INSTRUCTIONS TO MANAGER

November 6, 200X

Dear New Manager:

Welcome to your new position as resident manager. In performing your duties under our management agreement, please keep the following in mind:

1. Discrimination in rental housing on the basis of race, religion, sex, sexual preference, marital or familial status, age, national or ethnic origin, source of income, and any other unreasonable or arbitrary basis is illegal--whether you are accepting rental applications for vacant apartments or dealing with current residents. Your duties, in the event of a vacancy, are to advertise and accept rental applications in a non-discriminatory manner. This includes allowing all individuals to fill out applications and offering the unit on the same terms to all applicants. After you have collected all applications, please notify me at the phone number listed below. I will arrange to sort through the applications and make the final decision as to who occupies units.

2. Do not issue any rent increase or termination notices without my prior approval, unless a tenant's rent is more than five days past due and he or she is not withholding rent because of dissatisfaction with the apart-ment--for example, the tenant has made no complaints in the previous six months. In that case, you may, without prior approval from me, serve the tenant a Three-Day Notice to Pay Rent or Quit, using the blank forms I have given you. However, if you have any reason to think that the tenant may assert that the failure to pay rent is based on any defects in the rental unit, please contact me immediately. Do this even if you are convinced that the tenant's complaints are unfounded.

3. Treat all tenants who complain about defects, even trivial defects or ones you believe to be nonexistent, with respect. Enter all tenant complaints into the log book I have supplied to you. Respond to tenant complaints about the building or apartment units immediately in emergen-cies, and within 24 hours in nonemergencies. If you cannot correct or arrange to correct any problem or defect yourself, please telephone me immediately.

4. Except in serious life- or property-threatening emergencies, never enter (or allow anyone else to enter) a tenant's apartment without con-sent or, in his or her absence, unless you have given the proper notice. Proper notice is presumed to be 24 hours' notice, preferably in writing (48 hours' notice is required prior to conducting the initial move-out inspection requested by the tenant). You may enter in the tenant's ab-sence during ordinary business hours to do repairs or maintenance work, provided you have given the tenant a 24-hour notice in writing and

delivered personally, but posted on the door if necessary, and the tenant hasn't objected. Please call me if you have any problems gaining access to a tenant's apartment for maintenance or repairs.

5. When a tenant moves in, and again when he or she moves out, inspect the unit. Within a few days (at most) of the tenant giving or receiving a 30-day (or 60-day) notice of termination of tenancy, fill out and provide the tenant with a copy of the Move-Out letter, which explains the procedure for the return of security deposits. Conduct a move-out inspection with the tenant during the last two weeks of the tenancy, if the tenant requests it (try to arrange for one even if no request is made). Use the Landlord/Tenant Checklist to record damage and excessive wear and tear. After the tenant has moved, inspect again using the Landlord/Tenant Checklist to note unremedied (or new) damage or uncleanliness. Take a series of Polaroid or digital camera pictures at both inspections.

6. If you think a tenant has moved out and abandoned the apartment, do not enter it. Telephone me first.

7. Once a tenant has vacated an apartment and given you the key, itemize all cleaning costs and costs necessary to repair damages in excess of ordinary wear and tear. Give me a copy of this itemization, along with a notation of the amount of any back rent, the before and after Landlord/Tenant Checklist forms, and the departing tenant's forwarding address. Please make sure I see this material within a week after the tenant moves out, preferably sooner. I will mail the itemization and any remaining security deposit balance to the tenant within the required three-week period.

8. If you have any other problems or questions, please do not hesitate to call me. Leave a message on my answering machine if I am not at home.

Sincerely,

Terry Herendeen
Owner

 111 Maiden Lane, Fresno, CA
Address

 559-555-1234
Phone

   I have received a copy of this memorandum and have read and understood it.

Dated: Nov. 7, 200X   _Barbara Louis_
                                 Manager

In short, a landlord who knows the law but has a manager (or management company) who doesn't, could wind up in a lawsuit brought by prospective or former tenants. And many insurance companies do not pay for any loss or defend any lawsuit based on a manager's intentional misconduct, such as purposeful discrimination or retaliation against a tenant.

Here's how to minimize your liability for your manager's mistakes or illegal acts:

- Thoroughly check the background of all prospective managers. (See Chapter 12 for advice.)

- Limit the authority you delegate to your manager. If you specify the manager's responsibilities in writing, you reduce (but do not eliminate) your liability for manager misconduct that exceeds the authority you delegated. For example, a landlord who instructs a manager in writing only to accept rental applications, with the landlord actually selecting the tenant, is less likely to be held liable for a manager who, without authority, rents an apartment in a discriminatory fashion.

- Make sure your manager is familiar with the basics of landlord/tenant law. If you delegate more duties to your manager, such as authority to select tenants or serve three-day, 30-day, 60-day or 90-day notices, provide some legal guidelines. You might also give your manager this book to read and refer to. Written guidelines not only help the manager avoid legal trouble, but also demonstrate that you acted in good faith, which could be very useful should a tenant sue you based on your manager's misconduct. Your guidelines should dovetail with the manager's responsibilities laid out in the Residential Rental Property Management Agreement.

Above is a sample set of instructions for a manager with fairly broad authority. Obviously, if your manager is given more limited authority, your instructions should also be more limited.

Antidiscrimination training. You may wish to have your manager attend antidiscrimination training sessions given by local fair housing groups or landlord associations. This will help the manager avoid illegal discrimination and shows that you are making efforts to comply with antidiscrimination laws.

- Make sure your landlord's insurance covers illegal acts of your employees. No matter how thorough your precautions, you may still be liable for your manager's illegal acts—even if your manager commits an illegal act in direct violation of your instructions. To really protect yourself, purchase a good landlord's insurance policy. (We show you how in Chapter 12.)

- Keep an eye on your manager and listen to your tenants' concerns and complaints. If you suspect problems—for example, poor maintenance of the building or sexual harassment—do your own investigating. Try to resolve problems and get rid of a bad manager before problems accelerate and you end up with an expensive tenants' lawsuit.

THE HIGH COST OF A BAD MANAGER: SEXUAL HARASSMENT IN HOUSING

If tenants complain about illegal acts by a manager, pay attention. The owners of a Fairfield, California apartment complex learned this lesson the hard way—by paying more than a million dollars to settle a tenants' lawsuit.

The tenants, mostly single mothers, were tormented by an apartment manager who spied on them, opened their mail, and sexually harassed them. They were afraid to complain, for fear of eviction. When the tenants did complain to the building's owners, the owners refused to take any action—and the manager stepped up his harassment in retaliation.

Finally, tenants banded together and sued, and the details of the manager's outrageous and illegal conduct were exposed. The owners settled the case before trial for $1.6 million.

SAMPLE DISCLOSURE NOTICES

Notice: Address of Manager of Premises

Muhammad Azziz, 1234 Market Street, Apartment 1, San Jose, CA, phone (408) 555-6789, is authorized to accept rent and manage the residential premises at 1234 Market Street, San Jose, CA. Rent is accepted at this address Monday through Friday, 9 AM to 5 PM. If you have any complaints about the condition of your unit or common areas, please notify Mr. Azziz immediately. He is authorized to act for and on behalf of the owner of the premises for the purpose of receiving all notices and demands from you, including legal papers (process).

Notice: Address of Owner of Premises

Rebecca Epstein, 12345 Embarcadero Road, Palo Alto, CA, phone (650) 555-0123, is the owner of the premises at 1234 Market St., San Jose, CA. If you have any complaints about the condition of the unit or common areas, please notify Ms. Epstein immediately.

E. NOTIFYING TENANTS OF THE MANAGER

You are legally required to give tenants the manager's name, address, and phone number, since the manager is someone who is authorized to accept rent from tenants and legal documents for you. (CC §§ 1961-1962.7.) If rent is accepted in person, you must also state the days and hours when the manager will accept it. This information must be in writing, whether the tenant has a written lease or rental agreement or an oral rental agreement. (See Chapter 2, Section C.) It is included in our lease and rental agreements in Clause 23.

If you hire a manager after the lease is signed, you'll need to notify your tenants that the manager is authorized to receive legal papers from tenants, such as termination of tenancy notices or court documents in an eviction lawsuit. Two sample disclosure notices are shown above.

If you don't provide your address and phone number (or someone else's who's authorized to receive legal documents on your behalf), your manager will be the only person deemed to be your agent for the purpose of service of legal notices—whether you like it or not. Also, the tenant will be legally able to serve legal notices by certified mail (no return receipt required) rather than by personally delivering them to the manager. This means that a current or former tenant can serve lawsuit papers on you simply by mailing them, by certified mail, to your manager.

EXAMPLE

Three of your tenants have written rental agreements that don't give your name, phone number and address or name anyone to receive legal notices on your behalf. Three other tenants have oral agreements with your manager, Mike, who refused to disclose your name and address, which is not posted on the premises.

The tenants sue you over housing code violations, including defective heaters and a leaking roof that Mike never told you about. They serve the lawsuit papers (summons and complaint) on Mike, who is your agent for service of process because you didn't comply with the disclosure law. Mike throws the papers away without telling you about them, and neither you nor he appears in court. All the tenants win because you were properly served—through your agent—and didn't appear in court.

F. FIRING A MANAGER

Unless you have made a commitment (oral or written contract) to employ a manager for a specific period of time, you have the right to terminate the employment at any time. But you cannot do it for an illegal reason, such as:

- race, age, ethnic, or gender discrimination, or
- retaliation against the manager for calling your illegal acts to the attention of authorities.

EXAMPLE

You order your manager to dump 20 gallons of fuel oil at the back of your property. Instead, the manager complains to a local environmental regulatory agency, which fines you. If you now fire the manager, you will be vulnerable to a lawsuit for illegal termination.

To head off the possibility of a wrongful termination lawsuit, be prepared to show a good reason for the firing. It's almost essential to back up a firing with written records documenting your reasons. Reasons that may support a firing include:

- performing poorly on the job—for example, not depositing rent checks promptly, or continually failing to respond to tenant complaints
- refusing to follow instructions—for example, allowing tenants to pay rent late, despite your instructions to the contrary

- possessing a weapon at work
- being dishonest or stealing money or property from you or your tenants
- endangering the health or safety of tenants
- engaging in criminal activity, such as drug dealing
- arguing or fighting with tenants
- behaving violently at work, or
- unlawfully discriminating or harassing prospective or current tenants.

Ideally, a firing shouldn't come suddenly or as a surprise. Give your manager ongoing feedback about job performance and impose progressive discipline, such as an oral or written warning, before termination. Do a six-month performance review (and more often, if necessary), and keep copies. Solicit comments from tenants a few times a year and if comments are negative, keep copies.

For more information on how to handle problem employees—including how to avoid hiring them in the first place—see Nolo's *Dealing With Problem Employees*, by Amy DelPo and Lisa Guerin (Nolo).

G. EVICTING A MANAGER

If you fire a manager, you may also want that person to move out of your property, particularly if the manager occupies a special manager's unit or the firing has generated (or resulted from) ill will. How easy it will be to get the fired manager out depends primarily on whether you have separate management and rental agreements.

1. Separate Management and Rental Agreements

If you and the tenant-manager signed separate management and rental agreements, firing the manager will not affect the tenancy. The ex-manager will have to keep paying rent but will no longer work as manager.

To evict the former manager, you will have to give a normal 30-day or 60-day written termination notice, subject to any just-cause eviction requirements in rent control cities. (See Chapter 18.) All rent control cities do allow eviction of fired managers, though some cities impose restrictions on it. If the tenant has a separate fixed-term lease, you cannot terminate the tenancy until the lease expires.

2. Single Management/Rental Agreement

What happens to the tenancy when you fire a manager depends on the kind of agreement you and the manager had.

a. If the Manager Occupied a Special Manager's Unit

If you fire a manager who occupies a specially constructed manager's unit (such as one with a reception area or built-in desk) that must be used by the manager, your ability to evict the ex-manager depends on:

- the terms of the management/rental agreement, and

- local rent control provisions.

If the agreement says nothing about the tenancy continuing if the manager quits or is fired, termination of the employment also terminates the tenancy. That means you can evict the ex-manager without a separate tenancy-termination notice. In that case, no written notice is required to terminate the tenancy, unless one is required under the agreement. (See CCP § 1161(1).)

The just-cause eviction provisions of any applicable rent control law, however, may still require a separate notice or otherwise restrict your ability to evict a fired manager.

b. If the Manager Didn't Occupy a Manager's Unit

If the manager was simply compensated by a rent reduction, and there is no separate employment agreement, there may be confusion as to whether the rent can be "increased" after the manager is fired. (This is one reason we recommend against this kind of arrangement.)

If an ex-manager refuses to pay the full rent, you will have to serve a Three-Day Notice to Pay Rent or Quit, demanding the unpaid rent. (See Chapter 16.) If that doesn't get results, you'll have to follow up with an eviction (unlawful detainer) lawsuit.

3. Eviction Lawsuits

If you want to evict a former manager, we recommend that the eviction lawsuit be handled by an attorney who specializes in landlord/tenant law.

Eviction lawsuits against former managers can be extremely complicated. This is especially true if the management agreement requires good cause for termination of employment or a certain period of notice. (Our form agreement requires neither.) Such lawsuits can also be complicated where a single combined management/rental agreement is used or if local rent control laws impose special requirements.

HANDLING REQUESTS FOR REFERENCES

If another landlord asks you for a reference for someone you employed but later fired as manager, just follow this bit of folk wisdom: If you can't say something good, don't say anything at all. In light of the potential for being named in a slander suit, it's best to simply decline to give any information about a former manager (or tenant) rather than say anything negative. Besides, if you politely say, "I would rather not discuss Mr. Jones," the caller will get the idea. ∎

7

GETTING THE TENANT MOVED IN

Legal disputes between landlords and tenants have gained a reputation for being almost as strained and emotional as divorce court battles. Many disputes are unnecessary and could be avoided if—right from the very beginning—both landlord and tenant understood their legal rights and responsibilities. A clearly written lease or rental agreement, signed by all adult occupants, is the key to starting a tenancy. (See Chapter 2.) But there's more to getting new tenants moved in. You should also:

- Inspect the property, fill out a Landlord/Tenant Checklist, and take pictures of the unit.

- Prepare a move-in letter highlighting important terms of the tenancy.

- Collect rent and security deposit checks.

A. INSPECT AND PHOTOGRAPH THE UNIT

It is absolutely essential for you and prospective tenants (together, if at all possible) to check the place over for damage and obvious wear and tear, by filling out a Landlord/Tenant Checklist form and taking photographs of the rental unit.

1. Filling Out the Landlord/Tenant Checklist

A Landlord/Tenant Checklist, inventorying the condition of the rental property, is an excellent device to protect both you and your tenant when the tenant moves out and wants the security deposit returned. Without some record as to the condition of the unit, you and the tenant are all too likely to get into arguments about things like whether the kitchen linoleum was already stained or the bedroom mirror was already cracked at the time the tenant moved in.

The checklist will also be useful when you perform the initial move-out inspection, if requested by the tenant (which will give the tenant a chance to clean or repair, and avoid deductions). And, coupled with a system to regularly keep track of the rental property's condition, the checklist can also be useful if tenants withhold rent, claiming the unit needs

substantial repairs. (See Chapter 11 for instructions and forms to periodically update the safety and maintenance of your rental properties.) A sample Landlord/Tenant Checklist is shown below.

You'll find a tear-out version of the Landlord/Tenant Checklist in Appendix B. The CD-ROM that accompanies this book also includes the form.

When you look at the Checklist we've prepared for you, you'll see that we have filled out the first column with rooms and elements in these rooms. If you happen to be renting a 1-bedroom, 1-bath unit, our preprinted form will work just fine. However, chances are that your rental has additional (or fewer) rooms; or you may want to note and follow the condition of one aspect of a rental (say, the loft or the hot tub) that is not on our form. No problem! Once you load the CD-ROM that comes with this book into your computer, you can change the entries in the first column of the Checklist, and you can add rows. For example, you may want to add a row for a third bathroom (and list the toilet, sink, and shower), another bedroom, a service porch, and so on; or you may want to add room elements, such as a trash compactor, fireplace, or dishwasher. Consult the instructions for your word processing program for instructions on how to add a row to a table.

How to Fill Out the Checklist

You and the tenants should fill out the checklist together. If you can't do this together, complete the form and then give it to the tenant to review. The tenant should make any changes and return it to you.

The checklist is in two parts. The first side covers the general condition of each room. The second side covers the condition of any furnishings provided, such as a living room lamp or bathroom shower curtain.

If your rental property has rooms or furnishings not listed on the form, you can note this in "Other

Areas," or cross out something that you don't have and write it in. If you are renting out a large house or apartment or providing many furnishings, you may want to attach a separate sheet.

If your rental unit does not have a particular item listed, such as a dishwasher or kitchen broiler pan, put "N/A" (not applicable) in the "Condition on Arrival" column.

Mark "OK" in the space next to items that are in satisfactory condition.

Make a note—as specific as possible—on items that are not working or are in bad condition. For example, don't just write "needs fixing" if a bathroom sink is clogged. It's just as easy to write "clogged drain," so that later the tenant can't claim to have told you about a leaky faucet that he claims was there from the start.

The second column, "Condition at Initial Move-Out Inspection," is where you'll note any damage or needed cleaning when you go through the unit, at the tenant's request, prior to his moving out. If you like, you can also record the expected deductions that you'll make if the tenant doesn't remedy the noted problems.

The last two columns—Condition on Departure and Actual or Estimated Cost of Cleaning, Repair/Replacement—are for use when the tenant moves out and you need to make deductions from the security deposit for items that need to be repaired, cleaned, or replaced. (See Chapter 20 for details on recordkeeping and security deposits.)

After you and the tenants agree on all of the particulars, you all should sign and date the form on both sides, as well as any attachments. Keep the original for yourself and attach a copy to the tenant's lease or rental agreement. (See Clause 11 of our form agreements.)

Be sure the tenant also checks the box on the bottom of the first page of the checklist stating that the smoke detector—required for new occupancies by state law—was tested in his presence and shown to be in working order. This section on the checklist also requires the tenant to test the smoke detector monthly and to replace the battery when necessary.

By doing this, you'll limit your liability if the smoke detector fails and results in fire damage or injury. (See Chapter 11 for details on the landlord's responsibility to provide smoke detectors and maintain the property and Chapter 12 for a discussion of the landlord's liability for injuries to tenants.)

Be sure to keep the checklist up to date if you repair, replace, add, or remove items or furnishings after the tenant moves in. Both you and the tenant should initial and date any changes.

2. Take Pictures of the Property

Taking photos or videotapes of the unit before the tenant moves in is another excellent way to avoid disputes over a tenant's responsibility for damage and dirt. When the tenant leaves, you'll be able to compare "before" and "after" pictures. This will help if a tenant sues you for not returning the full security deposit. Nothing is better in the defense of a tenant's security deposit lawsuit than a landlord's pictures showing that the unit was immaculate when the tenant moved in and a mess at move-out. Photos/videos can also help if you have to sue a former tenant for cleaning and repair costs above the deposit amount.

It's best to take "before" photographs with a Polaroid or other camera that develops pictures automatically; the tenant can then date and sign or initial the pictures on the spot. Otherwise, use a camera that automatically imprints the date on each photo. If possible, you should repeat this process with "after" pictures, to be signed or initialed by the tenant as part of your established move-out procedure (described in Chapter 20).

B. SEND NEW TENANTS A MOVE-IN LETTER

A move-in letter should dovetail with the lease or rental agreement (see Chapter 2) but cover day-to-day issues, such as how and where to report maintenance problems (covered in detail in Chapter 11). It should also spell out the role of the manager, if any. A move-

Landlord/Tenant Checklist
GENERAL CONDITION OF RENTAL UNIT AND PREMISES

1234 Fell Street
Street Address

Apt. 5   San Francisco
Unit Number   City

	Condition on Arrival	Condition on Initial Move-Out Inspection	Condition on Departure	Actual or Estimated Cost of Cleaning, Repair/Replacement
LIVING ROOM				
Floors & Floor Coverings	OK			
Drapes & Window Coverings	OK			
Walls & Ceilings	OK			
Light Fixtures	OK			
Windows, Screens & Doors	back door scratched			
Front Door & Locks	OK			
Smoke Detector	OK			
Fireplace	N/A			
Other				
KITCHEN				
Floors & Floor Coverings	cigarette burn hole (1)			
Walls & Ceilings	OK			
Light Fixtures	OK			
Cabinets	OK			
Counters	discolored			
Stove/Oven	OK			
Refrigerator	OK			
Dishwasher	OK			
Garbage Disposal	N/A			
Sink & Plumbing	OK			
Smoke Detector	OK			
Other				

	Condition on Arrival	Condition on Initial Move-Out Inspection	Condition on Departure	Actual or Estimated Cost of Cleaning, Repair/Replacement
DINING ROOM				
Floors & Floor Covering	OK			
Walls & Ceilings	crack in ceiling			
Light Fixtures	OK			
Windows, Screens & Doors	OK			
Smoke Detector	OK			
Other				
BATHROOM				
Floors & Floor Coverings	OK			
Walls & Ceilings	OK			
Windows, Screens & Doors	OK			
Light Fixtures	OK			
Bathtub/Shower	tub chipped			
Sink & Counters	OK			
Toilet	OK			
Other				
Other				
BEDROOM				
Floors & Floor Coverings	OK			
Windows, Screens & Doors	OK			
Walls & Ceilings	OK			
Light Fixtures	dented			
Smoke Detector	OK			
Other				
Other				
Other				

OTHER AREAS	Condition on Arrival	Condition on Initial Move-Out Inspection	Condition on Departure	Actual or Estimated Cost of Cleaning, Repair/Replacement
Heating System	OK			
Air Conditioning	N/A			
Lawn/Garden	N/A			
Stairs & Hallway	N/A			
Patio, Terrace, Deck, etc.	OK			
Basement	OK			
Parking Area				
Other				
Other				
Other				
Other				
Other				

☒ Tenants acknowledge that all smoke detectors and fire extinguishers were tested in their presence and found to be in working order, and that the testing procedure was explained to them. Tenants agree to test all detectors at least once a month and to report any problems to Landlord/Manager in writing. Tenants agree to replace all smoke detector batteries as necessary.

NOTES:

FURNISHED PROPERTY

	Condition on Arrival	Condition on Initial Move-Out Inspection	Condition on Departure	Actual or Estimatead Cost of Cleaning, Repair/Replacement
LIVING ROOM				
Coffee Table	two scratches on top			
End Tables	N/A			
Lamps	OK			
Chairs	OK			
Sofa	OK			
Other				
Other				
KITCHEN				
Broiler Pan	N/A			
Ice Trays	OK			
Other				
Other				
DINING AREA				
Chairs	OK			
Stools	N/A			
Table	leg bent slightly			
Other				
Other				
BATHROOM				
Mirrors	OK			
Shower Curtain	OK			
Hamper	N/A			
Other				

	Condition on Arrival	Condition on Initial Move-Out Inspection	Condition on Departure	Actual or Estimated Cost of Cleaning, Repair/Replacement
BEDROOM				
Beds (single)	OK			
Beds (double)	N/A			
Chairs	OK			
Chests	N/A			
Dressing Tables	OK			
Lamps	OK			
Mirrors	OK			
Night Tables	N/A			
Other	N/A			
Other				
OTHER AREAS				
Bookcases				
Desks				
Pictures	hallway picture frame chipped			
Other				
Other				

Use this space to provide any additional explanation:

Landlord/Tenant Checklist completed on moving in on _____ May 1 _____, 20 OX .

_____ Ira Eppler _____ and _____ Chloe Gustafon _____

Landlord/Manager

Tenant

Tenant

Tenant

Landlord/Tenant Checklist completed at Initial Move-Out Inspection on _____, 20 ___ .

_____ and _____

Landlord/Manager

Tenant

Tenant

Tenant

Landlord/Tenant Checklist completed on moving out on _____, 20 ___ .

_____ and _____

Landlord/Manager

Tenant

Tenant

Tenant

SAMPLE MOVE-IN LETTER

April 29, 200X

Dear Mr. O'Hara:

Welcome to Happy Hill Apartments. We hope you will enjoy living here.

It is our job to provide you with a clean, undamaged, pleasant place to live. We take our job seriously. This letter is to explain what you can expect from the Management and what we'll be looking for from you.

1. Rental Agreement: Your signed copy is attached. Please let us know if you have any questions. A few things we'd like to highlight here:

- There is no grace period for the payment of rent (see Clause 6 for details, including late charges). Also, we don't accept postdated checks.
- If you want someone to move in as a roommate, please contact us. If your rental unit is big enough, we will arrange for the new person to fill out a rental application and, if it's approved, for all of you to sign a new rental agreement.
- *(for a month-to-month rental:)* To terminate your month-to-month tenancy, you must give at least 30 days' written notice to Management. Management may also terminate the tenancy, or change its terms, on 30 days' written notice.
- *(for a fixed-term lease:)* You occupy the premises under a fixed-term lease. You are responsible for all rent payments through the lease term, even if you move out before the lease expires. During the lease term, your rent cannot be increased, nor can other terms of your tenancy be changed.
- Your security deposit is only to be applied, by the owner, to costs of cleaning, damages, or unpaid rent

after you move out. You may not apply any part of the deposit, during your tenancy, toward any part of your rent in the last month of your tenancy. (See Clause 8 of your agreement.)

2. Manager: Sophie Beauchamp (Apartment #15, phone 555-1234) is your resident manager. You should pay your rent to her and promptly let her know of any maintenance or repair problems (see #4, below) and any other questions or problems. She's in her office every day from 8 A.M. to 10 A.M. and from 4 P.M. to 6 P.M. and can be reached by phone other times.

3. Landlord/Tenant Checklist: By now, Sophie Beauchamp should have taken you on a walk-through of your apartment to check the condition of all walls, drapes, carpets, appliances, etc. These are all listed on the Landlord/Tenant Checklist, which you should have carefully gone over and signed. When you move out, we will ask you to check each item against its original condition as indicated on the Checklist.

4. Maintenance/Repair Problems: You have a right to expect repairs to be made promptly. To help us accomplish this, the Management will give you Maintenance/Repair Request forms to report to the manager any problems in your apartment or the building or grounds, such as a broken garbage disposal. Keep several forms handy. (Extra copies are available from the manager.)

Except in an emergency, all requests for repairs should be made on this form during normal business hours. In case of emergency, or when it's not convenient to use this form, call the manager at 555-1234.

5. Semi-Annual Safety and Maintenance Update: It's our goal to keep your unit and the common areas in excellent condition. To help us do this, we'll ask you to fill out a

form every six months, to report any potential safety hazards or maintenance problems that otherwise might be overlooked. Please take the time to fill this out and send it back with your rent check.

6. Annual Safety Inspection: Once a year, we will inspect the condition and furnishings of your rental unit and update the Landlord/Tenant Checklist.

7. Insurance: We highly recommend that you purchase insurance, because tenants face many of the same risks that homeowners do:

- You could lose valuable property through theft or fire.
- You could be sued if someone is injured on the premises you rent.
- If you damage the building itself (say you start a fire in the kitchen and it spreads), you could be responsible for large repair bills.

Contact your insurance agent for more information on renters' insurance.

8. Moving Out: It's a little early to bring up moving out, but please be aware we have a list of items that should be cleaned before we conduct a move-out inspection. If you decide to move out, please ask the manager for a copy of our Move-Out Letter, explaining what is required and describing our procedures.

9. Telephone Number Changes: Please notify us if your home or work phone number changes, so we can reach you promptly in case of an emergency.

Please let us know if you have any questions.

Sincerely,
Tony Giuliano
Tony Giuliano, Owner

in letter can be changed from time to time as necessary. A sample is shown above. You should tailor this letter to your particular needs (for example, if your property is subject to local rent control or you don't employ a resident manager).

Along with your move-in letter, you may want to document the keys and passes that you're giving the new tenant. Our form, Key and Pass Receipt and Agreement, lists the common keys and passes landlords distribute, and gives you a place to add others. The form also advises the tenant not to copy or share these items, that you'll charge a lockout fee if you have to help tenants who have lost their keys, and that you will charge a reasonable fee for replacing lost or damaged keys or passes. Be reasonable when setting lockout and replacement fees (don't think of these as profit-generating moments).

You'll find a blank, tear-out version of the Key and Pass Receipt and Agreement in Appendix B. The CD-ROM that accompanies this book also includes this form.

C. Cash Rent and Security Deposit Checks

You don't want to get stuck with a tenant who's going to bounce checks to you. And if the new tenant's first rent or deposit check bounces, you might have to undertake time-consuming and expensive legal proceedings to evict a tenant who's paid you nothing.

To avoid this, never sign a rental agreement, let a tenant move furniture into your property or give him a key until you have the tenant's cash, or a certified check or money order, for the first month's rent and security deposit. An alternative is to cash a tenant's check at the bank before the move-in date. (While you have the tenant's first check, photocopy it for your records; the information on it can be helpful if you ever need to bring legal action.)

Responsible tenants, who prefer to plan ahead, will pay the rent and sign the lease at least several days before the move-in date; you can give the tenant a copy of the lease and the keys when the check clears or you receive cash or certified funds.

Clause 5 of our Lease and Rental Agreement forms requires tenants to pay rent on the same day of each month, with rent to be prorated between a move-in date (if it's other than the first) and the end of that month. For example, with a monthly rent of $900 due on the first of the month, a tenant who moves in on June 21 should pay ten days' prorated rent of $300 when she moves in, before the full $900 July rent is due.

As a general rule, if the prorated rent for that first partial month is less than half a month's rent, you should request a more substantial amount up front. The reason for this is simple: A few tenants might impress you in person and look good on their applications, but yet are unable to come up with all the rent when due. Such individuals often look for rentals that require only a few hundred dollars up front; they don't worry about how they'll pay the rent later, hoping to find roommates by the time the rent comes due. You stand to lose heavily if you allow a person like this to move in on $300 prorated rent for the last ten days of the month and hope he'll come up with the regular $900 monthly rent on the first of the following month. If he doesn't come up with the full rent, and it takes you up to a month to evict him, you're out a month's rent plus eviction costs, a sum larger than any security deposit—which should be used to compensate you for the damage and mess this tenant may leave behind.

Insisting on a substantial up-front payment helps ferret out such individuals. There are a few ways to do this:

• Require the prorated rent of less than half a month plus the next month's entire rent, plus the security deposit. (The deposit can be either two or three times the monthly rent amount, depending on whether the rental unit is furnished or unfurnished; see Chapter 5.) For example, your tenant who moves in on June 21 and pays $300 for the rent through June 30 should also be asked to pay in advance the $900 rent for July and the security deposit.

• Insist on an entire month's rent up front and then prorate the second month. For example, the tenant who moves in on June 21 would first pay the full $900 rent for July. Then, come July 1, the $300 rent for June 21 through 30 is due.

• Simply require rent payments on the day of the month that the tenant moved in, so that a tenant who moves in on the 21st will always pay rent on the 21st.

We recommend the first way—accepting the prorated rent if it is more than half a month's rent or, if it is less than that, the prorated amount plus another month's rent. It's easier and keeps the rent due on the convenient and customary first of the month. ■

8

Lawyers, Legal Research, Eviction Services, and Mediation

Generally, California landlords can deal with most routine legal questions and problems without a lawyer. Just the same, there are times when good advice from a specialist in landlord tenant law will be helpful, if not essential—for example, in complicated evictions or lawsuits by tenants alleging that dangerous conditions or wrongful acts caused injury.

This chapter recommends a strategy to most efficiently and effectively use legal services:

- First, keep up to date on landlord/tenant law so that you can anticipate and avoid many legal problems. Check the Nolo website at www.nolo.com for important updates on California landlord/tenant law. Don't forget to check for updates for this book, as instructed in "Read This First," right after the title page. Remember, however, that updates are kept on the site for current editions only. If you're using an old edition, it's time to upgrade!

- Second, use mediation services to settle disputes and head off lawsuits.

- Third, consider typing services as an alternative to lawyers in standard eviction cases.

- Fourth, know the best way to go about hiring a lawyer and negotiating fees.

Related Topics

To avoid legal problems in the first place, read these chapters and follow these guidelines:

- Screen tenant applicants carefully: Chapter 1

- Use a clear, unambiguous written rental agreement or lease: Chapter 2

- Make sure your manager knows landlord/tenant law: Chapter 6

- Clarify tenants' responsibilities and grievance/repair procedures with a move-in letter: Chapter 7

- Establish a system for reporting and handling repairs: Chapter 11.

A. LEGAL RESEARCH TOOLS

Using this book is a good way to educate yourself about the laws that affect your business—but one book is not enough by itself. At one time or another, you'll need to do some further research in the law library or online.

1. Local Ordinances

If you are a landlord in a city with a rent control ordinance, you need a copy of the ordinance, as well as all rules issued by the rent board covering rent increases and hearings. The Rent Control Chart in Appendix C lists website addresses for those cities that have posted their ordinances online.

Even if your rental property is not in a rent-controlled area, you should be aware of any local ordinances that affect your business—for example, your city may require that you pay interest on tenants' security deposits. You'll find local ordinances online by going to a site maintained by the Seattle Public Library at www.spl.org (choose the Databases and Websites link, then Government, then Law and Legal, and finally, Municipal Codes Online). Or, use the site maintained by the Institute of Governmental Studies in Berkeley, at www.igs.berkeley.edu. Choose the Library link, then the California Local Codes List.

2. State Laws

It's essential that you also have access to current versions of the California statutes that regulate the landlord/tenant relationship. They are collected in volumes called codes.

The *California Civil Code* (CC) contains most of California's substantive landlord/tenant law, primarily in Sections 1940 through 1991. It includes laws governing minimum building standards, payment of rent, change and termination of tenancy, privacy, security deposits, and abandoned property, to name a few.

The *California Code of Civil Procedure* (CCP) is a set of laws explaining how people enforce legal rights in civil lawsuits. Eviction lawsuit procedures are

contained in Sections 1161 through 1179 of the Code of Civil Procedure. Also of interest are the small claims court procedures, covered in Sections 116.110 through 116.950.

These codes are available in many public libraries and all county law libraries (found in county courthouses). However, because it's so important that you have immediate access to the laws that affect your business, we recommend that you buy copies of your own. They are sold in a number of different editions and are available at any law bookstore.

Remember that you'll need a new volume every year—the state legislature tinkers with landlord/tenant laws every session. *Never* rely on an old set of statutes.

If you have Internet access, it's simple to read the statutes online. Go to Nolo's website at www.nolo.com and choose the State Laws link in the Legal Research Center. When you read the statutes online, you're almost always assured of reading the latest versions of the laws (but check the state's disclaimer pages to make sure that the information is current). For information on pending legislation, go to the website maintained by the Legislative Council, at www.leginfo.ca.gov.

3.   State Regulations

Many rules that California landlords must comply with are in the California Code of Regulations. These rules are made by various state agencies charged by the legislature to give specificity to laws that the legislature has passed (and the governor has signed). For example, state law requires landlords to provide hot water, but the specifics of that obligation (how hot?) are in the Code of Regulations.

The Code of Regulations is in every law library, but it's far easier to look at it online. Go to http://ccr.oal.ca.gov and use the table of contents to find Title 25, Housing and Community Development. By looking through the various subheadings, you'll find rules that apply to housing and rental housing in particular. For example, the rule regarding hot water (it must be at least 110 degrees Fahrenheit) is in § 32 in Division 1, Chapter 1, Subchapter 1, Article 5. Other rules, such as plumbing and mechanical codes, are also in the Code of Regulations.

4.   Federal Statutes and Regulations

Congress has enacted laws, and federal agencies such as the U.S. Department of Housing and Urban Development (HUD) have adopted regulations, covering discrimination, wage and hour laws affecting employment of managers', and landlord responsibilities to disclose environmental health hazards. We refer to relevant federal agencies throughout this book and suggest you contact them for publications that explain federal laws affecting landlords, or copies of the federal statutes and regulations themselves.

We include citations for many of the federal laws affecting landlords throughout this book. The U.S. Code is the starting place for most federal statutory research. It consists of 50 separate numbered titles. Each title covers a specific subject matter. Two versions of the U.S. Code are published in annotated form: The *United States Code Annotated* (U.S.C.A.) (West Publishing Co.) and the *United States Code Service* (U.S.C.S.) (Bancroft-Whitney/Lawyer's Coop). Most law libraries carry both, and they are available online via Nolo's website.

Most federal regulations are published in the Code of Federal Regulations (C.F.R.), organized by subject into 50 separate titles.

You can access the United States Code and the Code of Federal Regulations at the U.S. House of Representatives Internet Law Library, at http://uscode.house.gov.

5. Court Decisions

Sometimes it isn't enough to read a statute—you also need to read the decisions of appeals courts, which explain what the statute means. These decisions are written by higher courts that hear appeals of decisions in trial courts, and state why the appeals court agrees or disagrees with the ruling of the trial court. Sometimes these case decisions are extremely important. For example, Civil Code Sections 1941 through 1942 set minimum housing standards. The 1974 case of *Green v. Superior Court* interpreted those statutes to allow tenants in substandard housing to withhold rent—without paying to make repairs themselves—even though no law specifically provides for this type of rent withholding. (See Chapter 11 for a discussion of this issue.)

The best way to learn of the existence of written court decisions which interpret a particular law is to first look in an "annotated code." An annotated code is a set of volumes of a particular code, such as the Civil Code or Code of Civil Procedure, that contains not only all the laws (as do the regular codes), but also a brief summary of many of the court decisions interpreting each law. These annotated codes—published by West Publishing Company (*West's Annotated California Codes*—blue volumes) and by Bancroft-Whitney (*Deering's California Codes*—brown volumes)—can be found in any county law library or law school library in the state. Some public libraries also have them. Unfortunately, you won't find annotated codes for free online—but it's probably just a matter of time until these helpful additions will be available.

These annotated codes have comprehensive indexes by topic, and are kept up to date each year with paperback supplements ("pocket parts") stuck in a pocket inside the back cover of each volume. To keep up to date on new laws and court decisions, look at these pocket parts each year (they're published in January and February) for Civil Code Sections 1940-1991 and Code of Civil Procedure Sections 1161 through 1179.

If a case summarized in an annotated code looks important, you may want to read the actual court opinion. To find it, you'll need the title of the case, the year of the decision and the "citation" following each brief summary of the court decision. The citation is a sort of shorthand identification for the set of books, volume, and page where the case can be found.

One set of volumes, the *Official Reports of the California Courts of Appeal,* shows decisions of the lower appellate courts, which include the Courts of Appeal (one for each of six districts in the state) and the Superior Court Appellate Department (one for each county). The Courts of Appeal hear appeals of cases brought in Superior Court (involving more than $25,000). Courts of Appeal decisions are abbreviated "Cal. App.," "Cal. App. 2d," "Cal. App. 3d," and "Cal. App. 4th," representing the first, second, third and fourth series of volumes. Superior Court Appellate Departments hear appeals of cases brought in Superior Court involving $25,000 or less, and those decisions are listed in the "Supplement" of each volume of the official reports. These cards are therefore abbreviated "Cal. App. 2d Supp.," "Cal. App. 3d Supp.," and "Cal. App. 4th Supp."

A second set of volumes, the *Official Reports of the California Supreme Court,* lists decisions of the California Supreme Court, the state's highest court, which reviews selected cases of the Courts of Appeal. Supreme Court decisions are abbreviated "Cal.," "Cal. 2d," "Cal. 3d," or "Cal. 4th," representing the first, second, third, and fourth series of volumes.

California appellate and Supreme Court decisions are also published by the West Publishing Company in the *California Reporter* (abbreviated "Cal. Rptr." and "Cal. Rptr. 2d," respectively, for the first and second series) and *Pacific Reporter* (abbreviated "P." or "P.2d").

CALIFORNIA'S TRIAL AND APPELLATE COURTS
SAMPLE CASE CITATIONS

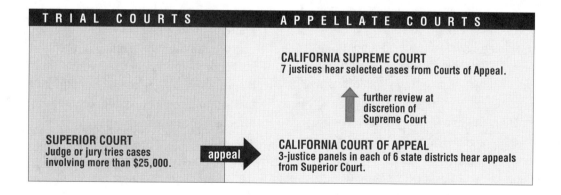

Green v. Superior Court, 10 Cal. 3d 616, 11 Cal. Rptr. 704, 517 P.2d 1168 (1974)

- case name
- volume number
- 3rd series of *Official Reports of the California Supreme Court*
- page number
- volume number
- the case also appears in *Calif. Reporter,* the unofficial reports
- page number
- volume number
- the case is also listed in 2nd series of *Pacific Reporter*
- page number
- year of decision

Glaser v. Myers, 137 Cal. App. 3d 770, 187 Cal. Rptr. 242 (1982)

- case name
- 3rd series of *Official Reports of the California Courts of Appeal,* Volume 137, page 770
- the case is also listed in *Calif. Reporter,* the unofficial reports, Volume 187, page 242
- year of decision

TRIAL COURTS	APPELLATE COURTS
	CALIFORNIA SUPREME COURT 7 justices hear selected cases from Courts of Appeal.
	further review at discretion of Supreme Court
SUPERIOR COURT Judge or jury tries cases involving more than $25,000.	**appeal →** **CALIFORNIA COURT OF APPEAL** 3-justice panels in each of 6 state districts hear appeals from Superior Court.

Note. Small claims court is a division of superior court. A defendant who loses in small claims court can request a new trial in superior court. (From there, no further appeal is allowed, except at the Court of Appeal's discretion.) A plaintiff who loses in small claims has no right of appeal.

You can read California cases online, too. Appellate and Supreme Court opinions are available free at www.findlaw.com. Choose the "States" sublink under "Laws: Cases and Codes" and click on California. You'll eventually come to screens that allow you to enter search terms (such as the case name or citation), which will lead you to the opinion you're looking for.

LEGAL RESEARCH HELP

We don't have space here to show you how to do your own legal research in anything approaching a comprehensive fashion.

To go further, we recommend an excellent resource: *Legal Research: How to Find and Understand the Law*, by Stephen Elias & Susan Levinkind (Nolo), which gives easy-to-use, step-by-step instructions on how to find legal information. (See order information at the back of this book.)

B. MEDIATING DISPUTES WITH TENANTS

Mediation is a technique where a neutral third party helps people settle differences themselves, without going to court. Unlike a judge in court or an arbitrator in a formal hearing, a mediator does not impose a decision on the parties, but facilitates a compromise. Generally, mediation works well in situations where people want to settle their disputes so they can work together in the future. In a landlord/tenant context, mediation can be extremely helpful in areas such as disputes about noise, the necessity for repairs, a tenant's decision to withhold rent because defects have not been repaired, rent increases, privacy, and security deposits. Many large landlords find that an established mediation procedure is an invaluable way to head off lawsuits.

At the mediation session, each side gets to state his or her position, which often cools people off considerably and frequently results in a compromise. If the dispute is not resolved easily, however, the mediator may suggest ways to resolve the problem, or may even keep everyone talking long enough to realize that the real problem goes deeper than the one being mediated. For example, if a tenant has threatened rent withholding because of a defect in the premises, you may learn that the tenant's real grievance is that your manager is slow to make repairs. This may lead to the further discovery that the manager is angry at the tenant for letting his kids pull up his tulips.

At any rate, mediation often works, and if it doesn't, you haven't lost much. If mediation fails, you can still fight it out in court. In fact, if you or the tenant have already filed suit in small claims court, you may find that the judge will insist that you try mediation before presenting your case in court. Call you county's small claims court clerk to find out if this is the way your court works.

Mediation is most effective when there's an established procedure tenants and landlords can use. Here's how to set one up.

1. Find a mediation group that handles landlord/tenant disputes. There are many mediation programs throughout the state, and almost all California cities receive federal funds to arrange for mediators to handle disputes between landlords and tenants. For more information, call city hall or the rent board in rent-controlled cities, and ask for the staff member who handles "landlord/tenant mediation matters" or "housing disputes." That person should refer you to the public office or private agency that attempts to informally resolve landlord/tenant disputes before they reach the court stage. Many mediation groups are city- or county-funded and do not charge for their services.

You can also contact one of the respected mediation organizations, such as the American Arbitration Association, or a neighborhood dispute resolution center, such as San Francisco's Community Boards Program, and arrange for this group to mediate landlord/tenant disputes.

If you and the tenant are involved in a discrimination dispute that has escalated to the point where the tenant has filed a complaint with the state's Department of Fair Employment and Housing, you can take advantage of their free and very successful mediation service. For more information, see their website at www.dfehmp.ca.gov.

2. Explain procedures for lodging complaints to every tenant. A move-in letter (see Chapter 7) would be a good place to do this. Make sure tenants know they can request mediation for disputes which escalate to the point where normal face-to-face compromise techniques prove to be of no avail, whether over privacy, rent withholding because of allegedly defective conditions, or whatever. Emphasize the fairness of the mediation process.

3. If possible, split the cost (if any) of a mediation. (If this isn't acceptable to the tenant, and you pay the total mediation cost, make sure your tenant realizes that the mediator has no power to impose a decision.)

For more information on mediation, see *Mediate, Don't Litigate,* by Peter Lovenheim and Lisa Guerin (Nolo). This book explains the mediation process from start to finish, including how to prepare for mediation and draft a legally enforceable agreement.

C. NONLAWYER EVICTION SERVICES

Filing and following through with an eviction lawsuit involves filling out a number of legal forms. And once the forms are filed with the court, they must then be served on the tenant—a task that isn't always easy. You can do it yourself, using *The California Landlord's Law Book: Evictions,* or you can hire a lawyer. There is also a third route: getting help with the paperwork, filing and service from an eviction service run by non-lawyers, known as "legal typing services" or "independent paralegals." They exist in most metropolitan areas.

For a flat fee that is usually much lower than what lawyers charge, and often at a faster pace, eviction services take the basic information from you, prepare most of the initial paperwork, file the necessary papers in court and have the tenant served with the Summons and Complaint.

Typing services aren't lawyers. They can't give legal advice about the requirements of your specific case and can't represent you in court—only you or your lawyers can present your case in court. You must decide what steps to take in your case and the

information to put in the needed forms. A nonlawyer eviction service can, however:

- provide written instructions and legal information you need to handle your own case

- provide the appropriate eviction forms and fill them out according to your instructions

- type your papers so they'll be accepted by the court, and

- arrange for filing the eviction forms in court and serving them on the tenant. (In the case of *People v. Landlords' Professional Services,* 215 Cal. App. 3d 1599 (1989), the court ruled that an eviction service whose nonlawyer employees gave oral legal advice was unlawfully practicing law. The court, however, said eviction services could legally give customers forms and detailed self-help legal manuals, fill out the forms as directed by the customers, and file and serve the papers.)

Most typing services handle only routine cases. If the tenant contests the eviction suit—which happens less than one-fourth of the time—the eviction service won't be able to help you in court. At this point, you must represent yourself in court or hire your own lawyer to take over. The eviction service may have a lawyer on its staff whom you can hire or may refer you to a lawyer.

To find an eviction service, check with a landlords' association or look in the telephone book under "Eviction Services" or "Paralegals."

Be sure the eviction service or typing service is reputable and experienced, as well as reasonably priced. (The cost should not exceed $100 for the service, plus another $100 for court filing fees and sheriff's fees.) Ask for references and check them. As a general matter, the longer a typing service has been in business, the better.

Also, an eviction service must be registered and bonded as an "unlawful detainer assistant." (B&P §§ 6400-6415.) If the service isn't registered, don't use it. The court forms that an eviction service prepares require you to state under penalty of perjury whether an "unlawful detainer assistant" helped you, and you must give the eviction service's name, address, and registration number.

D. FINDING A LAWYER

Throughout this book, we point out specific instances when an attorney's advice or services may be useful, including complicated eviction, discrimination, and personal injury lawsuits.

Finding a good, reasonably priced lawyer is not always an easy task. If you just pick a name out of the telephone book, you may get an unsympathetic lawyer, or one who will charge too much, or one who's not qualified to deal with your particular problem. If you use the attorney who drew up your family will, you may end up with someone who knows nothing about landlord law. This sorry result is not necessarily inevitable—there are competent lawyers who charge fairly for their services.

As a general rule, experience is most important. You want a lawyer who specializes in landlord/tenant law. The best way to find a suitable attorney is through some trusted person who has had a satisfactory experience with one. Your best referral sources are other landlords in your area and your local landlords' association.

The worst referral sources are:

- Heavily advertised legal clinics, which are less likely to offer competitive rates for competent representation in this specialized area. While they may offer low flat rates for routine services such as drafting a will, it's less common to see legal clinics charge reasonable flat fees for other specific services. It is not unusual for legal services to advertise a very low basic price and then add to it considerably, based on the assertion that your particular problem costs more.

- Referral panels set up by local bar associations. While they sometimes do minimal screening before qualifying the expertise of lawyers in landlord/tenant law, usually the emphasis is on the word "minimal." You may get a good referral from these panels, but they sometimes refer people to inexperienced practitioners who don't have enough clients and who use the panel as a way of generating needed business.

Once you get a good referral, call the law offices that have been recommended and state your problem. Find out the cost of an initial visit. You should be able to find an attorney willing to discuss your problems for $75. If you feel the lawyer is sympathetic to your concerns and qualified to handle your problem, make an appointment to discuss your situation.

Beware of lawyers who advertise "free consultations." As your own business experience doubtless tells you, the world provides little or nothing of value for free. This is doubly true when it comes to buying legal help. Lawyers who will see you for nothing have every motive to think up some sort of legal action that requires their services. If you insist on paying fairly for an attorney's time, you are far more likely to be advised that no expensive legal action is needed.

Here are some things to look for in your first meeting:

- Will the lawyer answer all your questions about the lawyer's fees and experience in landlord/tenant matters and your specific legal problem? Stay away from lawyers who make you feel uncomfortable asking questions.

- Is the lawyer willing to assist you when you have specific questions, billing you on an hourly basis when you handle your own legal work—such as evictions? Is the lawyer willing to answer your questions over the phone and charge only for the brief amount of time the conversation lasted? Or will you have to make a more time-consuming (and profitable) office appointment? If the lawyer tries to dissuade you from representing yourself in any situation, or won't give any advice over the phone despite your invitation to bill you for it, find someone else. There are plenty of lawyers who will be very happy to bill you hourly to help you help yourself.

• If you want someone to represent you in an eviction lawsuit, does the lawyer charge a flat fee, or an hourly fee with a maximum? Most evictions, especially for nonpayment of rent, are routine and present little trouble, even when contested by the tenant. Many attorneys charge reasonable flat fixed rates, such as $250 to $350, to handle eviction lawsuits. If the lawyer's hourly rate exceeds $100, with no upper limit, you can do better elsewhere.

• If your property is in a rent-controlled city, does the lawyer practice in or near that city and know its rent control laws and practices?

• Does the lawyer represent tenants, too? Chances are that a lawyer who represents both landlords and tenants can advise you well on how to avoid many legal pitfalls of being a landlord.

E. PAYING A LAWYER

If you do need a lawyer, find one who does not object to your doing as much legal work as you want and who will charge a reasonable hourly rate for occasional help and advice. While this isn't impossible, it may be difficult, because some lawyers may not want to accept piecemeal work.

Most lawyers charge $100 to $200 an hour. How you pay your lawyer depends on how often you need legal services.

1. Large Landlord With Regular Legal Needs

If you own more than a dozen rental units and do not wish to handle all your own evictions from start to finish (even if uncontested), you will probably want

to work out a continuing relationship with the lawyer, and you should have more than enough leverage to set up a relatively economical arrangement. There are several ways to go:

• Pay the attorney a modest monthly retainer to work with you and represent you in court in routine eviction cases as needed. (Other types of cases, such as where a tenant sues for damages, are so time-consuming that representation is not included in such retainer agreements.) You can usually get a lot of service for a reasonable pre-established rate.

• Negotiate a fee schedule for various kinds of routine services, based on the lawyer handling all your work. Since you will probably provide a fair amount of business over the years, this should be substantially below the lawyer's normal hourly rate.

• Do the initial legal work in evictions and similar procedures yourself, but turn over to a lawyer cases that become hotly contested or complicated. If this is your plan, look for a lawyer who doesn't resent your doing some of your own legal work and who won't sock you with a high hourly rate for picking up a case you began.

2. Small Landlord With Occasional Legal Needs

If you are a very small landlord, you expect (and hope) that you will have little continuing need for a lawyer. The drawback to needing only occasional legal help is that a lawyer has little incentive to represent you for a reasonable fee when you get into occasional legal hot water. But it's possible to find a lawyer who specializes in landlord/tenant law who will charge you the same prices larger landlords get. And who knows, the lawyer may hope that you will expand your business and become a more profitable client in the future.

Note on attorney fees clause in lawsuits. If your lease or written rental agreement has an attorney fees provision (see Clause 22 of our forms), you are entitled to recover your attorney fees if you win a lawsuit concerning that lease or rental agreement, based on the terms of that agreement. There's no guarantee, however, that a judge will award attorney fees equal to your attorney's actual bill, or that you will ultimately be able to collect the money from the tenant or former tenant. Also, as discussed in Chapter 2, an attorney fees clause in your lease or rental agreement works both ways. Even if the clause doesn't say so, you're liable for the tenant's attorney fees if you lose. (CC § 1717.) (Your landlord's insurance policy will not cover such liability where the lawsuit is unrelated to items covered by the policy, such as eviction lawsuits by the landlord and security deposit refund suits by the tenant.)

F.   RESOLVING PROBLEMS WITH YOUR LAWYER

If you see a problem emerging with your lawyer, nip it in the bud. Don't just sit back and fume; call or write your lawyer. Whatever it is that rankles, have an honest discussion about your feelings. Maybe you're upset because your lawyer hasn't kept you informed about what's going on in your lawsuit against your tenant for property damage, or maybe your lawyer has missed a promised deadline for reviewing your new system for handling maintenance and repair problems. Or maybe last month's bill was shockingly high, or you question the breakdown of how your lawyer's time was spent.

Here's one way to test whether a lawyer-client relationship is a good one—ask yourself if you feel able to talk freely with your lawyer about your degree of participation in any legal matter and your control over how the lawyer carries out a legal assignment. If you can't frankly discuss these sometimes sensitive matters with your lawyer, fire that lawyer and hire another one. If you don't, you'll surely waste money on unnecessary legal fees and risk having legal matters turn out badly.

Remember that you're always free to change lawyers. If you do, be sure to fire your old lawyer before you hire a new one. Otherwise, you could find yourself being billed by both lawyers at the same time. Also, be sure to get all important legal documents back from a lawyer you no longer employ. Tell your new lawyer what your old one has done to date, and pass on the file.

But firing a lawyer may not be enough. Here are some tips on resolving specific problems:

- If you have a dispute over fees, the local bar association may be able to mediate it for you.

- If a lawyer has violated legal ethics—for example, conflict of interest, overbilling, or not representing you zealously—the State Bar of California may discipline or even disbar the lawyer. Although lawyer oversight groups are typically biased in favor of the legal profession, they will often take action if your lawyer has done something seriously wrong.

- When a lawyer has made a major mistake—for example, missing the deadline for filing a case—you can sue for malpractice. Many lawyers carry malpractice insurance, and your dispute may be settled out of court.

YOUR RIGHTS AS A CLIENT

As a client, you have the following rights:

- courteous treatment by your lawyer and staff members

- an itemized statement of services rendered and a full advance explanation of billing practices

- charges for agreed-upon fees and no more

- prompt responses to phone calls and letters

- confidential legal conferences, free from unwarranted interruptions

- up-to-date information on the status of your case

- diligent and competent legal representation, and

- clear answers to all questions. ■

9

DISCRIMINATION

At one time, a landlord could refuse to rent to someone, or evict a month-to-month tenant on 30 days' notice, simply because he didn't like the tenant's skin color, religion, or national origin. All sorts of groups, including African-Americans, Asians, Jews, Hispanics, unmarried couples, gays, families with children, and the disabled, were routinely subjected to discrimination.

Fortunately, the days of legal invidious discrimination are long gone. Several federal, state, and local laws provide severe financial penalties for landlords who discriminate on the basis of race, religion, sex, age, and a number of other categories. And the categories named in the various statutes are not the only groups that are protected—the California Supreme Court has prohibited discrimination based on "personal characteristics" or "personal traits," meaning a person's geographical origin, personal beliefs, or physical attributes. (*Harris v. Capital Growth Investors XIV,* 52 Cal. 3d 1142, 278 Cal. Rptr. 614 (1991).)

This chapter reviews information you need to know to avoid illegally discriminating:

- legal reasons to turn down prospective tenants, such as a bad credit history or too many tenants for the size of the premises

- illegal types of discrimination and major laws and court cases, including recent developments in the field such as expanded protection for families with children

- tenants' legal remedies, in state and federal courts, for discrimination, and

- special rules applying to landlords who share their premises with tenants.

A. LEGAL REASONS FOR REFUSING TO RENT TO A TENANT

The most important decision a landlord makes, save possibly for deciding whether to purchase rental property in the first place, is the choice of your tenants. Chapter 1 recommends a system for carefully

screening potential tenants in order to select people who will pay rent on time, maintain your property and not cause you any problems. Here we focus more closely on making sure that your screening process does not precipitate a costly charge of discrimination.

Remember that only certain kinds of discrimination in rental housing are illegal, such as selecting tenants on the basis of religion or race. (See Section C, below.) You are legally free to choose among prospective tenants as long as your decisions are based on valid and objective business criteria, such as an applicant's ability to pay the rent and properly maintain the property. For example, you may legally refuse to rent to prospective tenants with bad credit histories, unsteady employment histories, or even low incomes that you reasonably regard as insufficient to pay the rent. Why? Because these criteria for tenant selection are reasonably related to your right to run your business in a competent, profitable manner (sometimes called your "legitimate or valid business interests"). And if a person who fits one or more obvious "bad tenant risk" profiles happens to be a member of a minority group, you are still on safe legal ground as long as:

- you are consistent in your screening and treat all tenants more or less equally—for example, you always require a credit report for prospective tenants

- you are not applying a generalization about people of a certain group to an individual, and

- you can document your legal reasons for not renting to a prospective tenant.

But pay attention to the fact that judges, tenants' lawyers, and government agencies that administer and enforce fair housing laws know full well that some landlords try to make up and document legal reasons to discriminate, when the real reason is that they just don't like people with a particular racial, ethnic, or religious background. So, if you refuse to rent to a person who happens to be African-American, has children, or speaks only Spanish, be sure you document your legitimate business reason specific to that individual (such as insufficient income or a history of eviction for nonpayment of rent). Be prepared to show that your tenant advertising, screening, and selection processes have been based on objective criteria and that a more qualified applicant has always gotten the rental unit.

This section discusses some of the common legal reasons you may choose or reject applicants based on your business interests. A valid occupancy limitation (such as overcrowding) can also be a legal basis for a refusal, but since this issue is fairly complicated, we have devoted a separate section to the subject. (See Section D, below.)

To protect yourself in advance, always document your reasons for rejecting a tenant. A tenant whom you properly reject may nevertheless file a discrimination complaint with a fair housing agency. (See Section E, below, for details on the complaint procedure.) Recognizing this, you want to be able to prove that you had a valid business reason for refusing to rent to the particular person, such as negative references from a previous landlord or poor credit history. This means you need to routinely

document your good reasons for rejecting all potential tenants before anyone files a discrimination claim. (We discuss how to document why you chose—or rejected—a particular tenant in Chapter 1.)

OBJECTIVE CRITERIA—WHAT DO THEY LOOK LIKE?

"Objective criteria" are tenancy requirements that are established before a prospective tenant even walks in the door, and are unaffected by the personal value judgments of the person asking the question. For example, a requirement that an applicant must never have been evicted for nonpayment of rent is "objective" because it is a matter of history and can be satisfied by a clear "yes" or "no." "Subjective criteria," on the other hand, have no preestablished correct answers, and the results of the questions will vary depending on the landlord who poses the question—for example, a requirement that the applicant present "a good appearance" has no predetermined "right" answer and will be answered differently by each landlord who asks the question. Subjective criteria are always suspicious in a housing context because their very looseness allows them to mask deliberate illegal discrimination.

So much for theory. Here are a few examples of allowable, objective criteria for choosing tenants:

- two positive references from previous landlords

- sufficient income to pay the rent, and

- a signed waiver allowing landlord to investigate applicant's credit history.

---

1. Credit Record and Income

You can legitimately refuse to rent to a prospective tenant who has a history of nonpayment of rent or whom you reasonably believe would be unable to pay rent in the future.

Here's some advice on how to avoid charges of discrimination when choosing tenants on the basis of income or credit history.

Do a credit check on every prospective tenant and base your selection on the results of that credit check. Accepting or rejecting tenants based on objective criteria tied to a credit report is the best way to protect yourself against an accusation that you're using a bad credit history as an excuse to illegally discriminate against certain prospective tenants. For example, if you establish rules saying you won't rent to someone with bad credit or who is evicted by a previous landlord for nonpayment of rent (information commonly found in credit reports), be sure you apply this policy to all tenants.

Avoid rigid point systems that rank prospective tenants on the basis of financial stability and other factors. Some landlords evaluate prospective tenants by giving each one a certain number of points at the outset, with deductions for bad credit and negative references and additional points for extremely good ones. Points are also awarded based on length of employment and income. The person with the highest score gets the nod. Point systems give the illusion of objectivity, but because the weight you give each factor is, after all, subjective, they can still leave you open to charges of discrimination.

Don't discriminate against married or unmarried couples by counting only one spouse's or partner's income (typically the man's). Always consider the income of both persons living together, married or unmarried, in order to avoid the accusation of marital status or sex discrimination (discussed in Section C, below).

Don't give too much weight to years spent at the same job, which can arguably discriminate against certain occupations. For example, software designers and programmers commonly move from one employer to another. If you insist that an applicant have a minimum number of years with the same employer, you may open yourself up to a charge that you are discriminating against applicants based on their "personal characteristics or traits," which is against the law.

2. Negative References From Previous Landlords

You can legally refuse to rent to someone based on what a previous landlord or manager has to say—for example, that the tenant was consistently late paying rent, broke the lease, or left the place a shambles.

3. Civil Lawsuits Involving a Tenant

Background reports typically indicate whether the applicant has been involved in civil lawsuits, such as an eviction or breach of contract suit. For many landlords, an eviction lawsuit is a red flag. Can you reject a tenant on this basis? It depends.

If a former landlord has filed—and won—an eviction lawsuit against the applicant, you have solid grounds to reject this person. Be careful, however, if the credit report indicates that the applicant, not the former landlord, won the eviction suit, or that the case was settled without stating clearly who won. (California used to prohibit a credit reporting agency from noting that an applicant was involved in an eviction lawsuit unless the landlord clearly won the lawsuit or the case was settled with a statement noting that the landlord prevailed. (CC § 1785.13(a)(3).) However, the Court of Appeal ruled that this law was unconstitutional as an abridgment of free speech. *U.D. Registry v. State of California* (Cisneros), 34 Cal. App. 4th 107 (1995).)

A tenant who has not been found liable by a court of law has not done anything wrong, even though you may suspect that the person is a troublemaker who just got lucky. In most situations, however, if the applicant is truly a poor prospect, the information you get from prior landlords and employers will confirm your suspicions, and you can reject the applicant on these more solid grounds (negative references).

The background report may also indicate that the applicant is now, or has been, involved in another type of civil lawsuit—for example, a custody fight, a personal injury claim, or a dispute with an auto repair shop. If the legal matter has nothing to do with the applicant's rental history, ability to pay the rent, or satisfy your other tenancy requirements, you are on shaky ground if you base a rejection solely on that basis.

4. Criminal History

Understandably, many landlords wish to know about an applicant's prior criminal history. Can you reject an applicant because she has a conviction for drunk driving, or murder, or drug use? What if there was an arrest but no conviction?

a. Convictions

If an applicant has been convicted for criminal offenses, you are probably, with one exception, entitled to reject on that basis. After all, a conviction indicates that the applicant was not, at least in that instance, a law-abiding individual, which is a legitimate criterion for prospective tenants. The exception, however, involves convictions for past drug use: As explained in Section C, below, past drug addiction is considered a disability under the Fair Housing Amendments Act, and you may not refuse to rent to someone on that basis—even if the addiction resulted in a conviction. (People with convictions for the sale or manufacture of drugs, or current drug users, are not, however, protected under the Fair Housing Act.)

b. Megan's Law

Not surprisingly, most landlords do not want to rent to tenants with convictions for violent sexual offenses or any sexual offenses against children. Checking a prospective tenant's background by ordering an investigative background report, as explained in Chapter 1, Section D3, is one way to find out about a person's criminal history. Self-reporting is another: Rental applications, such as the one in this book, typically ask the applicant whether he or she has ever been convicted of a crime and, if so, to provide the details.

"Megan's Law" may be able to further assist you in determining whether an applicant has a prior conviction for any sexual offense against a minor or a violent sexual offense against an adult. This law requires certain convicted sexual offenders to register with local law enforcement officials, who give the information on their whereabouts to a database maintained by the state. (Calif. Penal Code § 290.4.) The information is used or accessed in three ways:

- local law enforcement officials have the discretion to notify people who live near offenders who are "high risk" or "serious"

- any person can call a toll-free number and ask whether a certain individual is on the list, and

- people can view the information at local law enforcement agencies or police departments serving populations of 200,000 or more.

By law, it is illegal to use the information in a way to intimidate or harass any person. Local agencies may require you to state why you are asking for the information.

If you check the Megan's Law database, be aware that it has promised far more than it actually delivers. The law depends in large part on voluntary registration, and the not-surprising result is that California has lost track of nearly half of its sex offenders, according to data released by the state. ("Officials Admit Megan's Law Database Is Missing Thousands," *San Francisco Daily Journal,* January 8, 2003, p. 3.) In short, use the database as only one of your screening tools. Hopefully, the other methods we recommend that you use to learn about prospective tenants will, taken together, give you a complete and accurate picture.

The state maintains a website with information on how to use the database at http://caag.state.ca.us/ megan/. Here, you can read more about the law and download written request forms (which allow you to search or inquire about several names), learn which local law enforcement offices offer viewing, and read a set of frequently asked questions.

c. Arrests

A more difficult problem is posed by the person who has an arrest record but no conviction. For starters, California law strictly forbids a consumer credit reporting agency (the agency doing the background check) from reporting an arrest unless there was a resulting conviction. (CC § 1785.13(a)(6).) Moreover, even convictions that are more than seven years old cannot be reported at all. These restrictions apply to all credit reporting agencies preparing reports for use in California, even if the agency itself is based in another state.

State law does not, however, limit the right of an individual, as opposed to a credit reporting agency, from asking the question or going to the courthouse and asking to examine public records. If you do this and discover that an applicant has an arrest record, what should you do with this information?

Remember, many arrests result in the charges being dropped, and some defendants are acquitted at trial. A person who was mistakenly arrested or acquitted by a jury is not necessarily going to be a bad tenant. Think carefully before you base a rejection on an arrest record alone, especially if the arrest is old or involves a crime unrelated to good-tenant criteria. Be particularly careful if the applicant is also a member of a racial, ethnic, or other group that is protected by the fair housing laws. And keep in mind that if the rest of your background check (involving former landlords and employers) has been thorough, chances are that you will come up with solid information that you can use to reject an applicant without fear of a fair housing claim.

LEGAL RESTRICTIONS ON ACCESS TO ARREST RECORDS

The continued validity of state law (CC § 1785.13(a)(6)) forbidding a credit reporting agency from reporting arrests that did not result in a conviction remains in doubt in light of the holding of *U.D. Registry v. State of California (Cisneros)*, 34 Cal. App. 4th 107 (1995). That case concerned CC § 1785.13(a)(3), which limits the reporting of unlawful detainer actions to situations when the landlord prevailed or there was a settlement statement indicating that the landlord won. The Court of Appeal ruled that the limitation was a violation of the reporting company's right of free speech, since the fact of the unlawful detainer action (and its outcome) was contained in public records available to anyone. Logic would suggest that the same reasoning could be applied to records of arrest that resulted in charges but no conviction. These facts are contained in court records that are accessible to anyone who goes to the courthouse and asks to examine court dockets. Why should a background reporting agency be limited in ways that the general public is not? Check the Update service on the Nolo website, www.nolo.com, for future developments.

EXAMPLE

When the bank on Main Street was robbed, the police broadcast a description of the robber as a young white male with brown hair, wearing jeans, and driving a tan Camaro. Andrew was stopped because he and his car fit this description, and he was arrested and eventually stood trial. He was acquitted by the jury when his attorney was able to show that the fingerprints left by the robber did not match Andrew's.

When Andrew applied for an apartment a few years later, the landlord went to the local county courthouse and asked to examine the criminal records of the last several years. He read about Andrew's arrest, trial, and acquittal. Because Andrew was acquitted and had solid references from prior landlords and employers, the landlord disregarded the fact of the arrest and offered him the apartment.

5. Immigration Status

Until recently, it was not clear whether landlords could inquire as to their applicants' immigration status (and in New York City, landlords are prohibited from asking such questions). HUD has clarified this issue at least with respect to federal law, pointing out that discrimination based solely on a person's immigration status is not illegal. Therefore, asking applicants to provide documentation of their citizenship or immigration status during the screening process does not violate the Federal Fair Housing Act. ("Response to concerns about housing security following September 11, 2001," posted on the HUD website at www.hud.gov:80/offices/fheo/library/sept11.cfm.)

And what about California law? As you know from reading other sections of this chapter, California's antidiscrimination laws are broader than their federal counterparts. So far, however, our state courts and legislature have not directly addressed the question of "immigration status discrimination." Even if they were to disapprove of the practice of questioning immigration status, it's not clear that such a decision or rule would stand up, in view of the apparent intent by the federal government to have the final say regarding the country's response to the threat of terrorism. We suggest that, if you question applicants about their immigration status, be sure to demand proof from *all* applicants, not just those whom you suspect might come from countries that harbor terrorists. Otherwise, you may find yourself facing a charge of ethnic origin discrimination.

6. Incomplete or Inaccurate Rental Application

Your carefully designed application form will do its job only if the applicant provides you with all the necessary information. Obviously, if you can reject an

applicant on the basis of negative references or bad credit history, you can reject them for failing to allow you to check their background, or if you catch them in a lie.

7. Inability to Meet Legal Terms of Lease or Rental Agreement

It goes without saying that you may legally refuse to rent to someone who can't come up with the security deposit or meet some other condition of the tenancy, such as the length of the lease.

8. Pets

You can legally refuse to rent to people with pets, and you can restrict the types of pets you accept. You can also, strictly speaking, let some tenants keep a pet and say no to others—because "pet owners," unlike members of a religion or race, are not as a group protected by antidiscrimination laws. However, from a practical point of view, an inconsistent pet policy is a bad idea because it can only result in angry, resentful tenants.

Keep in mind that you cannot refuse to rent to someone with an animal if that animal is a properly trained "service" dog for a blind, deaf, or physically disabled person. (For a discussion of renting to pet owners, see Clause 13 of our form lease and rental agreements in Chapter 2. Also, see Chapter 12, Section A, which covers landlord liability for injuries caused by tenants' pets.)

B. Sources of Discrimination Laws

Now that we have discussed the permissible reasons to reject an applicant or treat tenants differently, it is time to turn to the impermissible reasons that constitute fair housing violations. First, let's set the stage by explaining the sources of the antidiscrimination laws.

Landlords in California are subject to at least two, and sometimes three or four, tiers of law dealing with illegal discrimination. On the federal side, you are bound by the federal Fair Housing Act (and its 1988 Amendments) and the Civil Rights Act of 1964 (specifically, Title VII of that Act). In addition, all California landlords are subject to the Unruh Act and the Fair Employment and Housing Act, plus provisions in the Business and Professions Code that proscribe unfair competition. (Although you might not think of it this way, courts consider illegal discrimination to be an illegal business practice, too.) Finally, some landlords are subject to local ordinances (enacted by their county or their city) that, either directly or indirectly, forbid additional types of housing discrimination. The chart entitled "Illegal Discrimination," below, summarizes these laws and the discriminatory practices they forbid.

Why is it important to understand that landlords are subject to many laws regulating their relationship with tenants? The obvious answer is that being subject to the laws of several legislative bodies makes you vulnerable to challenges from each of the agencies charged with carrying out these laws. In other words, an act of discrimination may expose you to challenges from the federal government (via the federal Department of Housing and Urban Development, or HUD), the state government (via the California Department of Fair Employment and Housing, or DFEH) or your county or city government (via the office charged with enforcing housing regulations). Under the state's unfair competition laws, you may even be sued by government officials or private citizens who were not themselves the target of the discriminatory incident. (B&P §§ 17200 et seq.) These statutes have been used by the attorney general, district attorneys, nonprofit organizations and even the Consumers' Union to file suit to stop discriminatory practices, even though neither they nor their members were directly affected by the discrimination.

C. FORBIDDEN TYPES OF DISCRIMINATION

Essentially, any discrimination that is not rationally related to a legitimate business reason is illegal. Courts and administrative agencies can assess substantial financial penalties for unlawful discrimination and can order a landlord to rent to a person who was discriminated against.

Even an innocent owner whose agent or manager discriminates without the owner's knowledge can be sued and found liable. (To protect yourself, make sure your manager knows the law. See Section G, below, and Chapter 6, Section D.) Even if you unintentionally violate the federal Fair Housing Act or the state Fair Employment and Housing Act, you can be found liable. In other words, if your behavior has a discriminatory impact on a protected class of persons, your personal intentions are irrelevant.

You might be under the impression that antidiscrimination laws apply only to your decision to accept or reject a prospective tenant. The laws' reach is much broader, however, and affects almost every aspect of your business. If a prospective tenant falls within one of the protected categories described in this section, antidiscrimination laws prohibit you from taking any of the following actions:

- advertising or making any statement that indicates a limitation or preference based on race, religion or any other protected category

- falsely stating that a rental unit is unavailable

- setting more restrictive standards for selecting certain tenants

- refusing to negotiate for a rental agreement or lease

- providing inferior housing conditions, privileges or services

- terminating a tenancy for a discriminatory reason

- providing or suggesting different housing arrangements (commonly known as "steering")

- refusing to allow a disabled person to make "reasonable modifications" to his living space, or

- refusing to make "reasonable accommodations" in rules or services for disabled persons.

An individual who suspects discrimination may file a complaint with HUD or the DFEH, or sue you in federal or state court. See Section E, below.

EXAMPLE 1

An owner, Osgood, rents apartments in his six-unit apartment building without regard to racial or other unlawful criteria. His tenants include an African-American family and a single Latin American woman with children. Osgood sells his building to Leo, who immediately gives only these two tenants 30-day notices. Unless Leo can come up with a valid nondiscriminatory reason for evicting these minority tenants, they can successfully defend an eviction lawsuit Leo brings on the basis of unlawful discrimination. The tenants can also sue Leo for damages in state or federal court.

EXAMPLE 2

Now, let's assume that Leo, having lost both the eviction lawsuits and the tenants' suits for damages against him, still tries to discriminate by adopting a less blatant strategy—adopting an inconsistent policy of responding to late rent payments. When Leo's white tenants without children are late with the rent, he doesn't give them a Three-Day Notice to Pay Rent or Quit until after a five-day grace period, while nonwhite tenants receive their three-day notices the day after the rent is due. In addition, Leo is very slow when nonwhite tenants request repairs. These more subtle means of discrimination are also illegal, and Leo's tenants have grounds to sue him for damages on account of emotional distress, plus punitive damages of up to three times that amount and attorney fees. Leo's tenants also have grounds to defend any eviction lawsuit Leo brings against them.

INFORMATION ON FAIR HOUSING LAWS

For more information on the rules and regulations of the Fair Housing Act, contact HUD's California office at 450 Golden Gate Avenue, San Francisco 94102. Phone: 415-436-6550; to order publications, call 800-767-7468 (TTY: 800-877-8339). For information on state fair housing laws, contact the Department of Fair Employment and Housing at 1515 Clay Street, Suite 701, Oakland 94612. Phone: 800-233-3212; 510-622-2945; www.dfeh.ca.gov. You'll also find good online information at www.housing.org, maintained by Project Sentinel, a Northern California nonprofit organization with consumer education projects, a free mediation service for landlords and tenants and authority to investigate reports of housing discrimination.

For information on local housing discrimination laws, contact the headquarters of your local government, such as your city hall or county courthouse.

HOW FAIR HOUSING GROUPS UNCOVER DISCRIMINATION

Landlords who turn away prospective tenants on the basis of race, ethnic background or other group characteristics obviously never come out and admit what they're doing. Commonly, a landlord falsely tells a person who's a member of a racial minority that no rentals are available, or that the prospective tenant's income and credit history aren't good enough. From a legal point of view, this can be a dangerous—and potentially expensive—tactic. Here's why: Both HUD and fair housing groups that are active in many areas are adept at uncovering this discriminatory practice by having "testers" apply to landlords for vacant housing. Typically, a tester who is African-American or Hispanic will fill out a rental application, listing certain occupational, income and credit information. Then, a white tester will apply for the same housing, listing information very similar—or sometimes not as good—as that given by the minority applicant.

A landlord who offers to rent to a white tester, and rejects—without valid reason—a minority applicant who has the same (or better) qualifications, is very likely to be found to be guilty of discrimination. Such incidents have resulted in many hefty lawsuit settlements. Fortunately, it's possible to avoid the possibility of legal liability based on discrimination by adopting tenant screening policies that don't discriminate and applying them evenhandedly. (See Section A, above.)

In the sections that follow, we'll look at each of the categories of illegal discrimination and explore their obvious and not-so-obvious meaning. These are the "hot buttons" that can get you into trouble with a fair housing agency.

1. Race or Religion

Fortunately, the amount of overt racial and religious discrimination has lessened over the last several decades. This is not to say, however, that discrimination doesn't exist, especially in subtle forms. And unfortunately, housing agencies and the courts may see "discrimination" where your intent was completely well intentioned. Below, we'll look at some of the common examples of both intentional (but subtle) discrimination and of unintended discrimination.

a. Intentional, Subtle Discrimination

It goes without saying that you should not overtly treat tenants differently because of their race or religion—for example, renting only to members of your own religion or race is obviously illegal. Deliberate discrimination should not be cavalierly dismissed, however, as something practiced by insensitive oafs. Unexpected situations can test your willingness to comply with antidiscrimination laws and can reveal subtle forms of intentional discrimination that are just as illegal as blatant discrimination. Consider the following scenario.

EXAMPLE

Several tenants in Creekside Apartments reserved the common room for a religious occasion. Creekside management learned that the tenants were members of a supremacist religion that believes in the inferiority of all nonwhites and non-Christians. Creekside was appalled at the thought of these ideas being discussed on its premises, and denied the group the use of the common room. The tenants who were members of this group filed a discrimination complaint with HUD on the basis of freedom of religion. HUD supported the religious group and forced Creekside to make the common room available. Creekside wisely sent all tenants a memo stating that making the common room available reflects management's intent to comply with fair housing laws and not their endorsement of the principles urged by any group that uses the room.

As the above example illustrates, religions that are outside the mainstream are protected under the discrimination laws.

Don't make decisions on the basis of how applicants sound over the phone. Academic studies show that people can often identify a person's ethnic background based on short phone conversations. Researchers tested this theory on unsuspecting landlords, some of whom rejected large numbers of African-American applicants compared to equally qualified white callers. Fair housing advocacy groups, described in "How Fair Housing Groups Uncover Discrimination," above, can be expected to use this tactic as a way to build a case against landlords whom they suspect of regular, illegal discrimination.

b. Unintended Discrimination

Unintended discriminatory messages may be conveyed when advertisements feature statements such as "next to the Catholic church" or "Sunday quiet times enforced." (Both ads may be understood as suggesting that only Catholics or Christians are welcome as tenants.) The same considerations apply to your dealings with your tenants after they have moved in. Conscientious landlords should carefully review tenant rules, signs, newsletters, and all communications to make sure that they cannot be construed in any way to benefit, support, or discriminate against any racial or religious group. The examples and advice we give below may seem "politically correct" in the extreme, but take our word for it, they are based on actual fair housing complaints, and deserve to be taken seriously.

- The apartment complex newsletter invites everyone to a "Christmas party" held by the management. Non-Christian tenants might feel that this event is not intended for them and therefore that they have been discriminated against. A better approach: Call it a "Holiday Party" and invite everyone.

- Management extends the use of the common room to tenants for "birthday parties, anniversaries and Christmas and Easter parties." A better idea: Invite your tenants to use the common room for special celebrations, rather than list specific holidays.

- In an effort to accommodate your Spanish-speaking tenants, you translate your move-in letter and house rules into Spanish. Regarding the use of alcohol in the common areas, the Spanish version begins, "Unlike Mexico, where drinking may be condoned in public places, alcoholic beverages may not be consumed in common areas. ..." Because this phrase applies a racial generalization, it may well become the basis for a fair housing complaint.

- The metropolitan area where you own residential rental property contains large numbers of both Spanish-speaking and Cantonese-speaking people. Advertising in only Spanish, or translating your lease into only Cantonese, will likely constitute a fair housing violation because it suggests that members of the other group are not welcome.

2. Ethnic Background and National Origin

Like discrimination based on race or religion, discrimination based on national origin is illegal, whether it's practiced openly and deliberately or unintentionally. Though a landlord may not openly state that he doesn't like certain ethnic or national groups and therefore will not rent to them, this is not the end of the story. A landlord who is motivated by a valid business concern, but who chooses tenants in a way that singles out people of a particular nationality, may be found to have acted in a discriminatory way. Let's see how a misguided attempt to choose financially stable, long-term tenants can amount to discrimination against a nationality.

You may legally reject a tenant who has a shadowy financial background and has broken prior leases by suddenly leaving the property. (Section A, above, discusses these types of objective criteria for choosing tenants.) It is common knowledge that many illegal aliens do not have verifiable financial histories, and they can be picked up and deported at any moment. In order to save the cost of a reference check, can you simply ask a Latino for his or her immigration papers or proof of citizenship?

The answer is "No," and the reason lies in the impact this practice will have upon Latinos as a whole (or any other group treated this way by the landlord). If you make it a practice to ask only Latinos for their immigration papers, you can be sure that a legal Latino (who after all is the only one likely to complain to a fair housing agency) will interpret your actions as sending a negative message to Latinos in general: Latinos are not welcome because you view all of them as presumptively poor, illegal aliens. A fair housing agency or court of law would probably agree that this is illegal discrimination.

On the other hand, if you require all prospective tenants to supply satisfactory proof of their identity and eligibility to work (as well as meeting your other criteria), you will get the needed information, but in a nondiscriminatory way. In fact, a directive from HUD specifically allows you to ask about immigration status, but cautions you to ask all applicants. (See Section A5, above, for more on HUD's directive.)

For advice on verifying the legal status of prospective tenants, contact the U.S. Citizenship and Immigration Services (USCIS). To locate a local USCIS office, check the phone book under U.S. Department of Justice, or go to their website at http://uscis.gov.

If you ask one person a question, ask everyone. It cannot be emphasized enough that questions on a prospective tenant's legal status must be put to all applicants, not just the ones who you suspect are illegal, and not just the ones who are applying to live in one of your buildings in a certain part of town.

3. Familial Status

Discrimination on the basis of familial status includes not only affirmatively refusing to rent to families with children or to pregnant women, but also trying to accomplish the same goal by setting overly restrictive space requirements (limiting the maximum number of people permitted to occupy a rental unit), thereby preventing families with children from occupying smaller units.

Section D, below, discusses how to establish reasonable occupancy standards. The fact that you can legally adopt occupancy standards, however, doesn't mean you can use "overcrowding" as a euphemism for refusing to rent to tenants with children, if you would rent to the same number of adults. A few landlords have adopted criteria that for all practical purposes forbid children under the guise of preventing overcrowding—for example, allowing only one person per bedroom, with a couple counting as one person. Under these criteria, a landlord would rent a two-bedroom unit to a husband and wife and their one child, but would not rent the same unit to a mother with two children. This practice, which has the effect of keeping all (or most) children out of a landlord's property, would surely be found illegal in court and would result in monetary penalties.

It would also be illegal to allow children only on ground floors, or to designate certain apartments as separate adult units and family units.

It is essential to maintain a consistent occupancy policy. If you allow three adults to live in a two-bedroom apartment, you had better let a couple with a child (or a single mother with two children) live in the same type of unit, or you leave yourself open to charges that you are illegally discriminating.

EXAMPLE

Jackson owned and managed two one-bedroom units in a duplex, one of which he rented out to three flight attendants who were rarely there at the same time. When the other unit became vacant, Jackson advertised it as a one-bedroom, two-person apartment. Harry and Sue Jones and their teenage daughter were turned away because they exceeded Jackson's occupancy limit of two people. The Jones family filed a complaint with HUD, whose investigator questioned Jackson regarding the inconsistency of his occupancy policy. Jackson was convinced that he was in the wrong, and agreed to rent to the Jones family and to compensate them for the humiliation they had suffered as a result of being refused.

ILLEGAL DISCRIMINATION

State law, and in some cases federal law, absolutely forbids discrimination on the following grounds, regardless of a landlord's claim of a legitimate business need.

Type of Discrimination	Civil Rights Act of 1964 (1)	Fair Housing Act and Fair Housing Amendments Act (2)	Unruh Act (CA) (3)	Fair Employment & Housing Act (CA) (4)	Court Decisions (see footnotes)	Local Ordinances
Race	X	X	X	X		X
Ethnic background		X	X	X		
National origin		X	X	X		
Religion		X	X	X		X
Sex		X	X	X		X
Gender identity				X		
Marital status			X	X	(5)	X
Age and families with children		X	X		(6)	X
Disability		X	X	X	(7)	X
Sexual orientation			X	X	(8)	X
Receipt of public assistance				X	(9)	
Personal characteristic or trait			X		(10)	

(1) 42 U.S.C. § 1982.

(2) 42 U.S.C. §§ 3601-3619, 3631.

(3) CC §§ 51-53, 54.1-54.8.

(4) Government Code §§ 12926, 12955-12988. For specific prohibition of discrimination on the grounds of marital status, see *Atkisson v. Kern County Housing Authority*, 58 Cal. App. 3d 89 (1976); and *Hess v. Fair Employment and Housing Commission*, 138 Cal. App. 3d 232 (1982).

(5) *Smith v. Fair Employment and Housing Commission*, 12 Cal. 4th 1143, 51 Cal. Rptr. 2d 700 (1996); and *Hess v. Fair Employment and Housing Commission*, 138 Cal. App. 3d 232 (1982).

(6) *Marina Point, Ltd. v. Wolfson*, 30 Cal. 3d 721 (1982), construes the Unruh Act to prohibit discrimination against families on the sole basis that they have children.

(7) *Giebeler v. M & B Associates*, 2003 WL 22119329, ____ F.3d ____ (2003). If a prospective tenant is disabled and therefore unable to work, but has a financially qualified cosigner who will agree in writing to pay the rent, refusal to accept the tenant, based on an inflexible policy against cosigners, could constitute illegal discrimination based on disability.

(8) *Beaty v. Truck Insurance Exchange*, 6 Cal. App. 4th 1455 (1992).

(9) 59 Ops. Cal. Atty. Gen. 223. However, a landlord may legally refuse to rent to a tenant who fails to meet minimum-income criteria, so long as the same test is applied equally to all applicants regardless of their source of income. *Harris v. Capital Growth Investors XIV*, 52 Cal. 3d 1142 (1991). But as to disabled prospective tenants who don't meet this criteria, see (7), above.

(10) *Harris v. Capitol Growth Investors XIV*, 52 Cal. 3d 1142 (1991).

You cannot legally refuse to rent on account of a woman's pregnancy (whether she is single, married, or with an unmarried cohabitant). Doing so is illegal discrimination based on sex. (Gov. C. § 12926(p); see Subsection C5 below.) When the birth of a child would result in exceeding your uniformly applied and reasonable occupancy standards, you should proceed with caution and contact an attorney knowledgeable in this area.

Finally, do not inquire as to the age and sex of any children who will be sharing the same bedroom. This is their parents' business, not yours. (The General Counsel for HUD wrote in a July 1995 memo that consideration by a landlord of the age and sex of tenant children was a violation of the Fair Housing Act with respect to sex discrimination.)

4. Marital Status

Under California law, landlords may not discriminate on the basis of marital status. This means that you cannot refuse to rent to single renters because you'd rather have married people in your building; nor may you refuse to rent to married tenants because you want a "singles only" environment.

But what about renting to people who appear to be a couple but who aren't married? Can a landlord who believes that cohabitation is morally wrong refuse to rent to unmarried couples? The answer is a firm "No." (*Smith v. Fair Employment & Housing Commission,* 12 Cal. 4th 1143, 51 Cal. Rptr. 2d 700 (1996).)

5. Age

The federal Fair Housing Act does not expressly use the word "age," but nevertheless discrimination on the basis of age is definitely included within the ban against discrimination on the basis of familial status. The Unruh Act, on the other hand, explicitly forbids discrimination on the basis of age. While the issue of age discrimination usually arises in the context of families with children, it is also present in the practice of some landlords to rent to only "youthful" applicants,

or to set quotas of young versus elderly tenants in order to preserve a certain "mix" of residents. Sometimes called "reverse discrimination," choices made on the basis of advanced age are as illegal as those based on youth. Housing reserved exclusively for senior citizens, which must meet strict requirements, is exempted. (CC § 51.3 defines senior citizen housing as that reserved for persons 62 years of age or older, or a complex of 150 or more units (35 in nonmetropolitan areas) for persons older than 55 years. The federal law definition is almost identical (42 U.S.C. § 3607).)

A charge of age discrimination could arise in situations where the landlord's intentions are well meaning but his methods are suspect. For example, we are often reminded that ours is an aging society, and that with the increase in the number of older adults comes the need for appropriate housing. Some older tenants may not, however, be able to live completely independently—for example, they may rely on the regular assistance of a nearby adult child or friend. Can you, as the landlord, refuse to rent to an older person solely because you fear that her frailty or dimming memory will pose a threat to the health or safety of the rest of your tenants?

The answer to this question is "No." You may feel that your worry about elderly tenants is well founded, but unless you can point to an actual incident or to facts that will substantiate your concern, you cannot reject an elderly applicant on the basis of your fears alone. For example, you could turn away an older applicant if you learned from a prior landlord or employer that the person regularly forgot to lock the doors, failed to manage his income so that he was often late in paying rent, or demonstrated an inability to undertake basic housekeeping chores. In other words, if the applicant has demonstrated that he or she is unable to live alone, your regular and thorough background check should supply you with those facts, which are legally defensible reasons to refuse to rent. If you reject an applicant solely on your "hunch" that the person will never be able to make it alone, you are setting yourself up for a fair housing complaint. As for your stylistic preference for youthful tenants, this is age discrimination in its purest form, and it will never survive a fair housing complaint.

EXAMPLE 1

Nora's 80-year-old mother, Ethel, decided that it was time to find a smaller place and move closer to her daughter. Ethel sold her home and applied for a one-bedroom apartment at Coral Shores. Ethel had impeccable references from neighbors and employers and an outstanding credit history. Nonetheless, Mike, the manager of Coral Shores, was concerned about Ethel's age. Fearful that Ethel might forget to turn off the stove, lose her key, or do any number of other dangerous things, Mike decided on the spot not to rent to her. Ethel filed a fair housing complaint, which she won on the basis of age discrimination.

Learning from his experience with Ethel, Mike, the manager at Coral Shores, became more conscientious in screening tenants. The following example shows how he avoided another lawsuit on age discrimination.

EXAMPLE 2

William was an elderly gentleman who decided to sell the family home and rent an apartment after his wife passed away. He applied for an apartment at Coral Shores. Since William had no "prior rental history," Mike, the manager, drove to William's old neighborhood and spoke with several of his former neighbors. Mike also called William's personal references. From these sources, Mike learned that William had been unable to take care of himself the last few years, having been completely dependent on his wife. Mike also learned that, since his wife's death, William had made several desperate calls to neighbors and family when he had been unable to extinguish a negligently started kitchen fire, find his

keys, and maintain basic levels of cleanliness in his house. Mike noted these findings on William's application and declined to rent to him on the basis of these specific facts.

You may also find yourself in the situation of having rented to someone who has lived alone competently for years but who, with advancing age, appears to be gradually losing the ability to live safely by himself. Determining the point when the tenant should no longer live alone is a judgment call that will vary with every situation, and we cannot provide a checklist of "failings" that will suffice for everyone. There is, however, one universal ground rule that will, by now, sound pretty familiar: You cannot evict merely on the basis of the person's elderly status, nor can you base your actions solely on your fears of what that person might do. You must be able to point to real, serious violations of the criteria that apply to all tenants before you can take action against an elderly violator.

Elderly tenants may also qualify as disabled tenants, who are entitled to accommodation under the law. An elderly tenant who, because of her age, cannot meet one of your policies may be entitled to special treatment because she also qualifies as someone disabled. (See the discussion of discrimination on the basis of disability in Section 7.) In other words, you may not be able to use an elderly tenant's inability to abide by one of the terms of the tenancy as the basis of an eviction—instead, you may be expected to adjust your policy in order to accommodate her disability. For example, an elderly tenant who is chronically late with the rent because of her sporadic disorientation might be entitled to a grace period or a friendly reminder from the landlord or manager when the rent is due; whereas a nondisabled tenant who is chronically late with the rent may be a proper candidate for eviction.

RENTING TO MINORS

You may wonder whether the prohibition against age discrimination applies to minors (people under age 18). If the minor applicant is "legally emancipated"—which means that the young person must be legally married, have a court order of emancipation, or be in the military—he or she has the same status as an adult. This means you will need to treat the applicant like any other adult. In short, if the applicant satisfies the rental criteria that you apply to everyone, a refusal to rent to a minor could form the basis of a fair housing complaint. On the other hand, if the applicant is not emancipated, it's probably not legal for the person to be on their own in the first place; and in any event, chances are that the applicant's credit history or financial status will not meet your requirements. The person could be rejected on that basis.

6. Sex

Sex discrimination sometimes takes the form of refusing to rent to single women with a certain income, but renting to men with similar incomes, though this is rare. It can also take the form of refusing to rent to a pregnant woman, whether she is single or with a cohabitant or spouse. (Gov. C. Sec. 12926(p); for more on this, see the discussion on Familial Status discrimination in Section C3 above.) Sex discrimination also sometimes takes the form of sexual harassment—refusing to rent to a person who resists a landlord's or manager's sexual advances, or making life difficult for a tenant who has resisted such advances.

What is sexual harassment in a rental housing context? Courts have defined it as:

• a pattern of persistent, unwanted attention of a sexual nature, including the making of sexual remarks and physical advances, or a single instance of highly egregious behavior. A manager's repeated requests for social contact or constant remarks concerning a tenant's appearance or behavior could constitute sexual harassment, as could a single extraordinarily offensive remark, or

• a quid pro quo, in which a tenant's rights are conditioned upon the acceptance of the owner's or manager's attentions. For example, the manager who refuses to fix the plumbing until the tenant agrees to a date is guilty of sexual harassment. This type of harassment may be established on the basis of only one incident.

EXAMPLE

Oscar, the resident manager of Northside Apartments, was attracted to Martha, his tenant, and asked her repeatedly for a date. Martha always turned Oscar down and asked that he leave her alone. Oscar didn't back off, and began hanging around the pool whenever Martha used it. Oscar watched Martha intently and made suggestive remarks about her to the other tenants. Martha stopped using the pool and filed a sexual harassment complaint with HUD, claiming that Oscar's unwanted attentions made it impossible for her to use and enjoy the pool. Oscar refused to consider a settlement when the HUD investigator spoke to him and Martha about his actions. As a result, HUD pursued the case in court, where a federal judge awarded several thousand dollars in damages to Martha.

Sexual harassment awards under the Civil Rights Act have no limits. Owners and managers who engage in sexual harassment risk being found liable under Title VII of the 1964 Civil Rights Act, which also prohibits sexual discrimination. There are no limits to the amount of punitive damages that can be awarded in Title VII actions. Punitive damages are generally not covered by insurance, and it is far from clear whether even actual damages in a discrimination case (that is, nonpunitive damages, such as pain and suffering) will be covered, either. See Section H, below, for a discussion of insurance coverage in discrimination cases.

7. Disability

The federal Fair Housing Act and the state's Unruh and Fair Employment and Housing Acts prohibit discrimination against people who:

- have a physical or mental disability (including, but not limited to, hearing, mobility and visual impairments, chronic alcoholism or mental illness, AIDS, AIDS-Related Complex, HIV-positive status, and mental retardation) that substantially limits one or more major life activities

- have a history or record of such a disability, or

- are regarded by others as though they have such a disability.

You may be shocked to see what is—and what is not—considered a disability. Although it may seem strange, an alcoholic is considered disabled. Does this mean that you must rent to a drunk? What about past, and current, drug addiction? Let's look at each of these issues.

a. Alcoholism

You may encounter an applicant, let's call him Ted, who passes all your criteria for selecting tenants but whose personal history includes a disquieting note: Employers and past landlords let you know they suspect that Ted has a serious drinking problem that is getting worse. However, as far as you can tell, Ted has not lost a job or a place to live due to his drinking problem. Can you refuse to rent to Ted for fear that he will drink away the rent, exhibit loud or inappropriate behavior, or damage your property? No, you cannot, unless you can point to specific acts of misbehavior or financial shakiness that would sink any applicant, regardless of the underlying cause. Your fear alone that this might happen (however well founded) will not legally support your refusal to rent to Ted. In a nutshell, you may not refuse to rent to an alcoholic simply because of his status as an alcoholic— you must be able to point to specific facts other than his status as an alcoholic that render him unfit as a tenant.

EXAMPLE

Patsy applied for an apartment one morning and spoke with Carol, the manager. Patsy said she would have to return that afternoon to complete the application form because she was due at an Alcoholics Anonymous meeting. Carol decided on the spot that she did not want Patsy for a tenant, and she told Patsy that the unit "had just been rented," which was a lie. (Patsy saw a newspaper ad for the unit the next week.) Patsy filed a complaint with HUD, alleging that she was an alcoholic who had been discriminated against. Because Carol could not point to any reason for turning Patsy away other than her assumption that Patsy, as an alcoholic, would be a bad tenant, the judge awarded Patsy several thousand dollars in damages.

The fact that alcoholism is classified as a disability does not mean that you must rent (or continue to rent) to every alcoholic. The law only prohibits you from turning away (or evicting) an alcoholic solely because he fits into this classification. If you do a thorough background check and discover that the applicant has shown an inability to pay the rent or a tendency to damage property, you may refuse to rent on those bases, just as you would refuse to rent to a nonalcoholic who had the same history. Similarly, if an alcoholic damages your property or interferes with your other tenants' ability to quietly enjoy their property, he is a candidate for eviction, just as would be any tenant who exhibited this behavior. Consider the following scenario, which is what Carol should have done.

EXAMPLE

Same facts as above, except that Carol went ahead and took an application from Patsy later that day and checked her references. Patsy's former landlord told Carol that Patsy had refused to pay for damage from a fire she had negligently caused; Patsy's employment history showed a pattern of short-lived jobs and decreasing wages. Carol noted this information on Patsy's application form and, as she would have done for any applicant with a similar background, Carol rejected Patsy. Patsy filed a complaint with HUD, again claiming discrimination on the basis of her alcoholism. When the HUD investigator asked to see Patsy's application and questioned Carol about her application criteria for all applicants, he concluded that the rejection had been based on legally sound business reasons and was not, therefore, a fair housing violation.

When dealing with suspected alcoholism, mental problems, or drug use, recognize that rejecting on these bases alone is illegal. Do a thorough investigation: If you discover that the applicant has negative references or a poor credit or employment history, use these factors as the basis for your rejection.

b. Drug Use

Under the Fair Housing Act, a person who has a past drug addiction is classed as someone who has a record of a disability and, as such, is protected under the fair housing law. You may not refuse to rent to someone solely because he is an ex-addict, even if that person has felony convictions for drug use. Put another way, your fear that the person will resume his illegal drug use is not sufficient grounds to reject the applicant. If you do a thorough background check, however, and discover a rental or employment history that would defeat any applicant, you may reject the person as long as it is clear that the rejection is based on these legal reasons.

On the other hand, someone who currently uses illegal drugs is breaking the law, and you may certainly refuse to rent to him—particularly if you have good reason to suspect the person is dealing drugs. (See Chapter 12 for a discussion of legal problems you face by allowing current drug users to live in your property.) Also, if the applicant has felony convictions for dealing or manufacturing illegal drugs, as distinct from convictions for possession of drugs for personal use, you may use that history as a basis of refusal.

c. Mental or Emotional Impairments

Like alcoholics or past drug users, applicants and tenants who have (or appear to have) mental or emotional impairments must be evaluated based on their financial stability and histories as tenants, not on their mental health status. Unless you can point to specific instances of past behavior that would make a prospective tenant dangerous to others, or unless you have other valid business criteria for rejecting the person, a refusal to rent could result in a fair housing complaint.

d. Questions and Actions That May Be Considered to Discriminate Against the Disabled

You may not ask a prospective tenant if she has a disability or illness, or ask to see medical records. If it is obvious that someone is disabled—for example, the person is in a wheelchair or wears a hearing aid—it is illegal to inquire how severely he is disabled.

Unfortunately, even the most innocuous, well-meaning question or remark can get you into trouble, especially if you decide not to rent to the person. What you might consider polite conversation may be taken as a probing question designed to discourage an applicant.

EXAMPLE

Sam, a Vietnam veteran, was the owner of Belleview Apartments. Jim, who appeared to be the same age as Sam and who used a wheelchair, applied for an apartment. Thinking that Jim might have been injured in the Vietnam War, Sam questioned Jim about the circumstances of his disability, intending only to pass the time and put Jim at ease. During their conversation, Sam learned that Jim had not been in Vietnam. When Jim was not offered the apartment—he did not meet the financial criteria that Sam applied to all applicants—he filed a complaint with

HUD, alleging discrimination based on his disability. Sam was unable to convince the HUD investigator that his questions were not intended to be discriminatory and, on the advice of his attorney, Sam settled the case for several thousand dollars.

A manager's or landlord's well-intentioned actions, as well as his words, can become the basis of a fair housing complaint. For example, it is illegal to "steer" applicants to units that you, however innocently, think would be most appropriate. For example, if you have two units for rent—one on the ground floor and one three stories up—do not fail to show both units to the applicant who is movement impaired, however reasonable you think it would be for the person to consider only the ground floor unit.

e. The Rights of Disabled Tenants

You must also concern yourself with the Fair Housing Act after you have rented a home to a disabled person. The Fair Housing Act requires that you:

* *accommodate* the needs of a disabled tenant, at your expense (42 U.S.C. § 3604(f)(B) (1988)), and

* allow disabled tenants to make reasonable *modifications* of their living unit at their expense if that is what is needed for the person to comfortably and

safely live in the unit. (42 U.S.C. § 3604(f)(3)(A) (1988).)

We'll look briefly at each of these requirements.

Accommodation. Landlords and managers are expected to adjust their rules, procedures or services in order to give a person with a disability an equal opportunity to use and enjoy a dwelling unit or a common space. Accommodations include such things as:

* providing a close-in, spacious parking space for a wheelchair-bound tenant

* allowing a guide dog or other "service dog" in a residence that otherwise disallows pets

* allowing a special rent payment plan for a tenant whose finances are managed by someone else or by a government agency

* arranging to read all communications from management to a blind tenant, and

* providing a tub and clothesline for a mentally ill tenant whose anxiety about machines makes her unable to use the washer and dryer.

Does your duty to accommodate disabled tenants mean that you must bend every rule and change every procedure at the tenant's request? Generally speaking, the answer is "No": A landlord is expected to accommodate "reasonable" requests, but he need not undertake changes that would seriously impair his ability to run his business.

Modification. Where your duty to accommodate ends, your obligation to allow the tenant to modify may begin. A disabled person has the right to modify his living space to the extent necessary to make the space safe and comfortable, as long as the modifications will not make the unit unacceptable to the next tenant or the disabled tenant agrees to undo the modification when he leaves, subject to reasonable wear and tear. Examples of modifications undertaken by a disabled tenant include:

* lowering counter tops for a wheelchair-bound tenant

* installing special faucets or door handles for persons with limited hand use

- modifying kitchen appliances to accommodate a blind tenant, and

- installing a ramp to allow access to a wheelchair.

You are not obliged to allow a disabled tenant to modify his unit at will, without your prior approval. You are entitled to ask for a reasonable description of the proposed modifications, proof that they will be done in a workmanlike manner and evidence that the tenant is obtaining any necessary building permits. Moreover, if a tenant proposes to modify the unit in such a manner that will require restoration when the tenant leaves (such as the repositioning of lowered kitchen counters), you may require that the tenant pay into an interest-bearing escrow account the amount estimated for the restoration. (The interest belongs to the tenant.)

If a tenant asks to modify his dwelling to accommodate a disability, you may ask for substantiation that the person does, indeed, have the claimed impairment that the proposed modification addresses. Requesting a letter from the tenant's physician describing the impairment and why the modifications are necessary would not violate the Fair Housing Act. Remember, however, that this is very different from asking that person before renting to him to describe and verify his disability: This is illegal!

f.   The Americans With Disabilities Act (ADA)

The federal Americans With Disabilities Act, commonly known as the "ADA," provides widespread protection to disabled people in the realm of employment and public and commercial accommodations. (42 U.S.C. § 12101 et seq.) Landlords who employ workers are subject to its requirements, but the impact of the ADA doesn't stop here. The ADA applies to two additional areas, even for landlords who are not employers:

- **Common areas and areas open to the public.** Areas of common use, such as the lobby and passageways, including the rental office, must comply with the ADA, whereas rental units are subject to the federal Fair Housing Act, the Unruh Act and the state Fair Employment and Housing Act.

- **Telecommuters or persons with home business offices.** The ADA exempts facilities covered by the federal Fair Housing Act, but the exemption may not apply when the residence is also used as a commercial site. Under federal law, even something as simple as a business call from a home office to another state could constitute an act of "commerce," thus bringing the home office within the purview of the ADA. The requirements of the ADA apply only to new construction, or when alterations are made in the existing building. (Landlords are not required to "retrofit" existing structures.) Of major importance to the landlord is the interpretation by the U.S. Department of Justice that the accessibility requirements extend not only to the commercial site itself (the home office), but to entryways, doorways, hallways, and restrooms if these aspects of the building are used by the telecommuter's or home worker's business invitees.

The implications of the ADA's requirements are significant. Unlike the federal Fair Housing Act, there is nothing in the ADA that requires the landlord to allow modification of the structure at the tenant's expense. The ADA simply mandates that the structure be in compliance; it is up to the landlord and the tenant/home office worker to work things out between themselves. Keep these considerations in mind if a tenant proposes to set up a home office.

FILL YOUR ACCESSIBLE UNITS

The National Apartment Association (NAA) maintains a website that connects owners of already accessible residential units with disabled tenants seeking housing: www.aptsforrent.com/naac. Owners complete a form listing the accessible features of their rental units—for example, lowered counters or the presence of a ramp. A tenant who calls the NAA can request a database search for an appropriate match. The service is free to landlords and tenants.

NEW BUILDINGS AND THE DISABLED

The Fair Housing Amendments Act (42 U.S. C. §§ 3604(f)(3)(C) and 3604(f)(7)) imposes requirements on new buildings of four or more units that were first occupied after March, 1991. All ground floor units and every unit in an elevator building must be designed or constructed so that:

- the main building is accessible and on an accessible route

- the public and common areas are "readily accessible to and usable by" the disabled, including parking areas (a good rule of thumb is to reserve 2% of the spaces)

- entryway doorways have 36" of free space *plus* shoulder and elbow room; and interior doorways are at least 32" wide

- interior living spaces have wheelchair-accessible routes throughout, with changes in floor height of no more than 1/4"

- light switches, outlets, thermostats, and other environmental controls are within the legal "reach range" (15" to 48" from the ground)

- bathroom walls are sufficiently reinforced to allow the safe installation of "grab bars," and

- kitchens and bathrooms are large enough to allow a wheelchair to maneuver within the room (40" turning radius minimum) and have sinks and appliances positioned to allow side or front use.

8. Sexual Orientation

It is illegal to discriminate on the basis of someone's sexual orientation in California. "Sexual orientation" includes heterosexuality, homosexuality, and bisexuality. (Government Code § 12920 and following.)

9. Gender Identity

As of January 1, 2004, it is against state law to discriminate on the basis of a person's gender or gender identity. (Calif. Government Code § 12926). This means that you may not refuse to rent to someone who has changed, or is in the process of changing, his or her gender, through hormone treatment, surgery, or both. In practical terms, if an applicant's dress and mannerisms don't match your expectation for that individual's stated gender identity, you cannot legally refuse to rent on that basis.

WHAT'S IT ALL ABOUT?

California law prohibits discrimination on the basis of sex, sexual orientation, and gender identity. Are you confused by these terms? You're not alone. Here's what they mean:

- **Sex.** Landlords cannot refuse to rent to someone (or set different policies) on the basis of that person's sex. For example, you can't decide that you'll not have women living in the ground floor units, nor can you turn down male applicants because you think that men will cause more wear and tear than women.

- **Sexual orientation.** You can't discriminate against people who are gay, lesbian, or bisexual, or whom you think are gay, lesbian, or bisexual.

- **Gender identity.** You cannot discriminate against people who have changed their gender, which means that they have transitioned from the gender they were assigned at birth to the opposite gender. Transgendered individuals transition to their new persona by dressing and acting according to their chosen gender, and often by taking hormones or having surgery.

Most savvy landlords will focus on an applicant's ability to pay the rent, credit history, and rental history. If you do the same, the applicant's manner and private life won't concern you

10. Smoking

Discrimination against smokers is not specifically prohibited by any civil rights law, and no California court has ruled that such discrimination is prohibited. Because "smokers," as a class, are not a specifically protected group, would it be legal for a landlord to turn away a smoker, or charge higher rent, or designate certain apartments as "nonsmoking" only? (Remember, each of these acts would be illegal if systematically practiced against members of a particular race, religion, ethnicity, or other protected group.) Or, to look at it from another perspective, would discrimination against smokers constitute discrimination on the basis of a person's "personal characteristics" or "personal trait" (discussed in more detail in Section 13, below), which is illegal under the Unruh Act?

There is no clear answer to this question, and we can only suggest how a court might approach the issue. Let's start by remembering the point made many times in Section A, above, when discussing legal reasons to discriminate: If a valid business reason underlies your housing decision, and if you apply the criterion across the board to every applicant and tenant, the mere fact that a particular individual happens to belong to a protected class will not turn your decision into an act of illegal discrimination. When we apply this principle to the question of smokers, a number of ideas come to mind in defense of a "No Smokers" policy:

- **Smoke = expense.** Smoke damages carpets, drapes, and paint. If this type of damage is considered "normal wear and tear," which you pay for, you will end up with greater repair and replacement costs by renting to a smoker. But you cannot "build in" the cost of smoke-damaged premises by tacking it onto a security deposit, since the maximum amount of the deposit is limited by state law. (See Chapter 5.) Therefore, you could make a strong argument that smokers create added maintenance and repair costs, which constitutes a valid business reason to charge a higher rent, limit the number of smokers' units, or prohibit smoking in common areas or altogether.

- **Smoke = liability.** The health dangers from secondhand smoke are understood and acknowledged. Indeed, California has a statewide law forbidding smoking in most workplaces and in restaurants (local restrictions may be even stricter). (Labor Code § 6404.5) It would seem illogical to require a restaurant to prohibit smoking, but not allow a landlord to make the same rule. And if a pile of stinking garbage constitutes a nuisance, over which the landlord can be successfully sued, why not the pervasive, unpleasant, and unhealthy stench from stale smoke in the apartment lobby or laundry room?

Remember, no court case has specifically upheld the landlord's right to limit his premises to nonsmokers, or to otherwise apply different rental terms and conditions to smokers. Whether such a practice would pass the "legitimate business interest" test, or whether it would run afoul of the prohibition against discrimination on the basis of one's "personal characteristic," is yet to be known.

11. Waterbeds

State law forbids an owner of property built after January 1973 from refusing to rent to a tenant simply because she has a waterbed. (CC § 1940.5.) However, the landlord may insist on strict standards (discussed under Clause 20 in Chapter 2) in leases and rental agreements.

12. Public Assistance

You may not refuse to rent to a person simply because he is receiving public assistance. You may, however, refuse to rent to persons whose incomes fall below a certain level, as long as you apply that standard across the board. For example, if you require all prospective tenants to have a $1,000 monthly income before you will consider renting to them, the fact that this excludes welfare recipients who receive only $700 a month does not constitute illegal discrimination under the Unruh Act. (In *Harris v. Capital Growth Investors XIV*, 52 Cal. 3d 1142 (1991), the California Supreme Court ruled that a landlord who insisted a tenant's monthly income equal three times the rent did not unlawfully discriminate in violation of the Unruh Act.) In addition, you cannot *exclude* any welfare or other assistance payments an applicant may receive when computing the applicant's total income, for purposes of your income-to-rent ratio. Using the example above, if an applicant receives a subsidy of $400 and has other income that, added to the subsidy, meets or exceeds your income requirements, you cannot disregard the subsidy.

Finally, you would be guilty of unlawful discrimination if you normally rented to tenants regardless of income, but set an income requirement for public assistance recipients; or if you refused to rent to a person who qualified under your guidelines solely because he received welfare.

13. Personal Characteristics or Traits

After reading the above list outlining the types of discrimination forbidden by California and federal law, you might be tempted to assume that it is legal to discriminate for any reason not mentioned by name in a state, federal, or local law. For example, because none of the civil rights laws specifically prohibits discrimination against men with beards or long hair, you might conclude that such discrimination is permissible. This is not true.

Even though California's Unruh Civil Rights Act contains only the words "sex, race, color, religion, ancestry, or national origin" to describe types of discrimination that are prohibited, illegal discrimination is not limited to these categories. The California Supreme Court has ruled that discrimination on the basis of an individual's "personal characteristic or trait" is also illegal. This means that you may not discriminate on the basis of a current or prospective tenant's geographical origin, physical attributes, or personal beliefs. (*Harris v. Capital Growth Investors XIV*, 52 Cal. 3d 1142 (1991).)

NOTE ON LOW-INCOME TENANTS

Many tenants with low incomes may qualify for federally subsidized housing assistance, the most common being the Section 8 program of the federal Department of Housing and Urban Development (HUD). ("Section 8" refers to Section 8 of the United States Housing Act of 1937, 42 U.S.C. § 1437(f).) That program subsidizes tenants' rents by paying part of the rent directly to the landlord. The local housing authority, landlord, and tenant enter into a one-year agreement, which includes a written lease supplied by the county housing authority. The tenant pays up to 30% of his monthly income to the landlord, and the housing authority pays the landlord the difference between the tenant's contribution and what it determines is the market rent each month.

Section 8 offers several advantages to the landlord:

• The larger part of the rent is paid on time every month by the housing authority, and the tenant's portion is low enough so that he doesn't have too much trouble paying on time, either.

• If the tenant doesn't pay the rent and you have to evict him, the housing authority guarantees the tenant's unpaid portion, and also guarantees payment for damages to the property by the tenant, up to a certain limit.

Section 8's disadvantages are that:

• The housing authority's determination of what is market rent is often low.

• The landlord is locked into a tenancy agreement for one year, and can't terminate the tenancy except for nonpayment of rent or other serious breach of the lease. Even then, 90 days' notice is required (CC § 1954.535.) (Evictions based on grounds other than nonpayment of rent are difficult.)

You have the right to decide not to participate in the Section 8 program without violating any anti-discrimination laws. Call the housing authority in the county where your property is located if you wish to participate in the Section 8 program. They will refer eligible applicants to you and will prepare the necessary documents (including the lease) if you decide to rent to an eligible applicant.

What does this tell a landlord who hates lawyers and decides never to rent to one, or who doesn't approve of long-haired men? In a word, it ought to tell him that discrimination on these grounds, since it is based on the person's appearance or occupation (which are personal characteristics or traits), is against the law. We come once again to the landlord's guiding light for housing decisions: Only valid business reasons, applied uniformly to all tenants, will make it past a fair housing complaint.

EXAMPLE

Sara owns a small apartment complex in a university town. She has had a recurring problem renting to students, many of whom have abandoned their leases, flaunted her policies regarding unauthorized cotenants, and caused inordinate wear and tear. Since many of the student tenants come from out of state, suing them successfully in small claims court has been difficult. Deciding that renting to students is a poor business practice, Sara adopts a "no out-of-state students" policy.

Sara's policy is an invitation to a fair housing complaint. Prospective student tenants could argue that her approach constitutes discrimination on the basis of a personal characteristic (being a student) and geographic origin (coming from out of state), both of which are against the law under the Supreme Court's interpretation of the Unruh Act. But what about Sara's experience with student tenants? Is there a legal way to protect her business?

The answer to Sara's problems lies in tightening up her procedures with respect to all applicants. For example, if she requires everyone to provide several references from prior landlords, she should to be able to weed out the applicants who are likely to break the lease and leave. In order to be fair to those students who have no rental history, Sara might accept employer references or require the students' parents to cosign the lease. The lease should make it clear

that the presence of unauthorized, long-term guests is grounds for eviction; it is up to Sara to be vigilant and make sure that this rule is not ignored.

D. OCCUPANCY LIMITS

The fact that discrimination against families with children is illegal does not mean you have to rent a one-bedroom apartment to a family of five. You can legally establish reasonable space-to-people ratios, but you cannot use overcrowding as a pretext for refusing to rent to tenants with children, if you would rent to the same number of adults.

A few landlords have adopted criteria that for all practical purposes forbid children under the guise of preventing overcrowding—for example, allowing only one person per bedroom, with a couple counting as one person. Under these criteria, a landlord would rent a two-bedroom unit to a husband and wife and their one child, but would not rent the same unit to a mother with two children. This practice has the effect of keeping all (or most) children out of a landlord's property and for this reason is likely illegal. At the least, it's strong evidence of an intent to discriminate.

One court has already ruled against a landlord who did not permit more than four persons to occupy three-bedroom apartments. (*Zakaria v. Lincoln Property Co.*, 185 Cal. App. 3d 500, 229 Cal. Rptr. 669 (1986).) In *Smith v. Ring Brothers Management Corp.*, 183 Cal. App. 3d 649, 228 Cal. Rptr. 525 (1986), another court held that a rule precluding a two-child family from occupying a two-bedroom apartment violated a local ordinance similar to state law.

The state Fair Employment and Housing Commission has ruled that a Los Angeles apartment owner who limited occupancy to one person per bedroom—when state health and safety laws would have allowed as many as ten people in a two-bedroom apartment there—had clearly intended to exclude children. The tenants who had been denied an apartment and complained to the state were awarded $2,500 each.

OCCUPANCY LIMITS AND THE UNIFORM HOUSING CODE

The Uniform Housing Code (the UHC) is part of California's state housing law, and is intended to prevent the unhealthy and dangerous results of overcrowding. (Calif. Health & Safety Code § 17922(a)(1).) The UHC addresses the question of occupancy in terms of the size of the rental's bedrooms. A room that the landlord has "designed or intended" to be used as a bedroom (Calif. Civil Code § 1941.2(a)(5)) must be at least 70 square feet for one person, plus an additional 50 square feet for each additional occupant:

- One person: 70 square feet
- Two people: 120 square feet, and
- Three people: 170 square feet (UHC § 503).

Cities are free to adopt their own occupancy specifications, and some (notably San Francisco) have allowed for more occupants per bedroom.

You may be wondering what happens when a rental bedroom is too small, in terms of square feet, to permit application of the "two per bedroom plus one" rule. For example, in a city that has not adopted its own occupancy standards (and is thus subject to the UHC rules), can the landlord prohibit three people from occupying a one-bedroom apartment if the bedroom is less than 170 square feet?

We are not aware of any California cases that have settled this question—but we can offer some guidelines based on a federal appellate court's conclusions and our own common sense. As long as the square-foot guidelines that you are following were developed and are applied in order to prevent overcrowding, and not as a means to weed out families, it's likely that a court would consider them reasonable. And if a landlord applies square-foot guidelines equally to all tenants (not to just families, for example), we don't see why he couldn't vary the two-per-bedroom-plus-one rule in appropriate situations. This was the conclusion reached by a federal appellate court in Ohio (*Fair Housing Advocates Ass'n, Inc. v. City of Richmond Heights, Ohio*, 209 F.3d 626 (6th Cir., 2000)).

This said, we urge you to apply a good dose of common sense. Unless you are prepared for a time-consuming and potentially expensive challenge by disappointed tenants (who may find willing advocates in a fair housing advocacy group), think long and hard before you refuse to rent a smallish one-bedroom unit to a couple with one child, or a two-bedroom unit to a family with three children, even if each bedroom falls slightly below the 170 square foot minimum. It's unlikely that you'll be challenged by the health and safety authorities if three children occupy one somewhat too small room; it's more likely that you'll face a fair housing complaint if you refuse to rent to this family. In instances of severe over-crowding, of course, you'll need to follow the law, but again, be sure that you don't "draw the line" in a manner that consistently excludes families but not groups of adults.

The Fair Employment and Housing Commission is the enforcement arm of the California Department of Fair Employment and Housing (DFEH). The DFEH (one of the places a tenant can complain about discrimination; see Section E, below) will investigate a complaint for possible filing with the Commission based on a "two-plus-one" rule: If a landlord's policy is more restrictive than two persons per bedroom plus one additional occupant, it is suspect. Thus, a landlord is asking for trouble when she insists on no more than two people in a one-bedroom unit, four in a two-bedroom unit, six in a three-bedroom unit and so on. However, a landlord who draws the line by refusing to rent to more than three people to a one-bedroom, five to a two-bedroom and seven to a three-bedroom unit will be on safe ground.

Are there any situations in which you can safely go below the "two per bedroom plus one" rule? In a word, rarely. You will have to be able to convincingly argue that physical limitations of your infrastructure (such as a limited plumbing system or an extraordinarily small dwelling) justify an occupancy standard that is lower than the state rule. Very few landlords have done so successfully. (*Pfaff v. U.S. Dept. of Housing and Urban Development*, 88 F.3d 739 (9 Cir. 1996).)

It is equally important to maintain a consistent occupancy policy. If you allow three adults to live in a two-bedroom apartment, you had better let a couple with a child live in the same type of unit, or you leave yourself open to charges that you are illegally discriminating.

Children born to tenants. In a nonrent-controlled city, you can evict tenants with month-to-month rental agreements by giving a 30-day notice, provided you do not have an illegal discriminatory motive. Be careful, though, if your reason for evicting is that a tenant has given birth or adopted. You should not evict for this reason unless the new arrival results in illegal overcrowding under the two-plus-one rule. You also should realize that any tenants, particularly ones who are expecting a child, are likely to be upset if you ask them to move. They may scrutinize your rental policies and practices toward families with children, and may initiate a complaint with the Department of Fair Employment and Housing or even file a lawsuit.

You may be within your rights to insist on a reasonable rent increase after a child is born, provided:

- Your tenant has only a month-to-month rental agreement rather than a lease fixing rent for a specific period.

- Your property is not subject to rent control. (Some cities, including San Francisco, rule out childbirth as a rationale for a rent increase.)

- The rent increase is reasonable and truly based on the number of occupants in the property.

E. LEGAL PENALTIES FOR DISCRIMINATION

A landlord who unlawfully discriminates against a tenant or prospective tenant may end up in state or federal court or before a state or federal housing agency facing allegations of discrimination.

Showing you how to defend a housing discrimination lawsuit is beyond the scope of this book. With the exception of a suit brought in small claims court, you should see an attorney if a tenant sues you or files an administrative complaint against you for discrimination. Contact your insurance company if a lawsuit or claim is filed against you. You may be entitled to a defense (and perhaps coverage for a settlement or verdict as well) under your comprehensive general liability policy.

A tenant may complain about illegal discrimination by filing a lawsuit in state or federal court, or by filing an administrative complaint with the U.S. Department of Housing and Urban Development (HUD) or the California Department of Fair Employment and Housing (DFEH). Commonly, the federal courts require that the tenant first file a complaint with HUD. Discrimination on grounds not prohibited by federal law, such as marital status or sexual orientation, can generally be taken only to the state court or to California's Department of Fair Employment and Housing. Similarly, HUD usually, but not always, requires that the tenant first file a complaint with the state agency.

State and federal courts and housing agencies that find that discrimination has taken place have the power to:

- Order a landlord to rent a particular piece of property to the person who was discriminated against.

- Order the landlord to pay the tenant for "actual" or "compensatory" damages, including any higher rent the tenant had to pay as a result of being turned down, and damages for humiliation, emotional distress, or embarrassment. In 1991, the California Supreme Court ruled that the state Fair Employment and Housing Commission cannot award actual damages based on humiliation, emotional distress, and so on, and that only courts can award these types of damages. (*Walnut Creek Manor v. Fair Employment and Housing Commission*, 54 Cal. 3d 245, 284 Cal. Rptr. 718.) Still, the Commission can award damages based on higher rent the tenant had to pay, and punitive damages of up to $1,000 for each illegal act. Also, this ruling is not binding on federal agencies, and the state and federal courts may still award these types of damages.

• Make the landlord pay punitive damages (extra money as damages for especially outrageous discrimination) and the tenant's attorney fees.

Under the federal Fair Housing Act, which covers discrimination based on sex, race, religion, disability, family status, and national or ethnic origin, punitive damages may be as high as $11,000 for a first violation and $55,000 for a third violation within seven years. For racial discrimination, however, higher punitive damages are allowed under the Civil Rights Act of 1964. (*Morales v. Haines*, 486 F.2d 880 (7th Cir. 1973); *Lee v. Southern Home Sites Corp.*, 429 F.2d 290 (5th Cir. 1970).) The state's Fair Employment and Housing Commission's power to award punitive damages is limited to $1,000 per violation.

Under California's Unruh Civil Rights Act, triple actual damages may be awarded in a lawsuit for a violation of discrimination laws, and at least $250 must be awarded if you go to court and win. Small claims courts can award damages of up to their maximum jurisdictional amounts of $5,000. For more information on small claims courts, see *Everybody's Guide to Small Claims Court in California*, by Ralph Warner (Nolo).

If you wish to know more about complaint procedures, contact HUD or the DFEH. See sidebar, "Information on Fair Housing Laws" in Section C, above.

F. OWNER-OCCUPIED PREMISES AND OCCASIONAL RENTALS

Even small-scale landlords are subject to the fair housing laws. Regularly renting out a single apart-

ment or house, or even half of an owner-occupied duplex, constitutes the operation of a business to which the Unruh Act applies. An owner-occupant of a duplex, triplex, or larger complex is governed by civil rights laws in the renting of the other unit(s) in the building, even though he or she lives in one of the other units, because the owner-occupant is renting out property for use as a separate household, where kitchen or bathroom facilities aren't shared with the tenant. See *Swann v. Burkett*, 209 Cal. App. 2d 685 (1962), and 58 Ops. Cal. Atty. Gen. 608 (1975). The state Fair Employment and Housing Act applies as well. The federal Fair Housing Acts apply only to owner-occupied properties of four or more units (in practical terms, however, this exemption for smaller owner-occupied properties is somewhat irrelevant, since the applicable state laws are more protective than their federal counterparts).

But what about owners who rent to single boarders, or who are onetime or occasional landlords? If you're in one of these categories, certain fair housing requirements may not apply, provided you meet certain requirements, as explained in the two sections below.

1. Rentals to Single Boarders in Single-Family Homes

We have all seen advertisements like this, in newspapers and newsletters and on supermarket bulletin boards: "Widow seeks single, older Christian lady to share her home as a boarder. …" Based on what you know about illegal housing discrimination, you might wonder how these advertisements escape prosecution. Isn't the ad above a perfect example of marital, age, religious, and sexual discrimination?

The answer is "Yes." But the reality of the situation is that few spurned boarders, and certainly fewer government agencies, are interested in suing one-person landlords and forcing them to accept a housemate not of their choosing. And state housing law (Government Code §§ 12955(c) & (d) and § 12927(c)) does, in any event, make housing preferences like the example above perfectly legal as long as there is:

- only one boarder, and

- no discriminatory advertising.

The ban against discriminatory advertising means that the owner must not make any discriminatory "notices, statements or advertisements." As you might expect, this requirement has proved to be quite unworkable. How can the widow communicate her preferences for her boarder without making any "notices, statements or advertisements"?

Perhaps in response to this absurdity, the legislature amended the state Fair Employment and Housing Law to provide that advertisements for a boarder of a certain sex will not be considered a discriminatory act. (Government Code § 12927(2)(B).) In other words, the widow mentioned above would be on solid ground if she mentions only her desire for a female roommate; but her stated preferences for an elderly, single Christian would still, theoretically, be a violation of the fair housing laws.

2. Occasional Rentals

State fair housing laws also apply to someone who rents out his home on a one-time or even occasional basis. What if you rent out your home while on a temporary job assignment in another state, or while your family takes an extended summer vacation? What if you're a teacher who rents out your home during every sabbatical—an occasional but regular rental situation?

Unfortunately, the answers to these questions are not very clear. On the one hand, the Unruh Act applies only to "business establishments," which would seem to exclude the sporadic or onetime rental, but possibly not the infrequent-but-regular rental. Before a landlord quickly decides that he is not subject to Unruh, however, it would be prudent to remember that the California Supreme Court has been mandated to apply Unruh "in the broadest sense reasonably possible." (*Burks v. Poppy Construction Company*, 57 Cal. 2d 463, 20 Cal. Rptr. 609 (1962).) Moreover, the Fair Employment and Housing Act applies generally to "owners," and is not restricted to business establishments.

What should the careful landlord conclude regarding his fair housing duties? We recommend that you comply with all of the fair housing laws, in your advertisements, statements, and practices.

G. MANAGERS AND DISCRIMINATION

If you hire a manager, particularly one who selects tenants, make certain that person fully understands laws against housing discrimination. (See Chapter 6 on landlord liability for a manager's conduct and strategies for avoiding problems in this area.)

You should always let your tenants know that you, as well as your manager, intend to abide by the law, and that you want to know about and will address any fair housing problems that may arise. While this will not shield you from liability if you are sued due to your manager's conduct, it might (if you are lucky) result in the tenant's initial complaint being made to you, not a fair housing agency. If you hear about a manager's discriminatory act and can resolve a complaint before it gets into "official channels," you will have saved yourself a lot of time, trouble, and money.

One way to alert your tenants and prospective tenants to your commitment to the fair housing laws is to include in all ads, applications, and other material given to prospective tenants a section containing your antidiscrimination stance. Prepare a written policy statement as to the law and your intention to abide by it. Post this statement in the manager's office or somewhere on the premises, and give a copy to all prospective tenants.

SAMPLE STATEMENT ON EQUAL OPPORTUNITY IN HOUSING

FROM: Shady Dell Apartments

TO: All Tenants and Applicants

It is the policy of the owner and manager of Shady Dell Apartments to rent our units without regard to a tenant's race, ethnic background, sex, age, religion, marital or family status, physical disability, or sexual orientation. As part of our commitment to provide equal opportunity in housing, we comply with all federal, state, and local laws prohibiting discrimination. If you have any questions or complaints regarding our rental policy, call the owner at (phone number).

If, despite your best efforts, you suspect that your manager—whether on purpose or inadvertently—is using unlawful discriminatory practices to select or deal with tenants, you should immediately resume control of tenant selection and property management yourself. Alternatively, this may be the time to shield yourself from potential liability and engage the services of an independent management company, who in most cases will be responsible for their own actions.

H. INSURANCE COVERAGE FOR DISCRIMINATION CLAIMS

Despite your best efforts to avoid discriminating in the selection and treatment of your tenants, you may find yourself the subject of a fair housing claim. Will your insurance policy cover the cost of defending the claim and, if you lose, the cost of the settlement or judgment? The answers to these questions depend entirely on two highly variable factors: the wording of your insurance policy and the court decisions, if there are any, about the meaning of the words. In short, there are no answers that will apply to everyone, but we can alert you to the issues that arise in every situation. At the very least, knowing how insurance companies are likely to approve or deny defense and judgment costs should help you evaluate your own policy.

In this section we'll review the kinds of insurance coverage that most owners are likely to carry. Next, we'll discuss the key insurance terms ("bodily injury," "occurrence" and "personal injury") that are called into question when coverage for discrimination is involved. It is beyond the scope of this book to conclusively analyze every possible policy, but at the very least it will be clear to every landlord that since insurance coverage for discrimination claims is far from assured, your need to prevent fair housing violations in your business must be taken extremely seriously.

Chapter 12, Section G discusses broad types of liability insurance, coverage for managers and other employees and coverage for injuries suffered as a result of defective conditions on the property.

1. Typical Liability Insurance Policy

Most owners of residential rental property carry a comprehensive liability insurance policy, which typically includes business liability coverage. With this type of coverage, the insurance company agrees to pay on your behalf all sums that you are legally obligated to pay as damages "for bodily injury, property damage or personal injury caused by an occurrence to which this insurance applies." The policy will generally define the three key terms "bodily injury," "occurrence," and "personal injury." The meaning of these terms in the context of a discrimination claim will determine whether the insurance company will cover any particular defense and the claim. Let's look at them more closely.

THE INSURANCE COMPANY'S DUTY TO DEFEND: BROADER THAN THE DUTY TO COVER

When you purchase liability insurance, you have bought two things: the promise of the insurance company to defend you if you are sued for an act that arguably falls within the coverage of the policy, and their promise to settle or pay the damage award if you lose. But sometimes (as is the case in fair housing claims), it is unclear whether, assuming you lose the case, your policy covers the conduct that gave rise to the claim. When this happens, your insurance company will usually defend you, but they may reserve the right to argue about whether they are obligated to pay the damages if the case is lost.

---

2. Definition of "Bodily Injury"

Discrimination complaints rarely include a claim that the victim suffered a physical injury at the hands of the landlord or manager. It is far more likely that the tenant or applicant will sue for the emotional distress caused by the humiliation of the discriminatory act. Is a claim for emotional distress covered under the policy's definition of "bodily injury?"

"Bodily injury" is typically defined as injury, disease, or sickness. In a case alleging a violation of the federal fair housing laws brought in federal court in California, the owner and the insurance company argued about whether the policy could cover the injury that the plaintiff (the tenant) was claiming. The owner was able to convince the court that the policy would apply to the tenant's claim of emotional distress because the tenant had physical manifestations (dry throat and stomach cramps) that accompa-

nied the mental distress. (*State Farm Fire & Cas. Co. v. Westchester Investment Co.*, 721 F.Supp. 1165 (CD CA 1989).) In short, the court concluded that, if proved, the emotional distress was an "injury" because there were more than mental symptoms. Keep in mind, however, that this ruling applies only to federal fair housing cases. California state courts, which typically hear state claims (those brought under the state Fair Employment and Housing Act, Unruh and others), are not bound by this federal court ruling.

3. Definition of "Occurrence"

Your insurance company will defend and pay out on a claim if it is caused by an occurrence to which the policy applies. An "occurrence" is typically defined as an accident, the results of which are neither expected nor intended from the standpoint of the insured (the property owner). So, even if you make it past the emotional-distress-isn't-bodily-injury hurdle, your insurance company may successfully deny coverage if it can convince a judge that an act of discrimination is not an "occurrence" under the policy.

It doesn't take much brainwork to see how an insurance company can argue that an act of discrimination—like turning away a minority applicant—cannot be considered an "occurrence" because it is by definition intentional, not accidental. In California, courts have ruled that an intentional act is not an "accident" that would bring the action within the policy. (*Commercial Union Insurance Company v. Superior Court of Humboldt County*, 196 Cal. App. 3d 1205, 242 Cal. Rptr. 454 (1987); see also *Royal Globe Insurance Company v. Whitaker*, 181 Cal. App. 3d 532, 226 Cal. Rptr. 435 (1986).)

In one case, however, where it was the manager's act of discrimination that formed the basis of the complaint, the owner was able to successfully argue that the alleged negligent supervision of the manager constituted the "accident" necessary to bring the conduct within the scope of the policy. (*State Farm Fire & Cas. Co. v. Westchester Investment Co.*, 721 F.Supp. 1165 (CD CA 1989).) This theory wouldn't work if the owner herself were the one who allegedly committed the fair housing violation.

4. Definition of "Personal Injury"

Now that we've explained how an insurance company might deny coverage because the discrimination complaint claims nonphysical, intentional injury, we have some possibly better news. Insurance policies also typically provide coverage for "personal injury," or an injury that arises out of the conduct of your business. Personal injuries typically include false arrest, libel, slander, and violation of privacy rights; they also include "wrongful entry or eviction or other invasions of the right of private occupancy." As you can see from this definition, personal injuries include items that are neither bodily injuries nor accidental. And the definition includes some offenses, like libel, that seem somewhat similar to discrimination. Why, then, wouldn't a discrimination claim be covered under a policy's definition of "personal injury?"

The answer lies in the legal meaning of the phrase "wrongful entry or eviction or other invasions of the right of private occupancy," which is part of the definition of "personal injury." Does an act of discrimination fit within this phrase? Very few courts have addressed this question, let alone answered it, but of those that have, the answers have been quite mixed. For example, coverage has been denied on the grounds that "discrimination" is a specific wrong and, had the insurance company intended to cover discrimination, it would have specifically mentioned it (as it did with the terms libel, eviction, and the others). Coverage for discrimination claims by prospective tenants (such as applicants who have been turned away) has, however, been allowed by one federal court in California in a case alleging a

violation of the federal Fair Housing Act. (*State Farm Fire & Cas. Co. v. Westchester Investment Co.*, 721 F.Supp. 1165 (CD CA 1989).)

In sum, there are at least three ways that insurance companies can deny coverage, if not also the defense, of a fair housing claim and award: They can claim that the discriminatory act resulted in emotional distress, which is not a type of bodily injury; they can argue that an act of discrimination was intentional, and thus not an accidental occurrence to which the policy applies; and they can argue that discrimination is not one of the personal injuries that are covered by the policy. We suggest that you give the matter some thought when choosing a broker and negotiating your policy; but by far the best use of your energy is to make sure that your business practices do not expose you to these claims in the first place.

DISCRIMINATION AND PUBLIC POLICY

An insurance company will occasionally argue that it should not have to cover a landlord's intentional acts of discrimination because discrimination is an evil act that someone should not be able to insure against. While this argument has some persuasive aspects—discrimination is, indeed, contrary to public policy—it falls apart when you acknowledge that all sorts of other intentional bad acts (like libel and slander) are perfectly insurable. Courts have not been persuaded by the "public policy" argument.

10

Cotenants, Subtenants, and Guests

Conscientious landlords go to a lot of trouble to screen prospective tenants. All those sensible precautions, however, may do you no good if unapproved tenants move in, in addition to or in place of the people you chose. You may have trouble getting the new tenants to pay rent or pay for damage to the unit. And, if worse comes to worst, you may have a tough time evicting them.

Fortunately, you can usually avoid these problems, and others, by spelling out cotenants' and subtenants' rights and responsibilities in your lease or rental agreement.

COMMON DEFINITIONS

Cotenants. Two or more tenants who rent the same property under the same lease or rental agreement, both being jointly liable for the rent and other terms of the agreement. Roommates and couples who move in at the same time are generally cotenants. (See Section A.)

Subtenant. Someone who rents all or part of the premises from a tenant (not the landlord). The tenant continues to exercise some control over the rental property, either by occupying part of the unit or intending to retake possession at a later date. (See Section B.)

Sublease. A written or oral agreement by which a tenant rents to a subtenant. (See Section B.)

Roommates. Two or more unrelated people living under the same roof and sharing rent and expenses. (See Section C.) A roommate may be a cotenant or a subtenant.

Assignment. The transfer by a tenant of all his rights of tenancy to another who is the "assignee." (See Section D.)

Our form agreements (Chapter 2) spell out these respective rights and responsibilities by:

- limiting the number of people who can live in the rental property (Clause 3)

- allowing only the persons whose names appear on the lease or rental agreement, along with their minor children, to live in the property (Clauses 1 through 3)

- requiring the landlord's written consent in advance for any sublet, assignment of the lease or rental agreement, or for any additional people to move in (Clause 10)

- allowing tenants' guests to stay no more than ten days in a six-month period (Clause 3).

A. RENTING TO MORE THAN ONE TENANT

When two or more people rent property together, and all sign the same rental agreement or lease (or enter into the same oral rental agreement when they move in at the same time), they are cotenants. Each cotenant shares the same rights and responsibilities under the lease or rental agreement. Neither cotenant may terminate the other's tenancy.

1. Cotenants' Responsibilities

In addition to having the same rights and responsibilities, each cotenant is independently obligated to abide by the terms of the agreement. All cotenants are legally responsible to the landlord.

a. Paying Rent

Each cotenant, regardless of agreements they make among themselves, is liable for the entire amount of the rent.

EXAMPLE

James and Helen sign a month-to-month rental agreement for an $800 apartment. They agree between themselves to each pay half of the rent. After three months, James moves out without notifying Helen or the owner, Laura. As one of two cotenants, Helen is still legally obligated to pay all

the rent (although she might be able to recover James's share by suing him in small claims court).

Laura has three options if Helen can't pay the rent:

• Laura can give Helen a Three-Day Notice to Pay Rent or Quit, and follow through with an unlawful detainer (eviction) lawsuit if Helen fails to pay the rent or move within the three days.

• If Helen offers to pay part of the rent, Laura can legally accept it, but Helen is still responsible for the entire rent. (It's common for roommate cotenants to offer only "their portion" of the rent, when in fact they're all jointly liable for it all; see Chapter 3 for a detailed discussion of accepting partial rent payments.)

• If Helen wants to stay and find a new co-tenant, Laura can't unreasonably withhold her approval. She should, however, have the new cotenant sign a rental agreement. (See Section C, below.)

b. Violations of the Lease or Rental Agreement

In addition to paying rent, each tenant is responsible for any cotenant's action that violates any term of the lease or rental agreement—for example, if one co-tenant seriously damages the property, or moves in an extra roommate or a pit bull, contrary to the lease or

rental agreement, all cotenants are responsible. The landlord may terminate the entire tenancy with the appropriate three-day notice, even though some of the cotenants objected or weren't consulted by the prime offender.

If you have to evict a tenant for a breach other than for nonpayment of rent (in which case you would evict all the tenants), you must decide whether to evict only the offending cotenant or all of them. Your decision will depend on the circumstances. You obviously don't want to evict an innocent cotenant who has no control over the troublemaker who just brought in a pit bull—assuming the innocent one can still shoulder the rent after his roommate is gone. On the other hand, you may wish to evict all cotenants if they each share some of the blame for the problem.

2. Disagreements Among Cotenants

Usually, cotenants orally agree among themselves to split the rent and to occupy certain parts of the property, such as separate bedrooms. Not infrequently, this sort of arrangement goes awry. If the situation gets bad enough, the tenants may start arguing about who should leave, whether one co-tenant can keep the other out of the apartment, or who is responsible for what part of the rent.

The best advice we can give landlords who face serious disagreements between cotenants is not to get involved, as a mediator or otherwise. If one or more cotenants approach you about a dispute, explain that they must resolve any disagreements among themselves. Remind them that they are each legally obligated to pay the entire rent, and that you are not affected by any agreement they have made among themselves.

If one tenant asks you to change the locks to keep another cotenant out, tell the tenant that you cannot legally do that. If the tenant fears violence from a co-tenant, refer the tenant to the local superior court, where the tenant can seek a restraining order. A landlord may not lock out one tenant unless a court has issued an order that the tenant stay out.

B. SUBTENANTS AND SUBLETS

A subtenant is a person who rents all or part of the property from a tenant and does not sign the rental agreement or lease with the landlord. A subtenant is someone who either:

- rents (sublets) an entire dwelling from a tenant who moves out temporarily—for the summer, for example, or

- rents one or more rooms from the tenant, who continues to live in the unit.

If a tenant moves out permanently and transfers all his rights under the lease or rental agreement to someone else, that new tenant is not a subtenant; this person is an "assignee." (See Section D, below, on assignments.)

1. Subtenants' Responsibilities

The tenant functions as the subtenant's landlord. The subtenant is responsible to the tenant for whatever rent they've agreed on between themselves. The tenant, in turn, is the one responsible to the landlord for the rent. Even a tenant who has temporarily moved out and sublet the property is liable to the landlord—this is true even if the landlord, for convenience, accepts rent from the subtenant. Doing so does not make the subtenant the landlord's tenant.

A subtenant has an agreement only with the tenant. This is true even if the subtenant is approved by the landlord. Because the subtenant does not have a separate agreement with the landlord, he does not have the same legal rights and responsibilities as a tenant (described in Section A, above).

The subtenant's right to stay depends on the tenant's right to stay. So if you can legally evict the tenant, then you can evict the subtenant. (See Section C2, below.) For example, if the lease or rental agreement prohibited the tenant from subleasing without the landlord's consent, and the tenant brought in a subtenant anyway, the tenant would be in breach of the lease. The landlord could evict the tenant for this

breach, and since the subtenant's right to stay depends on the tenant's right to stay, the landlord could evict the subtenant, also.

See Section C, below, for a discussion of how a subtenant can gain the same legal rights as a tenant.

2. If a Tenant Wants to Sublet

Our lease and rental agreement require the tenant to obtain the landlord's written consent in advance in order to sublet or bring in additional people to live in the unit. (See Chapter 2, Clause 10.) This will let you control who lives in your property. (If you want to collect damages against a tenant with a lease or rental agreement who leaves early, you cannot unreasonably withhold your consent to sublet. See Chapter 19 for a discussion of this concept of the landlord's obligation to mitigate damages.)

Suppose you wish to accommodate a tenant who wants to sublet for six months while she is out of the area, and you approve of the proposed subtenant. You may want to insist on signing a written agreement with the new person for the six-month period that the original tenant plans to be away. That makes the new person a regular tenant who is liable to you for the rent, not a subtenant who is liable to someone else (the tenant).

You should also get the original tenant to sign a document, such as the sample below, stating that the original tenant agrees to terminate his tenancy. This will terminate the tenancy so that you can rent the property to the new tenant. Then, when the first tenant returns and the second leaves, you can again rent to the first, using a new agreement.

If the original tenant is uneasy about you renting to the subtenant directly, and asks you how he will get the unit back if the new tenant is reluctant to leave at the end of six months, as long as your lease or rental agreement prohibits subletting, your answer should be a polite version of, "That's your problem." Think of it this way: By asking you the question, your tenant admits that he doesn't completely trust the

SAMPLE TERMINATION OF TENANCY AGREEMENT

Termination of Tenancy Agreement

I, _____ name of tenant _____, agree that my tenancy at

_____ address _____, entered into

on _____ date of original agreement _____, 200X, will terminate ____ effective date of termination ____, 200X.

Date:_____   _____ signature of tenant _____
                               Tenant

---

new tenant, even though he selected that person. You don't want to be in the middle of this type of situation. It's better that the original tenant bear the brunt of any problem—if there is one—than you.

If, on the other hand, you want to hold the original tenant's place and allow him to come back after the six months, you may decide to consent to the sublet. Although the subtenant won't be liable to you for the rent, you can still evict the subtenant if the rent isn't paid. If the rent continues to be paid but the subtenant won't leave after the six months, it's up to the tenant to evict the subtenant.

House sitters are subtenants. Even if your tenant doesn't collect rent from a house sitter, that person is legally still a subtenant. Treat a house sitter the way you'd treat any proposed subtenant: Remind the tenant that your written consent is required and, if you have any qualms about the ability of the tenant to keep paying the rent, insist that the house sitter become a regular tenant, as explained above.

C. WHEN A TENANT BRINGS IN A ROOMMATE

Suppose love (or loneliness) strikes your tenant and he wants to move in a roommate? Assuming your lease or rental agreement restricts the number of people who can occupy the unit (as ours does in Clause 3), the tenant must get your written permission for additional tenants.

1. Giving Permission for a New Roommate

Obviously, your decision to allow a new cotenant should be based on whether you believe the new person will be a decent tenant. If your tenant proposes to move in a new person who has a good credit record and isn't otherwise objectionable, and there is enough space in the unit, you may want to allow the new roommate. (See Chapter 9, Section D for overcrowding standards which you may lawfully impose.) If the new occupant is a spouse or registered domestic partner and there's no problem with overcrowding, be careful before you say no. Refusal to allow your tenant to live with a spouse or registered domestic partner could be considered illegal discrimination based on marital status.

SAN FRANCISCO'S MASTER TENANTS

A San Francisco ordinance has created the legal category of "master tenant" in shared housing situations. A master tenant (or tenants) is the person who signs the lease or rental agreement with and is responsible to the landlord. This master tenant then has the legal authority to rent to others, unless, of course, the lease or rental agreement (as ours do) prohibits subletting without the landlord's prior written consent.

We do not believe that it's wise for a San Francisco landlord to get into a master tenant/sub-tenant situation for two reasons: First, a subtenant is responsible only to the master tenant for rent, and not to the owner. As a property owner, you are better protected when all occupants of the property are jointly liable to you, as cotenants on the same lease, for all the rent. Second, the law in this area is complicated by conflicting rent board rules.

You should insist that all cotenants sign a lease or rental agreement with you, and if one or more leaves, deal directly with their replacements.

a. Raising the Rent

When an additional tenant comes in, it is perfectly reasonable for you to raise the rent (or the security deposit), if it is allowed under local rent control laws. To accomplish this, have both the original and new occupants sign a new lease or rental agreement at the higher rent, as cotenants. Failing that, if it's a month-to-month rental agreement, you could increase the rent by a 30-day notice (60 days' for a rent increase over 10%), provided you don't care about the new occupant being a subtenant who is not liable to you directly. Obviously, more people living in a residence means more wear and tear and higher maintenance

costs in the long run. Also, a rent increase when an additional tenant moves in should cause little hardship to the current occupants, who will now have someone else to pay part of the rent. The new rent should be in line with rents for comparable units occupied by the same number of persons.

If the existing tenant has a fixed-term lease, you will have to change the lease to raise the rent. As long as the lease allows a set number of tenants and requires your permission before the tenant moves in new people, you can legally withhold your permission until the lease is changed to provide a reasonable rent increase. If the property is subject to rent control, however, you may need to petition the local rent control board for permission to increase the rent based on an increased number of occupants. (For more on rent control, see Chapter 4.)

b. Prepare a New Rental Agreement or Lease

If you allow a new person to move in, make sure the newcomer becomes a full cotenant. You'll need to prepare a new lease or rental agreement for signature by all tenants. Do this before the new person moves in, to avoid the possibility of a legally confused situation.

EXAMPLE

Chung, the landlord, rents to Suzy. Olaf moves in later without signing a rental agreement or lease. Because Olaf has not entered into a contract with Chung, he starts with no legal rights or obligations to Chung. His obligations to Suzy, as her subtenant, depend on their agreement regarding the rent and Olaf's right to live in the apartment. Suzy is completely liable for the rent and for all damage to the premises, whether caused by Olaf or herself, because she, not Olaf, entered into a contract with Chung. Olaf would only be liable for damage he negligently caused, if Chung could prove that Olaf was the one who caused the damage.

2. Guests and New Occupants You Haven't Approved

Our rental agreement and lease allow guests to stay overnight up to ten days in any six-month period, without your written permission. (See Clause 3.) The value of this clause is that a tenant who tries to move someone in for a longer period has violated the lease or rental agreement, which gives you grounds for termination (discussed below).

If a tenant simply moves a roommate in on the sly—despite the fact that your lease or rental agreement prohibits it—or it appears that a "guest" has moved in clothing and furniture and has begun to receive mail at your property, take decisive action right away. If you don't take action, the roommate will turn into a subtenant—one you haven't screened or approved of.

A subtenant, despite not having all the rights of a tenant, is entitled to the same legal protection, if you try to evict, to which a tenant is entitled. Such an individual must be:

- served a separate Three-Day Notice to Pay Rent or Quit

- named in an eviction lawsuit
- served with legal papers.

An unauthorized subtenant creates a lot more hassle for you in the event of an eviction, and a tremendous hassle if you never learn the subtenant's name. (For details on the eviction process, see Chapter 18 and *The California Landlord's Law Book: Evictions*.)

You may want to make the roommate or guest a cotenant by preparing a new lease or rental agreement. You may also increase the rent or the security deposit unless that's prohibited by any applicable rent control ordinance. If you do not want to rent to the guest or roommate and if that person remains on the premises, or if that person refuses to sign a lease or rental agreement (asking to be a "permanent guest"), make it clear that you will evict all occupants based on breach of the occupancy terms of the lease.

If your tenant has a month-to-month tenancy in an area where there is no rent control, and the tenant is not renting under a federal housing program, you can always give the tenant a 30-day notice to leave, without giving any reason. (We discuss terminations of tenancy in Chapter 18.)

If your property is in a rent-controlled area requiring just cause for eviction, see Chapter 4 and Chapter 18, Section C. Generally, moving in an illegal tenant should qualify as just cause to get rid of the tenant under most rent control ordinances, because it is a significant violation of the terms of the tenancy. However, you can't evict a tenant until you first give notice of the problem (in this case, the additional person) and a chance to cure it (get the new person to leave).

Don't discriminate against guests. You cannot legally object to a tenant's frequent overnight guests based on your religious or moral views. (See Chapter 9.) It is illegal to discriminate against unmarried couples, including gay or lesbian couples, in California.

D. IF A TENANT LEAVES AND ASSIGNS THE LEASE TO SOMEONE

A lease or rental agreement gives a tenant certain rights—the most important, obviously, is to live in the premises. If the tenant permanently gives or sells all these rights to someone else, it's called an "assignment," because the tenant has legally assigned all her rights to someone else. For example, a tenant who signs a year lease may leave after six months and assign the rest of the term to a new tenant.

The lease and rental agreements at the back of this book (Clause 10) forbid assignments without the owner's consent.

Assignments aren't quite as bad as sublets, however, as far as a landlord is concerned. The new occupant (assignee) is directly responsible to the landlord for everything the original tenant was liable for—even without an agreement between the assignee and the landlord. (CC § 822.) The previous occupant (assignor) remains liable to the landlord also, unless the landlord agrees otherwise in writing.

Nevertheless, even if your lease or rental agreement allows a tenant to assign his rights, it's better to have the new tenant sign a new lease or written rental agreement. That will make your legal relationship with the new tenant clear.

If you unreasonably withhold your consent for a tenant to assign her rights—for example, six months left under a year-long lease—you may lose your right to recover the rest of the rent due under the lease. A landlord is obligated to limit the original tenant's responsibility for the remaining rent by renting to a suitable new tenant as soon as possible. (This is discussed in detail in Chapter 19.) If you turn down an acceptable prospect found by the tenant, you won't have a strong case if you want to sue the original tenant for not paying the rent for the rest of the lease term. ■

11

THE LANDLORD'S DUTY TO REPAIR AND MAINTAIN THE PROPERTY

The tenant's responsibility to pay rent depends on the landlord's fulfilling his legal duty to maintain the property and keep it in good repair. Obviously, then, keeping up rental property should be something every landlord takes seriously.

This chapter describes the specific housing standards and laws landlords must follow, and outlines strategies for dealing with tenants who threaten to or do withhold rent because of the property's condition. It also provides practical advice on how to stay on top of your repair and maintenance needs, and minimize financial penalties and legal problems.

Related Topics

- Lease and rental agreement provisions on landlords' and tenants' responsibilities for repair and maintenance: Chapter 2

- Delegating maintenance and repair responsibilities to a manager: Chapter 6

- Highlighting repair and maintenance procedures in a move-in letter and using a Landlord/Tenant Checklist to keep track of the premises before and after the tenant moves in: Chapter 7

- Landlord's liability for a tenant's injuries from defective and dangerous housing conditions: Chapter 12

- How to avoid illegal retaliatory evictions after tenants complain about housing conditions or withhold rent: Chapter 15

- Conducting a final inspection of the rental unit for cleaning and damage repair before the tenant moves out: Chapter 20

- Evicting a tenant who damages the property: Chapter 18.

A. State and Local Housing Standards

Several state and local laws set housing standards for residential rental property. These laws require landlords to put their rental apartments and houses in good condition before renting them, and keep them that way while people live there. Here is a list of the laws you need to know about.

California's State Housing Law. Also known as the State Building Standards Code, this law lists property owners' general obligations to keep residential property in livable condition. (Health and Safety Code §§ 17900 through 17997.8, including regulations contained in Title 25 of the California Code of Regulations.) It refers, in turn, to very specific housing standards contained in the Uniform Housing Code enforced by local governments.

Industry codes. Several "industry codes" also set habitability standards. Most cities and counties have adopted and enforce the Uniform Housing Code (UHC), which contains very specific housing standards—for example, regarding the heating system. The UHC is available in most libraries and may be purchased from the purchased from the International Code Council (ICC). The Los Angeles District Office is at 5360 Workman Mill Road, Whittier, CA 90601-2298, 800-284-4406. The ICC website is at www.iccsafe.org. A few cities, including Los Angeles, have enacted ordinances with additional requirements. (Besides the UHC, there are Uniform Building, Plumbing, and Mechanical Codes, and a National Electrical Code.) Check with the building inspector or health department of the city or county where you own rental property to see which local laws apply to your property.

Civil Code Sections 1941.1-.3. This state statute lists the minimum legal requirements for a rental dwelling to be "tenantable," or legal to rent to tenants. If your property doesn't meet these requirements— for example, if it has a leaking roof—a tenant may be excused by a judge from paying all or part of the rent. (See Section F, below.) Many of the Section 1941.1-.3 requirements overlap those set forth in the State Housing Law and local ordinances. (For example, Civil Code § 1941.1 requires only that "hot water" be available, while the UHC requires that the water heater be able to heat the water to 110° Fahrenheit.)

Civil Code Section 1941.4 and Public Utilities Code Section 788. These statutes make residential landlords responsible for installing a telephone jack in each of their rental units and placing and maintaining inside phone wiring.

Health and Safety Code Section 13113.7.
This state statute requires all units in multiunit buildings to have smoke detectors.

Health and Safety Code Section 13220. This state statute requires landlords to provide information on emergency procedures in case of fire to tenants in multistory rental properties. The statute applies to apartment buildings that are two or more stories high and contain three or more rental units that open into an interior hallway or lobby area. Landlords must post emergency information on signs using international symbols at every stairway area and in other specified places throughout the building.

B. ENFORCEMENT OF HOUSING STANDARDS

The State Housing Law and local housing codes are enforced by the building department of the city (the county, in unincorporated areas). Violations creating immediate health hazards, such as rats or broken toilets, are handled by the county health department. Fire hazards, such as trash in the hallways, are dealt with by the local fire department.

If you establish a system for tenants to regularly report on maintenance and repair needs, and if you respond quickly when complaints are made (we show how in Section J, below), you may never have to deal with these local agencies.

1. Inspections by Local Agencies

A local building, health, or fire department usually gets involved when a tenant complains. The agency inspects the building and, if problems are found, issues a deficiency notice that requires the owner to remedy all violations, including any the tenant didn't complain about. Owners of residential rental property in Los Angeles County who have received certain deficiency notices from local building or health department officials must register their substandard property with the county within ten days. A landlord who fails to comply can face civil and criminal penalties—including not being able to evict a tenant

of the property for nonpayment of rent. (Health & Safety Code §§ 17997 to 17997.5.)

In some cases, a tenant's complaint about a single defect can snowball, with the result that several agencies require the landlord to make needed repairs. For example, say a tenant complains to the health department about a lack of heat. During its inspection, the health department observes an unsafe stove and an unventilated bathroom. The health department notifies the fire department about the stove and tells the building department about the bathroom, which results in inspections by both departments.

DELEGATING REPAIR AND MAINTENANCE RESPONSIBILITIES TO TENANTS

Any lease or written rental agreement provision by which a tenant agrees to give up his rights to a habitable home is illegal and unenforceable. (*Green v. Superior Court*, 10 Cal. 3d 616 (1974).) Nor can a landlord escape his duty to keep rented property in good repair and properly maintained by trying to make it the tenant's responsibility.

But the tenant and landlord can agree that the tenant is solely responsible for repairs and maintenance in exchange for lower rent. (CC § 1942.1. Also see *Knight v. Hallsthammar*, 29 Cal. 3d 46 (1981).) (See Clause 17 of our form lease and rental agreements in Chapter 2.) Major maintenance and repair duties are rarely, however, appropriate candidates for delegation, since these jobs will generally involve a significant amount of money and will require expertise that the average tenant is not likely to possess. In any delegation situation, monitor the situation to make sure that proper materials and procedures are chosen by your tenant-repairperson.

See Section F, below, for a discussion of a tenant's rights to withhold rent and sue when a landlord fails to keep the rental property in a habitable condition. For a related topic—setting repair and maintenance responsibilities for a resident manager—see Chapter 6, Section A.

Housing Standards Under State Law

Rental housing standards established by Civil Code §§ 1941.1-.3, the State Housing Law and its implementing regulations and the Uniform Housing Code (UHC) include:

- A structure that is weatherproof and waterproof; there must be no holes or cracks through which wind can blow, rain can leak in, or rodents can enter (CC § 1941.1).

- A plumbing system in good working order (free of rust and leaks), connected to both the local water supply and sewage system or septic tank. The landlord is not responsible for low pressure, contamination, or other failures in the local water supply—his obligation is only to connect a working plumbing system to the water supply (CC § 1941.1).

- A hot water system capable of producing water of at least 110 degrees Fahrenheit (CC § 1941.1 and UHC).

- A heating system that was legal when installed (CC § 1941.1), and which is maintained in good working order and capable of heating every room to at least 70 degrees Fahrenheit (UHC).

- An electrical system that was legal when installed, and which is in good working order and without loose or exposed wiring (CC § 1941.1). There must be at least two outlets, or one outlet and one light fixture, in every room but the bathroom (where only one light fixture is required). Common stairs and hallways must be lighted at all times (UHC).

- A lack of insect or rodent infestations, rubbish, or garbage in all areas (CC § 1941.1). With respect to the living areas, the landlord's obligation to the tenant is only to rent out units that are initially free of insects, rodents, and garbage. If the tenant's housekeeping attracts pests, that's not the landlord's responsibility. However, the landlord is obliged to keep all common areas clean and free of rodents, insects, and garbage at all times.

- Enough garbage and trash receptacles in clean condition and good repair to contain tenants' trash and garbage without overflowing before the refuse collectors remove it each week (CC § 1941.1).

- Floors, stairways, and railings kept in good repair (CC § 1941.1).

- The absence of lead paint hazards (deteriorated lead-based paint, lead-contaminated dust or soil, or lead-based paint disturbed without containment (CC § 1941.1; H&S § 17920.10). See Chapter 12, Section F for more information on lead hazards.)

- Deadbolt locks on certain doors and windows, effective July 1, 1998 (CC § 1941.3). Your duty to provide locks is explained in more detail in Chapter 12, Section B.

- Ground fault circuit interrupters for swimming pools (effective July 1, 1998), and antisuction protections on wading pools, excepting single-family residence rentals (effective January 1, 1998 for new pools and January 1, 2000 for existing pools) (H&S §§ 116049.1 and 116064).

Each rental dwelling must, under both the UHC and the State Housing Law, have the following:

- A working toilet, wash basin, and bathtub or shower. The toilet and bathtub or shower must be in a room that is ventilated and allows for privacy.

- A kitchen with a sink, which cannot be made of an absorbent material such as wood.

- Natural lighting in every room through windows or skylights having an area of at least one-tenth of the room's floor area, with a minimum of 12 square feet (three square feet for bathroom windows). The windows in each room must be openable at least halfway for ventilation, unless a fan provides for ventilation.

- Safe fire or emergency exits leading to a street or hallway. Stairs, hallways, and exits must be litter free. Storage areas, garages, and basements must be free of combustible materials.

- Every apartment building having 16 or more units must have a resident manager (25 California Code of Regulations § 42).

Civil Code § 1941.4 and Public Utilities Code § 788 make residential landlords responsible for installing a telephone jack in their rental units, and for placing and maintaining inside phone wiring.

Health and Safety Code § 13113.7 requires smoke detectors in all multiunit dwellings, from duplexes on up. Apartment complexes must also have smoke detectors in the common stairwells.

Some cities don't wait for tenants to complain. As discussed in Chapter 13, Section B, they routinely inspect rental property for compliance with local law.

State and local agencies don't enforce Civil Code § 1941.1, which requires a rental unit to be "tenantable." It is enforced by the tenant through the withholding of rent and other remedies, as described in Section F, below.

2. Failure to Comply With Repair Orders

If you fail to make any repairs demanded by local officials, the city or county may bring a lawsuit, or even criminal charges, against you. Violations of the State Housing Law are misdemeanors, punishable by a fine of up to $1,000 ($5,000 for a second offense within five years) or up to six months' imprisonment, or both. (Health and Safety Code §§ 17995-17995.5.) For very serious violations due to "habitual neglect of customary maintenance" that endanger "the immediate health and safety of residents or the public" within a five-year period, the maximum penalty is a $5,000 fine and up to a year in jail. (In 1987, a Los Angeles slumlord with a history of failing to make needed repairs was sentenced to two years in jail. *People v. Avol,* Los Angeles County Superior Court No. CR-A23579 (1987).)

You may be required to pay "relocation benefits" to tenants who must move in order for you to effect repairs. (Health and Safety Code § 17980.7.) (The tenant's right to move out is discussed in Section H, below.) If the court finds that the substandard conditions constitute a nuisance (a serious threat to safety or morals), it may order the building to be razed or removed. You may even be disallowed from claiming state income tax write-offs associated with the property, including interest, taxes, and depreciation on the building. (California Revenue and Taxation Code § 24436.5.)

In addition to penalties assessed by governmental agencies, the tenant may sue you if you don't make necessary repairs. (Section I, below, discusses lawsuits by tenants for defective conditions.) Tenants can ask the judge to order the landlord to make repairs (and reduce rent until repairs are completed), or even to appoint a receiver who would be authorized to collect rents, manage the property and supervise the necessary repairs. Even after the repairs are completed and the receiver discharged, the court can order you to report to it concerning the condition of the building for up to 18 months. (Health and Safety Code § 17980.7.)

A tenant may also withhold rent if you fail to make necessary repairs. In fact, if you haven't made repairs within 35 days after being ordered to by a government agency, the tenant is automatically entitled to withhold rent. (See Sections F and G, below.)

Under the Rent Escrow Account Program (REAP), Los Angeles tenants may in some circumstances pay rent directly into a city-managed escrow account if the owner fails to make repairs ordered by the local building or health department within 60 days after receiving written notice to repair. Both the city and county of Sacramento have similar ordinances, but they are seldom used.

If you discover a meth lab (or the remnants of one) in a tenant's unit, be extremely careful and thorough in your clean-up efforts. The chemicals used to make this illegal drug are extremely dangerous and harmful to health. See "Clean Meth Labs Carefully," in Chapter 18, Section B3.

C. MAINTENANCE OF APPLIANCES AND OTHER AMENITIES

State and local housing laws deal with basic living conditions only—heat, water, and weatherproofing, for example. They do not deal with "amenities"— other facilities that are not essential but make living a little easier. Examples are drapes, washing machines, swimming pools, saunas, parking places, intercoms, and dishwashers. The law does not require the landlord to furnish these things, but a landlord who does might be required to maintain or repair them— not by state and local housing laws, but by her own promise to do so.

The promise might be express or implied. When the lease or rental agreement says that the landlord

THE LOS ANGELES RENT ESCROW ACCOUNT PROGRAM [REAP]

If the repairs ordered by the local building or health department aren't completed on time, the Department of Housing Preservation and Production requests the owner to appear at an informal conference to explain the delay. If the Department of Housing isn't satisfied, a REAP advisory committee, consisting of representatives of the housing, building and fire departments, can recommend that the City Council impose a rent escrow. A landlord can appeal this recommendation to a hearing officer. If the hearing officer also recommends imposition of the escrow, the matter then goes to the City Council for the ultimate decision.

If the City Council orders it, tenants may pay their rents into the city escrow program. As long as tenants do so, they cannot be evicted for nonpayment of rent. (Needless to say, a 30-day notice of termination of tenancy [or even of a rent increase] would seem retaliatory at this stage, and Los Angeles's rent control law requires a landlord to show just cause for eviction.) Also, a landlord whose building has been put under REAP is prohibited from passing on the costs of repairs in the form of higher rents, as is normally allowed under Los Angeles's rent control ordinance.

With city authorization, repairs can be paid for by the escrow program administrator out of the escrow. However, taxes and mortgage payments cannot be made out of the escrow. After all required repairs have been made, any money left over is returned to the landlord, minus an administrative fee.

Obviously, the best way to avoid REAP is to quickly respond to repair orders by local authorities. Failing that, be cooperative and conciliatory at the informal conference, stressing your willingness to make needed repairs. If any of the problems were caused by tenants, you should point that out. If your building is recommended for REAP and you believe some of the defects were caused by tenants, you should see an attorney about appealing for a formal hearing before a hearing officer.

will repair or maintain certain items, such as appliances, the promise is express. When the landlord (or a manager or agent) says or does something that seems to indicate the landlord would be responsible for repairing or maintaining an item or facility, the promise is implied. Here are some typical examples of implied promises.

EXAMPLE 1

Tina sees Joel's ad for an apartment, which says "heated swimming pool." After Tina moves in, Joel stops heating the pool regularly because his utility costs have risen. Joel has violated his implied promise to keep the pool heated. (Joel should avoid ad language that commits him to such things.)

EXAMPLE 2

When Joel's rental agent shows Tom around the building, she goes out of her way to show off the laundry room, saying, "Here's the laundry room—it's for the use of all the tenants." Tom rents the apartment. Later the washing machine in the laundry room breaks down, but Joel won't fix it. Joel has violated his implied promise to maintain the laundry room appliances in working order.

EXAMPLE 3

Tina's apartment has a built-in dishwasher. When she rented the apartment, neither the lease nor the landlord said anything about who was to repair the dishwasher if it broke. The dishwasher has broken down a few times and whenever Tina asked Joel to fix it, he did. By doing so, he has established a "usage" or "practice" that the landlord—not the tenant—is responsible for repairing the dishwasher.

If you violate an express or implied promise relating to the condition of the premises, the tenant may sue you for money damages, usually in small claims court. The tenant cannot repair the appliance and deduct the cost from the rent (see Section E, below). Keep in mind that you can't label an essential piece of equipment an "amenity" and hope to avoid either your duty to supply it or the consequences (such as a tenant's rent withholding) if you fail to. (In *Secretary of HUD v. Layfield*, 88 Cal. App. 3d Supp. 28 (1979), a court allowed rent withholding because of the landlord's failure to provide security, even though the lease had no express promise of security.)

Don't decrease services. A decrease in promised services may be considered an illegal rent increase. (See Chapter 14, Section F.)

D. THE TENANT'S RESPONSIBILITIES

State law also requires tenants to use rented premises properly and keep them clean. Specifically, Civil Code §§ 1941.2-.3 require the tenant to:

- **Keep the premises as "clean and sanitary as the condition of the premises permits."** For example, a tenant whose kitchen had a rough, unfinished wooden floor that was hard to keep clean would not be able to keep the floor bright, shiny, and spotless.

- **Properly operate gas, electrical, and plumbing fixtures.** Examples of abuse include overloading an electrical outlet, flushing large foreign objects down the toilet, and allowing bathroom fixtures to become filthy.

- **Refrain from damaging or defacing the premises or allowing anyone else to do so.**

- **Use living and dining rooms, bedrooms, and kitchens for their proper respective purposes.** For example, the living or dining room should not regularly be used as a makeshift bedroom.

- **Report broken door or window locks in the dwelling unit.** Tenants are specifically charged with the duty to alert you of malfunctioning locks in their units. If a tenant has not notified you of a

problem, and you in fact are unaware of the broken device, you will not be liable for a violation of the state law.

In addition, under Civil Code § 3479, every tenant is prohibited from disturbing her neighbor's peaceful enjoyment of his property. This is known as refraining from creating or allowing a "nuisance," which is discussed more fully in Chapter 12.

To protect yourself, make sure your lease or rental agreement spells out basic tenant obligations. (See Clause 11 of our form agreements in Chapter 2.)

A tenant's isolated or minor violation of these duties will not relieve a landlord from his obligations to provide a habitable dwelling. (The landlord is still responsible for the condition of the premises and can be prosecuted for violating housing standards.) However, if a tenant is in "substantial violation" of any of these requirements, and this violation "substantially contributes" to the untenantable condition (or "substantially interferes" with the landlord's obligation to make the dwelling tenantable), the landlord is relieved from his duty to repair the condition. The tenant cannot withhold rent or sue the landlord if the tenant has contributed to the poor condition of the premises. (CC §§ 1929, 1941.2 and 1942 (c).)

EXAMPLE

Lance complains to his landlord, Gary, about a defective heater. When Gary's repairperson goes to fix the heater, he is confronted by an overwhelming smell of garbage and mildewed laundry. Lance cannot sue Gary for failing to fix the heater until and unless Lance cleans house, even though the foul smell didn't cause the heater to break. Lance's failure to keep the place clean and sanitary obviously interferes substantially with his landlord's attempt to fix the heater.

To protect a landlord against a tenant's careless damage to the property, our lease and rental agreements make the tenant financially responsible for repair of damage caused by the tenant's negligence or misuse. (See Clause 18, Chapter 2.) That means, where the tenant or his friends or family cause damage—for example, a broken window, a toilet clogged with children's toys, or a refrigerator that no longer works because the tenant defrosted it with a carving knife—it's the tenant's responsibility to make the repairs or to reimburse the landlord for doing so.

EXAMPLE

By his own sorrowful admission, Terry, angry over the loss of his job, puts his fist through a window. As a result, a cold wind blows in, cooling off Terry, if not his temper. Terry can't withhold rent to make his landlord fix the window, since Terry caused the problem in the first place. However, under state and local law, Terry's landlord is still responsible for fixing the window, after which he can and should bill Terry for the repair.

If a tenant refuses to repair or pay for the damage he caused, you can sue the tenant, normally in small claims court, for the cost of the repairs. If the tenancy is from month to month in a nonrent-controlled area, you may also want to consider a 30-day termination notice (or a 60-day notice if the tenant has lived there one year or longer). If the damage is very severe, such as numerous broken windows or holes in the wall, you can use a three-day notice and sue for eviction on the basis that the tenant has "committed waste" to the property. (See Chapter 18, Section B, and *The California Landlord's Law Book: Evictions.*)

You could also evict based on the tenant's breach of the lease or rental agreement provision forbidding damage to the premises (Clause 18), but you would have to give the tenant a chance to correct the problem. On the other hand, if you proceed under the theory that the tenant has committed waste, your three-day notice need not give this option—except in some rent-controlled cities. (CCP § 1161(4).) In any eviction case based on a three-day notice, you must also be able to establish that the damage was truly caused by the tenant's neglect, or you will lose the case and have to pay the tenant's court costs and attorney fees.

E. THE TENANT'S RIGHT TO REPAIR AND DEDUCT

Under certain circumstances a tenant can, without your permission, have a defect repaired and withhold the cost of the repairs from the following month's rent. (CC § 1942.) (A tenant can also just move out of an untenantable premise—see Section H, below.)

This is commonly called the "repair-and-deduct" remedy. It is subject to the following restrictions:

- The defect must be related to "tenantability." In other words, the problem must be at least somewhat serious and directly related to health or safety. Examples are broken heaters, stopped-up toilets, broken windows, and the absence or malfunctioning of legally required door and window locks.

- The defect or problem must not have been caused by the careless or intentional act of the tenant or a guest. Thus, a tenant cannot use this remedy to replace a window he broke himself.

- The amount the tenant withholds must be less than one month's rent.

- The tenant can use this remedy no more than twice in any 12-month period.

- Before having the repair done, the tenant must give the landlord or manager "reasonable" notice of the problem, either orally or in writing.

Of all these rules, the rule that the tenant give "reasonable" notice is the one most open to interpretation. According to Civil Code § 1942(b), reasonable notice is presumed to be 30 days. But it can be a lot less for an urgent problem, such as a defective heater in winter, a leaky roof during the rainy season, or a stopped-up toilet in a one-bath unit any time.

EXAMPLE 1

In July, Pam tells her landlord, Lorraine, that she was treated to some April showers in her living room three months earlier, due to a leaky roof. Unless it suddenly starts raining regularly in the middle of summer, this problem, though serious, isn't urgent. Pam must wait at least 30 days before she can take the repair into her own hands.

EXAMPLE 2

On a cold Monday in January, Frank tells his landlord, Regina, that the heater no longer works. By Wednesday night, Regina still hasn't fixed the heater. In the meantime, Frank and his family must sleep in a 45 degree apartment. So on Thursday, after only two days, Frank has the heater fixed, at a cost of $100. In February, Frank deducts this amount from his rent. Regina sues to evict Frank for nonpayment of rent. The judge decides that two days' notice was reasonable under the circumstances, and Regina loses. She must pay not only her own court costs and attorney fees, but Frank's as well.

EXAMPLE 3

Phil complains to his landlord, Linton, that the kitchen sink faucet drips slightly. Under their rental agreement, the tenant is not allowed to do any repairs on the rental unit. Although the duty to fix the faucet is Linton's, the problem does not pose a serious health or safety threat. Consequently, Phil cannot use the repair-and-deduct remedy.

If it comes to a fight, reasonable notice will be defined by a judge, not by the landlord. And going to court over this sort of dispute, unless the tenant's behavior was truly outrageous, is not a productive way to arrive at a decision. (Section G, below, discusses other options when a tenant repairs and deducts rent.)

COMMON MYTHS ABOUT RESPONSIBILITIES FOR REPAIRS

Paint. No law requires a landlord to repaint the interior every so often. So long as the paint isn't actually flaking off, it should comply with the law. The situation is different, however, if you are dealing with lead-based paint. (We discuss landlord liability for health problems caused by exposure to lead paint in Chapter 12, Section F.)

Drapes and Carpets. As for carpets and drapes, so long as they're not sufficiently damp or mildewy to constitute a health hazard, and so long as carpets don't have dangerous holes that could cause someone to trip and fall, you aren't legally required to replace them.

Windows. Quite a few landlords think a tenant is responsible for all broken windows. This is not true. A tenant is responsible only if the tenant or a guest intentionally or carelessly broke the window. If the damage was outside the tenant's control, however—for example, because a burglar, vandal or neighborhood child broke a window—you are responsible for fixing the window.

Your best bet is to set up a good responsive maintenance system and stick to it. We discuss this in more detail in Section J, below. And remember, in deciding whether the tenant acted unreasonably, consider how much it would have cost you to make the same repair. Obviously, a tenant who pays $200 for a simple toilet repair that should have cost only $40 is acting more unreasonably than one who paid $80 for a repair you could have accomplished for $50.

F. THE TENANT'S RIGHT TO WITHHOLD RENT WHEN THE PREMISES AREN'T HABITABLE

The repair-and-deduct remedy isn't the only legal way a tenant can withhold part or all of the rent from a landlord who doesn't properly maintain residential property. A tenant can also legally refuse to pay all or part of the rent if the unit falls short of the minimum requirements for a habitable dwelling as set forth in Civil Code § 1941.1 and other applicable housing and industry codes. In addition, one court decision seems to have expanded tenants' rights by allowing them to withhold rents for deficiencies not even addressed by building or housing statutes. (For example, in *Secretary of HUD v. Layfield,* 88 Cal. App. 3d Supp. 28 (1979), an appellate court ruled that a tenant could withhold rent if the landlord failed to provide adequate security patrols, even though there is no law requiring security guards.)

1. What Justifies Rent Withholding

Under California law, every landlord makes an implied promise that a dwelling will be fit for human habitation—whether or not that promise is written down in a lease or rental agreement. (*Green v. Superior Court,* 10 Cal. 3d 616 (1974).) If the landlord does not keep the place in a habitable condition at all times, he is said, in legal jargon, to have "breached the implied warranty of habitability." That breach justifies the tenant's withholding of rent.

For a tenant to legally withhold rent, the problems must not have been caused by the tenant, and the following must be true:

- The defects must be serious ones that threaten the tenant's health or safety.

- The tenant must have given the landlord reasonable notice of the problem. (*Hinson v. Delis,* 26 Cal. App. 3d 62 (1972).)

a. Severity of Problems

A tenant can withhold rent only if the premises have "substantial" defects. Examples of substantial defects are a bathroom ceiling that has collapsed and not been repaired; rats, mice, and cockroaches infesting the building; lack of heat or hot water; the presence of lead paint hazards in sufficient concentration (and extent); or the absence or malfunctioning of required

door and window locks. Fairly trivial defects, such as leaky water faucets or cracked windows or plaster, aren't enough to violate the implied warranty of habitability. And, a landlord's breach of the duty to provide a tenantable dwelling rarely excuses the tenant's duty to pay all of the rent due under the lease.

EXAMPLE

Wilbert rents a two-bedroom apartment from Molly for $600 a month. Because the toilet makes an occasional running sound until Wilbert jiggles the handle, Wilbert withholds an entire month's rent. Molly gives Wilbert a three-day notice and follows this with an eviction lawsuit. The judge decides that because the problem wasn't substantial, Wilbert had no right to withhold the rent, and gives Molly a judgment for the $600 rent, court costs, and possession of the property. (Because Molly handled her own case, she is not eligible for attorney fees.)

b. Notification of the Landlord

A tenant who wants to withhold rent must first notify the landlord or manager of the problem. There are, however, no precise notice requirements—for example, that the notice be in writing or delivered a certain way. And, unlike the rules with the repair-and-deduct remedy, there is also no definite rule as to how much time the landlord has to fix the problem after receiving notice of it, except that 35 days is too long under any circumstances. (CC §§ 1942.3 and 1942.4.) In other words, the tenant can give the notice orally or in writing, but before withholding rent on account of a defect, she must give the landlord a "reasonable" time to respond. If the question ends up in court, what's reasonable will be decided by a judge.

Some tenants make false claims to try to get out of paying some rent or avoid being evicted. For example, a tenant who is simply unable to pay the rent calls the health department to complain about—and exaggerate the effect of—a minor plumbing problem that the tenant previously tolerated and never complained about to the landlord. The best way to thwart these kinds of tenants is to establish and follow a good maintenance and inspection system. (See Section J, below.)

2. How Much Rent a Tenant Can Legally Withhold

If you do not fix a serious problem within a reasonable time, the tenant can withhold rent. But how much? Theoretically, the tenant can withhold as much rent as the defect lowers the value of the property. But as a practical matter, the tenant can withhold as much rent as the landlord—or a judge, if the case gets to court—will allow under the circumstances. A judge will make a decision based on an estimate of the rental value of the premises, in light of the seriousness of the defect.

Judges use various criteria to determine what's a reasonable amount of rent to withhold. Under the "percentage reduction" approach, the judge figures what percentage of the dwelling was rendered unfit, and reduces the rent accordingly. (For example, if a leaky roof made one room of a four-room apartment unlivable, the rent would be reduced by 25%.) Another method is to calculate the value of the dwelling in its defective state, subtract that amount from the fair market value of the rental (usually the agreed-upon rent) and allow the withholding of the resulting difference. Most courts use the percentage reduction approach.

EXAMPLE

For $900 a month, Lou rents a two-bedroom house to Ken. The house is heated by two wall heaters, one in the kitchen and one in a bedroom, which is somewhat isolated in a separate wing. In mid-November, the bedroom heater stops working, and Ken notifies Lou immediately. This leaves one end of the house, including one of the two bedrooms and a bathroom, chilly and uncomfortable. On December 1, the heater is still not fixed, so Ken refuses to pay Lou any rent. Lou finally fixes the heater on December 15 and demands the rent. Ken claims he only owes $450, half the rent for December. Lou takes the $450 but insists on the other $450, giving Ken a three-day notice to pay up or get out, followed by an unlawful detainer (eviction) lawsuit when Ken doesn't respond.

After hearing the case, the judge decides that Ken gave adequate notice to Lou regarding a substantial defect affecting the tenantability of the house, and that Lou should have fixed the problem by December 1. Since half the house was livable for the first half of December, Ken should also pay half of that half-month's rent, or $225, in addition to what he already paid. However, because Ken was correct in withholding rent, he wins the suit and can stay in his apartment if he pays Lou the $225, and Lou must pay Ken's court costs and attorney fees. However, if Ken doesn't pay the additional $225, Lou wins, getting a judgment for the $225, possession of the property and court costs.

In other situations, the judge might base a decision on the testimony of a real estate expert who knows about what the property would rent for, with all its defects. Or, a judge may even guess at an amount due the tenant as compensation for the inconvenience or annoyance of putting up with a problem—such as water leaking into the living room during winter months—and subtract that from the monthly rent.

Tenants who successfully withhold rent must pay the adjusted rental value within a reasonable time, or they will lose the unlawful detainer action. A tenant who has convinced a judge that a substantial defect justified his withholding some or all of the rent must pay the reasonable rental value of the premises up to the date of trial or risk losing possession. The rent must be paid within a "reasonable time," but in any event no more than five days after the date of the court's judgment (if the judgment is made by mail, then five days plus another five-day extension period provided by law). (CCP § 1013.) In other words, unless he is ready to pay the accrued adjusted rent, the tenant will lose the unlawful detainer action even though he has established a breach of the warranty of habitability. (CCP § 1174.2(a)(1) & (2).)

If you do end up in court, be prepared to prove the following:

- The claimed defect was not so serious or substantial as to render the property untenantable.

- Even if the defect was substantial, you were never given adequate notice and a chance to fix it. (At this point, you should present your detailed complaint procedure to the court and show, if possible, that the tenant didn't follow it.)

- Assuming there was a substantial defect that wasn't fixed within a reasonable time (perhaps you were away and your manager screwed up), this defect justifies the withholding of only a small amount of rent because it didn't inconvenience the tenant much. For example, although an inoperable heater is a substantial defect, it won't cause the tenant too much discomfort in the summer; or perhaps a tenant who used a portable electric heater instead wasn't badly inconvenienced.

Court fights over rent withholding are covered in Section G2, below.

G. The Landlord's Options If a Tenant Repairs and Deducts or Withholds Rent

When confronted with a tenant who withholds all or part of the rent, whether justifiably or not, most landlords almost reflexively turn to a lawyer to bring an eviction lawsuit. But even if you eventually get the tenant evicted, it is often only after considerable cost. In most eviction suits, the lawyers are the only clear winners. Even if you get a judgment for unpaid rent and attorney fees, these amounts often turn out to be uncollectible.

If you feel your tenant improperly deducted the costs of repairs from the rent or withheld rent—perhaps by giving you little or no notice—try working things out with the tenant. Failing that, if you feel strongly enough about it, sue the tenant for the deducted part of the rent, in small claims court or in an eviction lawsuit.

1. Working Out a Compromise

If you think the tenant is wrong but sincere, and is not simply trying to make up an excuse for not paying rent, you may want to go along with the tenant's withholding or repair-and-deduct proposal. If, for example, the tenant uses the repair-and-deduct remedy, but you feel you were never given adequate notice and could have had the problem fixed for $50 less than the tenant paid, it may make sense to drop the matter. Trying to evict the tenant will cost far more, and you may not win the suit.

This isn't to say you should roll over and accept any silly scheme a tenant invents. Set up a meeting with the tenant to review your repair procedures. Listen to any grievance the tenant has, and make sure that the next time there is a problem, you will be notified promptly. Obviously, if a tenant persists in being unreasonable, you will eventually have to get more assertive.

You may want to try to work out a compromise with the tenant. A compromise would certainly include repairing any defect having to do with any of the tenantability factors listed in Section A, above. You might also give the tenant a prorated reduction in rent for the period between the time the tenant notified you of the defect and the time it was corrected.

For example, suppose a leaky roof during a rainy month deprives a tenant of the use of one of his two bedrooms. If the tenant gave you notice of the leak and you did not take care of the problem quickly, the tenant might be justified in deducting $300 from the $800 rent for that month. However, if the tenant didn't tell you of the problem until the next month's rent was due, a compromise might be reached where the tenant bears part of the responsibility, by agreeing to deduct only $100 from the rent.

The first step in working towards a compromise with the rent-withholding tenant is to make a phone call. Dropping over unannounced to talk may threaten the tenant and put him in a defensive posture. If you're reluctant to call, you might want to try a letter. See the sample letter below.

If you can't work something out with the tenant, consider mediation, where a neutral third party can help you arrive at a solution. Many cities have community organizations (sometimes called "boards") that conduct mediation between landlords and tenants. These organizations can be extremely helpful in resolving disputes over the amount of rent (if any) it is reasonable to withhold, the condition of the premises, or the need for repairs. (We discuss mediation in some detail in Chapter 8.)

Many organizations that offer mediation also conduct arbitration, if the parties can't reach an agreement. In arbitration, a neutral third party makes a decision—just like a judge in court, but after a much less formal hearing. In binding arbitration, the parties agree in advance, in writing, to abide by the decision. If you and the tenant agree to binding arbitration, an informal hearing is held. Each person tells his or her side of the story, and an arbitrator reaches a decision, which is enforceable in court.

2. Court Fights Over Rent Withholding

Rent withholding almost always comes before a judge in the context of an unlawful detainer (eviction) lawsuit. In response to the tenant's failure to pay rent, the landlord serves a Three-Day Notice to Pay Rent or Quit and, when the tenant fails to do either, files suit.

A tenant normally has the burden of convincing a judge that the withholding was reasonable, unless the landlord took more than 35 days to fix any defect that a local health or building inspection department official insisted be repaired following an inspection. (CC §§ 1942.3 and 1942.4.) In this case, the burden falls on the landlord to prove the tenant was wrong to withhold rent.

Here's how judges typically rule on rent withholding:

- If the judge rules that the tenant had no right to withhold any rent at all, the landlord will win a judgment for the unpaid rent, court costs (and attorney fees if the rental agreement had an attorney fees clause), and possession of the property. The tenant's eviction will be ordered.

- If the judge decides that the tenant had the right to withhold rent and withheld the correct amount (having paid the balance to the landlord), the judge will rule for the tenant, who will be able to stay in the property. In addition, the landlord will be responsible for paying the tenant's court costs and attorney fees if the lease or rental agreement has an attorney fees clause.

- If the judge decides that the tenant had a right to withhold rent, but not as much as the tenant withhheld, it's a little more complicated. The judge will normally order the tenant to pay the difference, sometimes giving the tenant up to five days to do so. If the tenant pays the landlord within the time the judge allows, he gets to stay, wins the lawsuit, and can even get a judgment against the landlord requiring the landlord to pay court costs. (The tenant is considered the winner because the tenant had a valid complaint, even if he did withhold too much rent. The tenant isn't penalized for having been unable to guess the right amount of rent to withhold.) (See CCP § 1174.2 and *Strickland v. Becks,* 95 Cal. App. 3d Supp. 18, 157 Cal. Rptr. 656 (1979). This rule also applies to attorney fees if the applicable lease or rental agreement has an attorney fees clause. This is because CC § 1717(a) says that attorney fees provided for in a written contract are considered "costs of suit," and so are treated the same way as costs in this respect.)

- On the other hand, if the tenant doesn't pay the difference between how much rent he withheld and what he should have withheld, the landlord will then win a judgment for that amount, possession of the property, court costs, and attorney fees, if the lease or rental agreement has an attorney fees

SAMPLE LETTER SUGGESTING COMPROMISE ON RENT WITHHOLDING

May 3, 200X

Tyrone McNab
Villa Arms, Apt. 4
123 Main Street
Monterey, California

Dear Mr. McNab:

I am writing you in the hope we can work out a fair compromise to the problems that led you to withhold rent. You have rented a unit at the Villa Arms for the last three years and we have never had a problem before. Let's try to resolve it.

To review briefly, on May 1, Marvin, my resident manager at Villa Arms, told me that you were refusing to pay your rent because of several defective conditions in your apartment. Marvin said you had asked him to correct these problems a week ago, but he hasn't as yet attended to them. Marvin states that you listed these defects as some peeling paint on the interior wall of your bedroom, a leaky kitchen water faucet, a running toilet, a small hole in the living room carpet, and a cracked kitchen window.

I have instructed Marvin to promptly arrange with you for a convenient time to allow him into your apartment to repair all these problems. I am sure these repairs would already have been accomplished by now except for the fact that Hank, our regular repairperson, has been out sick for the last ten days.

Because of the inconvenience you have suffered as a result of the problems in your apartment, I am prepared to offer you a prorated rebate on your rent for ten days, this being the estimated length of time it will have taken Marvin to remedy the problems from the day of your complaint. As your monthly rent is $450, equal to $15 per day, I am agreeable to your paying only $300 rent this month.

If this is not acceptable to you, please call me at 555-1234 during the day. If you would like to discuss any aspect of the situation in more detail, I would be pleased to meet with you at your convenience. I will expect to receive your check for $300, or a call from you, before May 10.

Sincerely,

Sandra Schmidt

Sandra Schmidt

clause and the landlord was represented by an attorney. (See Chapter 18 for more on eviction lawsuits.)

A judge who determines that the tenant properly withheld rent based on a defect in the property may (1) order the landlord to repair it within a set period of time, (2) require the landlord to come back to court to show proof the repairs have been made, and (3) reduce the future rent the tenant will have to pay until repairs are made. (CCP § 1174.2(a)(3)-(5).) The judge can also order the landlord to pay the tenant's attorneys fees (even in the absence of a written lease or rental agreement with an attorney's fees clause), if the landlord failed to make necessary repairs within 35 days of receiving a notice from a health or building department official. (CC § 1942.4 (b), CCP § 1174.21.) In a suit brought by the tenant, the judge can also award "special damages" of $100 to $5,000.

EXAMPLE

Tillie Brooks stops paying her $750 monthly rent to Lenny Swoboda in January because Lenny didn't repair a leaky roof. Lenny serves Tillie with a three-day notice, then files an unlawful detainer (eviction) lawsuit when Tillie still refuses to pay. Tillie defends, and wins. The judge reduces the rent to $500 a month and orders Tillie to pay $500 to Lenny for January's rent in order to stay. Tillie pays and stays. The judge also orders Lenny to show written proof from the Health Department that he fixed the roof at another hearing 30 days later. He also reduces the rent to $500 a month until such time as Lenny shows proof of repairs. After 30 days, if Lenny doesn't fix the problem, the judge can keep the rent reduced indefinitely, and can exercise what amounts to continuing supervision over the property until the repairs are made.

Retaliatory evictions and rent increases are illegal. Occasionally, a landlord, faced with a troublesome tenant who seems to be unreasonably asserting his legal remedies to the letter of the law—whether in the form of a complaint to local officials or the deduction of repair costs from the rent—gives the tenant a notice terminating the tenancy or raising the rent. A tenant can defend against this sort of eviction or rent increase on the basis that the landlord is illegally retaliating against him for exercising his rights. (CC § 1942.5. Also, in the cases of *S.P. Growers Assn. v. Rodriguez,* 17 Cal. 3d 719 (1976) and *Vargas v. Municipal Court,* 22 Cal. 3d 902 (1978), the California Supreme Court upheld the right of a tenant who sued a landlord to defend a subsequent eviction on the basis that it was motivated by the landlord's intent to retaliate against the tenant for having brought suit.)

For a detailed discussion of retaliatory evictions, see Chapter 15.

H. THE TENANT'S RIGHT TO MOVE OUT

In several circumstances, tenants have the right to move out because of defective conditions in the premises.

1. Asking Tenants to Move So Repairs Can Be Made

Local authorities may sue a landlord who fails to repair code violations in a reasonable time. If a court rules that the property's conditions "substantially endanger the health and safety of residents," and if the landlord must ask tenants to move in order to make repairs, the landlord must:

- provide the tenant with comparable temporary housing nearby or, if that's not possible, pay the difference between the old rent and the tenant's new rent elsewhere, for up to four months

- pay the tenant's moving expenses, including packing and unpacking costs

- insure the tenant's belongings in transit, or pay for the replacement value of property lost, stolen, or damaged in transit

- pay the tenant's new utility connection charges, and

- give the tenant the first chance to move back into the old place when repairs are completed. (Health and Safety Code § 17980.7.)

2. The Tenant's Right to Move Out of Untenantable Premises

If there is a problem that allows a tenant to use the repair-and-deduct remedy (see Section E, above), the tenant also has the option of simply packing up and leaving without further notice if the landlord fails to fix the problem in a reasonable time. (CC § 1942.) The tenant is not responsible for payment of any rent from the time the repair should have been made, even if due under a long-term lease. In addition, the tenant is entitled to a prorated refund of any rent paid in advance that covers the time during which the unit was in disrepair, and compensation for living in substandard housing.

EXAMPLE

On January 1, Lionel leases his house to Lisa for a year, and Lisa pays the first month's rent of $900. On February 1, Lisa pays the rent again, but the next day, the water heater springs a leak. Lisa tells Lionel about the problem, but Lionel does nothing. Several more anguished calls from Lisa, who has no hot water, produce no action. After fifteen days, Lisa simply packs up and leaves. She is probably acting reasonably and legally under the circumstances.

Not only is Lisa relieved of any further obligation under the lease, but she's also entitled to a refund of $450, representing the prorated rent for the second half of the month, plus her security deposit (less any lawful deductions). In addition, Lisa is entitled to a further rent reduction on account of having no hot water for the half month she was there. If Lionel and Lisa can't agree on this figure, a judge will have to decide when Lisa takes Lionel to small claims court.

3. Destruction of the Premises

As California residents know all too well, natural disasters such as earthquakes, fires, and floods are a common threat. Also, despite your successful efforts to maintain a safe building, you cannot isolate your property from destructive forces that might start elsewhere, such as a fire that spreads from the neighboring property. If part or all of your rental property is destroyed in one of these events, what are your obligations to your tenants?

Landlords and tenants may address this issue in their lease or rental agreement and agree on the following questions between themselves:

- Who will determine whether the property is totally destroyed?

- Who will decide whether the totally destroyed premises are to be rebuilt, and how quickly must that decision be made?

- Even if there is only partial destruction, who will decide whether the tenant may consider the premises unfit?

- If you repair a partially destroyed building and the tenant remains, who will decide how much rent the tenant must pay?

- How much time will you have to complete repairs?

Clause 18 (Damage to the Premises) of our form rental agreement and lease (see Chapter 2) addresses these questions and provides guidelines in the event that there is total or partial destruction of your rental property. If you and your tenants have not, however, considered these issues in advance and specified solutions in your lease or rental agreement, some guidelines are provided by law.

Under California law, unless you and the tenant have agreed otherwise, total destruction of the premises cancels the rental or lease contract. The tenant's obligation to pay rent ceases, and the landlord's duty to provide housing is also extinguished. (CC § 1933(4).) You do not need to return advance payments of rent. (*Pedro v. Potter*, 197 Cal. 751 (1926).)

But what about partial destruction? State law provides that the lease or rental agreement will be considered terminated if:

- the destruction is not the fault of the tenant

- the landlord had reason to believe, when the lease or rental agreement was signed, that the destroyed portion or aspect of the rental premises was a "material inducement" to the tenant (that is, a major reason why the tenant rented the premises), and

- the tenant gives notice to the landlord that he considers the lease to be over because of the destruction of an important aspect of the premises. (CC § 1932(2).)

EXAMPLE

Sandra wanted a rental with a large, fenced yard that would be a safe play area for her three small children. When she saw Alex's duplex, she was delighted at the spacious backyard and told him that it was the perfect answer to her needs. When he offered to show her another duplex that had no yard but a larger interior, she declined and told him that her most important requirement was the yard, and that she would make do with smaller rooms. Sandra signed a year's lease in late fall.

The weather that winter was exceptionally severe, and the rainstorms caused the hill behind Sandra's home to slide, burying the backyard in a foot of mud and crushing the fences. Although the house itself escaped damage, the yard was ruined. Sandra wrote to Alex to tell him that she considered the lease to be over, since the backyard, now unusable, was a major reason for her decision to rent. Sandra moved out and although she did not recover the balance of that month's rent, she was not responsible for any future rent. She got her entire security deposit back when Alex examined the house and determined that there was no damage beyond normal wear and tear.

I. THE TENANT'S RIGHT TO SUE FOR DEFECTIVE CONDITIONS

As we have explained in Sections E and F, above, the landlord's failure to maintain rental property may result in the tenant's use of the rent withholding or repair-and-deduct remedies. When this happens, landlords often move to evict based on the tenant's failure to pay rent, and the tenant defends by pointing to the substandard conditions and arguing that he used the remedy appropriately.

A landlord who fails to maintain property can also be sued by a tenant. (*Landeros v. Pankey*, 39 Cal. App. 4th 1167 (1996).) This is true even if the tenant has withheld rent or was the subject of an eviction lawsuit. By failing to repair defective conditions, the theory goes, the landlord breached an implied term of the lease or rental agreement—that is, to provide a habitable dwelling. The tenant, whether he remains in the property or moves out, can sue the landlord for breaking the lease contract, and can ask for the following:

- partial or total refund of rent paid while conditions were substandard
- the value, or repair costs, of property lost or damaged as a result of the defect—for example, furniture ruined by water leaking through the roof
- compensation for personal injuries—including pain and suffering—caused by the defect
- an order requiring the landlord to repair the defects, with rent reduced, until the landlord shows proof to the court that the defects have been remedied (CC § 1942.4(c)), and
- attorney fees, even if the lease or rental agreement does not have an attorney fees clause. (Our form agreements do—see Clause 22 in Chapter 2.)

In the sections that follow, we'll explain the various ways that tenants can initiate lawsuits against landlords.

1. Lawsuits Authorized by Statute

Landlords who have failed to maintain their property in accordance with the habitability requirements of Section 1941.1-.3 of the Civil Code may be sued by a tenant if all the following requirements are met (CC § 1942.4.):

- The dwelling "substantially lacks" any of the habitability standards as set forth in Civil Code § 1941.1-.3—for example, hot water and heating systems. (See Section A, above.)
- A housing officer has inspected the premises and has given written notice to the landlord (or her agent) that the condition must be repaired.

- At least 35 days have passed since the notice was issued, the defect has not been remedied, and there is no "good cause" for the delay.

- The defect was not caused by the tenant's act or failure to maintain the dwelling in good order. (See Section D, above, for a discussion of the tenant's obligations.)

Tenants typically use this statutory remedy—suing the landlord—when they decide to remain in the dwelling unit (despite its defects) and do not want to withhold rent and risk eviction if they lose the unlawful detainer lawsuit brought by the landlord.

Tenants may bring lawsuits of this type in small claims court if their claims do not exceed $5,000. The tenant may be awarded special damages of up to $5,000 as well, if the defective conditions caused unique hardship or losses to the tenant. If the defective conditions constitute a nuisance, the court may order the landlord to abate (cease) the nuisance, and the court may hold on to the case until it is satisfied that the threat to the tenant's health or safety has been removed. Finally, the winning party will get attorney's fees and costs (irrespective of whether this provision is included in the lease contract).

EXAMPLE

Lucy rented the top-story apartment in a building owned by Mike. During January, the roof above Lucy's bedroom leaked, causing water to saturate the walls and resulting in extensive mildew. Lucy notified Mike of the leaking roof, but got no action. She then called the local health inspector, who came out to inspect her bedroom. The inspector declared that the leaking roof violated the state requirement that rental premises be adequately waterproofed, and ordered Mike to fix the roof. Three months later, the roof still leaked and Lucy sued Mike under Section 1942.4 of the Civil Code. She was able to recover:

- actual damages of several hundred dollars, representing the difference between the stated rent and the rental value of the apartment without a bedroom (since Lucy had been unable to use her bedroom because of the leaking roof)

- special damages of $1,000, representing the dry-cleaning costs for Lucy's clothes, the value of her damaged art on the walls, and the value of her ruined carpet, and

- attorney fees and costs.

2. Lawsuits for Rent Refunds

In some situations, tenants can sue landlords without first going to the local health department for an inspection and repair order, as explained in Section 1, above. A tenant who has moved out, in particular, has little interest in forcing the landlord to repair the habitability defect. Instead, a tenant who has left may file a garden-variety breach of contract lawsuit against the landlord for losses caused by the landlord's failure to provide habitable housing.

To win a breach of contract lawsuit, the tenant must establish that:

- a substantial defect in the premises rendered it uninhabitable

- the landlord was notified within a reasonable time of the tenant's discovery of the defect, and

- the landlord was given a reasonable time to correct the defect but failed to do so.

The winning tenant will collect a rent refund, equal to the amount by which the stated, agreed-upon rent exceeds the value of the damaged premises. For example, if a two-bath apartment rented for $500 per month, but a leak in one of the bathrooms made that room unusable, reducing the unit to a one-bath apartment, the damages would be the difference between $500 and the rental value of a one-bath unit. Also, the landlord will have to pay the tenant's court costs and attorney fees if the lease or rental agreement has an attorney fees clause.

3. Lawsuits for Emotional Distress

Landlords who fail to maintain habitable rental property may be vulnerable to lawsuits that charge them with the intentional or negligent infliction of emotional distress—even in the absence of actual physical injury caused by the defect. (Claims for emotional distress can also accompany lawsuits where there has been a physical injury, as is explained in Chapter 12.) Tenants who sue for emotional distress must show that the landlord's failure to repair was particularly extreme or outrageous because of the landlord's:

- **Recklessness.** The landlord wantonly failed to fix a significant problem, which would cause mental distress to any tenant, or

- **Willfulness.** The landlord's failure to repair the substantial defect was intentional, done with the knowledge that the tenant was susceptible to emotional torment.

EXAMPLE

Randy complained to his landlord, Al, about the leaking toilet in his apartment. Al checked the bathroom and confirmed that, indeed, the seal was broken and sewage was leaking into the room, but he did not fix it. After a week had passed, Randy decided to use the repair-and-deduct remedy, so he had the problem fixed and deducted the repair costs from his next month's rent.

Al was furious when he received less than the full rent. He accosted Randy and told him to pay up "or else we'll handle this like real men, the way we used to in the old days." Randy felt he was being threatened, and felt fearful every time he left his apartment. Eventually, he was unable to leave his apartment at all. Randy sued Al for intentional infliction of emotional distress. The jury agreed with Randy and awarded him a judgment of several thousand dollars.

Managers can be personally liable for emotional distress. When tenants sue for general and special damages for habitability defects (rent refunds and the value of ruined property), the landlord is financially responsible, even if the manager had been given the repair responsibility. If the tenant claims that the manager caused emotional distress, however, the manager's liability may be shared with the landlord, and the manager himself may be responsible for a percentage of the damages.

4. Lawsuits for Maintaining a Nuisance

If the landlord's failure to maintain the property in a habitable condition results in an offensive or injurious condition, the tenant may sue for the maintenance of a private nuisance. (CC §§ 3479 and 3501.) Put another way, if the defects substantially interfere with the tenant's use or enjoyment of the property, a nuisance may exist. A tenant who sues over a private nuisance is limited to recovering for the value of his lost use of his property—but not for physical or mental suffering. (If the tenant claims that the nuisance has caused physical or mental anguish, he must use the public nuisance statutes, which are discussed in Chapter 12, Section A.)

Whether a habitability defect is so severe as to constitute a nuisance is always a question for the jury. Factors considered include the number of people affected, the nature of the neighborhood and the surroundings, the duration and frequency of the behavior, the harm alleged, and the seriousness of the disturbance. A court that decides that a nuisance exists may order the landlord to fix the problem and compensate the tenant for having put up with the situation. If the landlord's conduct was intentional (and not merely negligent), the tenant may get punitive damages as well, which are monetary awards intended to punish the landlord for his malicious or willful behavior.

EXAMPLE

John and Mary rented a duplex from their landlord Len, who lived in the second half of the building. Under their rental agreement, John and Mary shared use of the driveway and yards with Len.

When he retired, Len started to collect and repair old cars. Because he did not have a garage, Len used the backyard and driveway to store and work on his cars. The presence of Len's cars made it impossible for John and Mary to use the yard or driveway, and they were constantly plagued by the stench of car exhaust and oil and the unsightly view of many old junkers. After unsuccessful attempts to get Len to remove the cars, John and Mary sued him in small claims court, alleging that the presence of the junkyard on their property constituted a private nuisance. The court agreed that the cars made it impossible for John and Mary to enjoy the yard and use the driveway, and ordered Len to remove the cars. The court also ordered Len to compensate John and Mary for the fact that their enjoyment and use of the property had been impaired.

A landlord may not retaliate against a tenant who files a lawsuit and stays in the property. It may seem inconsistent for a tenant to take the extreme step of suing his landlord and expect to remain on the property. Nevertheless, a tenant who sues and stays is exercising a legal right, and retaliation, such as with a rent increase or termination notice, is illegal and will give the tenant yet another ground on which to sue. (See CC § 1942.5 and Chapter 15 for a discussion of retaliatory eviction.)

J. AVOID RENT WITHHOLDING AND OTHER TENANT REMEDIES BY ADOPTING A HIGH-QUALITY REPAIR AND MAINTENANCE SYSTEM

A landlord's best defense against rent withholding hassles or tenant lawsuits is to:

- establish and communicate clear, easy-to-follow procedures for tenants to ask for repairs
- document all complaints
- respond quickly when complaints are made, and
- make annual safety inspections.

1. Recommended Repair and Maintenance System

Follow these steps to avoid maintenance and repair problems with tenants:

- Clearly set out landlord's and tenant's responsibilities for repair and maintenance in your lease or rental agreement. (See Clause 11 of our form agreements in Chapter 2.)
- Use the written Landlord/Tenant Checklist form in Chapter 7 to check over the premises and fix any problems before new tenants move in.
- Don't assume your tenants know how to handle routine maintenance problems such as a clogged toilet or drain. Make it a point to explain the basics

---

WHEN DOES LEGAL BUT ANNOYING BEHAVIOR BECOME A "NUISANCE"?

Landlords often hear complaints from tenants about annoying behavior of other tenants—for example, someone whose putting practice results in golf balls sailing onto the other tenants' patios. Or, a tenant may complain about his upstairs neighbor who arises every morning at 5 a.m. and clumps about in heavy work boots. While such annoying behavior will generally not violate the warranty of habitability, it still may create legal headaches for landlords.

It's unlikely that one tenant's annoying behavior is serious enough for another tenant to successfully sue you for the maintenance of a private nuisance. But rather than risk a court battle, address tenants' complaints quickly and reasonably, using the complaint handling system we recommend in Section J, below. And if problems persist, you may need to evict the tenant with the annoying behavior.

Clause 16 of our form lease and rental agreements in Chapter 2 prohibits tenants from causing disturbances or creating a nuisance—that is, behavior that prevents neighbors from fully enjoying the use of their own homes.

when the tenant moves into the unit. In addition, include a brief list of maintenance do's and don'ts as part of your move-in materials. For example:

- how to avoid overloading circuits

- proper use of garbage disposal

- location and use of fire extinguisher

- problems tenant should definitely not try to handle, such as electrical repairs.

• Encourage tenants to immediately report plumbing, heating, weatherproofing or other defects, or safety or security problems—whether in the tenant's unit or in common areas such as hallways and parking garages. A Maintenance/Repair Request form (discussed in Section 3, below) is often useful in this regard. Give every tenant a copy of your complaint procedure and safety and maintenance system. This should be part of a move-in letter, described in Chapter 7.

• Keep a written log (or have your property manager keep one) of all complaints (including those made orally) and correspondence and how and when they were handled. This should include a box to indicate your immediate and any follow-up responses (and subsequent tenant communications), as well as a space to enter the date and brief details of when the problem was fixed. The Maintenance Repair/Request form, below, can serve this purpose.

• Keep a file for each apartment or unit with copies of all complaints and repair requests from tenants and your response. As a general rule, you should respond in writing to every tenant repair request (even if you also do so orally).

• Handle repairs (especially urgent ones) as soon as possible, but definitely within the time any state law requires. Notify the tenant by phone and follow up in writing if repairs will take more than 48 hours, excluding weekends. Keep the tenant informed—for example, if you have problems scheduling a plumber, let your tenant know with a phone call or a note.

• Twice a year, give your tenants a checklist on which to report any potential safety hazards or

maintenance problems that might have been overlooked. See the Semi-Annual Safety and Maintenance Update, described in Section K, below. Respond promptly and in writing to all requests, keeping copies in your file.

• Once a year, inspect all rental units, using the Landlord/Tenant Checklist as a guide. See Annual Safety Inspection, described in Section K, below. (Keep copies of the filled-in checklist in your file.)

• Especially for multiunit projects, place conspicuous notices in several places around your property about your determination to operate a safe, well-maintained building, and list phone numbers for tenants to call with maintenance requests.

• As part of every written communication, remind tenants of your policies and procedures to keep your building in good repair. Be sure to include a brief review of the complaint procedure. For example, at the bottom of all routine notices, rent increases and other communications, a landlord might remind tenants of the following:

"The management's policy is to properly maintain all apartment units and common areas. If you have any questions, suggestions, or requests regarding your unit or the building, please direct them to the manager between 9 a.m. and 6 p.m., Monday through Saturday, either by calling 555-9876 or by dropping off a completed Maintenance/Repair Request form at the manager's office. In case of emergency, please call 555-6789 at any time."

2. Benefits of Establishing a Repair and Maintenance System

This system gives you several benefits. First, it allows you to fix little problems before they grow into big ones. It also helps you communicate with tenants who do have legitimate problems and creates a climate of cooperation and trust that can work wonders in the long run.

And at least as important, it provides you with an excellent defense when it comes to those few unreasonable tenants who seek to withhold or reduce rent for no adequate reason other than their disinclination to pay. (In addition, if you need to establish that the repair problem is phony, you may want to have the repairperson who looked at the "defect" come to court to testify about it.) You may still have to go to court to evict them, but your carefully documented procedures will constitute a "paper trail" to help you accomplish this with a minimum of time and expense.

If you regularly solicit comments about the condition of your rental property, a tenant who doesn't report a problem will have a hard time in court if the tenant later refuses to pay the rent because of your failure to repair that problem. If you make it your normal business practice to log all verbal repair requests from tenants and save all written requests, the absence of a request or notification of one is evidence that the tenant has made no complaints.

Finally, this kind of repair and recordkeeping system can also help keep down your potential liability to your tenants. If you're sued for injuries suffered as a result of allegedly defective conditions on your property, your chances of losing are less because, in many situations, injured persons must prove not only that they were hurt, but that you were negligent (unreasonably careless). This can be difficult to do if you adopt an extremely responsive repair scheme and stick to it. (Landlord liability for injuries is discussed in Chapter 12.)

EXAMPLE

Geeta owns a 12-unit apartment complex and encourages her tenants to request repairs in writing, using the Maintenance/Repair Request form shown below. Most tenants use the form. Geeta routinely saves all tenants' filled-out forms for at least one year, and she also keeps a log of all verbal repair requests. One month, Ravi doesn't pay his rent, even in response to Geeta's three-day notice. When Geeta files an eviction suit, Ravi claims he withheld rent because of a leaky roof and defective heater Geeta supposedly refused to repair. At trial, Geeta describes her complaint handling and recordkeeping system and even brings her logs and files to court. She testifies

that she has no record of ever receiving a complaint from Ravi. The judge has reason to doubt Ravi ever complained, and rules in Geeta's favor.

3. Resident's Maintenance/Repair Request Form

One way to assure that defects in the premises will be reported by conscientious tenants—while helping to refute bogus tenant claims about lack of repairs—is to include a clause in your lease or rental agreement requiring tenants to notify you of repair and maintenance needs. (See Clause 11 of our form agreements in Chapter 2.) Make the point again and describe your process for handling repairs in your move-in letter to new tenants. (See Chapter 7.)

Many tenants will find it easiest (and most practical) to call the landlord or manager with a repair problem or complaint, particularly in urgent cases. Make sure you have an answering machine, voice mail, or other service available at all times to accommodate tenant calls. Check your messages frequently when you're not available by phone.

We also suggest you provide all tenants with a Maintenance/Repair Request form. Give each tenant five or ten copies when they move in, and explain how the form should be used to request specific repairs (see the sample, below). Be sure that tenants know to describe the problem in detail and to indicate the best time to make repairs. Make sure tenants know how to get more copies. Your manager (if any) should keep an ample supply of the Maintenance/Repair Request form in her rental unit or office.

You (or your manager) should complete the entire Maintenance/Repair Request form or keep a separate log for every tenant complaint (including those made by phone). (See Section 4, Tracking Tenant Complaints, below.) Keep a copy of our form or your log in the tenant's file, along with any other written communication. Be sure to keep good records of how and when you handled tenant complaints, including reasons for any delays and notes on conversations with tenants. For a sample, see the bottom of the Maintenance/Repair Request form (labeled For Management Use). Also, see Section 5, Responding to

Tenant Complaints, below, for additional advice. You might also jot down any other comments regarding repair or maintenance problems you observed while handling the tenant's complaint.

You'll find a tear-out version of the Resident's Maintenance/Repair Request in Appendix B. The CD-ROM that accompanies this book also includes this form.

A sample Maintenance/Repair Request form is shown below. You'll see that the repairperson has also made a note to return and fix a separate problem—a good way to keep on top of repair duties. But keep in mind that if you do make notes of this kind, it's important that you follow up and do the work. If you don't and the tenant later complains about unattended repairs —and resorts to repair-and-deduct or rent withholding—your note will be the best evidence that you knew about the problem but didn't attend to it.

4. Tracking Tenant Complaints

Most tenants will simply call you when they have a problem or complaint, rather than fill out a Maintenance/Repair Request form. For recordkeeping purposes we suggest you fill out this form, regardless of whether the tenant does. It's also a good idea to keep a separate chronological log or calendar with similar information on tenant complaints.

5. Responding to Tenant Complaints

You should respond almost immediately to all complaints about defective conditions by talking to the tenant and following up (preferably in writing). Explain when repairs can be made or, if you don't yet know, tell the tenant that you will be back in touch promptly. This doesn't mean you have to jump through hoops to fix things that don't need fixing or to engage in heroic efforts to make routine repairs. It does mean you should take prompt action under the circumstances—for example, immediate action

should normally be taken to cope with broken door locks or security problems. Similarly, a lack of heat or hot water (especially in winter in cold areas) and safety hazards such as broken steps or exposed electrical wires should be dealt with on an emergency basis.

One way to think about how to respond to repair problems is to classify them according to their consequences. Once you consider the results of inaction, your response time will be clear:

- **Personal security and safety problems = injured tenants = lawsuits.** Respond and get work done immediately if the potential for harm is very serious, even if this means calling a 24-hour repair service or having you or your manager get up in the middle of the night to put a piece of plywood over a broken ground floor window.

- **Major inconvenience to tenant = seriously unhappy tenant = tenant's self-help remedies (such as rent withholding) and vacancies.** Respond and attempt to get work done as soon as possible, or within 24 hours, if the problem is a major inconvenience to the tenant such as a plumbing or heating problem.

- **Minor problem = slightly annoyed tenant = bad feelings.** Respond in 48 hours (on business days) if not too serious.

Yes, these deadlines may seem tight and, occasionally, meeting them will cost you a few dollars extra, but in the long run you'll be way ahead. (See Section 2, above, for a discussion of the benefits of establishing a good repair and maintenance system.)

Respect tenants' privacy. To gain access to make repairs, the landlord can enter the rental premises only with the tenant's consent, or after having given written and reasonable notice, presumed to be 24 hours. See Chapter 13 for rules and procedures for entering a tenant's home to make repairs and how to deal with tenants who make access inconvenient for you or your maintenance personnel.

Resident's Maintenance/Repair Request

Date: _August 29, 200X_

Address: _392 Main St., #401, Modesto_

Resident's Name: _Mary Griffin_

Phone (home): _555-1234_   Phone (work): _555-5678_

Problem: _Garbage disposal doesn't work_

Best time to make repairs: _Best times are after 6 p.m. or Saturday morning_

Comments : _____

I authorize entry into my unit to perform the maintenance or repair requested above, in my absence, unless stated otherwise above.

Mary Griffin
Resident

. . . .

FOR MANAGEMENT USE

Work done: _Fixed garbage disposal (removed spoon)_

Time spent: _1/2_ hours

Date completed: _August 3_, 20_OX_

Unable to complete on _____, 20____, because: _____

Notes and comments: _Faucet drips—needs follow-up call_

August 9, 200X   _Hal Ortiz_
Date   Landlord/Manager

If you're unable to take care of a repair right away, such as a dripping faucet, and if it isn't so serious that it requires immediate action, let the tenant know when the repair will be made. It's often best to do this orally (a message on the tenant's answering machine should serve), and follow up in writing by leaving a notice under the tenant's door. If there's a delay in handling the problem (maybe the part you need to fix the oven has to be ordered), explain why you won't be able to act immediately.

You'll find a tear-out version of the Time Estimate for Repair in Appendix B. The CD-ROM that accompanies this book also includes this form.

A sample Time Estimate for Repair is shown below. Notice that the form allows you to notify the tenant of the expected day and time for the repair. Under California law, even when tenants ask you to perform repairs, you must still give them proper notice, or advance warning, of your intended entry, and you may enter only on certain days and during certain hours. If you provide the required information (and stick to it), you will have satisfied your duty to give notice of your entry. Chapter 13 explains tenants' rights of privacy and the rules governing when, and for what purposes, you may enter.

If a tenant threatens to withhold rent, respond promptly in writing (see sample letter in this section), telling him either:

- when the repair will be made and the reasons why it is being delayed—for example, a replacement part may have to be ordered, or

- why you do not feel there is a legitimate problem that justifies rent withholding—for example, point out that the worn flooring may be annoying, but the floor is still intact and not dangerous.

At this point, you might also consider suggesting that you and the tenant mediate the dispute. (See Section G1, above.)

Be careful not to retaliate against complaining tenants. When landlords are confronted by tenants asking that repairs be made, they sometimes—especially when they feel the particular tenant is unreasonable or otherwise unpleasant—look around for some tenant misconduct to justify not making the repair. This is a mistake, unless the tenant's failure to maintain the property is fairly outrageous. It can result in legal problems that are out of proportion to the maintenance problem. A landlord's tit-for-tat response may escalate into rent withholding on the part of the tenant, necessitating a nasty eviction lawsuit. Even if a landlord is legally right and is judged so in court, the time and expense involved are unlikely to be worth it.

The better response is usually to fix the problem and try to work out a clear maintenance plan with the tenant for the future. If this fails, you may want to think about trying to get rid of the tenant. This is fairly easy to do, unless you are in a jurisdiction containing a rent control law with a just-cause-for-eviction provision or have a long-term lease. Still, you must be careful that your move to end the tenancy cannot be legally interpreted as retaliating against the tenant for making a legitimate complaint. (See Chapter 15 for rules on retaliatory evictions.)

LIMITS ON USING HANDYMEN

Repair work that will cost over $500 per contract (labor and materials) must be done by a licensed contractor. You may use a handyman to do less-expensive work, but the handyman must disclose to you, in writing, that he or she is not a licensed contractor. Penalties for violating this law fall upon the worker, not the hiring firm or individual. (B&P §§ 7028.6 and 7030).

Time Estimate for Repair

Stately Manor Apartments
_____

October 10, 200X
_____
Date

Jane Walker
_____
Tenant

123 Main Street, Apt. 12
_____
Street address

San Jose, California
_____
City and State

Dear _Ms. Walker_____,

                            Tenant

On _October 8, 200X_____, you notified us of the following problem in your rental unit:

The pilot light on the gas stove doesn't work.
_____

_____

We have investigated the problem and have found:

The pilot light element is broken and is out of stock locally. We have ordered it and we expect it will

be delivered on October 15, 200X.
_____

We expect to have the problem corrected on _October 17_____, 20 _OX_.

Unless we hear from you to the contrary, we will enter your unit between 1 pm and 4 pm on

the above date to perform the needed work.
_____

_____

_____

We regret any inconvenience this interval may cause. Please do not hesitate to point out any other problems that may arise.

Sincerely,

Fred Tebbets
_____
Landlord/Manager

SAMPLE LETTER WHEN TENANT THREATENS TO WITHHOLD RENT

Robin Lee
123 Davis Place
Venice, California

July 21, 200X

Bruce Moore
456 Springsteen Square
Apartment 7
Los Angeles, California

Dear Mr. Moore,

This is in response to your letter of July 19, in which you suggested the possibility of withholding your next month's rent if the bathroom toilet is not repaired.

I have ordered the replacement parts necessary to prevent the stopper from improperly seating and allowing water to run from the tank to the bowl. An order was necessary through ABC Plumbing Supply because it's an old toilet, requiring special parts, and the part is not available locally. I expect to receive the part within one week. Until then, the toilet still flushes and is usable, despite the running sound it makes.

As you will recall, I came to check the toilet on three occasions and found it perfectly operable. I suspect that the stopper only occasionally does not seat properly into the hole separating the toilet tank from the bowl. In any event, a jiggle on the flush handle when the toilet makes a running sound will correct the problem on the few occasions when the stopper fails to seat. The problem is a minor one that does not make your unit uninhabitable, and therefore does not justify rent withholding under California law. Accordingly, should you withhold rent on this basis, I will have no choice but to give a three-day notice to pay rent or leave the premises, followed by an eviction suit if you fail to comply.

Sincerely,

Robin Lee

Robin Lee
Landlord/Manager

K. TENANT UPDATES AND LANDLORD'S REGULAR SAFETY AND MAINTENANCE INSPECTIONS

Encouraging your tenants to promptly report problems as they occur should not be your sole means of handling your maintenance and repair responsibilities. Here's why: If tenants are not conscientious, or if they simply don't notice that something needs to be fixed, the best reporting system will not do you much good. To back it up, you need to force the tenant (and yourself) to take stock at specified intervals. In Section 1, below, we'll explain the tenant update system, and in Section 2 we'll discuss the landlord's annual safety inspection. Make sure your lease or rental agreement and move-in letter cover these updates and inspections as well.

1. Tenant's Semi-Annual Safety and Maintenance Update

You can (nicely) insist that your tenants think about and report needed repairs by giving them a Semi-Annual Safety and Maintenance Update on which to list any problems in the rental unit or on the premises—whether it's low water pressure in the shower, peeling paint, or noisy neighbors. Asking tenants to return this Update twice a year should also help you in court if you are up against a tenant who is raising a false implied warranty of habitability defense, particularly if the tenant did not note any problems on his most recently completed Update. As with the Maintenance/Repair Request form, be sure to note how you handled the problem on the bottom of the form.

You'll find a tear-out version of the Semi-Annual Safety and Maintenance Update in Appendix B. The CD-ROM that accompanies this book also includes this form.

2. Landlord's Annual Safety Inspection

Sometimes even your pointed reminder (by use of the Semi-Annual Update) that safety and maintenance issues need to be brought to your attention will not do the trick: If your tenant can't recognize a problem even if it stares him in the face, you'll never hear about it, either. In the end, you must get into the unit and inspect for yourself.

Landlords should perform annual safety and maintenance inspections as part of their system for repairing and maintaining the property. For example, you might make sure that items listed on the Semi-Annual Safety and Maintenance Update—such as smoke detectors, heating and plumbing systems, and major appliances—are in fact in safe and working order. If a problem develops with one of these items, causing injury to a tenant, you may be able to defeat a claim that you were negligent by arguing that your periodic and recent inspection of the item was all that a landlord should reasonably be expected to do. (Chapter 12 discusses in detail the consequences to a landlord if a tenant or guest is injured on the property.)

A landlord cannot insist on such inspections against the tenant's will, even if a lease or rental agreement clause so provides. This is because the law does not allow the landlord to enter the dwelling against the tenant's will—even on 24 hours' notice—solely to perform inspections. (CC § 1954.) Any lease or rental agreement provision allowing for this is illegal and unenforceable. (CC § 1953(a)(1).) Also, evicting a tenant who refused to allow such an inspection would constitute illegal retaliatory eviction. (CC § 1942.5(c).)

However, most tenants will not object to yearly safety inspections if you're courteous about it—giving 24 hours' notice and trying to conduct the inspection at a time convenient for the tenant. If you encounter hesitation, just point out that you take your responsibility to maintain the property very seriously. Remind the tenant that you'll be checking for plumbing, heating, electrical, and constructional problems that the tenant might not notice, which could develop into bigger problems later if you're not allowed to check them out.

Semi-Annual Safety and Maintenance Update

Please complete the following checklist and note any safety or maintenance problems in your unit or on the premises.

Please describe the specific problems and the rooms or areas involved. Here are some examples of the types of things we want to know about: garage roof leaks, excessive mildew in rear bedroom closet, fuses blow out frequently, door lock sticks, water comes out too hot in shower, exhaust fan above stove doesn't work, smoke alarm malfunctions, peeling paint, and mice in basement. Please point out any potential safety and security problems in the neighborhood and anything you consider a serious nuisance.

Please indicate the approximate date when you first noticed the problem and list any other recommendations or suggestions for improvement.

Please return this form with this month's rent check. Thank you.—THE MANAGEMENT

Name: _____ Mary Griffin _____

Address: _____ 392 Main St., #401 _____

_____ Modesto, California _____

Please indicate (and explain below) problems with:

☐ Floors and floor coverings _____

☐ Walls and ceilings _____

☐ Windows, screens, and doors _____

☐ Window coverings (drapes, mini-blinds, etc.) _____

☐ Electrical system and light fixtures _____

☒ Plumbing (sinks, bathtub, shower, or toilet) _____ Water pressure low in shower _____

☐ Heating or air conditioning system_____

☒ Major appliances (stove, oven, dishwasher, refrigerator) _____ Exhaust fan doesn't work _____

☐ Basement or attic _____

☒ Locks or security system _____ Front door lock sticks _____

☐ Smoke detector _____

☐ Fireplace _____

☐ Cupboards, cabinets, and closets _____

☐ Furnishings (table, bed, mirrors, chairs) _____

☐ Laundry facilities _____

☐ Elevator _____

☐ Stairs and handrails _____

☐ Hallway, lobby, and common areas _____

☐ Garage _____

☐ Patio, terrace, or deck _____

☒ Lawn, fences, and grounds _ *Shrubs near back stairway need pruning* _____

☐ Pool and recreational facilities _____

☐ Roof, exterior walls, and other structures _____

☐ Driveway and sidewalks _____

☐ Neighborhood _____

☒ Nuisances _____ *Tenant in #502 often plays stereo too loud* _____

☐ Other _____

_____

Specifics of problems: _____

_____

_____

_____

_____

Other comments: _____

_____

_____

_____

_____

_____

_____ *February 200X* _____ *Mary Griffin* _____

Date   Tenant

· ·

FOR MANAGEMENT USE

Action/Response: _ *Fixed shower, exhaust fan, and sticking front door lock on February 15. Pruned shrubs* _

_ *on February 21. Spoke with tenant in #502 about keeping stereo low on February 2.* _

_____

_____

_____

_____

_____

_____

_____ *February 22, 200X* _____ *Terri Zimet* _____

Date   Landlord/Manager

L. TENANTS' ALTERATIONS AND IMPROVEMENTS

Your lease or rental agreement probably includes a clause prohibiting tenants from making any alterations or improvements without your express, written consent. (See Clause 17 of our lease or rental agreement forms in Chapter 2.) For good reason, you'll want to make sure tenants don't change the light fixtures, replace the window coverings, or install a built-in dishwasher unless you agree first.

But in spite of your wish that your tenants leave well enough alone, you're bound to encounter the tenant who goes ahead without your knowledge or consent. On the other hand, you may also hear from an upstanding tenant who would, indeed, like your consent to the tenant's plan to install a bookshelf or closet system. To know how to deal with unauthorized alterations or straightforward requests, you'll need to understand some basic rules.

Disabled tenants have rights to modify their living space that may override your ban against alterations without your consent. See Chapter 9 for details. Similarly, tenants' legal rights to telecommunications access (cable hookups, satellite dishes, and other antennae) will affect your ability to control the installation of access equipment, as explained below in Sections M and N.

1. Improvements That Become Part of the Property

Anything your tenant attaches to a building, fence, deck, or the ground itself (lawyers call such items "fixtures") belongs to you, absent an agreement saying it's the tenant's. This is an age-old legal principle, and it's described in Civil Code § 1019. This means when the tenant moves out, you are legally entitled to refuse any offer to remove the fixture and return the premises to its original state.

When a landlord and departing tenant haven't decided ahead of time as to who will own the fixture, the dispute often ends up in court. Judges use a variety of legal rules to determine whether an object—an appliance, flooring, shelving, or plumbing—is something that the tenant can take away or is a permanent fixture belonging to you. Here are some of the questions judges ask when separating portable from nonportable additions:

- **Did your tenant get your permission?** If the tenant never asked you for permission to install a closet organizer, or asked but got no for an answer, a judge is likely to rule for you—particularly if your lease or rental agreement prohibits alterations or improvements.

- **Did the tenant make any structural changes that affect the use or appearance of the property?** If so, chances are that the item will be deemed yours, because removing it will often leave an unsightly area or alter use of part of the property. For example, if a tenant modifies the kitchen counter to accommodate a built-in dishwasher and then takes the dishwasher out, you will have to install another dishwasher of the same dimensions or rebuild the space. The law doesn't impose this extra work on landlords, nor does it force you to let tenants do the return-to-original work themselves.

- **Is the object firmly attached to the property?** In general, additions and improvements that are nailed, screwed, or cemented to the building are likely to be deemed "fixtures." For example, hollow-wall screws that anchor a bookcase might convert an otherwise free-standing unit belonging to the tenant to a fixture belonging to you. Similarly, closet rods bolted to the wall become part of the structure and would usually be counted as fixtures. On the other hand, shelving systems that are secured by isometric pressure (spring-loaded rods that press against the ceiling and floor) involve no actual attachment to the wall and for that reason are not likely to be classified as fixtures.

- **What did you and the tenant intend?** Courts will look at statements made by you and the tenant to determine whether there was any understanding as to the tenant's right to remove an improvement.

In some circumstances, courts will even infer an agreement from your actions—for instance, if you stopped by and gave permission to install what you referred to as a portable air conditioner, or helped lift it into place. By contrast, if the tenant removes light fixtures and, without your knowledge, installs a custom-made fixture that could not be used in any other space, it is unlikely that the tenant could convince a judge that she reasonably expected to take it with her at the end of her tenancy.

IMPROVEMENTS THAT PLUG OR SCREW IN

The act of plugging in an appliance doesn't make the appliance a part of the premises. The same is true for simple connectors or fittings that join an appliance to an electrical or water source. For example, a refrigerator or free-standing stove remains the property of the tenant. Similarly, portable dishwashers that connect to the kitchen faucet by means of a coupling may be removed.

---

2. Responding to Improvement and Alteration Requests

If a tenant approaches you with a request to alter your property or install a new feature, chances are that your impulse will be to say no. But perhaps the request comes from an outstanding tenant whom you would like to accommodate and would hate to lose. Instead of adopting a rigid approach, consider these alternatives.

Option One: Is the improvement or alteration one that is easily undone? For example, if your tenant has a year's lease and you plan to repaint at the end, you can easily fill and paint any small holes left behind when the tenant removes the bookshelf bolted to the wall (and you can bill for the spackling costs, as explained below). Knocking out a wall to install a wine closet is a more permanent change and not one you're likely to agree to.

Option Two: Is the improvement or alteration an enhancement to your property? For example, a wine closet might actually add value to your property. If so, depending on the terms of the agreement you reach with your tenant, you may actually come out ahead.

Before you accommodate your tenant's requests, decide which option makes sense in the circumstances and which you prefer. For example, you may have no use for an air conditioner attached to the window frame, and your tenant may want to remove it at the end of the tenancy. You'll need to make sure that the tenant understands that she is responsible for restoring the window frame to its original condition, and that if her restoration attempts are less than acceptable, you will be justified in deducting from her security deposit the amount of money necessary to do the job right. (And if the deposit is insufficient, you can sue her in small claims court for the excess.) On the other hand, a custom-made window insulation system may enhance your property (and justify a higher rent later on) and won't do your tenant any good if she takes it with her. Be prepared to hear your tenant ask you to pay for at least some of it.

If you and the tenant reach an understanding, put it in writing. As shown in the sample agreement regarding tenant alterations below, you will want to carefully describe the project and materials, including:

- whether the improvement or alteration is permanent or portable

- the terms of the reimbursement, if any, and

- how and when you'll pay the tenant, if at all, for labor and materials.

Our agreement makes it clear that the tenant's failure to properly restore the premises, or removal of an alteration that was to be permanent, will result in deductions from the security deposit or further legal action if necessary.

You'll find a tear-out version of the Agreement Regarding Tenant Alterations to Rental Unit in Appendix B. The CD-ROM that accompanies this book also includes this form.

Agreement Regarding Tenant Alterations to Rental Unit

_____Iona Lott_____ (Landlord)

and ____Doug Diep_____ (Tenant)

agree as follows:

1. Tenant may make the following alterations to the rental unit at _____75A Cherry Street,_____
   Pleasantville, California. _____ :

   1. Plant three rose bushes along walkway at side of residence.

   2. Install track lighting along west (ten-foot) kitchen wall.

2. Tenant will accomplish the work described in Paragraph 1 by using the following materials and procedures:

   1. Three bare-root roses, hybrid teas, purchased from Jackson-Perky and planted in
      March.

   2. "Wallbright" track lighting system purchased from "Lamps and More," plus necessary
      attachment hardware.

3. Tenant will do only the work outlined in Paragraph 1 using only the materials and procedures outlined in
   Paragraph 2.

4. The alterations carried out by Tenant:

   [X] will become Landlord's property and are not to be removed by Tenant during or at the end of the tenancy, or

   [ ] will be considered Tenant's personal property, and as such may be removed by Tenant at any time up to
   the end of the tenancy. Tenant promises to return the premises to their original condition upon removing
   the improvement.

5. Landlord will reimburse Tenant only for the costs checked below:

   [X] the cost of materials listed in Paragraph 2

   [X] labor costs at the rate of $ _____10_____ per hour for work done in a workmanlike manner
   acceptable to Landlord up to _____10_____ hours.

6. After receiving appropriate documentation of the cost of materials and labor, Landlord shall make any payment called for under Paragraph 5 by:

[X] lump sum payment, within ____10____ days of receiving documentation of costs, or

[ ] by reducing Tenant's rent by $ _____ per month for the number of months necessary to cover the total amounts under the terms of this agreement.

7. If under Paragraph 4 of this contract the alterations are Tenant's personal property, Tenant must return the premises to their original condition upon removing the alterations. If Tenant fails to do this, Landlord will deduct the cost to restore the premises to their original condition from Tenant's security deposit. If the security deposit is insufficient to cover the costs of restoration, Landlord may take legal action, if necessary, to collect the balance.

8. If Tenant fails to remove an improvement that is his or her personal property on or before the end of the tenancy, it will be considered the property of Landlord, who may choose to keep the improvement (with no financial liability to Tenant), or remove it and charge Tenant for the costs of removal and restoration. Landlord may deduct any costs of removal and restoration from Tenant's security deposit. If the security deposit is insufficient to cover the costs of removal and restoration, Landlord may take legal action, if necessary, to collect the balance.

9. If Tenant removes an item that is Landlord's property, Tenant will owe Landlord the fair market value of the item removed plus any costs incurred by Landlord to restore the premises to their original condition.

10. If Landlord and Tenant are involved in any legal proceeding arising out of this agreement, the prevailing party shall recover reasonable attorney fees, court costs and any costs reasonably necessary to collect a judgment.

February 10, 200X   _Iona Lott_
Date   Landlord

February 10, 200X   _Doug Diep_
Date   Tenant

M. CABLE TV

Major changes in technology have expanded entertainment services available from cable TV. Tenants are often eager to take advantage of the offerings, but do not always realize that doing so usually involves installation of wires, cables, or other hardware.

The legal issues surrounding cable access are a bit more complicated than the rules you encounter when a tenant asks for permission to install a bookcase or paint a room. The federal government has something to say about your tenants' rights, as explained in the Federal Telecommunications Act of 1996 (47 U.S.C. §§ 151 and following). In this Act, Congress decreed that all Americans should have as much access as possible to information that comes through a cable or over the air on wireless transmissions. The Act makes it very difficult for state and local governments, zoning commissions, homeowners' associations, and landlords to impose restrictions that hamper a person's ability to take advantage of these new types of communications.

1. Previously Unwired Buildings

Most residential rental properties are already wired for cable. In competitive markets especially, you'll have a hard time attracting tenants if you do not give them the option of paying for cable. However, in the event that your property does not have cable, you may continue to resist modernity and say "No" to tenants who ask you for access. Don't be surprised if, in response, your tenant mounts a satellite dish on the balcony, wall or roof. See Section N, below, for your ability to regulate these devices.

2. Buildings With Existing Contracts

Many multifamily buildings are already wired for cable. In competitive markets, landlords have been able to secure attractive deals with the service providers, passing savings on to tenants. Many landlords have signed "exclusive" contracts, whereby they promise the cable provider that they will not allow other providers into the building.

Here is where things get a bit tricky. In the residential context (but not in commercial rentals), federal law allows landlords to enter into exclusive deals, as does California. Even if you don't have an exclusive contract, you're under no obligation to allow other companies into your property. Although an incumbent cable company can in theory share its wires with other providers, they typically don't want to make their hardware available to competitors. You are not obliged to allow a hodge-podge of wires throughout your building, which may happen if several companies run cable. (*Cable Arizona v. Coxcom, Inc.*, 261 F.3d 871 (9th Cir. 2001).)

N. SATELLITE DISHES AND OTHER ANTENNAS

Wireless communications have the potential to reach more people with less hardware than any cable system. Tenants who enjoy watching sports programs are often eager to have a satellite dish antenna, which will deliver far more programs than cable. But there is one essential piece of equipment: A satellite dish with wires connecting it to the television set or computer.

Small and inexpensive dishes, two feet or less in diameter, are now available. Wires can easily be run under a door or through an open window to an individual TV or computer. Predictably, tenants have attached dishes to balconies, windowsills, railings, and even the roof. Landlords are upset at the unappealing sight of wires and equipment that ruin a building's "curb appeal." They are concerned that dishes may fall and cause injuries and that their installation may damage weatherproofing of walls and roofs and interfere with electrical or plumbing systems.

Fortunately, the Federal Communications Commission (FCC) has provided considerable guidance on residential use of satellite dishes and other antennas (Over-the-Air Reception Devices Rule, 47 C.F.R. § 1.4000, further explained in the FCC's Fact Sheet, "Over-the-Air Reception Devices Rule"). Basically, the FCC prohibits landlords from imposing restrictions that unreasonably impair tenants' abilities to install, maintain, or use an antenna or dish that meet criteria described below. Here's a brief overview of the FCC rule.

For complete details on the FCC's rule on satellite dishes and other antennas, see www.fcc.gov/mb or call the FCC at 888-CALLFCC. The FCC's rule was upheld in *Building Owners and Managers Assn. v. FCC*, 254 F.3d 89 (D.C. Cir. 2001).

1. Devices Covered by the FCC Rule

The FCC's rule applies to video antennas, including direct-to-home satellite dishes that are less than one meter (39.37 inches) in diameter, TV antennas, and wireless cable antennas. These pieces of equipment receive video programming signals from direct broadcast satellites, wireless cable providers, and television broadcast stations. Antennas up to 18 inches in diameter that transmit as well as receive fixed wireless telecom signals (not just video) are also included.

Exceptions: Antennas used for AM/FM radio, amateur ("ham"), and Citizen's Band ("CB") radio, or Digital Audio Radio Services ("DARS") are excluded from the FCC's rule. You may restrict the installation of these types of antennas, in the same way that you can restrict any modification or alteration of rented space.

2. Permissible Installation

Tenants may place dishes or other antennas only in their own, exclusive rented space, such as inside the rental unit or on a balcony, terrace, deck, or patio. The device must be wholly within the rented space (if it overhangs the balcony, you may prohibit that placement). Also, you may prohibit tenants from drilling through exterior walls, even if that wall is also part of their rented space.

Tenants *cannot* place their reception devices in common areas, such as roofs, hallways, walkways, or the exterior walls of the building. Exterior windows

are no different from exterior walls—for this reason, placing a dish or other antenna on a window by means of a series of suction cups is impermissible under the FCC rule (obviously, such an installation is also unsafe). Tenants who rent single-family homes, however, may install devices in the home itself or on patios, yards, gardens, or other similar areas.

3. Restrictions on Installation Techniques

Landlords are free to set restrictions on how the devices are installed, as long as the restrictions are not unreasonably expensive or are imposed for safety reasons or to preserve historic aspects of the structure. You cannot insist that your maintenance personnel (or professional installers) do the work. Nor can you require your tenants to submit their installation plans to you for prior approval, unless the reason for the prior review is a safety concern or to preserve the historical integrity of the property. (*In re Frankfurt*, 16 FCC Rcd. 2875 (2001).)

a. Expense

Landlords may not impose a flat fee or charge additional rent to tenants who want to erect a satellite dish or other antenna. On the other hand, you may be able to insist on certain installation techniques that will add expense—as long as the cost isn't excessive and reception will not be impaired. Examples of acceptable expenses include:

- insisting that an antenna be painted green in order to blend into the landscaping, or

- requiring the use of a universal bracket which future tenants could use, saving wear and tear on your building.

b. Safety Concerns

You can insist that tenants place and install devices in a way that will minimize the chances of obvious accidents and will not violate safety or fire codes. For example, you may prohibit placement of a satellite dish on a fire escape, near a power plant, or near a walkway where passers-by might accidentally hit their heads. You may also insist on proper installation techniques, such as those explained in the instructions that come with most devices. What if proper installation (attaching a dish to a wall) means that you will have to eventually patch and paint a wall? Can you use this as reason for preventing installation? No—unless you have legitimate reasons for prohibiting the installation, such as a safety concern. You can, however, charge the tenant for the cost of repairing surfaces when the tenant moves out and removes the device.

If you set restrictions on placement or installation based on safety concerns, it's important to specifically explain how the restriction meets a particular safety concern, unless the reason for the restriction is obvious. For example, it's obvious that requiring an antenna to be securely fastened meets the safety concern that it not fall down and injure people or property. However, it's not self-evident why requiring installation on only one side of the building furthers legitimate safety concerns. You'll need to articulate exactly why that restriction is necessary for safety.

Be consistent in setting rules for tenant improvements. Rules for mounting satellite dishes or other antennas shouldn't be more restrictive than those you establish for artwork, flags, clotheslines, or similar items. After all, attaching these telecommunications items is no more intrusive or invasive than bolting a sundial to the porch, screwing a thermometer to the wall, or nailing a rain gauge to a railing. For general guidance, see the discussion in Section L, above, of tenants' alterations and improvements.

Require tenants who install antennas to carry renters' insurance. If the installation (or removal) causes damage to your property, you can charge the tenant or use the security deposit to cover the repair costs. Renters' insurance should cover the cost, too, which will save you the hassle of collecting from the tenant or dipping into (and having to replenish) the deposit. And if a device falls or otherwise causes personal injury, the policy will cover a claim.

c.   Preserving Your Building's Historical Integrity

It won't be easy to prevent installation on the grounds that doing so is needed to preserve the historical integrity of your property. You can use this argument only if your property is included in (or eligible for) the National Register of Historic Places, the nation's official list of buildings, structures, objects, sites, and districts worthy of preservation for their significance in American history, architecture, archaeology, and culture. For more information on how to qualify for the Register, see www.cr.nps.gov/places.htm.

4.   Placement and Orientation

Tenants have the right to place an antenna where they'll receive an "acceptable quality" signal. As long as the tenant's chosen spot is within the exclusive rented space, not on an exterior wall or in a common area as discussed in Section 2, above, you may not set rules on placement—for example, you cannot require that an antenna be placed only in the rear of the rental property if this results in the tenant's receiving a "substantially degraded" signal or no signal at all.

Reception devices that need to maintain line-of-sight contact with a transmitter or view a satellite may not work if they're stuck behind a wall or below the roofline. In particular, a dish must be on a south wall, since satellites are in the southern hemisphere. Tenants who have no other workable exclusive space may want to mount their devices on a mast, in hopes of clearing the obstacle. They may do so, depending on the situation:

- **Single-family rentals.** Tenants may erect a mast that's 12 feet above the roofline or less without asking your permission first—and you must allow it if the mast is installed in a safe manner. If the mast is taller than 12 feet, you may require the tenant to obtain your permission before erecting it—but if the installation meets reasonable safety requirements, you should allow its use.

- **Multifamily rentals.** Tenants may use a mast as long as it does not extend beyond their exclusive rented space. For example, in a two-story rental a mast that is attached to the ground-floor patio and extends into the air space opposite the tenant's own second floor would be permissible. On the other hand, a mast attached to a top-story deck, which extends above the roofline or outward over the railing, would not be protected by the FCC's rule—a landlord could prohibit this installation because it extends beyond the tenant's exclusive rented space.

5. How to Set a Reasonable Policy

The FCC has ruled that tenants do not need your permission before installing their antennas—as long as they have placed them within their exclusive rented space and otherwise abided by the rules explained above. (*In re Frankfurt*, 16 FCC Rcd. 2875 (2001).) This means that you won't get to review a tenant's plans before the tenant installs a dish or antenna—though you can certainly react if you find that the FCC's standards have not been met.

The smart thing to do is to educate your tenants beforehand, in keeping with the FCC's guidelines, so that you don't end up ripping out an antenna that has been placed in the wrong spot or attached in an unsafe manner. In fact, the FCC directs landlords to give tenants written notice of safety restrictions, so that tenants will know in advance how to comply. We suggest that you include guidelines in your Rules and Regulations, or as an Attachment to your lease or rental agreement. For guidance on developing sound policies, see the FCC's website at www.fcc.gov/mb.

6. Supplying a Central Antenna for all Tenants

Faced with the prospect of many dishes and antennas adorning an otherwise clean set of balconies, you may want to install a central dish or other antenna for use by all.

If you install a central antenna, you may restrict the use of antennas by individual tenants only if your device provides:

- **Equal access.** The tenant must be able to get the same programming or fixed wireless service that he could receive with his own antenna.

- **Equal quality.** The signal quality to and from the tenant's home via your antenna must be as good or better than what the tenant could get using his own device.

- **Equal value.** The costs of using your device must be the same or less than the cost of installing, maintaining, and using an individual antenna, and

- **Equal readiness.** You can't prohibit individual devices if installation of a central antenna will unreasonably delay the tenant's ability to receive programming or fixed wireless services—for example, when your central antenna won't be available for months.

If you install a central antenna after tenants have installed their own, you may require removal of the individual antennas, as long as your device meets the above requirements. In addition, you must pay for the removal of the tenant's device and compensate the tenant for the value of the antenna.

7. How to Handle Disputes About the Use and Placement of Satellite Dishes and Other Antennas

In spite of the FCC's attempts to clarify tenants' rights to reception and landlords' rights to control what happens on their property, there are many possibilities for disagreements. For example, what exactly is "acceptable" reception? If you require antennas to be painted, at what point is the expense considered "unreasonable"?

Ideally, you can try to avoid disputes in the first place, by setting reasonable policies. But, if all else fails, here are some tips to help you resolve the problem with a minimum of fuss and expense.

a. Discussion, Mediation and Help From the FCC

First, approach the problem the way you would any dispute—talk it out and try to reach an acceptable conclusion. Follow our advice in Chapter 8, Section B for settling disputes on your own—for example, through negotiation or mediation. You'll find the information on the FCC website very helpful. The direct broadcast satellite company, multichannel distribution service, TV broadcast station, or fixed wireless company may also be able to suggest alternatives that are safe and acceptable to both you and your tenant.

b. Get the FCC Involved

If your own attempts don't resolve the problem, you can call the FCC and ask for oral guidance. You may also formally ask the FCC for a written opinion, called a Declaratory Ruling. For information on obtaining oral or written guidance from the FCC, see the FCC website at www.fcc.gov/mb. Keep in mind that unless your objections concern safety or historic preservation, you must allow the device to remain, pending the FCC's ruling.

c. Go to Court

When all else fails, you can head for court. If the satellite dish or other antenna hasn't been installed yet and you and the tenant are arguing about the reasonableness of your policies or the tenant's plans, you can ask a court to rule on who's right (just as you would when seeking the FCC's opinion). You'll have to go to a regular trial court (not small claims court) for a resolution of your dispute, where you'll ask for an order called a "Declaratory Judgment." Similarly, if the antenna or dish *has* been installed and you want a judge to order it removed, you'll have to go to a regular trial court and ask for such an order. Unfortunately, the simpler option of small claims court will usually not be available in these situations because most small claims courts handle only disputes that can be settled or decided with money. They tend to shy away from issuing opinions about whether it's acceptable to do (or not do) a particular task.

Needless to say, going to regular trial court means that the case will be drawn out and expensive. You could handle it yourself, but be forewarned—you'll need to be adept at arguing about First Amendment law and divining Congressional intent, and you'll have to be willing to spend long hours in the library preparing your case (before proceeding, at the very least read the cases already decided by the FCC, which you'll find on their website, referenced above). In the end, you may decide that it would have been cheaper to provide a buildingwide dish (or good cable access) for all tenants to use.

12

THE LANDLORD'S LIABILITY FOR DANGEROUS CONDITIONS, CRIMINAL ACTS, AND ENVIRONMENTAL HEALTH HAZARDS

As a property owner, you are responsible for keeping the premises safe for tenants and their guests. You must also be sure that conditions on the property don't bother neighbors. If you fall short in either of these obligations, you could be faced with a lawsuit from an injured tenant or angry neighbor. In the legal world, this area of the law is known as "premises liability," and it is fertile ground for creative plaintiffs' lawyers.

Landlords may be liable for physical injuries caused by faulty premises, such as a broken step, inadequate lighting, or substandard wiring. Tenants can sue for past and future medical bills, lost earnings, and pain and suffering in small claims court (up to $5,000), or superior court (where the sky's the limit).

A tenant or a neighbor may sue the landlord for damages for maintaining a legal nuisance—a serious and persistent condition that adversely affects the tenant's (or neighbor's) enjoyment of their property—even if no physical injury occurs. For example, a tenant, plagued by the stench of garbage scattered about because the landlord hasn't provided enough garbage cans for the apartment building, can sue the landlord for the annoyance and inconvenience of putting up with the smell. Under a relatively new understanding of the term "nuisance," a tenant—or a neighbor or group of neighbors—can sue a landlord for tolerating the presence of a drug-dealing tenant.

Landlords are also being sued with increasing frequency by tenants injured by criminals. You may be found liable if a rape or other assault occurs on your property and the jury finds that you failed to provide adequate security. The average settlement in these types of cases is very high, and the average jury award (when cases go to trial) is even higher. In some situations, you may even be held responsible for the violent acts of your own employees or tenants.

An explanation of premises liability would not be complete without a discussion of landlords' liability under federal law for tenant injuries due to environmental hazards such as asbestos, lead, radon, and carbon monoxide.

We don't have the space here to show you how to fight a personal injury or nuisance lawsuit brought by a tenant. If you are sued, unless the suit is filed in small claims court, you'll need a lawyer. (See Chapter 8 for advice on choosing a lawyer. For advice on small claims court, see *Everybody's Guide to Small Claims Court,* by Ralph Warner (Nolo).)

We do, however, give you an overview of the legal and practical issues involved, which will help you reduce the likelihood that you will be sued or found liable for tenant injuries. We also discuss the importance of liability insurance to limit your potential financial loss, should you end up facing a claim or in court.

Related Topics

- Lease and rental agreement provisions on landlords' and tenants' responsibilities for damage to premises, repairs, and liability-related issues: Chapter 2

- How to minimize your liability for your manager's mistakes or illegal acts: Chapter 6

- Landlord's liability for intentional discrimination: Chapter 9

- How to comply with state and local housing laws and avoid safety and maintenance problems: Chapter 11

- Liability for invasion of privacy: Chapter 13

- Liability for retaliatory conduct against the tenant: Chapter 15

- Liability for illegal evictions: Chapter 17.

A. Legal Standards for Liability

As a general rule, a landlord is liable to a tenant for an injury caused by a defect in the premises if the landlord failed to exercise reasonable care in the maintenance of the property.

An injured tenant may sue a landlord under several different legal theories, the most common being negligence. In the sections that follow, we're going to explain what this means. You may be wondering why you should take the time and energy to read what looks like a short course in landlord/tenant law—after all, if you conduct your business carefully and always maintain your property, you probably won't get into trouble and shouldn't need to master the fine points of legal theory. In one sense, you're right: If you prefer, you can review our repair and maintenance suggestions in Chapter 11, Sections J and K; or skip ahead to Section C for advice on how to avoid liability for criminal incidents on your property.

However, if you stick with us, you will see why understanding the theoretical basis for holding landlords liable for tenant injuries is important. Here are just a few ways this knowledge will help landlords:

- **Evaluate existing situations.** Understanding how injured tenants may successfully present their cases to the courts will help you to identify—and correct—potentially dangerous situations in your own rental property before an accident occurs.

- **Recognize redflag situations.** Even a thoroughly conscientious landlord needs to understand that certain kinds of injuries pose a much greater risk for landlord liability and, consequently, deserve much more preventive attention. This may require you to allocate your repair and maintenance resources accordingly.

- **Appreciate the rules of the game.** Unfortunately, there is no foul in lawyer-land like football's "piling on": A single injury can give rise to multiple reasons why the landlord should be held responsible, any one of which will be sufficient to win the tenant's case. If you understand the rules by which the personal injury lawsuit game is played, you are in a good position to establish sound repair and maintenance procedures and explain to managers and tenants why they're necessary.

Our goal in this chapter is not to frighten you, but rather to convince you that it makes sense to develop a comprehensive and responsive maintenance and repair system designed to reduce, if not eliminate, tenant injuries and to keep you out of court.

1. Negligence: The Landlord's Careless Acts

Negligence is the most common legal theory under which injured tenants or guests sue landlords. Negligence is behavior that is unreasonable, considering all the circumstances. If someone sues you alleging an injury caused by your negligence, a judge will first decide whether you owed the injured person a duty to refrain from acting negligently. If the judge decides that you owed that person a "duty of due care," as it's called in legalese, the injured person (the plaintiff) will then be allowed to take his case to the jury. At this point, the plaintiff will have to convince the jury that you failed to live up to your duty of due care, that your failure caused his injury, and that he is truly injured and deserves a certain amount of money in compensation.

a. Duty of Due Care

If a tenant is injured on your rental property and sues you, he must first convince the judge that you owed him a duty to refrain from acting negligently. Judges will ask the following four questions when asked to make that determination:

1. Control: How much control did the landlord have over the situation? In most cases, you will be held responsible for an injury if you were legally obligated to maintain and repair the injury-causing factor. For example, a landlord normally has control over a stairway in a common area, and if its disrepair causes a tenant to fall, the landlord may be held liable. The landlord also has control over the building's utility systems, and if their malfunction causes injury (like scalding water from a broken thermostat), he may likewise be held responsible.

Common areas and building systems are not the only areas the landlord controls. If you have established control over an area that might otherwise be controlled by the tenant, you may be responsible for injuries. For example, the lease may forbid the tenant from making repairs inside her apartment. From the landlord's point of view, this is a wise policy because it prevents shoddy or expensive repairs by inept tenants. This policy does, however, have a flip side: Having prevented the tenant from addressing interior repair problems, the landlord is now responsible—that is, the landlord retains control. If you fail to make repairs (or do a faulty job), you will be liable for any consequent injuries. For example, a tenant who is injured in her apartment by a broken electrical switch will have a strong case against the landlord who prohibited interior repairs, knew about the problem, and failed to fix it.

Finally, you may be surprised to learn that you may have "control" even if you don't own the injury-causing defect. If you know about a dangerous condition on adjacent property and realize that your tenants are likely to encounter it, and if you have the ability to warn your tenants about it or fence off the dangerous condition, your failure to do so may expose you to liability. For example, a landlord who was repeatedly told by some of his tenants about the broken and dangerous condition of a water meter box in the front lawn was found by the California Supreme Court to have a duty to warn and protect all tenants, even though the utility box belonged to the water company and in spite of the evidence that, in fact, the lawn was planted on city property! (*Alcaraz v. Vece,* 14 Cal. 4th 1149 (1997).)

2. Likelihood: How likely was it that an accident would occur? You will be responsible for an injury if it can be shown that it was foreseeable. A judge will consider whether any reasonable person in the position of the landlord should have realized that an injury was likely to happen. For example, common sense would tell you that loose handrails will lead to accidents, but it would be unusual for injuries to result from peeling wallpaper.

In California, a landlord's duty of due care extends not only to his tenants (who will be the most likely to be injured), but to the tenants' guests, delivery persons, repairpersons, and even trespassers. (The California Supreme Court ruled that a landlord has the same duty of care to maintain the property regardless of whether the person injured is a tenant, guest, or visitor. *Rowland v. Christian,* 69 Cal. 2d 108, 70 Cal. Rptr. 97 (1968).)

3. Burden: How difficult or expensive would it have been for the landlord to reduce the risk of injury? The chances that you will be held responsible for an accident are greater if an inexpensive and easy response to the situation could have averted the accident. In other words, could something as simple as warning signs and caution tape have prevented the accident, or would you have had to do major structural remodeling to reduce the likelihood of injury?

4. Seriousness: How serious an injury was likely to result from the problem? If a major injury was the likely result, you are expected to take the situation more seriously. By contrast, if the problem was only likely to cause a minor annoyance (even if in fact it caused a more serious injury), then your duty to fix it is less.

To understand how these four questions apply to your duty to refrain from acting negligently, let's look at some typical situations. In each, you'll see how the basic questions of control, likelihood, burden, and seriousness work together to help the judge decide whether the landlord owes the injured tenant a duty of due care. You'll also understand how, for every incident, there are no clear, universal answers.

EXAMPLE 1

Mark broke his leg when he tripped on a loose step on the stairway leading from the lobby to the first floor. The step had been loose for several months. Should the case go to court, Mark will point to the fact that the landlord was legally responsible for (in control of) the condition of the common stairways, that it was highly foreseeable (likely) to any reasonable person that someone would slip on a loose step, that securing the step was a simple and inexpensive repair (not a burden) and that the probable result (falling and injuring oneself on the stairs) is a serious matter. In this situation, the landlord's position appears weak. The best he could hope for would be to show that Mark, through inattention or carelessness, somehow brought the injury on himself. (See the Section A1d discussion of comparative negligence, below.)

EXAMPLE 2

Lee slipped on a marble that had been dropped in the hallway outside his apartment by another tenant's child just a few minutes earlier. Lee twisted his ankle and lost two weeks' work. Lee will have a difficult time establishing that his landlord acted unreasonably under the circumstances. Although the landlord is responsible for the condition of the common hallways, he obviously does not have complete control over what his tenants negligently leave behind. The likelihood of injury from something a tenant drops is slim (especially assuming the landlord checks the condition of the corridors at regular intervals), and the burden on the landlord to eliminate all possible problems at all times by constant sweeping of the halls is unreasonable. Finally, the seriousness of the likely injury as a result of not sweeping constantly is open to great debate.

EXAMPLE 3

James suffered a concussion when he hit his head on an overhead beam in the apartment garage. He had been loading items onto the roof rack of his truck. James will have a more difficult time convincing a judge or jury that the landlord should be held responsible for his injury. Although the landlord is, certainly, in charge of the parking garage, he probably won't be held responsible for the relatively unusual activity (loading items onto a truck roof) that led to James's injury. Or, put another way, the likelihood of injury from a low beam is slim, since most people don't climb on the roofs of trucks, and

those who do normally see the beam and avoid it. As to eliminating the condition that led to the injury, it's highly unlikely a court would expect the landlord to rebuild the garage, but it's possible that a judge might think it reasonable to paint the beams a bright color and post warning signs. After all, injury from low beams is likely to be to the head, which is a serious matter.

b. Responsibility for Injuries

If a judge decides that you owed an injured person (tenant, guest, worker, or trespasser) a duty of due care, you are not automatically liable for the injury. The person suing you (the plaintiff, usually the tenant) must then take the case before a jury and convince them that:

- **You didn't fulfill your duty.** The injured person must show that you failed to live up to your duty—for example, that the landlord in Example 1 above did not in fact fix the broken step. In his defense, the landlord might be able to prove that he fixed the step (fulfilling his duty) but that the repair materials failed through no fault of his own.

- **The accident was caused by your failure to exercise due care, and not by some other cause.** Even if the tenant can convince the jury that you breached your duty of due care, the tenant will have to convince the jury that the accident was a result of your failure and not, for example, because the plaintiff himself was careless.

- **There was a real injury caused by the accident.** Before a plaintiff can get monetary damages, he will have to prove that he has a real injury that was caused by the incident and not the result of, say, a previous accident.

Here are some actual examples of injuries for which juries have held a landlord liable:

- Tenant falls off stairway due to a defective handrail. (*Brennan v. Cockrell*, 35 Cal. App. 3d 796, 111 Cal. Rptr. 1221 (1973).)

- Tenant trips over a rock on a common stairway not properly maintained by the landlord. (*Henrouille v. Marin Ventures*, 20 Cal. 3d 512, 143 Cal. Rptr. 247 (1978).)

- Tenant injured or property damaged by fire resulting from defective heater or wiring. (*Evans v. Thompson,* 72 Cal. App. 3d 978, 140 Cal. Rptr. 525 (1977); and *Golden v. Conway,* 55 Cal. App. 3d 948, 128 Cal. Rptr. 69 (1976).)

- Tenant's child on tricycle run over by car on public street adjacent to steep driveway on landlord's property, where children often rode tricycles and sped down the hill into the street. (*Barnes v. Black,* 71 Cal. App. 4th 1473, 84 Cal. Rptr. 2d 634 (1999).)

The responsibility for safe residential rental property cannot be passed on to a manager or contractor. Under California law, your duty to repair and maintain your property cannot be delegated—in other words, you cannot escape liability for failing to maintain your property in a safe condition by making managers or independent contractors responsible for repair and maintenance. For example, you cannot avoid responsibility for the improper maintenance of elevators, water heaters, or roofs, even though you have hired or contracted with someone else to maintain them. (*Brown v. George Pepperdine Foundation,* 23 C2d 256, 143 P2d 929 (1943); *Knell v. Morris,* 39 C2d 450, 247 P2d 352 (1952); *Poulsen v. Charlton,* 224 Cal. App. 2d 262, 36 Cal. Rptr. 347 (1964).) Also, if the work involves a "peculiar," or inherent, risk of injury (like building demolition or major construction), an independent contractor's negligence will be laid upon the landlord. (Restatement 2d Torts § 416.)

Landlord liability for injuries to tenants by third parties and issues involving drug-dealing tenants are discussed in Sections B, D, and E, below.

FENCES AND OTHER DANGEROUS CONDITIONS

You are not required to fence off your property, even if it is adjacent to a busy thoroughfare or dangerous open spaces. (*Brooks v. Eugene Berger Management Corp.,* 215 Cal. App. 3d 1611, 264 Cal. Rptr. 756 (1989).) However, once you have erected a fence around your property, you will be expected to maintain it and can be held liable if its deterioration leads to an injury. The rules change, however, with respect to dangerous conditions that are especially attractive to children: Landlords are expected to make these dangerous sites (called "attractive nuisances") inaccessible or remove them. In particular, fences around swimming pools are required by many local ordinances, and their absence, low height, or poor repair is considered negligence *per se,* discussed below in Section A1c.

---

c. Negligence *Per Se:* Landlord Liability for Violating a Law

When a tenant is injured because the landlord violated a law designed to protect tenants, the landlord is presumed to be negligent. Lawyers call this "negligence *per se.*" From a practical point of view, this means that all the questions that a judge considers regarding the landlord's duty to act reasonably in a straightforward negligence case (questions about foreseeability, seriousness of the probable injury, moral blame, and so on) are skipped. The only way that the defendant (the landlord) can escape liability is to prove that his violation of the law was not the cause of the injury, or that there was really no injury at all, or that somehow the plaintiff (usually the tenant) brought the accident upon himself.

Probably the most common example of landlords' negligence *per se* is failure to install smoke alarms when required by state or local law. For example, a tenant who suffers injury or damage as the result of a fire that would have been extinguished sooner but wasn't because the landlord violated a law requiring smoke detectors in the building does not have to convince a court that the landlord was negligent. The

LANDLORD LIABILITY FOR DOG BITES AND OTHER ANIMAL ATTACKS

You may be liable for the injuries caused by your tenants' animals, be they common household pets or more exotic, wild animals.

Dangerous domestic pets. Landlords who are aware that their tenants are keeping vicious or dangerous domestic pets, such as a vicious pit bull, may be held liable if the animal injures another person on the property. An injured person would have to show two things:

- that the landlord actually knew (or, in view of the circumstances, must have known) of the animal's dangerous propensities, and

- that the landlord could have prevented the injury. For example, the landlord could have evicted the tenant with the dangerous pet (on the grounds that the animal's presence constituted a danger to other tenants or guests).

To add insult to injury, a landlord's liability insurance policy may not cover him if the tenant had posted a "Beware of Dog" sign. Some insurance carriers have successfully argued that this type of warning sign indicates that the tenant expected (or even intended) that the dog would cause injury. Intentional assaults are not covered by insurance.

Dangerous exotic pets. The situation is a little different with respect to wild animals kept as pets: Unlike the accepted practice of keeping conventional pets, who aren't always dangerous, the keeping of wild animals is considered an "ultrahazardous activity," which the law considers always dangerous. While the landlord needs to know about the vicious tendencies of domestic animals before he will be held liable, the landlord will be presumed to know of the dangerous aspects of a wild animal *as soon as he learns that the animal is on the property.* Thus, if your tenant keeps a monkey and you know about it

(or, in the exercise of reasonable care, should know about it), a court will assume that you understood the dangers presented, and you may be liable if the animal causes injury and you failed to take steps to prevent it.

You may wonder how your responsibility to prevent tenants from keeping wild animals squares with your inability to enter your tenant's home without his consent in order to inspect. (See Chapter 13 for legal rules regarding tenants' privacy rights.) If a wild animal is kept without your knowledge, you probably will not be held liable. In practical terms, however, this is rarely going to be the case: One court that ruled on an attack by a tenant's monkey noted that the manager had received complaints about wild animal noises but had failed to follow up. The court ruled that the manager was put on notice that the no-pets clause in the monkey owner's lease was being violated and therefore, irrespective of tenant privacy protections, had the right and duty to investigate. His failure to do so was negligence. (*Jendralski v. Black,* 176 Cal. App. 3d 897, 222 Cal. Rptr. 396 (1986).)

law assumes the landlord was negligent because he violated the law.

All multiple-unit dwellings, from duplexes on up, must have smoke detectors installed. (Health & Safety Code § 13113.7.) Violation is also a criminal offense.

Other examples of negligence *per se* include:

- failure to equip rental units with deadbolt locks as required by state law and any local ordinances (see the discussion of the duty to maintain secure premises in Chapter 11), and

- failure to abide by other safety laws, including the provision of fire extinguishers and the installation and maintenance of interior sprinklers.

TENANTS CAN'T SIGN AWAY THEIR RIGHT TO SUE LANDLORDS FOR NEGLIGENCE

You cannot protect yourself from lawsuits brought by tenants by putting a clause in leases and rental agreements absolving yourself in advance for injuries suffered by a tenant as a result of your negligence. Known as "exculpatory clauses," these provisions are not legal or enforceable. (CC § 1953.)

---

d. Defenses to Negligence Charges

Even if a landlord has been negligent in failing to correct a problem that caused harm to a tenant or guest, there are still a few defenses and partial defenses available in some situations.

Comparative negligence. If the injured tenant or visitor was also guilty of negligence—for example, if he was drunk, or didn't watch his step when he tripped on a rock on the landlord's poorly maintained common stairway—the landlord's liability is proportionately reduced. For example, if a judge or jury ruled that a tenant who had suffered $10,000 in damages was equally (50%) as negligent as the landlord, the tenant would recover only $5,000.

Assumption of the risk. A person who knows the danger of a certain action and decides to take the chance anyway is said to "assume the risk" of injury. If the person is injured as a result, there's no entitlement to recover anything, even if another person's negligence contributed to the injury.

EXAMPLE

A tenant falls and is injured when he takes a shortcut over a sidewalk that has fallen into disrepair and is littered with broken pieces of cement. The tenant knew that the sidewalk was dangerous but sues the landlord, claiming that the landlord was negligent for not fixing the sidewalk. Because the tenant knew the possible risk of walking on the dangerous sidewalk, he might not win a lawsuit against a landlord based on the landlord's negligence.

2. Breach of Warranty and Fraud

If you make an express promise in a written lease or rental agreement, such as to make even minor interior repairs, you are very likely to be held liable to a tenant who is injured if:

- you simply didn't make the repair and the defect caused injury

- you made the repair but did so in a shoddy way, causing injury, or

- the tenant was injured when he resorted to attempting the repair himself.

STRICT LIABILITY/LIABILITY WITHOUT FAULT: WILL IT APPLY TO OWNER-BUILDERS?

Between 1985 and 1995, landlords in California were subject to the rule of strict liability—meaning that they were liable for injuries caused by hidden defects in the property, present at the time the lease was signed. The law made even careful, conscientious landlords liable for hidden defects that even the most thorough inspection would not reveal. (The classic case involved a landlord who purchased a building in which the shower doors in the rental units were made of non-safety glass. In spite of his careful inspection of the premises, and the fact that it would have taken an expert to determine that the tiny logo on the doors indicated that the glass was not shatterproof, the landlord was held liable when a tenant fell against a door and severely cut himself.)

In 1995, the California Supreme Court overturned the rule of strict liability, in most situations returning California landlords to the standard of negligence (which is the standard applied in 48 other states). (*Peterson v. Superior Court* (Banque Paribas), 10 Cal. 4th 1185 (1995).)

The court decision left open the possibility that strict liability would continue to apply to the landlord who is also the builder of the premises. If you are the original builder of your rental property, you need to understand that, if a tenant is injured due to a hidden defect in the property that was present at the time the tenant signed the lease, you may be held liable regardless of your best efforts to properly repair and maintain the premises.

EXAMPLE

Tom's lease included a clause prohibiting him from doing any interior repairs. When the lifting mechanism of his double-hung window broke, Tom reported the problem to his landlord Len. Len did nothing, leaving Tom to swelter in the summer heat. After repeated requests for repairs, Tom raised the window and attempted to secure it with a bar, but the window fell and severely injured his hand. Len was found liable on the grounds that, having obligated himself to perform interior repairs, he ought to have done so in a reasonably timely manner. Moreover, Tom's resort to self-help was entirely reasonable under the circumstances.

Even without a written lease or rental agreement provision, a landlord who advertises or tells current or prospective tenants about some special feature of the property, such as an immaculate laundry facility, is likely to be held liable if a soapy puddle next to the washing machine causes a tenant to slip and fall.

3. Reckless or Intentional Acts

A landlord who injures someone as the result of an intentional or reckless act—for example, assaulting a tenant or jerry-rigging an electrical repair instead of calling an electrician—is liable for the injury or property damage. "Recklessness" generally means extremely careless behavior regarding an obvious defect or problem. A landlord who has been aware of a long-existing and dangerous defect but neglects to correct the problem is guilty of recklessness, not just ordinary carelessness.

Intentional injuries are rarer, but they do occur. For example, if the landlord or manager harasses or verbally abuses the tenant, causing the tenant extreme emotional distress, the tenant may sue for compensation for emotional upset and mental suffering, as well as medical bills, lost wages, and future lost wages. Tenants who sue for emotional distress must show that the landlord's failure to repair was particularly extreme or outrageous.

In cases of reckless or intentional acts, a judge or jury may award "punitive" damages—extra money over and above the amount required to compensate the victim for his actual damages, such as medical bills. Punitive damages are designed to punish a person guilty of injuring someone through reckless or intentional conduct, with an eye toward preventing similar conduct in the future. (CC § 3294.) In California, punitive damages are not covered by insurance, and a landlord who is hit with a punitive damages award will always have to pay for it out of his own pocket.

EXAMPLE

Andrew rented a split-level duplex from Ellen. Andrew told Ellen that the carpet covering the three interior stairs was loose and dangerous, and needed to be replaced or repaired. Ellen planned to replace all of the carpeting when Andrew's lease expired in a few months, and didn't want to waste time and money repairing carpet that was just going to be ripped out. Despite Andrew's repeated requests, Ellen refused to repair the carpet. Andrew was injured when the carpet pulled out and he fell down the steps.

Andrew sued Ellen for recklessly and willfully failing to repair and maintain the rental property. He collected several thousand dollars for his past and future medical bills, loss of earnings, and pain and suffering. Because the jury found that Ellen acted intentionally and recklessly, they assessed punitive damages against her, which she had to pay for out of her own pocket.

Managers can be independently sued for emotional distress. When tenants sue for general and special damages for habitability defects (like asking for a rent refund and the value of ruined property when the roof leaks), the person who pays is the landlord, even if the manager had been given the repair responsibility. (Liability of the landlord for defects in the property that do not cause injury is discussed in Chapter 11.) If the tenant claims that the manager caused emotional distress, however, the manager may be liable together with the landlord. Chapter 6 discusses an owner's liability for his manager's acts.

4. Lawsuits for Maintaining a Public Nuisance

The habitability requirements of housing laws and court decisions are not the only repair and maintenance requirements imposed on landlords. You may not create or tolerate any situation that is injurious to health, indecent or offensive to the senses, or an obstruction to the free use of one's property. If you create or allow such a situation to develop, and if an entire neighborhood or community is affected, you are liable for maintaining a public nuisance. (CC § 3491.) Unlike the theory of private nuisance discussed in Chapter 11, Section I, tenants who sue under the public nuisance statutes can recover for mental suffering as well as the interference with their enjoyment of their property. As with the claim of emotional distress discussed above in Section 3, the complaining tenants or neighbors need not claim that they were physically touched by the offensive behavior.

Public nuisance lawsuits are increasingly being filed against landlords whose tenants have established drug-using or -selling operations on the premises, a topic discussed in detail in Section E, below. This is not the only use of the public nuisance remedy, however. The consequences of lawful activity may also rise to the level of a public nuisance. For example, a tenant's nightly jam session with twelve of his closest musician friends, continuing into the wee hours, may not be illegal, but it may interfere with his neighbors' abilities to sleep and cause them physical and mental suffering. Whether the music constitutes a public nuisance will depend on the evidence presented to the judge and the judge's view of the seriousness of the conduct and the harm caused.

If a court decides that a nuisance exists, it may order the landlord to fix the problem and compensate the neighbors or other tenants for the interference and suffering the nuisance caused. If the landlord's conduct was intentional (and not merely negligent), the tenants can get punitive damages as well.

B. LANDLORD'S RESPONSIBILITY TO PROTECT TENANTS FROM CRIME

A landlord's duty to keep premises safe includes taking reasonable measures to protect tenants and visitors from foreseeable assault. If your negligence results in injury to a tenant or visitor from a criminal act by a stranger, another tenant, or an employee, you may be liable.

1. Understanding What Basic "Security" Means

Obviously, home security is a very general concept, covering everything from locks on doors and windows to landscaping and lights to environmental design. And, of course, multiunit buildings have a number of additional security considerations, needing to limit access to the premises and keep common areas safe. People are continually coming and going, and there are many common areas of the building where an attacker could hide. Excellent lighting will be needed, for example, in stairwells, elevators, laundry rooms, basements, parking garages, and outdoor walkways.

To understand what the law requires of a multi-unit landlord, we'll start with a discussion of the basic security measures ("reasonable precautions") that every landlord must take to protect his tenants. The source of this universal duty is the landlord's implied warranty that the premises are habitable, and the requirement that the landlord maintain the property in a tenantable condition (CC § 1941) and exercise due care (CC § 1714(a)). (See Chapter 11, Section A.) In addition, state law requires locks on certain doors and windows. (CC § 1941.3). In other words, landlords must take both specific and reasonable measures to guard against criminal, as well as accidental, harm to their tenants.

These general requirements may be amplified by specific safety measures specified by local codes. For example, the building code in your city may go further than the state law requiring you to provide secure entryways and windows. Your duty to provide secure housing starts with requirements like these but usually doesn't end there, although landlords are most often found liable when criminals have gained access through broken locks and windows.

You may also be bound to provide what we'll call "enhanced" security measures, either because of what you have promised in your lease, rental negotiations, or ads, or because of what you know about the unique problems of your property or tenants. (Section 2, below, covers enhanced security measures.) For example, if you have proudly advertised that your building has security personnel and an intercom system, the law is likely to impose a duty on you to continue to maintain these features. If a crime occurs when these features are either nonfunctional or missing, you are likely to be held liable. Similarly, if you know that criminal incidents have occurred on your property in the past, you may be required to beef up your security systems, especially if it is reasonably foreseeable that the same activity may occur again.

a. Security Duties Imposed by State Law

You must provide deadbolt locks on main exterior doors (except for sliding doors), existing common area doors and gates and certain windows. (CC§ 1941.3.) The law requires:

- A deadbolt lock that is at least $13/16$th of an inch long for each main entry door. A thumb-turn lock in place on July 1, 1998 will satisfy the requirement (but a $13/16$th of an inch deadbolt must be installed whenever the lock is repaired or replaced). If you use other locking mechanisms, they must be inspected and approved by a state or local government agency in order to satisfy the requirements of the law.

- Locks that comply with state or local fire and safety codes in existing doors or gates that connect common areas (such as lobbies, patios and walkways) to rental units or an area beyond the property (such as a main front door).

- Window locks on louvered and casement windows. Prefabricated windows with their own opening and locking mechanisms are exempt, as are those that are more than 12 feet above the ground. However, a window that is over 12 feet from the ground, but less than six feet from a roof or any other platform, must have a lock.

b. Basic Security Duties Imposed by Local Ordinances

Most building and housing codes adopted by local governments are rich with specific rules designed to minimize the chances of a criminal incident on residential rental property—for example, by requiring peepholes, deadbolts, and specific types of lighting on the rental property. On the other hand, some local ordinances give the landlord little specific guidance, requiring "clean and safe" housing but not filling in the meaning of these terms. If your local codes are not equipment specific, you will need to do some independent homework: realistically assess the crime situation in your locality and implement security that provides reasonable protection for your tenants.

EXAMPLE

The housing code in the city where Andrew owned rental property included several sections that dealt with minimum standards for apartment houses. One of the sections specified that parking garages and lots be maintained in a "clean and safe" condition. The garage in Andrew's apartment house was dark (because there were not enough lights) and fairly easily accessible from the street (because the automatic door worked excruciatingly slowly). When a tenant was assaulted by someone who gained entry through the substandard garage door, Andrew was sued and found partially liable for the tenant's injuries.

c. How the Landlord's Duty of Due Care Relates to Security

Learning what the local laws require isn't the only way a rental property owner can discover the basic security measures needed on her property. Basic security duties also derive from the property owner's general duty to act reasonably under the circumstances—or, put another way, to act with due care. Earlier in this chapter we saw that landlords must refrain from acting negligently and causing accidental injury to their tenants. For example, common areas must be maintained in a clean and safe condition so that they do not create a risk of accidents. In the area of security, too, you must take reasonable precautions to further your tenants' safety from criminal assaults.

Whether you have acted reasonably with respect to your tenants' safety from crime is analyzed in the same way as are your actions protecting tenants from structural defects. In Section A, above, we explained that several factors are considered before a judge decides that the landlord had a duty to protect a tenant from accidental harm: the degree of control that the landlord has over the situation, the foreseeability of the injury, the severity of the probable injury, and the burden on the landlord that a duty to protect would entail. A judge asks the same questions when a tenant is injured by the act of a criminal. If the questions are answered in favor of the tenant, the judge will conclude that the landlord owed him a duty of care, and the rest of the case (whether the landlord actually breached that duty, whether his breach caused the incident, and whether the tenant was injured) will go to the jury. The questions asked by the judge are:

- **How much control did the landlord have over the situation?** Did the breach in security occur in a common area (over which the landlord traditionally exercises exclusive control) such as a hallway, or in the tenant's own apartment? If in a common area, the landlord's responsibility is heightened. If the crime was perpetrated on the sidewalk outside the building, are there reasonable measures the landlord could have taken to minimize the chances of this happening?

- **How likely, or foreseeable, was it that a crime would occur?** Was it an isolated event, or yet another in a string of neighborhood crimes? Had there been prior criminal incidents on the property itself? A landlord who knows that an offense is likely (because of a rash of break-ins or prior crime on the property) may be expected, as part of basic security, to take at least some reasonable steps to guard against future crime. (See Section 2, below, for a fuller discussion of the role of the landlord's knowledge as it relates to enhanced security.)

- **How difficult or expensive would it have been to reduce the risk of crime?** For instance, would locks and lighting have discouraged most would-be assailants, or would the landlord have had to do major structural remodeling to reduce the chance of crime? If a relatively cheap or simple measure would have made a significant difference in the likelihood of crime, it is likely that the landlord will be held to a duty of due care.

- **How serious was the probable injury?** When assessing negligence in the context of an accidental injury, courts consider the seriousness of the probable (not the actual) injury. When it comes to the question of a criminal assault, however, the seriousness of probable injury is usually assumed: Very few judges or juries would consider an assault to be a minor matter.

To understand how these four questions work together to jointly determine whether a landlord has a duty to provide basic security, let's look at two examples that illustrate how the question of due care is completely dependent on the facts of each situation.

EXAMPLE 1

Sam was accosted outside the entryway to his duplex by a stranger who was lurking in the tall, overgrown bushes in the front yard next to the sidewalk. Both the bushes and the lack of exterior floodlights near the entryway prevented Sam from seeing his assailant until it was too late. The judge decided that the landlord owed a duty of due care to Sam, on the theory that the landlord controlled the common areas outside the duplex; that it was foreseeable that an assailant would lurk in the bushes and that, because there had been many previous assaults in the area, it was also probable that another assault would occur. Finally, the judge put all this together and concluded that the burden of preventing this type of assault was small in comparison to the risk of injury. It was then up to the jury to decide whether the landlord had breached this duty, whether this breach caused the injury, and whether Sam actually suffered any injuries.

EXAMPLE 2

Max was assaulted and robbed in the open parking lot next to his apartment house. Several muggings had recently been reported in the neighborhood. The lot was thoroughly lit by bright floodlights, but it was not fenced and gated. The judge in Max's case found that the landlord owed a duty of due care toward Max, since the lot was under the landlord's control, an assault seemed reasonably foreseeable in view of the recent nearby muggings, and the burden of securing the area was not overwhelming. When the jury got the case, however, they decided that the landlord had not, in fact, breached his duty of due care, for they decided that the bright lights were all that a reasonably conscientious landlord should be expected to provide in the circumstances.

2. Landlord's Responsibility to Provide Enhanced Security

Knowing the security requirements of your local laws, and being generally familiar with how the courts have ruled on cases holding landlords responsible for criminal acts against their tenants, is a good start. Your next step is to understand how your responsibilities may be increased by both your own acts and factors beyond your control:

- If you promise security features beyond the basics, you may well have to provide them. This includes your written promises (in the lease or rental agreement) and your oral representations about the security you provide—and even your representations about security in your advertisements.

- Although crimes against your tenants may be beyond your control, if your property is in a high-crime area, and especially if there have been crimes on the premises before, your duty to provide security will rise accordingly.

In the sections that follow, we'll explore how your basic security duties can be enhanced, either by virtue of your own promises or actions (Section a, below) or because of the nature of the surrounding neighborhood or the prior occurrence of crime on the premises (Section b, below).

a. Offering or Agreeing to Provide Additional Security

Your advertisements, written promises in the lease, and oral representations made to a prospective tenant can trigger security responsibilities beyond the basics.

Be careful what you advertise or promise. The desire for secure housing is often foremost in the minds of prospective tenants, and landlords know that the promise (advertisement) of safe housing is often a powerful marketing tool. During discussions with interested renters, you will naturally be inclined to point out security locks, outdoor lighting, and burglar alarms, since these features may be as important to prospective tenants as a fine view or a swimming pool.

Take care, however, that your written or oral descriptions of security measures are not exaggerated: Not only will you have begun the landlord/tenant relationship on a note of insincerity, but your descriptions of security may legally obligate you to actually provide what you have portrayed. And if you fail to do so, or fail to conscientiously maintain promised security measures in working order (such as outdoor lighting or an electronic gate on the parking garage), and if this lack of security is found by a court or jury to be a material factor in a crime on the premises, you may well be held liable for a tenant's injuries. This is true even though you might not have been found liable if you hadn't made the promise in the first place.

EXAMPLE

The manager of Jeff's apartment building gave him a thorough tour of the building before he moved in. Jeff was particularly impressed with the security locks on the gates of the high fence at the front and at the rear of the property. Confident that the interior of the property was accessible only to tenants and their guests, Jeff didn't hesitate to take his kitchen garbage to the disposal area at the rear of the building late one evening. There he was accosted by an intruder who had gained entrance through a small side gate that did not have a lock. Jeff's landlord was held liable on the grounds that his manager's representations regarding the locked gates had created a false sense of security which led Jeff to do something (going out at night to a remote area of the building) he might not otherwise have done.

Ads That Invite Lawsuits

Advertisements like the following will come back to haunt you if a crime occurs on your rental property:

- "No one gets past our mega security systems. A highly trained guard is on duty at all times."

- "We provide highly safe, highly secure buildings."

- "You can count on us. We maintain the highest standards in the apartment security business."

Be especially careful what you promise in writing. The simple rule of following through with what you promise, discussed above in the context of ads and oral promises, is even more crucial when it comes to written provisions in your lease or accompanying documents. Why? Because the fact that you have made the promise is preserved in black and white, in your own lease, whereas there is always room for interpretation when an oral representation forms the basis of the promise. For example, if your lease or rental agreement promises something either as vague as "safe and secure premises," or as specific as an electronic security system or a doorman after dark, you will be hard pressed to deny this promise if it is brought up against you in court. If you have failed to follow through with the written promise, you will likely find that a court will hold you liable for criminal acts that were made possible through your lapse.

EXAMPLE

The tenant information packet given to Mai when she moved into her apartment stressed the need to keep careful track of door keys: "If you lose your keys, call the management and the lock will be changed immediately." When Mai lost her purse containing her keys, she called the management company right away but was unable to reach them because it was Sunday morning and there was no weekend or after-hours emergency procedure. That evening, Mai was assaulted by someone who got into her apartment by using her lost key. Mai sued the owner and management company on the grounds that they had failed to live up to the standard they had set for themselves (to change the locks promptly) and were therefore partially responsible for the assailant's entry. The jury agreed and awarded Mai a large sum.

Be careful to maintain what you have already provided. Your actions can obligate you as much as an oral or written statement. If you "silently" provide enhanced security measures (such as security locks or a nighttime guard)— that is, you make these features available without enumerating them in the lease, in advertisements or through oral promises— you may be bound to continue and maintain these features, even though you never explicitly promised to do so.

Many landlords react with understandable frustration when their well-meaning (and expensive) efforts to protect their tenants actually have the effect of increasing their level of liability. But the answer to this frustration is not to cut back to the bare minimum for security. Instead, turn a practical eye to the big picture: Over time, you are better off (legally safer) using sophisticated security measures (thereby ensuring contented, long-term tenants and fewer legal hassles) than you would be by offering the bare minimum and trusting to fate, the police, and hopefully the savviness of the tenants to keep crime at bay. But at least from the point of view of future liability for criminal acts, the less you brag about your security measures, the better.

Be careful how you handle complaints. Take care of complaints about a dangerous situation or a broken security item immediately, even if the problem occurs in the middle of the night or at some other inconvenient time. Failure to do so may increase your liability should a tenant be injured by a criminal act while the security system is out of service or the window or door lock broken. A court may even consider your receipt of the complaint as an implicit promise to do something about it. In short, if you get a complaint about a broken security item—even one you didn't advertise—you should act immediately to:

- fix it, or
- if it's impossible to fix it for a few days or weeks, alert tenants to the problem and take other measures. For example, if your front door security system fails and a necessary part is not immediately available, you might hire a security officer.

Section C5, below, provides more advice for how to respond to tenants' complaints about security.

b.   Security in Response to the Neighborhood

Your duty to provide enhanced security may have nothing to do with what is required by law or what you promise or provide. Your liability for damage and injuries caused by a criminal act can also be based on the prevalence of crime in your area, particularly the prior occurrence of crime on your rental property and your failure to take steps to reduce the risk of future crimes.

EXAMPLE

Allison rented an apartment in Manor Arms after being shown the building by the resident manager, who assured her that the building was "safe." A month after moving in, Allison was assaulted by a man who stopped her in the hallway and claimed to be a building inspector. Unbeknownst to Allison, other similar assaults had occurred in the building, and the manager even had a composite drawing of the suspect. Allison's assailant was captured and proved to be the person responsible for the earlier crimes as well. Allison sued the building owners, claiming that they were negligent in failing to warn her of the specific danger posed by the repeat assailant and in failing to beef up their security (such as hiring a guard service) after the first assault. The judge found that the landlords owed Allison a duty of care to protect and warn her of the danger; the jury found that the owners had breached that duty and that Allison was injured as a result.

Here are some actual cases in which landlords have been held liable for tenants' injuries and property damage caused by third parties on the property. All involved situations that the landlord might have guarded against. (See Section E, below, for related cases of landlord liability involving drug-dealing tenants.)

- Tenant's visitor killed in dim, empty parking area with broken security system and a history of violent crimes. (*Gomez v. Ticor,* 145 Cal. App. 3d 622, 193 Cal. Rptr. 622 (1983).)

- Tenant robbed and assaulted in dimly lit common area where landlord knew or should have known about earlier robberies and assaults. (*Penner v. Falk,* 153 Cal. App. 3d 858, 200 Cal. Rptr. 661 (1984); and *Isaacs v. Huntington Memorial Hospital,* 38 Cal. 3d. 112, 211 Cal. Rptr. 356 (1985).)

C. How to Protect Your Tenants From Criminal Acts While Also Reducing Your Potential Liability

The job of maintaining rental units that are free from crime—both from the outside and, in the case of multiunit buildings, from within—can be a monumental task. Sometimes, your duty to protect your tenants can even seem to conflict with your duty to respect your tenants' rights to privacy and autonomy. How will you know if the premises are safe unless you perform frequent inspections of individual rental units—which you can't legally insist upon—and the common areas? How will you know about the activities of your tenants unless you question them thoroughly regarding their backgrounds and livelihoods, or unless you watch them carefully?

We recommend a seven-step preventive approach to effectively and reasonably protect your tenants and, at the same time, reconcile your need to see and know (and thus to protect) with your duty to respect tenants' privacy:

Step 1: Meet or exceed basic legal requirements for safety devices, such as deadbolt locks, good lighting, and window locks. (See Chapter 11, Section A.)

Step 2: Educate your tenants about crime problems and prevention strategies. Make it absolutely clear that they—not you—are primarily responsible for their own protection.

Step 3: Provide and maintain adequate enhanced security measures based on an analysis of the vulnerability of your property and neighborhood. If your tenants will pay more rent if you make the building safer, you are foolish not to do it.

Step 4: Don't hype your security measures.

Step 5: Conduct regular inspections of your properties to spot any problems (and ask tenants for their suggestions).

Step 6: Quickly respond to your tenants' suggestions and complaints.

Step 7: If an important component of your security systems breaks, be prepared to fix it on an emergency basis and provide appropriate alternative security.

These steps will not only limit the likelihood that criminal activity will occur on your property, but also reduce the risk that you will be found responsible if a criminal assault or robbery does occur there.

1. Provide Adequate Security Measures

A landlord who wants to improve the way his property looks knows that there are several steps towards discovering what needs to be done and how to do it. For example, he might study the property and make a list of possible improvements. Also, he might hire a professional designer or landscaper as a consultant or copy other properties that have achieved the "look" he is after. Finally, before spending a fortune, the sensible landlord will measure the cost of any potential improvement project against both his available funds and any increase in the property's rental or sales value.

The landlord who wants to improve the security of his property follows a very similar course: personal inspection, attention to what has worked in nearby properties, professional advice (including input from the local police and your insurance company) and a cost/benefit analysis will result in a sensible approach to providing safe housing.

The steps are the same for all kinds of housing and neighborhoods—whether you rent a duplex or single-family home in a low-crime suburban area or a multiunit apartment building in a dangerous part of town.

a. Start With Your Own Personal Inspection

Walk around your property and as you assess the different areas, ask yourself two questions:

- Would I, or a member of my family, feel reasonably safe here, at night or alone? and,
- If I were a thief or assailant, how difficult would it be to gain access and approach a tenant?

Schedule your assessment walks at different times of the day and night—you might see something at 11:00 p.m. that you wouldn't notice at 11:00 a.m.

At the very least, we recommend the following sensible security measures for every multiunit rental property:

- Exterior lighting directed at entrance ways and walkways should be activated by motion or on a timer. (Do not rely on managers or tenants to manually operate the lights.) The absence or failure of exterior lights is the single most common allegation in premises liability cases brought against landlords.
- Make sure you have good, strong interior lights that come on automatically, in hallways, stairwells, doorways and parking garages.
- Sturdy deadbolt door locks and solid window and patio door locks (including bars) are essential, as

are peepholes at the front door. (Best to install two—one at eye level for an adult and another at a level appropriate for a child.)

- Intercom and buzzer systems that allow the tenant to control the opening of the front door from the safety of his apartment are also obviously a good idea for many types of buildings.
- Shrubbery/landscaping needs to be designed and maintained so that it is neat and compact. It should not obscure entry ways nor afford easy hiding places adjacent to doorways or windows.
- Where necessary, a 24-hour door person is a good idea. In some areas, this is essential and may do more to reduce crime outside your building than anything else. Spread over a large number of units, this may cost less than you think.
- Driveways, garages, and underground parking areas need to be well lit and as secure (inaccessible to unauthorized entrants) as possible. Fences and automatic gates may be a virtual necessity in some areas of some cities. There are several trade magazines in the rental housing industry that often give good, practical information on available equipment.
- Elevators are an ideal space for a fast-acting assailant: While his victim is neatly confined to a small space, he can quickly accomplish his dirty deed. Limiting access to the elevators by requiring a pass key and installing closed-circuit monitoring reduce the chances that an assailant will choose this site.
- A 24-hour internal security system with cameras and someone monitoring them is often effective in deterring all but the most sophisticated criminals. Though these systems are expensive, some tenants will bear the extra cost in exchange for the added protection.

EXAMPLE

An assailant studied an upscale apartment building and waited until it was clear that large numbers of people were arriving for a party. When he entered the lobby, he told the guard that he, too, was headed for the party upstairs. Because the guard had not been given a list of invited guests and told to ask for identification from every party-goer, the assailant was allowed into the building, where he assaulted a woman in the laundry room. Had the owner or manager instructed his tenants to supply the guard with lists of guests, and told the guard that no one should be admitted without confirmation, the unfortunate incident would not have happened. The landlord was held partially liable for the tenant's injuries.

SHOULD YOU USE A DOORMAN OR SECURITY GUARD?

Security guards, or doormen, are appropriate in some situations. The presence of an alert human can make an empty lobby more inviting to a tenant and less attractive to a prospective criminal. But bear in mind that the "security" provided is only as good as the individual doing the job. If you hire a firm, choose carefully and insist on letters of reference and proof of insurance. You can also hire your own guard, but this tends to get complicated very quickly, since you will be responsible for his or her training and weapons used (if any). It is essential to remember that, even with the best-trained and most visible security personnel, you must continue to pay attention to other aspects of security.

---

b. Consider the Neighborhood as Well as Your Property

The extent of your security measures depends somewhat on the nature of the neighborhood and the property itself. If there have been no incidents of crime in your area, you have less reason to equip your property with extensive prevention devices. On the other hand, residential crime is a spreading, not receding, problem, and you certainly do not want one of your tenants to be "the first to be raped or robbed on your block." Especially if there have been criminal

incidents in the neighborhood, talk to the neighbors and the police department about what measures have proven to be effective.

The physical aspects of the neighborhood, as well as its history, can be important indicators of the risk of crime on your property. Properties adjacent to late-night bars and convenience stores often experience more burglaries and assaults than housing that is removed from such establishments. In some cities, proximity to a freeway on-ramp (an effective avenue of escape) may increase the risk of crime.

SECURITY FOR A HOUSE OR DUPLEX

Single-family housing and duplexes present opportunities for security that may not be appropriate in multifamily residences. For example, it may be wise to provide an alarm that is hooked up to a security service. Also, while yard maintenance may be the tenants' responsibility, you may need to supervise the job to make sure that bushes and trees are trimmed so that they do not obscure entryways or provide convenient hiding spots for would-be criminals.

---

c. Get Advice From Professionals

Increasingly, as the problems of urban crime escalate, the police will work together with you to develop a sound approach and educate tenants. Contact the local police department and ask for help in assessing the vulnerability of your property. Many police departments will send an officer to your property, and some will also meet with tenants to advise them on ways to recognize, avoid, and report suspicious behavior.

Another professional resource is your own insurance company. Many companies provide free consultation on ways to deter crime, having figured out that in the long run it's cheaper to offer preventative advice than to pay out huge awards to injured clients. For example, drawing on its experience with prior claims generated by security breaches, your company might be able to suggest equipment that has (and has not!) proven to be effective in preventing break-ins and assaults.

The obvious resource for advice is the private "security industry" itself. As the amount of residential crime has gone up, so too have the number of companies that specialize in providing security services. Listed in the telephone book under "Security Systems," these firms will typically provide an analysis of your situation before recommending specific equipment—whether it be bars on windows or an internal electronic surveillance system. Even if you do not ultimately engage their services, a professional evaluation may prove quite valuable as you design your own approach. Speak with other landlords or housing authorities to make sure that you choose a reputable outfit to examine your property.

When a Tenant Wants to Supply Additional Security

Some tenants may be dissatisfied with your security measures, even if you've fully complied with state and any local laws, and may want to install additional locks or an alarm system to their unit at their expense. Clause 17 of our form lease and rental agreements forbids the tenant from rekeying or adding locks or a burglar alarm system without your written consent. If you provide such consent, make sure the tenant gives you duplicate keys, instructions on how to disarm the alarm system, and the name and phone number of the alarm company, so that you can enter in case of emergency. Think carefully before you refuse your tenant permission to install extra protection: If a crime occurs that would have been foiled had the security item been in place, you will obviously be at a disadvantage before a judge or jury.

Key Control

The security of your rental property extends from the locks on rental unit doors to the keys to those doors. Don't let keys get into the wrong hands:

- Keep all duplicate keys in a locked area, identified by a code that only you and your manager know. Several types of locking key drawers and sophisticated key "safes" are available. Check ads in magazines that cater to the residential rental industry, or visit a local lock shop.

- Strictly limit access to master keys by allowing only you and your manager to have them.

- Keep strict track of all keys provided to tenants and, if necessary, to your employees.

- Rekey every time a new tenant moves in.

- Give some thought to the problem of the front door lock: If it is operated by an easy-to-copy key, there is no way to prevent a tenant from copying the key and giving it to others or using it after he moves out. Consider using locks that have hard-to-copy keys; or (with small properties) rekey the front door when a tenant moves. There are also easy-to-change card systems that allow you to change front door access on a monthly basis or when a tenant moves.

- Give keys only to people you know and trust. If you have hired a contractor whom you do not know personally, open the unit for him and return to close up when he is done. Keep in mind that often even known and trusted contractors hire day laborers whose honesty is yet to be proven.

- Don't label keys with the rental unit number or name and address of the apartment building.

d. Evaluate the Effectiveness of Security Measures Against Their Cost

The best security measures on the market will do you no good if, to pay for them, you have to raise rents so high that you end up with no tenants to protect. Short of going bankrupt (or getting out of the business altogether), the best approach is to provide the amount of security that is economically feasible. And, of course, no matter how much security you provide, you'll want to let your tenants know that no security can be counted on as foolproof, and that it's up to them to be wary. (See Section 3, below.) This at least puts your tenants on notice that they cannot entirely depend on you to ensure their safety. And, should an unfortunate incident occur on your property, you will be able to argue to a jury not only that you did the best you could in the circumstances, but that you were honest with your renters as to the limitations of your measures.

2. Be Candid About Security Problems

Your candid disclosures regarding the safety problems of your neighborhood and the limited effectiveness of the existing security measures may help shield you from liability if a criminal incident does occur on your property. (See Section B, above.) From the tenants' point of view, such disclosures serve to alert them to the need to be vigilant and to assume some responsibility for their own safety. If you do not disclose the limitations of the security you provide (or if you exaggerate) and a crime does occur, one of the first things your tenant will say (to the police, his lawyer, and the jury) is that he was simply relying upon the protection you had assured him would be in place.

3. How to Educate Your Tenants

Few neighborhoods, particularly in urban areas, are free of crime, although, obviously, some areas are more dangerous than others. In Section 1, above, we recommend that you identify the vulnerabilities of your particular neighborhood—for example, by talking to the police. Don't keep this information to yourself, but make your tenants savvy to the realities of life in your neighborhood. We recommend a two-step process:

- Alert tenants to the specific risks associated in living in your neighborhood (problems are worst Friday and Saturday night between 10 p.m. and 11 a.m.) and to what they can do to minimize the chances of assault or theft (avoid being on the street or in outside parking areas alone).

- No matter how secure your building, warn tenants of the *limitations* of the security measures you have provided.

EXAMPLE

Paul recently moved into his apartment and had been told by the manager that doormen were on duty "all the time." One afternoon, he opened his door to someone who identified himself as a "building inspector" who needed to check his hot water heater. Paul was assaulted and robbed by this individual, and sued his landlord. At trial, he explained that he would never have opened the door but for the assurances of the manager that the doormen would screen visitors at any hour. (In fact, the service was in place only from 6 p.m. to 6 a.m.) Paul was able to convince the jury that the landlord bore part of the blame for the attack.

This approach allows you to "cover your bases" by both disclosing the risks and frankly informing the tenants that you have not (and cannot) ensure their safety in all possible situations. If, despite your best efforts, a tenant is assaulted on your property, you can point out that you disclosed as much as you knew about a potentially risky situation.

a. Identify Specific Risks

Making certain your tenants are aware of the possible dangers inherent in any urban living situation is a good start to their education, but it should not be the end of it. Follow through with information specific to your property. Here are some ideas:

- If there have been incidents of crime in the area (and especially in your building), inform your tenants (but be careful to maintain the confidentiality of the victim). It's best to do this at the start of the tenancy, when you first show the rental unit to prospective tenants.

• Update your information on the security situation in your building as necessary. For example, let tenants know if there has been a crime in or near the building by sending them a note or posting a notice in the lobby.

• If you have hired a professional security firm to evaluate your rental property, share the results of their investigation with your tenants.

• Encourage tenants to set up a neighborhood watch program. (Many local police departments will come out and meet with citizens attempting to organize such a program.)

• Encourage tenants to report any suspicious activities or security problems to you, such as loitering, high numbers of late-night guests, or broken locks.

b. Explain the Limitations of Your Security Measures

An important component of your disclosures to tenants involves disabusing them of any notion that you are their guardian angel. Let them know where your security efforts end, and where their own good sense (and the local police force) must take over. Specifically:

• Explain what each security measure will and will not do. For example, if the windows in each unit of your building can be locked only if they are fully closed, warn tenants that they may need to choose between ventilation and security.

• Highlight particular aspects of the property that are, despite your efforts, vulnerable to the presence of would-be assailants or thieves. For instance, a fast-moving person could, in most situations, slip into a garage behind an entering car despite the fact that it has a self-closing door. Pointing this out to your tenant may result in more careful attention to the rearview mirror or a second thought about whether to come and go at late hours.

• Place signs in any potentially dangerous locations that will remind tenants of possible dangers and the need to be vigilant. For example, you might post signs in the parking garage, the laundry room, and common walkways: "Caution. Take steps to protect yourself from crime."

• Suggest safety measures. For example, tenants arriving home after dark might call ahead and ask a neighbor to be an escort.

Giving your tenants information on how they, too, can take steps to protect themselves will also help if you are sued. If a tenant argues that you failed to disclose a dangerous condition, you will be able to show that you have done all that could be expected of a reasonably conscientious landlord.

4. Maintain Your Property and Conduct Regular Inspections

Start by understanding that landlords are most often found liable for crime on their property when the criminal has gained access through broken doors or locks. Not only is the best security equipment in the world useless if it has deteriorated or is broken, but the very fact that it's not in operation can be enough to result in a finding of landlord liability. By contrast, a jury is far less likely to fault a landlord who can show that reasonable security measures were in place and operational, but were unable to stop a determined criminal.

Inspect your property frequently, so that you discover and fix problems before an opportunistic criminal comes along. At the top of your list should be fixing burned-out exterior flood lights and broken locks. Overgrown shrubbery that provides a convenient lurking spot can be easily detected by a thorough and regular walk-through by the owner or manager, and should be regularly cut back. Rather than trusting your memory or intuition as to what you should inspect and when you last did it, devise a checklist designed specifically for that property (perhaps in conjunction with a security or insurance expert), and conduct regular inspections. Enlist your tenants to help you spot and correct problems. In spite of your personal or even professional inspection of the property, remember that the people who actually live in your rental property will generally know first about security and repair problems. One good approach is to post several notices in central locations, such as elevators and main lobbies, asking tenants to promptly report any security problems, such as broken locks or windows. If you rent a duplex or house, periodically meet with your tenants and discuss any changes in the neighborhood and/or the structure of the building.

Chapter 11, Sections J and K, provides a detailed system for inspecting rental property and staying on top of repair and maintenance needs.

5. Respond to Your Tenants' Complaints Immediately

Respond immediately to your tenants' complaints about broken locks or concerns about security problems and suspicious activities. Keep in mind that a serious breach in your security measures has much greater potential liability consequences than a garden-variety maintenance problem. That's why we recommend a truly fast response. For example, a stopped-up sink is certainly inconvenient to the tenant, and may result in rent abatement or repair-and-deduct measures if not fixed for a period of days or weeks (see Chapter 11), but it rarely justifies a four-alarm response by the landlord. On the other hand, a broken lock or disabled intercom system is an invitation to crime and needs to be addressed pronto. If you fail to do so and a crime occurs, your chances of being held liable increase dramatically.

Consider the following all-too-common scenarios, and our suggested response:

- The glass panel next to the front door was accidentally broken late one afternoon by a departing workman. The landlord, conscious of the fact that this created a major security problem, called a 24-hour glass replacement service to get it replaced immediately.

- The intercom system failed due to a power surge following an electrical storm. The landlord hired a 24-hour guard for the two days it took to repair the circuitry.

- Several exterior floodlights were knocked out by vandals throwing rocks at 6:00 p.m. A tenant who

had been encouraged by management to report problems of this nature called the landlord. The landlord alerted the police and asked for an extra drive-by during the night, posted signs in the lobby and the elevator, closed off the darkened entrance and advised tenants to use an alternate, lighted entry way instead. The floodlights were repaired the next day and equipped with wire mesh screen protection.

Establishing complaint procedures will help prevent crime on your rental property by alerting you to security problems. (See Chapter 11, Section J for details.) Such procedures will also be of considerable value to you in limiting your liability, should you be sued by a tenant whose assailant gained access via a broken window lock that the tenant failed to disclose to you.

D. PROTECTING TENANTS FROM EACH OTHER (AND FROM THE MANAGER)

Section B, above, focused on the landlord's duty to take reasonable measures to avert foreseeable crime on the premises by unknown, third-party criminals. This section will explore your responsibility when one of the tenants, your manager, or any other employee is responsible for criminal activity on the premises. (Tenants who engage in illegal drug trafficking are discussed in Section E, below.) Like your duty to protect tenants from crime at the hands of unknown, third-party assailants, this duty is limited to what is reasonably foreseeable and to what a reasonable person in your position would do.

1. Landlord's Responsibility for Tenants' Criminal Acts

A tenant who is injured by another tenant may sue you, claiming that you knew, or should have known, of the other tenant's continuing criminal predisposition, and you:

- were negligent in renting to the person in the first place

- were negligent in not evicting the troublemaker, or
- at the very least, were negligent in not warning others about the individual.

Tenants who sue their landlord in these types of lawsuits face an uphill task. They must convince a jury of two things—that it is reasonable to expect a landlord to discover the details of his tenants' pasts, and that a landlord can predict and control tenants' behavior as well. Landlords usually win these cases, but not always. In one case, the landlord knew of a tenant's bizarre behavior and that she owned a gun. This knowledge, however, did not give the landlord reason to anticipate that this tenant would get into an argument with and fatally shoot another tenant. Moreover, the court noted that the landlord could not reasonably have been expected to discover the precise details of the tenant's mental condition, nor control her behavior. (*Davis v. Gomez*, 207 Cal. App. 3d 1401, 255 Cal. Rptr. 743 (1989).)

You are far more likely to be found liable under the legal theory of negligence for a tenant's injuries when the injured party can show that the incident was foreseeable and could have been avoided had you taken simple and precautionary measures—for example, by evicting a tenant whom you believe may physically harm another tenant. In the face of re-peated threats and assaultive behavior by one tenant toward another, a landlord who knew about the situation but took no action against the first tenant was liable to the second tenant when she was as-saulted again by the first tenant. (*Madhani v. Cooper*, 106 Ca.App.4th 412 (2003).)

Keep in mind that your duty to rid your property of dangerous types extends to tenants' guests, includ-ing unauthorized occupants, whose presence (and dangerous propensities) you know about. For ex-ample, in one case a court ruled that a landlord could be liable for the stabbing of a tenant's young child by the adult son (an unauthorized occupant) of other tenants, because complaints had been made in vain by other tenants concerning the son's menacing actions—including an attempt to force entry into another's apartment unit. (*Valencia v. Michaud*, 81 Cal. App. 4th 190, 94 Cal. Rptr. 2d 268 (2000).)

EXAMPLE

Al had a quick temper and a mean disposition, and he particularly disliked Larry, who rented an apartment in the same building. Al had threatened Larry several times. Their landlord knew about these threats but did nothing—he didn't try to evict Al, post extra security guards, or even discuss the situation with him. When Al attacked Larry, Larry sued the landlord. Larry claimed that the landlord's knowledge of the situation and his ability to take some steps to protect Larry made the landlord partially responsible for the attack. A jury agreed and awarded damages to Larry.

PROTECT YOURSELF, TOO

Landlords and managers need to remember to take precautions for their own personal safety. In addition to being subject to many of the same risks to which your tenants are exposed, there are added special considerations that come with your job. Regardless of whether you live on the rental property:

- Promptly deposit rent checks and money orders. Do not accept cash.

- When you show a vacant apartment, consider bringing someone with you. A would-be assailant may be deterred by the presence of another person who could overpower him or identify him later. If you must show apartments by yourself, at least alert a family member or friend to the fact that you are showing a vacant unit, and when you expect to be done.

- Especially if your building is in a relatively high crime area, carry a small alarm device (such as beeper-sized box that emits a piercing alarm when its pin is removed), and consider carrying a cellular phone. Many cellular service providers offer "emergency only" service that is relatively inexpensive.

- Work on vacant units during the day and be alert to the fact that, although keeping the front door open (to the building or the unit) may be convenient as you go to and fro for materials and equipment, it is also an invitation to someone to walk right into the building.

---

2. Landlord's Responsibility for Managers' Criminal Acts

The person you hire as your manager will occupy a critical position in your business. Your manager will interact with every tenant, and will often have access to tenants' personal files and their homes. If your manager commits a crime, for example, using a key to enter a tenant's apartment and steal her stereo, you

may be held liable if you knew (or should have known) that this event was reasonably foreseeable. It follows that extreme caution must be exercised in your choice of a manager. (See Chapter 6 for advice on choosing a manager.)

Whether you will be found legally liable for a manager's crimes will usually turn on whether you acted "reasonably under the circumstances" in hiring and supervising the manager. You are likely to be sued for negligent hiring if:

- you have failed to investigate your manager's background to the full extent allowed by law

- it can be shown that a proper investigation would have revealed a past criminal conviction that would have rendered the applicant unsuitable for the job, and

- the manager's offense against the tenant is one that is reasonably related to a past conviction or assaultive incident.

EXAMPLE

Martin needed to hire a new manager for his large apartment complex when Sandy, his longtime manager, suddenly left. Pressured by the need to replace Sandy fast, Martin hired Jack without checking his background or information provided on the application form. Martin took Jack at his word when he said that he had no felony convictions. Several months later, Jack was arrested for stealing stereo equipment from a tenant's home, which he entered using the master key. Martin was successfully sued when the tenant learned that Jack had two prior felony convictions for burglary and grand theft.

As the manager's employer, you may also be held liable if your manager's negligence makes it possible for another person to commit a crime against a tenant. For example, if your manager is careless with rental unit keys, and this carelessness allows a criminal to obtain and use a tenant's key, you will be held responsible on the grounds that you failed to properly supervise the manager.

3. How to Protect Tenants From Each Other (and From the Manager)

Here we discuss several practical steps that you can take both to avoid the occurrence of trouble by a tenant or manager and, in the event that problems do erupt, to limit your exposure to lawsuits.

a. Screen Tenants and Managers Carefully

Careful tenant selection is by far the best approach to choosing tenants who are likely to be law-abiding and peaceful citizens. Chapter 1 recommends a comprehensive system for screening prospective tenants, including checking out references from past landlords and employers. Thorough screening will give you a fairly complete idea as to a prospective tenant's legitimate source of income and temperament, and will help you select tenants who will be less likely to cause you any legal or practical problems later. We recommend the same careful screening for potential managers.

b. Respond Quickly to Complaints About Other Tenants or the Manager

In addition to choosing tenants carefully, be sure you establish a system to respond to tenants' complaints and concerns about other tenants or the manager, the same way you handle repair complaints. A system of this kind will enable you to respond quickly to inappropriate tenant or manager behavior—for example, by evicting the tenant or firing the manager. A complaint-handling system will serve an additional, perhaps unexpected function: If a manager or tenant does, despite your best selection efforts, prove suddenly to be dangerous or unreliable and you are sued, and if you have complete business records that show that there were no prior complaints regarding his behavior, the absence of any complaints will bolster your claim that you acted reasonably under the circumstances (by continuing to rent to or hire the individual) because you had no inkling that trouble was likely.

c. Do Not Tolerate Tenants' Disruptive Behavior

Although there is no way you can be absolutely certain that the tenants you select will not create problems in your building, you are clearly in a position to act swiftly against those who exhibit antisocial behavior once they have moved in. You do not want to establish a police state in your building, but you do want to emphasize your expectation that all tenants (and their families and guests) will conduct themselves in a law-abiding manner, or face the threat of prompt termination. Your lease or rental agreement is the most effective place to make this point. It should contain an explicit written provision stating that tenants who "violate any law or ordinance, including laws prohibiting the use, possession, or sale of illegal drugs, commit waste or nuisance, or annoy, disturb, inconvenience, or interfere with the quite enjoyment and peace and quiet of any other tenant or nearby resident" will be terminated and evicted if necessary, and you should consistently enforce it. (See Clause 16, Prohibitions Against Violating Laws and Causing Disturbances, of our form agreements in Chapter 2.)

Your response to a disruptive tenant should be carefully designed to fit the problem. Some situations involving disruptive tenants call for prompt efforts to terminate. If the tenant causes problems before you are able to get him out and you are sued, you can at least argue that you acted as quickly as possible to get rid of him. On the other hand, if the behavior is merely annoying and not serious enough to sustain a termination, mediation might be warranted as a first step. In each situation, you will have to consider the seriousness of the risk and the likelihood that a court will uphold your attempt to end the tenancy. See Chapter 8, Section B for information on mediation.

E. Landlord Liability for Drug-Dealing Tenants

It's an understatement to say that tenants who engage in illegal activity on your property—by dealing drugs, storing stolen property, engaging in prostitution, or participating in gang-related activity—present you with a host of problems. In this section, we focus on

HOW MUCH CAN YOU FIND OUT ABOUT A TENANT'S PAST?

Your questions about a tenant's past criminal activity, drug use, or mental illness may be limited both legally and practically. In Chapter 9 we discuss these issues in detail. In brief:

Criminal activity. It is impossible for a private landlord to obtain complete official information about an applicant's criminal past. Under state law, you may check the Department of Justice's database of registered sexual offenders—if the applicant is on the list, you'll find out (but the value of the database has been seriously questioned, as explained in Chapter 9, Section A4). But information about other convictions is harder to obtain. The Department of Justice is authorized to release a person's criminal history only to specified state agencies or individuals. (Penal Code § 11105.) Only government housing authorities may obtain limited information. (Penal Code § 11105.03.) Individuals and private background reporting services, however, may examine county courthouse records and report anything of public record (such as a conviction). (Chapter 1 discusses background reporting services.) The thoroughness and reliability of such services will vary.

There is nothing, however, to prevent you from asking an applicant for a criminal history. Even if you can legally ask the question, however, it will be difficult (on a practical level) to confirm the truthfulness of the answers, since court records, although a matter of public knowledge, must be examined in person. Also, in California there are many record-sealing procedures available to people convicted of misdemeanors and even felonies who have satisfied certain post-conviction behavior requirements. One of the effects of sealing a record often includes an individual's right to answer "No" to any questions about the sealed or dismissed conviction.

Drug and alcohol use. Under the Fair Housing Amendments Act, past drug addiction and alcoholism are classified as a handicap. It is illegal under federal law to refuse to rent to someone on the basis of their past drug addiction. Landlords may, however, ask prospective tenants about current drug use and refuse to rent on that basis. Also, it is not a violation of federal law to inquire as to past convictions for dealing or manufacturing illegal drugs, and to refuse to rent to someone on that basis.

Mental illness. Under the Fair Housing Amendments Act, it is illegal to refuse to rent to someone solely on the grounds that they are, have been, or are regarded as being mentally ill. However, if the mental impairment makes the person ineligible on any of your established criteria for all prospective tenants—for instance, the illness prevents the person from holding a steady job, he has no acceptable guarantor for the rent, and he therefore cannot meet your financial stability requirements—you may refuse to rent to him.

the most common problem (drug dealing), but our discussion applies equally to the other illegal activities.

1. The Cost of Renting to Drug-Dealing Tenants

Increasingly over the last decade, stricter laws and court decisions have made landlords who fail to sufficiently monitor the activities of their tenants liable, especially if a tenant is found to be engaging in a continuing illegal activity such as drug dealing. In addition, your failure to act quickly—for example, by failing to evict drug-dealing tenants—can result in these practical and legal problems:

- Good tenants who pay rent on time and maintain the rental property may be difficult to find and keep, and the value of your property will plummet.

- Using the theory of "constructive eviction," good tenants, trying to avoid drug-dealing tenants, may be able to legally move out without notice and before a lease runs out. They will argue that the presence of the illegal activity has, for all practical purposes, evicted them, in that the problems associated with drug dealing prevent them from the "quiet enjoyment" of their home.

- Tenants injured or annoyed by drug dealers, both in the building and neighborhood, may withhold rent or sue you for violating anti-nuisance laws and building codes.

- Local, state or federal authorities may levy stiff fines against you for allowing the illegal activity to continue—as high as $25,000 (H&S § 11571 et seq.).

- Law enforcement authorities may choose to pursue criminal penalties against both the tenants and you as landlord for knowingly allowing the activities to continue.

- As an extreme but relatively uncommon consequence, the presence of drug dealers may result in your rental property being confiscated under one of two powerful tools developed by society to deal with crime: public nuisance abatement laws and forfeiture laws. A judge can even order an owner to live on the property until the nuisance—the drug dealing—has stopped. (Health & Safety Code § 11571.)

Be vigilant or be sorry. In some situations, the government will fine you and seize property with only the barest of knowledge on the landlord's part as to the nefarious activities of the tenants. Some landlords may suspect—or even know full well—that illegal drug dealing is taking place on their rental property, but do nothing—out of either inertia, fear of reprisals from drug dealers, or the attitude that they're unlikely to get in trouble. Whatever the reason for inaction, landlords need to understand their legal responsibilities towards their tenants and neighbors and the impact of allowing drug dealing on their rental property. It clearly behooves landlords to learn how to avoid substantial fines or the risk of losing rental property by acting very quickly and decisively to eliminate drug-dealing and other illegal activities on their property.

2. Rent Withholding

Although no statute specifically allows it, one court has said that tenants may withhold rent if the landlord fails to protect their security. (*Secretary of HUD v. Layfield,* 88 Cal. App. 3d. Supp. 28 (1979).) (See Chapter 11, Section F for details on tenants' withholding rent.) A landlord who does nothing about a tenant's drug dealing is certainly open to this accusation.

Even if the landlord tried to evict the complaining tenants for nonpayment of rent, a court could well rule that the tenants were within their rights to withhold rent until the property again became reasonably safe and peaceful.

3. Lawsuits Against Landlords

Government officials, tenants, and neighbors who are affected by the crime that surrounds a drug dealer's home may also sue the landlord who does nothing to stop drug dealing on the property. These lawsuits typically charge the landlord with the maintenance of a "public nuisance"—an illegal, noxious state of affairs that interferes with the neighbors' enjoyment of their property. Penalties include:

- speedy clean-up and eviction by the municipal authorities, with the cost charged to the landlord or filed as a lien against the property (Government Code § 38773)

- temporarily closing the property even before the trial on the charge of maintaining a nuisance, which may include relocation costs for law-abiding tenants charged to the landlord (H&S § 11573.5)

- placing rents in an escrow account controlled by the court (H&S §11573.5)

- orders to provide improved interior and exterior lighting, security guards, capital improvements (such as security gates), signs, membership in neighborhood associations, attendance at property management training programs, and cosmetic improvements to the property

- closure of the property for a year if the existence of the nuisance is proved at trial (H&S § 11581)

• sale of the property to pay the costs of eviction and clean-up (Penal Code § 11231; H&S § 11585).

In recent years, exasperated neighbors have brought individual nuisance lawsuits against landlords in small claims court—and won. Clusters of such claims (at a maximum of $5,000 per claim) can quickly add up to tens—or even hundreds—of thousands of dollars.

In 1993, 75 neighbors plagued by the crime, noise and fear generated by a crack house in Berkeley won a total small claims court judgment of $218,325 against the owner of the apartment building where drug dealing occurred. (*San Francisco Chronicle,* December 27, 1993.)

In another example, a group of San Francisco neighbors successfully sued the city Housing Authority for allowing drug dealing and related crime to flourish on its property. They won a total of $25,500. (*San Francisco Chronicle,* November 2, 1990.)

Also, tenants may sue the landlord in federal court under the federal Racketeering Influenced Corrupt Organizations (RICO) Act, if they can prove the landlord is tolerating drug dealing. (*Spinosa v. University Students Cooperative Assn.,* 939 F.2d 808 (9th Cir., 1991).)

Many cities have laws aimed at getting drug-dealing tenants evicted. The laws make it easier for landlords to evict, and they punish landlords who sit by while drug dealing goes on in their property. A city may even force the sale of property where illegal drug activities occur in violation of state law. In 1993, a superior court judge ordered a Berkeley homeowner to sell her property within 60 days and pay the city $68,300 in legal fees and penalties assessed for crack cocaine manufacturing and drug dealing on the property. (*San Francisco Chronicle,* December 27, 1993.)

Federal or local law enforcement authorities can take legal action to have housing used by drug dealers seized and turned over to the government, even if the owner's part in the crime is just to ignore it. The federal law is the Comprehensive Drug Abuse Prevention and Control Act of 1970 (21 U.S.C. § 881). The state law is the Uniform Controlled Substances Act (Uniform Controlled Substances Act, § 505, 9 (Part II) U.L.A. 1, 883 (1988 & Supp. 1990).) In 1988, the San Mateo County district attorney brought just such a suit against the owner of a 60-unit drug haven in the city of East Palo Alto. The owner was fined $35,000 in civil penalties and had to shut the building down and pay tenants' relocation expenses.

ACTIVITIES THAT ARE ALWAYS CONSIDERED NUISANCES

State law has declared that certain acts are automatically deemed "nuisances," which means that a plaintiff need not convince a judge in every case that the activities are injurious to public health or morals. These nuisances *per se* include:

• illegal gambling, lewdness, prostitution, or a bathhouse permitting conduct that is capable of transmitting AIDS (Penal Code §§11225 et seq.)

• illegal liquor sale (Penal Code §§ 11200 et seq.)

• use or sale of controlled substances (illegal drugs) (H&S §§ 11570 et seq. and Civil Code § 3479)

• criminal street gang activities (Penal Code § 186.22a).

---

4.   What You Can Do to Prevent Drug Lawsuits and Seizures

Landlords who have been careful to manage their property so as to minimize the possibility that tenants will be burglarized or assaulted (by strangers or other tenants) have gone a long way toward preventing the development of situations that lead to abatement and nuisance actions. If you follow these steps, it is unlikely that a tenancy will deteriorate to the point that neighbors or the government feel it is necessary to step in and take over:

• Carefully screen potential renters to avoid renting to drug dealers. (See Chapter 1.)

• Keep the results of your background checks that show that your tenants' rent appeared to come from legitimate sources (jobs and bank accounts).

• Don't accept cash rental payments.

- Include a clause in your lease or rental agreement prohibiting drug dealing and other illegal activity. (See Clause 16 of our form lease and rental agreements in Chapter 2.)

- Promptly evict tenants who deal drugs or engage in other illegal activity. If a local rent control law or the lease requires "just cause" for eviction, you must be able to prove (to a rent control board or a court) that the tenant was engaging in illegal activity. Chapter 18, Section B.3 discusses how to evict a drug-dealing tenant.

- Make your presence and interest in keeping drug dealing out of the building or neighborhood known among your renters.

- Respond to tenant and neighbor complaints about drug dealing on the rental property.

- Be aware of heavy traffic in and out of the rental premises.

- Inspect rental premises and improve lighting and security.

- Get advice from police and security professionals immediately upon learning of a drug-related problem.

- Consult with security experts to determine whether you have done all that one could reasonably expect to discover and prevent illegal activity, such as drug dealing on your property.

F. LIABILITY FOR ENVIRONMENTAL HAZARDS

In our discussion of property owners' responsibility for dangerous conditions, we have addressed accidental injuries resulting from the landlord's failure to maintain and repair the rental premises (Section A); injuries and losses caused by assailants and other criminals, as well as other tenants or employees (Sections B and D); and problems caused by tolerating a legal nuisance, such as a drug-dealing operation (Section E). As if the list of potential liabilities isn't long enough, we must add yet another: injury from environmental health hazards. Landlords are increasingly likely to be held liable for tenant health prob-

lems resulting from exposure to environmental hazards in the rental premises, even if the landlord didn't cause—or even know about—the danger. This liability is based on many of the same legal theories discussed already in this chapter, such as negligence and negligence per se (negligence that is automatic when a statute is broken).

This section provides an overview of the legal and practical issues involving landlord liability for environmental health hazards. We focus primarily on asbestos and lead, because these problems are most likely to be encountered by rental property owners. We provide an explanation of mold, the latest environmental danger to appear on the scene. We also include a brief discussion on other environmental hazards, including radon and carbon monoxide.

1. Landlord Liability for Asbestos Exposure: OSHA Regulations

Exposure to asbestos has long been associated with increased risk of certain forms of cancer, particularly for workers in the asbestos manufacturing industry or in construction jobs involving the use of asbestos materials. More recently, the danger of asbestos in people's homes has also been acknowledged.

Homes built before the mid-1970s often contain asbestos insulation around heating systems, in ceilings, and in other areas. Until 1981, asbestos was also widely used in many other building materials, such as vinyl flooring and tiles. Asbestos that has begun to break down and enter the air—for example, when it is disturbed during regular maintenance or renovation work—has the potential to become a significant health problem to tenants.

The EPA uses the term "friable" to describe the culprit—material containing less than 1% asbestos, which can be pulverized or crumbled by hand pressure when dry. Common examples of friable construction materials include acoustic "popcorn" ceilings, heating and air conditioning duct wrap, paper backing of linoleum, and wall texturing compounds.

Until quite recently, however, private owners of residential rental property had no obligation to test for the presence of asbestos. A landlord whose tenant developed an asbestos-related disease could successfully defend himself if he could convince the judge or jury that he did not know of the presence of asbestos on his rental property.

Landlords' protection from liability for asbestos exposure all but evaporated on October 1, 1995, when the U.S. Occupational Safety and Health Administration (OSHA) issued a 200-page regulation setting strict workplace standards for the testing, maintenance, and disclosure of asbestos. OSHA's regulations require property owners in general industry, construction work, and shipyards to install warning labels, train staff, and notify people who work in areas that might contain asbestos. In certain situations, owners must actually test for asbestos.

Rental property owners are considered to be part of "general industry" as understood by OSHA, and must adhere to the regulations for general industry in their role as employers of maintenance personnel. This includes large landlords who employ maintenance staff (or managers who do maintenance work), and small-scale landlords who have no employees but who do hire outside contractors for repair and maintenance jobs. OSHA regulations apply to any building constructed before 1981, and apply even if the property owner doesn't plan to remodel or otherwise disturb the structure. Unless the owner rules out the presence of asbestos by having a licensed inspector test the property, it will be presumed that asbestos is present, and the regulations will apply.

> ## PROPOSITION 65 DISCLOSURES
>
> Landlords who employ ten or more employees must comply with California's Proposition 65. (Health & Safety Code §§ 25249 and following.) The law does not require you to test for asbestos or other specified harmful chemicals, but if you know that your property contains them, you must inform your tenants. If you're not sure (which is the case for most owners), disclose this, too. You don't have to make any formal disclosures if the property has been tested and has received a clean bill of health.

a. Levels of OSHA's Protective Requirements

OSHA protections vary according to the level of asbestos disturbed by the activity being done. For example, workers who are involved in the removal of large amounts of asbestos receive maximum protection, whereas those who merely perform superficial custodial tasks need less.

• **Asbestos exposure in custodial work.** Employees and contractors whose work involves direct contact with asbestos or materials that are presumed to include it—for example, certain types of floors and ceilings—or who clean in areas near asbestos are subject to OSHA regulations designed for "general industry." The handyman employee who washes asbestos tiles in the lobby of a pre-1981 building, or who installs, replaces and tests smoke alarms that are embedded in acoustic-tile ceilings made with asbestos, would fall within this category. The general industry regulations require the worker to receive two hours of instruction (including appropriate cleaning techniques) and to use special work procedures under the supervision of a trained superior. The general industry standard does not require testing for asbestos. Of course, if it is known that high levels of asbestos are present, even custodial tasks must be performed with appropriately higher levels of protection, such as special masks and clothing.

- **Asbestos exposure in renovation or repair work.** A stricter set of procedures is triggered by any intentional disturbance of asbestos or asbestos-containing materials (for example, in heating systems or ceilings). This invariably happens when asbestos materials are subject to repair or renovation. At this level of activity, the landowner must test for the presence of asbestos. OSHA's "construction standard" requires exposure assessment (air monitoring for asbestos), sixteen hours of worker training per year, oversight by a specially trained person, and respiratory protection in some situations. In addition, employers must conduct medical surveillance of certain employees and maintain specified records for many years. So, for example, a decision to replace that ugly, stained acoustic-tile ceiling would require, first, that the material be tested, followed by worker protection measures that are appropriate to the level of exposure expected by the professional tester.

b. How OSHA Regulations Affect Tenants

You may still be wondering what OSHA's workplace regulations for asbestos have to do with your obligations to your tenants, who are not, after all, your employees or hired contractors. The answer, simply put, is that once the genie is out of the bottle, you cannot put him back in. When you comply with OSHA's testing and maintenance requirements for your employees or contractors, and your professional tester discovers that asbestos—a health risk—is either airborne or about to become so, you cannot pretend that you do not know that it is present with respect to your tenants as well. The presence of asbestos, regardless of how you found out about it, becomes simply an undisclosed, hidden, and dangerous defect that you are obligated to disclose to tenants.

If asbestos is present on your property and a tenant's lawyer can show that it caused the tenant's illness, you may be found liable on legal theories in addition to failing to disclose a known hidden defect. For example, the presence of airborne asbestos may be argued as a breach of the implied warranty of habitability, which would give the tenant the opportunity to break the lease and move out without notice, pay less rent, withhold the entire rent, or sue to force the landlord to bring the dwelling up to a habitable level.

There is no escaping OSHA's asbestos regulations under the theory that what you don't know about can't cause legal problems. Owners of residential rental property may think that they can escape the clutches of OSHA's asbestos regulations by personally doing minor repair and maintenance and hiring independent contractors (whom they hope will ignore the testing requirement) to do the major jobs. This may work for a while, until the first law-abiding contractor, who acknowledges his independent duty to protect his employees, lists asbestos testing as a part of his bid. The results of the tests will, of course, confer knowledge on the part of the owner.

KEY ASPECTS OF OSHA ASBESTOS REGULATIONS

Our discussion of the impact of the OSHA regulations on residential rental property owners is not intended to give you all the necessary information to conduct renovations and otherwise manage your business safely and within the requirements of the regulations. You'll need to get a copy of the actual regulations for that. (See "Resources: Asbestos.") Briefly, however, you should at least know the following:

Buildings affected. The regulations apply to pre-1981 structures, and if a newer structure contains asbestos, the regulations apply to it as well.

Where asbestos is likely to be found. The regulations cover two classes of materials: those that definitely contain asbestos (such as certain kinds of flooring and ceilings), and those that the law presumes to contain asbestos. The second class is extremely inclusive, describing, among other things, any surfacing material that is "sprayed, troweled on, or otherwise applied." Under this definition, virtually every dwelling must be suspected of containing asbestos.

What work is covered. The regulations apply to custodial work and to renovation and repair work. Mere custodial work does not require the stringent training and precautions that are triggered by renovation work. It is not clear at this time how some typical apartment management tasks (such as mopping asbestos tile floors, deep cleaning of a rental unit before a new tenant moves in, and routine maintenance of painted surfaces) will be classed. To be on the safe side, it would be wise to assume that these tasks are covered, and to prepare your employees accordingly.

RESOURCES: ASBESTOS

For further information on asbestos rules, inspections, and control, contact the nearest office of the U.S. Occupational Safety and Health Administration (OSHA) or call 800-321-OSHA (6742).

OSHA has developed interactive computer software called "Asbestos Advisor" that will walk you through questions designed to help identify asbestos in your property and suggest the most sensible solution. It is available at the OSHA website at www.osha.gov.

c. How Landlords Can Limit Liability for Asbestos

Limiting your liability for asbestos-related injuries (to tenants and workers alike) begins with your understanding a fundamental point: Unless you perform detailed testing to rule out the presence of asbestos, every pre-1981 structure must be treated as if it does contain asbestos. Acknowledging that you must follow the OSHA procedures for custodial and renovation/repair work should trigger the following actions:

- Get a copy of the OSHA regulations, which explain in detail what we have touched upon here. (See "Resources: Asbestos.")

- Realize that almost any repair and maintenance work you do—no matter how small—may involve asbestos materials. Test for the presence of asbestos in advance for the benefit of workers and tenants.

- Make disclosures to tenants if you learn of the presence of asbestos, even if its presence is not yet a problem. For example, if there is asbestos in the walls but it is not a health problem, point out that it is not likely to pose a danger, and that you will monitor the situation.

- Where possible, don't disturb asbestos. The conventional wisdom is that unless the asbestos material has begun to break down and enter the air, it is usually best to leave it alone and monitor it. This may mean that it simply may not make economic sense to do certain types of remodeling jobs. Seek an expert's opinion before taking action.

- If you learn that asbestos material is airborne and a health hazard, seek an expert's advice on how to remedy the situation. When removal of 100 square feet or more is necessary, hire certified asbestos-removal specialists, and check to make sure the debris is legally disposed of in approved hazardous waste disposal sites.

- Make sure tenants don't make repairs to or otherwise invade any spaces containing asbestos, such as walls and ceilings. This might even consist of hanging pictures or otherwise making small holes. Absurd as this might seem, remember that you are accomplishing two things with your cautious approach: You are protecting your tenants' health, and you are making it harder for a lawsuit-happy tenant to file a frivolous claim. Require your tenants to report any deterioration to you. Monitor the asbestos situation as part of regular safety and maintenance procedures. (See Chapter 11, Sections J and K.)

2. Landlord Liability for Lead Exposure: Title X

Exposure to lead-based paint dust and chips and lead water pipes may lead to serious health problems, particularly in children. Brain damage, attention disorders, and hyperactivity have all been associated with lead poisoning. Landlords who are found responsible for lead poisoning may face liability for a child's lifelong disability. Jury awards and settlements for lead poisoning are typically enormous, because they cover remedial treatment and education of a child for the rest of his life, and include an award for the estimated lifelong loss of earning capacity caused by the injury. The cost of a typical "slip and fall" injury pales in comparison to some of the multimillion-dollar jury awards and settlements for lead poisoning.

Buildings constructed before 1978 are likely to contain some source of lead, be it lead-based paint, lead pipes, or lead-based solder used on copper pipes. (In 1978, the federal government required the reduction of lead in house paint; lead pipes are generally only found in homes built before 1930, and lead-based solder in home plumbing systems was banned in 1988.) Pre-1950 housing in poor, urban neighborhoods that has been allowed to age and deteriorate is by far the greatest source of lead-based paint poisonings.

To help combat the health problems caused by lead poisoning, the Residential Lead-Based Paint Hazard Reduction Act (42 U.S.C. § 2852d) became law in 1992. Commonly referred to as Title X (Ten), the goal of this law is "lead hazard reduction," which will be accomplished by evaluating the risk of poisoning in each housing situation and taking the appropriate steps to reduce the hazard. Much of Title X is directed to federal housing and federally financed private housing—that is, federally owned and managed housing (known as "HUD housing") and federally subsidized private housing.

Title X also addresses private rental housing. The Occupational Safety and Health Administration (OSHA) and the Environmental Protection Agency (EPA) have written regulations explaining the law (24 Code of Federal Regulations Part 35 and 40 Code of Federal Regulations Part 745). Compliance with Title X became effective for all landlords as of December 6, 1996.

a. Disclosure of Lead Paint Hazards

You must inform tenants, before they sign or renew a lease or rental agreement, of any information you possess on lead paint hazards on the property, including individual rental units, common areas and garages, tool sheds, other outbuildings, signs, fences, and play areas. If your property has been tested (which must be done only by a state-certified lead inspector), you must show a copy of the report, or a summary written by the inspector, to tenants.

With certain exceptions (listed below), you must give every new (or renewing) tenant a disclosure sheet, even if you have not tested for lead paint hazards. You can use the disclosure form developed by the EPA, or you can design your own, as long as it meets the EPA requirements.

WHAT'S A LEAD-PAINT HAZARD?

A "lead hazard" includes deteriorated lead-based paint, lead contaminated dust or soil, or the results of disturbing lead paint without containing the dust. The suspect paint, dust, or soil will become a legal hazard depending on two measurements: the concentration of lead and the area that's affected.

Concentration. The chart below shows the minimum concentrations that will establish a lead hazard.

Lead in Paint Hazard Levels	Lead in Bare Soil Hazard Levels	Lead in Dust Hazardous Levels
Lab test results of 5,000 ppm (parts per million) or 0.5% or more (by weight)	Lab test results of 400 ppm or more in bare soil in areas where children play	Dust from interior floors with 50 micrograms of lead per square foot (50 μg/ft²) or more
XRF test results of 1.0 milligrams of lead per square centimeter (1.0 mg/cm²) or more	Lab test results of 1,000 ppm or more in all other areas	Dust from interior horizontal window surfaces with 250 micrograms of lead per square foot (250 μg/ft²) or more
		Dust from exterior floors and exterior horizontal window surfaces with 800 micrograms of lead per square foot (800 μg/ft²) or more

Source: California Department of Health Services, www.dhs.ca.gov/childlead.

Area Affected. Soil, paint, or dust with sufficient lead will become a legal hazard if it is present in an area that is equal to, or bigger than:

- two square feet in any one interior room or space

- twenty square feet on exterior surfaces, or

- ten percent of the surface area on the interior or exterior of a component such as window sills, baseboards, and trim.

Finally, if lead-based paint is "deteriorated" or "disturbed" and is associated with a person with a blood lead level over 10 micrograms per deciliter, it's a lead hazard, no matter what the concentration of the dust, soil, or paint or the size of its presence. (Health & Safety Code § 17920.10.)

HOW LEAD POISONING OCCURS

When the dangers of lead-based paint were first discovered, the ingestion of lead-based paint chips was considered the most common means of poisoning. While this source (or "vector") for lead poisoning certainly exists, it is now widely acknowledged that airborne lead-laden dust caused by the deterioration of exposed lead-based paint is the greater culprit. Falling on window sills, walls and floors, this dust makes its way into the human body when it is stirred up, becomes airborne, and is inhaled, or when it is transmitted directly from hand to mouth. Exterior lead-based house paint is also a potential problem in that it can slough off walls directly into the soil and be tracked into the house.

An equally powerful source of lead-based dust is the dust that results from renovations or remodeling, including, unfortunately, those projects undertaken to rid the premises of the lead-based paint. Lead poisoning can also occur by drinking water that contains leached-out lead from lead pipes, or from broken-down lead solder used in copper pipes.

Children between the ages of 18 months and five years are the most likely to become lead-based paint victims. Their poisoning is detected when they become ill or, increasingly, in routine examinations of presymptomatic children where elevated blood levels of lead easily appear.

You'll find a tear-out version of the EPA's Disclosure of Information on Lead-Based Paint or Lead-Based Paint Hazards form (in English and in Spanish) in Appendix B. The CD-ROM that accompanies this book also includes this form.

What about tenants who began renting before December 6, 1996: Must you provide disclosure forms for them, too? Your compliance obligations depend on whether the current tenant has a lease or is renting on a month-to-month basis:

- **Tenants with leases.** You need not comply with Title X until the lease ends and the tenant renews or stays on as a month-to-month tenant.

- **Month-to-month tenants.** You should have given month-to-month tenants a disclosure statement when you collected your first rent check dated on or after December 6, 1996.

As you'll see, the disclosure form has a place for the tenant to initial, indicating that the tenant has received the form. Make a copy of the initialed form and keep it safely in your records for at least three years. If a federal or state agency questions whether you're complying with the disclosure law, you'll have a cabinet full of signed forms as evidence. And, if a tenant claims to have developed symptoms of lead poisoning and points to your property, you'll want to have proof that you disclosed what you knew.

b. Information on Lead Hazards

You must give all tenants the lead hazard information booklet "Protect Your Family From Lead in Your Home," written by the EPA. You may reproduce the booklet in a legal-size, 8½ x 14-inch format, and attach it to the lease or rental agreement. The graphics in the original pamphlet must be included. Or, you may use California's pamphlet, approved by the EPA, *Environmental Hazards: A Guide for Homeowners, Buyers, Landlords and Tenants.* See "Resources: Lead," below, for information on these booklets.

You'll find a tear-out version of the EPA booklet "Protect Your Family From Lead in Your Home" in Appendix B. The CD-ROM that accompanies this book also includes this form.

LEAD INSPECTIONS

While lead inspections are not required by federal law, you may voluntarily arrange an inspection in order to certify that your property is leadfree and exempt from federal regulations. (See list of exemptions, below.) Also, if you take out a loan or buy insurance, your bank or insurance company may require a lead inspection.

Professional lead inspectors don't always inspect every unit in large, multifamily properties. Instead, they inspect a sampling of the units and apply their conclusions to the property as a whole. Giving your tenants the results and conclusions of a buildingwide evaluation satisfies the law, even if a particular unit was not tested. If, however, you have specific information regarding a unit that is inconsistent with the buildingwide evaluation, you must disclose it to the tenant.

c. Penalties

The EPA doesn't deploy the lead police to make sure that landlords deliver a lead hazard information booklet and disclosure statement to every tenant. However, the EPA will respond if a tenant calls and complains. This will probably result in no more than a letter or call from the inspectors, since the EPA will not cite you unless your noncompliance with the laws is willful and continuing. But a landlord who continues to ignore Title X may find himself subject to the penalties of up to $10,000. You may have to pay substantial damages to a tenant who is injured by lead and who could have taken steps to avoid the exposure had you warned him of its known presence.

RENTAL PROPERTIES EXEMPT FROM TITLE X REGULATIONS

These rental properties are exempt from the federal Title X regulations:

- Housing for which a construction permit was obtained, or on which construction was started, after January 1, 1978. Older buildings that have been completely renovated since 1978 are not exempt, even if every painted surface was removed or replaced.

- Housing certified as leadfree by a state-accredited lead inspector. Lead free means the absence of any lead paint, even paint that has been completely painted over and encapsulated.

- Lofts, efficiencies, studios, and other "zero-bedroom" units, including dormitory housing and rentals in sorority and fraternity houses. University-owned apartments and married student housing are not exempted.

- Short-term vacation rentals of 100 days or fewer.

- A single room rented in a residential home.

- Housing designed for persons with disabilities (as explained in HUD's Fair Housing Accessibility Guidelines, 56 Code of Federal Regulations § 9472, 3/6/91), unless any child less than six years old resides there or is expected to reside there.

- Retirement communities (housing designed for seniors, where one or more tenant is at least 62 years old), unless children under the age of six are present or expected to live there.

Cities and counties may have their own lead laws imposing additional requirements on property owners. For example, the City and County of San Francisco strictly regulates how lead paint may be worked on and removed. Check with your local

IT MAKES SENSE TO TEST FOR LEAD

Unless your rental property was built after 1978, consider testing your rental property for lead. Here are seven good reasons why:

1. **It's cheaper than a lawsuit.** Lead hazard control (as discussed below) is much less burdensome than going through a lawsuit, let alone living with the knowledge that a child's health has been damaged.

2. **Deliberate ignorance won't shield you from a lawsuit.** Even though the EPA regulations do not require testing, ignorance of the condition of your property may not shield you from liability in a lawsuit brought by an injured tenant. At some point, a court may rule that the danger of lead paint in older housing is so well known that owners of older housing will be presumed to know of the danger. Should this "imputed knowledge" of the hazard ever be attributed to you, a jury will have a difficult time believing that you were truly ignorant. Moreover, an injured tenant may be able to show the court that it was likely that you were, in fact, apprised of the lead problem—through your attendance at seminars for landlords, subscriptions to periodicals aimed at property owners, and even reading this book!

3. **You can't legally avoid renting to children.** Recognizing that children are the ones most at risk for lead poisoning, you cannot simply refuse to rent to tenants with children—this is illegal discrimination under federal and state law. (See Chapter 9, Section C3.)

4. **You can't avoid responsibility by attempting a clever legal dodge.** You cannot count on a clause in your lease or rental agreement attempting to shift responsibility for lead-based injuries from the landlord to the tenant to protect you. This type of clause (called an "exculpatory clause," in legalese) will not be upheld by a California court. Ironically, if you make liability for lead poisoning a subject of an exculpatory clause, and the clause is not upheld in court, you will have effectively established that you were aware of the lead problem. (Why else would you have written such a clause?)

5. **Eventually, you'll have to test to satisfy a seller or a lender.** If you attempt to refinance or sell your rental property, you will find that most major lenders will require lead testing before a loan is approved.

6. **Your insurance company may eventually require it.** You can expect that your own insurance company may soon require lead testing as a condition of issuing a policy. Lead poisoning cases are incredibly expensive—for example, in two New York cases recently, injured tenants were awarded $7 million and $10million. It is only a matter of time before the insurance industry nationwide realizes that it cannot continue to blindly insure all properties against lead poisoning. (Consider the reaction of the insurance industry to earthquakes and wildfires in California, where coverage for these disasters is now often difficult to procure.)

7. **Your tenant may address the problem on his own.** Effective January 1, 2003, the presence of lead paint hazards on residential rental property joined the ranks of problems that render property "untenantable." (CC §1041.1; H&S § 17920.10; see "What's a Lead-Paint Hazard?," above.) This means that a tenant can use the repair-and-deduct remedy or withhold rent if hazards are present and you don't do anything about them. You'll want to avoid withheld rent or serious repairs undertaken by persons you haven't hired.

building department for any lead paint laws that might apply to residential property owners.

LEADED MINI-BLINDS

Some imported mini-blinds from China, Taiwan, Indonesia, and Mexico are likely to contain lead, but are not banned by the Consumer Product Safety Commission. If your property has leaded mini-blinds, you do not have to disclose this fact unless you know that the blinds have begun to deteriorate and produce lead dust. To avoid problems, use mini-blinds from other sources or different kinds of window coverings.

Your insurance company may not cover you if a tenant is injured by lead that you knew about and failed to deal with. Insurance policies uniformly deny coverage for losses that you knew (or should have known) were likely. If you understand the effect of lead on the human body, once you know about the presence of lead on your property, you can reasonably expect poisonings. Facing a lawsuit without insurance will probably end your business.

d. Why Landlords Should Test for Lead

Before the advent of Title X and the EPA regulations concerning disclosure of lead in residential rental property, landlords who suspected that there might be lead lurking in the tenants' paint or water faced a difficult choice:

- Landlords who had their property tested and learned that lead was present had thereby gained the knowledge that their property had a dangerous defect. As a result, these landlords placed themselves at increased legal risk for tenant lawsuits unless they took prompt and effective remedial action.

- On the other hand, landlords who didn't test had to live with the nagging suspicion that their property might be making their tenants sick and damaging the development of children exposed to lead.

Although the EPA regulations do not require a landlord to test for lead, practical considerations point strongly in that direction. It comes down to this:

- If your rental property was built after 1978, it is unlikely to have lead poisoning problems, and you've probably got nothing to worry about.

- If your property was built before 1978 (particularly pre-1950 housing in poor condition), you should consider having the property inspected—especially if you rent to families with children under the age of six.

In sum, as with many landlord problems discussed in this book, there is no effective way to hide a serious lead problem over the long run. Your best bet is to tackle it directly on your own terms, before you are forced to do so. The next section explains how to go about getting information on testing and reducing one of the most serious lead hazard risks—lead-based paint.

e. How to Clean Up Lead-Based Paint

Lead is relatively easy to detect—you can buy home use kits that contain a simple swab that turns color when drawn over a lead-based surface. Knowing how much lead is present and how to best clean it up, however, are subjects for the experts. It is beyond the scope of this book to present detailed remediation or clean-up instructions, if only because each situation will require a specific response. We can, however, give you an overview of the current thinking on the issue.

The most important thing to understand when faced with a lead paint problem is that sometimes the wholesale removal of the paint, or even sanding and repainting, may not be the best solution. This is because these types of renovations often create and release tremendous amounts of lead dust, the deadliest vector for poisoning. Unless the job is done by trained personnel, the well-intentioned removal of lead paint may actually create a far bigger problem than originally existed. California has training and licensing requirements for lead abatement professionals.

Drastic measures may be needed when the underlying structure itself is so deteriorated that safety requires a from-the-bottom-up approach, but this is rarely the case. The most effective response to lead-based paint is usually a program consisting of these steps:

1. Inspect for deteriorated paint. Pay close attention to areas that get the most use (floors and window channels), and determine whether lead is present. An environmental engineer will be able to tell you how much lead is present at floor level and above, which will alert you as to whether your property exceeds the amounts allowable by law.

2. Clean up lead-contaminated dust with a good vacuum cleaner and detergent that is specifically designed to pick up lead. Regular household cleaners, even TSP, do not do a very effective job of capturing lead, nor will a standard vacuum cleaner be able to filter out the microscopic lead particles. Consider using a lead-specific cleanser ("Ledizolv" is one such product) and buying or renting a "HEPA" vacuum (a "high efficiency particle arresting" vacuum, often available for rent from hardware stores or equipment rental agencies). If you are dealing with lead dust, wear a mask and disposable protective clothing.

3. Repaint with non-lead-based paint to provide a strong, cleanable surface.

4. Educate your tenants on how to identify, control and clean up any lead dust that might still be present. The EPA's "Protect Your Family From Lead in Your Home," a pamphlet you will be required to give to each resident under Title X, will help you in this respect.

5. Monitor lead dust situations. Design your periodic safety inspections (discussed in Chapter 11,

Section K) so that you keep on top of any deterioration of lead-based surfaces.

6. Do as much as possible, within the recommendations of your experts, to prevent the accumulation of lead dust. Theoretically, some lead dust problems might be containable by frequent, lead-specific, and thorough cleaning, rather than repainting. There are some professional cleaning companies that specialize in lead dust cleaning. It is risky, however, to entrust that specialized housecleaning job to your tenants, even if you are prepared to give them the appropriate vacuum cleaners and detergents. You cannot, from a practical point of view, adequately monitor their housekeeping practices. Instead, prevent the accumulation of lead dust by painting over lead paint, if possible, even if this solution appears more costly than dust maintenance. It will certainly cost less than a lawsuit.

3. Renovations and Lead Hazards

When you renovate occupied rental units or common areas in buildings constructed before 1978, EPA regulations require that current tenants receive lead hazard information before the renovation work begins. (40 CFR §§ 745.80-88.) The regulations were developed under the federal Toxic Substances Control Act (15 U.S.C. §§ 2681-2692). The EPA has written a helpful booklet, "The Lead-Based Paint Pre-Renovation Education Rule," which you can download from their website. See "Resources: Lead," below.

The obligation to distribute lead information rests with the "renovator." If you hire an outside contractor to perform renovation work, the contractor is the renovator. But if you, your property manager, your superintendent, or other employees perform the renovation work, the landlord is the renovator and must give out the required information.

The type of information that the renovator must give to tenants depends on where the renovation is taking place. If an occupied rental unit is being worked on, you must give the tenant a copy of the EPA pamphlet "Protect Your Family From Lead In Your Home." If common areas will be affected, you will have to distribute a notice to every rental unit in the building.

a. What Qualifies as a Renovation?

According to EPA regulations, a "renovation" is any change to an occupied rental unit or common area of your building that disturbs painted surfaces. Here are some examples:

- removing or modifying a painted door, wall, baseboard, or ceiling

- scraping or sanding paint, or

- removing a large structure like a wall, partition, or window.

   Not every renovation triggers the federal law, though. There are four big exceptions:

- **Emergency renovations.** If a sudden or unexpected event, such as a fire or flood, requires you to make emergency repairs to a rental unit or to your property's common areas, there's no need to distribute lead hazard information to tenants before work begins.

- **Minor repairs or maintenance.** Minor work that affects two square feet or less of a painted surface is also exempt. Minor repairs include routine electrical and plumbing work, so long as no more than two square feet of the wall, ceiling, or other painted surface gets disturbed by the work.

- **Renovations in lead-free properties.** If the rental unit or building in which the renovation takes place has been certified as containing no lead paint, you're not required to give out the required information.

- **Common area renovations in buildings with three or fewer units.** Only buildings with four or more units are required to give tenants information about common area renovations.

   Repainting a rental unit in preparation for a new tenant doesn't qualify as a "renovation" unless accompanied by sanding, scraping or other surface preparation activities that may generate paint dust. Minor "spot" scraping or sanding can qualify for the "minor repairs and maintenance" exception if no more than two square feet of paint is disturbed on any surface to be painted. (EPA Interpretive Guidance, Part I, May 28, 1999.)

b. Give Out EPA Pamphlet When Renovating Occupied Rental Units

Before starting a renovation to an occupied rental unit, the renovator must give the EPA pamphlet "Protect Your Family From Lead In Your Home" to at least one adult occupant of the unit being occupied, preferably the tenant. This is the same one you gave new tenants when they signed their lease or rental agreement. This requirement applies to all rental properties, including single-family homes and duplexes, unless the property has been certified lead-free by an inspector.

   You may mail or hand deliver the pamphlet to the tenant. If you mail it, you must get a "certificate of mailing" from the post office dated at least seven days before the renovation work begins. If you hand deliver it, have the tenant sign and date a receipt acknowledging that the pamphlet was received before renovation work began in the unit. Make sure the tenant will receive the pamphlet 60 days (or fewer) before the work begins (delivering the pamphlet more than 60 days in advance won't do).

c. Give Out Notice When Renovating Common Areas

If your building has four or more units, the renovator —you or your contractor—must notify tenants of all "affected units" about the renovation and tell them how to obtain a free copy of the EPA pamphlet "Protect Your Family From Lead In Your Home." (40 CFR § 745.85(b)(2).) In most cases, common area renovations will affect all units in your property, meaning that all tenants must be notified about the renovation. But when renovating a "limited use common area" in a large apartment building, such as the 16th floor hallway, you need only notify those units serviced by, or in close proximity to, the limited use common area. The EPA defines large buildings as those having 50 or more units.

   To comply, the renovator must deliver a notice to every affected unit describing the nature and location of the renovation work, its location, and the dates you expect to begin and finish work (see a sample "Common Area Renovations Notice," below). If you can't provide specific dates, you may use terms like "on or about," "in early June," or "in late July" to describe expected starting and ending dates for the renovation. The notices *must be delivered within 60 days before work begins*. The notices may be slipped under apartment doors or given to any adult occupant of the rental unit. (You may not mail the notices, however.) After the notices are delivered, keep a copy in your file, together with a note describing the date and manner in which you delivered the notices to rental units.

d. Penalties

Failing to give tenants the required information about renovation lead hazards can result in harsh penalties. Renovators who knowingly violate the regulations can get hit with a penalty of up to $27,500 per day for each violation. Willful violations can also result in imprisonment.

Common Area Renovations Notice

March 1, 200x

Dear Tenant,

Please be advised that we will begin renovating the hallways on or about March 15, 200x. Specifically, we will be removing and replacing the baseboards, wallpaper, and trim in the 2nd, 3rd, and 4th floor corridors, and sanding and repainting the ceilings. We expect the work to be completed in early May, 200x.

You may obtain a free copy of the pamphlet "Protect Your Family From Lead In Your Home" from Paul Hogan, the building manager. Paul may be reached at (212) 555-1212.

We will make every attempt to minimize inconvenience to tenants during the renovation process. If you have questions about the proposed renovation work, feel free to contact Mr. Hogan or me.

Very truly yours,

Lawrence Levy

Lawrence Levy, Manager

RESOURCES: LEAD

Information on the evaluation and control of lead dust, and copies of the "Protect Your Family From Lead in Your Home" pamphlet, may be obtained from the regional offices of the federal EPA or by calling the National Lead Information Center at 800-424-LEAD. Information (including pamphlets on renovation and a parents' guide) is also available from the EPA on its website: www.epa.gov/lead.

The U.S. Department of Housing and Urban Development (HUD) issues a pamphlet entitled "Guidance on the Lead-Based Paint Disclosure Rule, Parts I and II," which may be obtained by contacting your nearest HUD office. You can also get this information online from the HUD Lead Office website at www.hud.gov/offices/lead. Click the "Lead Paint Disclosure Rule" link. The U.S. Occupational Safety and Health Administration (OSHA) has developed interactive software, "Lead in Construction," that will help you assess the lead problems on your property and design appropriate responses. You can access the program by going to the OSHA website at www.osha.gov. In the Search window, type in "Lead in Construction" and choose the hit that corresponds to software.

HUD also maintains a "Lead Listing" of names, addresses, and phone numbers of trained lead paint contractors (for testing and abatement) in every state. Call 1-888-LEAD-LIST or access the list on the Web at www.leadlisting.org.

For a copy of the California Department of Health Services' *Environmental Hazards: A Guide for Homeowners, Buyers, Landlords, and Tenants*, or a list of state-certified lead inspectors, contact the Department of Health Services at 800-597-LEAD. Their website is www.dhs.ca.gov/childlead.

The lead paint renovation rules can be found at 40 Code of Federal Regulations Part 745, Federal Register Vol. 63, No. 104, pp. 29908–29921.

 Require renovation contractors to give out required information. The federal disclosure requirements apply to "renovators." When you hire an outside contractor to perform renovations in rental units or common areas, the contractor is responsible for giving out the required information. To avoid any misunderstandings, make sure your renovation contract or work agreement specifically requires the contractor to provide all required lead hazard information to tenants as provided under federal law and regulations.

4. Landlord Liability for Exposure to Radon

Radon is a naturally occurring radioactive gas that is present throughout the atmosphere. Exposure to large concentrations of radon is associated with lung cancer. It can enter and contaminate a house built on soil and rock containing uranium deposits, or enter through water from private wells drilled in uranium-rich soil. Radon becomes a lethal health threat when high levels are trapped in tightly sealed homes that have been insulated to keep in heat or have poor ventilation, when it escapes from building materials that have incorporated uranium-filled rocks and soils (like certain types of composite tiles or bricks), or when it is released into the air from aerated household water that has passed through underground concentrations of uranium. Problems occur most frequently in areas where rocky soil is relatively rich in uranium and in climates where occupants keep their windows tightly shut—to maintain heat in the winter and air conditioning in the summer.

Homes in California are not at great risk for excessive radon concentrations. The state's Department of Health Services estimates that only two percent of the housing stock has significant problems. Housing in parts of the Sierra Nevada mountains, portions of the inland valleys, Santa Barbara and Ventura Counties and the Los Angeles basin are statistically more likely to have radon difficulties than elsewhere. But this does not mean that other locations are immune— any site can have dangerous radon levels.

Fortunately, there are usually simple, inexpensive ways to dispel radon levels in buildings. Ventilation measures will effectively disperse the gas in most situations. These measures range from the obvious

(open the windows and provide cross ventilation) to the somewhat complex (sealing cracks in the foundation, or sucking radon out of the soil before it enters the foundation and venting it into the air above the roof through a pipe). According to the EPA, a typical household radon problem can be solved for $500 to $2,500.

Is radon contamination something that should concern you? Should you test your property? There are currently no laws that require a private landlord to detect and remedy the presence of radon. And, admittedly, your chances of a problem are low. This does not necessarily mean, however, that under certain circumstances you could not be found liable for radon exposure. If you know that other properties in your area or neighborhood contain worrisome levels of radon gas, you are courting trouble if, in fact, radon is a problem on your property and a tenant sues you for an increased risk of cancer. The tenant will argue that you were negligent in refusing to heed the obvious signs of danger. In short, the ostrich approach will not protect you if a jury decides that any reasonable person in your position would have taken steps to confront the possibility of a radon problem.

RESOURCES: RADON

The California Department of Health Services, Indoor Air Quality Program, gives consumers lots of information about radon and how to detect it on their website, www.dhs.ca.gov/radon.

Additional information on the detection and removal of radon is available from the EPA's national radon hotline at 800-767-7236. You can ask for a copy of their booklet, "Consumer's Guide to Radon Reduction."

You will have to do a little work to find out whether your property is affected by dangerous levels of radon. Your city planning department or your insurance broker may know about local geology and radon dangers. If you decide to test, consider starting with the inexpensive do-it-yourself kit available from the Department of Health Services (see "Resources: Radon," below). If you decide to hire a professional, use an inspector certified by the EPA. Testing takes at least three days, and sometimes months. If testing indicates high radon levels, be sure to warn tenants and correct the problem.

5. Mold

Mold is the newest environmental hazard driving lawsuits against rental property owners. Across the country, tenants have won multimillion dollar cases against landlords for significant health problems—such as rashes, chronic fatigue, nausea, cognitive losses, hemorrhaging, and asthma—allegedly caused by exposure to "toxic molds" in their building. In a typical case, the Delaware Supreme Court in May 2001 upheld a $1.4 million award to two tenants who suffered asthma and other health problems caused by mold that grew when the landlord refused to fix leaks in their apartment.

Mold is also among the most controversial of environmental hazards now in the news. There is considerable debate within the scientific and medical community about which molds, and what situations, pose serious health risks to people in their homes. In fact, the scientific evidence increasingly shows that it's very unlikely that exposure to most molds will cause more than an allergic reaction in some people.

There is no such debate among plaintiff's lawyers, however, and juries have increasingly found landlords legally liable for tenant health problems associated with exposure to mold. As a result, it is crucial that you understand how to identify and avoid problems with mold in your rental property—before you find yourself in court.

a. Where Mold Is Found

Mold comes in various colors and shapes. The villains—with names like stachybotrys, penicillium, aspergilus, paecilomyces, and fusarium—are black, white, green, or gray. Some are powdery, others shiny. Some molds look and smell disgusting; others are barely seen—hidden between walls, under floors and ceilings, or in less accessible spots such as basements and attics.

Mold often grows on water-soaked materials, such as wall paneling, paint, fabric, ceiling tiles, newspapers, or cardboard boxes. However, all that's really needed is an organic food source, water, and time. Throw in a little warmth and the organism will grow very quickly, sometimes spreading within 24 hours.

Humidity sets up prime growing conditions for mold. Buildings in naturally humid climates of Texas, California, and the South have experienced more mold problems than residences in drier climates. But mold can grow irrespective of the natural climate when moisture is present. Here's how:

- Floods, leaking pipes, windows, or roofs may introduce moisture that will lead to mold growth in any structure—in fact, these are the leading causes of mold.

- Tightly sealed buildings (common with new construction) may trap mold-producing moisture inside.

- Overcrowding, poor ventilation, numerous over-watered houseplants, and poor housekeeping may also contribute to the spread of mold.

Unsightly as it may be, most mold is not harmful to tenants' health—for example, the mold that grows on shower tiles is not dangerous. It takes an expert to know whether a particular mold is harmful or just annoying. Your first response to discovering mold shouldn't be to call in the folks with the white suits and ventilators. Most of the time, proper clean-up and maintenance will remove mold. Better yet, focus on early detection and prevention of mold as discussed below.

b. Laws on Mold Affecting Landlords

A landlord's responsibilities regarding mold have not been clearly spelled out in building codes, ordinances, statutes, and regulations. The main reason for the lack of standards is that the problem has only recently been acknowledged. Some states have responded to mold problems in schools, but addressing residential issues has been slow to come.

California is the first state to take steps towards establishing permissible mold standards. The Toxic Mold Protection Act of 2001 (H&S §§ 26100 and following) authorizes the state's Department of Health Services (DHS) to adopt, if feasible, permissible exposure levels ("PELs") for indoor mold for sensitive populations, such as children and people with compromised immune systems or respiratory problems. If this is not feasible, the DHS may develop guidelines for determining when the presence of mold is a health threat. In addition, the California DHS will develop identification and remediation standards which will guide contractors, owners, and landlords in how to inspect for mold and safely remove it.

When the Department issues its findings, they will be posted on the Department's website at www.dhs.ca.gov. Once those standards are developed, a landlord who is aware of mold concentrations in a residential unit will be required to notify current and prospective tenants of the presence of such concentrations. (See the DHS website, given below in "Resources: Mold.")

San Francisco has added mold to its list of nuisances, thereby allowing tenants to sue landlords under private and public nuisance laws if they fail to clean up serious outbreaks. (San Francisco Health Code § 581.) See Chapter 11, Section I for information on nuisance laws.

c. Landlord Liability for Tenant Exposure to Mold

With little law on the specific subject of mold, landlords must look to their general responsibility to maintain and repair rental property (the subject of Chapter 11) for guidance. Your legal duty to provide and maintain habitable premises naturally extends to fixing leaking pipes, windows, and roofs—the causes of most mold outbreaks. If you don't take care of leaks and mold grows as a result, you may be held responsible if a tenant can convince a judge or jury that the mold has caused a health problem. Your position, legally, is really no different from what happens if you fail to deal with any health or safety hazard on your property. For example, if you know

about (but fail to fix) a loose step, you'll foot the bill if someone is injured as a result of tripping on the step.

You are less likely to be held legally responsible when mold grows as the result of your tenant's behavior, such as keeping the apartment tightly shut, creating high humidity, and failing to maintain necessary cleanliness. You cannot be expected to police your tenant's lifestyle (in fact, California's privacy statute prevents you from making unannounced inspections, as explained in Chapter 13). When a tenant's own negligence is the sole cause of injury, the landlord is not liable.

d. Prevention: The Best Way to Avoid Mold Problems

As we've stressed many times in this book, the issue for landlords is not who will win in court, but how you can avoid getting dragged into a lawsuit, even one that you would probably win. Your efforts should be directed squarely at preventing the conditions that lead to the growth of mold. This requires maintaining the structural integrity of your property (the roof, plumbing, and windows) and adopting a thorough and prompt system for detecting and handling problems. (Chapter 11 explains how in great detail.)

The following steps are especially important if you live in a humid environment or have encountered mold problems in the past.

1. Check over the premises and fix mold problems before new tenants move in. Fill out the Landlord/Tenant Checklist form in Chapter 7 and follow the advice on inspecting rental property at the start of a tenancy.

2. Make sure that every tenant understands the risks of poor housekeeping practices and recognizes the factors that contribute to the growth of mold. Use your lease or house rules to educate tenants about sensible practices to reduce the chances of mold—or to fix problems should they arise. Give tenants specific advice, such as how to:

• ventilate the rental unit

• avoid creating areas of standing water—for example, by emptying saucers under houseplants, and

• clean vulnerable areas, such as bathrooms, with cleaning solutions that will discourage the growth of mold.

The EPA website, mentioned below, includes lots of practical tips for discouraging the appearance of mold in residential settings.

3. Encourage tenants to immediately report specific signs of mold, or conditions that may lead to mold such as plumbing leaks and weatherproofing problems.

4. Make all necessary repairs and maintenance to clean up or reduce mold—for example:

• Consider installing exhaust fans in rooms with high humidity (bathrooms, kitchens, and service porches), especially if window ventilation is poor in these areas.

• Provide tenants with dehumidifiers in chronically damp climates.

• Reduce the amount of window condensation by using storm windows or double-glazed windows.

• Quickly respond to tenant complaints or your own observations and clean up mold as discussed in Subsection e, below.

These preventive steps will do more than just decrease the chances that mold will begin to grow. They will also reduce the ability of tenants to make you legally liable for health problems resulting from mold caused by the tenants' poor housekeeping or failure to alert you to problems.

EXAMPLE

The shower tray in Jay's bathroom began to leak, allowing water to penetrate walls, floors, and ceilings below. Sydney, Jay's landlord, had repeatedly stressed the need for ventilation and proper housekeeping and encouraged all his tenants, including Jay, to promptly report maintenance problems. Jay ignored Sydney's recommendations and willingness to do repairs, even though Sydney always took care of maintenance problems promptly. Mold grew in the bathroom and Jay developed a cough and a rash.

Jay will have a tough time holding Sydney legally responsible for his health problems, simply because he failed to take advantage of Sydney's proven readiness to address the problem, which would have avoided the harm.

e. How to Clean Up Mold

Although reports of legal settlements and jury verdicts are alarming, the fact is that most mold is relatively harmless and easily dealt with. Most of the time, a weak bleach solution (one cup of bleach per gallon of water) will remove mold from nonporous materials. You and your tenants should follow these commonsense steps to clean up mold:

• Use gloves and avoid exposing eyes and lungs to airborne mold dust (if you disturb mold and cause it to enter the air, use masks).

• Allow for frequent work breaks in areas with plenty of fresh air.

• Clean or remove all infested areas, such as a bathroom or closet wall. Begin work on a small patch and watch to see if workers develop adverse health reactions, such as nausea or headaches. If so, call in a construction professional who is familiar with working with hazardous substances.

• Don't try removing mold from fabrics such as towels, linens, drapes, carpets, and clothing—you'll have to dispose of these infested items.

• Contain the workspace by using plastic sheeting and enclosing debris in plastic bags.

For more information, check out the sites noted in "Resources: Mold," below.

People with respiratory problems, fragile health, or compromised immune systems should not participate in clean-up activities. If your tenant raises health concerns and asks for clean-up assistance, provide it—it's a lot cheaper than responding to a lawsuit.

WHAT'S "TOXIC" MOLD?

Molds are naturally occurring organisms that have been with us for all time, and not all of them are bad (think of blue cheese, for example). But what about "toxic" mold? Where does that fit in?

While they are growing, some molds produce metabolic products, or toxins, that discourage or prevent bacteria or other fungi from growing in the same area. When those metabolic products also cause health problems in animals or humans, they are called mycotoxins. Mycotoxins are natural products from molds that may cause a toxic response in vertebrates when small amounts are eaten, inhaled, or touched.

Molds that are capable of generating toxins (called "toxigenic mold") do not always produce them in every situation. Scientists believe that certain very specific conditions must be present for a toxigenic mold to actually produce toxins, such as the right combination of temperature, moisture, type of material the mold is growing on and, perhaps, competition from other microorganisms.

Source: California Department of Health Services

ELECTROMAGNETIC FIELDS

Electromagnetic fields (EMFs) are one of the most controversial of the household "environmental hazards" that concern landlords.

Power lines, electrical wiring, and appliances emit low-level electric and magnetic fields. The intensity of both fields are thousands of times lower than the natural fields generated by the electrical activity of the human heart, brain, and muscles. The further away you are from the source of these fields, the weaker their force.

The controversy surrounding EMFs concerns whether exposure to them increases a person's chances of getting certain cancers—specifically, childhood leukemia. Although some early research raised the possibility of a link, recent studies have discounted it. For example, a 1999 review by the U.S. National Institutes of Health concluded that the scientific evidence suggesting that EMF exposures pose any health risk was weak. The same conclusion was reached in 2001 by the U.K. National Radiation Protection Board. Interestingly, the scientific inquiry into the health consequences of EMFs has shifted to studying the effects of cell phone reception and use.

Still, your tenants may be worried about the presence of EMFs. Practically speaking, a tenant's only option is to move. If the tenant has a month-to-month rental agreement or the lease is up, she can easily move on without legal repercussions. But what about a tenant who decides mid-lease that the EMFs are intolerable? Legally, she would be justified in breaking a lease or rental agreement only if the property presents a significant threat to her health or safety. (Breaking a lease when the property is unfit is explained at length in Chapter 11.) Given the lack of evidence regarding the danger from EMFs, it is unlikely that a court would decide that their presence makes your property unlivable.

Electromagnetic Fields Resources. The National Institute of Environmental Health Sciences and the U.S. Department of Energy publish an excellent article entitled "Questions and Answers About EMF" (1995). You can read it online by going to the National Institute website at www.niehs.gov. Use the search feature and type in EMF.

f.   Testing for Toxicity

If you or your tenants discover mold on the property, should you test it to determine the nature of the mold and its harmfulness? Most of the time, no. You're much better off directing your efforts to speedy clean-up and replacement of damaged areas. Knowing the type of mold present and whether it produces mycotoxins will not, in most cases, affect the appropriate method of clean-up.

Properly testing for mold is also extremely costly. Unlike your ability to detect lead paint by using a swab kit, you cannot perform a reliable mold test yourself. (Over-the-counter kits, which cost around $30, provide questionable results.) A professional's basic investigation for a single-family home can cost $1,000 or more. And to further complicate matters, there are relatively few competent professionals in this new field—unlike lead and asbestos inspectors who must meet state requirements for training and competence, there are no state or federal certification programs for mold busters.

This said, it will be necessary to call in the testers if you are sued. In that event, your insurance company will hire lawyers who will be in charge of arranging for experts. If you are facing the threat of a tenant's lawsuit, it's time to contact your insurance broker.

g.   Insurance Coverage of Mold Problems

If structural aspects of your property have been ruined by mold and must be replaced, especially if there's a lawsuit on the horizon brought by ill tenants, contact your insurance broker immediately. Your property insurance may cover the cost of the clean-up and repairs, but only if the damage is from an unexpected and accidental event, such as a burst pipe, wind-driven rain, sewerage backup or unanticipated roof leak. Damage due to mold in a chronically damp basement will probably not be covered under your policy. If mold grows as a result of a flood, you may also be out of luck—flooding is normally excluded from most property insurance coverage.

Your liability policy may also cover you if you are sued by ill tenants. But watch for the insurance industry to try to wiggle out as the amount of litigation grows (and their claims rise). Carriers have claimed that mold falls within the "pollution exclusion" (most policies will not cover you if you commit or allow pollution—for example, there's no coverage if you are sued by a tenant who is hurt by your deliberate dumping of solvents onto the property). Sadly, many insurers are now simply exempting damage due to mold from standard liability insurance policies when they renew the policy. Read your policy (and check with your broker) to learn whether mold-related claims are allowable under your policies.

RESOURCES: MOLD

For information on the detection, removal, and prevention of mold, see the EPA website at www.epa.gov/iaq. See their document "Mold Remediation in Schools and Commercial Buildings" (which includes multifamily properties). Publications written with the homeowner in mind are available from the California Department of Health Services at www.cal-iaq.org. This site includes many helpful links to other states' health departments and to academic and scientific studies on the subject of mold. New York City's Department of Health has developed guidelines for indoor air quality, which any landlord would be wise to consult. You can read them online at www.ci.nyc.ny.us (use the site's search function and enter the word "mold").

---

6.   Landlord Liability for Carbon Monoxide Poisoning

Carbon monoxide (CO) is a colorless, odorless, lethal gas. Unlike radon, whose deadly effects work over time, CO can build up and kill within a matter of hours. And, unlike any of the environmental hazards discussed so far, CO cannot be covered up or managed.

When CO is inhaled, it enters the bloodstream and replaces oxygen. Dizziness, nausea, confusion, and tiredness can result; high concentrations bring on unconsciousness, brain damage, and death. It is possible for someone to be poisoned from CO while sleeping, without waking up. Needless to say, a CO problem must be dealt with immediately.

a. Sources of Carbon Monoxide

Carbon monoxide is a by-product of fossil fuel combustion. Electric appliances cannot produce it. Common home appliances, such as gas dryers, ranges, water heaters, or space heaters; oil furnaces, fireplaces, charcoal grills, and wood stoves all produce CO. Automobiles and gas gardening equipment also produce CO. If appliances or fireplaces are not vented properly, CO can build up within a home and poison the occupants. In tight, "energy-efficient" apartments, indoor accumulations are especially dangerous.

AVOIDING CARBON MONOXIDE PROBLEMS

- Check chimneys and appliance vents for blockages.

- In your tenant rules and regulations, prohibit the indoor use of portable gas grills or charcoal grills.

- Warn tenants never to use a gas range, clothes dryer, or oven for heating.

- Prohibit nonelectric space heaters, or specify that they must be inspected annually. Tenants can get recommendations from fuel suppliers.

- Check the pilot lights of gas appliances as part of your regular maintenance routine. They should show a clear blue flame; a yellow or orange flame may indicate a problem.

---

b. Preventing Carbon Monoxide Problems

If you have a regular maintenance program, you should be able to spot and fix the common malfunctions that cause CO buildup. But even the most careful service program cannot rule out unexpected problems like the blocking of a chimney by a bird's nest or the sudden failure of a machine part.

Fortunately, relatively inexpensive devices, similar to smoke detectors, can monitor CO levels and sound an alarm if they get too high. If you install one, make sure it is UL certified.

Unlike smoke detectors, which are required by many local ordinances, CO detectors are not legally required. But that doesn't mean that you wouldn't be wise to install one. Detectors that are connected to the interior wiring of the house and backed up with emergency batteries are best.

RESOURCES: CARBON MONOXIDE

Local natural gas utility companies often have consumer information brochures available to their customers. The Chimney Safety Institute of America, 2155 Commercial Drive, Plainfield, IN 46161, 800-536-0118, will provide copies of brochures on carbon monoxide and chimney safety. For more information, visit their website at www.csia.org.

---

c. Responsibility for Carbon Monoxide

Most CO hazards are caused by a malfunctioning appliance or a clogged vent, flue, or chimney. It follows that the responsibility for preventing a CO build-up depends on who is responsible for the upkeep of the appliance:

- **Appliances.** Appliances that are part of the rental, especially built-in units, are typically your responsibility, although the tenant is responsible for intentional or unreasonably careless damage. For example, if the pilot light on the gas stove that came with the rental is improperly calibrated and emits high amounts of CO, you must fix it. On the other hand, if your tenant brings in a portable oil space heater that malfunctions, that is his responsibility.

- **Vents.** Vents, chimneys, and flues are part of the structure, and their maintenance is typically your job. In single-family houses, however, it is not unusual for landlords and tenants to agree to shift maintenance responsibility to the tenant. As always, write down any maintenance jobs that you have delegated—if an accident occurs, you'll be able to prove that responsibility had been shifted to and accepted by the tenant.

G. LIABILITY, PROPERTY, AND OTHER TYPES OF INSURANCE

A well-designed insurance program can protect your rental property from many types of perils, including damage to the property caused by fire, storms, burglary, and vandalism. A thorough program will also include liability insurance, covering injuries or losses suffered by others as the result of defective conditions on the property. Equally important, liability insurance covers the cost (lawyer's bills) of defending personal injury lawsuits.

This section provides advice on choosing liability and property insurance. For a more detailed discussion on insuring your rental property business, see *Legal Guide for Starting & Running a Small Business,* by Fred S. Steingold (Nolo).

1. Choosing Liability Insurance Coverage

As we've discussed throughout this chapter, you can be legally liable for people injured and for others' damaged property because you or your manager didn't use reasonable care. Because an injured person can collect not only for lost wages and medical bills but also for such intangibles as pain, suffering, and emotional distress, a single personal injury verdict against your business has the potential to wipe it out.

Here are some specific tips on choosing liability insurance, something all landlords should buy. Advice on property insurance in general and working with an insurance agent are covered in the sections below.

a. Purchase High Levels of Liability Coverage

Liability policies are designed to cover you against lawsuit settlements and judgments up to the amount of the policy limit, plus the cost of defending the lawsuit. (A few policies, however, consider the cost of defense as part of the limits of the policy.) They provide coverage for a host of common perils, such as tenants falling and getting injured on a defective staircase. Liability policies usually state a dollar limit per occurrence and an aggregate dollar limit for the policy year. For example, your policy may say that it will pay $300,000 per occurrence for personal injury or a total of $1 million in any one policy year.

Depending on your property, buying more coverage is a very good idea, especially in large metropolitan areas where personal injury damage awards can be very high.

b. Purchase "Commercial General Liability" Coverage

Make sure your liability policy covers not only physical injury but also includes coverage or protection for libel, slander, discrimination, unlawful and retaliatory eviction, and invasion of privacy suffered by tenants and guests.

If the policy does not specifically include these types of claims, you may still be covered if one of these charges is filed against you. As explained in detail in Chapter 9, Section H, California courts have not clearly ruled that the standard language in every commercial liability policy (which uses terms like "bodily injury" and "personal injury") must be understood to include libel, discrimination, and so on. Ask your insurance agent whether the underwriters for your policy have extended coverage for libel and discrimination claims. If they have, get it in writing or write a "letter of understanding" to your agent yourself, setting out your understanding that the company will cover such claims. If the answer is "No" or the agent cannot tell you, consider shopping for another agent.

c. Terrorism Insurance

The huge losses caused by the events of September 11, 2001, produced a predictable response from insurance companies: They began writing liability and property policies that specifically excluded coverage for losses due to acts of terrorism. Congress reacted by passing the Terrorism Risk Insurance Act, which will help ensure that property owners have access to adequate terrorism insurance at affordable rates. Much like the federal flood insurance scheme, the law requires insurance companies to offer coverage (for an additional premium) and to void any clauses in existing policies that exclude coverage (if you want coverage under an existing policy, you're now entitled to buy it). Federal funds of up to $100 billion will be available to cover up to 90% of any loss—this is known as "gap" insurance, giving you a deep pocket (the federal government) in case of a catastrophic loss. Importantly, it protects you from punitive damages unless the injured person can prove that you encouraged the act of terrorism. (15 U.S.C § 6701 and following.)

LIMITING YOUR LIABILITY

If you run your landlording business as a sole proprietorship or a partnership, you and the business are indistinguishable when it comes to debts. That means that you are personally responsible for any debts that you incur as a result of your business operations—including liability for an injured tenant. Your own house, your personal bank account, any business properties, and other assets could all be seized to pay off a big settlement or jury award.

There are ways, however, to protect personal assets from being used to pay business debts. The most common method is to incorporate your landholding business and conduct all of your business as a corporation, not as an individual. That way, if a debt arises out of the corporation's activities, only the corporation's assets are liable for the debts. For example, say you create the ABC Corporation to own an apartment building in a troubled neighborhood. If the corporation is sued successfully for a crime that occurred on the property, only the corporation's assets can be used to pay the settlement or judgment. Your personal assets, or other business assets not owned by the ABC Corporation, won't be vulnerable. The effectiveness of this corporate shield depends on whether you consistently treat the corporation separately from your personal and other business affairs, and if you follow state laws prohibiting commingling of corporate and personal assets.

Another way to limit your personal liability is to run your business as a limited liability company, which is a relatively new form of business. Incorporating or forming a limited liability company also gives you advantageous tax consequences. See *Form Your Own Limited Liability Company*, by Attorney Anthony Mancuso (Nolo), and *LLCMaker*, a software program, also by Anthony Mancuso (Nolo). Ordering information is at the back of this book.

d. Purchase Nonowned Auto Liability Insurance

Be sure to carry liability insurance not only on your own cars and trucks, but also on your manager's personal car or truck if his or her vehicle will be used for business purposes. Nonowned auto insurance will protect you from liability for accidents and injuries caused by your manager or other employee while running errands for you in their own vehicle. Remember, however, that this is liability coverage only and does not cover collision or other damage caused to your employee's car.

Check the driving record carefully of any manager or employee who will be using your vehicle or doing business errands using their own cars. When you interview a prospective manager or employee who will be driving as part of the job, ask for a current copy of the applicant's driving record, which can be easily and inexpensively obtained from the Department of Motor Vehicles. Chapter 6, Section A discusses how to screen and hire potential managers.

2. Punitive Damages and Other Common Insurance Exclusions

Punitive damages are monetary awards that are intended to punish you for willful or malicious behavior, rather than to compensate the injured person. As you might expect, the insurance industry would like to be able to exclude punitive damages from coverage, but they have never adopted a standard-form exclusion clause. (Insurance policies are typically made up of prewritten, commonly used clauses that are used by virtually every insurance company.) If an insurance policy does not specifically state whether punitive damages will be covered (and most do not), it will be up to the courts to decide whether standard policy language covers punitive awards.

California courts will not require insurance companies to cover punitive damages awarded in a lawsuit for intentional acts, such as beating up a tenant. (Illegal discrimination or retaliation is also treated by some insurers as being an intentional act not covered by the policy, but most liability insurers will at least pay for the defense of such lawsuits.) However, punitive damages are almost never awarded in landlord/tenant cases involving accidental injuries. Also, as a general rule, landlords won't be liable for punitive damages if they refrain from extreme neglect and intentional wrongs against tenants and others.

3. Property Insurance

In choosing property coverage, there are four main questions to consider.

a. What Business Property Is Insured?

Be sure your insurance covers all the property you want protected. In addition to the entire building, does your insurance cover additions under construction? Outdoor fixtures, such as pole lights? Washing machines and other appliances? Property used to maintain the building, such as gardening equipment and tools? Boilers and heavy equipment? Personal business property such as computers used in managing your rental business?

Make sure your tenants know that your insurance does not cover loss or damage (caused by theft or fire) to tenants' personal property. Tenants will need their own renters' insurance to cover these losses. Clause 19 of our form lease and rental agreements in Chapter 2 discusses renters' insurance.

b. What Perils Will the Property Be Insured Against?

Be sure you know under what conditions you will be entitled to receive payment from the insurance company. Coverage of damage caused by fire is common in the most basic policies, while damage from mudslides, windstorms, and the weight of snow may be excluded. Almost every new (or renewed) policy excludes mold. Earthquake insurance on the building itself and flood insurance are typically separate. They are often expensive and have very high deductibles, but they still are good options if your building is highly susceptible to earthquake or flood damage. Whatever policy you decide on, read it carefully before you pay for it—not just when you've suffered a loss.

Be sure to check out "loss of rents" insurance, which will reimburse you for the loss of rents from rental units that have been sidelined—for example, due to a fire or other calamity covered under your underlying property insurance. This coverage will kick in even if you are able to move the tenant to another, vacant unit.

c. What Dollar Amount of Insurance Should You Carry?

Obviously, the higher the amount of coverage, the higher the premiums. You don't want to waste money on insurance, but you do want to carry enough so that a loss wouldn't jeopardize your business.

Be sure to carry enough insurance on the building to rebuild it. But there's no need to insure the total value of your real property (the legal term that includes land and buildings), because land doesn't burn. Especially if you're in an area where land is very valuable, this is a big consideration. If you're in doubt as to how much it would cost you to rebuild, have an appraisal made so you know that your idea of value is realistic. Because the value of the building and other property may increase, it's wise to get a new appraisal every few years. Your insurance agent should be able to help you do this.

d. Should You Buy Coverage for Replacement Cost or for the Present (Actual Cash) Value of the Property?

We recommend that you keep your fire insurance coverage equal to the cost of replacing your property. This may well be more than your bank or mortgage company requires you to purchase. But remember, land won't burn, so it's less than your property's total value. Historically, in the event of a loss a basic fire

insurance contract covered the actual cash value of the property, not its full replacement value. Today, policies are routinely available with replacement cost coverage. This is the coverage you want.

e. Code Upgrade Insurance

Plain "cost of replacement" coverage, which replaces the existing building should it be destroyed, won't be adequate should you need to bring an older building up to code after a fire or other damage. The problem is that legal requirements adopted since the building was constructed will normally require that a stronger, safer, more fire-resistant building be constructed. Doing this can cost far more than simply replacing the old building. To cope with this possibility, you need a policy that will not only replace the building but pay for all legally required upgrades. This coverage is called "Ordinance or Law Coverage" and is hardly ever included in a policy unless the policyholder specifically asks for it.

4. Working With an Insurance Agent

Here are some tips for choosing an insurance agent:

- **Find and work with a knowledgeable insurance agent—one who takes the time to analyze your business operations and come up with a sensible program for your company.** Get recommendations from people who own property similar to yours, or from real estate people with several years' experience—they will know who comes through and who doesn't. Working with an agent who knows your business is advantageous because that person is already a fair way along the learning curve when it comes to helping you select affordable and appropriate insurance.

- **Steer clear of an agent who, without learning the specifics of your property and business, whips out a package policy and claims it will solve all your problems.** While there are some excellent packages available that may meet your needs, neither you nor your insurance agent will know for sure until the agent asks you a lot of questions and thoroughly understands your business. If the agent is unable or unwilling to tailor your coverage to your particular business, find someone else.

- **Be frank with your agent when discussing your business.** Reveal all areas of unusual risk. If you fail to disclose all the facts, you may not get the coverage you need or, in some circumstances, the insurance company may later take the position that you misrepresented the nature of your operation and, for that reason, deny you coverage for exceptional risks.

- **Make sure you have a clear understanding of what your insurance policy covers and what's excluded.** Does the policy exclude damage from a leaking sprinkler system? From a boiler explosion? From an earthquake? If so, and if these are risks you face, find out if they can be covered by paying a small extra premium.

Landlords with managers and other employees will need workers' compensation insurance. (See Chapter 6, Section B.)

5. Saving Money on Insurance

This section is based on the sensible premise that few landlords can really afford to adequately insure themselves against every possible risk. You need to decide what types of insurance are really essential and how much coverage to buy. Many factors affect this decision, including the condition and location of the rental property. While choosing insurance is not always an easy task, here are some guidelines that should help.

a. Set Priorities

Beyond any required coverage for your business, ask these questions: What insurance do I really need? What types of property losses would threaten the viability of my business? What kinds of liability lawsuits might wipe me out? Use your answers to tailor your coverage to protect against these potentially disastrous losses. Get enough property and liability coverage to protect yourself from common claims. Buy insurance against serious risks where the insurance is reasonably priced.

b. Keep Costs Down by Selecting High Deductibles

Deductibles (the amount of money you must pay out of pocket before insurance coverage kicks in) are used primarily for real and personal property insurance, including motor vehicle collision coverage. The difference between the cost of a policy with a $250 deductible and one with a $500 or $1,000 or even higher deductible is significant—particularly if you add up the premium savings for five or ten years. Consider using money saved with a higher deductible to buy other types of insurance where it's really needed. For example, the amount you save by having a higher deductible might pay for loss of rents coverage.

c. Reduce the Likelihood of Insurance Claims Through Preventive Measures

Good safety and security measures, such as regular property inspections, may eliminate the need for some types of insurance or lead to lower insurance rates. In addition to following the steps we recommend in this chapter and in Chapter 11, ask your insurance agent what you can do to get a better rate.

Although how to protect against some types of risks may be obvious to you, how to protect against many others won't be. Get help from people who are experienced in identifying and dealing with risks. One excellent resource is your insurance company's safety inspector; your insurance agent can tell you whom to contact. Another good approach is to ask your tenants to identify all safety risks, no matter how small. (See Chapter 11, Sections J and K.)

d. Comparison Shop

No two companies charge exactly the same rates; you may be able to save a significant amount by shopping around. But be wary of unusually low prices—they may be a sign of a shaky company. Or it may be that you're unfairly comparing policies that provide very different types of coverage. Make sure you know what you're buying. And review your coverage and rates periodically. ■

13

LANDLORD'S RIGHT OF ENTRY AND TENANT'S PRIVACY

Next to disputes over rent or security deposits, the most emotional misunderstandings between landlords and tenants involve conflicts between a landlord's right to enter the property—to maintain, repair, show for sale or rent, or just plain inspect it—and a tenant's right to be left alone. What is so unfortunate is that many of these problems are unnecessary—they could easily be avoided if landlord and tenant understood and followed existing legal rules and common sense.

We can't help you if one of your tenants turns paranoid every time you want to inspect the furnace or fix the plumbing. We *can* make sure you know your legal rights and responsibilities, as well as offer you several management strategies that have worked well for other landlords.

The tenant's duty to pay rent is conditioned on the landlord's proper repair and maintenance of the premises. (See Chapter 11.) This means that, of necessity, a landlord must keep fairly close tabs on the condition of the property. For this reason, and because it makes good sense to allow landlords reasonable access to their property, the law clearly recognizes the right of a landlord to enter the premises under a number of defined circumstances.

This doesn't mean a landlord can enter a tenant's home at any time for any reason. Once you rent residential property in California, you must respect it as your tenant's home. You may enter it only under certain circumstances, which we discuss below. If you don't follow the legal rules regarding a tenant's privacy rights, the tenant could sue you or withhold rent. And an owner can be held liable for his property manager's disrespect of the tenant's right of privacy, even if the owner never knew about the manager's conduct.

Related Topics

- Recommended lease and rental agreement clauses for a landlord's access to rental property, and illegal provisions regarding a landlord's rights of entry and inspection: Chapter 2

- How to make sure your manager doesn't violate tenants' right of privacy: Chapter 6

- Tenants' right of privacy and landlord's policy on guests: Chapter 10

- Procedures for respecting tenants' right of privacy while handling tenant complaints about safety and maintenance problems and conducting an annual safety inspection: Chapter 11

- Privacy issues regarding evictions: Chapter 15

- Entering premises which have been abandoned by a tenant: Chapter 19.

A. THE LANDLORD'S RIGHT OF ENTRY

State law allows a landlord to legally enter rented premises while a tenant is still in residence in these situations (CC § 1954.):

- pursuant to court order

- to deal with an emergency

- when the tenant gives permission

- to make needed or agreed-upon repairs (or assess the need for them), or to provide needed or agreed-upon services

- to show the property to prospective new tenants, mortgagees, workers, contractors, or actual or potential purchasers

- to conduct an initial move-out inspection, if requested by the tenant (who has a right to be present at the inspection). The initial move-out inspection is covered in detail in Chapter 20, Section B, and

- when the tenant has abandoned or surrendered the premises.

A landlord's right to entry cannot be expanded, or the tenant's privacy rights waived or modified, by any provision in a lease or rental agreement. (CC § 1953(a)(1).)

In most instances—except emergencies, abandonment (that is, when the tenant moves out without notifying the landlord), and invitation by tenant—a landlord can enter only during normal business hours and then only after reasonable notice, presumed to be 24 hours (except when scheduling an initial move-out inspection, as explained above, when 48 hours' notice is required). A few clarifying points:

- **In writing.** In most situations, landlords and managers must give notice of intent to enter in writing. The notice must include the date, approximate time, and purpose of the entry. (Use the Notice of Intent to Enter Dwelling Unit form in Appendix B.) If you mail the notice (as opposed to giving it personally to the tenant or other occupant, or putting it on, under, or near the door), you must give six days' notice. You need not give notice when entering in an emergency, with the tenant's permission, or when the tenant has abandoned the property. A fourth exception to the written notice requirement applies when the property is for sale and you've notified the tenant of this in writing within the past 120 days, in which case 24 hours' verbal notice is sufficient.

- **Oral notice.** You and the tenant may agree orally to your entry to make agreed repairs or provide agreed services, as long as the agreement includes the date and approximate time of the entry, which must be within one week of the agreement. You don't have to use a written notice in this situation. (CC § 1954(d)(3).)

- **When you may enter.** Normal business hours, customarily, are 9 a.m. to 5 p.m., Monday through Friday, but the statute doesn't give specific hours and days. You may want to change the permissible hours of entry to fit your particular needs. Our form lease and rental agreements define normal business hours as 9 a.m. to 6 p.m. Monday through Friday, and 10 a.m. to 1:00 p.m. Saturday. (See Clause 14 in our form lease and rental agreements in Chapter 2.)

1. Entry in Case of Emergency

A landlord or manager can enter the property without giving notice to respond to a true emergency that threatens injury or property damage if not corrected immediately. For example, a fire, gas, or serious water leak is a true emergency which, if not corrected, will result in damage, injury, or even loss of life.

Here are some examples of situations in which it would be legal for the landlord or manager to enter without giving the tenant notice:

- A tenant tells your on-site manager she hears screams coming from the apartment next door. After calling the police, your manager uses her passkey to enter and see what's wrong.

- Your manager sees water coming out of the bottom of a tenant's back door, but the tenant has changed the locks. It's okay to break in, to find the water leak.

- Smoke is pouring out the tenant's window. You call the fire department and use your master key—or break in if necessary—to deal with the fire.

On the other hand, a landlord's urge to repair an important but nonlife- or property-threatening defect (say a stopped-up drain) isn't a true emergency that allows entry without proper notice.

To facilitate your right of entry in an emergency, you are entitled to have a key to the premises, including keys to any locks the tenant may add. To avoid misunderstandings in this area, we recommend that you state this right in the lease or rental agreement. (See Clause 14 in our sample agreement forms in Chapter 2.)

Don't change locks. It is unwise to change a lock installed by a tenant without permission, even if you immediately give the tenant a key. This invites a lawsuit and false claims that you tried to lock the tenant out or stole the tenant's possessions.

But what if the tenant installs a security system or burglar alarm? If these systems involve alterations to the property—even cutting a hole in a door for a deadbolt lock—they can be restricted with a lease provision that forbids alterations without the landlord's consent. (See Clause 17 of our form lease and rental agreements.)

Clause 17 also requires the tenant to provide instructions on how to disarm any burglar alarm system, if the landlord so requests. Not all landlords will want to know how to disarm tenant-installed security systems, given the idiosyncrasies of all the alarm systems on the market. In addition, if a tenant's goods are stolen and the alarm doesn't function, a landlord may wish he did not know the code or have the key.

The decision is yours. If an emergency occurs and you have to enter and shut off the alarm but don't know how, rest assured: All you really need to know is the name and phone number of the alarm company, which is commonly printed on the alarm box itself. Call the alarm company and explain the situation.

If you do have to enter a tenant's apartment in an emergency, be sure to leave a note explaining the circumstances and the date and time you entered.

2. Entry With the Permission of the Tenant

A landlord can always enter rental property, even without 24 hours' notice, if the tenant agrees without pressure or coercion. If problems are only occasional and you have no special needs of entry, you can probably rely on a friendly telephone call to the tenant asking for permission to enter. (Don't be too insistent, lest the tenant claim you coerced this permission out of him.) Be sure, however, that this oral agreement isn't more than one week before your intended (and actual) entry.

If the tenant agrees, but has been difficult and not always reliable in the past, you might even want to cover yourself by documenting his apparent willingness by sending him a confirmatory thank-you note afterwards, and keeping a copy for yourself. If this is met with unease or outright hostility, you should send a formal 24-hour notice. (See Section 3, below.)

If you have a maintenance problem that needs regular attending to—for example, a fussy heater or temperamental plumbing—you might want to work out a detailed agreement with the tenant covering entry.

3. Entry to Make Repairs

State law allows you and your repairperson to enter the tenant's home "to make necessary or agreed repairs, decorations, alterations, or improvements [and to] supply necessary or agreed services. ..." (CC § 1954.) In this situation, however, you must enter only during normal business hours and must give the tenant written "reasonable notice." It is always wise to give your tenant at least 24 hours' notice if possible. However, if there is a good reason—for example, a repairperson is available to make urgently needed repairs on a few hours' notice—you can legally give a reasonable but shorter notice. Under the statute, the 24-hour notice period is presumed to be reasonable, but it is not absolutely required.

EXAMPLE

If Marcus, a landlord, arranges to have a repairperson inspect a wall heater at 2 p.m. on Tuesday, he should notify his tenant, Georgia, in writing on or before 2 p.m. on Monday, explaining when, and why, he will be entering her home. But if Marcus can't contact Georgia until 6 p.m.—for example, she can't be reached at home or at work—less than 24 hours' notice is probably okay (but it should still be in writing). Of course, if Georgia consents to Marcus's plan, the notice period is not a problem. (See Section 2, above.)

If you can't reach the tenant at home or at work to give 24 hours' notice of your intention to enter, you can leave the notice at the tenant's home, with a responsible person. Or, post a note detailing your plan on the tenant's front door, keeping a copy for your own records. A sample letter is shown below.

SAMPLE LETTER REQUESTING ENTRY

November 19, 200X

Elliot Faust
123 Parker Street
Apartment 4
Berkeley, CA

Dear Mr. Faust:

Please be advised that in response to your complaint regarding the heater in your apartment, the management has arranged to have it repaired tomorrow, on Tuesday, November 20, at 2:00 p.m. Because we were unable to reach you at home or work to obtain your consent, I am leaving this note on your door.

Sincerely,

Melba Tharpe

Melba Tharpe, Manager

Now, if the tenant doesn't receive the notice, it's because she didn't return home and you couldn't reach her at work, in which case, a 24-hour notice would have been impractical anyway.

In many situations, the 24-hour notice period will not be a problem, as your tenant will be delighted that you are making needed repairs and will cooperate with your entry requirements. However, as every long-time landlord knows, some tenants are uncooperative when it comes to providing reasonable access to make repairs, at the same time that they are extremely demanding that repairs be made. If you must deal with a tenant who is a stickler for her legal right of privacy, you should give at least 24 hours' written notice of your intent to enter rather than try to shorten this period.

Avoid tenant claims that you or your repairperson is a thief. Give plenty of notice—this gives your tenant the chance to hide valuables. Try to arrange repairs when the tenant is home, or only authorize people you trust to enter alone. Carefully check references of plumbers and other repairpeople.

A fill-in-the-blank notice for entry to make repairs is shown below, and a blank, tear-out form is in Appendix B. You must use this or a similar form or other written notice to satisfy the law's requirement that you deliver notice in writing.

Problems may arise if the repairperson shows up late—for example, if he's supposed to come at 4 p.m. and doesn't show up until 8 a.m. the next morning. A tenant who has been seriously inconvenienced is likely to be hostile and to stand on her rights. If it isn't possible to get the repairperson to come on time in the first place, call the tenant and explain the problem, and ask permission to enter later on. If the tenant denies permission, you'll have to give a second 24-hour notice.

a. Entry to Inspect for Needed Repairs

As a general rule, the landlord may not insist on entering rented property simply to inspect it. A lease or rental agreement provision that allows this may be of no legal effect, as an unlawful waiver by the tenant of his or her right to privacy. On the other hand, since the law allows entry to keep the property maintained and repaired, occasional periodic inspections—such as one every six or twelve months to see whether anything needs to be repaired or improved—are probably okay, provided the tenant is given at least 24 hours' notice. But a landlord wishing to conduct an inspection should back off if the tenant objects. (See Chapter 11, Section K for a discussion of annual safety inspections. Also see Section B, below, for a discussion of local building inspections.)

Don't use the right to inspect improperly. A landlord can't use his right to access to harass or annoy the tenant. Repeated inspections, even when 24-hour notice is given, are an invitation to nonpayment of rent or a lawsuit. To clear up any uncertainty in this regard, your rental agreement or lease should spell this out, as do our sample agreements. (See Clause 14 in Chapter 2.) Also, we recommend an annual safety inspection (see Chapter 11), to be mentioned in a move-in letter in (Chapter 7).

Waterbed exception. If the tenant has a waterbed, a landlord may inspect its installation periodically to make sure it complies with the standards a landlord may legally impose. (CC § 1940.5(g).)

b. Entry During Tenant's Extended Absence

You should be on safe legal ground to enter rental property during a tenant's extended absence, as long as there is a genuine need to protect the property from damage. You should enter only if something really needs to be done—that is, something that the tenant would do if he were home, as part of his obligation to keep the property clean, safe, and in good repair. (See Chapter 11, Section D for a discussion of tenant repair and maintenance responsibilities.) For example, if the tenant leaves the windows wide open just before a driving rainstorm, you would be justified in entering to close them.

Require tenants to report extended absences. To protect yourself and make sure your tenant knows what to expect, be sure your lease or rental agreement requires tenants to inform you when they will be gone for an extended time, such as two weeks. The rental document should include your intent to enter the premises during these times if necessary. (See Clause 15 of the form agreements in Chapter 2.)

Notice of Intent to Enter Dwelling Unit

Civil Code § 1954

To: _____ Anna Rivera _____,
                                        Name

Tenant(s) in possession of the premises at _____ 123 Market Street, Apt. #14 _____,
                                                        Street Address

City of ____ Los Angeles _____, County of _____ Los Angeles _____, California.

PLEASE TAKE NOTICE that on _____ January 7 _____, 20 _OX_,

between _____ a.m./p.m. and _____ a.m./p.m.

the undersigned Landlord, or the Landlord's agent, will enter the said premises for the following reason:

☒ To make or arrange for the following repairs or improvements: _____
_____ fix garbage disposal _____

_____

_____

_____

☒ To exhibit the premises to:

    ☐ a prospective tenant or purchaser

    ☒ workers or contractors regarding the above repair or improvement,

    ☐ Other: _____

☐ To conduct an initial move-out inspection, as requested by you (48 hours' notice required) (Calif. Civil Code § 1950.5(f)(1).)

If you wish to be present, you may make the appropriate arrangements. If you have any questions or if the above-stated date or time is inconvenient, please notify the undersigned at ____ (213) 555-7899 _____.
                                                                              Phone Number

Marlene Morgan _____   January 5, 200X _____
Landlord/Manager   Date

4.   Entry to Show Property

You may enter rented property to show it to prospective tenants toward the end of a tenancy or to prospective purchasers if you wish to sell the property, and to mortgagees, workers, or contractors. You must, however, comply with the business hours and notice provisions discussed above. If you've planned ahead, you can dispense with the written notice requirement, as long as you've already sent the tenant written notice, within the last four months, that you intend to sell and show the property and that you or your agent will be contacting the tenant verbally in order to make arrangements (see Subsection b, below). You still must give 24 hours' oral notice, however.

Below is a sample fill-in-the-blank notice that can be used for this type of situation, as well as for entry to make repairs.

You'll find a tear-out version of the Notice of Intent to Enter Dwelling Unit in Appendix B. The CD-ROM that accompanies this book also includes this form.

a.   Showing Property to Prospective New Tenants

A landlord who doesn't plan to renew a tenant's about-to-expire lease, or who has given or received a notice terminating a month-to-month tenancy, may show the premises to prospective new tenants during the last few weeks of the outgoing tenant's stay. It is not a good idea, however, to show property if a dispute exists over whether the current tenant has a right to stay. If there's a chance the dispute will end up in court as an eviction lawsuit, the current tenant may be able to hang on for several weeks or even months. Insisting on showing the property in this situation only causes unnecessary friction, and you will be unable to tell the new tenants when they can move in.

Our contracts include a clause to protect you from liability if you must delay a new tenant's move-in date after you've signed a lease or rental agreement. (Clause 12 in Chapter 2.)

b.   Showing Property to Prospective Buyers

You may also show potential buyers or mortgage companies your property—whether a rented single-family house, condominium unit, or multiple-unit building. Remember that 24 hours is presumed to be reasonable notice to your tenant.

Problems usually occur when an overeager real estate salesperson shows up on the tenant's doorstep without warning, or calls on very short notice and asks to be let in to show the place to a possible buyer. In this situation, the tenant is within his right to say politely but firmly, "I'm busy right now—try again in a few days after we've set a time convenient for all of us." Naturally, this type of misunderstanding is not conducive to good landlord/tenant relations, not to mention a sale of the property. Make sure the real estate salespeople you deal with understand the law and respect your tenants' rights to advance notice.

Selling a house occupied by a tenant isn't easy on anyone. At times, you will want to show the place on short notice. And you may even want to have an occasional open house on weekends. Your tenants, on the other hand, are liable to feel threatened by the change in ownership. From their point of view, any actions you take to show the house to strangers may seem like an intolerable intrusion.

As in other nonemergency situations when you want to enter a rental, your notice must be in writing. However, if you have sent the tenant a letter within the previous 120 days saying the property is being sold, and that you or your agent may be contacting her verbally to request entry to show the property, the 24-hour notice may be verbal (in person or over the phone). Where verbal notice is given in this situation, it still should be 24 hours' notice. In addition, you or your agent must "leave written evidence of entry inside the unit." (C.C. § 1954(d).) A real estate agent's business card will probably satisfy this requirement.

Even if you have sent such a letter, we still recommend that you give written notice wherever possible. That's becuse the best way to achieve your ends is with the cooperation of the tenant. One good plan is to meet with the tenant in advance and offer a reasonable rent reduction in exchange for cooperation—for example, two open houses a month and showing the unit on two-hour notice, as long as it doesn't occur more than three times a week. However, you should realize that this type of agreement is in force only so long as the tenant continues to go along with it. Technically, any written agreement changing the rent is really an amendment to the rental agreement, and rental agreement clauses under which tenants give up their privacy rights are void and unenforceable if it comes to a court fight. This may be one situation when an informal understanding that the rent be lowered so long as the tenant agrees to the frequent showings may be better than a written agreement.

c.   Putting For Sale or For Rent Signs or Lockboxes on the Property

Occasionally, friction is caused by landlords who put For Sale or For Rent signs on tenants' homes, such as a For Sale sign on the lawn of a rented single-family house. Even if a landlord is conscientious about giving 24 hours' notice before showing property, putting a sale or rental sign on the property is virtually an invitation to prospective buyers or renters to disturb the tenant with unwelcome inquiries.

Be particularly careful with For Sale signs. Tenants who like where they are living often justifiably feel threatened and insecure about a potential sale. A new owner may mean a rent increase or eviction notice if the new owner wants to move in herself. In this situation, if your tenant's privacy is ruined by repeated inquiries, the tenant may resort to rent withholding or sue you for invasion of privacy, just as if you personally had made repeated illegal entries.

Keep in mind that in the age of computerized multiple-listing services, many real estate agents commonly sell houses and other real estate without ever placing a For Sale sign on the property, except when an open house is in progress. If you or your real estate agent must put up a sign advertising sale or rental of the property, make sure it clearly warns against disturbing the occupant and includes a telephone number to call. A good compromise is a sign which says "Shown by Appointment Only" or "Do Not Disturb Occupant." If your real estate agent refuses to accommodate you, find a new one that will respect your tenants' privacy and keep you out of a lawsuit.

Don't use a lockbox. Under no circumstances should an owner of occupied rental property that is listed for sale allow the placing of a key-holding "lockbox" on the door. This is a metal box that attaches to the front door and contains the key to that door. It can be opened by a master key or, in some cases, a numeric code, held by area real estate salespeople. Since a lockbox allows a salesperson to enter in disregard of the 24-hour notice requirement, it should not be used—period. A lockbox will leave you wide open to a tenant's lawsuit for invasion of privacy, and possibly liable for any property the tenant claims to have lost.

5.   Entry to Conduct a Requested Initial Move-Out Inspection

As we'll see in Chapter 20, a tenant who will be vacating the property has a right to an initial move-out inspection (and to be present at that inspection), when you or your manager point out any problems that will have to be remedied in order for the tenant to receive as much of a security deposit refund as possible. (CC § 1950.5(f).) Once you and the tenant have agreed on a time for this inspection (or if you can't agree, once you've decided on a date and time), you must notify the tenant in writing and give 48 hours' notice. (This requirement exists even when the tenant has agreed to, and thus knows of, the date and time, *unless* the tenant signs a written waiver of the 48-hour written notice.) When giving notice of an initial move-out inspection, check the appropriate box on the "Notice of Intent to Enter Dwelling Unit" form and give it to a tenant or other responsible person; or put it on, under, or near the front door. (For more details on how to prepare for and conduct the inspection, see Chapter 20.)

6. Entry After the Tenant Has Abandoned the Premises or Moved Out

To state the obvious, a landlord may enter the premises at any time after the tenant has moved out. It doesn't matter whether the tenant left voluntarily after giving back the key, or involuntarily after the sheriff or marshal evicted the tenant following a successful eviction lawsuit.

In addition, a landlord who believes a tenant has abandoned the property—that is, skipped out without giving any notice or returning the key—may legally enter. Chapter 19 explains the legal procedure for entry if you are not absolutely sure your tenant has left permanently.

HOW TO COMPLY WITH THE LAW ON TENANTS' PRIVACY

Don't:

- enter a tenant's home without giving 24 hours' notice—except in a true emergency

- conduct too-frequent inspections

- enter a tenant's home alone, without witnesses, or

- enter a tenant's home against his wishes.

B. ENTRY BY OTHERS

This section describes situations when other people, such as municipal inspectors, may want entry to your rental property.

1. Health, Safety, or Building Inspections

While California sets guidelines for your entry to rental property, the rules are different when it comes to entry by state or local health, safety, or building inspectors.

a. Neighbor's Complaints

If inspectors have credible reasons to suspect that a tenant's rental unit violates housing codes or local standards—for example, a neighbor has complained about noxious smells coming from the tenant's home or about his 20 cats—they will usually knock on the tenant's door and ask permission to enter. Except in the case of genuine emergency, your tenant has the right to say no.

Inspectors have ways to get around tenant refusals. A logical first step (maybe even before they stop by the rental unit) is to ask you to let them in. If you follow the letter of the law, you'll say no, because the purpose of their entry (to investigate a complaint) is not one of the enumerated reasons for permissible entry (remember, you can enter only for the reasons stated in the Civil Code). If inspectors can't convince the tenant, their next step will probably be to get a search warrant based on the information from the tenant's neighbor. (The warrant satisfies the "court order" requirement for entry, under the law.) The

Fred, it's announce first, then break down the door

inspectors must first convince a judge that the source of their information—the neighbor—is reliable, and that there is a strong likelihood that public health or safety is at risk. Inspectors who believe that a tenant will refuse entry often bring along police officers who, armed with a search warrant, have the right to do whatever it takes to overcome the tenant's objections.

b. Random Inspections

Fire, health, and other municipal inspectors some-times randomly inspect apartment buildings even if they don't suspect noncompliance. These inspections are allowed under some local ordinances in California. To find out whether your city has a program of random building inspections, call your city manager's or mayor's office.

Your tenant has the right to say no to a random building inspection. But this will buy only a little time, since the inspector will almost surely have a judge issue a search warrant, allowing him to enter to check for fire or safety violations. Again, if there is any expectation that your tenant may resist, a police officer will usually accompany the inspector.

An inspector who arrives when the tenant is not home may ask you to open the door on the spot, in violation of California state privacy laws. If the inspector has come with a warrant, you can probably give consent, since even the tenant couldn't prevent entry. But if the inspector is there without a warrant, think twice before allowing entry. Cautious landlords will ask an inspector without a warrant to enter after they have given the tenant reasonable notice (presumed to be 24 hours', in writing) under state law, and only with the tenant's consent.

c. Inspection Fees

Many cities impose fees for inspections, on a per unit or building basis or a sliding scale based on the number of your holdings. Some fees are imposed only if violations are found. If your ordinance imposes fees regardless of violations, you may pass the inspection cost on to the tenant in the form of a rent hike. It's not illegal to do this, and even in rent-controlled cities, the cost of an inspection might justify a rent increase, though you will probably have to petition the rent board for permission. (See Chapter 14 for information on how you may legally increase rents.)

If your ordinance imposes a fee only when violations are found, you should not pass the cost on to the tenant if the noncompliance is not the tenant's fault. For example, if inspectors find that you failed to install state-mandated smoke alarms, you should pay for the inspection; but if the tenant has allowed garbage to pile up in violation of city health laws, the tenant should pay the inspector's bill.

2. Police

Even the police may not enter a tenant's rental unit unless they can show you or your tenant a recently issued search or arrest warrant, signed by a judge. The police do not need a search warrant, however, if they need to enter to prevent a catastrophe, such as an explosion or imminent crime; or if they are in hot pursuit of a fleeing criminal or on the trail of important evidence of a serious crime.

C. Other Types of Invasions of Privacy

Entering a tenant's home without consent isn't the only way a landlord can interfere with the tenant's privacy. Here are a few other common situations, with advice on how to handle them.

1. Allowing Others to Enter

Occasionally a landlord or manager will be faced with a very convincing stranger who will tell a heart-rending story: "I'm Nancy's boyfriend and I need to get my clothes out of her closet now that I'm moving to New York," or, "If I don't get my heart medicine that I left in this apartment, I'll die on the spot," or "I'm John's father and I just got in from the North Pole, where a polar bear ate my wallet and I have no other place to stay." The problem arises when you can't contact the tenant at work or elsewhere to ask whether it's okay to let the desperate individual in.

A story may be legitimate—still, it doesn't make sense to expose yourself to potential liability should you get taken in by a clever con artist. There is always a chance that the person is really a smooth talker whom your tenant has a dozen good reasons to want kept out.

Never let a stranger into your tenant's home without your tenant's permission. A landlord may not, for example, consent to a warrantless police search of premises occupied by a tenant. (*People v. Escudero,* 23 Cal. 3d 800, 806 (1979); *People v. Roman,* 227 Cal. App. 3d 674, 278 Cal. Rptr. 44 (1991).)

If you do let a stranger in, your tenant can sue you for any damage or loss incurred. Even if you have been authorized to allow a certain person to enter, it is wise to ask the stranger for identification. Although this no-entry-without-authorization policy may sometimes be difficult to adhere to in the face of a convincing story, stick to it. You have much more to lose in admitting the wrong person into the tenant's home than you would have to gain by letting in someone who's "probably okay."

2. Giving Information to Strangers

As a landlord, you may be approached by strangers, including creditors, banks, and perhaps even prospective landlords, to provide credit or other information on your tenant. Resist your natural urge to be helpful, unless the tenant has given you written permission to release this sort of information. You have nothing to gain, and possibly a lot to lose, if you give out information that your tenant feels constitutes a serious violation of her privacy. And if you give out incorrect information—even if you believe it to be accurate—you can really be in a legal mess if the person to whom you disclose it relies on it to take some action that negatively affects your tenant.

EXAMPLE

If you tell others that a tenant has filed for bankruptcy (and this isn't true), and the tenant is damaged as a result—for example, he doesn't get a job—

the tenant has grounds to sue you for defamation (libel or slander).

Some landlords feel that they should communicate information to prospective landlords, especially if the tenant has failed to pay rent or maintain the premises or has created other serious problems. If you do give out this information, make sure you are absolutely factual and that the information you provide has been requested. If you go out of your way to give out negative information—for example, you try to blackball the tenant with other landlords in your area—you definitely risk legal liability for libeling your tenant and interfering with the tenant's contractual rights.

Beware of gossipy managers. A number of landlords we know have had serious problems with on-site managers who have gossiped about tenants who, for example, paid rent late, were served with a three-day notice, had overnight visitors, or drank too much. This sort of gossip may seem innocent, but if flagrant and damaging, can be an invasion of privacy for which you can be liable. So, impress on your managers their duty to keep confidential all sensitive information about tenants.

EXAMPLE

Your resident manager, Moe, tells Jerry that his ex-girlfriend Wendy "went out for the evening with the same guy she's had over here every other night." As a result, Jerry makes Wendy's life miserable for the next few weeks—or months. Wendy sues Moe—and you—for invading her privacy and subjecting her to Jerry's abuse.

3. Calling or Visiting Tenants at Work

Should you need to call your tenant at work (say when his Uncle Harry shows up and asks to be let into his apartment), try to be sensitive to whether it's permissible for him to receive personal calls. While some people work at desks with telephones and have bosses who don't get upset about occasional personal calls, others have jobs that are greatly disrupted by any phone call. A general rule seems to be that the more physical the type of the work, the more tyrannical employers are about prohibiting personal phone calls at work.

Under no circumstances should you continue to call a tenant at work who asks you not to do so. This is especially true when calling about late rent payments or other problems.

Never leave specific messages with your tenant's employer, especially those that could reflect negatively on the tenant. A landlord who leaves a message like, "Tell your deadbeat employee I'll evict her if she doesn't pay the rent" can expect at least a lot of bad feeling on the part of the tenant and, at worst, a lawsuit for slander or invasion of privacy.

As for visiting the tenant at work—say to collect late rent—this is something you should avoid unless invited. What it boils down to is that no matter what you think of your tenant, you should respect the sensitive nature of the tenant's relationship with her employer.

There may be times you'll need to contact the tenant at work if you can't find the tenant at home after repeated tries—for example, to serve notice of a rent increase (Chapter 14) or an eviction notice (Chapter 18).

4. Undue Restrictions on Guests

A few landlords, overly concerned about tenants moving new occupants into the property, go a little overboard in keeping tabs on the tenants' legitimate guests who stay overnight or for a few days. Often their leases, rental agreements, or rules and regulations require a tenant to "register" any overnight guest.

Our form agreements limit guests' visits to no more than ten days in any six-month period, to avoid having a guest turn into an illegal subtenant. While

landlords should be concerned about persons who begin as guests becoming permanent unauthorized residents (see Chapter 10), it is overkill to require a tenant to inform his landlord of a guest whose stay is only for a day or two. Keep in mind that just because you own your tenants' homes, you don't have the right to restrict their social lives or pass judgment upon the propriety of their visitors' stays. Extreme behavior in this area—whether by an owner or a management employee—can be an invasion of privacy for which you may be held liable.

5. Spying on a Tenant

As a result of worrying too much about a tenant's visitors, a few landlords have attempted to interrogate tenants' visitors, knock on their tenants' doors at odd hours to see who answers, or even peek through windows. Needless to say, this sort of conduct can render a landlord liable for punitive damages in an invasion of privacy lawsuit. As far as talking to tenants' guests is concerned, engaging in anything more than pleasant hellos or nonthreatening small talk is legally out of bounds. If you think your tenant's activity with respect to guests is a problem, make an appointment with the tenant and talk about it.

D. WHAT TO DO WHEN TENANTS ARE UNREASONABLE

Occasionally, a landlord who gives reasonable notice of intent to enter the tenant's home for legitimate purposes is still adamantly refused entry by the tenant. If you repeatedly encounter unreasonable refusals to let you or your employees enter the premises during normal business hours for one of the reasons listed earlier in this chapter, you can legally enter anyway, provided you do so in a peaceful manner. However, for practical reasons, a wise landlord faced with a tenant who is unreasonably asserting her right to privacy will not enter alone. It's just common sense to bring someone along who can later act as a witness in case the tenant claims some of her property is missing.

Another problem landlords face is that some tenants have their locks changed. No statute or court decision addresses whether a tenant is within her rights to change the locks without giving the landlord an extra key. This would seem to be illegal, because it restricts your right of access in a true emergency or when you have given proper notice. As noted above, our lease and rental agreements require landlord key access, as well as notice of any change of locks or the installation of any burglar alarms. (See Clause 17 in Chapter 2.)

If you have a serious conflict over access with an otherwise satisfactory tenant, a sensible first step is to meet with the tenant to see if the problem can be resolved. If you come to an understanding, follow up with a note to confirm your agreement. Here's an example:

> This will confirm our conversation of _____(date)_____ regarding access to your apartment at _____ _____(address)_____ for the purpose of making repairs. The management will give you 24 hours' advance written notice, giving you the approximate time of entry and the purpose of the entry, and will enter only during business hours or weekdays. The person inspecting will knock first, then enter with a passkey if no one answers.

If this doesn't work, try mediation by a neutral third party. (See Chapter 8.)

If attempts at compromise fail, you can evict the tenant. You can give the tenant a 30- or 60-day notice to leave if the tenancy is one from month to month in a nonrent-controlled city. If you rent under a lease or in an area requiring just cause for eviction, you must use a three-day notice to shape up or leave, if the lease or rental agreement contains an appropriate right-of-entry provision. The cause justifying eviction is the tenant's breach of that provision. (Clause 14 in our written lease and rental agreements, Chapter 2.) As we explain in Chapter 18 and in *The California Landlord's Law Book: Evictions*, you're much better off

giving a month-to-month tenant a 30-day or 60-day termination notice stating no reason (at least in non-rent-controlled cities where you don't need just cause for eviction), rather than using a three-day notice that gives the tenant the chance of contesting the reason for eviction stated on the notice.

If you contemplate an eviction lawsuit against the tenant, make sure you can document your position. Keep copies of any correspondence and notes of your conversations with the tenant.

E. Tenants' Remedies If a Landlord Acts Illegally

Conscientious landlords should be receptive to tenants' complaints that their privacy is being violated and work out an acceptable compromise.

If you violate a tenant's right to privacy, and you can't work out a compromise, the tenant has several options.

Withholding rent because the landlord has denied the tenant "quiet enjoyment" of the premises. A tenant may withhold a portion of the next month's rent, claiming you have violated the tenant's right to quiet enjoyment of the property. (*Guntert v. Stockton*, 55 Cal. App. 3d 131 (1976).) (See Clause 16 of our form lease/rental agreement in Chapter 2.) Quiet enjoyment of rental real property means that a tenant has the same right to enjoy her home free from interference by her landlord (or anyone else) as does a homeowner. If the tenant withholds rent, you have two choices:

- Accept a tenant's nonpayment of whatever part of the rent she felt she deserved as compensation for your invasion or privacy, or

- Bring an eviction suit based on nonpayment of rent.

Chapter 11 includes a detailed discussion of rent withholding, specifically as it relates to habitability. The basic issues are the same for invasion of privacy.

Suing the landlord in court. A tenant can also bring a lawsuit, asking for money damages. It's easy for a tenant to press a claim for $5,000 or less in small claims court without a lawyer. Tenants can sue for a larger amount in superior court.

Depending on the circumstances, the legal theories by which a tenant can sue a landlord for unlawful entry include:

- trespass

- invasion of privacy and harassment. If the landlord's behavior is a "significant and intentional" privacy violation, they can be liable for up to $2,000 for each such violation. (See Chapter 17, Section B; and Civil Code § 1940.2.)

- breach of implied covenant of quiet enjoyment (*Guntert v. Stockton,* 55 Cal. App. 3d 131 (1976).)

- intentional infliction of emotional distress. (In a suit by a tenant alleging that a landlord was guilty of the intentional infliction of emotional distress, the court ruled that it was necessary to prove four things: (a) outrageous conduct on the part of the landlord; (b) intention to cause or reckless disregard of the probability of causing emotional distress; (c) severe emotional suffering; and (d) actual suffering or emotional distress. *Newby v. Alto Riviera Apartments,* 60 Cal. App. 3d 288 (1976).) And

- negligent infliction of emotional distress.

Moving out without liability for further rent. Finally, you should know that repeated abuses by a landlord of a tenant's right of privacy give a tenant under a lease a legal excuse to break it by moving out, without liability for further rent. Also, unlawful entry into a tenant's home—even by the landlord—can be considered a criminal trespass. ■

14

RAISING RENTS AND CHANGING OTHER TERMS OF TENANCY

Alandlord's freedom to raise rent or change other terms of the tenancy depends primarily on whether the tenant has a lease or a rental agreement (written or oral) for a month-to-month or other periodic tenancy. For the most part, a lease fixes the terms of tenancy for the length of the lease, while the terms of a periodic tenancy can be changed by giving the tenant proper written notice.

This chapter explains the rules for raising rents and changing other terms of a month-to-month or other periodic tenancy. These rules normally don't apply to long-term leases—the rent may be increased only when the lease expires.

Related Topics

- Legal rules regarding when, where, and how rent is due; late charges and returned check charges; partial and late rent payments: Chapter 3

- Local rent control ordinances, including property covered, administration and hearings, registration requirements, rent formulas, security deposits, vacancy decontrol, and just cause evictions: Chapter 4

- Landlord liability for retaliatory rent increases: Chapter 15

- Legal rules and procedures for terminating tenancies: Chapter 18.

A. BASIC RULES TO CHANGE OR END A TENANCY

If you rent using a rental agreement (whether oral or in writing) for a month-to-month or other periodic tenancy, you or your tenant can terminate the tenancy by giving written notice to the other (except, of course, in some cities that have rent control ordi-

nances requiring the landlord to have just cause to evict.) (See Chapter 4, Section H.)

The length of the notice period is normally determined by the interval between rent payments (one month, two weeks, and so on), unless the rental agreement specifies a longer or shorter notice period necessary to terminate the tenancy. In other words, a landlord can normally change the terms of a month-to-month tenancy on 30 days' written notice, a week-to-week tenancy on seven days' notice, and so on. (CC §§ 827(a), 827(b)(1).)

To increase the rent or otherwise change the terms of the tenancy, the landlord must normally give a month-to-month tenant 30 days' written notice. However, you must give 60 days' notice for a rent increase that, combined with others you've imposed during the year, raises the rent more than 10% of the lowest rent charged within 12 months before the effective date of the increase. (CC § 827(b)(2).) Section B, below, explains this rule in more detail.

RENT INCREASES AND FIXED-TERM LEASES

What happens when a fixed-term lease ends? Strictly speaking, the tenant must move, unless you either enter into a new lease or continue to accept rent. As a practical matter, many landlords let their tenants stay without signing a new lease.

If you continue to accept monthly rent, the tenancy becomes a periodic one (usually month to month) with the rent due at the same interval as called for under the lease. You can now raise the rent, change one or more of the terms of the tenancy, or terminate the now month-to-month tenancy by giving the tenant a written 30-day notice (60 days if the rent increase is over 10%), following the same rules discussed in this chapter for periodic tenancies.

Why do you have to change the terms of the lease by written notice if the lease has run out? Because state law provides that when a lease ends and the tenant stays on with the landlord's consent, all its terms continue in effect except those that have to do with the lease term itself. (CC § 1945.)

Example: Les rents a house from Owsley under a one-year lease that runs from January through December. The lease provides that the $900 monthly rent is payable on the first day of the month, and that pets are not allowed. The lease expires on December 31, and Owsley elects to continue the tenancy by accepting another $900 from Les in the next month of January. The tenancy is now month to month, with all other terms the same (rent is still $900 and pets are not allowed). If Owsley wants to raise the rent or change the terms of what is now a written month-to-month rental agreement, he'll have to give Les a 30-day notice to that effect. And if the rent increase is more than 10% (more than $90), Owsley will have to give 60 days' notice.

Once again, end-of-lease rent increases, as well as your right to insist the tenant leave at the end of the lease term, are subject to local rent control ordinances that may restrict rent increases even after a lease expires; and cities with just cause eviction provisions may allow the tenant to stay on, even though the lease has expired. (See Chapter 4.)

If the tenant has a fixed-term lease—one that expires on a particular future date—you cannot raise the rent during the lease term, unless the lease allows it. (This type of provision is rarely seen in residential leases, which customarily are for terms of six or twelve months.) However, at the end of the term, the rent can be increased.

B. RENT INCREASE RULES

The rules for increasing rent vary, depending on whether or not your property is under rent control.

1. No Rent Control

In areas without rent control, there is no limit to the amount a landlord can increase the rent of a month-to-month or other periodic tenant. Similarly, there is no restriction on the period of time between rent increases. You can legally raise the rent as much and as often as good business dictates. Of course, common sense should tell you that if your tenants do not perceive your increases as being fair, you may end up with vacant rental units or a hostile group of tenants looking for ways to make you miserable.

You can't, however, legally raise a tenant's rent as retaliation—for example, in response to a legitimate complaint or rent-withholding action (see Chapters 11 and 15) or as a discriminatory action (see Chapter 9). One way to protect yourself from charges that ordinary rent increases are retaliatory or discriminatory is to adopt a sensible rent increase policy and stick to it. For example, many landlords raise rent once a year in an amount that more or less reflects the increase in the Consumer Price Index.

Other landlords use a more complicated formula that takes into account other rents in the area, as well as factors such as increased costs of maintenance or rehabilitation. They make sure to inform their tenants about the rent increase in advance and apply the increase uniformly to all tenants. Usually, this protects the landlord against any claim of a retaliatory rent increase by a tenant who has coincidentally made a legitimate complaint about the condition of the premises.

EXAMPLE

Lois owns two multiunit complexes. In one of the complexes, Lois raises rents uniformly, at the same time, for all tenants. In the other apartment building (where she fears tenants hit with rent increases all at once will organize and generate unrest), Lois does things differently: She raises each tenant's rent in accordance with the Consumer Price Index on the yearly anniversary of the date each tenant moved in. Either way, Lois is safe from being judged to have retaliatorily increased rents, even if a rent increase to a particular tenant follows on the heels of a complaint from that tenant.

Of course, any rent increase given to a tenant who has made a complaint should be reasonable—in relation to the previous rent, what you charge other similarly situated tenants, and rents for comparable property in the area—or you are asking for legal trouble.

EXAMPLE

Lonnie has no organized plan for increasing rents in his 20-unit building, but simply raises them at random. On November 1, he raises the rent for one of his tenants, Teresa, without remembering her recent complaint about her heater. Teresa was the only one to receive a rent increase in November. In this situation, Teresa has a strong retaliatory rent increase case against Lonnie, simply because an increase that seemed to single her out happened to coincide with her exercise of a legal right. If the increase made her rent higher than those for comparable units in the building, she will have an even better case.

For a discussion of landlord liability for retaliatory rent increases and tenant lawsuits against the landlord, see Chapter 15.

2.   Rent Control

In cities with rent control, rent increases are governed by additional limitations. If your property is located in a city with rent control, you should check that city's ordinance to see whether it applies to your property. (See Chapter 4 for a detailed discussion of rent control.)

If a rent control ordinance does affect your property, check it for the following:

- **The maximum yearly rent increase.** The ordinance may allow periodic increases of either a fixed percentage or a percentage tied to a consumer price index, or the local rent board may establish the amount of the increase each year, in which case you will have to inquire. In cities that keep track of permissible rent control levels by requiring the landlord to register the property, state law requires the rent board, on request, to notify the landlord and tenant of the permissible rent increase. (CC § 1947.8.)

- **Whether the landlord must obtain permission from a rent board for a higher increase than set out by the ordinance or board.** This is generally required in moderate and strict rent-controlled cities. In some cities with mild rent control, a landlord can raise rents at will, with the tenant having the burden to object to increases above the approved formula increase.

- **Whether the ordinance requires that a rent increase notice contain specific information, such as a reason for the increase, in addition to normal state law notice requirements.** You may also want to contact a local landlords' association, or perhaps a lawyer who routinely represents landlords and is familiar with requirements of the locality's rent control law.

3.   30-Day or 60-Day Notice?

Every landlord who raises the rent must think twice about whether to use a 30-day or 60-day notice.

Especially if you raise the rent frequently during the year, you'll need to pay attention to the "10% Rule." That rule tells you that if the total of all your rent increases over the past 12 months is equal to or less than 10% of the lowest rent charged during that time, 30 days' notice will suffice. But if the total increase is more than 10% of any monthly rent charged during the previous year, you must use a 60-day notice. Follow these steps and use our Rent Increase Worksheet to know which notice period to use:

Step 1. Calculate when the new rent will take effect if you use a 30-day notice. For now, assume a 30-day period will suffice. Determine when the new rent will kick in based on proper delivery of your rent increase notice. (See Section D, below, for information on how to deliver the notice.)

Step 2. Check the tenant's rent rate history. Count back 12 months from the effective date of the increase (you got that date in Step 1, above). Look at the rent the tenant was charged for each of those 12 months and choose the lowest rent.

Step 3. Calculate 10% of the lowest rent paid. Multiply the lowest rent paid (you identified that figure in Step 2) times .1 to get your "10% Figure."

Step 4. Calculate the Total Rent Increase over the past 12 months. If the current increase is the only increase during the previous 12 months, the answer is simple—the increase is the one you're considering now. But if you increased the rent at other times during these months, add up all of the increases plus the current one to get the Total Rent Increase.

Step 5. Compare the 10% Figure from Step 3 with the Total Rent Increase in Step 4. If the Total Rent Increase is the same or lower than 10% of the lowest rent paid, you can stick with your 30-day notice. But if the total is higher, your notice must specify 60 days. In other words, your effective date, calculated in Step 1, must be lengthened by 30 days.

The examples below illustrate how this process works. As you'll see, the tricky situations arise when landlords raise the rent frequently within any 12-month period.

You'll find a tear-out version of the Rent Increase Worksheet in Appendix B. The CD-ROM that accompanies this book also includes this form.

Landlords subject to rent control may need to comply with the 60-day notice requirement in certain situations. Normally, your increases will be well below the 10% threshold, since the local rent board regulates them (and no board is likely to approve an increase that high!) However, if you have banked prior increases or get permission to impose a capital expenditures increase, the total may well exceed 10% of the lowest rent charged in the previous 12 months. Chapter 4 explains rent control in detail. Be sure to consult your ordinance before announcing *any* rent increase.

EXAMPLE 1

Len rents a house to Tom for $1,000 a month. Len wants to raise the rent $100, to $1,100, effective February 1. Len looks back at how much rent Tom has paid for the 12 months preceding Feb. 1. Tom has paid $1,000 for each of those months. Len does the math and figures out that 10% of $1,000 is $100. Since the increase isn't *more* than 10% of the lowest rent paid in the 12 months preceding the February 1 target date, Len can safely use a 30-day notice (of course, he has to serve it correctly).

EXAMPLE 2

Len rents another house to Tanya for $1,000 a month. On April 1, he decides to raise Tanya's rent by $150, and he wants the increase to take effect May 1. Len looks at the rent rates Tanya paid for the 12 months preceding May 1, and sees that she paid

$1,000 for every month. Again, 10% of $1,000 is $100. Since $150 is more than $100, Len realizes that he cannot use a 30-day notice, and must instead give her 60 days. In short, his rent increase can't take effect (assuming he delivers it according to law) until June 1.

EXAMPLE 3

Len rents a third house to Carol for $850 a month. He wants to raise Carol's rent by $50, to $900, and he wants that increase to take effect September 1. He looks at Carol's rent rate history for the 12 months previous to September 1 and sees that, from the previous September to January, Carol paid only $800 (he raised her rent $50 in January). He multiplies $800 times .1 to get his 10% Figure—it's $80.

Next, Len calculates the total rent increase. He adds the January increase of $50 to the current increase of $50 to get a total increase of $100. Since this figure is over $80, his 10% Figure, he realizes that he must give Carol a 60-day notice. Assuming he delivers it properly, his increase cannot take effect until October 1.

If you find these calculations somewhat confusing, you're not alone. To be on the safe side, it would be wise to always use a 60-day notice. At the very least, be sure to time your rent increases to take effect on the date the rent is due (this will make it easier to figure the monthly rent history). Use the Rent Increase Worksheet, which is shown below as Len would have filled it out for Carol, our third example above.

You must always deliver the notices according to law. Your planned "effective date" won't work for you if you don't communicate the increase in the legal manner—if your notice is "defective," as lawyers would say. Read Section D, below, very carefully to make sure that you can deliver the notice in time to meet your target effective date. In particular, note that if you use ordinary mail to deliver the notice, you'll have to add five days.

It's important to understand the consequences of delivering a 30-day notice when a 60-day notice is called for. Although the statute doesn't specify the results, it's a good bet that a judge will find the short notice ineffective—in other words, as if you never delivered the notice at all. Put another way, it's not likely that a court will fix your error by adding the needed 30 days. You'll have to start over and will not be able to collect the new rent as soon as you'd hoped.

EXAMPLE

Sally decided to raise Spencer's rent by $100, from $650 to $750. On May 1, she gave him a 30-day notice. Spencer knew that he would be entitled to 60 days' notice if the increase (combined with any others he'd had over the past 12 months) was over 10% of the lowest rent charged during those 12 months. Sally didn't know the law.

Spencer's rent had been a steady $650 from June 1 of the preceding year to now. He knew that any increase over $65 (that's 10% of $650) required a 60-day notice. He reasoned that her notice was simply ineffective, and when June 1 arrived, he gave Sally a rent check for $650.

Sally looked at the amount and demanded the new rent, then listened incredulously as Spencer explained the law. She argued that he should just "tack on" 30 days to her notice, making the rent increase effective July 1. Spencer refused and Sally wisely decided to start over, by delivering a proper 60-day notice on June 1. Sally won't see her new rent until August 1—if she'd done it right from the start, the increase would have kicked in on July 1.

Do not simply post the rent increase notice on the tenant's door. This does not constitute legally effective service of the notice. You must either deliver it personally or mail it, as explained below.

Rent Increase Worksheet

1. Tenant's name _Carol Tenant_

2. Effective date of increase (assumes proper service of a 30-day notice): _____
   September 1, 2001

3. Lowest rent paid from _September 1, 2000_ (12 months prior to effective date of increase) to effective date of increase: $ _____ _800.00_

4. **10% Figure** is 10% of lowest rent paid: ___ _800.00_ _____(rent in Step 3) x .1 = _____ _$80_ ____ .

5. Total rent increases from _September 1, 2000_ (12 months prior to effective date of increase) to and including current increase:

Increase #1: _____ _$50_ _____ (date) $ _Feb. 1, 2001_ _____

Increase #2: _____ (date) $ _____

Increase #3: _____ (date) $ _____

Current Increase: _____ _$50_ _____ (date) $ _Sept. 1, 2001_ _____

Total Rent Increase: $_____ _100_ _____

6. Compare the **10% Figure** with the **Total Rent Increase.**

☐ **Total Rent Increase** is the same or lower than the **10% Figure:** Use a 30-day notice which, if served properly, will allow you to collect the increased rent on the effective date you chose in Step 1.

☒ **Total Rent Increase** is greater than the **10% Figure**: Use a 60-day notice which, if properly served, will allow you to collect the increased rent 30 days after the date you specified in Step 1.

New effective rent increase date: _____ _October 1, 2001_ _____

C. PREPARING A NOTICE TO RAISE RENT

A notice raising the rent of a tenant who occupies a unit under an oral or written rental agreement with a periodic tenancy—for example, month to month or week to week—must be in writing and must clearly state the following:

- the name of the tenant

- the full address of the property, including street, city, and county

- the amount of the new rent

- the amount of the new security deposit (if increased)

- when the change is to go into effect. This can be no sooner than 30 days for a month-to-month tenancy (60 days for increases over 10%). But it can be longer, even if the lease or rental agreement doesn't require this. You can give a tenant as much additional notice as you want.

- prorated rental rate (see Section E, below)

- the date the rent increase notice is given, and

- the signature of the owner or manager.

Prepare your rent increase notice on a form called Notice of Change of Terms of Tenancy. A sample is shown below. You'll find a tear-out version in Appendix B. The CD-ROM that accompanies this book also includes this form.

Deposits. We noted in Chapter 5 that if you wish to raise the amount of a tenant's deposit when you raise the rent, you must specifically state that you are doing this. To accomplish this, check the box marked "Other" on the Notice of Change of Terms of Tenancy form and indicate the amount of the new deposit. We discuss the maximum amount you can charge for a deposit for furnished and unfurnished units in Chapter 5.

D. HOW THE NOTICE IS SERVED ON THE TENANT

The law is very strict on how a notice changing the terms of tenancy must be served on a tenant. It is not enough that you mail the notice or simply post it on the door, unless the tenant admits to receiving it—something you can never count on. Here are the two legal methods of service for a 30-day notice.

1. Personal Service

The best type of service of the 30-day notice is to simply hand your tenant the notice. Handing the notice to any other person, such as someone who lives with your tenant but is not listed as a cotenant on the written rental agreement, is not sufficient, except as described in Section D3, below.

For personal service to be legally effective, it is not necessary that your tenant accept the notice in her hand, and you or your manager (or whoever serves the notice) should not attempt to force the tenant to take the notice. It is enough that you make some sort of personal contact with your tenant and offer her the notice. If your tenant refuses to accept the notice, simply lay it down at her feet and walk away. Service is legally effective.

2. Mailing a Rent Increase Notice

You can serve a rent increase notice by ordinary first class mail addressed to the tenant at the premises. We advise you not to use certified mail requiring a return receipt, which will not reach a tenant who declines to accept and sign for the certified letter. Of course, you can still serve your rent increase by personal service or substituted service, which are explained below in Section D3.

If you choose to mail the notice instead of delivering it personally to the tenant or his sub, you must give the tenant an additional five days' notice of the rent increase. (CC § 827(b)(1)(B)(2) & (3); CCP § 1013.) This means giving 35 days' notice for a

Notice of Change of Terms of Tenancy

To: _____ Duc Mihn _____,
Name

Tenant(s) in possession of the premises at __1234 Market Street, Apt. #5_____,
Street Address

City of _____Sacramento_____, County of _____Sacramento_____, California.

The terms of tenancy under which you occupy these premises are changed as follows:

☒ The monthly rent will be increased to $_____700_____, payable in advance.

☒ Other: ____The amount of the security deposit is raised to $1,400, an increase of $100____

The change in terms of tenancy shall be effective:

☒ _____March 1_____, 20_OX_
Date

☐ On the 30th day following service on you of this notice. If the change of terms of tenancy is an increase in rent, the amount due on the next following due date, prorated at the current rental rate prior to the 30th day, and prorated at the increased rate thereafter, is $_____.

☐ [Rent increase over 10%] On the 60th day following service on you of this notice. If the change of terms of tenancy is an increase in rent, the amount due on the next following due date, prorated at the current rental rate prior to the 60th day, and prorated at the increased rate thereafter, is $_____.

_Dana Wickham_____   January 17, 200X_____
Landlord/Manager   Date

10%-or-less increase and 65 days' notice of an over-10% increase.

Be very sure to understand that if you want to change other terms of the tenancy besides the rent, such as the amount of the security deposit or a pets rule, you must use personal or substituted service. Mail service is available *only* for rent changes.

EXAMPLE 1

In Example 1 above, if Len increases Tom's rent by 10%, effective July 1, Len must mail the notice to Tom on or before May 26—35 days prior to July 1st.

EXAMPLE 2

In Example 2 above, where Len increases Tanya's rent by 15% effective June 1, he must mail it on March 27 in order to give Tanya the 65 days' notice required by law.

3. Effect of Improper Service

Once the tenant acknowledges receiving the notice or pays the increased rent, the tenant gives up the right to complain about any legal insufficiency in the manner the 30-day or 60-day notice was served, and the rent increase becomes effective, even if the service of the notice is technically improper. This is true regardless of the tenant's reason for acquiescing to the increase—whether she didn't know the notice had to be served a certain way, was too concerned about maintaining good relations with her landlord to raise the issue, or simply didn't care.

EXAMPLE

On May 28, Natalie mails a notice telling her tenant Linda her rent will be increased from $1,100 to $1,200 a month, effective July 1. Natalie mails the notice by ordinary first class mail. Linda pays the increased rent on July 1 and every month after, but learns in December that the law required that she be given 35 days' notice. Linda got only 34 days' notice. Linda demands that Natalie give her back the $100 increase she paid during each of those months. Natalie doesn't have to give a refund, since Linda, by paying the increase, gave up her right to insist on technically legal service of the notice.

Avoid informal rent increases. In practice, rents are often increased by a simple agreement between the landlord and tenant (or even a simple acquiescence on the tenant's part), even though this rent increase procedure does not comply with legal requirements. If the tenant responds by paying the increased rent, for even a month, he has given up the right to object to the increase. In effect, the tenant's failure to assert his right not to pay the increase is an implied agreement that the rent has been increased. Even if you know your tenants well and believe they will go along with a rent increase, we believe it is a poor business practice to rely on oral notice alone. As a courtesy, you may wish to tell your tenant of the increase personally, perhaps explaining the reasons— although reasons aren't legally necessary, except in areas covered by rent control. (See Chapter 4.) However, you should also follow up with a proper written notice. Good business practice requires written notice and documentation of all important decisions.

Here is a checklist which should help you follow correct procedures when you are about to raise your tenant's rent.

<hr>

CHECKLIST TO RAISE RENT

• Determine that your tenancy is from month-to-month or some other shorter period. As part of doing this, make sure your agreement doesn't require a 60- or 90-day notice period. (No increases are allowed during the term of a lease unless specified in the lease.)

• Find out if any local rent control laws prevent or limit your proposed increase.

• Decide when you want the increase to take effect. At least 30 days' notice is required for a month-to-month tenancy. Use the Rent Increase Worksheet, explained in Section B, above, to make sure that you can safely use a 30-day notice. If your increase (including any others within the past year) is more than 10% of the lowest rent paid within the 12 months prior to the increase effective date, you'll have to use 60 days.

• Fill out the blank Notice of Change of Terms of Tenancy in Appendix B. Sign the notice and make a copy for your files.

• Give the notice personally to the tenant, or use substituted or posting-and-mailing service.

<hr>

E. WHEN THE RENT INCREASE TAKES EFFECT

One of the legal misconceptions tenants are prone to make is the belief that a rent increase can legally take effect only at the beginning of a rental term. This is not true. The increase will take effect 30 or 60 days after you serve the tenant with a 30- or 60-day notice of the increase. For example, in the case of a month-to-month tenancy, where the rent is paid in advance on the first day of each month, a 30-day notice can increase the rent effective June 10, if served 30 days earlier on May 10. (See CC § 827(a)(1).) However, if you increase rent in the middle of a month, the rent for that month must be prorated, and the calculations are a little tricky. For this reason, many landlords find it easier to raise the rent as of the first of the full month after the notice is properly given, even though this may mean you give the tenant more than 30 or 60 days' notice.

If you do wish to prorate, here is the proper way to do it. Assume you wish to raise the rent of a tenant who has a written rental agreement with rent payable on the first of each month, by giving notice on the 10th of the month. Assuming you, in fact, give the tenant a notice on the 10th of May, increasing the rent from $500 to $550, the rent increase is effective June 9 (May has 31 days, but it's best to use a 30-day month, no matter how many days the month has). This would mean that the tenant would owe rent prorated at $500/month from June 1 through June 8, plus rent prorated at $550 per month from the 9th through the 30th. Remember, the rent is due on the first of the month, because rent is payable in advance. This works out to $537.10. Again, it may be more trouble figuring out how this number is calculated than it's worth.

F. CHANGING TERMS OTHER THAN RENT

If you rent to tenants under a periodic tenancy, the law allows you to change the terms of the agreement other than the amount of rent. Any rental agreement provision can be modified or even added in this way, as noted in Clause 4 of our form rental agreement. (See Chapter 2.) For example, the landlord could, with a 30-day notice, impose a pool fee, change the rules or fees for parking, or reduce the number of people allowed to live in a unit. Similarly, a landlord who originally allowed a month-to-month tenant to have a pet could give a 30-day notice imposing a new provision forbidding pets.

1. Preparing the Notice

The form you use to raise the rent can be used to change terms other than rent. (See Notice of Change of Terms of Tenancy in Section D, above.) But instead of checking "The monthly rent will be increased to $ _____ , payable in advance," check "Other" and write in the change you wish to make. For example:

- "Tenant may not keep pets in or on the premises."

- "Tenant may park only one motor vehicle in the parking lot behind 111 Navelier St."

- "Tenant must pay $25 per month for use of the indoor garage. Payment to be made with the monthly rent."

Just as some cities' rent control ordinances regulate the amount by which landlords can raise rents, some ordinances also prevent a landlord from otherwise changing the terms of the tenancy, particularly by reducing services while keeping the rent the same. For example, San Francisco's rent control ordinance was interpreted to prevent several landlords from taking back their tenants' rights to park in previously allowed parking spaces or beginning to charge parking fees. If your property falls under a rent control ordinance, check to see if it restricts changes in terms other than rent. Also prohibited by local rent control laws, as well as by state law, are changes in rental agreement terms that purport to have the tenant give up legal rights. (CC §1953(b).) In other words, the illegal and unenforceable rental agreement and lease terms discussed in Chapter 2, Section F are no more effective if accomplished by a Notice of Change of Terms of Tenancy than they would be if included in the original lease or rental agreement.

The notice should specify the following information:

- the tenant's name

- the full address of the property, including street, city, and county

- the change of terms, spelled out as carefully as if you were inserting it as

an additional clause in a rental agreement for the first time

- when the change of terms is effective, giving at least 30 days' notice in the case of a tenancy from month to month

- the date the notice is given, and

- the signature of the owner or manager.

A sample notice follows. It should be served in the same manner as a notice increasing the rent, namely by personal service (or substituted or posting-and-mailing service, if necessary).

You'll find a tear-out version of Notice of Change of Terms of Tenancy in Appendix B. The CD-ROM that accompanies this book also includes this form.

2. Serving the Notice

The notice should be served by personal service, explained above in Section D1.

3. Service of Notices Changing Other Tenancy Terms

Although a notice increasing a residential tenant's *rent* can be mailed, this is not true of notices changing other terms of the tenancy. For example, a notice changing the rent due date or stating that pets will no longer be allowed cannot be mailed. Such notices, if not served personally (as explained in Section D, above), should be served using one of the following methods.

a. Substituted Service on Another Person

If the tenant to whom you're attempting to give the notice never seems to be home, and you know where he works, you must try to personally serve him at his place of employment. If you are unable to locate the tenant at his workplace, the law allows you to use

Notice of Change of Terms of Tenancy

To: _____ Jean Friedman _____ ,
                                    Name

Tenant(s) in possession of the premises at _____ 456 Main Street, Apartment 7 _____ ,
                                                        Street Address

City of __ Los Angeles __ , County of __ Los Angeles __ , California.

The terms of tenancy under which you occupy these premises are changed as follows:

☐ The monthly rent will be increased to $_____ , payable in advance.

☒ Other: __ Tenant may not keep pets, including dogs and cats, on the premises. __

_____

The change in terms of tenancy shall be effective:

☒ _____ April 1 _____ , 20 __ OX __
              Date

☐ On the 30th day following service on you of this notice. If the change of terms of tenancy is an increase
  in rent, the amount due on the next following due date, prorated at the current rental rate prior to the
  30th day, and prorated at the increased rate thereafter, is $_____ .

☐ (Rent increases over 10% from last 12 months) On the 60th day following service on you of this notice. If
  the change of terms of tenancy is an increase in rent, the amount due on the next following due date,
  prorated at the current rental rate prior to the 60th day, and prorated at the increased rate thereafter, is
  $_____ .

_____ Felicia Alou _____   _____ January 31, 200X _____
Landlord/Manager   Date

"substituted service" in lieu of personally giving the notice to the tenant.

Substituted service simply means that you give the 30-day notice to a "substitute" person of "suitable age and discretion," preferably an adult, at your tenant's home or business, with instructions to that person to give the notice to the tenant. (However, if no adult is available, giving the notice to a teenage resident of the tenant's household is sufficient. *Lehr v. Crosby,* 123 Cal. App. 3d Supp. 1 (1981).) Substituted service must be followed with a mailed notice to the tenant's home to be effective.

To serve the notice this way, you must:

- try to personally serve the tenant at his home, but not succeed

- try to personally serve him at work, but not succeed

- leave a copy of the notice with an adult at home or work, and

- mail another copy to the tenant at home by ordinary first class mail. (CCP § 1162(2).)

Substituted service requires two notices. Service of the notice is not legally complete until you both leave a copy with the substitute and mail a second copy to the tenant at home.

b. Posting- and Mailing-Service

If you can't find a tenant on whom you wish to serve the 30-day notice, and you can't find anyone else at home or work (or if you don't know where the tenant is employed), you may serve the notice using a procedure known as "posting and mailing." (People in the business call it "nail and mail.") To do this, you tack or tape a copy of the notice to the front door of the rental unit and mail a second copy to the tenant at that address. In order to serve the notice this way, you must do the following, in the order indicated:

- try to personally serve the tenant at home, and not succeed

- try to serve the tenant at work and not succeed

- post a copy of the notice on the front door of the property, and

- mail another copy to the tenant at home by first class mail. (CCP § 1162(3).)

Again, service of the notice is not complete until you have followed through by mailing a second copy of the notice. ■

15

RETALIATORY RENT INCREASES AND EVICTIONS

It is illegal for a landlord to retaliate against a tenant who has exercised his tenant rights as specified by state law, or who has complained to a federal, state, or local agency about the habitability of the rental unit. The statute extends even beyond the exercise of strictly *tenant* rights—the exercise of "any rights under the law" are protected. Landlords may not reduce services, give (or even threaten to give) a rent increase or termination notice, or do anything else that works to the tenant's disadvantage. (CC § 1942.5.) The general idea is that tenants should not be punished by landlords just because they are invoking their legal rights or remedies.

Our goal in this chapter is twofold: First, we want you to clearly understand how the law defines retaliatory evictions and retaliatory rent increases. Second, and more important, we want you to know how to anticipate and avoid the legal problems that can be created by the few tenants who will try to maneuver you into the position of appearing to violate their rights.

Unfortunately, this chapter is essential reading for all landlords, even those of you (the great majority, certainly) who have no intention of ever illegally retaliating against any tenant for exercising legal rights. The problem is that the laws have been written so broadly that all sorts of innocently motivated conduct can form the basis for either a lawsuit against

the landlord for damages, or a successful defense against a landlord's unlawful detainer action.

In other words, a well-meaning ignorance of the law can cause you many problems, especially if you are dealing with a dishonest tenant who is determined to misuse the law to try to avoid paying rent. If you know your legal rights and learn to take sensible advance steps to nullify and counter a tenant's hostile urges, you should have few legal problems.

If you own property in areas with rent control laws that contain just-cause-for-eviction provisions, you should refer to Chapter 4. This is not to say that retaliatory rent increases and terminations are legal in rent-controlled areas. To the contrary, most rent-controlled ordinances have antiretaliation provisions that are even stricter than state law; in fact, some local ordinances even provide criminal penalties. It's just that the question of whether rent increases and terminations are retaliatory, and therefore illegal, seldom comes up in most rent control areas, where more stringent local laws restrict rent increases and terminations of every kind, retaliatory or not.

A. TYPES OF RETALIATION THAT ARE PROHIBITED

As we've discussed in preceding chapters, residential tenants have a number of legal rights and remedies. Because tenant protection laws would be meaningless if a landlord could legally retaliate against a tenant who asserts legal rights, the law forbids such retaliation. For example, the right of a month-to-month tenant to complain to the local fire department about a defective heater would be worth little if the landlord, angry about the complaint, could retaliate with an immediate 30-day or 60-day termination or rent increase notice. Recognizing this, the California Legislature and courts have made it illegal for a landlord to attempt to penalize a tenant in any way simply because the tenant has attempted to exercise a legal right that works to the landlord's disadvantage.

Under the theory that to be forewarned allows you to be forearmed, we list some key tenants' rights here and give a few examples where landlords are commonly accused of retaliating against the tenant:

- For tenants on a fixed-term lease: the right to refuse to pay a rent increase before the end of the lease term—unless the lease provides for periodic rent increases: Chapter 14

- For month-to-month tenants: the right to insist on a written notice of 30 days (60 days for some rent increases) before submitting to any change in terms of tenancy: Chapter 14

- The right to be free from discriminatory treatment based on factors such as race, religion, sex, disability, and marital status, and to complain to administrative agencies, or even courts, when a tenant feels her rights are being violated: Chapter 9

- The right to live in premises free of defects that might endanger a tenant's health or safety, including the right to complain to local authorities or to withhold rent in appropriate cases, or even to file a lawsuit against a landlord who fails to keep the premises in proper repair: Chapter 11

- The right to exercise the "repair-and-deduct" remedy (by deducting the cost of habitability-related repairs from the rent after giving the landlord written or oral notice and a reasonable time to remedy the problem) within the past six months, unless the notice states a valid reason for terminating the tenancy: Chapter 11

- The right to privacy and freedom from having the landlord enter the property without notice or for improper reasons: Chapter 13

- The right to engage in political activity of any kind, including the right to organize or take part in a tenants' organization or other tenant protests. A tenant who actively campaigns for local candidates whom property owners find obnoxious, or who campaigns for a rent control ordinance, has an absolute right to do so without fear of intimidation.

The above list is for illustration only. There are many more situations in which a tenant can assert a particular right and the landlord's subsequent efforts to evict the tenant or raise the rent on account of it will be considered illegal. This is true no matter how unpleasantly conveyed, ill-founded, or just plain wrong the tenant's gripe is. After all, the issue isn't whether the tenant had a good reason to act as he did, but whether his act was the exercise of a legal right and whether the landlord's subsequent act was a form of retaliation. Thus, tenants have prevailed on retaliatory eviction grounds in situations as diverse as the tenant's refusal to lie for the landlord at a trial and the tenant's calling the police for a crime committed by a manager. (See *Barela v. Superior Court,* 30 Cal. 3d 244, 178 Cal. Rptr. 618 (1981); and *Custom Parking, Inc. v. Superior Court,* 138 Cal. App. 3d 90, 187 Cal. Rptr. 674 (1982).)

B. PROVING RETALIATION

Both landlords and tenants commonly have misconceptions about the timing and proof required for tenants to raise the defense of retaliation.

1. Retaliation for Complaints to Government Agencies

It is illegal to retaliate against a tenant who has made a complaint about housing conditions, either to the landlord or to a health or building inspection department, no matter how unfounded or frivolous the tenant's complaint may have been. If the tenant has withheld rent to protest bad housing conditions, or makes use of the "repair-and-deduct" remedy, it is considered a form of illegal retaliation to follow this with a 30-day or 60-day termination or rent increase notice.

If a tenant whose rent is paid up complains to a government agency about defects in the premises, and if the landlord subsequently raises rent, decreases services, or evicts the tenant within 180 days, retaliation is presumed. If the tenant goes to court, the landlord must prove that the action was not retaliatory. (CC § 1942.5(a).) After 180 days, the tenant can still sue, but retaliation is no longer presumed.

Aside from limitations in any applicable rent control ordinance, a landlord can legally raise the rent or terminate the tenancy at any time if there is a legitimate nonretaliatory reason. But, if challenged, the landlord will have to prove that his actions were not retaliatory.

2. Retaliation for Other Acts

If the tenant asserts any other legal right—that is, other than complaining to a government agency about defects in the premises—the tenant must prove retaliation is the motive for any rent increase, decrease in services, or eviction that follows. Under both statutory and common law, the tenant may raise the defense of retaliation or sue the landlord for retaliatory eviction at any time, and it doesn't matter whether or not the tenant is paid up in rent. (CC § 1942.5(c). Also, see *Glaser v. Meyers,* 137 Cal. App. 3d 770 (1982).) Even so, as time goes on, it becomes harder for the tenant to establish that the landlord still has a retaliatory motive.

A landlord's conduct can be proof of his motive. In deciding whether a landlord acted with a retaliatory motive, judges look at such things as:

- how soon the landlord responded with a rent increase or termination notice after the tenant exercised a legal right

- how the landlord treated the complaining tenant as compared to other tenants who didn't exercise their rights in the same way

- the overall reasonableness of the landlord's conduct, and

- whether the landlord appears to have had a legitimate reason for the actions.

How retaliation cases are fought out in court—either by a tenant defending an eviction lawsuit or by a tenant suing a landlord—is discussed in Section D, below.

C. AVOIDING CHARGES OF RETALIATION

Sometimes it seems that every time a tenant can't or won't pay a legitimate rent increase, they will claim you are guilty of retaliatory misconduct. The same sort of unreasonable reliance on tenant protection laws can occur when you seek to terminate the tenancy for a perfectly legitimate reason and the tenant doesn't want to move. How do you cope with this sort of cynical misuse of the law? As with most things legal, there is no single answer. However, if you are prepared to plan ahead, you should be able to minimize any legal problems.

You start with a great advantage when faced with a tenant who attempts to defeat your legitimate rent increase or tenancy termination with phony retaliation claims. As a business person, you have an opportunity to plan ahead—anticipate that some tenants will adopt these tactics and prepare to meet them. The tenant, on the other hand, must react on an ad hoc basis and often has just a superficial knowledge of the law.

How exactly do you plan ahead? First, realize that some tenants affected negatively by any course of action you plan, such as a rent increase or eviction notice—no matter how legal and justified—are likely to strike back, often more by reflex than by thought. Second, try to anticipate what they will do, and be prepared to avoid or counter their tactics. Here are a number of proven landlord techniques:

1. Set up clear, easy-to-follow procedures for tenants to ask for repairs and respond quickly when complaints are made, and conduct annual safety inspections. (We show you how in Chapter 11.) This sort of policy will go a long way toward demonstrating that a complaint is phony—for example, if a tenant faced with a rent increase or tenancy termination suddenly complains to an outside agency about some defect in the premises they rent, without talking to you first. Also, if your periodic inquiries result in complaints from several tenants, but you only evict one tenant, you can show you don't have a policy of retaliating against tenants who do complain.

2. Do not announce your intention to terminate a tenancy in advance. Telegraphing your intentions gives the tenant a chance to lodge a complaint. For example, suppose you tell the tenant on the 25th that you're going to give him a 30-day notice on the 31st. His complaint to the health department on the 28th—over a trivial defect—will be followed by your written notice dated the 31st. The short timespan between his complaint and your 30-day notice will appear to substantiate the tenant's claim of your supposed retaliatory intent. Similarly, if you and a tenant are at loggerheads and no compromise seems possible, move quickly. Don't give the tenant time to create a raft of phony retaliatory eviction defenses.

If you genuinely want to work things out with the tenant, extend the notice period—but do this after the established date of the notice to avoid any attempts of phony retaliation.

3. Even though the law (in nonrent control areas) says that a landlord doesn't need a reason to terminate a tenancy, be prepared to demonstrate that you do have a good reason to evict the tenant. In other words, in anticipation of the possibility that a tenant may claim that you are terminating the tenancy for retaliatory reasons, you should be prepared to prove that your reasons were valid and not retaliatory. When you think of it, this burden isn't as onerous as it might first appear. From a business point of view, few landlords will ever want to evict an excellent tenant. And assuming there is a good reason why you want the tenant out—for example, the tenant repeatedly pays the rent late in violation of the rental agreement—you only need document it. (See Chapter 18 for legitimate reasons for terminating tenancies.)

4. Have legitimate business reasons for any rent increases or other changes in the conditions of the tenancy, and make the changes reasonable. The best answer to a charge of retaliation is proof that your act was based on legitimate business reasons and was wholly independent of any exercise by tenants of their rights. Chapter 14 discusses how to adopt a sensible rent increase policy.

5. If a tenant withholds rent or makes a complaint for even an arguably legitimate reason, at or near the time you were going to raise the rent or give the tenant a 30-day or 60-day notice anyway, wait. First take care of the complaint. Next, let some time pass. Then, do what you planned to do anyway (assuming you can document a legitimate reason for your action). However, if you disagree with the right of the tenant to withhold rent, you can give the tenant a Three-Day Notice to Pay Rent or Quit, with an eye toward suing the tenant on the basis of rent nonpayment. (See Chapter 16 for a discussion of three-day notices.)

The delay may cost you a few bucks, or result in some inconvenience, or even cause you to lose some sleep while you gnash your teeth, but all of these are preferable to being involved in litigation over whether you retaliated for the tenant's complaint.

EXAMPLE

A tenant, Fanny, makes a legitimate complaint to the health department about a defective heater in an apartment she rents from Abe. Even though Fanny does so without telling Abe or his manager first, Fanny is still within her legal rights to make the complaint. About the same time Fanny files the complaint, neighboring tenants complain to Abe, not for the first time, about Fanny's loud parties that last into the wee hours of the morning. Other tenants threaten to move out if Fanny stays. In response to the neighboring tenants' complaints, Abe gives Fanny a 30-day notice (Fanny has rented from Abe for less than a year). She refuses to move, and Abe must file an unlawful detainer complaint. Fanny responds that the eviction was in retaliation for her complaint to the health department. A contested trial results. Perhaps Abe will win in court, but in this situation, there is a good chance he won't.

SAMPLE LETTER REMINDING TENANT OF COMPLAINT PROCEDURE

February 1, 200X

Fanny Hayes
123 State Street, Apt. 15
San Diego, CA

Dear Ms. Hayes:

As you know, Ms. Sharon Donovan, my resident manager at Sunny Dell Apartments, repaired the heater in your unit yesterday, on January 31.

Ms. Donovan informs me that she never received a complaint from you nor any request to repair the heater, and that she learned about the problem for the first time when she received a telephone call to that effect from Cal Mifune of the San Diego County Health Department. Apparently, you notified the Health Department of the problem without first attempting to resolve it with Ms. Donovan.

While you certainly do have a legal right to complain to a governmental agency about any problem, you should be aware that the management of Sunny Dell Apartments takes pride in its quick and efficient response to residents' complaints and requests for repairs.

In the future, we hope that you'll avail yourself of our complaint procedure if you have a problem with any aspect of your apartment. Simply fill out a Maintenance/Repair Request form, available from Ms. Donovan during her office hours of 9:00 a.m. to 6:00 p.m., Monday through Saturday. In case of an urgent request during the evening or on Sundays, you may call me at 555-1234.

Sincerely,

Abe Horowitz

Abe Horowitz, Owner

Now, let's look at how you might better handle this problem:

Step 1. Fix the heater.

Step 2. Write the tenant, reminding her of your established complaint procedures. Tell her that you consider this sort of repair a routine matter that didn't necessitate a complaint to a public agency.

A sample letter is shown above.

Step 3. Carefully document the noise complaints of the neighbors. If possible, get them in writing. Feel out the neighbors about whether they would testify in court if necessary.

In several cities with rent control ordinances that require just cause for eviction, you are required to give the tenant a preliminary written notice to cease whatever conduct you claim violates the lease or rental agreement. Only if the tenant fails to comply can you legally give him a three-day, 30-day, or 60-day notice to terminate the tenancy. If you rent in one of these areas, you'll need to modify the following letter to comply with the requirements of your rent control ordinance. See Chapter 18, Section C3.

Step 4. Write the tenant about the neighbors' complaints. The first letter should be conciliatory. Offer to meet with the tenant to resolve the problem, but also remind the tenant of the rental agreement (or lease) provision banning illegal conduct, and that excessive noise after a certain hour is a violation of city or county ordinances. If the first letter doesn't work, follow up with another letter, even if you don't think this will do any good either. These letters will help you greatly should a court fight develop later.

Below are two sample letters. Also, see Chapter 18, Section C for a fill-in-the-blank warning letter you can send a tenant in response to complaints from neighbors or other residents. The form warning letter in Chapter 18 may be useful in many types of situations—not just those where a tenant claims retaliation.

Step 5. If possible, wait a few months, during which you should carefully document any more complaints before giving the tenant a 30-day or 60-day notice.

This sort of preparatory work may influence the tenant not to claim you are guilty of retaliatory conduct. However, even if you do end up in court, you should win easily.

FIRST SAMPLE LETTER REGARDING NEIGHBORS' COMPLAINTS

February 15, 200X

Fanny Hayes
123 State Street, Apt. 15
San Diego, CA

Dear Ms. Hayes:

I am writing this letter to inform you that several of your neighbors have complained to Ms. Sharon Donovan, Sunny Dell Apartments' resident manager, on several occasions during late January and early February, when you apparently hosted several parties in your apartment. In addition to complaints regarding shouting and the playing of loud music until 2:00 a.m., it appears that several party guests littered beer cans and other debris in the balcony outside the entrances to your apartment and those of several other units.

It is very important to the management of Sunny Dell Apartments that our residents be able to enjoy the peace and quiet of their homes. While we have no objections to our residents hosting occasional parties, we would hope that such events would be conducted with due regard for other residents, some of whom are elderly people quite easily agitated by excessive noise and litter.

Accordingly, we request that when you host parties in your apartment, you keep the noise within reasonable levels, particularly after 10:00 p.m., and that you restrain your guests from littering the common areas. Thank you for your cooperation.

Sincerely,

Abe Horowitz

Abe Horowitz, Owner

SECOND SAMPLE LETTER REGARDING NEIGHBORS' COMPLAINTS

February 25, 200X

Fanny Hayes
123 State Street, Apt. 15
San Diego, CA

Dear Ms. Hayes:

On February 15, I wrote to inform you that several of your neighbors had complained about loud music until the early hours of the morning from frequent parties you have in your apartment. I also called your attention to complaints regarding litter scattered about by your party guests.

Since then, I have received several more similar complaints regarding parties given within the past ten days. Some of the persons complaining have indicated their intention to move should this conduct continue. You appear intent on ignoring both my warnings to you and complaints made directly to you by your neighbors. For example, I am told that on February 20, you refused to reduce the volume of very loud music played at 1:30 a.m. until the police were called to ask you to do so, and that the next morning your neighbors discovered 15 empty beer cans and bottles scattered about the entrance to your apartment.

Please be advised that Clause 16 of your rental agreement makes illegal conduct in and about the premises a violation of the agreement, and that making excessive noise during late hours is unlawful under provisions of our city ordinance. Accordingly, this sort of behavior is the type for which your tenancy may be terminated. Should I receive any more complaints of similar conduct by you or your guests, I will have no choice but to have Ms. Donovan give you a notice of termination of tenancy.

Sincerely,

Abe Horowitz

Abe Horowitz, Owner

D. LIABILITY FOR ILLEGAL RETALIATION

Here are the methods by which a tenant can assert that a landlord is guilty of unlawful retaliatory conduct. We believe you need to know what they are so you can avoid being accused of such conduct.

1. The Tenant's Defense to an Eviction Lawsuit

A tenant who believes her landlord has illegally retaliated against her for having exercised a legal right can use what is called an "affirmative defense" in an eviction lawsuit. In an eviction lawsuit, the tenant normally has the burden of proving that the landlord's motive was to retaliate against her. *Western Land Office v. Cervantes,* 175 Cal. App. 3d 724, 220 Cal. Rptr. 784 (1985). However, this opinion suggests that if a tenant exercises a right under the law, and the landlord serves her with a termination or rent increase notice within six months, the landlord must state on the notice a justification or reason for the termination or rent increase. See Chapter 18 for details on eviction lawsuits.

The issue of retaliation may come up in a tenant's affirmative defense when a landlord goes to court to enforce a 30-day or 60-day termination notice after the tenant refuses to move out, or to sue for nonpayment of rent because the tenant refuses to pay a rent increase she claims is retaliatory. The tenant says in effect, "Even if the landlord served me with the proper 30-day notice or an otherwise valid termination of tenancy (or rent increase), the landlord's action is invalid because she was retaliating against me for exercising a legal right."

Let's take two examples to show how this works.

EXAMPLE 1

On March 1, Abe gives his tenant Fanny (to whom he has rented for less than a year) a 30-day notice to move, effective April 1. Come April 1, Abe refuses to accept Fanny's offer of another month's rent of $400, telling her he expects her to move. Fanny refuses, claiming that Abe's notice was motivated by Fanny's January 25 complaint to the Health Department about the heater. If Abe wants to make Fanny move, he'll have to bring an eviction lawsuit, serving Fanny with a "summons" and "complaint." Fanny will then file an "answer," which states the "affirmative defense" that the notice was retaliatory. In this situation, the case will go to trial about May 10.

If Abe can convince the judge his real reason for giving Fanny the 30-day notice was her repeated loud parties that other tenants complained about, and that his motive wasn't to retaliate against Fanny, the judge will award Abe the prorated rent through May 10 ($400 for April, plus $133.33 for May 1-10), possession of the property, court costs, and attorney fees (if Abe hired an attorney and the lease or rental agreement contains an attorney fees clause). Only then will Fanny have to move.

If the judge thinks Abe's motive was to retaliate, Fanny can stay, getting a judgment against Abe for court costs and for attorney fees (if either party is entitled to them in the lease or rental agreement). However, once it's settled that Fanny stays, her rent for April and May ($800 total) will come due. If Fanny doesn't pay the rent, Abe can legitimately serve her a Three-Day Notice to Pay Rent or Quit, and sue again if the rent still remains unpaid.

EXAMPLE 2

On September 1, Dolores gives her tenant Kit a 30-day notice increasing Kit's rent from $800 to $850 per month. (Since the last rent increase was over a year ago, and the increase was less than 10%, a 60-day notice is not required.) On October 1, Kit hands Dolores a check for $800, refusing to pay the $50 increase on the basis that it was retaliatory. Kit, who began organizing a building tenants' union in July, is convinced the increase is Dolores's way of striking back. Dolores accepts the $800, but then gives Kit a three-day notice to pay the $50 or vacate. When Kit does neither, Dolores files suit based on nonpayment of rent, Kit answers with a retaliatory rent increase defense and the case goes to trial about November 15.

If Dolores wins, the judge will award her the unpaid $50 for October, plus the prorated rent of $425 through November 15, court costs, attorney fees if appropriate and, of course, possession of the property; Kit will have to move.

If Kit wins, the judge will order Dolores to pay Kit's court costs and attorney fees, if applicable. Since the decision is in Kit's favor, the judge has clearly decided the rent increase was retaliatory; thus, the proper rent is $800 after all. Of course, now that it's November and the case is over, with Kit staying on, he'll owe Dolores the $800 rent in November.

Although the above examples show both the tenants and the landlords fighting bitter court battles to the very end, the examples are intended only to show what the law provides for when taken to this extreme. This isn't to say that both parties can't try to compromise at any stage. Always keep in mind that a landlord's victory can sometimes be hollow. If, after spending hundreds (or even thousands) of dollars on lawyers and filing fees and going without rent while the lawsuit is pending, the landlord winds up with an empty apartment and a court judgment that is uncollectible because the tenant skipped town or is judgment proof (has no assets), the landlord has not gained much.

IS GOING OUT OF BUSINESS "RETALIATION"?

The steps you cannot take in response to a tenant's exercise of a legal right don't clearly include the most drastic step of all—going out of the rental business. In rent control cities with just-cause eviction protection, this is just what many landlords have done. For example, faced with continuing complaints to building inspectors, tenant organizing, and use of the repair-and-deduct remedy, a landlord may decide to chuck it all and put the property to another use or sell to a buyer who intends to occupy the property.

Landlords who take property off the market must follow the Ellis Act, which generally gives tenants 120 days to move out (the Ellis Act is explained in more detail in *The California Landlord's Law Book: Evictions*, by David Brown (Nolo)). If the tenant refuses to move, a landlord may begin an eviction proceeding. In a normal eviction proceeding, of course, a tenant's exercise of legal rights would defeat the eviction. But can a tenant assert the prohibition against retaliation in an Ellis eviction, and survive the eviction? No, as long as the landlord had a bona fide intent to get out of the rental business, his motive is irrelevant. (*Drouet v. Superior Court (Broustis)*, 31 Cal.4th 583 (2003).)

Keep in mind that even though the *defense* is not available (thus allowing the landlord to evict), a tenant can still sue for money damages that have resulted from a retaliatory eviction. The tenant can sue for actual damages plus punitive damages of up to $1,000 for each retaliatory act committed with fraud, oppression or malice. (Civ.Code §§ 1942.5(f) & (g).)

2. Tenant Lawsuits Against the Landlord

It's also important for all landlords to realize that a tenant who feels the landlord has illegally retaliated against her doesn't have to sit back and wait for the landlord to take the matter to court. The tenant can initiate a lawsuit. Many tenants' attorneys advise their clients to do just this in order to put the landlord at a psychological disadvantage. In effect, the tenant asks the court to rule that the landlord's conduct was retaliatory, and to bar the landlord from bringing an eviction suit.

The tenant can also ask for money. A tenant who sues a landlord and convinces a judge or jury that the landlord illegally retaliated against her for exercising a legal right can obtain a judgment for damages for emotional distress, mental pain and suffering, punitive damages, court costs, and attorney fees, even if the lease or rental agreement doesn't have an attorney fees clause. (See also CC § 1942.5(f), *Newby v. Alto Rivera Apartments,* 60 Cal. App. 3d 288, 131 Cal. Rptr. 547 (1976).) Potential liability in these suits can and does reach tens of thousands of dollars.

The defense of this sort of lawsuit is well beyond the scope of this book, and we strongly advise you to retain a lawyer. If you have a good landlord's insurance policy that protects you from so-called "illegal acts," this will cover you in this situation (except for the deductible amount and punitive damages), and you can turn your legal defense over to the insurance company. See Chapter 12 on landlord liability for tenantability-related defects, where landlord insurance is discussed in more detail. If you have no insurance, see Chapter 8 on how to find, compensate, and work with a lawyer.

It's also important to realize that a tenant doesn't have to bring a lawsuit before the landlord does in order to be able to obtain money damages. If the landlord brings an eviction suit and the tenant defends on the basis of retaliation and wins, the tenant, bolstered by her victory, can bring another suit for damages. In fact, the tenant who won the preceding eviction suit on the basis that the landlord illegally retaliated may be able to apply the rulings from the first lawsuit to the second one, so as to prevent the landlord from again denying and litigating the issue of retaliation. In other words, the only issue in the second suit will be how much the landlord owes the tenant. This is one more illustration of how important it is to not engage in retaliatory behavior or, in spite of these efforts, to win or settle any eviction suit where the tenant defends on the basis of retaliatory eviction. ■

16

THE THREE-DAY NOTICE TO PAY RENT OR QUIT

A landlord who is serious about having tenants pay their rent on time must be prepared to use the tools the law provides for enforcing payment. Ultimately, the landlord's most powerful weapon to assure payment of rent is the ability to file an eviction lawsuit against tenants who don't pay. Although we reserve discussion of how to bring an eviction lawsuit for *The California Landlord's Law Book: Evictions*, by David Brown (Nolo), there is one preliminary aspect of a rent-nonpayment suit that must be outlined here. This is the requirement that a landlord give the tenant three days' written notice to pay the rent or quit (leave). This chapter shows you how to give that notice.

Related Topics

- Laws regarding how much rent you can charge, where, how, and when rent is due; and accepting partial rent payments: Chapter 3

- How to end a tenancy with a 30-day notice and various other types of three-day notices: Chapter 18.

A. WHEN TO USE A THREE-DAY NOTICE

Many landlords resist handing out three-day notices. After all, preparing and serving a three-day notice involves at least a little bit of trouble, and it's easy to conclude that it is the first step in what is sure to be a nasty court eviction battle, something almost every landlord dreads.

First, you should realize that serving a Three-Day Notice to Pay Rent or Quit does not necessarily lead to a lawsuit. A three-day notice is a tool designed to get tenants to pay rent, not to evict them. Remember, an eviction lawsuit is generally something the tenant wants to avoid at least as much as you do. In fact, most tenants who receive a three-day notice do pay up within the three days.

In a few cases, tenants don't pay, which means the three-day notice becomes the first step in a court action. If this occurs, the judge will likely scrutinize the notice carefully. If the notice contains certain errors, you will lose an eviction lawsuit, perhaps having to pay the tenant's attorney fees. In other words, even though a three-day notice doesn't necessarily lead to an unlawful detainer suit, you usually don't know in advance whether a particular notice will be the first step in a lawsuit. It may be; you should therefore take pains to be sure all notices you prepare and serve are legally correct.

B. HOW TO DETERMINE THE AMOUNT OF RENT DUE

The most common type of defect in a three-day notice involves the landlord demanding more rent than is due, or demanding improper extras, such as late charges, check-bounce fees, interest, utility charges, or even past due installments promised by the tenant towards a security deposit.

These are costly mistakes: If the three-day notice demands the wrong amount, it does not legally terminate the tenancy. To win an eviction lawsuit against a tenant who fails to pay rent, the judge has to rule that the tenancy was properly terminated by your having served a valid three-day notice on the tenant, followed by the tenant's nonpayment within the three days. A tenancy isn't legally terminated unless the three-day notice to which a tenant fails to respond stated the proper rent amount and was legally correct in other respects. For example, a three-day notice demanding $1,450 from a tenant who owes only $1,400 isn't legally sufficient to terminate the tenancy even though the tenant does owe the $1,400, and a judge won't allow an eviction based on the incorrect rent amount.

To avoid making a mistake in your three-day notice, you should keep the following rules in mind:

Do not demand anything other than past due rent in a three-day notice. Do not include late charges, fees of any kind, interest, utility charges, or anything else in a three-day notice—even if a written lease or rental agreement says you're entitled to payment for such items and even if your rental agreement or lease calls these sums "additional rent" (this is an attempt to get around the rule just explained—it works in a commercial lease, but not a residential one). Does this mean that you cannot legally collect these charges? No. It simply means you can't legally include them in the three-day notice or recover them in an eviction lawsuit. You can deduct these amounts from the security deposit or sue for them later in small claims court. (See Chapter 20.)

Rent control note. If your three-day notice demands more rent than was legally due under the local rent control ordinance, the notice is defective. You can't evict a tenant for refusal to pay a rent increase that was illegal under a rent control ordinance, even if the tenant also refuses to pay the part of the rent that is legal under the ordinance. A three-day notice is also defective under a rent control ordinance if the landlord at any time collected rents in excess of those allowed under the ordinance and failed to credit the tenant with the overcharges, even if the landlord now charges the correct rent and seeks to evict only on nonpayment of the legal rent. Since the previously collected excess rents must be credited against unpaid legal rent, any three-day notice that doesn't give the tenant credit for previous overcharges is legally ineffective because it demands too much rent. Check your local rent control ordinance for any special requirements on three-day notices.

Rent is almost always due in advance for the entire rental period. (See Clause 4 of our form lease and rental agreements in Chapter 2.) For example, rent is due in advance on November 1 for the period November 1 through November 30. In other words, the amount of rent due is not appor-

tioned on the basis of the date the three-day notice is served, but is due for the whole month, on the first or other rent payment date. The only time rent must be apportioned as part of a three-day notice is when the tenancy terminates in the middle of the rental period, usually because of an earlier 30-day notice. For example, if the landlord gives a 30-day or 60-day notice on November 15, the tenancy should terminate on December 15. This means that on December 1, only 15 days' rent is due if the rental period begins on the first of the month. If the tenant fails to pay on the first, the landlord should serve a three-day notice demanding only prorated rent for the 15-day period. To do this, you must first arrive at a daily rental amount. This is easy. The daily rental is always taken to be the monthly rental divided by 30, even in months with 28, 29, or 31 days.

If the tenant has paid you part, but not all, of the rent due, your demand for rent must reflect the partial payment. See Chapter 3, Section F for a discussion of accepting partial rent payments after a three-day notice.

You do not have to credit any part of a security deposit to the amount of rent you ask for in the three-day notice. In other words, you have a right to wait until after the tenant has moved, to see if you should apply the deposit to cover any necessary damages or cleaning. (See Chapter 20.)

Here are a few examples of how rent is calculated in various situations.

EXAMPLE 1

Richard has been paying $500 rent to his landlord, Loretta, on the first of each month, as provided by a written rental agreement. On October 6, Richard still hasn't paid his rent, and Loretta serves him with a three-day notice to pay the $500 or leave. (Although Loretta has, in effect, given Richard the benefit of a five-day grace period, she didn't have to, and could have given Richard the notice on October 2.) Even though the rental agreement provides for a $10 late charge after the second day, Loretta should not list that amount in the three-day notice.

EXAMPLE 2

Dan's rent of $750 is due the 15th of each month for the period of the 15th through the 14th of the next month—in advance, of course. Dan's check for the period from October 15 through November 14 bounces, but his landlord Len doesn't discover this until November 15. Now, Dan not only refuses to make good on the check, but also refuses to pay the rent due for the November 15-through-December 15 period. It's now November 20. What should Len ask for in his three-day notice? Dan owes Len $750 for October 15–November 14 (the rent which was to have been covered by the bounced check), plus $750 for the period November 15–December 14. The three-day notice should demand payment of $1,500. Len should not add check-bouncing charges or late fees to the amount in the three-day notice. And even though Dan promises to leave in a few days, Len should demand rent for the entire period of November 15 through December 14.

EXAMPLE 3

Laurie gives Dean a 60-day notice (because Dean has rented from Laurie for over a year) on May 11, after Dean paid his May rent (due on May 1) nine days late. Because the 60-day notice will terminate Dean's tenancy on July 10, Dean will only owe rent for the first ten days of July, due on the first day of that month. In this situation, rent should be apportioned if it is necessary to send a three-day notice. In other words, if Dean doesn't pay up on July 1, the three-day notice Laurie gives Dean on July 2 should demand this ten days' rent, or 1/30th of the monthly rent ($350/30 = $11.66/day) for each of these days, a total of 10 x $11.66, or $116.60.

EXAMPLE 4

Renee is a month-to-month tenant who pays her landlord $600 rent on the first of each month. On June 30, she gives her landlord a 30-day notice saying she'll be leaving at the end of July. Her letter also says, "Please consider my $600 security deposit as the last month's rent for the month of July." Renee's landlord has no obligation to let Renee do this, and can serve her a three-day notice demanding July's rent of $600 on July 2, the day after it's due. As a practical matter, however, he might be wiser to ask Renee for permission to inspect the property to see if it is in good enough condition to justify the eventual return of the security deposit. If so, there is little to be gained by filing a three-day notice and then suing for unpaid rent, since by the time the case gets before a judge, the need to return the security deposit (this must be done within three weeks after Renee leaves) will cancel it out.

To summarize, to issue a correct three-day notice, demand only rent, due in advance and not prorated (except where the tenancy terminates in the middle of a rental period because of the service of an earlier 30-day or 60-day notice), and give credit for partial rent payments, but not for any part of the security deposit.

Note on habitability defenses. In arriving at the amount of rent due, you do not have to anticipate a claim by your tenant that she doesn't owe the entire rent because the property was "untenantable" for all or part of the time for which you claim rent. In other words, ask for the entire amount due under the terms of the lease or rental agreement. If the tenant doesn't pay (or the two of you don't work out a compromise settlement and you file an unlawful detainer lawsuit), it's up to the tenant to assert her habitability defense in court. However, if you expect a tenant to raise a habitability defense in court, we strongly urge you to read Chapter 11 before proceeding.

On the other hand, if a tenant has deducted from the rent the actual cost of repairs of a habitability-related defect and notified you of that earlier, you should give the tenant credit for the cost of repair, if the deduction is legitimate and proper. (See Chapter 11.)

C. HOW TO FILL OUT A THREE-DAY NOTICE

A sample Three-Day Notice to Pay Rent or Quit appears below, and a blank tear-out form is included in Appendix B and on the CD-ROM. You may tear out the form or use a copy, following the instructions that follow the sample form.

Pay close attention to the directions. Any mistake in the notice, however slight, may give your tenant (or her attorney) an excuse to contest or delay any eviction lawsuit you may ultimately bring if the tenant doesn't pay up in response to your notice. At worst, a mistake in the three-day notice may render your unlawful detainer lawsuit "fatally defective"—which means you lose, must pay the tenant's court costs and attorney fees (in addition to your own) and have to start all over again with a correct three-day notice.

For example, if you just demand the rent and do not set out the alternative of the tenant leaving, your notice is fatally defective. The notice must also include a statement that you will pursue legal action (or declare the lease or rental agreement "forfeited") if the tenant does not pay the entire rent or move.

Directions for Completing the Three-Day Notice to Pay Rent or Quit

Step 1. Fill in the Tenant's Name.

The first blank is for the name(s) of the tenant(s) to whom the three-day notice is addressed. Although this is technically not required, it is so customary to put the tenant's name on a three-day notice that to omit it could invite a delaying tactic from a tenant's attorney on the theory that the tenant might not have known it was for her. Be sure to list the names of the tenant(s) whose names are listed on a written lease or rental agreement, or with whom you orally entered into a rental agreement, plus the names, if known, of any other adult occupants of the property. (See Section D3, below.)

Step 2. Fill in the Address.

List the street address, city, and county. In addition, be sure to list the apartment number if your tenant lives in an apartment complex or in a condominium unit.

In the unlikely event the unit has no street address, you should use a legal description of the premises available from your deed to your property, along with an ordinary, understandable description of where the place is located—for example, "the small log cabin behind the third hill going north on River Road from Pokeyville." You can retype the notice to make room for the legal description or staple a separate property description as an attachment to the notice and type "the property described in the attachment to this notice" in place of the address.

Step 3. Fill in the Rent Due.

The next space is for you to fill in the amount of rent due. It is mandatory to state this figure accurately. (See Section B, above.) Although it is not legally required to indicate the rental period(s) for which the rent is due, it is customary, and some judges who are used to seeing it may question, or even reject, notices that don't include the dates.

Step 4. Fill in Payment Information.

The next spaces tell the tenant to whom, where, and how to pay the rent, as follows:

Under "RENT IS TO BE PAID TO," check the box next to "the undersigned" if the person who signs the notice (such as the manager or owner) will receive the rent. If someone else will receive the rent, check the box next to "the following" and list the name of that person.

Under "AT THE FOLLOWING ADDRESS," give the address where the rent should be paid (do not list a post office box unless you want the rent to be mailed to one). Give the telephone number of the person who will accept the rent.

Three-Day Notice to Pay Rent or Quit

To: _____Tyrone Jones_____,

                                       Name

all tenants, subtenants, adult occupants, and others in possession of the premises at _123 Market Street_____,

                                                             Street Address

____Apartment 4___, City of __San Diego_____, County of __San Diego_____, California.

PLEASE TAKE NOTICE that the rent on these premises occupied by you, in the amount of $___400_____, for

the period from _____August 1, 200X_____ to _____August 31, 200X_____, is now due and

payable.

YOU ARE HEREBY REQUIRED to pay this amount within THREE (3) days from the date of service on you of this

notice or to vacate and surrender possession of the premises. In the event you fail to do so, legal proceedings will

be instituted against you to recover possession of the premises, declare the forfeiture of the rental agreement or

lease under which you occupy the premises, and recover rents, damages, and costs of suit.

RENT IS TO BE PAID TO:

      [x] the undersigned, or

      [ ] the following person: _____

AT THE FOLLOWING ADDRESS: _____456 Trolley Street, San Diego_____, California, _____ (ZIP)

      phone: (619) __123-4567____

IN THE FOLLOWING MANNER:

      [x] In person. Usual days and hours for rent collection are: _Monday through Friday, 9:00 AM to 4:30 PM_

      [ ] by mail to the person and address indicated above

      [ ] by deposit to account _____ at _____, a financial institution located within 5 miles

         of your rental at _____,

         California

      [ ] by electronic funds transfer procedure previously established.

Carlos Austen _____   August 5, 200X _____

Landlord/Manager   Date

· ·

Proof of Service

I, the undersigned, being at least eighteen years of age, served this notice, of which this is a true copy, on

_____, one of the occupants listed above as follows:

☐ On _____, 20___, I delivered the notice to the occupant personally.

☐ On _____, 20___, I delivered the notice to a person of suitable age and discretion at the

    occupant's residence/business after having attempted personal service at the occupant's residence, and business, if

    known. On _____, 20___, I mailed a second copy to the occupant at his or her residence.

☐ On _____, 20___, I posted the notice in a conspicuous place on the property, after

    having attempted personal service at the occupant's residence, and business, if known, and after having been unable

    to find there a person of suitable age and discretion. _____, 20___, I mailed a second

    copy to the occupant at the property.

I declare under penalty of perjury under the laws of the State of California that the foregoing is true and correct.

_____   _____

                                                Date

Under "IN THE FOLLOWING MANNER," check one or more boxes indicating how the rent will be accepted. If you check "in person," be sure to list the days and hours when someone will be present to accept the rent. For example, the office hours for a resident manager might be "Monday through Friday, 9:00 AM through 5:00 PM." If you check "by mail …" only, rent is legally paid when mailed, regardless of when you receive it.

Do not omit any information on your three-day notice. Failure to include all of the information called for on the form may make the notice legally ineffective. If your tenant refuses to move and you attempt to evict on the basis of a legally defective three-day notice, you'll be tossed out of court and will have to begin all over, with a new three-day notice.

Step 5. Sign and Date the Notice.

The ultimatum language—that the tenant either pay the rent within three days or move out, or you'll bring legal action—and the "forfeiture" language are already included in the printed form. All you need to add are your signature and the date you signed it. The date is not legally required, but it helps to clarify when the rent was demanded. The date should not be the same day the rent was due, but at least one day later.

Be sure to make several copies for your records (the original goes to the tenant).

Step 6. Complete the Proof of Service Box on Your Copy of the Notice.

At the bottom of the Three-Day Notice to Pay Rent or Quit is a "Proof of Service" that indicates the name of the person served, the manner of service and the date(s) of service. You or whoever served the notice on the tenant should fill out the Proof of Service on your copy of the three-day notice and sign it. You do not fill out the Proof of Service on the original notice that is given to the tenant. If more than one person is served with the notice, there should be a separate Proof of Service (on a copy of the notice) for each person served. Save the filled-out Proof(s) of Service on the copies of the three-day notice—you'll need these to prove that you served the notice if you end up filing an eviction lawsuit.

D. SERVING THE THREE-DAY NOTICE ON THE TENANT

The law is very strict about when and how you give the three-day notice to your tenant(s). (See *Lydon v. Beach*, 89 Cal. App. 69 (1928) [notice can be served only after rent falls due], and CCP § 1162 [manner of service].) Even a slight departure from the rules may result in your losing any eviction lawsuit you bring if it is contested.

1. When to Serve the Notice

The Three-Day Notice to Pay Rent or Quit can be given to your tenant on any day after the rent was due, but not on the day it is due. For example, if the rent for a particular month is due on the first day of each month, if you give the notice to the tenant on that day, it will have no legal effect. Of course, if you allow a several-day grace period (remember, you don't legally have to) before serving the notice, you will have no problem.

If the rent comes due on a Saturday, Sunday, or holiday, a word of caution: Although the courts have recently ruled that a due date in a lease or rental agreement is not extended on account of falling on a weekend or holiday, despite laws that seemed to allow for such an extension, it still might be a good idea to wait until the day after the next business day to serve the three-day notice, if the rent comes due on a weekend or holiday. (*Gans v. Smull* (2003) 111 Cal.App.4th 985 (2003); see Chapter 3, Section B) This is good advice for several reasons.

- First, if the lease or rental agreement actually gives the tenant until the next business day to pay the rent—as do our form rental agreement and lease—then the rent really is not due until the next business day, usually on Monday. The three-day notice can't be served until the day after that—Tuesday.

- Second, if you wait until the day following the next business day to serve the three-day notice, you'll avoid having to respond in court to a likely argument by the tenant, who will assert that she had until the next business day to pay the rent. Under the authority quoted above, you should win, but there's no guarantee and it's better not to have to deal with complicated legal arguments even if you're right.

- Third, the myth of the supposed "grace period" of three to five days to pay the rent is so ingrained in most renters' minds that you stand a better chance of collecting your rent, following service of a three-day notice, if you wait and serve it about five days after the rent due date. As mentioned above, doing this will avoid your having to deal with the holiday-extension issue in court later on.

- Fourth, for all these reasons (and probably a few others), many judges will hesitate to order a tenant evicted, when the landlord seemingly jumped on the tenant with the three-day notice a single day after the rent was due. (That's why professional property management companies typically serve three-day notices on the sixth or seventh day after the rent due date specified in the lease or rental agreement.)

Bizarre as it sounds, if you give the notice even one day prematurely, but the tenant still didn't pay the rent during the two to three weeks he contested the lawsuit, you may still lose the case, anyway. The moral is simple—count your days carefully.

2. Who Should Serve the Three-Day Notice?

Anyone over the age of 18 can legally give or serve the three-day notice on the tenant. However, if you have to bring an eviction lawsuit against the tenant, that person may have to come to court to testify that he or she gave the tenant the notice, so make sure you pick someone who will be available.

You can legally serve the notice yourself, but it's often a better business practice to have it served by someone else. Many owners have their managers serve all three-day notices. That way, if the tenant refuses to pay the rent and contests the resulting eviction suit by falsely claiming he didn't receive the notice, you will not have to rely on your own testimony that you served the notice. Instead, you can present the testimony of someone not a party to the lawsuit, who is more likely to be believed by a judge. Of course, you must weigh this advantage against your time, trouble, or expense getting someone else to serve the three-day notice and, if necessary, appear in court.

3. Whom to Serve

If you rented your property to just one tenant, whose name alone appears on any written rental agreement or lease, you should serve that person with the three-day notice.

If you rented to more than one tenant, it's a good idea to serve separate copies of the three-day notice on each, even though it is legally sufficient for a landlord to serve just one of several cotenants who are all listed on a written lease or rental agreement. (*University of Southern California v. Weiss*, 208 Cal. App. 2d 759, 25 Cal. Rptr. 475 (1962).) We recommend serving everyone to minimize the possibility that any nonserved tenants will try to defend against any subsequent eviction lawsuit on the ground that they didn't receive the notice.

You normally have no obligation to serve the three-day notice on occupants who are not named in the written rental agreement or lease and with whom you've had no dealings in renting the property. However, if the tenant has rented to a subtenant (even illegally) and left, so that only one or more subtenants live there, you must serve the subtenants in addition to the tenant. (*Chinese Hospital Foundation Fund v. Patterson,* 1 Cal. App. 3d 627, 632, 8 Cal. Rptr. 795 (1969); see CCP § 1161(2).) Serve the nonresident tenant by substituted service (see Section 4, below). However, if the person has been living in your property for some time—for example, the lover or roommate of one of your tenants—and you have had contact with the person and treated them as a tenant (perhaps you even accepted rent from them), you should serve them with a three-day notice as well. We discuss who is and who is not a tenant in Chapter 10.

4. How to Serve the Notice on the Tenant

The law is very strict on how the three-day notice must be served on the tenant. (CCP § 1162.) It is not enough that you mail the notice or simply post it on the door. Here are the three legal methods of service for a three-day notice, listed in the order of preference.

Personal service. The best way to serve the three-day notice is to simply hand your tenant the notice. It isn't necessary that the tenant take the notice in his hand; if he refuses to do so, it may be dropped at his feet. Giving the notice to any other person, such as someone who lives with your tenant but is not listed as a cotenant on the written rental agreement, is not sufficient, except as described next under the heading "Substituted service on another person."

Substituted service on another person. If the tenant you're attempting to serve never seems to be home, and you know where she works, you should try to personally serve her at the place of employment. If you are unable to locate the tenant at either place, the law allows you to use substituted service in lieu of personally giving the notice to the tenant. That means you can leave a copy of the notice with an adult at the tenant's home or workplace and mail a second copy to the tenant at home. The first day of the notice's three-day period is the day after both these steps are accomplished.

Substituted service rules are contained in Chapter 14, Section D.

EXAMPLE

Andy should have paid his rent on the first of the month. By the fifth, you're ready to serve him with a Three-Day Notice to Pay Rent or Quit. When you try to personally serve it on him at home, a friend of Andy's answers the door, saying Andy's not home. You can't serve the notice on Andy's friend yet because you still have to try Andy's workplace—the one listed on the rental application Andy filled out when he moved in. You go to Andy's workplace only to find that Andy called in sick that day. You could either give the notice to one of Andy's coworkers, or go back and give it to his friend at home, with instructions to give it to Andy when they see him. After that, you mail another copy of the notice to Andy at home by ordinary first class mail. Service is complete only after all this has been done.

Posting-and-mailing service. If you can't find the tenant on whom you wish to serve the three-day notice, and you can't find anyone else at home or work (or if you don't know where the tenant is employed), you may serve the three-day notice through a procedure known as "posting and mailing" (also known as "nail and mail"). To do this, attach a copy of the three-day notice to the tenant's front door, and mail another copy, following the instructions in Chapter 14, Section D.

EXAMPLE

Lana's rent is due on the 15th of each month, but she still hasn't paid you by the 20th. You can never find her (or anyone else) at home, and you don't know where she works. Since there is no one on whom to personally or substitute serve the three-day notice, that leaves you with the posting-and-mailing alternative. You can tape one copy to the door of the property and mail a second copy to her at that address by regular first class mail. Begin counting the three days with the next day after both of these tasks are accomplished.

5. Counting the Three Days After Service

The date of service is the date you hand the tenant the notice, if you use personal service. If you left the three-day notice with someone else at the tenant's home (or office) and mailed another copy; or posted a copy on the premises and mailed another copy, the date of service is the date you took that action. It doesn't matter that the tenant didn't actually receive the notice until later. (*Walters v. Meyers*, 226 Cal. App. 3d Supp. 15 (1990).)

The tenant isn't entitled to additional time when you serve the three-day notice by substituted service and mailing or by posting and mailing. (*Losornio v. Motta*, 67 Cal. App. 4th 110, 78 Cal. Rptr. 2d 799

(1998).) To foreclose the possibility that the tenant might later claim he or she never received the notice, try to talk to the tenant—before you file an eviction lawsuit—and pin her down as to having received the notice. (Don't ask, "Did you get my three-day notice?" Ask, "When are you going to pay the rent I asked for in the three-day notice I left you?" If the tenant gives any answer other than, "I never got a notice!" you've got something to use in court if the tenant later claims that he never got your notice.

To count the three days, do the following:

- Ignore the date of service and start counting on the next day.
- Count three days.
- If the third day falls on a Saturday, Sunday, or holiday, ignore that day and move on to the next business day.

EXAMPLE 1

You serve the tenant with a three-day notice on Wednesday. To count the three days, do not count Wednesday; begin with Thursday. This makes Saturday the third day. But Saturday is a holiday, and so is Sunday. So the third day is Monday. Therefore, the tenant has until the end of Monday to comply. If you file your eviction lawsuit before Tuesday, it may be thrown out of court if the tenant raises the issue.

EXAMPLE 2

You serve the tenant on Friday. Saturday is the first day, Sunday is the second day, and Monday is the third day. Neither of the weekend days extends the three-day period.

E. IF THE TENANT OFFERS TO PAY RENT

If the tenant offers the rent in full any time before the end of the three-day period, you must accept it if it's offered in cash, certified check, or money order. If you've routinely accepted rent payments by personal check, you must accept a personal check in response to a three-day notice unless you notified the tenant otherwise in the notice itself. If you refuse to accept the rent (or if you insist on more money than demanded in the notice, such as late charges) and file your lawsuit anyway, your tenant will be able to contest it and win. (The only way to evict a month-to-month tenant who never pays until threatened with a three-day notice is to terminate the tenancy with a 30-day notice—see Chapter 18.)

If you accept rent (even a partial payment) after the three-day period, however, you waive your right to evict for the late payment. (*EDC Associates, Ltd. v. Gutierrez*, 153 Cal. App. 3d 169 (1984).)

F. IF THE TENANT WON'T PAY RENT (OR LEAVE)

Although one of the main purposes behind a Three-Day Notice to Pay Rent or Quit is to get the tenant to pay, you may be faced with a tenant who still won't or can't pay the rent within the three days. As we'll see in Chapter 17, it is illegal to harass the tenant in any way, even if she has no valid reason for not paying. Threatening or physically evicting a tenant or cutting off his or her utilities is illegal and may subject you to severe liability. The only legal way to evict a nonpaying tenant who won't move voluntarily is to file an eviction lawsuit, go to court, and obtain a judgment that the sheriff or marshal evict the tenant. Eviction lawsuits are discussed in Chapter 18 and in detail in *The California Landlord's Law Book: Evictions*, by David Brown (Nolo). ■

17

SELF-HELP EVICTIONS, UTILITY TERMINATIONS, AND TAKING TENANTS' PROPERTY

As any experienced landlord will attest, there are occasional tenants who do things so outrageous that the landlord is tempted to bypass normal legal protections and take direct and immediate action to protect his property. For example, after numerous broken promises to pay rent, a landlord may consider changing the locks and putting the tenant's property out in the street. Or, in a situation where the landlord is responsible for paying the utility charges, he may be tempted to simply not pay the bill in the hopes that the resulting lack of water, gas, or electricity will hasten the tenant's departure. When you realize how long a legal eviction can sometimes take, these actions can almost seem sensible.

If you are tempted to take the law into your own hands to force or scare a troublesome tenant out of your property, heed the following advice: *Don't do it!* Only the sheriff, marshal, or constable is legally allowed to physically evict a tenant, and then only after the landlord has obtained a court order allowing the eviction to take place. (We show you how to do this in *The California Landlord's Lawbook: Evictions*.) Evictions, or attempted evictions, by anyone else are illegal and may result in arrest, a lawsuit by the tenant for a great deal of money, or both. Obtaining such a court order and having the appropriate law enforcement officials carry out the eviction certainly entails some trouble, expense, and delay. This is a cost of the property rental business that can be minimized by proper selection of tenants and good management techniques, but can never be completely eliminated.

If you are sued by a tenant whom you forcibly evicted or tried to evict, the fact that the tenant didn't pay rent, left your property a mess, verbally abused you, or otherwise acted outrageously will not be a valid defense. You will very likely lose the lawsuit, and it will cost you far more than evicting the tenant using normal court procedures.

This chapter discusses the rules regarding forcible evictions, other coercive attempts to get tenants out and the taking of tenants' belongings, all of which are illegal.

EVICTING A LODGER

Civil Code § 1946.5 and Penal Code § 602.3 allow an owner-occupant of a house who is renting to no more than one roomer or lodger to insist—without going to court and filing an unlawful detainer lawsuit—that the local police evict the lodger for refusing to leave after expiration of a 30-day or 60-day notice. However, in practice it may be difficult to get your local police or sheriff to do so. Many simply don't know the law and will argue with you even if you show them the statute. Hiring an attorney to accompany you to the station house, and asking to speak with a senior officer, may do the trick.

Related Topics

- How to anticipate and avoid liability for retaliatory rent increases and evictions: Chapter 15

- The legal rules and procedures for evicting a tenant: Chapter 18.

A. FORCIBLE EVICTIONS

It is illegal for a landlord (or anyone else) to forcibly enter a tenant's residence or to peaceably enter the residence and then threaten or force the tenant out. (CCP §§ 1159 and 1160.) It's just as illegal for a landlord to knock on the tenant's door, be invited in, and then threaten to bodily evict the tenant, as it is for a landlord to kick down the door or break a window to enter the property. Or, to take another example, if a landlord simply tells a tenant, "I want you out," while accompanied by sufficiently numerous or large persons apparently capable of accomplishing the task, the landlord is courting serious legal trouble.

A landlord foolish enough to evict, or try to evict, by force or threat can be sued by the tenant under all sorts of legal theories, including trespass, assault, battery (if physical force is used against the tenant), and even intentional infliction of emotional distress. (*Newby v. Alta Rivera Apartments,* 60 Cal. App. 3d 288 (1976).) Enough said, we hope.

See Chapter 13 for a discussion of a landlord's rights of entry and tenant remedies if a landlord acts illegally and invades a tenant's privacy.

B. LOCKING OR DRIVING THE TENANT OUT WITHOUT FORCE

It is illegal for a landlord to use any of the following nonviolent methods to attempt to evict or drive out a tenant (CC § 789.3):

- locking the tenant out by changing the locks, attaching a "bootlock" to the door, or nailing the door shut

- removing doors or windows in the hope that the tenant will move out because of the resulting drafty and unsecured dwelling

- removing any of the tenant's property, or even the landlord's furniture rented as part of furnished premises, or

- shutting off any of the utilities (including gas, electricity, water, or elevator service) or causing them to be shut off by nonpayment when the landlord pays for the utilities.

Don't use lease clauses to try to get self-help rights. Even if your lease or rental agreement form contains a provision that purports to allow the landlord to break into the tenant's home, change the locks, recover property, shut off the utilities, or otherwise legally forgo the requirements of a lawful eviction, it is completely void and of no effect. (See Chapter 2, Section F.)

It's possible that not all utility cutoffs violate this law. For example, suppose a landlord who pays for the tenant's utilities properly gives a month-to-month tenant a 30-day or 60-day notice of change of terms of tenancy, which requires the tenant to put the utilities in his own name and pay for them. (This may not be permissible in certain rent-controlled cities.) If the tenant refuses and the landlord stops paying for the utilities, so as to result in a shutoff, the landlord's intent is not to illegally evict the tenant, but to enforce a proper change in terms. Still, this course is risky because a judge may conclude differently. Also, if it turns out that for any reason the change in the terms of the rental agreement is not effective—for example, the 30-day or 60-day notice was defective or found to be retaliatory in a later court action—the utility shutoff is at least a breach of contract for which the landlord can still be held liable.

In a lawsuit by a tenant against a landlord accused of unlawful lockout, property removal, or utility shutoff, a court may award the tenant all of the following:

- The tenant's "actual damages." This can include damages for inconvenience, emotional distress or humiliation, loss of property illegally removed by the landlord (or stolen or damaged by third persons after the landlord put the property outside), and loss of use of the premises. Examples include tenant losses for such things as meat spoiling in the refrigerator after the electricity is turned off, or motel bills if the tenant has to find a temporary place to live because the utilities were turned off.

- Punitive damages of up to $100 for each day, or fraction of a day, that the tenant is unable to stay in the premises or goes without utilities or without property removed by the landlord, with a minimum punitive damages liability of $250.

- Additional punitive damages if the landlord's conduct is especially outrageous, such as beating up the tenant or taking his property.

- A court-ordered award of attorney fees, even if the lease or rental agreement has no attorney fees clause.

- A restraining order, injunction, or other court order preventing the landlord, under penalty of contempt of court, from using any other illegal means to attempt to get the tenant out.

Illegal evictions are costly. In 1988, a jury awarded 23 tenants of a San Francisco residential hotel $1.48 million from their landlord, who had cut off water, entered tenants' rooms without notice, and threatened the tenants, most of whom were elderly or disabled. (The trial judge had tripled the amount based on the San Francisco rent control law. The landlord appealed the verdict, however, and the appellate court ruled that the San Francisco rent control ordinance does not allow tripling awards for mental anguish. *Balmoral Hotel Tenants Association v. Lee,* 226 Cal. App. 3d. 686, 276 Cal. Rptr. 640 (1990). Still, after the appeal, the judgment stood at a hefty half-million dollars.)

A tenant can bring suit in small claims court (for up to $5,000), or retain a lawyer and sue for much more.

As with suits for forcible eviction, a landlord cannot defend a suit for wrongful lockout, property removal, or utility shutoff on the basis that the tenant didn't pay the rent, promised to leave but didn't, or did something else even more outrageous. The legal system takes the view that a landlord (or a tenant, for that matter), when faced with the tenant's (or landlord's) wrong, cannot take the law into his own hands, then later excuse himself because of the other's original misconduct. The place for the landlord to complain is in a separate suit against the tenant.

C. SEIZING THE TENANT'S PROPERTY AND OTHER HARASSMENT

You cannot take and sell tenants' personal belongings without a court order if they fail to pay the rent. While state law allows a way to get such a court order, it is of almost no practical value to a landlord. (CC §§ 1861-1861a, known as California's Baggage Lien Law.) First of all, the law applies mainly to persons residing in hotels and motels. Second, to obtain such an order, you must convince a judge that your tenant is about to destroy or remove his property—property on which you may have a lien in an actual innkeeper situation—from the premises. Even when the law applies, it requires that the tenant be given a hearing in court, separate from any hearing on the impending eviction case. Needless to say, the trouble and expense of doing this (not to mention the problems of getting a judge to sign the order) by far exceed any benefit you could obtain from being able to take the tenant's property. And even if you get the property, it's not likely to benefit you much; the tenant will probably be entitled to get most of it back.

It is also illegal for a landlord to do any of the following things to harass a tenant "for the purpose of influencing a tenant to vacate a dwelling" (CC § 1940.2):

- take the tenant's property in violation of Penal Code § 484 (a) (theft)
- commit extortion (threatening to injure the tenant or his property, or report him or a relative for supposedly committing a crime), in violation of Penal Code § 518
- threaten force or use other menacing conduct that interferes with the tenant's quiet enjoyment of the premises, so as to "create an apprehension of harm in a reasonable person" (CC §. 1940.2(a)(4)), or
- commit a "significant and intentional" violation of the tenant's privacy, in violation of CC § 1954 (see Chapter 13).

In a lawsuit by a tenant against a landlord accused of any of these things, a court may award the tenant a civil penalty of up to $2000 for each violation—in addition to the tenant's actual damages.

D. EFFECT OF LANDLORD'S FORCIBLE EVICTION ON A TENANT'S LIABILITY FOR RENT

Among the things that clearly excuse a tenant from paying the rent is eviction from the property or other interference with the tenant's right to "quiet enjoyment" of the premises. The tenant can also sue a landlord who interferes with the tenant's use of the property by forcibly evicting her, locking her out, removing her property or shutting off her utilities. And if the landlord himself sues to evict the tenant, it will be unclear how much rent the tenant still owes.

Here's an example, based on an actual case handled by one of the authors.

EXAMPLE

Albert, exasperated at Rosie's repeated excuses for not coming up with the $850 monthly rent for July and August, enters Rosie's apartment on August 6, changes the locks, puts Rosie's property and furniture in the hallway and shuts off the utilities. Rosie and her two children stay with friends until her lawyer gets a court order letting Rosie move back in on August 10. Rosie's lawyer got the court order as part of a lawsuit against Albert for actual and punitive damages (including punitive damages of $100 per day for each of the five days when she was locked out). Albert sees a lawyer, who advises him to do what he should have done in the first place—file an unlawful detainer suit after service of the proper Three-Day Notice to Pay Rent or Quit.

On August 12, Albert prepares and serves the three-day notice, which demands the full $1,700 rent for July and August. Rosie defends on the basis that the lockout reduced the rent actually due by an amount equal to five days' prorated rent, so that only $1,558 was due. At the unlawful detainer trial a month later, the judge rules that the three-day notice was defective because it erroneously demanded $1,700. Since it was defective, it didn't legally terminate Rosie's tenancy. Accordingly, Rosie wins, getting a judgment against Albert for attorney fees under the attorney fees clause in her rental agreement. Albert has to start all over again with a new and correct three-day notice and unlawful detainer lawsuit. He eventually gets Rosie out in October. Rosie, of course, hasn't paid any rent all this time, and Albert still has to defend against Rosie's lawsuit. In the end, Albert loses a few thousand dollars when you add up the judgment against him, attorney fees, and lost rent. ■

18

TERMINATING TENANCIES

A landlord who wants to be rid of a troublesome tenant (particularly one who pays the rent only in response to a three-day notice) generally will have to use a 30- or 60-day termination notice or a three-day notice that orders the tenant out. This chapter shows you how to legally terminate your tenant's tenancy by properly serving the appropriate termination notice. See *The California Landlord's Law Book: Evictions* for details on the specific legal process for filing an unlawful detainer lawsuit to evict the tenant who fails to move and/or pay rent in response to one of the types of notices described in this chapter.

Be meticulous in preparing notices. Landlords must strictly comply with all of the law's requirements when it comes to preparing and serving termination notices. (*Kwok v. Bergren,* 130 Cal. App. 3d 596, 599-600 (1982).) If you make even a small mistake in a required notice or the tenant doesn't receive the notice, the eviction itself might be invalid, and you may have to start the process over. Follow our directions carefully. If you're unsure about notice requirements or have any doubt about the language or validity of your termination notice, consult an attorney specializing in landlord/tenant law.

TERMINATION NOTICES AT A GLANCE

KIND OF TERMINATION NOTICE	WHEN USED
30-DAY NOTICE (NO REASON GIVEN)	To end month-to-month tenancy in nonrent control city, where the tenancy was for less than a year.
30-DAY NOTICE (WITH REASON FOR TERMINATION)	To end month-to-month tenancy that lasted less than a year in cities other than Los Angeles, in cities that require just cause for eviction and in government-subsidized tenancies. See Section C3, below.
60-DAY NOTICE (NO REASON GIVEN)	To end a month-to-month tenancy in a non-ent control city, where the tenancy was for one year or more.
60-DAY NOTICE (WITH REASON FOR TERMINATION)	To end month-to-month tenancy where tenant has occupied the premises for a year or more in a rent control city that requires "just cause" for eviction.
90-DAY NOTICE (WITH REASON FOR TERMINATOIN)	To end a govement-subsidized tenancy. See Section A, below.
THREE-DAY NOTICE (CONDITIONAL)	To end month-to-month or fixed-term tenancy when tenant has violated a term of the tenancy but must be given a chance to correct it. See Section B1, below (or Section C2 for cities that require just cause for eviction).
THREE-DAY NOTICE (UNCONDITIONAL)	To end month-to-month or fixed-term tenancy when tenant has violated a term of the tenancy which cannot be corrected in three days. May be preceded by warning letter demanding the tenant comply with terms of tenancy or face eviction notice. See Section B2, below (or Section C2 for cities that require just cause for eviction).
THREE-DAY NOTICE FOR NONPAYMENT OF RENT	To end month-to-month or fixed-term tenancy when tenant has paid rent late, primarily used in hope that tenant will stay and pay the rent. See Chapter 16.

Related Topics

- Lease and rental agreement provisions on grounds and procedures for ending tenancies: Chapter 2

- Evicting a manager: Chapter 6

- Highlighting termination rules and procedures in a move-in letter to the tenant: Chapter 7

- How to find and use legal help for evictions: Chapter 8

- Illegal reasons and procedures for terminating a tenancy: Chapters 9 (discrimination), 15 (retaliation) and 17 (forcible evictions)

- Starting the tenancy termination process for nonpayment of rent: Chapter 16

- Termination of month-to-month rental agreements and fixed-term leases by the tenant, including situations when the tenant leaves before the end of the term: Chapter 19.

EVICTING AN ACTIVE DUTY TENANT

If you're considering evicting an active duty military tenant, proceed carefully. The Servicemembers' Civil Relief Act (formerly known as the Soldiers' and Sailors' Civil Relief Act of 1940) requires you to obtain court permission before evicting a servicemember who:

- is a member of the Army, Navy, Air Force, Marines, or Coast Guard; or is a commissioned member of the Public Health Service or National Oceanic and Atmospheric Administration; or is a member of the National Guard who has been called to active service for more than a month at a time, and

- pays up to $2,400 per month in rent (this figure will be adjusted annually for inflation). (50 App. U.S.C.A. § 301.)

These protections also apply to a servicemember's family or dependent if the dependent can show the court the dependent's ability to comply with the lease has been "materially affected" by the servicemember's active duty. It's a misdemeanor to violate this Act.

A. THE 30-, 60-, OR 90-DAY NOTICE

As a general rule, a landlord may give a tenant with a month-to-month tenancy a 30-day termination notice for any reason, or for no reason at all. (CC § 1946.) There are, however, some important restrictions on the use of 30-day notices:

- **Tenants who have occupied the premises for one year or more.** State law requires a landlord to give 60 days' written notice when the tenant has occupied the premises for a year or more, although there are exceptions (see Section 2, below). (CC § 1946.1.)

- **Rent control cities that require just cause for eviction.** In the cities of Berkeley, Beverly Hills, East Palo Alto, Hayward, Los Angeles, Oakland, San Francisco, Santa Monica, Thousand Oaks, and West Hollywood, the 30- or 60-day termination notice must state the reason for termination. See Section C, below.

- **Subsidized housing.** When the landlord receives rent or other payments from a federal, state, or local program to assist low-income tenants, the form lease drafted by the government agency usually lists acceptable reasons for termination. In addition, the notice must give 90 days' notice and should state one of these reasons when terminating housing authority-assisted ("Section 8") tenancies or Housing and Urban Development- (HUD-) assisted tenancies. (CC § 1954.535.) (See Chapter 9, Section C for information on Section 8 tenancies.)

EVICTIONS IN SECTION 8 HOUSING

Tenants whose rent payments are subsidized by the federal government under the Section 8 program cannot be terminated during the term of their lease unless you have "good cause" for doing so. (24 C.F.R. §§ 882 and following.) The HUD lease addendum lists the good cause reasons, including a prohibition against criminal activity known as the "one strike" rule. This provision authorizes eviction for the one-time use or possession of a controlled substance in or near the tenant's rented premises, by the tenant or a guest. The landlord need not prove that the tenant participated in the use or possession or even knew about the presence of the drugs. (*Department of Housing and Urban Development v. Rucker*, 535 U.S. 125, 1225 S Ct. 1230 (2002.)

After the first year, you may terminate a Section 8 tenancy for any reason or no reason at all (as long as your motives are not discriminatory or retaliatory), as long as you give 90 days' notice. (CC § 1954.535.)

- **Discrimination.** Even if just cause for eviction isn't required, you can't evict because of race, religion, sex, marital status, having children, sexual preference, or other arbitrary reasons. (See Chapter 9 on discrimination.)

- **Retaliatory eviction.** You can never legally terminate a tenancy to retaliate against a tenant for exercising any right under the law, such as the tenant's right to complain about housing conditions or to organize other tenants into a tenants' union. (See Chapter 15 for details on illegal retaliation.)

1. When to Use a 30- or 60-Day Notice

Your reason for terminating a tenancy can become relevant, even though legally you aren't required to have one, if a tenant accuses you of discrimination or retaliation. In any eviction lawsuit based on termination by a 30- or 60-day notice, if the tenant claims your motive is to retaliate or discriminate, you will have to counter with the true nonretaliatory, nondiscriminatory reason for eviction. Make sure your reason for evicting any tenant is related to the smooth and peaceful operation of your rental business and cannot possibly be construed as either discriminatory or retaliatory.

Here are some valid reasons to give a 30- or 60-day notice in nonrent control cities:

- Your tenant is repeatedly late with the rent. You've given Three-Day Notices to Pay Rent or Quit several times, and the tenant has come through with the rent before the end of the third day. Your warnings to pay rent on time in the future have had no effect.

- The tenant has given you a number of bad checks. You've used three-day notices and the checks were made good, but it keeps happening.

- Your tenant repeatedly disturbs other tenants or neighbors by having loud and boisterous parties or playing a stereo at unreasonable levels. Other tenants are complaining to you.

- Your tenant is using illegal drugs in or about the property or, even worse, dealing in them. (We discuss evicting drug-dealing tenants in Section B3, below.)

- The tenant has damaged the property—for example, by causing holes in the wall or cigarette burns in the carpet.

- The tenant is extremely obnoxious or vulgar to you, your manager, or other tenants.

- Your tenant repeatedly violates a clause of your rental agreement, such as the "no pets" provision or a valid limit on the number of people living in the premises.

- You want the property vacant to remodel it.

- You're selling your rental property (a single-family dwelling, for example), and the new buyers want the tenants out.

- You want to move in yourself or want to rent the property to a close friend or relative.

Notice of Termination of Tenancy

To: _____ Jerry Hodges _____,

Name

all tenants, subtenants, adult occupants, and others in possession of the premises at _123 Market Street,_ ,

Street Address

Apartment 4 , City of _San Diego_ , County of _San Diego_ , California.

YOU ARE HEREBY NOTIFIED that effective __30__ DAYS from the date of service on you of this notice, the periodic tenancy by which you hold possession of the premises is terminated, at which time you are required to vacate and surrender possession of the premises. If you fail to do so, legal proceedings will be instituted against you to recover possession of the premises, damages, and costs of suit.

Carlos Luiz _November 14, 200X_

Landlord/Manager   Date

. . . .

Proof of Service

I, the undersigned, being at least eighteen years of age, served this notice, of which this is a true copy, on
_____, one of the occupants listed above as follows:

☐ On _____, 20____, I delivered the notice to the occupant personally.

☐ On _____, 20____, I delivered the notice to a person of suitable age and discretion at the occupant's residence/business after having attempted personal service at the occupant's residence, and business, if known. On _____, 20____, I mailed a second copy to the occupant at his or her residence.

☐ On _____, 20____, I posted the notice in a conspicuous place on the property, after having attempted personal service at the occupant's residence, and business, if known, and after having been unable to find there a person of suitable age and discretion. _____, 20____, I mailed a second copy to the occupant at the property.

I declare under penalty of perjury under the laws of the State of California that the foregoing is true and correct.

_____   _____

                                                                        Date

In some of these cases, you can also use a three-day notice. Section B5, below, discusses why you're usually better off using a 30- or 60-day notice—when you have a choice.

2. 60-Day Notice for Tenants of a Year or More

Since January 1, 2003, landlords must give 60 days' notice when terminating a month-to-month tenancy if the tenant has lived in the unit for a year or more. However, 30 days will suffice if all of the following conditions are met:

- the dwelling can be bought and sold as a separate unit, which means it's a single-family home or condominium unit

- the dwelling is being sold to an actual ("bona fide") purchaser (as opposed to being transferred to a relative for less than fair market price, for example)

- the buyer is an individual (not a legal entity such as a corporation, partnership, or REIT)

- the buyer intends in good faith to occupy the property for at least a year

- the buyer and seller have opened an escrow for the sale to be consummated, and

- the 30-day notice is given within 120 days of opening the escrow.

Unless all the above conditions are met, you must give a tenant who has occupied the property for a year or more at least 60 days' written notice to terminate a month-to-month or other periodic tenancy.

Importantly, a new buyer may give only one 30-day notice within this window. If that notice is withdrawn (or the buyer receives rent from the tenant after delivering the notice), the next notice must be a full 60-day notice.

3. Termination Notices for Government-Subsidized Tenancies

If you receive rent or other subsidies from federal, state, or local governments, or if your tenants receive assistance from a local housing authority under a Section 8 or other similar program, you may evict for certain reasons only. Acceptable reasons for termination are usually listed in the form lease drafted by the agency or in the agency's regulations.

To evict a subsidized tenant, we suggest that you use a 90-day notice, not a 30-day or 60-day notice. As this book goes to press, the California Supreme Court is considering whether all subsidized tenants are entitled to 90 days' notice, or whether only those in rent control cities are entitled to 90 days (if the latter, then those residing in nonrent control cities would be entitled to 30 days' or 60 days', depending on the length of their tenancy). (*Wasatch Property Management v. Delgrate,* Cal. Supreme Court No. S112386.) Until the Supreme Court rules, you would be wise to assume that the longest notice period is required. Check the Legal Updates section of the Nolo site (www.nolo.com) for the latest information. In the notice, specify the acts the tenant did, and when, that violated the lease or otherwise constitute good cause for eviction.

If you decide to terminate a Section 8 tenant because you no longer wish to participate in the program, simply say so on the termination form. Keep in mind, however, that you cannot terminate for this reason until that tenant's initial rental term, usually one year, has elapsed. In addition, during the 90-day period prior to termination, you cannot increase the rent or otherwise require any subsidized tenant to pay more than was paid under the subsidy.

You'll find tear-out versions of the 30-Day, 60-Day, and 90-Day Notice of Termination of Tenancy in Appendix B. The CD-ROM that accompanies this book also includes these forms.

4. Preparing the 30-, 60-, or 90-Day Notice

There are three termination forms in Appendix B, one each for 30-day, 60-day, and 90-day notices. Filling in whichever notice you need is not difficult. Each form normally requires (1) the name of the tenant, (2) the address of the rental property, (3) the date, and (4) your signature.

You will need to specify the reason for termination if (1) the property is in a rent control city that requires you to state a reason for terminating a tenancy, or (2) you are using a 90-day notice to terminate a government-subsidized tenancy. Follow the instructions in Section C3, below.

Be sure to make at least two copies for your records. The original goes to the tenant. Fill in the Proof of Service (indicating how, when, and by whom the notice was served) on the copy after giving the original to the tenant. See Chapter 16, Section D for directions on completing the Proof of Service.

Rental agreements providing for less than 30- or 60-days' notice are not valid. If your rental agreement has a provision reducing the applicable notice period required to terminate a tenancy, that provision is not enforceable.

5. Serving the Termination Notice

As with a Three-Day Notice to Pay Rent or Quit (see Chapter 16), you must follow specific procedures when serving a termination notice.

a. When to Serve a 30-, 60-, or 90-Day Notice

A Notice of Termination of Tenancy can be served on the tenant on any day of the month, unless the rental agreement requires it to be served on a certain day. For example, a 30-day notice served on March 17 terminates the tenancy effective 30 days later, on April 16. This is true even when rent is paid for a period running from the first to the last day of each month.

Simply count 30 days (or 60 days), regardless of whether the month has 28, 29, or 31 days. If the 30th (or 60th) day falls on a Saturday, Sunday, or holiday, the tenant has until the close of the next business day (usually Monday) to move.

It's usually best to serve the notice shortly after you receive and cash the tenant's rent check for the month. If the tenant paid rent on time, the notice will usually be given toward the beginning of the month, and the last day of legal tenancy will fall several days into the next month for a 30-day notice (or the month after that, for a 60-day notice). The advantage is that you will already have the rent for as much of the time as possible that the tenant can (legally) remain on the premises. In the case of a 30-day notice, if the tenant refuses to pay any more rent (for the day or two in the next month), you can just deduct it from the security deposit. (Chapter 20 shows how.)

If you want to, you may legally give the tenant *more* than the 30, 60, or 90 days' notice required. If you do this, cross out the "30," "60," or "90" on the appropriate form and fill in your longer notice period.

EXAMPLE 1

Cleve is habitually late with his rent, usually paying on the third day after receiving your three-day notices. You decide it's time for a change of tenants. On October 2, you knock on Cleve's door and ask for the rent. If you luck out and get him to pay, cash the check. (You may even want to do it at his bank, so that you get your money immediately.) After the check clears, promptly serve Cleve with his 30-day notice. (Since Cleve has rented from you for less than a year, you don't have to use a 60-day notice.) The last day of his tenancy will be in early November, and on November 1, he'll only owe you a few days' rent. Since you can't bring an eviction lawsuit asking for this amount without a three-day notice (which really isn't worth the trouble), you can deduct this amount from the security deposit when Cleve leaves.

Of course, if Cleve doesn't pay his rent on the second day of October, you can use a Three-Day Notice to Pay Rent or Quit. If he still doesn't pay within three days, you can sue for nonpayment of rent. (See *The California Landlord's Law Book: Evictions.*)

If a Notice of Termination of Tenancy terminates the tenancy in the middle of a month or rental period, the tenant will owe rent only for the period that ends on the 30th (or 60th) day.

EXAMPLE 2

Because of her constant loud parties, you serve your tenant, Rhoda, with a 30-day notice on August 13 (Rhoda has rented her place for less than a year). The last day of the tenancy should be the 30th day after that, or September 12. On September 1, Rhoda owes you rent only for those first 12 days of September. The rent for each day is the monthly rent, $600, divided by 30, or $20. The rent for the first 12 days of September is 12 x $20, or $240.

Don't accept rent for a period beyond the 30-day (or 60-day) period—if you do, you cancel the notice and will have to start all over again with a new one. (*EDC Associates, Ltd. v. Gutierrez,* 153 Cal. App. 3d 167, 171 (1984); *Highland Plastics, Inc. v. Enders,* 109 Cal. App. 3d Supp. 1, 11 (1980).) It is especially important to prorate rent accurately. Don't accept any rent at all if you collected "last month's rent" from the tenant.

EXAMPLE 3

Because of her frequent late rent payments, you gave Sujata a 30-day notice on January 22, terminating her tenancy effective February 21. The rent is $1,200 per month, due on the first of the month. When Sujata moved in, you accepted $1,200 as "last month's rent." You are legally bound to use it for the last month's rent. Sujata's last month's rent (and more) is already paid. If you accept any rent at all on February 1, Sujata will be able to claim that you voided the 30-day notice by accepting rent beyond the notice period. Your best bet is to hold onto the last month's

rent of $1,200, of which $840 is the actual rent for the first 21 days in February. The remaining $360 is handled like a security deposit, which you would have been wiser to call it in the first place. (See Chapter 5, Section E on security deposits.)

Many tenants served with a termination notice in the middle of a month or rental period will not be eager to pay rent for part of the next month (or months, in the case of a tenant who has lived in the unit for a year or more or a subsidized tenant). Their attitude may be, "You're evicting me anyway, so I'm not giving you anything." If you expect this reaction, talk to your tenant in advance and try to settle the issue amicably.

When needing to give 30 days' notice because the tenant occupied the property for less than a year, you might simply decide to take the unpaid rent for that last portion of the month out of the security deposit. But if you had to give 60 (or 90) days' notice, this is impractical because a tenant who stops paying rent would then be occupying the premises courtesy of his security deposit for a lot more than just a few days into the following month. The following example illustrates the bind you could be in when it comes to covering any damage after the tenant leaves.

EXAMPLE 4

Because Tim has been late with his $900 monthly rent for every one of the last eight months of his two-year occupancy, you decide to give Tim a 60-day notice. On September 8, he pays the rent, and you cash his check and give him the 60-day notice, so that the last day of Tim's tenancy will be November 7. (October has 31 days.) Tim, now angry, refuses to pay his October rent. Unfortunately, October's $900 rent plus November's prorated rent ($210 for November 1 through 7) totals $1,110, more than Tim's $1,000 security deposit. This leaves you with unpaid rent and nothing to cover cleaning and damages after Tim moves out.

THREE-DAY NOTICES AT A GLANCE

KIND OF TERMINATION NOTICE	WHEN USED
THREE-DAY NOTICE TO PAY RENT OR QUIT	Requires the tenant who is late in paying the rent to pay the rent or move within three days. Failure to do so allows the landlord to bring an eviction lawsuit against the tenant. (See Chapter 16.)
THREE-DAY NOTICE TO PERFORM COVENANT OR QUIT	Requires the tenant who has violated a lease or rental agreement provision to correct the problem (perform covenant) or move (quit) within three days. For example, if the tenant's lease forbids pets, this type of three-day notice requires the tenant to get rid of her pet or move within three days. If the tenant does correct the problem within the three-day period, the tenancy continues. If the tenant does not correct the problem within three days, the landlord may bring an eviction lawsuit. This lawsuit is very similar to a lawsuit based on a Three-Day Notice to Pay Rent or Quit after the tenant has failed to pay.
THREE-DAY NOTICE TO QUIT	Simply orders the tenant to leave and does not give the tenant the alternative of stopping his misbehavior. This type of notice can be used only if the tenant has sublet the premises, contrary to a lease or rental agreement provision; seriously and repeatedly disturbed neighbors or other tenants; seriously damaged the property; used the property for an illegal purpose; or violated the lease or rental agreement in a manner that cannot be corrected within three days. (See Section B2, below.)

When the tenant to whom you've given a termination notice refuses to pay future rent, your other option is to serve the tenant with a Three-Day Notice to Pay Rent or Quit, the second day after the next rent is due. (This is obviously the preferred route when dealing with a tenant who's received a 60-day or 90-day notice, as Example 4, above, illustrates.) If you gave the tenant a 30-day notice, the three-day notice should request the prorated rent that will come due in the next month or rental period. If you used a 60- or 90-day notice, the three-day notice should request the following month's rent.

EXAMPLE 5

In Example 2, above, Rhoda owed $240 in prorated rent for the first 12 days of September. On September 1, Rhoda refuses to pay. On September 2, you serve Rhoda a three-day notice demanding that she pay the $240 rent or leave. If she ignores it, you can file a lawsuit based on her refusal to pay on September 6 without having to wait until the day after the 30-day period (September 13) to sue. If you decide to do this, refer to *The California Landlord's Law Book: Evictions.*

EXAMPLE 6

In Example 4, above, Tim refused to pay October's rent of $900 after he was served a 60-day notice on September 8. On October 2 (assuming the rent due date of October 1st didn't fall on a Saturday or Sunday), you serve Tim with a Three-Day Notice to Pay Rent or Quit, seeking October's rent of $900.

Three-Day Notice to Perform Covenant or Quit

To: _____Glen Cagney_____,
Name

Tenant(s) in possession of the premises at _____123 Main Street, Apartment 4_____,
Street Address

City of _____San Jose_____, County of _____Santa Clara_____, California.

YOU ARE HEREBY NOTIFIED that you are in violation of the lease or rental agreement under which you occupy

these premises because you have violated the covenant to: _____refrain from keeping a pet on the premises_____

_____

_____

in the following manner: _____by having a dog and two cats on the premises (Clause 13)_____

_____

_____

YOU ARE HEREBY REQUIRED within THREE (3) DAYS from the date of service on you of

this notice to remedy the violation and perform the covenant or to vacate and surrender possession

of the premises.

If you fail to do so, legal proceedings will be instituted against you to recover possession of

the premises, declare the forfeiture of the rental agreement or lease under which you occupy the premises and

recover damages and court costs.

_____*Larry Smith*_____   _____November 6, 200X_____

Landlord/Manager   Date

· ·

Proof of Service

I, the undersigned, being at least eighteen years of age, served this notice, of which this is a true copy, on

_____, one of the occupants listed above as follows:

☐ On _____, 20____, I delivered the notice to the occupant personally.

☐ On _____, 20____, I delivered the notice to a person of suitable age and discretion at the
occupant's residence/business after having attempted personal service at the occupant's residence, and business, if
known. On _____, 20____, I mailed a second copy to the occupant at his or her residence.

☐ On _____, 20____, I posted the notice in a conspicuous place on the property, after
having attempted personal service at the occupant's residence, and business, if known, and after having been unable
to find there a person of suitable age and discretion. _____, 20____, I mailed a second
copy to the occupant at the property.

I declare under penalty of perjury under the laws of the State of California that the foregoing is true and correct.

_____   _____

Date

YOU ARE HEREBY NOTIFIED that you are in violation of the lease or rental agreement under which you occupy these premises because you have violated the covenant to:

pay agreed installments of the security deposits, in the amount of $50 per month on the first day of each

month (in addition to rent) until paid

in the following manner:

failing to pay the $50 on the first day of the month of December 200X

---

b. Who Should Serve the Notice?

The 30-, 60-, or 90-day notice may be served by any person over age 18, including you. See Chapter 16, Section D2 for some of the pros and cons of serving the notice yourself.

c. Whom to Serve

You should try to serve a copy of the notice on each tenant to whom you originally rented the property. However, as with a Three-Day Notice to Pay Rent or Quit, service of a Termination Notice on one of several cotenants who are listed together on a written lease or rental agreement is legally sufficient. (See Chapter 16, Section D3 for more on this.)

d. How to Serve the Notice

A Notice of Termination of Tenancy can be sent certified or registered mail, return receipt requested (but not just first class mail), without first trying to serve the tenant personally. (CC § 1946.1(e).)

This notice can also be served by:

- personal service
- substituted service on another person plus mailing, or
- posting and mailing, also known as "nail and mail."

These methods are explained in Chapter 16, Section D4.

B. THE THREE-DAY NOTICE IN CITIES THAT DON'T REQUIRE JUST CAUSE FOR EVICTION

Sometimes you may wish to use a three-day notice to terminate a tenancy, especially if the tenant has a fixed-term lease that doesn't expire for some time, as opposed to a month-to-month tenancy, in which a 30- or 60-day notice may be used. There are basically three types of three-day notices:

- Three-Day Notice to Perform Covenant or Quit
- Three-Day Notice to Pay Rent or Quit
- Three-Day Notice to Quit.

1. The Three-Day Notice to Perform Covenant or Quit

If a tenant violates a lease or rental agreement clause, you can serve a three-day notice demanding that the tenant leave or correct the violation. (CCP § 1161(3).) If the violation could be corrected within a reasonable period of time, the notice must give the tenant the option to correct the violation. If the violation is not correctable, the notice need only tell the tenant to leave within three days. (See Section B2, below.)

But tenants generally fail to respond to three-day notices that do give this option—other than Three-Day Notices to Pay Rent or Quit—so these notices are primarily a means for terminating a tenancy, with an eye toward initiating an eviction lawsuit.

Most lease or rental agreement violations are considered correctable. Those that are not considered correctable and for which the landlord therefore may serve an unconditional Three-Day Notice to Quit include subletting without your permission, extensively damaging the premises, causing a nuisance (repeatedly disturbing other tenants or neighbors), or having used the premises for an illegal purpose. By contrast, the tenant who violates a no-pets clause can correct the violation by getting rid of the pet; a tenant who refuses to pay an installment toward a security deposit that he agreed in the lease to pay can correct the violation by paying the installment.

Always give the tenant the benefit of the doubt on this one—if you're unsure, give the tenant the option of correcting the problem. If the tenant refuses to leave after getting your three-day notice and you have to file an eviction lawsuit, you don't want your case thrown out of court because you should have given the tenant the option in the notice but didn't.

Your Three-Day Notice to Perform Covenant or Quit should contain all of the following:

- The tenant's name

- A description of the rental property—the street address, apartment number (if any), city, and county

- A very specific statement as to how the tenant violated a particular provision of the rental agreement or lease. State that the tenant failed to "perform the covenant" (abide by a provision) of the lease or rental agreement, and cite the specific clause.

- A demand that the covenant be "performed" (for example, by getting rid of the pet) within three days, or that the tenant leave the premises within three days if the violation is noncorrectable

- A statement that you will pursue legal action (or declare the lease or rental agreement "forfeited") if the tenant does not cure the violation or move within the three days, and

- Your signature, or that of your manager.

Make at least two copies for your records.

Fill in the Proof of Service on the copy after giving the original to the tenant. See Chapter 16, Section D for directions on completing the Proof of Service.

You'll find a tear-out version of the Three-Day Notice to Perform Covenant or Quit in Appendix B. The CD-ROM that accompanies this book also includes this form.

Above is another example of language in a three-day notice—a situation when the tenant failed to make agreed payments toward a security deposit which was to be paid off over a period of time.

2. The Three-Day Notice to Quit

Only when a tenant's conduct is extreme, or when the lease violation can't be corrected in three days, can a three-day notice to quit just tell the tenant to leave in three days without giving the tenant the option of correcting the problem. (CCP § 1161(4).)

The unconditional Three-Day Notice to Quit can be used only in one of the following situations:

- **Noncorrectable violation.** If there is no way the violation could possibly be corrected in three days, you can use an unconditional three-day notice. The most common example is when a tenant has sublet all or part of the premises to someone else, contrary to the rental agreement or lease.

- **Nuisance.** The tenant is causing a nuisance on the premises, repeatedly annoying neighbors.

- **Extreme damage.** The tenant is causing a great deal of damage to the property (called "waste"). This means extreme problems such as holes punched in the wall or numerous windows broken. This doesn't include run-of-the-mill damage caused by carelessness, in which case the tenant must at least be given a chance to correct the problem.

- **Illegal use.** The tenant is using the property for an illegal purpose—like running a house of prostitution, dealing drugs (a special case, discussed in Section B3, below), or even operating a legitimate business in violation of local zoning laws.

OVERVIEW OF LEGAL EVICTION PROCESS

Here's an overview of the eviction process, which often takes more than a month or two depending on whether the tenant contests the eviction. See *The California Landlord's Law Book: Evictions,* for complete details.

1. The landlord terminates the tenancy by serving a termination notice on the tenant, which may be a Three-Day Notice to Pay Rent or Quit, a Three-Day Notice to Perform Covenant or Quit, an Unconditional Three-Day Notice to Quit, or a 30- or 60-Day Notice.

The notice must be prepared and served in accordance with state and local law. If the tenant pays rent, corrects the violation, or moves (depending on the particular notice), that's the end of the matter, but the tenant may still owe rent.

2. After the three, 30, or 60 days are up, and if the tenant hasn't paid the rent, corrected the violation or left, the landlord can begin an eviction lawsuit by filing an "unlawful detainer complaint" in superior court. The tenant must file a written response in court, usually within five days (plus applicable extensions).

3. If the tenant hasn't filed a written response in court by the deadline, the landlord wins. The court clerk issues a "Default Judgment for Possession of Premises" and "Writ of Possession," which the landlord takes to the sheriff or marshal.

If the tenant files a response, the court will set the case for trial. After trial (or if the case is decided summarily by a judge), if the landlord wins, the landlord gets a judgment for possession of the property and for rent and court costs. The landlord gets a "Writ of Execution" from the clerk and gives it, and eviction instructions, to the sheriff or marshal.

4. After several days, the sheriff or marshal gives the tenant written notice he'll be forcibly evicted within five days if he doesn't move out first.

5. After five more days, the sheriff or marshal forcibly evicts any tenants who have not left, and turns the property over to the landlord.

6. After eviction, if the landlord got a Default Judgment for Possession, the landlord can go back to court and get a judgment for rent and court costs.

LOS ANGELES PROSECUTORS MAY EVICT FOR YOU AT A PRICE

The legislature has established a pilot program for certain courts within Los Angeles County that authorizes the city attorney or district attorney to file an unlawful detainer action against tenants who are using rental property to sell, use, store, or make illegal drugs. (H&S § 11571.1.) The program applies to cases brought in Los Angeles County's downtown courthouses and in Van Nuys, Los Cerritos, and Long Beach. It will expire January 1, 2005, unless the legislature extends it.

Owners will be given 15 days' notice of the intended eviction lawsuit, and will be given an opportunity to proceed with the eviction on their own. If they decline, they will be expected to furnish relevant information about the tenants and their activities and must assign their right to evict to the city. Owners may be asked to cover up to $600 worth of the city's litigation costs. If the owners don't cooperate or respond within the 15 days, the city can join the owners as defendants in the eviction lawsuit. And if the city has to go this route and wins, the owner will be ordered to pay the city for the entire cost of bringing the lawsuit.

Heard enough? The message is clear: Take care of drug problems yourself, quickly. If you don't want to handle the eviction on your own, hire counsel. Don't end up footing the bill for the services of well-paid city attorneys.

Three-Day Notice to Quit

(Improper Subletting, Nuisance, Waste, or Illegal Use)

To: _____Eric Kahn_____ ,

Name

Tenant(s) in possession of the premises at ___1234 Francisco Street, Apartment 5_____ ,

Street Address

City of _____San Francisco_____ , County of _____San Francisco_____ , California.

YOU ARE HEREBY NOTIFIED that you are required within THREE (3) DAYS from the date of service on you of

this notice to vacate and surrender possession of the premises because you have committed the following

nuisance, waste, unlawful use, or unlawful subletting:

_____You have unlawfully sublet a portion of the premises to another person who now lives on the premises_____

____with you contrary to the provisions of your lease (Clause 10)._____

_____

_____

_____

_____

As a result of your having committed the foregoing act(s), the lease or rental agreement under which you occupy

these premises is terminated. If you fail to vacate and surrender possession of the premises within three days,

legal proceedings will be instituted against you to recover possession of the premises, damages, and court costs.

____*Lisa Kramer*_____   ___May 1, 200X_____

Landlord/Manager   Date

· ·

Proof of Service

I, the undersigned, being at least eighteen years of age, served this notice, of which this is a true copy, on

_____ , one of the occupants listed above as follows:

☐ On _____ , 20____ , I delivered the notice to the occupant personally.

☐ On _____ , 20____ , I delivered the notice to a person of suitable age and discretion at the

occupant's residence/business after having attempted personal service at the occupant's residence, and business, if

known. On _____ , 20____ , I mailed a second copy to the occupant at his or her residence.

☐ On _____ , 20____ , I posted the notice in a conspicuous place on the property, after

having attempted personal service at the occupant's residence, and business, if known, and after having been unable

to find there a person of suitable age and discretion. _____ , 20____ , I mailed a second

copy to the occupant at the property.

I declare under penalty of perjury under the laws of the State of California that the foregoing is true and correct.

_____   _____

                                                            Date

3. A Reason for Which You Must Evict— Drug Dealing

In cases of drug dealing, it's not a question of whether it's permissible to evict a tenant—it's imperative to do so. In fact, a landlord who fails to evict a tenant who deals illegal drugs on the property can face lawsuits from other tenants, neighbors, and local authorities. Many landlords have been held liable for tens of thousands of dollars in damages for failing to evict drug-dealing tenants; a landlord can also lose the property and can even be ordered by a judge to live there! (Chapter 12, Section E discusses penalties facing landlords who fail to evict drug-dealing tenants.)

If the tenant has a fixed-term lease rather than a month-to-month rental agreement, you will have to use a Three-Day Notice to Quit. Evictions for drug dealing may be a little more difficult if the tenant has a lease rather than a month-to-month rental agreement or lives in a rent-controlled city with just cause eviction provisions in its rent control ordinances. (See Section C, below.)

Terminating a tenancy when drug dealing is suspected is difficult. Except for termination of non-government subsidized month-to-month tenancies in cities that don't require just cause for eviction, the termination notice must state, often in detail, the reason the tenancy is being terminated. The tenant, faced with a written accusation of a serious crime, may refuse to move, thinking that to do so would be tantamount to admitting wrongdoing.

If the tenant fights the eviction in court, a landlord who must show just cause for eviction due to a rent control ordinance or government-subsidized tenancy will have to prove that the tenant is dealing drugs, most likely by indirect (circumstantial) evidence. For example, there may be suspiciously heavy traffic in and out of the unit. Other tenants and neighbors, who are in the best position to know about goings on in the suspected dealer's apartment, may be too intimidated to testify.

A landlord faced with a potentially difficult eviction of a suspected drug-dealing tenant should take these steps, especially when there must be just cause for terminating the tenancy:

- **Gather evidence.** Remind other tenants or neighbors that you have a strict no-drug-dealing policy (as reflected in Clause 16 of our lease and rental agreements in Chapter 2), and are determined to put a stop to any drug-related activity, but that you need proof to evict the tenant. Ask them to keep records of what they see, including dates and times when the same people go into the tenant's apartment for brief periods. Ask them if they would be willing to testify in court if necessary. Keep notes of your conversations with tenants and neighbors.

- **Contact the tenant.** Don't accuse a tenant of dealing drugs. Do say that you've received complaints about heavy traffic in and out of the unit and about disturbances that have been brought to your attention. Do not disclose the names or locations of the people who have complained. Tell the tenant that if it continues, you'll have no choice but to terminate the tenancy. Follow through with a letter, and keep a copy for your records. (We include a sample warning letter in Section C2, below.)

- **Tell the police.** If other tenants have been intimidated by the dealers or customers, make an appointment to see someone at the police station. Follow through with a letter to the chief of the local police agency, and keep a copy for your records. Send a copy to the local district attorney's office. If tenants want a building watch program, ask the police to help establish one.

- **Don't make an accusation of drug dealing on the termination notice unless that's the only way you can evict, and you can prove it.** For example, if the tenant is behind in the rent or has repeatedly disturbed neighbors (people go in and out all night), evict on one of those grounds.

CLEAN METH LABS CAREFULLY

Apartment owners are increasingly encountering illegal, clandestine methamphetamine (crystal meth) labs. According to one study, an estimated fifty percent of all labs are found on rental properties. The chemicals used to produce meth are toxic and very costly to clean up. While law enforcement authorities typically investigate and remove the chemicals, owners are ultimately responsible for decontamination procedures.

If you've evicted someone who ran a meth lab, understand that the acids, solvents, and other flammable and toxic chemicals used to make the drug may still lurk in appliances, rugs, walls, furniture, sinks, and ventilation systems. You need to make sure that the next occupants (or neighboring tenants) aren't exposed. Contact the state Department of Toxic Substances Control (www.dtsc .ca.gov). They are required to remove and dispose of hazardous materials found by law enforcement; and they are supposed to give property owners and residents information about risks posed by clandestine drug labs. (California H & S Code § 25354.5.) You may also need to hire a contractor who specializes in such clean-up, which will be expensive (but not as costly as a lawsuit brought by sickened tenants).

---

4.   Preparing the Three-Day Notice to Quit

The unconditional Three-Day Notice to Quit must contain the following:

- The tenant's name.

- A description of the premises—street address, apartment number (if any), city, and county.

- A demand that the tenant leave the premises within three days.

- A specific statement as to how and approximately when the tenant illegally sublet, caused a nuisance, damaged the premises, or illegally used the premises. This is the most important part of the notice, and must be drafted very carefully to clearly tell the tenant what the tenant is doing wrong. Also, remember that you may have to prove in court that the tenant violated the lease or rental agreement, if the tenant refuses to move. This is especially important when evicting tenants for illegal uses of the premises, such as drug dealing.

- An unequivocal statement that the lease is forfeited and that you will take legal action to remove the tenant if the tenant fails to vacate within the three days.

- Your signature, or that of your manager's, and the date.

- Fill in the Proof of Service stating how the three-day notice was served on the tenant. (You fill in the proof of service on the copy after having given the original to the tenant.) (See Chapter 16, Section D for directions on completing the Proof of Service.)

You'll find a tear-out version of the Three-Day Notice to Quit in Appendix B. The CD-ROM that accompanies this book also includes this form.

Here are examples of language you can use in Three-Day Notice to Quit:

- **Nuisance.** "You have committed a nuisance on the premises by having or allowing loud, boisterous parties at which music was played at an extremely high volume, and at which intoxicated guests milled about outside the front door to the premises and shouted obscenities at passersby on several nights between February 26 and 28, 200X."

- **Waste.** "You committed or allowed to be committed waste on the premises, in that you or your guests have punched holes in the doors and walls of the premises and broken the front living room window."

- **Illegal use.** "You have used the premises for an unlawful use by selling illegal controlled substances to visitors to the premises, between April 1, 200X, and the present."

5. Advantage of 30-Day/60-Day Notice Over Three-Day Notice

As described in Section B2, above, some reasons for eviction—such as making too much noise or damaging the property—may justify evicting with an unconditional Three-Day Notice to Quit. A landlord in a nonrent-controlled area who wants to evict a month-to-month tenant (whose rent is paid) will often be better off using a 30-day or 60-day notice.

If you can evict a tenant by using a three-day notice, why give the tenant with a month-to-month tenancy a break by using a 30-day or 60-day notice? Because it's good business, for several reasons:

- A tenant is far more likely to defend against an eviction lawsuit that gives her only three days to get out, rather than 30 or 60 days.

- If a tenant does force you to go to court, if your tenancy termination is based on a 30-day or 60-day notice, you don't even have to list the reason in the lawsuit papers (unless the tenant has a lease or government-subsidized tenancy, or the property is in a rent-controlled area requiring just cause for eviction). With a three-day notice, you must clearly tell the tenants what they are doing wrong; the slightest omission of necessary information could render the three-day notice invalid.

- Judges are more reluctant to allow a tenant to be evicted if you use a three-day notice for breaching the rental agreement or causing a nuisance or damage, than they are if you use a 30-day or 60-day notice.

6. Serving the Three-Day Notice

As with other types of notices, there are specific procedures for serving a three-day notice. Both kinds of three-day notices (conditional and unconditional) are served the same way.

a. When the Three-Day Notice Should Be Served

A Three-Day Notice to Perform Covenant or Quit or a Three-Day Notice to Quit can be served on a tenant on any day of the month. The only requirement is that the tenant's violations of the lease or rental agreement already have occurred. For example, if the tenant's third loud and boisterous party in a month occurred on April 15, and you're using the three disturbances as a basis for eviction, you can serve your Three-Day Notice to Quit on April 16.

If the tenant's violation of the lease or rental agreement involves a failure to do something else on a certain date, the notice should be served the day after that. For example, if a tenant must pay a security deposit installment that the lease or rental agreement says is due on the first day of the month, the tenant isn't late until the first business day after that date. If the day for the tenant to pay the money or otherwise perform the act falls on a Saturday, Sunday or holiday, he doesn't legally have to do it until the following business day.

It doesn't matter that you've earlier accepted the rent for a particular month when it comes to giving a tenant a three-day notice for a reason unrelated to rent. Just don't accept rent after you've become aware of the violation for which you'll be evicting.

EXAMPLE

Your tenant Rochelle paid you the $500 rent for her apartment on October 1, then had four loud and wild parties (which lasted to 2 A.M. despite protests from other tenants) on October 5, 6, 13, and 14. Your Three-Day Notice to Quit could be given on the 15th, asking Rochelle to leave by the 18th, even though you've accepted her rent through October 31. (This would be a situation in which you would probably want to give a conditional three-day notice—that is, tell the tenant to cease the offending conduct or leave.) This is because Rochelle, in creating a nuisance after having paid her rent, has legally forfeited her right not only to continue under the lease or rental agreement, but also to live there for the rest of the period for which she paid rent in advance. After that, your service of the three-day notice on her, plus waiting the three days, allows you to file an eviction lawsuit. However, if you accept rent in November—well after the loud parties occurred— you can't evict on that basis with a three-day notice.

b. Who Should Serve the Notice?

The three-day notice may be served by anyone over 18, you included.

c. Whom to Serve

You should try to serve a copy of the Three-Day Notice to Perform Covenant or Quit or Three-Day Notice to Quit on each tenant to whom you rented the property. You are not legally obligated to serve all cotenants on the same written lease or rental agreement. But you are required to serve all persons considered to be subtenants if the tenant has sublet (even illegally) and left. (See Chapter 16, Section D3.) Serving all adult occupants means you won't have to worry about a cotenant whom you didn't serve claiming she was a subtenant entitled to notice. We discuss who is and who is not a tenant in Chapter 10.

d. How the Notice Is Served

A Three-Day Notice to Quit may be served as follows:

- personal service
- substituted service on another person, plus mailing, or
- posting and mailing.

See Chapter 16, Section D4, for details on serving three-day notices. The rules for service are identical for all types of three-day notices.

e. Accepting Rent After the Notice Is Served

With conditional three-day notices, don't accept any rent unless the tenant has corrected the violation within three days—in which case, you can't evict and the tenant can stay. If the tenant doesn't correct the violation within three days, don't accept any rent unless you want to forget about evicting for the reason stated in the notice.

Acceptance of the rent will be considered a legal admission that you decided to forgive the violation and continue collecting rent rather than deal with the problem.

C. TERMINATION WHEN JUST CAUSE FOR EVICTION IS REQUIRED

Quite a few cities with rent control (Berkeley, Beverly Hills, East Palo Alto, Hayward, Los Angeles, Oakland, San Francisco, Santa Monica, Thousand Oaks, and West Hollywood) require a landlord to have just cause for terminating a month-to-month (or other periodic) tenancy.

In these cities, the notice (whether 30-day, 60-day, or three-day) must always specify in detail the reason for termination, but there are often other requirements as well. For example, San Francisco's ordinance requires that the notice state that tenant assistance is available from the rent control board (the address and phone number of the rent board must be included). Berkeley's ordinance requires that copies of all such notices be filed with the local rent board. Some cities restrict a landlord's ability to evict fired managers. (See Chapter 6.) Failure to comply with technical requirements of a rent control ordinance may result in your losing a subsequent eviction lawsuit and being held liable for the tenant's court costs and attorney fees.

Some of these cities require that the landlord's reason for terminating the tenancy be specified in either a 30-day, or 60-day or three-day termination notice.

If your property is subject to a rent control ordinance, obtain a copy of the ordinance and look for:

- allowable reasons for termination
- special requirements for what must be included in the termination notice, and
- requirements that you warn the tenants, in writing, before sending a termination notice.

1. Which Notice to Use

In rent-controlled cities requiring just cause for eviction, and where the tenancy is government-subsidized, you must have good cause to evict (even if the tenancy is from month to month), whether you use a three-day or other notice. In Section 8 government-subsidized tenancies, you must use a 90-day notice to evict for reasons other than nonpayment of rent. (See *Gallman v. Pierce,* 639 F. Supp. 472 (N.D. Cal. 1986).) But where the just cause requirement is imposed only by a rent control law, there is only a slight advantage to using the 30-day (or 60-day) notice when you have a choice. (See Section C3, below, for situations where you may only use a 30-day notice.) A tenant receiving a 30- or 60-day notice might more readily move, having more time within which to do so, than if only three days' notice is given. On the other hand, low-cost legal help to tenants is readily available from tenants' groups and other sources, and even tenants who receive the full 30-day or 60-day notice may stay and fight it out anyway.

2. Reasons Allowed for Termination With a Three-Day Notice

All rent-controlled cities allow evictions for, among other things:

- nonpayment of rent
- violation of a lease or rental agreement provision
- causing serious damage to the premises
- causing a nuisance, and
- illegal use of the premises.

a. Nonpayment of Rent

In rent-controlled cities, a Three-Day Notice to Pay Rent or Quit is not much different from areas without rent control. You can use the Three-Day Notice to Pay Rent or Quit in Appendix B, following the directions in Chapter 16. Be sure to check your local ordinance for any special requirements.

b. Violation of a Lease or Rental Agreement Provision

A Three-Day Notice to Perform Covenant or Quit, spelling out the lease or rental agreement violation and giving the tenant a chance to correct it, satisfies ordinance requirements that the tenant's misconduct be specified and that the tenant be given a chance to correct it. (This assumes the violation is correctable.) So, with the possible exception of a requirement that the notice include the local rent control board's name, address, and phone number, or that a copy be given to the board, a three-day notice based on a tenant's lease violation is no different in a rent-controlled city from in areas without rent control. Follow the directions in Section B1, above, for serving a Three-Day Notice to Perform Covenant or Quit.

c. Violation of Access Clause of a Lease or Rental Agreement

Many leases and rental agreements, including the forms in the back of this book, contain a clause requiring the tenant to provide the landlord access to the property as required by law—for example, to repair or maintain the premises. (See Chapters 2 (Clause 14) and 13.) Some rent control ordinances allow eviction both for rental agreement or lease violations and specifically for the tenant's refusal to allow the landlord property access—provided such refusal is a violation of the lease or rental agreement. The Three-Day Notice to Perform Covenant or Quit would include language like:

> "...you are in violation of the lease ... because you have violated the covenant to: allow Landlord access to the property as required by Civil Code Section 1954, following the giving of legal notice by the Landlord that he would conduct repairs to the premises on December 1, 200X, in the following manner: you refused to allow such access on December 3, 200X."

If the tenant still refuses you access over the next three days, you may want to begin an eviction lawsuit. You might also advise the tenant, in the notice or elsewhere, that California law makes it an infraction, punishable by a fine of up to $500, to refuse access to a property owner of record (or his agent) when the owner asserts a legal reason to enter. (Penal Code § 420.1)

Check your ordinance to make sure you comply with its requirement for such a notice.

Warning Notice (Complaints From Neighbors/Residents)

Date: _____December 16, 200X_____

Memorandum from Landlord/Manager to

_Bruce Wilson_____, Resident(s) of

Property at _____950 Ocean View St., Apt. 10_____

_____Santa Monica, California_____

Re: Complaints from neighbors/other residents

Several of your neighbors have complained to the management regarding to the following disturbance or condition:

_loud noises from parties in your apartment, until 3:00 a.m._____

_____

_____

Approximate date of occurrence: _____December 7, 8, 14, and 15, 200X_____

It is very important to the management that our residents be able to enjoy the peace and quiet of their homes. Disturbing or affecting neighbors is a violation of the terms of your lease/rental agreement. You are requested to take the following corrective action: _____

Keep noise within reasonable limits. No noise after midnight on weekends and 10:00 p.m. on weekdays.

_____

_____

If you have any questions, please contact _____Jason Knepps_____,

at _____Manager's Office-Apartment 1._____.

Sincerely,

_Jason Knepps_____
Landlord/Manager

Three-Day Notice to Quit

(Improper Subletting, Nuisance, Waste, or Illegal Use)

To: _____ Bruce Wilson _____ ,

Name

Tenant(s) in possession of the premises at _____ 950 Oceanview Street, Apartment 10 _____ ,

Street Address

City of _____ Santa Monica _____ , County of _____ Los Angeles _____ , California.

YOU ARE HEREBY NOTIFIED that you are required within THREE (3) DAYS from the date of service on you of this notice to vacate and surrender possession of the premises because you have committed the following nuisance, waste, unlawful use, or unlawful subletting:

_____ (1) You have continued, despite a written request to cease, dated December 16, 200X, to be so disorderly as to destroy the peace and quiet of other tenants, by having a loud party December 21, 200X, which lasted until 3 a.m. and at which very loud music was played until that time. Prior to this, you conducted four similar parties, on December 7th, 8th, 14th, and 15th. (2) You have failed, despite receiving a written request, to pay the reasonable cost of repairing a shattered window and holes in walls, caused by you or your guests at one more of such parties. _____

As a result of your having committed the foregoing act(s), the lease or rental agreement under which you occupy these premises is terminated. If you fail to vacate and surrender possession of the premises within three days, legal proceedings will be instituted against you to recover possession of the premises, damages, and court costs.

_____ Jason Knepps _____ _____ December 22, 200X _____

Landlord/Manager   Date

· ·

Proof of Service

I, the undersigned, being at least eighteen years of age, served this notice, of which this is a true copy, on _____ , one of the occupants listed above as follows:

☐ On _____ , 20 ___ , I delivered the notice to the occupant personally.

☐ On _____ , 20 ___ , I delivered the notice to a person of suitable age and discretion at the occupant's residence/business after having attempted personal service at the occupant's residence, and business, if known. On _____ , 20 ___ , I mailed a second copy to the occupant at his or her residence.

☐ On _____ , 20 ___ , I posted the notice in a conspicuous place on the property, after having attempted personal service at the occupant's residence, and business, if known, and after having been unable to find there a person of suitable age and discretion. _____ , 20 ___ , I mailed a second copy to the occupant at the property.

I declare under penalty of perjury under the laws of the State of California that the foregoing is true and correct.

_____ _____

                                                                          Date

d. Damage and Nuisance

Rent control ordinances typically allow eviction of tenants for excessively damaging the property or causing a nuisance. But most ordinances require that the tenant must first be notified of the problem in a written notice—often called a cease-and-desist notice—and be given a chance to correct the problem, no matter what it is.

EXAMPLE

Berkeley's ordinance allows eviction of a tenant for damaging the property (in excess of ordinary wear and tear) only if the tenant "has refused, after written notice, to pay the reasonable costs of repairing such damage and ceasing damaging premises." (This raises some interesting legal issues regarding how far a city may go in essentially altering state procedural laws governing three-day notices. In *Birkenfeld v. City of Berkeley,* 17 Cal. 3d 129, 148-151 (1976), the California Supreme Court stated that a more extensive digression from state law [requiring that an eviction certificate be issued by the rent board] was improper, while a less serious digression, like the one in this case, [requiring a 30-day notice to specify the reason for termination] was okay.)

To reconcile the ordinance with state law, you can use a Three-Day Notice to Perform Covenant or Quit. This gives the tenant an option to correct. However, we prefer another method, in which two notices are used. First, send a letter that demands that the tenant correct the problem, pay to repair the damage, or stop having loud parties. Second, should the tenant fail to correct the problem, serve an unconditional Three-Day Notice to Quit.

EXAMPLE

After paying the rent on December 1, Bruce held some wild holiday parties in his Santa Monica apartment on the 7th, 8th, 14th, and 15th. Other tenants repeatedly complained (eventually to the police) about Bruce's parties. At these parties, a drunken guest threw a beer bottle through the front window of the apartment. Santa Monica's rent control ordinance requires that (1) before terminating a tenancy for causing excessive damage, the landlord must give the tenant a chance to pay the cost of repairs, and (2) to terminate for disturbing neighbors, the disturbances must continue following a written notice to cease.

Here's a situation where you'd want to send a letter addressing both issues. (See the Sample Warning Letter (Tenant Damage or Nuisance), below.) This should be followed by serving Bruce with an unconditional Three-Day Notice to Quit if he doesn't pay for the damage and stop his raucous parties. It should be given to the tenant in the same way as a three-day notice is served. (See Section B6, above.) This type of warning letter can also be used in nonrent control situations where you have grounds for eviction, but feel the tenant's behavior will change given a warning notice. You can also use a fill-in-the-blank Warning Notice, which you can use the same way as a warning letter.

You'll find a tear-out version of the Warning Notice (Complaints from Neighbors/Residents) in Appendix B. The CD-ROM that accompanies this book also includes the form.

If Bruce fails to pay the money for repairs or has another wild party, you would prepare and serve the above unconditional Three-Day Notice to Quit (Just Cause for Eviction).

e. Illegal Use of the Premises

Some rent control ordinances neglect to mention this as a ground for eviction. Does this mean that you can't evict a tenant who, for example, runs a house of prostitution from the apartment? The answer, of course, is no. Virtually all written leases and rental agreements (including our form lease and rental

SAMPLE WARNING LETTER (TENANT DAMAGE OR NUISANCE)

December 16, 200X

Bruce Wilson
950 Oceanview St.
Monica Apartments, Apt. 10
Santa Monica, CA

Dear Mr. Wilson:

This letter is to advise you that the management of Monica Apartments intends to proceed to terminate your tenancy of the above premises if you continue to conduct yourself in a manner that seriously disturbs other tenants and results in the destruction of our property.

On December 7, 8, 14, and 15, you held loud and boisterous parties, which lasted until 3 a.m. and at which very loud music was played and guests spilled out into the street. The police were called on three of the four occasions. This conduct has destroyed the peace and quiet of other tenants. If this conduct does not cease, your tenancy will be terminated in accordance with local and state law.

On December 14 and/or 15, several of the party guests damaged our property, shattering the front window to your apartment and punching two holes in your bathroom wall. After a properly noticed inspection of the premises yesterday by myself and my maintenance person, I have concluded that the reasonable cost of repairing this damage is $350. If you fail to pay this sum to me within three days, your tenancy will be terminated in accordance with both local and state law.

Sincerely,

Jason Knepps

Jason Knepps
Manager

30-Day Notice of Termination of Tenancy
(Tenancy of Less Than One Year)

To: _____ Hope Swensen _____,
    Name

all tenants, subtenants, adult occupants, and others in possession of the premises at _____ 1234 Grove Street, _____
    Street Address

_____ Apartment 5 _____, City of _____ Berkeley _____, County of _____ Alameda _____, California.

YOU ARE HEREBY NOTIFIED that effective THIRTY (30) DAYS from the date of service on you of this notice, the periodic tenancy by which you hold possession of the premises is terminated, at which time you are required to vacate and surrender possession of the premises. If you fail to do so, legal proceedings will be instituted against you to recover possession of the premises, damages, and costs of suit.

_____ You have continued, following a written request to cease dated December 10, 200X, to refuse _____

_____ me access to the premises as required by Civil Code Section 1954, on 12/11/XX, 12/12/XX, and 12/13/XX, _____

_____ despite the fact that I gave you notice 24 hours in advance, in each case, of an intent to repair a _____

_____ defective heater. (Rent Stabilization Ordinance, Section 13 (a)(60).) _____

[OR]

_____ I wish to have my son, Orville Bergman, reside in the premises, there being no other vacant _____

_____ comparable unit in the property. (Rent Stabilization Ordinance, Sect ion 13 (a)(9).) _____

_____

_____ Olaf Bergman _____   _____ December 22, 200X _____
Landlord/Manager   Date

• •

Proof of Service

I, the undersigned, being at least eighteen years of age, served this notice, of which this is a true copy, on _____, one of the occupants listed above as follows:

☐ On _____, 20_____, I delivered the notice to the occupant personally.

☐ On _____, 20_____, I delivered the notice to a person of suitable age and discretion at the occupant's residence/business after having attempted personal service at the occupant's residence, and business, if known. On _____, 20_____, I mailed a second copy to the occupant at his or her residence.

☐ On _____, 20_____, I posted the notice in a conspicuous place on the property, after having attempted personal service at the occupant's residence, and business, if known, and after having been unable to find there a person of suitable age and discretion. _____, 20_____, I mailed a second copy to the occupant at the property.

I declare under penalty of perjury under the laws of the State of California that the foregoing is true and correct.

_____   _____
    Date

agreement) either specify that the property be used only as a residence, or that illegal use of the property is forbidden. An illegal activity, such as drug dealing, therefore constitutes a violation of the rental agreement. A Three-Day Notice to Quit could be used, and you need not give the tenant the alternative of stopping his misbehavior.

3. Reasons Allowed for Termination With a 30-Day or 60-Day Notice

All the reasons listed in Section C2, above, for which a tenant's tenancy can be terminated with a three-day notice under local ordinance, apply whether the tenancy is from month to month (or some other period) or for a fixed term.

The just cause eviction sections of most rent control ordinances also allow termination of the tenancy for other reasons. These reasons permit termination of a month-to-month tenancy (but not a tenancy under a fixed-term lease) by an unconditional 30-day (or 60-day) notice (Just Cause for Eviction), and include:

- The tenant refuses to allow the landlord access to the premises, but no lease or rental agreement clause requires the tenant to allow access.

- The landlord, after having obtained all necessary permits, intends to extensively remodel the premises, convert the dwelling to a condominium unit, or demolish the structure.

- The landlord (or a close relative) is intending to move into the dwelling.

a. Tenant Refusal to Allow Access

A three-day notice can be used to terminate tenancy where the tenant refuses to allow the landlord legal access to the property—provided such refusal is a violation of the lease or rental agreement. (See Chapter 13.) If the rental agreement doesn't have an access clause, however, a 30-day or 60-day notice must be used. This sort of notice should be preceded with a warning letter of the type mentioned in Section C2,

above. Also, the reason for termination should be stated in the notice. You might also advise the tenant, in the notice or elsewhere, that California law makes it an infraction, punishable by a fine of up to $500, to refuse access to a property owner of record (or his agent) when the owner asserts a legal reason to enter. (Penal Code § 420.1) A sample notice is shown above.

b. Remodeling, Conversion, or Demolition

Most rent control ordinances allow a month-to-month tenancy to be terminated by a 30-day or 60-day notice if the landlord wishes to extensively remodel the premises, convert the property into a condominium unit, or demolish it. The landlord must first obtain all permits necessary, and comply with other ordinances providing for notice to affected persons, the tenants included. The 30-day or 60-day notice should specify in detail the reason for termination, giving the date the permits were granted by the city or county.

Some landlords have abused ordinances that allow eviction for remodeling, either by claiming nonexistent needs for extensive remodeling, or failing to do the remodeling once the tenant left. In response, several cities have added safeguards to protect tenants. For example, Berkeley's ordinance requires a landlord seeking to evict a tenant for remodeling to give the tenant the right of first refusal to rerent the property when the remodeling is done, and even to house the tenant in the interim (at the same rent) if the landlord has any other vacant rental property in the city. Again, be sure to check your local ordinance for specific requirements.

c. Landlord or Close Relative to Move In

Most rent control ordinances allow a month-to-month tenancy to be terminated by 30-day (or 60-day) notice when the landlord wants to live in the property or move in a close relative. This basis for termination has had its share of abuse, with some landlords falsely claiming to have relatives interested in moving into the property, which would then be occupied by the relative for a very short time, if at all. Cities have tightened their ordinances to prevent abuse. For example, San Francisco's and Oakland's ordinances require the landlord or relative to move in within three months of the original tenant's move-out, and requires the landlord (or relative) to remain for at least 36 months.

Also, just cause for eviction ordinances now provide for heavy penalties against landlords who use a phony relative ploy, as does state law. (Chapter 4, Section H2, describes penalties for attempted violation of this type of rent control ordinance provision.)

D. TERMINATION WHEN NO NOTICE IS REQUIRED

Most just cause provisions of rent control ordinances also allow a landlord to evict a tenant who refuses to sign a new fixed-term lease after the old one expires. However, the new lease the landlord presents to the tenant must contain essentially the same terms as the old one, with no substantial change, and must not contain any clauses forbidden by state law (see Chapter 2, Section F) or local ordinance. This basis for eviction applies only where:

- A fixed-term lease expires on a certain date.

- The landlord has not accepted any rent after that date, and so has not converted the tenancy into a nonexpiring month-to-month tenancy, and

- The tenant has refused to sign a new lease essentially identical to the earlier one.

In this situation, the landlord does not have to give the tenant a written notice of any kind before filing an eviction lawsuit. This is because the tenancy ended of its own accord when the lease expired, and the tenant is refusing to extend it.

E. NOTIFYING TENANT OF INITIAL MOVE-OUT INSPECTION

When a residential tenancy terminates, you must notify the tenant before the end of the tenancy, in writing, of the tenant's right to request an initial move-out inspection. At this inspection, you or your manager go through the unit with the tenant, inspect for damage or wear beyond normal wear and tear, and advise the tenant of what needs to be done in order to obtain as much of a security deposit refund as possible. Your obligation to notify the tenant of this right applies regardless of who initiates the termination—when you terminate the tenancy with a 30-, 60-, or 90-day notice, when the tenant terminates, or when a fixed-term lease simply expires per its terms. You do not, however, have to notify a tenant of this inspection when you terminate using a three-day notice.

We suggest using the "Move-Out Letter" in Chapter 20, Section A for this purpose. Fill it out and mail it to the tenant within a few days after (1) you serve a 30-day, 60-day, or 90-day notice on the tenant, or (2) the tenant serves you with a written tenancy-termination notice. In situations where a lease will expire and you or your tenant have indicated you are not going to renew, fill it out and mail it as soon as it's clear that the tenant isn't renewing (or staying on with your permission, as a month-to-month tenant). ∎

19

WHEN A TENANT LEAVES: MONTH-TO-MONTH TENANCIES, FIXED-TERM LEASES, ABANDONMENT, AND DEATH OF TENANT

You might think, after reading Chapter 18, that many tenancies end with the landlord giving the tenant some sort of written termination notice. In fact, most tenancies end with the tenant leaving voluntarily. (Remember that although you're required to give the tenant a 60-day notice of termination if he has occupied the property for a year or more, the converse doesn't apply. A tenant need only give a landlord 30 days' notice to terminate a month-to-month tenancy.)

A. TERMINATION OF MONTH-TO-MONTH TENANCIES

Most tenancies end when the tenant decides to move and gives you 30 days' notice. If the rental agreement specifically allows for a shorter notice period, the tenant isn't required to give you a full 30 days' notice. (This is true regardless of state law, rent control ordinances, and rules regarding government-subsidized tenancies, all of which restrict only *the landlord's* ability to terminate the tenancy.)

This section discusses the tenant's liabilities and responsibilities when ending a month-to-month tenancy.

To make sure your tenant will give you the required 30 days' notice, highlight termination notice requirements in a move-in letter to new tenants. (See Chapter 7.)

1. Insisting on a Written Notice

The tenant's notice should be in writing, and should be personally served on you or your manager or mailed by certified mail. (CC § 1946.1.) In practice, many tenants mail the notice by ordinary first class mail, which is still legally effective so long as you receive it 30 or more days before the termination date.

If the tenant simply tells you that he will be leaving in 30 days or more, it's good business to insist that the notice be in writing. If the tenant doesn't do this, you should prepare and serve your own written 30 days' notice on the tenant. Why bother, if the tenant plans to leave anyway? Because if you don't,

you may be caught between the proverbial rock and a hard place if you sign a rental agreement for a new tenant to move in and the current tenant does not move as promised. If you signed a lease or rental agreement, or even orally promised your new tenant that she could move in, you will be liable to the new tenant for the full cost of temporary housing until the existing tenant leaves, unless the agreement has a clause limiting your liability if you can't deliver possession on the promised date. (Clause 12 of our forms has such a provision.).

EXAMPLE

Your current tenants, the Beckers, call and tell you they plan to move in 30 days. On the basis of their promise, you sign a rental agreement with new tenants, the Owenses, beginning the day after you expect the Beckers to depart. Unfortunately, that agreement has no clause limiting your liability for inability to deliver possession as promised. The Beckers later inform you (or you discover) that they won't leave as planned. Because the Beckers did not give you a written 30-day notice, you cannot sue to evict them. The best you can do is serve the Beckers with a 30-day (or 60-day) notice. If the Owenses must stay in a motel until the Beckers leave in 30 (or 60) days, you are responsible for the cost, which is certain to be more than the rent you will get from the Beckers. If, on the other hand, the Beckers had given you a written 30-day notice but failed to abide by it, you could have sued to evict them as soon as the 30 days were up.

2. Applying the Security Deposit to the Last Month's Rent

A month-to-month tenant may ask you to apply the security deposit toward the last month's rent, which the tenant tells you he won't be paying. You must abide by this request if you called all or part of the tenant's initial payment "last month's rent." But if you have not—wisely—described the up-front deposit in this way, you are not legally obliged to apply a security or other deposit to the last month's rent.

Why should you care if a tenant doesn't pay last month's rent if the deposit, no matter what it's called, covers the rent? The problem is that you can't know in advance in what condition the property will be left. If the tenant leaves the property a mess and has already applied the security deposit to last month's rent, obviously you will have nothing left to use to repair or clean the property.

You have two choices if you are faced with a tenant who tries to use a security deposit for last month's rent. Your first is simply to do nothing. In some circumstances, if you have good reason to believe that the particular tenant will in fact leave the property clean and undamaged, this may be the best thing to do.

Your second choice is to treat the tenant's nonpayment (or partial payment) of the last month's rent as an ordinary case of rent nonpayment. You can serve a Three-Day Notice to Pay Rent or Quit on the tenant as set out in Chapter 16, and file an eviction lawsuit if the tenant doesn't pay. But because it takes a minimum of three weeks to evict even in uncontested cases, this probably won't get the tenant out much sooner than he would leave anyway. However, you can get a court judgment for the unpaid last month's rent. This means you may apply the security deposit to pay for any necessary cleaning and repair costs, with any remainder applied to the judgment for nonpayment of rent. (We show how in Chapter 20.)

EXAMPLE

On December 31, Lee gives Sara 30 days' notice and asks her to take his last month's rent out of his deposit. Immediately, Sara serves Lee with a three-day notice to pay the remaining $450 rent or quit. Four days later, on January 8, Sara may bring suit. If Sara's suit is uncontested, she can get a default judgment on January 14 and perhaps get the sheriff or marshal to evict as soon as January 20. The money part of the judgment, assuming Sara can collect it, will compensate her for the rent, and she'll be free to use the deposit for its proper purpose— payment of repair and cleaning costs.

3. Accepting Further Rent After a 30-Day Notice Is Given

If you accept rent for any period beyond the termination date, you cancel the termination notice and create a new tenancy. This is true whether your tenant gave you a 30-day notice or you gave the tenant a 30-day or 60-day notice.

EXAMPLE

On April 15, George sends his landlord, Yuri, a 30-day termination notice. A few weeks later, however, he changes his mind and decides to stay. He simply pays the usual $500 monthly rent on May 1. If he were intent on leaving on May 15 as promised, he should be paying only 15 days prorated rent. Unwittingly, Yuri cashes the $500 check for the rent for all of May, even though she's already rerented to a new tenant who hopes to move in on the 16th. Not only will Yuri be powerless to evict George, but, if she wasn't careful about limiting her liability for inability to deliver possession as promised, she'll also be liable to the new tenant for failing to put the new tenant in possession of the property as promised.

If you've already accepted "last month's rent," do not accept rent for the last month of the tenancy. If you don't want to continue the tenancy as before, but are agreeable to giving the tenant a few days or weeks more, prepare a written agreement to that effect and have the tenant sign it.

4. Notifying Tenant of Initial Move-Out Inspection

As we saw in Chapter 18, Section A, you should mail your tenant a "Move-Out Letter" that advises tenants of their right to an initial move-out inspection and to be present at it. Be sure to mail the outgoing tenant the Move-Out Letter within a few days after the tenant gives you notice.

5. What to Do When the Tenant Gives Less Than 30 Days' Notice

A tenant may mail the notice two weeks before vacating, or may just say good-bye while handing you the keys. But a tenant's written termination notice isn't ineffective just because it gives you less than the full 30 days' notice. It is still a valid notice of termination, but you are entitled to rent money for the entire 30 days from the date of the notice. (There is one restriction on your right to the rent: If the tenant moves out less than 30 days after the notice is served, you must try to rerent the property before you can charge the tenant for giving you too little notice. This rule is discussed below.)

EXAMPLE

On August 25, Cara gives Simon a note saying she'll be moving out in ten days, on September 4. Simon is entitled to rent for 30 days from the date of the notice, through September 24. So on September 1, when Cara tries to get by with paying prorated rent for her four remaining days in September, Simon reminds her that he's entitled to 24 days' prorated rent. Of course, if Cara pays it, she'll have the right to stay through the 24th if she wishes. If Cara doesn't pay, which is likely (a threat of an eviction suit for rent nonpayment isn't likely to faze a tenant about to leave anyway), Simon can deduct the unpaid rent from her deposit. If the deposit won't cover this plus cleaning and damage costs, he'll have to take Cara to small claims court for the balance. (We discuss how to do this in Chapter 20.)

If a tenant leaves without giving you the 30 days' notice you're entitled to and doesn't pay rent for some or all of those days, you're entitled to the rent you've lost. But you can't collect double by charging the former tenant rent beyond the date she left, while at the same time collecting rent from a new tenant. In other words, if you immediately find a new tenant to replace the outgoing one who didn't give you the full 30 days' notice, and therefore suffer no financial loss as a result of the inadequate notice, you can't charge the outgoing tenant that extra rent. However, if there was a gap of a few days, during which time you had no

paying tenant, you are entitled to the prorated rent for those days, plus any costs of advertising the property. You may deduct these amounts from the outgoing tenant's deposit, as discussed in detail in Chapter 20.

If you can't collect double rent, both from the outgoing tenant who didn't give sufficient notice and from the new tenant, why should you bother getting a new tenant so quickly? Because the law requires you to take reasonable steps to minimize your losses. This is called "mitigation of damages." If you don't, and instead sit back and let the property lie vacant between the day the tenant vacates and the 30th day from the date of the notice, hoping to charge the rent for that period to the outgoing tenant's deposit, you may be in for an unpleasant surprise. You can't charge the former tenant if you didn't take reasonable steps to find a new tenant. (CC § 1951.2.)

EXAMPLE

On June 25, Rick, who rents from LaVerne on a month-to-month basis, says he'll be leaving on June 30. He's liable for the rent for another 25 days, through July 25. Rick's security deposit was $500. LaVerne charges him 25 days of prorated rent, or $375 (his monthly rent is $450), and because the property was clean and undamaged, returns the remaining $125 of the deposit. LaVerne makes no effort to rerent the place until July 26, almost four weeks after Rick leaves. Rick takes LaVerne to small claims court, suing for the $375. The judge may find that LaVerne should have made a reasonable effort to locate a new tenant. Based on the local housing market, which is extremely tight, the judge concludes that LaVerne probably could have found a new tenant within ten days if she listed the vacancy in the papers and with rental location agencies. The judge therefore allows LaVerne to keep only ten days' prorated rent, or $150, giving Rick a judgment for the $225 difference.

To summarize, if a month-to-month tenant gives you less than 30 days' written notice, you're entitled to:

- Thirty days' rent prorated from the date of the written notice, less

- Any rent you reasonably could have collected from a new tenant for the period between the day the outgoing tenant left and the end of the 30-day period, plus

- sAny reasonable advertising expenses incurred in finding that new tenant.

B. TERMINATION OF FIXED-TERM LEASES

As we discussed in Chapter 2, a lease lasts for a fixed term, typically six months or a year. During the term of the lease, neither you nor the tenant may terminate the tenancy unless the other party violates the lease by failing to fulfill his obligations. You would generally use a three-day notice to terminate a tenancy for violation of a lease provision. (See Chapters 16 and 18 for details.)

If, however, everything goes well, the lease simply terminates of its own accord at the end of the lease term. Unfortunately, however, this description of how a lease works is often more theoretical than real. This section of the chapter focuses on your rights and responsibilities as well as those of a tenant who leaves at the end of a lease term. This section also discusses problems that occur when a tenant breaks a lease simply by leaving before the end of the term.

A lease can convert to a month-to-month tenancy.
If you accept rent for a period beyond the date when a fixed-term lease ends, you've extended the tenancy on a month-to-month basis. To terminate the tenancy at this point, follow the rules for terminating a month-to-month tenancy. (See Chapter 18, Section A.)

1. Tenant Leaves at the End of the Lease Term

A fixed-term lease simply expires at the end of the term. The tenant may pick up and leave at the end of the lease term, without any further obligation. Any notice from the tenant, written or oral, indicating the tenant's intent to leave before the natural expiration of the lease term is of no legal effect other than to tell you that the tenant is planning to break the lease.

Under state law, the landlord may, without giving any advance notice to the tenant, insist he move out just as the lease expires. (*Black v. Black,* 77 Cal. App. 82 (1926).) However, this is not generally a good idea. First, in cities with just-cause eviction provisions in their rent control ordinances, the ordinances do not allow you to insist on a lease-holding tenant's departure, except for specified reasons, including when the tenant has refused to sign a new lease containing essentially the same terms. (See Chapter 18, Section C.)

In any case, even though no formal notice of termination is required, you should, as a practical matter, routinely give tenants a 30-day notice if you don't wish to continue the tenancy when the lease expires. Otherwise, as mentioned above, the lease will convert to a month-to-month tenancy. Although the tenant is theoretically required to leave at the end of the lease term, and you are not legally required to give notice that you don't intend to renew, it has become so customary for a tenant to stay on a month-to-month basis, in the absence of anything said to the contrary, that it's an essential business practice to advise your tenant at least a month in advance if you won't be renewing or even extending the lease.

As with a month-to-month tenancy, a tenant with a fixed-term lease may not legally refuse to pay the rent for the last month of occupancy and insist that you take it out of the security deposit, unless you have accepted a deposit specifically called "last month's rent." (See Section A2, above.)

As we saw in Chapter 18, Section A, you should mail your tenants a "Move-Out Letter" that advises them of the right to an initial move-out inspection, and to be present at it. This applies even where the lease is simply expiring. Be sure to mail the Move-Out Letter within a few days after it becomes clear that the fixed-term lease won't be renewed or that the tenant won't be staying on without a lease but with your permission (as a month-to-month tenant).

2. Tenant Leaves Before the End of the Term

A tenant who leaves (whether or not she notifies you that she's leaving) before the expiration of a fixed-term lease and refuses to pay the remainder of the rent due under the lease is said to have "broken the lease."

A tenant renting under a lease agrees at the outset to pay a fixed total rent: the monthly rent multiplied by the number of months the lease will last. Payment is normally made in monthly installments over the term of the lease. This means the tenant is liable for the entire rent for the entire lease term (except where the landlord breaches an important lease provision first). According to this rule, a landlord faced with a tenant leaving early could sue the tenant for the remaining rent that the landlord would have collected had the tenant not left early.

Make sure your tenant understands this long-term responsibility for rent in both the lease (see Clause 4 in Chapter 2) and move-in letter (Chapter 7).

But a tenant's liability for leaving too soon is limited by the landlord's duty to mitigate damages by finding a new rent-paying tenant as soon as reasonably possible. (CC § 1951.2.) This is true whether the tenancy is under a fixed-term lease or a month-to-month arrangement (as discussed in Section A4, above), but applies most powerfully in the lease situation.

EXAMPLE 1

Juan rented an apartment to Jorge in January for a term of one year, with monthly rent of $1,000. Everything went well until late September, when Jorge skipped out on the lease. Jorge is theoretically liable to Juan for $3,000—the rent for October, November, and December. However, if Juan mitigated these damages by taking out an ad and re-renting on October 15, Jorge will owe much less. If the new tenant pays $500 for the last half of October and $1,000 in November and December, Juan must credit the total $2,500 he got from the new tenant against Jorge's $3,000 liability. This leaves Jorge liable for only $500 for the unrented days, plus Juan's advertising costs of $20, for a total of $520.

EXAMPLE 2

Same example as above, but assume that after Jorge skips out in late September, Juan does nothing to re-rent the property, but sues Jorge in December for the three months' rent of $3,000. If Jorge can convince the court that Juan could have rerented the property after half a month at the same rent, the court will award Juan only the $500 he would have lost had he acted more diligently.

Of course, the landlord's duty to mitigate damages only gets the tenant off the hook if it's possible to get a satisfactory new tenant to pay the same amount of rent or more. Most of the time landlords can re-rent, but occasionally a landlord might have problems, as could be the situation with a soft market, student housing during the summer, or vacation rentals off season.

Often a tenant wishing to break the lease by leaving before it expires will approach the landlord and offer to find a suitable new tenant so that the flow of rent will remain uninterrupted. It is a good idea to cooperate with a tenant who suggests this. A landlord who refuses to cooperate by accepting an excellent new tenant is almost by definition refusing to mitigate damages, and may wind up with no recovery if he sues the outgoing tenant who broke the lease.

In this context, the mitigation-of-damages rule is, in effect, a hidden lease clause requiring the landlord to be reasonable about consenting to accept a new tenant to fill out the first tenant's lease term, even where the lease flatly prohibits a sublease. In fact, about the only criterion a landlord may legitimately use to reject a replacement tenant suggested by the outgoing one—that is, with an eye to still being able to collect damages from the departing tenant—is a bad credit or renting history. Of course, if the rental market is really tight in your area, and you can lease the unit easily at a higher rent, you may not care if a tenant breaks a lease, but will want to rent the property yourself and not bother with the tenant's help.

<table>
<tr><td>

SPECIAL RULES FOR TENANTS WHO ENLIST IN OR ARE CALLED TO ACTIVE DUTY

Tenants who enter active military service and certain portions of the Public Health Service, plus National Guard members who are called up for more than a month at a time, after signing a lease or rental agreement, have the right to get out of leases and rental agreements, irrespective of state law or the provisions in your rental documents (Servicemembers' Civil Relief Act (50 App. U.S.C.A §§ 501 and following). Tenants must mail written notice of their intent to terminate their tenancy to you or your manager.

- **Month-to-month rental agreements.** Once the notice is mailed or delivered, the tenancy will terminate 30 days after the day that rent is next due. For example, if rent is due on the first of June and the tenant mails a notice on May 28, the tenancy will terminate on July 1. If your agreement provides for shorter notice periods, these will control.

- **Leases.** A tenant who enters active military service after signing a lease may terminate the lease by following the procedure for rental agreements, above. For example, suppose a tenant signs a one-year lease in April and enlists October 10 (rent is due on the first of the month). If the tenant mails a termination notice on October 11, the lease terminates on December 1, 30 days after the first time that rent is due (November 1) following the mailing of the notice. This tenant will have no continuing obligation for rent past December 1.

The Servicemembers' Relief Act also restricts your ability to evict active duty servicepersons for nonpayment of rent. See *The California Landlord's Law Book: Evictions,* by David Brown (Nolo) for details.

</td></tr>
</table>

If you and the outgoing lease-breaking tenant do agree on a replacement tenant, you can legally proceed in one of two ways. You can: (1) agree to let the outgoing tenant sublet to the incoming one (in which case the outgoing tenant still remains responsible for the remainder of the rent under the lease if the new tenant doesn't pay), or (2) you may have the new tenant enter into a new lease with you (in which case you might even want to raise the rent a little, if local rent control ordinances permit). As we discuss in some detail in Chapter 10, we believe the second alternative is the more desirable because it makes the new tenant directly legally responsible to you.

To summarize, where your fixed-term tenant leaves before the end of the lease, you're entitled to:

- The remaining rent due under the lease, less

- Any rent you could have collected from a new tenant between the time the outgoing tenant left and the end of the lease term, plus

- Any reasonable advertising expenses incurred in finding a new tenant.

You can deduct the total of these three items, plus repair and cleaning charges, from the tenant's security deposit. (See Chapter 20.)

3. "Locking In" the Tenant Who Leaves Early

Landlords are understandably frustrated by the notion that they are expected to mitigate the tenant's losses when it is the tenant who has broken the lease by leaving early. There is a solution to this problem—called the "lock-in provision." (CC § 1951.4.) But, like most things legal, this solution is somewhat double-edged. Here's how it works:

You can "lock in" the tenant—that is, continue to expect rent to be paid as it comes due, without the duty to mitigate damages by finding another tenant—provided all of the following are true:

- the lease includes a provision that you will not unreasonably refuse an assignment or a sublease, and also states your intention to take advantage of the "lock-in provision" of the Civil Code, and

- the tenant has abandoned the lease without providing an acceptable substitute.

If you take advantage of the lock-in option, you may not take possession of the premises other than to secure the doors and windows and keep the property safe (for example, by shutting off the gas). Of course, if you do retake possession and rerent, then you must do so for the benefit of the absconding tenant—in other words, doing so will constitute an abandonment of the lock-in remedy.

This remedy is useful only in limited situations. To begin with, few landlords would want to leave their property vacant and unused, especially if vandalism is a likely problem. And, from a practical point of view, it may be impossible to collect the rent from a tenant who may be long gone. Finally, telling the tenant in the lease that you will not "unreasonably" refuse an assignment or sublease goes one step further than our suggested clause (Clause 10 in Chapter 2), which says merely that assignment or subleasing requires your written consent. Some tenants may take the promise not to be unreasonable as an invitation to sublet or assign, which is not the message you want to convey.

On the other hand, we can imagine certain situations when the lock-in remedy might be useful. Consider the landlord who rents in a university town, whose rentals typically run from September to September. A landlord whose tenant leaves in June will understandably not want to take the time and trouble to rent for two or three months, and knows that few applicants would be interested in a lease of that length. If the landlord knows that she can find and sue her departed tenant, and if she is comfortable leaving the residence unlived-in for a short amount of time, she may wish to hold the tenant to his lease by securing the unit, waiting until the lease expires, and then suing the old tenant for the unpaid rent. Remember, however, that the lock-in option is available *only* to the landlord who has alerted the tenant beforehand to the landlord's willingness to be reasonable with respect to a request to assign or sublet; and to her intention to invoke the lock-in remedy. Be sure to carefully follow the procedures described in Section C, short of rerenting the premises.

C. TERMINATION BY TENANT ABANDONING PREMISES

This section describes the legal way to regain possession of your rental property, without having to go to court, when you have reason to believe the tenant simply left without intending to come back, but didn't bother to tell you about it.

Often it's hard to tell whether a tenant has left for good. People do, after all, sometimes disappear for weeks at a time, going on vacations or elsewhere. And even when a tenant doesn't intend to come back, she may leave behind enough discarded clothing or furniture to make it appear that she may plan to return. (We discuss what to do with abandoned property in Chapter 21.)

Often the first hint you'll have that a tenant has abandoned the premises will be when you don't receive the rent. Or, you may get a call from a neighbor asking about a vacancy, or simply walk by a window and notice the lack of furniture. Unfortunately, the mere appearance that your rental property is no longer occupied doesn't give you the legal right to retake possession. It does, however, constitute legal justification to inspect the place for signs of abandonment. (See Chapter 13, on tenants' privacy.) And remember, you don't have to give 24 hours' advance notice of entering if it's "impracticable" to do so, which is certainly the case if no one's been around for days.

1. Rerent the Property

Once you've determined that your tenant has probably skipped out with no intention of returning, you have several choices. First and most obvious, you can assume that the tenant won't return, and proceed to clean up, dispose of any possessions left behind (see Chapter 21), and rerent the property. This is perfectly okay if the tenant doesn't come back, and may be your best bet if the tenant who has cleared out has not paid rent and has left nothing behind. However, it does involve some legal risk—the tenant might return to find the place rerented and her possessions gone. If you are too impatient, you could face heavy liability in a lawsuit. This is especially true if you retake possession during a time for which the departing tenant has paid rent.

2. Track Down the Tenant

Your second choice is to hunt down the tenant and ask whether the tenant intends to stay away or come back. Look at the tenant's rental application and phone each personal and business reference. If that doesn't work, try asking neighbors and, finally, the police.

Why should you go to so much trouble? Because this approach beats the third alternative, which, although it protects you from liability, requires you to go without rent for a little over a month. From a business standpoint, it's far better to track down the tenant and get her to admit she isn't coming back, allowing you to retake possession immediately, than to have to follow the legally correct procedure, which requires you to leave the place vacant for a month.

3. Formally Notify the Tenant of Plans to Terminate the Tenancy

The third procedure is the formal legal one. It requires that you try to notify the tenant in writing that you intend to terminate the tenancy as the result of the tenant's apparent abandonment of the premises. Unfortunately, you must wait until 14 days have passed without the tenant's having paid rent before you can initiate this procedure. (CC § 1951.3.) During this 14-day waiting period, you might as well prepare a Three-Day Notice to Pay Rent or Quit and serve it by posting and mailing. (See Chapter 16.) This way, if the tenant does show up later and indicates an intent not to leave after all, you can begin the unlawful detainer suit to get the tenant out if she won't pay the rent. However, in situations where the tenant doesn't show up, use of an unlawful detainer suit will be just as time-consuming as, and more costly than, the abandonment notice procedure discussed here. It involves mailing a notice to the tenant's address at the property (or any other known mailing address) on or after the 15th day of rent nonpayment. This notice should look like the sample below.

Mail the notice to the tenant by first class mail at the property, with extra copies mailed to any other address you have for the tenant.

INSPECTING ABANDONED PROPERTY

Here are some tips for inspecting property you suspect has been abandoned:

- Look in the refrigerator. Is it empty, or is most of the food spoiled?

- Check whether electricity and telephone service have been cut off.

- Look in closets to see if very little clothing remains behind.

If these conditions apply, the property might be abandoned.

You'll find a tear-out version of the Notice of Belief of Abandonment in Appendix B. The CD-ROM that accompanies this book also includes this form.

To preserve her right to the property, the tenant must provide you with a written statement that indicates an intent not to abandon; and must provide you with a mailing address at which she may be served by certified mail with an unlawful detainer suit. If you don't receive such a response by the 18th day after mailing the notice (not counting the day of mailing), you may retake possession of the premises. (If you served the notice personally, you need wait only 15, rather than 18, days before retaking possession. But if you had actually been able to serve the notice personally, you obviously would have long since asked the tenant if she intends to stay, and the whole notice procedure should be moot.) Just walk in and begin your usual preparation for rerenting. You don't have to go to the courthouse first. You should return or dispose of any of the tenant's abandoned possessions in the manner described in Chapter 21.

Notice of Belief of Abandonment

Civil Code Section 1951.3

To: _____ Alice Green _____ ,
                                                    Name

Tenant(s) in possession of the premises at _____ 123 Sendaro Street _____ ,
                                                                     Street Address

City of _____ Fresno _____ , County of _____ Fresno _____ , California.

This notice is given pursuant to Section 1951.3 of the Civil Code concerning the real property leased by you at the above address. The rent on this property had been due and unpaid for 14 consecutive days, and the landlord or his agent believes that you have abandoned the property.

The real property will be deemed abandoned within the meaning of Section 1951.2 of the Civil Code and your lease will terminate on _____ May 5 _____ , 20 _OX__ , a date not less than 18 days after the mailing of this notice, unless before such date the undersigned receives at the address indicated below a written notice from you stating both of the following:

(1) your intent not to abandon the real property

(2) an address at which you may be served by certified mail in any action for unlawful detainer of the real property.

You are required to pay the rent due and unpaid on this real property as required by the lease, and your failure to do so can lead to a court proceeding against you.

_____ April 15, 200X _____

Date

_____ *Ruth Clark* _____

Landlord (signature)

_____ Ruth Clark _____

Landlord (print)

_____ 456 State Street, Fresno, California _____

Street address

_____

D. WHAT TO DO WHEN SOME TENANTS LEAVE AND OTHERS STAY

When one of your tenants leaves and the other (whether a spouse, lover, or roommate) remains behind, good business practice, as well as sound legal reasons, requires that you take the change into account rather than ignore it. However, your best course of action, from a legal point of view at least, depends on the extent to which the person leaving is still responsible for the rent if the remaining tenant doesn't pay. We discuss the legal liability of cotenants and subtenants in detail in Chapter 10. Here we review this material briefly.

1. Cotenant Liability

When two or more people rent property together, and all sign the same rental agreement or lease (or enter into the same oral agreement when they move in at the same time), they are cotenants with equal rights to occupy the premises and equal responsibility for the rent. This is why it's best to have all adult occupants sign the lease or rental agreement. A cotenant who moves out and leaves a fellow cotenant behind is still legally liable for the rent due under the lease or rental agreement. This is true until the lease period expires (unless you agree to an earlier termination) or until the month-to-month tenancy is terminated by 30-day notice.

For example, if you sign a one-year lease with Jack and Elaine, and Elaine moves out, Elaine is still jointly liable with Jack for the rent for the time left on the lease. If Jack doesn't pay the rent, you can sue Elaine in small claims court for unpaid rent. It's important to remember, though, that this suit should be separate from any eviction suit—in which only occupants can be named as defendants. (See *The California Landlord's Law Book: Evictions.*)

If Jack and Elaine had a month-to-month rental agreement, Elaine would be liable for the monthly rent after leaving, unless she properly terminated the tenancy, as to herself, by giving you a 30-day notice. (This situation may differ, however, if Jack and Elaine

were married, and did not intend to separate permanently. Elaine might still be liable for the rent, even after giving such a 30-day notice, if she moved out but Jack stayed, because Elaine is legally responsible for her husband's necessities of life. Family Code § 914(a).)

Because the tenancy is one from month to month, Elaine can move out and terminate her obligation by giving you a 30-day notice. Still, as a practical matter, if Jack stopped paying rent after Elaine left without giving a proper notice, you would sue only Jack in an unlawful detainer proceeding, since, as noted above, you can sue only occupants of the premises in that kind of suit. If you could find Elaine, you could of course file a separate small claims suit against her for all unpaid rent.

2. Subtenant Liability

A subtenant is a person who rents all or part of the property from a tenant and does not sign a rental agreement or lease with the landlord. A subtenant is someone who either took over the property after the original tenant temporarily left, or one who simply lives with the tenant who has signed your lease or rental agreement.

If your lease or rental agreement prohibits subleasing, you can evict the tenant who brings in a subtenant for violating this lease term. If you don't evict, however, you normally have few legal rights vis-a-vis the subtenant who does not have a tenant/landlord relationship with you. As a result, you can't sue the subtenant for rent—either in small claims court or in an eviction suit. (You can bring an eviction lawsuit against the subtenant based on nonpayment of rent, but you can get a judgment against the subtenant only for possession of the property and court costs, not for the rent itself.) However, should you rent to a married couple and neglect to get both to sign the lease, the nonsigning spouse, although a subtenant, is liable for the rent, because each spouse is legally responsible for the necessities of life of the other. (Family Code § 914(a).)

3. When a Cotenant Leaves and a New Person Moves In

When a cotenant leaves and someone else moves in, you must act decisively. Although the departing tenant will still be liable for the rent unless you and the newcomer sign a new agreement, this will probably not be worth too much if your original tenant leaves for parts unknown. You are almost always better off to sign a lease or rental agreement with any new tenant if the replacement is acceptable. As an added advantage, it will be clear that the outgoing tenant is no longer entitled to possession of the property. This last point may be especially important where a couple (married or not) separates. If one of them leaves and then wants to come back—against the will of the other—you are powerless to keep that person out, if:

- the person who has left didn't terminate the month-to-month tenancy as to herself with a 30-day notice, or

- in the case of a lease, no new lease was entered into by the remaining tenant (on his own or with someone else as a co-tenant), or

- the couple is still married, even if a new agreement has been signed. (Under Family Code § 753, a spouse may not be excluded from the home of the other in the absence of a court order, even if a divorce is pending.)

If someone is moving in to replace the departing tenant, it's usually best to have the remaining tenant and the new tenant sign a new lease or rental agreement. The new roommate thus becomes jointly liable for the rent. If you live in a city with rent control, this may also be your chance to raise the rent if the remaining tenant was not part of the original group you rented to. Remember, in most rent control cities, you can raise the rent in shared housing only when all the original tenants move out. For more on vacancy decontrol, see Chapter 4.

But what happens if the new tenant isn't acceptable to you? If that person hasn't moved in, simply use your authority to deny permission to sublet. If the would-be tenant has moved in without your permission, promptly move to evict the tenant on the basis of his violation of the lease term prohibiting sublets. (You should also name the person moving in on the eviction action—see *The California Landlord's Law Book: Evictions.*) If you rent under a month-to-month tenancy, a simple 30-day notice is probably your best bet.

E. DEATH OF A TENANT

Occasionally, a landlord will be faced with the death of a tenant who lives alone. Because lawyers and public agencies are bound to be involved, you should be sure to comply with the law, even though your first urge may be to clear out the property and rent it as quickly as possible. You may also have questions about how to handle the tenant's belongings, what to do with the security deposit (including what to do if it's inadequate to cover unpaid rent or damage), and how much rent you are entitled to after learning of the tenant's death.

1. Secure the Premises

When you first suspect or learn of a death of a tenant, call the police or fire department. After the body is removed, you are required to take reasonable precautions to preserve the deceased tenant's property. Obviously, you don't want to be sued by the executor of the estate for giving away valuable property to relatives or to friends, to the detriment of the true heirs. If you can, contact the next of kin, but allow them to remove only personal effects (such as the deceased's clothing needed for the funeral). Keep everyone else out of the premises. If more than a negligible amount of property is in the dwelling, put a padlock on the door. Open it for the public administrator for the county, or to a court-appointed executor or administrator who can show you Letters Testamentary or Letters of Administration (legal mumbo-jumbo for papers signed by a judge appointing a legal representative for the deceased's estate).

DOMESTIC PARTNERS WHO DIE WITHOUT WILLS

If you rent to an unmarried couple, straight or gay, and one member of the couple dies without a will, you might be caught in a nasty crossfire between the blood relatives of the deceased and his or her domestic partner.

The chances for disputes will be lessened if your tenants are *registered* domestic partners who have filed a Declaration of Domestic Partnership with the secretary of state. (Probate Code §§ 8461 & 8462.) The surviving partner is like a surviving spouse, who will inherit the deceased's property as long as the deceased had no children. But if the deceased partner has living children, they will inherit a portion of the property.

If the domestic partnership is not registered, the blood relatives inherit automatically unless the survivor and the deceased had a contract to share ownership of all property. This is all pretty tricky stuff, made more so by your inability to know the details. If a lot of property is involved, your best bet is to check with your lawyer.

If the deceased tenant's total estate was small ($100,000 or less), or the tenant used probate-avoidance techniques such as a living trust, there may well be no official probate procedure and hence no court-approved executor or administrator. In this situation, if a family member of the deceased's appears and wants to take the property, you can safely release it if you receive a copy of the decedent's will establishing that the person in question is entitled to the property, along with a declaration under penalty of perjury signed by the person to whom the property has been left. (Probate Code § 13100.) If there is no will, however, and only a small amount of property remains on the premises, formal probate proceedings are unlikely and it's probably okay to release the property to close relatives—provided they sign a receipt for what they take. If you are in doubt, talk to a lawyer.

After all the deceased tenant's property is removed, consider making a claim to the deceased tenant's estate for any unpaid rent through the date the property remained on the premises. If a probate proceeding is initiated, you should submit a filled-out creditor's claim form (available from the court clerk) to the probate clerk of the superior court. You have four months in which to file your claim, beginning when the court officially appoints the estate's executor. If the estate doesn't go through probate (many small estates do not), the best you can do is bill the next of kin.

2. The Deceased Tenant's Security Deposit

You are entitled to use the deceased tenant's security deposit to cover unpaid rent, to remedy damage beyond normal wear and tear, and to do necessary cleaning (see Subsection 2 for more information on how much rent you are entitled to). To return any unused portion of the security deposit, follow the instructions for returning other tenant property in Subsection E1, above. If the deposit does not cover your necessary expenses, you'll need to make a claim on the deceased's estate (or bill the next of kin), as explained below in Subsection 3.

3. What Happens to the Lease or Rental Agreement?

You and the tenant's estate (or next of kin) will need to confront the question of what happens to the tenant's rental agreement or lease now that the tenant is dead—and in particular, whether you are entitled to rent past the date of the tenant's death. Some landlords may also encounter relatives or friends who will want to take over the tenant's unit. Must you allow them to do so? The answers depend on whether the tenant rented under a rental agreement or a lease.

a. Tenants with month-to-month rental agreements

Your deceased tenant's responsibility for rent will end 30 days after the date the tenant last paid rent. For example, if rent was payable on the first of every month and the tenant died on the tenth of September, the tenant's estate or next of kin is responsible for rent only for the month of September—as of October 1, the rental agreement is over and so is any obligation to pay rent. This result seems contrary to the normal rules of notice (which would suggest that the landlord is entitled to rent for 30 days after getting notice of the tenant's death, or though October 10 in our example), but it's the law in California nevertheless. (*Miller & Desatnik Management Co. v. Bullock*, 221 Cal.App.3d Supp. 13 (1990); CC § 1934.)

This rule will not prevent you, however, from being compensated by the estate if the tenant's belongings remain on the property after the next rent due date. This often happens while the legalities of who is entitled to what are being sorted out, and is sure to happen if the tenant dies right before the next rent payment was due. When the tenant's belongings remain in the unit, you're simply dealing with a "holdover tenant" situation, and you are entitled to rent for those days. You should consider making a claim to the estate for prorated rent through the date the property remains on your premises (this is how you'd ask for unpaid back rent, too).

If there's a probate proceeding, submit a creditor's claim form (available from the court clerk) to the probate clerk of the superior court. You have four months in which to file your claim, beginning when the court officially appoints the estate's executor. If the estate doesn't go through probate (many small estates do not), the best you can do is bill the next of kin.

Since the tenancy will legally end as of the next rent due date, you are under no legal obligation to accept a substitute tenant proposed by the deceased tenant's family or friends. If someone would like to move in, treat that person just as you would any other applicant, by evaluating the applicant's creditworthiness and rental history with the same care you use with any applicant.

b. Tenants with leases

Unlike the result described above in Subsection a, when a tenant with a lease dies, the lease is *not* terminated. Instead, you'll need to treat the situation as you would if the tenant had broken the lease by moving away mid-term. In other words, the tenant (now, the estate or next of kin) remains responsible for the rent through the end of the lease term, but you are obligated to use reasonable efforts to find a replacement tenant (your duty to mitigate damages is explained in detail in Chapter 19, Section B). (*Joost v. Castel*, 33 Cal.App.2d 138 (1939); CC § 1934.) When you begin receiving rent from the next tenant (or when you could have received rent, had you used reasonable efforts to find a replacement), the estate's responsibility for rent ends.

If your ex-tenant had a favorable lease—at a good rate and with significant time left on it—you may learn that a family member (or a friend) of the original tenant would like to assume the lease. Such people have no legal right to live in the deceased tenant's unit unless you give the official okay. Evaluate them as you would all applicants. If they pass your "good tenant" test, it would be wise to rent to them (if you don't and later have difficulty filling the unit, you'll have a hard time collecting rent from the estate past the date you rejected a perfectly acceptable candidate).

Single tenants with favorable leases in rent-controlled cities cannot pass them on to survivors. It's not uncommon for tenants to stay in rent-controlled units for many years, leaving only when they die. Unless the tenant lived in the unit with family members (or a registered domestic partner), the tenancy will end at the tenant's death. ■

20

RETURNING SECURITY DEPOSITS

As any small claims court judge will tell you, disputes over whether a landlord properly withheld all or part of a tenant's security deposit account for a large percentage of the landlord/tenant disputes that wind up in court. Even though landlords commonly win the suits they initiate, they sometimes don't gain very much given the time that goes into bringing the suit and the often difficult and time-consuming job of collecting the judgment. Your best protection against spending hours haggling in court over back rent, cleaning costs, and damage to your property is to follow the law scrupulously when you return security deposits. And make sure your tenant knows the law and your procedures on security deposits.

This chapter shows you how to conduct pre-move out inspections, itemize deductions, provide receipts for labor and materials, and refund security deposits as the law requires. It also covers the occasional necessity of taking a tenant to small claims court for unpaid rent, damage, or cleaning bills not covered by the deposit.

Related Topics

- How to avoid deposit disputes by using clear lease and rental agreement provisions: Chapter 2

- Highlighting security deposit rules in a move-in letter to new tenants; taking photographs and using a Landlord/Tenant Checklist to keep track of the condition of the premises before and after the tenant moves in: Chapter 7

- How much you can charge for security deposits, local requirements to pay interest on deposits, and the effect of sale of the property on an owner's liability for security deposits: Chapter 5

- How to increase security deposits: Chapter 14.

A. BASIC RULES FOR RETURNING DEPOSITS

The law allows you to make certain deductions from a tenant's security deposit, provided you do it correctly. The basic rule is this: Within three weeks after

a tenant who has paid a deposit leaves—whether voluntarily, by abandonment, or by eviction—you must mail the following to the tenant's last known address, or forwarding address if you have one:

- The tenant's entire deposit, or

- A written, itemized accounting of deductions for back rent and costs for necessary cleaning and damage repair, including receipts for labor and materials, together with a check for any deposit balance. (See CC § 1950.5(g).)

If you act in bad faith and keep a security deposit, or any portion of it, you may be liable for up to twice the amount of the deposit in statutory damages should the tenant sue you in small claims court, in addition to actual damages, including back rent improperly withheld. (CC § 1950.5(l).) The court may award damages whenever the facts warrant—regardless of whether the tenant has specifically requested relief. Also, judges are often skeptical about the legitimacy of a landlord's charges for cleaning and damages if the landlord never bothered to itemize these charges until the tenant raised the issue of getting the deposit back.

1. Security Deposits Defined

California law defines a security deposit as any money you collect from a tenant other than a legitimate credit check fee or the first month's rent, which you intend to use to cover unpaid rent or damage. (CC § 1950.5(b).) It specifically includes "last month's rent." In other words, whether you call your tenant's up-front money a fee, deposit or charge for "rent," "cleaning," "damage," or even "keys," you must account for it under the law applicable to refundable security deposits. Anything in a lease or rental agreement to the contrary is of no legal effect. (CC § 1953(a)(1).) (Chapter 5 discusses these rules in more detail.)

2. When You Rent to More Than One Tenant

When you rent to two or more cotenants under the same agreement (where their names are all listed on the written lease or rental agreement), you don't have to return or account for any of the deposit until all the tenants leave. In other words, you're entitled to the benefit of the entire deposit until the entire tenancy ends. Any question as to whether a departing cotenant is entitled to any share of the deposit he originally paid should be worked out between or among the co-tenants. Obviously, you can voluntarily work out an appropriate agreement with a departing tenant in this situation. But if you do, make sure you're adequately protected by the remainder of the deposit or require that the remaining tenants (or the new roommate, if there is one) bring the deposit up to an acceptable amount.

3. When a Tenant Is Evicted

With one exception, you must follow the legal procedures for returning and accounting for security deposits whether the tenant leaves voluntarily or involuntarily, with or without the threat or use of eviction proceedings. The exception concerns your duty to notify tenants of their right to a pre-move-out inspection when their tenancy ends as a result of your three-day or unconditional quit notice (see Section B, below).

Quite a few landlords are under the mistaken belief that they don't have to account for the deposit to a tenant who's been evicted by court order, apparently thinking the tenant's misconduct allows a landlord to pocket the entire deposit without further formality. This is not true. Even if you win a judgment in court against a tenant for several months' unpaid rent—more than the amount of the deposit— you still must notify the tenant in writing within three weeks after the tenant departs as to how you applied the deposit toward cleaning or damage charges, along with receipts, and the court judgment for rent. (See Section C, below.)

B. INITIAL MOVE-OUT INSPECTION AND RIGHT TO RECEIPTS

Since January 2003, tenants are entitled to a pre-move-out inspection, when you or your manager tell the tenant what defects, if any, need to be corrected in order for the tenant to optimize the security deposit refund. You are required to conduct this inspection if the tenant requests it. (CC § 1950.5(f).) Done in a conciliatory, nonthreatening way, this should alleviate any of the tenant's uncertainty concerning exactly what deductions (if any) will be made from the deposit. After all, a tenant unpleasantly surprised by the amount withheld from the deposit is more likely to take the matter to court. Here are the details on how to proceed.

You do not need to notify the tenant of a right to be present at a move-out inspection if you have served a three-day notice to pay rent or quit (or other three-day or unconditional quit notice based on some other breach), or if you are evicting on that basis. The need to tell the tenant of a right to be present at an initial move-out inspection applies only where the tenant should be leaving because you or the tenant gave the other a 30-day or 60-day or other regular notice of termination of tenancy—one that was not associated directly with a tenant's misconduct—or where a fixed-term lease expires and is simply not being extended. CC § 1950.5(f)(1).) Such a tenant is, however, entitled to receipts and invoices for deductions, as explained below.

As of January 1, 2004, you must also provide receipts for security deposit deductions when you refund the balance, if any, of the deposit. These receipts must include (or you must supply) the name, address, and phone number of the person doing the work or supplying the replacement item. Here are the fine points you'll need to know:

- **Applies to all tenants.** This law applies to tenants who leave as a matter of course at the end of a lease; to month-to-month tenants whose tenancy has terminated voluntarily or after receiving a 30- or 60-day notice from you; and to tenants who leave (or are evicted) following a termination for wrongdoing, such as nonpayment of rent.

- **Minimum amount.** The rule requiring receipts does not apply if the total deductions are $125 or less.

- **Materials you buy in bulk or on an ongoing basis.** If you deduct for a particular item that you purchase on an ongoing basis (such as rug shampoo that you buy regularly and in bulk), you must supply an invoice that documents the cost of the item, and figure the tenant's share.

- **Labor done by you or your employee.** Your statement must describe the work, the time spent, and include a reasonable hourly rate.

- **When you can't finish the job within 21 days of the tenant's departure or don't have invoices.** If you can't reasonably complete a repair within 21 days of the tenant's departure, or if you don't yet have the documents from a repairperson or company documenting the repair, you may deduct a good faith estimate of the eventual costs. You must, however, give the tenant the repairperson's name, address, and phone number. Within 14 days of getting the invoice, you must send it to the tenant in the same manner that you sent the original itemization.

Like the right to an initial move-out inspection, this right can be waived. However, the waiver must be signed at the same time or after a notice of termination has been given by you or the tenant or, if the tenancy is at an end because the lease is up, within 60 days of the lease's end. (In other words, you can't hand this waiver to the tenant at the start of the tenancy.) If you want to give your tenants the option of waiving their rights to receipts, the tenants must do so in writing, on a document that explains the gist of the law. We've designed a form, Tenant's Waiver of Right to Receipts and Invoices, that you can use.

Be aware that the tenant can rescind the waiver after receiving your itemized statement of deductions. The tenant has 14 days in which to request the same documentation that you would have supplied had the tenant never waived the right to receive it. Once you receive the request, you must comply within 14 days, by sending the documentation as if you were supplying it in the first place. The lesson here is clear: Keep all documents that substantiate security deposit deductions, even for tenants who have waived their

rights. You never know when tenants will change their minds.

1. Notify the Tenant

First, you must notify the tenant in writing of the right to request an initial inspection, at which the tenant has a right to be present. You are not legally required to tell tenants of their rights to receive invoices and receipts, but we think it's a good idea, if only so that you can ask them to waive that right if you choose to do so. A Move-Out Letter that explains your inspection procedures to the tenant—and gives this legally required notice—is shown below; it also includes information on the tenant's rights to receive invoices and receipts. We suggest that you attach the Tenant's Response Regarding Initial Move-Out Inspection and Tenant's Waiver of Right to Receipts and Invoices to this letter, to make it easy for tenants to ask for the inspection or to specifically decline it, and to waive the right to receipts. The letter also imparts some important legal information regarding your right to deduct for deficiencies that are not remedied, those that crop up after the inspection, and those that you can't see because the tenant's possessions are in the way. It also reminds the tenant that the tenant's right to perform repairs is contingent on any restrictions in the rental document regarding rights to make repairs (see Section 5, below). A filled-out sample is shown below, as is a sample of a completed invoice waiver.

You can complete the top portion (with the date you prepare the form, the tenant's name and address, and the date the tenancy will terminate). The tenant chooses the option he wants: an inspection that he'll attend, an inspection that you or your manager will do without him, or no inspection at all. Keep this form with the tenant's file for as long as you keep the rest of your tenant's paperwork. It will give you a paper trail should you ever need to prove that you gave the tenant notice of his rights and he declined to be present or to ask for an inspection. Your tenant can request an inspection without using this form, however—any written or verbal request will trigger your duty to inspect.

Move-Out Letter

July 5, 200X

Dear Resident:

We hope you have enjoyed living here.

Before vacating, be sure to thoroughly vacuum the floors (shampoo carpets, if necessary) and clean the walls, kitchen cabinets, stove and oven, refrigerator (which should be emptied of food, turned off, with the door left open), kitchen and bathroom sink, bathtubs, showers, toilets, plumbing fixtures, and _____ deck _____

You have the right to request an initial move-out inspection, at which time management will inspect your rental and, to the extent possible, identify damage, excessive wear and tear, and unacceptable uncleanliness that will have to be remedied in order to avoid deductions from your security deposit. You have the right to be present at that inspection if you choose, and we encourage you to do so. Problems that occur between the inspection and when you move out, or that were missed due to the presence of your possessions, can still form the basis of a deduction from your deposit.

If we need to deduct from your security deposit to cover needed repairs or to clean the rental unit, and if the total deduction (for labor and materials) is more than $125.00, we will give you copies of receipts and invoices for all work done and items purchased. If management or its employees do any of the work, we will bill you at a reasonable rate for that work. These invoices and bills will be included with an itemization of deductions and return of the balance, if any, of your security deposit, which you will receive within three weeks after you move out. (If management does not have these items in its possession when it itemizes and returns any balance, either because the work is yet to be completed or the invoices have not been received, we will include an estimate of the deductions, with the repairperson's name, address, and phone number, and send the actual bills to you within 14 days of receiving them.) You may waive your right to receive invoices (we will give you a form for this), and you may also rescind that waiver (and ask for invoices) if you do so within 14 days of receiving the itemization.

Please provide a forwarding address where we may mail your security deposit less any past due rent and minus any lawful deductions for the cost of necessary cleaning and repairs of damage in excess of ordinary wear and tear (with receipts and invoices for such deductions).

We will give you two written response forms, on which you can tell us whether you would like an initial move-out inspection and whether you would like to waive your right to copies of bills and receipts for any work done or items purchased, as explained above. If you have any questions, please contact me at _555-1234_____ .

Sincerely,

Denise Parsons
Landlord/Manager

Tenant's Response Regarding Initial Move-Out Inspection

Tenant: _____ Marie Williams _____

Rental Address: _____ 413 4th Street, #4 _____

_____ San Dimo, CA 94123 _____

Termination Date: _____ August 1, 200x _____

I understand that I have a legal right to an initial move-out inspection. (California Civil Code Section 1950.5.) The purpose of this inspection, which my landlord or manager will perform no earlier than two weeks before my termination date, is to give me a chance to avoid probable deductions from my security deposit. At the inspection, I'll be advised of intended deductions for deficiencies such as damage, excessive wear and tear, or the need to clean the rental unit. I understand that I may remedy these problems consistent with any repair rights or limitations that may be in my lease or rental agreement. I also understand that my landlord will reinspect when I leave, and may deduct for deficiencies that:

- have been noted in the initial inspection but have not been satisfactorily remedied

- could not be seen during the initial inspection due to the presence of my possessions in the rental unit, or

- have appeared since the date of the initial inspection.

Tenant, please initial one of the following:

_M.W._ I would like to be present at the inspection. Please contact me so that we can arrange for a mutually convenient time.

_____ I would like an initial inspection but do not wish to be present. Please give me 48 hours' notice of the day and time you will inspect.

_____ I do not wish to have an initial move-out inspection.

s/ _____ Andrew Liu _____

_____, Landlord/Manager

Andrew Liu

June 13, 200x
_____
Date signed by Landlord

June 15, 200x
_____
Date form given to Tenant

s/ _____ Marie Williams _____

_____, Tenant

Marie Williams

June 17, 200x
_____
Date signed by Tenant

Tenant's Waiver of Right to Receipts and Invoices
California Civil Code Section 1959.5(g)(4)(B)

Tenant: _____ Marie Williams _____

Rental Address: _____ 413 4th Street, #4 _____

_____ San Dimo, CA 94123 _____

Termination Date: _____ August 1, 200x _____

      I understand that I will receive a list of itemized deductions from my security deposit, for necessary cleaning and repairs to, or replacement of, items damaged beyond normal wear and tear. I also understand that I have the right to receive copies of documents, such as bills, invoices, and receipts, showing charges incurred and deducted by my landlord to repair or clean the premises. (California Civil Code Section 1950.5 (g)(2).) In particular,

- If my landlord or the landlord's employee does the work, the itemized statement will include the work performed, time spent, and a reasonable hourly rate.

- If others did the work, the statement will include a copy of the receipt, bill, or invoice sent by the repairperson, along with the person's address and phone number.

- If the landlord deducts for materials or supplies, the statement will include a copy of the bill, invoice, or receipt. If the material or item is one that the landlord purchases on an ongoing basis, the statement will include a copy of the bill, invoice, receipt, vendor price list, or other vendor document that will indicate the cost of the item used in the repair or for the cleaning of my rental unit.

      I now waive these rights to receive copies of invoices, bills, and receipts, as described above. Within 14 days of receiving my itemized statement I may, however, request documentation of all deductions from my security deposit, and I understand that the landlord will have 14 days after receiving my request in which to furnish such documentation to me, in the same manner in which the initial itemization was prepared and sent.

s/_____ *Marie Williams* _____   July 5, 200x _____

_____ Marie Williams _____, Tenant   Date

You'll find a tear-out version of the Move-Out Letter, the Tenant's Response Regarding Initial Move-Out Inspection, and Tenant's Waiver of Right to Receipts and Invoices in Appendix B. The CD-ROM that accompanies this book also includes these forms.

2. Give Notice of Your Inspection

If the tenant requests an inspection, you or your manager should contact the tenant to arrange for a date and time for the inspection to take place. The inspection must occur no sooner than two weeks before the anticipated move-out date. If you can't agree on a time, you still need to conduct an inspection, and you will just have to select a date and time yourself.

Even when you and the tenant agree on the date and time for the move-out inspection, you still need to give the tenant 48 hours' notice, in writing, of your intent to conduct the inspection. See Chapter 13, Section A, and use the Notice of Intent to Enter Dwelling Unit form referred to there. Conduct the inspection on the date and time indicated on the

notice. You must conduct the inspection even if the tenant doesn't show up for it, unless the tenant has withdrawn the request for the inspection.

3. Conduct and Document the Inspection

Whether you do the final inspection in the tenant's presence or not, we suggest that you do a thorough job. Bring two copies of the Landlord/Tenant Checklist that you (hopefully) filled out (and both signed) when the tenancy began (you'll need two because one must be left with the tenant). If you didn't use this Checklist at the beginning of the tenancy, use it now (obviously, you'll need to leave the first column blank). Attach any notes that you might have made when the tenant moved in.

At the inspection, check each element of the rental—for example, the refrigerator, doors, and bathroom walls—that's included on the Checklist. Note any problems in the "Condition at Initial Move-Out Inspection" column. Keep in mind that items marked "OK" initially may be damaged now; on the other hand, items that were already damaged may have been repaired or replaced by you since the tenant moved in (or, of course, they may still be damaged, in which case you cannot expect the tenant to repair or replace them). As you go through the unit

EXCERPT FROM LANDLORD/TENANT CHECKLIST—INITIAL MOVE-OUT INSPECTION

Landlord/Tenant Checklist
GENERAL CONDITION OF RENTAL UNIT AND PREMISES

572 Fourth St.   Apt. 11   Anytown, CA

Street Address   Unit Number   City

	Condition on Arrival	Condition on Initial Move-Out Inspection	Condition on Departure	Actual or Estimated Cost of Cleaning, Repair/Replacement
LIVING ROOM				
Floors & Floor Coverings	OK	red wine stain, 6" diameter, 2' from picture window. Needs to be removed	OK	Ø
Drapes & Window Coverings	Mini-blinds discolored	OK	Dirty	$30
Walls & Ceilings	OK	wall near light switch dirty. Needs to be cleaned.	Several holes in wall	$100
Light Fixtures	OK	OK	OK	Ø
Windows, Screens & Doors	Window rattles	picture window dirty, smeared. Needs to be washed inside & out	OK	Ø

and the list, be sure to note the condition of the elements as thoroughly as you can, and keep in mind any intervening repair history (if you've kept repair records, it's a good idea to bring them along). In the same column, after you describe the problem, clearly indicate what needs to be cleaned or repaired. See the sample, below, for an illustration on how one landlord might describe the problems and note the needed response.

When you've finished the inspection, you and the tenant should sign the Checklist at the end, in the space provided for the Initial Move-Out Inspection. Getting the tenant's signature here will establish, should you ever need to prove it, that you did indeed conduct the inspection.

4. Estimate Costs and Give Tenant the Required List and Law

After you've gone through the rental unit, you aren't required to specify how much you will deduct if the problems aren't rectified. However, discussing the expected dollar amounts may, in some situations, be a good idea. It will give the tenant the information he needs in order to decide whether to do the work himself or accept the deduction. Give the tenant one copy of the Landlord/Tenant Checklist, specifying repairs or cleaning that you propose to deduct for if the tenant doesn't correct the problems before moving.

You must also give the tenant a copy of a portion of the security deposit law, which explains how landlords may use a tenant's security deposit. Use our Notice of Tenants' Security Deposit Rights form, which is shown below, and attach it to the Checklist. Note that you can leave both items with the tenant, or with someone whom the tenant has apparently designated as his representative (such as a friend or relative). If the tenant did not show up and didn't supply a proxy, you can leave both documents in the unit in a safe and obvious place, such as the kitchen table.

5. Repairs by the Tenant—Or Not

The whole point of the initial inspection is to give the tenant time to remedy the problems you've identified as likely candidates for a deduction from the security deposit. In some instances, the remedy (such as waxing the kitchen floor or cleaning the refrigerator better) will be something you can reasonably expect the tenant to undertake and do well, and the only issue when he moves will be, did the tenant do an adequate job? Other problems that you might identify may not, however, have such an easy and obvious resolution. Here are some of the trickier issues you'll need to think about and plan ahead for:

- **Repairs that are dangerous.** In your initial inspection, you may discover the need for repairs or replacements that you would not want any tenant to undertake, because doing so would be dangerous for most people. For example, if your tenant's cooking adventures have rendered the oven element useless, it will need to be replaced—but most people would agree that no one but a trained appliance repairperson should attempt the job.

- **Repairs that require advanced skill.** Some repairs or replacements may not be so dangerous to perform, but the results of doing a poor job could be extremely harmful to others (or damaging to the property). For instance, if the tenant's kids have broken a window, it will need to be replaced—but removing glass and properly installing and glazing the new pane is a tricky job that, if done improperly, can result in a loose (and dangerous) window and ruinous leaks.

- **Repair or replace?** You and the tenant may disagree as to how to address a problem that you've identified. Your tenant may think that a quick fix is all that's needed; you may consider the deficiency beyond repair and a candidate for replacement. For instance, a hole in a hollow-core, natural-finish door can theoretically be patched, but the patch will show, the more so if the hole is large. Since wood putty and wood stain is cheaper than a new door, the tenant will want to repair the

Notice of Tenant's Security Deposit Rights

Dear _____Mr. Wong_____ (tenant),

Your landlord or his or her agent has performed an initial move-out inspection as requested by you pursuant to California Civil Code Section 1950.5. Attached to this Notice is an itemization of needed repairs, replacements, or cleaning which may, if not remedied, form the basis of deductions from your security deposit.

Civil Code Section 1950.5 provides that:

"1950.5(b): As used in this section, "security" means any payment, fee, deposit or charge, including, but not limited to, any payment, fee, deposit or charge, except as provided in Section 1950.6, that is imposed at the beginning of the tenancy to be used to reimburse the landlord for costs associated with processing a new tenant or that is imposed as an advance payment of rent, used or to be used for any purpose, including, but not limited to, any of the following:

(1) The compensation of a landlord for a tenant's default in the payment of rent.

(2) The repair of damages to the premises, exclusive of ordinary wear and tear, caused by the tenant or by a guest or licensee of the tenant.

(3) The cleaning of the premises upon termination of the tenancy necessary to return the unit to the same level of cleanliness it was in at the inception of the tenancy. The amendments to this paragraph enacted by the act adding this sentence shall apply only to tenancies for which the tenant's right to occupy begins after January 1, 2003.

(4) To remedy future defaults by the tenant in any obligation under the rental agreement to restore, replace or return personal property or appurtenances, exclusive of ordinary wear and tear, if the security deposit is authorized to be applied thereto by the rental agreement.

1950.5(d): Any security shall be held by the landlord for the tenant who is party to the lease or agreement. The claim of a tenant to the security shall be prior to the claim of any creditor of the landlord."

I have given this Notice and its attachment to _____ (tenant) or a person of apparent authority, suitable age, and discretion; or have left it in the rental unit in a safe and conspicuous place.

s/_____

_____, Landlord or agent   _____

                                                     Date

I have received this Notice and its attachment.

s/_____

_____, Tenant or recipient   _____

                                                     Date

problem; you'll want to buy a new door and deduct the cost from the deposit. Does your tenant have a "right" to fix the hole? Or, put another way, if you reject his patch job, buy a new door and deduct its cost from the deposit, can the tenant who sues you over the deduction expect to win?

Fortunately, some thought went into these issues when the legislation that created this inspection rule was passed, but we are the first to say that there are no totally satisfactory answers to the problematic scenarios described above. Buried deep in the statute are words that qualify the tenant's right to respond to needed repairs: "The purpose of the initial inspection shall be to allow the tenant an opportunity to remedy identified deficiencies, *in a manner consistent with the rights and obligations of the parties under the rental agreement*, in order to avoid deductions from the security." (CC § 1950.5(f)(1), emphasis added.) This means that if your rental agreement requires your consent before repairs are begun, and if your policies limit a tenant's repairs to nonstructural elements and only to items that do not require advanced skill or training, you're halfway there. You can safely remind the tenant that although a particular item or element of the rental will need to be repaired or replaced, he cannot attempt it on his own. An extra-careful landlord will explain this in writing to a tenant who proposes, for example, to pull out his toolbox and repair the broken microwave on his own. Lease or rental agreement language that makes repairs subject to your approval should also support you if you are sued over your rejection of a repair attempt that was off-limits, per your lease or rental agreement.

If your rental document says nothing about what a tenant may do in response to looming deductions, you may have some difficulty convincing him that he'll need to stand back and let you take care of the problem. It may also be difficult to argue successfully before a judge that you were within your rights to reject the tenant's repair attempts and fix or replace the deficiency yourself (deducting the expense from the deposit).

Similarly, your rental document can protect you somewhat from the well-meaning and even skilled tenant who wants to repair something that he's damaged beyond repair and which you'd rather replace, not repair. Again, the document needs to specify (as do our leases and rental agreements) that repairs may be undertaken only with the landlord's consent, and that this consent will be given only when it reasonably appears that the damaged item can be returned to its predamaged condition or appearance.

The limitations you build into your lease or rental agreement will help you avoid hassles over what a tenant can and cannot do; and they may help you defend yourself if you take certain deductions and are then sued by the tenant in small claims court. However, no amount of advance planning and lease language can assure that you won't end up with arguments, as the following example illustrates.

EXAMPLE

Roger and his landlord inspected Roger's apartment a few weeks before Roger's departure. The landlord found the following deficiencies:

- Dirty toilet (lime stains around the rim)
- Stains on living room rug, and
- Cigarette burns on the kitchen's Formica countertop.

Roger's lease said nothing about the types of repairs he could (and could not) undertake. He bought some industrial-strength lime remover and cleaned the toilet; he rented a rug shampooer and cleaned the rug; and he bought some epoxy and a set of color tints and patched the kitchen counter. When the landlord reinspected at the end of Roger's tenancy, he removed the intended deduction for cleaning the toilet but charged Roger for stain removal (he claimed the rug stains were still there) and for the cost of replacing the entire kitchen counter.

Roger sued his landlord over the return of his deposit—specifically, for the rug and counter deductions. The landlord's photos of the rug (taken when Roger moved out) convinced the judge that the cleaning deduction was legitimate. However, the judge ruled that the deduction for the kitchen counter burn holes was not warranted, since the lease did not include any restrictions as to what repairs a tenant might make. The landlord's argument—that the patches made an otherwise clean and unmarred counter look shabby—were unavailing.

Roger's landlord realized that, had he specified in his lease that repairs needed prior approval and would be approved only if the likely result would return the item to its original condition, he might have been able to avoid the court fight over the burn holes. He could have reminded Roger of this clause when they did their initial move-out inspection, and he could have told him not to attempt what would undoubtedly result in a shoddy job. Perhaps Roger would have argued and done the repair anyway (and sued when the landlord charged him for the replacement). But maybe they would have reached a compromise, with Roger agreeing to pay for part of the cost of a new countertop. One thing was for sure: having invested time, money, and a little artistic effort in the repair job, and then having filed a lawsuit, Roger was in no mood to compromise in court.

6. Deducting for Additional Damage or Repairs

You may be concerned about your ability to adequately inspect a rental unit while tenants are still living there. Understandably, you may be loath to start rummaging around a tenant's belongings in order to see every inch of the rental As a result, you may miss evidence of damage simply because furniture or clothing is covering it. Similarly, what about damage or uncleanliness that appears after your initial inspection?

California law specifically allows you to make proper deductions that you haven't noted during the initial inspection, as long as the damage or uncleanliness appeared after the inspection and before the end of the tenancy. Similarly, you can deduct if the problem was not identified during the inspection due to the presence of a tenant's possessions. (CC § 1950.5(f)(5).)

7. The Consequences of Not Doing an Initial Move-Out Inspection

If you don't comply with the initial move-out inspection requirements, you may find yourself in small claims court, sued by a tenant who disagrees with the deductions from his deposit and is righteously angry that he didn't get a chance to address the deficiencies. Of course, even if you comply fully with the inspection procedure but end up deducting for damage or cleaning that was not remedied, you can still be sued; but if you skip the initial inspection step, you're more likely to lose than if you had included it. For example, if you deduct $150 for dirty drapes, a small claims judge may disallow the deduction because you didn't give the tenant fair warning, at a initial move-out inspection, of the need to clean the drapes.

C. FINAL INSPECTION

As soon as possible after the tenant has vacated the rental, you or your manager should conduct a final inspection. Pull out your Checklist again and go over the unit, noting any deficiencies in the "Condition on Departure" column. Note any item that needs cleaning, repair, or replacement in the third column (Condition on Departure). At this point, don't fill out the final column, "Actual or Estimated Cost of Cleaning, Repair/Replacement." You'll enter these figures after you've done the work or replaced damaged items, and have bills or receipts for these costs. (If you don't have bills by the time you need to return the deposit—within three weeks of the tenant's departure—you can enter reasonable estimates.) Section F, Preparing an Itemized Statement of Deductions, explains how to include bills and receipts in your itemized statement.

In Chapter 7, we recommend that you photograph or videotape the premises before the tenant moves in. You should do the same when the tenant leaves, to make before and after comparisons.

Finally, if you have any reason to expect a tenant to take you to court over deductions you plan to make from a security deposit, have the unit examined by another, more neutral person, such as another tenant in the same building. This person should be available to testify in court if necessary.

D. DEDUCTIONS FOR CLEANING AND DAMAGES

You may deduct the following amounts from the tenant's deposit.

1. Costs of Cleaning

The reasonable costs of cleaning include taking care of such things as flea infestations left behind by the tenant's dog, cleaning the oven, removing decals from walls, getting rid of mildew in the bathroom, and defrosting the freezer.

As you can imagine, many landlord/tenant disputes over deductions from security deposits deal with whether or not it was reasonable for the landlord to clean the premises after the tenant moves. The only "bright line" test is a somewhat limited one: For tenancies that began on or after January 1, 2003 (either month to month or with a lease), you may

expect the rental to be returned only as clean as it was when the tenancy began. (CC § 1950.5(b)(3).) We think this means that if the rental was only "broom clean" when it was rented, that's all you can demand now. "How Clean is Clean?," below, gives more illustrations. After reading the chart, you may wisely conclude that when a prior tenant leaves a messy campsite, it behooves you to clean it up (and deduct from the security deposit for your efforts!) before turning it over to the next tenant—otherwise, you'll end up with a perpetually dirty unit at turnover time.

This rule will help landlords and tenants understand the legal standard they are supposed to use when evaluating a rental's cleanliness. While helpful, this standard won't, of course, forestall arguments over whether the tenant *actually* returned the unit in the same condition.

For tenancies that predate January 1, 2003, we suggest that you adopt the same standard. It's fair to both you and the tenant. If the unit needs to be additionally cleaned to make it rentable, that should be done on your dime and considered part of the cost of doing business. You shouldn't expect to cover your turnover expenses by dipping into the security

---

HOW CLEAN IS CLEAN?

Rentals that began on or after January 1, 2003, must be returned in the same level of cleanliness that existed when the tenancy began. Below are some examples of what this means.

Condition When Tenancy Began	What the Tenant Should Do
Kitchen cabinets lined with used shelf-lining paper	Tenant need not remove/replace paper, even if he replaced original linings with his own.
Shower clean but grout stained and drain sluggish	Clean the shower but leave grout stains and slow drain
Windows dirty	Need not wash windows
Living room rug vacuumed but stained	Tenant should vacuum but does not have to steam clean old stains (should clean any new ones, however)
Oven spattered and greasy	Tenant should do minimal work on oven, leaving it no worse than it was when he got there
Large plastic bags with prior tenant's garbage left in carport next to garbage receptacles	Bag refuse and place it next to garbage receptacles.

deposits of departing tenants, and if you attempt to do so blatantly, a judge is likely to disallow it. In practical terms, this means that you can't, as a standard policy, charge a tenant for cleaning carpets, drapes or walls or repainting. (If repainting badly smudged walls is cheaper and more effective than cleaning, however, you can charge for repainting. See Section 2a, below.)

You may charge only for cleaning that is actually necessary. Items for which cleaning is often necessary—and costly—include stained carpets, drapes (particularly smoke-contaminated ones), furniture (for furnished premises) and dirty stoves, refrigerators, and kitchen and bathroom fixtures. That's why we highlight these trouble spots in our move-out letter.

You can deduct a reasonable hourly charge if you or your employees do any necessary cleaning. Several large management companies we know cost out cleaning time at $20 per hour, and this is accepted by small claims courts. You can justify this rate as follows: Maintenance people get $8–$10 per hour. With benefits, this adds up to nearly $15 per hour. Supervisors who must schedule maintenance and inspect the unit (this could be you) are paid a higher hourly rate although they work on any one unit for a shorter period of time.

If you have cleaning done by an outside service, be sure to keep their bill and have the service itemize the work. By and large, small claims courts accept cleaning charges unless they are clearly unreasonable.

However, if you pay teenagers the minimum wage to do the work, you can expect trouble in court if you have charged the tenant a $20 hourly rate. Also, it's wise to try to patronize only those cleaning services whose employees are willing to testify for you, or at least send a letter describing what they did in detail, if the tenant sues you in small claims court, contesting your deposit deductions.

2. Repairing Damage to Property

You may deduct the cost of fixing damage, but not of fixing ordinary wear and tear. Almost as common as disputes over cleaning are those over whether or not damages were due to ordinary wear and tear. Some typical areas of disagreement concern repainting, carpets, and fixtures.

Damages over and above ordinary wear and tear include obvious sorts of things, such as cigarette burns, holes in walls, and broken tiles; but also more subtle breakage, such as broken refrigerator parts, missing broiler pans, water damage from hanging plants, and urine stains from animals. See Section D1, above, for advice on determining the costs of repairing damage.

a. Repainting

Landlords and tenants often argue about whether normal deterioration or the tenant's carelessness makes repainting necessary. Basically, this depends on the condition of the premises and how long the tenant has occupied them. One landlord we know uses, with excellent success, the following approach when a tenant moves out and repainting is necessary: If the tenant has occupied the premises for six months or less and the unit needs repainting, the full cost of repainting (labor and materials) is subtracted from the deposit. If the tenant lived in the unit between six months and a year, and the walls are dirty, two-thirds of the painting cost is subtracted from the deposit. Tenants who occupy a unit for between one and two years and leave dirty walls are charged one-third of the repainting cost. No one who stays for two years or more is ever charged a painting fee. No matter how dirty the walls become, the landlord would always repaint as a matter of course if more than two years had passed since the previous painting. Obviously, a general rule of this type is only that, and must be modified occasionally to fit particular circumstances

What about actual damage to walls? Generally, minor marks or nicks are ordinary wear and tear, but large marks or paint gouges are the responsibility of the tenant. A large number of picture, hook or tack holes in the wall or ceiling that require filling with plaster, or otherwise patching and repainting, are usually damage that goes beyond ordinary wear and tear.

b. Cleaning Carpets or Drapes

Moderate dirt or spotting on a carpet or drapes, even if you can't get the stains out, is probably just ordinary wear and tear if the tenant has occupied the unit for a number of years. On the other hand, you would be justified in deducting from the security deposit for large rips or indelible stains in a carpet. The basic approach to take is to determine whether the tenant has damaged or substantially shortened the life of something that does wear out. If the answer is yes, you may charge the tenant the prorated cost of the item, taking into account how old it was, how long it might have lasted otherwise, and the cost of replacement. For example, if your tenant has ruined an eight-year-old rug that had a life expectancy of 10 years, and for which a replacement would cost $1,000 at today's prices, you would charge the tenant $200 for the two years of life that would have remained in the rug had the tenant not ruined it.

c. Removing Fixtures

Many lease and rental agreements (including ours, in Clause 17) forbid tenants from repairing or altering the premises—for example, by installing fixtures. If the tenant leaves behind a row of bolted-to-the-wall bookshelves, contrary to the provisions of the rental agreement, you can remove them, restoring the property to the same condition as before they were installed, and subtract the cost from the tenant's security deposit. You do not have to return the bookcases to the tenant because, after all, you've only removed something that has become part of the premises and hence your property.

E. DEDUCTIONS FOR UNPAID RENT

After deducting legitimate cleaning and damage charges from a tenant's security deposit, you can also deduct any unpaid rent.

1. Month-to-Month Tenancies

If a tenant leaves owing rent, figure the exact amount by prorating the monthly rent for the number of days the tenant failed to pay.

> **EXAMPLE**
>
> Your tenant pays you the rent of $600 for March—supposedly his last month—but stays until April 5 without paying anything more. You are entitled to deduct 5/30ths (or 1/6th) of the total month's rent, or $100, from the security deposit.

If the tenant gave less than the required 30 days' notice before leaving, you are entitled to rent for the entire 30 days, unless you rerent, or reasonably could have rerented, within the 30 days.

> **EXAMPLE**
>
> After having paid her $600 monthly rent on October 1, your tenant Sheila informs you on the 15th that she's leaving on the 25th, thus giving you only ten days' notice when you're entitled to 30. You're entitled to rent through the 30th day, counting from October 15, or November 14, unless you found—or reasonably could have found—a new tenant in the meantime. (We discuss your responsibility to try to find a replacement tenant in these circumstances in Chapter 19. Unless the departing tenant produces a satisfactory new tenant who will begin paying rent immediately, it is generally (but not always)

assumed that it is reasonable to take up to 30 days to find a new tenant and get them moved in.) Since the rent is paid through October 31, Sheila owes you the prorated rent for 14 days in November. At $600 per month or $20 a day, this works out to $280, which can be deducted from Sheila's security deposit.

2. Leases

If a tenant leaves before a fixed-term lease expires, you are entitled to the balance of the rent due under the lease, less any rent you receive from new tenants before the end of the lease term, or could receive if you make a diligent effort to rerent the property. If your tenant leaves more than one month early, your duty to cut your losses by finding a new tenant is usually taken seriously by courts. In other words, if you withhold more than one month's rent from the tenant's deposit and you are challenged in court, a judge is likely to want to know why you couldn't re-rent the property. (See Chapter 19, Section A for a discussion of a landlord's duty to find a new rent-paying tenant as soon as possible.)

EXAMPLE

On January 1, Will leased his house to Anthony and his family for $1,200 a month. On June 30, Anthony moves out, even though six months remains on his one-year lease, making him responsible for a total rent of $7,200. Will rerents the property on July 10, this time for $1,250 a month (prorated at $833 for the last 20 days in July), so that he'll receive a total rent of $7,083 through December 31. Because this sum is $117 less than the $7,200 he would have received from Anthony had he lived up to the lease, Will may deduct $117 from Anthony's deposit. If Will spent a reasonable amount of money to find a new tenant (for newspaper ads, rental agency commissions, and so on), he could also deduct these costs from the deposit.

3. Court Judgments for Unpaid Rent

If you sue to evict and obtain a judgment for rent through the date of the judgment, you can subtract:

- the amount of judgment, and
- prorated rent for the period between the date of the judgment and the date the tenant actually leaves.

EXAMPLE

You sue a tenant who fails to pay May's rent of $450, and get a judgment on June 10 for rent prorated through that date. The tenant doesn't leave until the 17th, when the sheriff comes and puts him out. You can deduct the following items from the deposit:

- costs of any necessary cleaning and damage
- judgment for rent through June 10, and
- the extra week's rent (seven days at $15/day, or $105) for the week between judgment and eviction.

Before you subtract the amount of a court judgment for unpaid rent, deduct for cleaning and damage costs and any rent not included in the judgment. The reason is simple: A judgment can be collected in all sorts of ways—for example, you can garnish the former tenant's wages or attach a bank account—if the security deposit is not large enough to cover it. However, you are much more limited when it comes to collecting money the tenant owes you for damage and cleaning if you don't have a judgment for the amount. If you don't subtract them from the deposit, you'll have to file suit in small claims court.

But if you subtract the amount for cleaning, damage and any unpaid rent not covered in the judgment first, you will still have the judgment if the deposit isn't large enough to cover everything.

EXAMPLE 1

Amelia collected a security deposit of $1,200 from Timothy, whom she ultimately had to sue to evict for failure to pay rent. Amelia got a judgment for $160 court costs plus $1,000 unpaid rent through the date of the judgment. Timothy didn't leave until the sheriff came, about five days later, thus running up an additional prorated rent of $100 not reflected in the $1,160 judgment. Timothy also left dirt and damage that cost $1,000 to clean and repair.

Amelia (not having read this book) first applied the $1,200 security deposit to the $1,160 judgment, leaving only $40 to apply toward the rent of $100, which was not reflected in the judgment, as well as the cleaning and repair charges, all of which totaled $1,100. Therefore, Amelia must now sue Timothy for the $1,060 he still owes her.

EXAMPLE 2

Now, let's assume that Monique was Timothy's landlord in the same situation. But Monique applied Timothy's $1,200 deposit first to the cleaning and damage charges of $1,000 and then to the $100 rent not reflected in the judgment. This left $100 to apply to the $1,160 judgment, the balance of which she can collect by having the sheriff garnish Timothy's wages or by attaching his bank account.

F. PREPARING AN ITEMIZED STATEMENT OF DEDUCTIONS

You must send the tenant a written itemized explanation of any deductions within three weeks after a tenant who has paid a deposit leaves. You must also supply receipts and invoices unless the tenant has waived the right to receive these documents. We have included three forms, which vary according to the types of deductions you are making. Blank, tear-out copies are in Appendix B.

Remember, if your property is located in a city such as San Francisco, Los Angeles, Berkeley or Santa Monica,

which requires you to pay interest on a tenant's entire deposit, you must also refund this amount. See the chart in Chapter 5 which summarizes the features of cities requiring interest on security deposits.

1. Returning the Tenant's Entire Deposit

If you are returning a tenant's entire security deposit, (including interest, if required), simply send a brief letter like the one below.

You'll find a tear-out version of the Letter for Returning Entire Security Deposit in Appendix B. The CD-ROM that accompanies this book also includes the form.

2. Itemizing Deductions for Repairs and Cleaning

If you are making deductions from the tenant's security deposit only for cleaning and repair, use the form Security Deposit Itemization (Deductions for Repairs and Cleaning). A sample is shown below.

For each deduction, list the item and the dollar amount, and attach receipts to the Itemization. If your receipts are not very detailed, add more information—for example, "carpet cleaning, $160, required by several large grease stains and candle wax embedded in living room rug," or "plaster repair, $400, of several fist-sized holes in bedroom wall"—especially if you feel your tenant will dispute your deductions. (Sections B1 and B2, above, will help you determine proper amounts to deduct for repairs and cleaning.)

Be sure to include the repairperson's address and phone number, if it's not on the invoice or bill; and if you're billing for your own time or that of an employee, include the work, the time spent, and a reasonable hourly rate. You must also include vendor lists or other documentation if you charge for materials that you buy in bulk or on an ongoing basis (such as cleaning supplies).

Letter for Returning Entire Security Deposit

November 5, 200x

Gerry Fraser

976 Park Place

Sacramento, CA

Dear Gerry   :

Here is the itemization, as required by Civil Code Section 1950.5, of your $ 1,500 security deposit on the property at 976 Park Place ,

which you rented from me on a month-to-month basis on March 1, , 20 OX and vacated on September 30 , 20 OX.

As you left the rental property in satisfactory condition, I am returning the entire amount of your security deposit of $ 1,500 .

Sincerely,

Tom Stein

Landlord/Manager

**Security Deposit Itemization
(Deductions for Repairs and Cleaning)**

Civil Code Section 1950.5

Date: _November 8, 200X_

From: _Rachel Tolan_

123 Larchmont Lane

Oceanside, California

To: _Lena Coleman_

456 Penny Lane, #101

San Diego, California

Property Address: _789 Cora Court, Oceanside, California_

Rental Period: _January 1, 200X, to October 31, 200X_

1. Security Deposit Received $ _600_

2. Interest on Deposit (if required by lease or law): $ _N/A_

3. Total Credit (sum of lines 1 and 2) $ _600_

4. Itemized Repairs and Related Losses (receipts, bills, or invoices attached, unless previously waived):

   Repainting of living room walls, required by crayon

   and chalk marks

   Total Repair Cost: $ _260_

5. Necessary Cleaning (receipts, bills, or invoices attached, unless previously waived):

   Sum paid to resident manager for 4 hours

   cleaning at $20/hour: debris-filled garage,

   dirty stove and refrigerator

   Total Cleaning Cost: $ _80_

6. Amount Owed (line 3 minus the sum of lines 4 and 5)

   ☐ a. Total Amount Tenant Owes Landlord: $ _____

   ☒ b. Total Amount Landlord Owes Tenant: $ _260_

Comments: _A check for $260 is enclosed._

Security Deposit Itemization
(Deductions for Repairs, Cleaning, and Unpaid Rent)
Civil Code Section 1950.5

Date: _December 19, 200X_

From: _Timothy Gottman_

8910 Pine Avenue

Pacific Grove, California

To: _Monique Todd_

999 Laurel Drive

Monterey, California

Property Address: _456 Pine Avenue #7, Pacific Grove, California_

Rental Period: _January 1, 200X, to October 31, 200X_

1. Security Deposit Received $ _1,200_

2. Interest on Deposit (if required by lease or law): $ _N/A_

3. Total Credit (sum of lines 1 and 2) $ _1,200_

4. Itemized Repairs and Related Losses (receipts, bills, or invoices attached, unless previously waived):

   Carpet repair $160, drapery cleaning $140, plaster

   repair $400, painting of living room $100 (receipts

   attached)

   Total Repair Cost: $ _800_

5. Necessary Cleaning (receipts, bills, or invoices attached, unless previously waived):

   Sum paid to resident manager for 10 hours cleaning

   at $20/hour: debris-filled garage, dirty stove and

   refrigerator

   Total Cleaning Cost: $ _200_

6. Defaults in Rent Not Covered by Any Court Judgment (list dates and rates):

   5 days at $20 day from November 6 to November 11

   (date of court judgment of date of physical eviction)

   Total Rent Defaults: $ _100_

7. Amount of Court Judgment for Rent, Costs, Attorney Fees: $ _____ 1,160 _____

8. Other Deductions:

Specify: _____

_____

_____ $ _____

9. Amount Owed (line 3 minus the sum of lines 4, 5, 6, 7, and 8)

   [X] a. Total Amount Tenant Owes Landlord: $ _____ 1,060 _____

   [ ] b. Total Amount Landlord Owes Tenant: $ _____

Comments: _____ The security deposit has been applied as follows: $1,000 for damage and cleaning charges, $100 for defaults in rent (not covered by any court judgment) and the remaining $100 towards payment of the $1,160 court judgment. This leaves $1,060 still owed on the judgment. Please send that amount to me at once or I shall take appropriate legal action to collect it.

3. Itemizing Deductions for Repairs, Cleaning, and Unpaid Rent

Use the form Security Deposit Itemization (Deductions for Repairs, Cleaning, and Unpaid Rent) if you have to deduct for unpaid rent as well as cleaning and repairs. A sample is shown below. You still must itemize the deduction even if you have a judgment against the tenant larger than the deposit. For instructions on itemizing deductions for repairs and cleaning, see Section 2, above. Heed the advice regarding repairpersons' names and addresses, as well as documenting your own labor and materials, as explained just above in Subsection a.

You'll find a tear-out version of the Security Deposit Itemization (Deductions for Repairs and Cleaning) in Appendix B. The CD-ROM that accompanies this book also includes the form.

This form also includes spaces for you to include unpaid rent not covered by a court judgment (line 6) and the amount of a court judgment you won in an eviction lawsuit (line 7). (Section C, above, shows you how to figure these amounts.)

It's better to deduct cleaning and damage costs from the security deposit before deducting any court judgment charges. (See Section C3, above.)

If there's a court judgment involved, explain how you applied the deposit in the Comments section at the bottom of the itemization form. This makes it clear that you are demanding the balance owed, and that you can still collect any part of the judgment not covered by the security deposit.

4. Mailing the Security Deposit Itemization

Your security deposit itemization should be mailed to the tenant's last known address or forwarding address, along with a check for any balance you owe, within three weeks of the tenant's departure. If the tenant hasn't left you a forwarding address, mail the itemization and any balance to the address of the rental property itself. That, after all, is the tenant's last address known to you.

If your former tenant has left a forwarding address with the post office, it will forward the mail. If you put "Address Correction and Forwarding Requested" on the envelope, as in the itemization itself, the Postal Service will notify you of the new address, for a nominal fee. This will help if the tenant's deposit doesn't cover all proper deductions and you want to sue in small claims court. (See Section H, below.) It will also help you collect any judgment you have against the tenant.

If the tenant has left no forwarding address, the letter will come back to you. The postmarked envelope is your proof of your good-faith attempt to notify the tenant. It should protect you from the danger of being assessed up to twice the amount of the deposit in damages that a judge is empowered to assess you if the tenant later takes you to small claims court.

G. Small Claims Lawsuits by the Tenant

No matter how meticulous you are about properly accounting to your tenants for their deposits, sooner or later you may be sued by a tenant who disagrees with your assessment of the cost of cleaning or repairs. Because virtually all residential security deposits are less than $5,000, almost all such suits are brought in small claims court. ($5,000 is the maximum award available in small claims court.)

This section suggests several strategies for dealing with small claims suits over security deposits, including how to prepare and present a case in small claims court. For more information on small claims court procedures, see *Everybody's Guide to Small Claims Court in California,* by Ralph Warner (Nolo).

SAMPLE SETTLEMENT AGREEMENT

Settlement Agreement

Lionel Washington, "Landlord," and LaToya Jones, "Tenant," hereby agree as follows:

1. Landlord rented the premises at 1234 State Avenue, Apartment 5, Los Angeles, California, to Tenant on July 1, 200X, pursuant to a written rental agreement for a tenancy from month to month.

2. Under the Agreement, Tenant paid Landlord $1,000 as a security deposit.

3. On October 31, 200X, Tenant vacated the premises.

4. Within three weeks after Tenant vacated the premises, Landlord itemized various deductions from the security deposit totaling $380 and refunded the balance of $620 to Tenant.

5. Tenant asserts that she is entitled to the additional sum of $300, only $80 of the deductions being proper. Landlord asserts that all the deductions were proper and that he owes Tenant nothing.

6. To settle the parties' entire dispute, and to compromise on Tenant's claim for return of her security deposit, Landlord pays to Tenant the sum of $150, receipt of which is hereby acknowledged by Tenant, as full satisfaction of her claim.

Lionel Washington   December 1, 200x
_____   _____
Lionel Washington, Landlord/Manager   Date

LaToya Jones   December 1, 200x
_____   _____
LaToya Jones, Tenant   Date

1. When a Tenant May Sue

A tenant may file suit three weeks after leaving the premises if the tenant doesn't receive a deposit refund (with an itemization of what the deposit was used for) and accompanying receipts and invoices. If you return part of a deposit sooner than three weeks, a tenant who does not agree with your charges will most likely express that dissatisfaction by way of a letter or phone call demanding that you refund more than you did. This sort of demand is a requirement before anyone can begin a small claims suit. (CCP § 116.4(a) requires a person suing in small claims court to state under penalty of perjury that the claimant "has demanded payment.")

After making a demand, the tenant can bring suit immediately. A tenant who is going to sue will probably do it fairly promptly, but has at least two years to do so. The statute of limitations for a tenant's suit to recover a security deposit is two years if a landlord's failure to refund a deposit is viewed as a breach of an oral agreement (CCP § 339). Tenants have four years if a written lease or rental agreement is involved and a judge decides that failure to return a deposit is such a breach (CCP § 337.) Don't throw out any photos showing damage or dirt—you may need them.

2. Try to Settle a Potential Lawsuit

If you receive a demand letter from a tenant, your best bet is to try to work out a reasonable compromise with the tenant. Be open to the idea of returning more of the deposit to the tenant, even if you believe your original assessment of the cost of repairs and cleaning was more than fair and you feel you will surely win in court. As a businessperson, it usually doesn't make sense for you to spend a morning in court to argue over $50, $100, or even $200.

SPLITTING THE DIFFERENCE WITH TENANTS

One landlord we know with thousands of units experiences about 250 move-outs each month. He receives about ten complaints per month about the amount charged against deposits; charges vary widely with the circumstances, but average about $175. This landlord's general policy is to offer to settle for 50% of the disputed amount. He does this not because he thinks his original assessment was wrong, but because he finds that coming to a settlement with a tenant costs a lot less than fighting in court. However, if the settlement offer isn't accepted promptly by the tenant, he fights to win and almost always does.

If you and the tenant can't arrive at a reasonable compromise, you may wish to get help from a local landlord/tenant mediation service, described in Chapter 8, Section B.

If you arrive at a compromise settlement with your former tenant, you should insist that your payment be accepted as "full satisfaction" of your obligation to return the deposit. The term "full satisfaction" simply means that this is the end of the matter, and that the tenant agrees not to demand any more money (any subsequent lawsuit for more money would probably be thrown out). The best approach is to prepare and have the tenant sign a brief settlement agreement, such as the sample above. You could shorten this agreement by simply using the first two lines and the material in paragraph 6, along with the signature lines.

It is no longer possible to force a settlement by writing on the check you mail to the tenant the words "paid in full" or similar wording. If the tenant crosses out such a notation on the check before cashing it, or even fails to cross it out because he didn't notice the wording, the tenant still may sue for any balance he claims is due. (CC § 1526.)

SAMPLE DECLARATION

Declaration of Paul Stallone, Cleaner

I, Paul Stallone, declare:

1. I am employed at A & B Maintenance Company, a contract cleaning and maintenance service located at 123 Abrego Street, Monterey, California. Gina Cabarga, the owner of an apartment complex at 456 Seventh Street, Monterey, California, is one of our accounts.

2. On May 1, 200X, I was requested to go to the premises at 456 Seventh Street, Apartment 8, Monterey, California, to shampoo the carpets. When I entered the premises, I noticed a strong odor, part of what seemed like stale cigarette smoke. An odor also seemed to come from the carpet.

3. When I began using a steam carpet cleaner on the living room carpet, I noticed a strong smell of urine. I stopped the steam cleaner, moved to a dry corner of the carpet, and pulled it from the floor. I then saw a yellow color on the normally white foam-rubber pad beneath the carpet, as well as smelled a strong urine odor, apparently caused by a pet (probably a cat) having urinated on the carpet. On further examination of the parts of the carpet, I noticed similar stains and odors throughout the carpet and pad.

4. In my opinion, the living room carpet and foam-rubber pad underneath need to be removed and replaced and the floor should be sanded and sealed.

I declare under penalty of perjury under the laws of the State of California that the foregoing is true and correct.

Dated: June 15, 200X   *Paul Stallone*
                            _____
                            Paul Stallone, Cleaner

3. Preparing for a Small Claims Court Hearing

If you don't reach a compromise and the tenant sues, the first official notification of the lawsuit you will receive will be a copy of the tenant's "Claim of Plaintiff" form. This will either be sent by certified mail or personally delivered. It will notify you of the date, time, and place of the small claims court hearing.

It's still not too late at this stage to try to work out a settlement by paying part of what the tenant's suing for. However, if you compromise at this stage, insist that the tenant sign a dismissal form. This form, called a Request for Dismissal, is available from the small claims clerk.

You don't have to file any papers with the court clerk unless you want to countersue for money you feel the tenant owes you. Normally, you would want to do this only if you kept the tenant's entire deposit and demanded that he pay you more. Obviously, you'll look silly if you refunded part of the deposit, admitting the tenant only owes you the amount withheld, and then change your mind and sue for more. You can, however, defend against the tenant's suit and still initiate your own later.

Before your court hearing, gather your evidence. The landlord always has the burden of proving the premises needed cleaning or were damaged. (CC § 1950.5(k).) Unless you prove that the place was dirty or damaged, all a former tenant needs to prove to win is that a residential tenancy existed, that the tenant paid you a deposit, and that you didn't return all of it. It is essential that you show up in court with as many of the following items of evidence as you can:

- Three copies of the Landlord/Tenant Checklist, which you should have filled out with the tenant when the tenant moved in, again at the initial move-out inspection, if the tenant requested one, and again when the tenant moved out. (See Chapter 7 and Section B, above.) This is particularly important if the tenant admitted, on the Checklist, to the presence of damaged or dirty conditions.

- Photos or a video of the premises before the tenant moved in, which show how clean and undamaged the place was.

- Photos or a video after the tenant left, which show a mess or damage.

- An itemization of hours spent by you or your repair or cleaning people on the unit, complete with the hourly costs for the work.

- Damaged items small enough to bring into the courtroom (a curtain with a cigarette hole would be effective).

- Receipts for professional cleaning (particularly of carpets and drapes) and repair.

- One, or preferably two, witnesses who were familiar with the property, who saw it just after the tenant left, and who will testify that the place was a mess or that certain items were damaged. People who helped in the subsequent cleaning or repair are particularly effective witnesses. You can use written statements or declarations under penalty of perjury, but they aren't as effective as live testimony. A sample written statement is shown above.

4. The Small Claims Court Hearing

In small claims court, people don't sit in a witness box. They normally stand behind a table facing the judge and explain their version of the dispute. In some courts, however, judges use other procedures, such as requesting that all parties and witnesses approach the judge's bench and explain what went on in conversational tones.

Here is how a small claims hearing would probably begin:

Clerk: "Calling the case of *Wendy Tanaka v. Linda Lu.*"

Judge: "Well, Ms. Tanaka, since you're the plaintiff, please tell me your version of the facts first."

Wendy Tanaka: "I moved into apartment A at 1700 Walnut St. in Costa Mesa in the spring of 200X. I paid my landlady here my first month's rent of $900, plus a $900 security deposit. When I moved out, she withheld $540 of this, returning only $360. As I believe this constitutes a willful denial of my rights under Civil Code Section 1950.5, I am asking for not only the $540 she owes me, but $200 in punitive damages, for a total of $740. Here is a copy of the rental agreement [HANDS IT TO THE CLERK], which specifically states my deposit is to be returned to me if the apartment is left clean and undamaged.

When I moved into apartment A, it was a mess. It's a nice little apartment, but the people who lived there before me were sloppy. The stove was filthy, as was the bathroom, the refrigerator, the floors, and just about everything else. But I needed a place to live and this was the best available, so I moved in despite the mess. I painted the whole place—everything. My landlady gave me the paint, but I did all of the work. And I cleaned the place thoroughly, too. It took me three days. I like to live in a clean house."

Judge: [LOOKING AT ONE OF THE TENANT'S WITNESSES] "Do you have any personal knowledge of what this apartment looked like?"

Witness: "Yes, I helped Wendy move in and move out. I simply don't understand what the landlady is fussing about. The place was a mess when she moved in, and it was clean when Wendy moved out."

Judge: "Ms. Lu, you may now tell your side of the story. I should remind you that you have the burden of proving that the amounts you withheld were reasonable."

Linda Lu: "Your Honor, it is true, as Ms. Tanaka testified, that the people who lived in the apartment before her were sloppy. They left things a mess, but my manager and I cleaned it up the day before Ms. Tanaka actually moved in. Here are several photographs we took after the previous tenant moved out [HANDS PHOTOS TO CLERK]. My manager, Bennie Owens, and I spent a long day cleaning the place before Ms. Tanaka moved in. We took this second set of photos to show the contrast after we cleaned it. Anyway, the point is that these photos [HANDS TO THE CLERK] also show the apartment just before Ms. Tanaka moved in. Also, when Ms. Tanaka moved in, she signed this inventory sheet [HANDS TO CLERK] indicating that all parts of the premises were clean and undamaged, right after she and Bennie Owens—

who is here to testify—inspected the premises together.

When I learned that Ms. Tanaka was terminating her tenancy, I sent her my standard Move-Out Letter, which advised her of her right to an initial move-out inspection and her right to attend. She told me she wanted an inspection and to be present, so I gave her 48 hours' written notice of the day and time. She didn't show up for the inspection, and I left this second inventory sheet (handing it to the clerk) on her kitchen table, to allow her to take care of the mildewed refrigerator, dirty oven, dirt-stained area in the hall carpet and candle wax embedded in the bedroom carpet. I still didn't hear from her in response to this list.

It's true that Ms. Tanaka did some painting, but this was in exchange for a reduction of her first month's rent of $150 and our supplying the paint. Mr. Owens will also testify to his inspection of the premises after Ms. Tanaka left, and will present the pictures he took on the day she left. But before he does, I should add that Ms. Tanaka gave me only ten days' verbal notice, on October 15, before she left the apartment on October 25. Her rent was paid through the 31st, but I was unable to rerent the property until November 10, despite the ads I put in the paper as soon as she gave me her notice. Because she didn't give me the full 30 days' notice, I charged her ten days prorated rent of $150 for the rent I didn't receive within the 30-day period, as well as $120 for cleaning the apartment. I believe this was reasonable under the circumstances."

Judge: [LOOKING AT BENNIE OWENS] "What do you have to add, Mr. Owens?"

Bennie Owens: "Well, Your Honor, I did inspect the premises with Ms. Tanaka when she first moved in. She stated everything looked fine and signed the Landlord/Tenant Checklist I gave her. When she moved out on October 25, I went into the apartment and took these pictures. [HANDS THEM TO THE CLERK TO GIVE TO THE JUDGE]. Although the place wasn't a real mess, it still wasn't clean enough to rerent right away, either. The pictures I took clearly show mildew in the refrigerator and a dirty oven. They also show a large dirt-stained area in the hall carpet, as well as a foot-square area where candle wax was embedded in the bedroom carpet. I hired a professional cleaning service to clean the refrigerator, stove, and carpet. Here's the receipt [HANDS TO CLERK]. The total was $120."

After you and your witnesses have presented your evidence as in the above example, the judge may ask a few questions and may announce a decision right there. Or, the judge may take the matter "under submission," and notify you of the result by mail. If you lose the small claims case, you must pay the judgment within 20 days (unless you appeal), or the tenant will be able to attach your bank account or other property, or even to put a lien on the property.

A plaintiff who loses cannot appeal. As a defendant, however, you have the right to appeal an adverse small claims decision to the superior court and have a new trial, where you may be represented by an attorney (not allowed in small claims court). Before you do so, however, you should consider that the superior court judge will more than likely lean toward affirming the decision of the small claims judge. Finally, if the judge feels that you appealed the case just to harass or delay the plaintiff, and that you had no valid defense, you may have to pay the plaintiff's attorney fees up to $1,000. The tenant can also ask to be compensated for any actual loss of earnings and any transportation and lodging expenses that he incurred by having to answer your appeal. (CCP § 116.790.)

Nothing that happens in small claims court affects the validity of any judgment you may already have (for example, from an earlier eviction suit) against the tenant. So, if you got a judgment against a tenant for $1,200 for unpaid rent as part of an eviction action, this judgment is still good, even though a tenant gets a judgment against you for $200 in small claims court based on your failure to return the deposit.

H. If the Deposit Doesn't Cover Damage and Unpaid Rent

If the security deposit doesn't cover the rent, cleaning, or repair costs a former tenant owes you, you may wish to file a lawsuit. In this situation, small claims court is both faster and easier to use than superior court as long as your claim doesn't exceed $5,000, the small claims court limit.

Here we discuss only the basics of suing a tenant for back rent or damages not covered by the tenant's deposit. If you decide to go to court, we recommend *Everybody's Guide to Small Claims Court in California*, by Ralph Warner (Nolo).

1. The Demand Letter

If you decide that it is worthwhile to go after your tenant for money owed, your first step is to write a letter asking the tenant to pay the amount of your claim. Although this may seem like an exercise in futility, the law requires that you make a demand for the amount before filing in small claims court. (CCP § 116.320(b)(3).) Your written itemization of how you applied the tenant's security deposit to the charges, which requests payment of the balance, is such a demand. (See Section D, above.) We suggest that you resend it if you're planning to sue.

2. Collection Agencies

If you don't want to sue in small claims court, consider hiring a licensed local collection agency to try to collect from the tenant. The agency usually keeps about one-third of what it collects for you. If it can't collect, it can hire a lawyer to sue the ex-tenant. Lawyers working for collection agencies may not sue in small claims court, however, and must sue in superior court. Many collection agencies pay all court costs, hoping to recover them if and when they collect the resulting judgment. In exchange, however, collection agency commissions often rise to 50% or more if they've hired a lawyer to sue.

Of course, turning a matter over to a collection agency doesn't necessarily mean you wash your hands of the matter. The collection agency still takes direction from you. If the tenant defends against a lawsuit filed by a collection agency's lawyer, you must be involved in the litigation. The only way to walk away from it completely is to sell the debt (back rent or damage compensation) to the collection agency, which may pay you only a fraction of the amount owed.

3. Should You Sue?

Before you rush off to your local small claims court to file a claim against your former tenant, ask yourself three questions:

- Do I have a valid case? (If you are a landlord with many rental units and use a local small claims court regularly, make particularly sure the cases you bring are good ones. You do not want to lose your credibility with the court in future cases by even *appearing* to be unfair.)

- Can I locate the former tenant?

- Can I collect a judgment if I win?

If the answer to any of these questions is no, think twice about initiating a suit.

Pay particular attention to the third question, about how you will collect a judgment. The best way to collect any judgment against your ex-tenant is to garnish the tenant's wages. If the tenant is working, there is an excellent chance of collecting if payment is not made voluntarily. You can't, however, garnish a welfare, social security, unemployment, pension, or disability check. So, if the person sued gets the bulk of her income from one of these sources, you may be wasting your time unless you can identify some other asset that you can efficiently get your hands on.

Bank accounts, motor vehicles, and real estate are other common collection sources. But people who run out on their debts don't always have much in a bank account (or they may have moved the account to make it difficult to locate), and much of their personal property may be exempt under California debt protection laws. For example, equity in motor vehicles owned by the debtor is exempt up to $1,900, and the tools of a person's trade are exempt up to $5,000. Ordinary and reasonably necessary household furnishings, appliances, and clothing are all exempt, as is money in bank accounts that can be traced to exempt assets, such as disability and unemployment benefits. (These exemption amounts change from time to time, but they only go up.) (See *How to Collect When You Win a Lawsuit in California,* by attorney Robin Leonard (Nolo).)

4. How to Sue in Small Claims Court

If you decide a small claims court suit is worthwhile, you can file suit in the judicial district in which your premises are located or in which the tenant now resides, whichever is most convenient for you.

To start your case, go to the small claims clerk's office, pay a small filing fee (which you can recover if you win), and fill out a form called "Plaintiff's Statement to Clerk." When you have completed the form, give it to the court clerk, who will use it to type out a Claim of Plaintiff form and assign your case a number. You will be asked to sign this form under penalty of perjury. A copy of the Claim of Plaintiff will go to the judge, and another must be served on the defendant.

If the person you're suing lives in the same county in which the suit is brought, your hearing date should be between 10 and 40 days from the time the papers are filed. If the defendant lives outside of the county where you bring suit, the case will be heard between 30 and 70 days from that date. (CCP § 116.4.)

When you file your papers, arrange with the clerk for a court date that is convenient for you. You need not take the first date the clerk suggests. Be sure to leave yourself enough time to get a copy of the Claim of Plaintiff form served on the defendant. The defendant is entitled to receive service of the Claim of Plaintiff form at least five days before the date of the court hearing, if the tenant is served within the county in which the courthouse is located. If the defendant is served in a county other than the one where the trial will take place, he must be served at least 15 days before the trial date. (If you fail to serve your papers properly on the defendant in time, there is no big hassle—just notify the clerk, get a new court date, and try again.)

Small claims court sessions are usually held between 9 A.M. and 3 P.M. on working days. Larger counties are required to hold at least one evening or Saturday session per month. Ask the clerk for a schedule.

All the persons you name as defendants in a small claims case must be served with the papers. This can often be done by certified mail. The clerk of the court does the mailing for you. The fee is modest and is recoverable if you win. This method of service is both cheap and easy, but its success depends on the defendant signing for the letter. Some people never accept certified mail, knowing instinctively, or perhaps from experience, that nothing good ever comes by certified mail. The consensus among court clerks is that about 40% of certified mail services are accepted. The Claim of Plaintiff can also be served on each defendant personally, using the sheriff, the marshal, a private process server, or any adult (except you). Or, you can use substituted service, which involves giving a copy of the papers to a person at the defendant's home or workplace with a second copy mailed to the defendant there. (CCP § 415.20.) (See Chapter 18 for a discussion of different forms of service.)

SEND YOUR MANAGER TO COURT

In some situations, you may send your manager to small claims court instead of appearing yourself. (CCP §116.540.) Here's how it works:

- **If you employ a property manager who manages the property that is the subject of the lawsuit, you can send the manager in your place.** You must employ the manager primarily to manage the property, not to handle small claims lawsuits. This manager can appear if you are the plaintiff or the defendant. If you send your manager to court, give him a signed, dated declaration that he is authorized to appear for you, that he is the manager for the property involved and that he is not employed solely to represent you in court.

- **If you do not employ a manager with duties as described above, you must appear yourself.** However, there's an exception for owners who live out of state: If you are sued in small claims court (that is, you are the defendant, not the plaintiff), you may send someone in your place as long as (1) you do not pay that person, and (2) he or she has appeared in small claims court on behalf of others no more than four times in the calendar year. Instead of sending a proxy, a nonresident landlord-defendant may submit a declaration to the court to serve as evidence; or you may send a declaration as well as a stand-in. Equip your proxy with a signed declaration that he is authorized to appear for you, that he is unpaid, and that he has appeared as a proxy no more than four times in the calendar year.

Once you've obtained your court date and had your former tenant served with the Claim of Plaintiff, you are ready to prepare for trial. See Section E3 of this chapter, above, on small claims suits over deposits, and *Everybody's Guide to Small Claims Court in California,* by Ralph Warner (Nolo).

At the small claims hearing, you should offer a copy of your demand letter and Security Deposit Itemization to the judge, noting that you're doing so for the purpose of showing that you made the required demand before suing. Although the judge will pay more attention to what you say in court rather than what you said in the demand letter, a coherent set of facts in writing certainly doesn't hurt.

If the tenant is suing you but has not demanded payment of the security deposit, as legally required, point this out to the judge, who may dismiss the suit on that basis. ■

21

PROPERTY ABANDONED BY A TENANT

This chapter outlines the proper steps to take to deal with property left behind by tenants who have moved out, so that you can prepare the premises for the next tenant. Obviously, you want to protect yourself from claims by the tenant who has moved out that you have destroyed or stolen the tenant's property. In legal jargon, this is known as "unlawful conversion." Conversion occurs when you take someone else's property and convert it to your own use or benefit, either by selling it or otherwise disposing of it, or using it yourself.

A. HANDLING, STORING, AND DISPOSING OF PERSONAL PROPERTY

Whether a tenant vacates voluntarily or with the aid of the sheriff or marshal, landlords all too often must not only clean up and repair damage, but also dispose of a pile of junk. You're much more likely to face this problem when the tenant was evicted and wasn't allowed to take everything. The belongings of evicted tenants are not put into the street. The law enforcement officer performing an eviction will allow the tenant to carry out a few armloads of personal possessions, leaving the remainder to be locked in the premises and stored by you until the tenant can arrange to take them away.

Removing obvious trash is normally no problem, but even here you must exercise care. If you toss a moth-eaten book in the dumpster and it turns out to have been a valuable first edition, you could have problems.

As a general rule, the more valuable the property left behind by a tenant, the more formalities you must comply with when disposing of it. In rare instances, you may have a judgment against a tenant for unpaid rent or damages to your premises, and this tenant has left behind valuable property that she never claims. If so, you can safely have the property sold and the money applied to pay your judgment, but only if you follow the legal procedures outlined in this chapter.

You cannot touch a tenant's property until you have legally gained possession of the premises. This occurs when a tenant finally leaves voluntarily, whether or not she gives you the keys; or when the tenant is physically evicted by the sheriff, marshal, or constable. If you gained possession of the property after having heard nothing from the tenant for 18 days since mailing a Notice of Belief of Abandonment (see Chapter 19), you should understand that your mailing of the abandonment notice relating to the real property—the premises—has nothing to do with any personal property abandoned inside. In other words, it only allows you to enter legally after the premises were abandoned, not dispose of property. You may dispose of property only after following the procedures described in this chapter.

1. If the Tenant Demands His Property

Ideally, a tenant who has left property behind after moving out will contact you about reclaiming it. If not, try to contact the tenant to pick up the property. If you can't reach him, look through the tenant's rental application and phone personal or business references listed there.

By all means, if a tenant is willing to pick up his property, return everything to him, even if he owes you money. If a tenant owes you money—for example, back rent—you cannot insist that he pay you before you return his property. You can, however, deduct back rent from any security deposit. But remember that the basic rule for returning deposits within three weeks after the tenant leaves applies in situations where the tenant has abandoned—regardless of whether the tenant has left property behind. (See Chapter 20 for details on returning security deposits.)

There's one exception, however: You may insist the tenant pay your costs of moving and storing the property before you return his belongings. If you've kept the property on the premises the tenant vacated, you have the right to insist on being paid the prorated daily rental value for keeping the property on your premises and/or any out-of-pocket costs you incur after that for renting storage space. You can also subtract the value of your time for packing the tenant's property up in the first place.

However, in most situations where there is not a lot of property, we recommend that you give the tenant his belongings and forget about any charges, particularly if you didn't incur any out-of-pocket expenses. It's just not worth it to get in fights over $75 worth of used books, records, and old clothes. If you insist on too high a storage charge and the tenant refuses to pay it, you will end up having to keep or sell the tenant's property. As a result, the tenant may sue you, raising the possibility that a judge may hold you liable for the entire value of the property because your storage charge wasn't reasonable in the first place. Under state law (CC § 1965), a landlord who fails to promptly return a tenant's belongings may be liable for the value of the property plus $250 and the tenant's attorney fees.

The process by which a tenant demands his property is supposed to work this way:

- The tenant moves out, leaving personal belongings behind.

- Within 18 days, the tenant writes the landlord demanding the return of his property.

- Within five days after receiving the tenant's demand, the landlord must either return the tenant's property or notify the tenant by letter (addressed to the tenant at the return address specified in the demand letter) itemizing in detail the amount of moving and/or storage charges, which the landlord demands as a condition of returning the tenant's property. (As stated above, however, we think it's less hassle to simply return the property, without insisting on moving or storage charges.)

- The tenant then has three days to pay the landlord's moving and storage charges (if any) and reclaim the property.

If the tenant does not reclaim the property after all this, the landlord will not be liable under state law. However, the landlord will then have to proceed as described in the following section.

2. If the Tenant Doesn't Demand His Property

A tenant truly interested in keeping his belongings usually won't leave anything behind. (Even tenants evicted by the sheriff or marshal usually manage to move themselves and their belongings out a day or two before the scheduled eviction date.) So, when a tenant leaves personal property, it's usually junk that has been intentionally left behind. Unfortunately, you can face serious liability for disposing of the junk, unless you use a Notice of Right to Reclaim Abandoned Property, as shown below. (See CC §§ 1980-1991.)

If, after a tenant has left, you discover property in addition to obvious trash or garbage, follow these steps:

Step 1. Take an inventory of the abandoned property and write down a list of everything you find. An objective witness (tenant or neighbor) is valuable here if you want to protect yourself from any charge that you have not done this honestly. Don't open locked trunks or suitcases or tied boxes; just list the unopened container. You may, however, open other containers to check for items of value, since your method of disposing of the property depends on its total value.

Step 2. Decide whether the value of all the property—what you could get for it at a well-attended flea market or garage sale—is more than $300.

Step 3. Regardless of the items' value, send the tenant a Notice of Right to Reclaim Abandoned Property. There is no time limit for doing this, but you may not legally dispose of the property until you begin the process with this notice. A sample is shown below.

You'll find a tear-out version of the Notice of Right to Reclaim Abandoned Property in Appendix B. The CD-ROM that accompanies this book also includes this form.

On the Notice of Right to Reclaim Abandoned Property, you list:

1. The name of the tenant (and any other person you believe has an interest in the property).

2. The address of the premises.

3. A description of the property. If there are too many items of property to list on the form, you can list them on a separate sheet of paper labeled "Attachment A." The property must be described "in a manner reasonably adequate to permit the owner of the property to identify it." (CC § 1983(b).) Merely describing it as "household goods" is insufficient.

4. A place where the tenant can claim the property.

5. The value of the property, by checking the appropriate box on the form as to whether the property, in your opinion, is worth more or less than $300.

6. Your signature and date the Notice was mailed.

FIXTURES BELONG TO YOU

If a tenant attaches something more or less permanently to the wall, such as bookshelves bolted or nailed in, it is called a "fixture." The general rule, in the absence of a lease provision or later agreement between you and the tenant that provides otherwise, is that a fixture installed by the tenant becomes a part of the premises and belongs to the landlord. That means a tenant who attaches bookshelves to a wall, using bolts, nails, or other fasteners is legally required to leave the shelves in place when she leaves. (In practice, tenants may remove the fasteners and patch the wall. Usually, landlord prefer this, and may chose to deduct from the deposit the cost of repainting, if it's necessary.) Fixtures that have not been removed are the landlord's property, and do not have to be returned to the tenant.

Mail the notice to the tenant's last known residence, which will, of course, usually be the address of your residential rental property. The postal service will forward the notice if the tenant has left a forwarding address.

You must surrender the property if the tenant contacts you within 18 days after you mailed the notice. If you haven't mailed a notice, you must surrender the property within 18 days after the tenant has left. Again, before returning the tenant's property, you have the right to charge moving and storage costs (not exceeding the prorated daily rental value for keeping the property on your premises), and/or any out-of-pocket costs you incur for renting storage space. However, as we mentioned, it may not be worth the hassle and risk to insist on these charges.

Don't demand more than moving and storage charges. Even if the tenant owes you a substantial sum for back rent or damages, you may not insist on payment of that amount as a condition of returning the tenant's property, even if you've obtained a court judgment. In order to properly keep the property to have it sold and applied against such a judgment, you must have the sheriff seize the property and auction it off. The costs of doing this may exceed the value of the property, however.

a. Property Worth Less Than $300

If your former tenant or other owner of the property left behind doesn't contact you within 18 days of your mailing the Notice of Right to Reclaim Abandoned Property, you may keep, sell, give away, use, or do anything else you wish with the property, if it is all worth less than $300. (CC § 1988.) In other words, it's yours. To recover from you for wrongfully disposing of the property, the tenant would have to convince a probably skeptical judge that the property was worth over $300 and that your belief that it was worth less was unreasonable.

Several landlords we know routinely put all the material left behind by the tenant, when the total value obviously does not exceed $300, in large plastic

Notice of Right to Reclaim Abandoned Property
Civil Code Section 1984

To: _____ Scott Gold _____,
                                    Name

When the premises at _____ 123 Alameda Avenue #4 _____
                                                    Street Address

City of _____ Santa Monica _____, County of _____ Los Angeles _____, California,

were vacated, the following personal property remained: one Sony color TV, one green couch, shirts and pants, small coffee table, standing lamp

☐ Continued on Attachment "A" hereto.

You may claim this property at: _____ 246 Great Street _____.

City of _____ Los Angeles _____, County of _____ Los Angeles _____, California.

Unless you pay the reasonable cost of storage for all the above-described property, and take possession of the property that you claim not later than eighteen (18) days after the date of mailing of this notice indicated below, this property will be disposed of pursuant to Civil Code Section 1988.

☐ Because this property is believed to be worth less than $300, it will be kept, sold, or destroyed without further notice if you fail to reclaim it within the time limit indicated.

☒ Because this property is believed to be worth more than $300, it will be sold at a public sale after notice has been given by publication, if you fail to reclaim it within the time limit indicated. You have the right to bid on the property at this sale. After the property is sold and the cost of storage, advertising, and sale is deducted, the remaining money will be turned over to the county. You may claim the remaining money at any time within one year after the county receives the money.

Date of Mailing _____ December 16, 200X _____

                        Marilyn Winters
Landlord/Manager

                        123 Alameda Avenue #1
Street address

                        Santa Monica, California

bags, which they tag and keep in their own storage room for six months or so. A few times a year, they give everything that hasn't been claimed to Goodwill Industries, the Salvation Army, or some other non-profit organization that operates second-hand stores.

b. Property Worth More Than $300

Very seldom will a departing tenant leave behind personal effects worth more than $300. Indeed, one management company that handles several thousand units, and has done so for 30 years, tells us that they have only had this occur once. In the rare event this does occur, you must arrange for the property to be sold at a public auction, and you must publish a notice in the newspaper announcing the auction. (CC § 1988.)

The ad must be published after the 18-day period for the tenant to claim the items has expired, and at least five days before the date of the auction. Although your estimate of value can be based on flea market or garage sale values, actually holding a flea market or garage sale does not comply with the law, which requires a "public sale by competitive bidding." You must hire a licensed and bonded public auctioneer. (See the "Auctioneer" listings in the Yellow Pages of your telephone directory.)

Place your ad in the legal section of a local newspaper. The newspaper must be one of "general circulation" that has paid subscribers in the county. Most daily newspapers qualify; weekly "throwaway" newspapers delivered free of charge and that depend on advertising for all their revenue do not. (See Government Code § 6066, and CC § 1988(b) and (c) for how to advertise and handle the proceeds of a public sale.) Basically, the ad must describe the property in the same way you described it in the Notice of Right to Reclaim Abandoned Property.

Proceeds from the sale go first to pay your reasonable costs of storage, advertising, and sale. You must pay the balance to the county within 30 days of the sale, unless you have a judgment for unpaid rent, in which case you can keep the amount necessary to pay the judgment. (To do this, however, you will have to take the judgment and a "Writ of Execution," available from the court clerk, to the sheriff or marshal and give them the appropriate fee and written instructions to "levy" on the funds in the county's control. Ask the sheriff's or marshal's office for details.) In the unlikely event that money is left over, ask the county clerk for instructions, including a form to account for the sale proceeds. The county gets to keep the money if the tenant or other owner of the property doesn't claim it within a year.

Why should you go to all this trouble? After all, no law enforcement agency will prosecute you for failing to comply with this law. But following this procedure will protect you from any liability in the event the tenant or other owner of the property left behind shows up later and sues you for unlawful conversion of her property. (CC § 1989(c).) Also, if the property is worth a lot more than $300, there may be enough money left over from the proceeds of the sale, after subtracting your costs for storage, advertising, and conducting the auction, to apply to any judgment you have against the tenant.

EXAMPLE

After Donna went to court and obtained a judgment for eviction and $1,000 back rent against her tenant, Abbie, Abbie simply took off for parts unknown. Strangely enough, Abbie left behind a good-quality color TV, a piano and a starving Persian cat. Donna sent Abbie a Notice of Right to Reclaim Abandoned Property, to which Abbie didn't respond. Donna then advertised and arranged a public auction, which brought in $750. Donna applied the auction proceeds as follows: $100 for storage charges, including care and feeding of the cat and prorated rental value for the days Abbie's property was on the premises; $100 for the cost of running the legal ad; and the auctioneer's $200 fee. This left $350 for Donna to have the sheriff apply against her $1,000 judgment.

Be careful how you use auction proceeds. If the tenant owes you money—even for back rent—you can't use the proceeds of the sale to pay the tenant's debt unless you have a court judgment. This is because the proceeds, after subtracting costs of storage, advertising and sale, are still the tenant's property. You are not allowed to take someone else's property except to pay off a judgment.

In the above example, to enforce her judgment, Donna should instruct the auctioneer to hold the funds in Abbie's name. Donna should then have the clerk of the court that issued the judgment issue a Writ of Execution, which Donna would, in turn, take to the local sheriff or marshal, with appropriate instructions to levy on the funds held by the auctioneer. As a practical matter, if Donna simply takes the excess auction proceeds and applies them toward the judgment (and accounts for it properly to the tenant if and when Abbie shows up later), it's unlikely a judge would penalize Donna, assuming her accounting was honest. And even if a judge did rule that Donna's action was improper, Donna still would have the right to offset her judgment against the tenant's claims for any wrongful disposition of the property.

B. MOTOR VEHICLES LEFT BEHIND

Occasionally, a departing tenant will leave an inoperable "junker" automobile in the parking lot or garage. Unfortunately, motor vehicles are a special category of personal property to which the procedures listed in Section A, above, do not apply. If the tenant has used the street in front of your property, or the property itself, as a junk yard, you should call the local police, giving the vehicle's license number, make, and model, and indicate where it's parked. If the car is parked on the street, the police will arrange to have it towed away 72 hours later, placing a notice to that effect on the windshield. (Vehicle Code § 22651(k).)

If the vehicle is parked on your property, you can arrange to have it towed away within 24 hours after notifying the police, if the vehicle "lacks an engine, transmission, wheels, tires, doors, windshield, or any other major part or equipment." (Vehicle Code § 22658(a)(3).) Otherwise, the police may still arrange for the vehicle's removal after an officer determines it is abandoned and tags it. (Vehicle Code §§ 22523(b) and 22669.)

Cities have slightly different ordinances to cover this situation. In some, there is a small charge, but in many others, the city recovers towing and storage costs from the sale of the car. Several landlords have reported that the police are slow to pick up motor vehicles abandoned on private property and try to tell landlords that it's their responsibility to do a lien sale through the Department of Motor Vehicles. If a car is worth a fair amount, this is a viable alternative, as you can use the money you get from the sale to satisfy any judgment you have against the tenant. But it involves a fair amount of paperwork and is often more trouble than it's worth.

Your best approach is usually to insist that the police help you. Get a copy of the local abandoned property ordinance and refer to it if the police resist. ■

APPENDIX A

HOW TO USE THE CD-ROM

The tear-out forms in Appendix B are included on a CD-ROM in the back of the book. This CD-ROM, which can be used with Windows computers, installs files that can be opened, printed, and edited using a word processor or other software. It is *not* a stand-alone software program. Please read this Appendix and the README.TXT file included on the CD-ROM for instructions on using the Forms CD.

Note to Mac users: This CD-ROM and its files should also work on Macintosh computers. Please note, however, that Nolo cannot provide technical support for non-Windows users.

HOW TO VIEW THE README FILE

If you do not know how to view the file README.TXT, insert the Forms CD-ROM into your computer's CD-ROM drive and follow these instructions:

- Windows 9x, 2000, Me, and XP: (1) On your PC's desktop, double click the My Computer icon; (2) double click the icon for the CD-ROM drive into which the Forms CD-ROM was inserted; (3) double click the file README.TXT.

- Macintosh: (1) On your Mac desktop, double click the icon for the CD-ROM that you inserted; (2) double click on the file README.TXT.

While the README file is open, print it out by using the Print command in the File menu.

Two different kinds of forms are contained on the CD-ROM:

- Word processing (RTF) forms that you can open, complete, print, and save with your word processing program (see Section B, below), and
- Forms (PDF) that can be viewed only with Adobe Acrobat Reader 4.0 or higher. You can install Acrobat Reader from the Forms CD (see Section C,

below). These forms are designed to be printed out and filled in by hand or with a typewriter.

See Appendix B for a list of forms, their file names, and file formats.

A. INSTALLING THE FORM FILES ONTO YOUR COMPUTER

Before you can do anything with the files on the CD-ROM, you need to install them onto your hard disk. In accordance with U.S. copyright laws, remember that copies of the CD-ROM and its files are for your personal use only.

Insert the Forms CD and do the following:

1. Windows 9x, 2000, Me, and XP Users

Follow the instructions that appear on the screen. (If nothing happens when you insert the Forms CD-ROM, then (1) double click the My Computer icon; (2) double click the icon for the CD-ROM drive into which the Forms CD-ROM was inserted; and (3) double click the file WELCOME.EXE.)

By default, all the files are installed to the \CA Landlord Rights Forms folder in the \Program Files folder of your computer. A folder called "CA Landlord Rights Forms" is added to the "Programs" folder of the Start menu.

2. Macintosh Users

Step 1: If the "CA Landlord Rights CD" window is not open, open it by double clicking the "CA Landlord Rights CD" icon.

Step 2: Select the "CA Landlord Rights Forms" folder icon.

Step 3: Drag and drop the folder icon onto the icon of your hard disk.

B. Using the Word Processing Files to Create Documents

This section concerns the files for forms that can be opened and edited with your word processing program.

All word processing forms come in rich text format. These files have the extension ".RTF." For example, the form for the Consent to Background and Reference Check discussed in Chapter 1 is on the file CONSENT.RTF. All forms, their file names, and file formats are listed in Appendix B.

RTF files can be read by most recent word processing programs, including all versions of MS Word for Windows and Macintosh, WordPad for Windows, and recent versions of WordPerfect for Windows and Macintosh.

To use a form from the CD to create your documents, you must: (1) open a file in your word processor or text editor; (2) edit the form by filling in the required information; (3) print it out; (4) rename and save your revised file.

The following are general instructions on how to do this. However, each word processor uses different commands to open, format, save, and print documents. Please read your word processor's manual for specific instructions on performing these tasks.

Do not call Nolo's technical support if you have questions on how to use your word processor.

Step 1: Opening a File

There are three ways to open the word processing files included on the CD-ROM after you have installed them onto your computer:

- Windows users can open a file by selecting its "shortcut" as follows: (1) Click the Windows "Start" button; (2) open the "Programs" folder; (3) open the "CA Landlord Rights Forms" subfolder; (4) open the "RTF" subfolder; and (5) click on the shortcut to the form you want to work with.

- Both Windows and Macintosh users can open a file directly by double clicking on it. Use My Computer or Windows Explorer (Windows 9x, 2000, Me, or XP) or the Finder (Macintosh) to go to the folder you installed or copied the CD-ROM's files to. Then, double click on the specific file you want to open.

- You can also open a file from within your word processor. To do this, you must first start your word processor. Then, go to the File menu and choose the Open command. This opens a dialog box where you will tell the program (1) the type of file you want to open (*.RTF); and (2) the location and name of the file (you will need to navigate through the directory tree to get to the folder on your hard disk where the CD's files have been installed). If these directions are unclear, you will need to look through the manual for your word processing program—Nolo's technical support department will *not* be able to help you with the use of your word processing program.

WHERE ARE THE FILES INSTALLED?

Windows Users

- RTF files are installed by default to a folder named \CA Landlord Rights Forms\RTF in the \Program Files folder of your computer.

Macintosh Users

- RTF files are located in the "RTF" folder within the "CA Landlord Rights Forms" folder.

Step 2: Editing Your Document

Fill in the appropriate information according to the instructions and sample agreements in the book. Underlines are used to indicate where you need to enter your information, frequently followed by instructions in brackets. *Be sure to delete the underlines and instructions from your edited document.* If you do not know how to use your word processor to edit a document, you will need to look through the manual for your word processing program—Nolo's technical support department will *not* be able to help you with the use of your word processing program.

EDITING FORMS THAT HAVE OPTIONAL OR ALTERNATIVE TEXT

Some of the forms have check boxes before text. The check boxes indicate:

- Optional text, where you choose whether to include or exclude the given text.

- Alternative text, where you select one alternative to include and exclude the other alternatives.

If you are using the tear-out forms in Appendix B, you simply mark the appropriate box to make your choice.

If you are using the Forms CD, however, we recommend that instead of marking the check boxes, you do the following:

Optional text

If you **don't want** to include optional text, just delete it from your document.

If you **do want** to include optional text, just leave it in your document.

In either case, delete the check box itself as well as the italicized instructions that the text is optional.

Alternative text

First delete all the alternatives that you do not want to include.

Then delete the remaining check boxes, as well as the italicized instructions that you need to select one of the alternatives provided.

Step 3: Printing Out the Document

Use your word processor's or text editor's "Print" command to print out your document. If you do not know how to use your word processor to print a document, you will need to look through the manual for your word processing program—Nolo's technical support department will *not* be able to help you with the use of your word processing program.

Step 4: Saving Your Document

After filling in the form, use the "Save As" command to save and rename the file. Because all the files are "read-only," you will not be able to use the "Save" command. This is for your protection. *If you save the file without renaming it, the underlines that indicate where you need to enter your information will be lost and you will not be able to create a new document with this file without recopying the original file from the CD-ROM.*

If you do not know how to use your word processor to save a document, you will need to look through the manual for your word processing program—Nolo's technical support department will *not* be able to help you with the use of your word processing program.

C. USING PDF FILES TO PRINT OUT FORMS

Electronic copies of useful forms are included on the CD-ROM in Adobe Acrobat PDF format. You must have the Adobe Acrobat Reader installed on your computer (see below) to use these forms. All forms, their file names, and file formats are listed in Appendix B.

These forms cannot be filled out using your computer. To create your document using these files, you must: (1) open the file; (2) print it out; and (3) complete it by hand or typewriter.

INSTALLING ACROBAT READER

To install the Adobe Acrobat Reader, insert the CD into your computer's CD-ROM drive and follow these instructions:

- Windows 9x, 2000, Me, or XP: Follow the instructions that appear on screen. (If nothing happens when you insert the Forms CD-ROM, then (1) double click the My Computer icon; (2) double click the icon for the CD-ROM drive into which the Forms CD-ROM was inserted; and (3) double click the file WELCOME.EXE.)

- Macintosh: (1) If the "CA Landlord Rights CD" window is not open, open it by double clicking the "CA Landlord Rights CD" icon; and (2) double click on the "Acrobat Reader Installer" icon.

If you do not know how to use Adobe Acrobat to view and print the files, you will need to consult the online documentation that comes with the Acrobat Reader program.

Do *not* call Nolo technical support if you have questions on how to use Acrobat Reader.

to the folder you created and copied the CD-ROM's files to. Then, double click on the specific file you want to open.

- You can also open a PDF file from within Acrobat Reader. To do this, you must first start Reader. Then, go to the File menu and choose the Open command. This opens a dialog box where you will tell the program the location and name of the file (you will need to navigate through the directory tree to get to the folder on your hard disk where the CD's files have been installed). If these directions are unclear, you will need to look through Acrobat Reader's help—Nolo's technical support department will *not* be able to help you with the use of Acrobat Reader.

WHERE ARE THE PDF FILES INSTALLED?

- Windows Users: PDF files are installed by default to a folder named \CA Landlord Rights Forms\PDF in the \Program Files folder of your computer.

- Macintosh Users: PDF files are located in the "PDF" folder within the "CA Landlord Rights Forms" folder.

Step 1: Opening PDF Files

PDF files, like the word processing files, can be opened one of three ways.

- Windows users can open a file by selecting its "shortcut" as follows: (1) Click the Windows "Start" button; (2) open the "Programs" folder; (3) open the "CA Landlord Rights Forms" subfolder; (4) open the "PDF" folder; and (5) click on the shortcut to the form you want to work with.

- Both Windows and Macintosh users can open a file directly by double clicking on it. Use My Computer or Windows Explorer (Windows 9x, 2000, Me, or XP) or the Finder (Macintosh) to go

Step 2: Printing PDF files

Choose Print from the Acrobat Reader File menu. This will open the Print dialog box. In the "Print Range" section of the Print dialog box, select the appropriate print range, then click OK.

Step 3: Filling in PDF files

The PDF files cannot be filled out using your computer. To create your document using one of these files, you must first print it out (see Step 2, above), and then complete it by hand or typewriter. ∎

APPENDIX B

File Name	Form	Chapter
Warning.rtf	Warning Notice (Complaints From Neighbors/Residents)	18
Abandonment.rtf	Notice of Belief of Abandonment	19
MoveOut.rtf	Move-Out Letter	20
Response.rtf	Tenant's Response Regarding Initial Move-Out Inspection	20
DepositRights.rtf	Notice of Tenant's Security Deposit Rights	20
Waiver.rtf	Tenant's Waiver of Right to Receipts and Invoices	20
DepositReturn.rtf	Letter for Returning Entire Security Deposit	20
Itemization1.rtf	Security Deposit Itemization (Deductions for Repairs and Cleaning)	20
Itemization2.srtf	Security Deposit Itemization (Deductions for Repairs, Cleaning, and Unpaid Rent)	20
Reclaim.rtf	Notice of Right to Reclaim Abandoned Property	21

Rental Application

Separate application required from each applicant age 18 or older.

THIS SECTION TO BE COMPLETED BY LANDLORD

Address of Property to Be Rented: _____

_____

Rental Term: ☐ month to month ☐ lease from _____ to _____

Amounts Due Prior to Occupancy

First month's rent .... $_____

Security deposit .... $_____

Credit-check fee .... $_____

Other (specify): _____ $_____

TOTAL .... $_____

Applicant

Full Name—include all names you use(d): _____

Home Phone: ( )   Work Phone: ( )

Social Security Number: _____   Driver's License Number/State: _____

Other Identifying Information: _____

Vehicle Make: _____ Model: _____ Color: _____ Year: _____

License Plate Number/State: _____

Additional Occupants

List everyone, including children, who will live with you:

Full Name   Relationship to Applicant

_____

_____

_____

_____

Rental History

Current Address: _____

Dates Lived at Address: _____   Reason for Leaving: _____

Landlord/Manager: _____   Landlord/Manager's Phone: ( )

Previous Address: _____

Dates Lived at Address: _____   Reason for Leaving: _____

Landlord/Manager: _____   Landlord/Manager's Phone: ( )

Previous Address: _____

Dates Lived at Address: _____   Reason for Leaving: _____

Landlord/Manager: _____   Landlord/Manager's Phone: (____) _____

Employment History

Name and Address of Current Employer: _____

_____   Phone: (____) _____

Name of Supervisor: _____   Supervisor's Phone: (____) _____

Dates Employed at This Job: _____   Position or Title: _____

Name and Address of Previous Employer: _____

_____   Phone: (____) _____

Name of Supervisor: _____   Supervisor's Phone: (____) _____

Dates Employed at This Job: _____   Position or Title: _____

Income

1. Your gross monthly employment income (before deductions): $ _____

2. Average monthly amounts of other income (specify sources): $ _____

_____

_____

TOTAL: $ _____

Credit and Financial Information

Bank/Financial Accounts	Account Number	Bank/Institution	Branch
Savings Account:			
Checking Account:			
Money Market or Similar Account:			

Credit Accounts & Loans	Type of Account (Auto loan, Visa, etc.)	Account Number	Name of Creditor	Amount Owed	Monthly Payment
Major Credit Card:					
Major Credit Card:					
Loan (mortgage, car, student loan, etc.):					
Other Major Obligation:					

Miscellaneous

Describe the number and type of pets you want to have in the rental property: _____

_____

Describe water-filled furniture you want to have in the rental property: _____

_____

Do you smoke?   ☐ yes ☐ no

Have you ever: Filed for bankruptcy? ☐ yes ☐ no   Been sued? ☐ yes ☐ no

Been evicted? ☐ yes ☐ no   Been convicted of a crime? ☐ yes ☐ no

Explain any "yes" listed above: _____

_____

References and Emergency Contact

Personal Reference: _____   Relationship: _____

Address: _____

Phone: (____) _____

Personal Reference: _____   Relationship: _____

Address: _____

Phone: (____) _____

Contact in Emergency: _____   Relationship: _____

Address: _____

Phone: (____) _____

I certify that all the information given above is true and correct and understand that my lease or rental agreement may be terminated if I have made any material false or incomplete statements in this application. I authorize verification of the information provided in this application from my credit sources, credit bureaus, current and previous landlords and employers, and personal references. I understand that if I have initiated a "security freeze" on my credit information with any of the credit reporting agencies, I will promptly lift the freeze for a reasonable time so that my credit report may be accessed by the Landlord/Manager; and I understand that if I fail to do so, the Landlord/Manager may consider this an incomplete application. (CC § 1785.11.2.) This permission will survive the expiration of my tenancy.

_____

Date   Applicant

Notes (Landlord/Manager): _____

_____

_____

_____

Consent to Background and Reference Check

I authorize _____
to obtain information about me from my credit sources, current and previous landlords and employers, and
personal references, to enable _____ to evaluate my rental application. I authorize my credit
sources, credit bureaus, current and previous landlords and employers, and personal references to disclose to
_____ information about me that is
relevant to _____ 's decisions regarding my application and tenancy. This
permission will survive the expiration of my tenancy.

_____

Name

_____

Address

_____

Phone Number

_____   _____

Date   Applicant

Application Screening Fee Receipt

This will acknowledge receipt of the sum of $ _____ by _____
[Property Owner/Manager] from _____ [Applicant] as part of his/her
application for the rental property at _____[Rental
Property Address].

As provided under California Civil Code Section 1950.6, here is an itemization of how this
$ _____ screening fee will be used:

Actual costs of obtaining Applicant's credit/screening report $ _____

Administrative costs of obtaining credit/screening report and checking Applicant's references and
background information $ _____

Total screening fee charged $ _____

_____   _____
Date   Applicant

_____   _____
Date   Owner/Manager

Disclosures by Property Owner(s)

The owner(s) of property located at _____

_____

_____

make(s) the following disclosure(s) to prospective tenant(s) and/or employee(s):

_____

_____

_____

_____

_____

_____

_____

_____

_____

_____

_____

_____

_____

_____

_____

_____ _____
Owner's Signature   Date

I have read and received a copy of the above Disclosures by Property Owner(s).

_____ _____
Signature   Date

_____ _____
Signature   Date

Tenant References

Name of Applicant:_____

Address of Rental Unit:_____

Previous Landlord or Manager

Contact (name, property owner or manager, address of rental unit): _____
_____

Date: _____

Questions

When did tenant rent from you (move-in and move-out dates)? _____

What was the monthly rent? _____

Did tenant pay rent on time? _____

Was tenant considerate of neighbors—that is, no loud parties and fair, careful use of common areas? _____
_____

Did tenant have any pets? If so, were there any problems? _____
_____

Did tenant make any unreasonable demands or complaints? _____
_____

Why did tenant leave? _____
_____

Did tenant give the proper amount of notice before leaving? _____

Did tenant leave the place in good condition? Did you need to use the security deposit to cover damage?
_____

Any particular problems you'd like to mention? _____
_____
_____

Would you rent to this person again? _____
_____

Other Comments: _____
_____
_____
_____
_____
_____

Employment Verification

Contact (name, company, position): _____

Date: _____

Salary: _____ Dates of Employment: _____

Comments: _____

_____

_____

_____

_____

_____

_____

_____

Personal Reference

Contact (name and relationship to applicant): _____

Date: _____ How long have you known the applicant? _____

Would you recommend this person as a prospective tenant? _____

Comments: _____

_____

_____

_____

_____

_____

_____

Credit and Financial Information

_____

_____

_____

_____

_____

Notes, Including Reasons for Rejecting Applicant

_____

_____

_____

_____

Notice of Denial Based on Credit Report Information

To:

_____

Applicant

_____

Street Address

_____

City, State, and Zip Code

THIS NOTICE is to inform you that your application to rent the property at _____ [rental property address] has been denied because of [check all that apply]:

❏ Insufficient information in the credit report provided by _____ [name, address, and telephone number of consumer credit reporting agency providing credit report; include toll-free telephone number if this is a national credit reporting agency]

❏ Negative information in the credit report provided by _____ [name, address, and telephone number of consumer credit reporting agency providing credit report; include toll-free telephone number if this is a national credit reporting agency]

The consumer credit reporting agency noted above did not make the decision not to rent to you and cannot explain why your application was rejected. It only provided information about your credit history.

Providing this notice meets the requirements of the federal Fair Credit Reporting Act as amended by the Fair and Accurate Credit Transactions (FACT) Act of 2003 (15 U.S.C. §§ 1681 and following). You have the right under this Act to obtain a free copy of your credit report from the consumer credit reporting agency named above, if your request is made within 60 days of this notice or if you have not requested a free copy within the past year (15 U.S.C. § 1681(j)). You also have the right to dispute the accuracy or completeness of your credit report and add your own "consumer statement" (up to 100 words) to the report (15 U.S.C. § 1681(i)). For more information, contact the above-named consumer credit reporting agency.

_____

Date

_____

Owner/Manager

Receipt and Holding Deposit Agreement

This will acknowledge receipt of the sum of $_____ by _____

_____ ("Landlord") from _____

_____ ("Applicant") as a holding deposit to hold vacant the

rental property at _____

_____, until

_____ at _____. The property will be rented to Applicant on a

_____ basis at a rent of $_____ per month, if Applicant signs Landlord's written

_____ and pays Landlord the first month's rent and a $_____

security deposit on or before that date, in which event the holding deposit will be applied to the first month's

rent.

This Agreement depends upon Landlord receiving a satisfactory report of Applicant's references and credit

history. Landlord and Applicant agree that if Landlord offers the rental unit but Applicant fails to sign the

Agreement and pay the remaining rent and security deposit, Landlord may retain from this holding deposit a sum

equal to the prorated daily rent of $_____ per day until the unit is rerented, plus a $_____

charge to compensate Landlord for lost rents and the time and expense incurred by the need to rerent.

_____   _____

Applicant   Date

_____   _____

Landlord   Date

Month-to-Month Residential Rental Agreement

1. **Identification of Landlord and Tenants.** This Agreement is made and entered into on _____, 20_____, between _____ ("Tenants") and _____ ("Landlord"). Each Tenant is jointly and severally liable for the payment of rent and performance of all other terms of this Agreement.

2. **Identification of Premises and Occupants.** Subject to the terms and conditions set forth in this Agreement, Landlord rents to Tenants, and Tenants rent from Landlord, for residential purposes only, the premises located at _____, California ("the premises"). The premises will be occupied by the undersigned Tenants and the following minor children: _____

   _____

3. **Limits on Use and Occupancy.** The premises are to be used only as a private residence for Tenants and any minors listed in Clause 2 of this Agreement, and for no other purpose without Landlord's prior written consent. Occupancy by guests for more than ten days in any six-month period is prohibited without Landlord's written consent and will be considered a breach of this Agreement.

4. **Defining the Term of the Tenancy.** The rental will begin on _____, 20____, and will continue on a month-to-month basis. This tenancy may be terminated by Landlord or Tenants and may be modified by Landlord, by giving 30 days' written notice to the other, or 60 days' notice by Landlord to Tenant, in accordance with Civil Code Section 827 or 1946.1 (subject to any local rent control ordinances that may apply).

5. **Amount and Schedule for the Payment of Rent.** Tenants will pay to Landlord a monthly rent of $_____, payable in advance on the _____ day of each month, except when that day falls on a weekend or legal holiday, in which case rent is due on the next business day. Rent will be paid to

   _____

   at _____,

   or at such other place as Landlord may designate.

   a. The form of payment will be ❑ cash ❑ personal check ❑ certified funds or money order ❑ credit card ❑ automatic credit card debit ❑ bank debit

   ❑ b. [Check if rent will be accepted personally, not by mail.] Rent is accepted during the following days and hours: _____

   ❑ c. [Check if rent will be paid by electronic funds transfer.] Rent may be paid by electronic funds transfer to account number _____ in the name of _____

       Account Number   Account Holder

   at _____, _____ branch, a financial institution located at

     Institution   Branch

   _____, telephone (____) - _____ .

   Bank Address   Telephone

6. **Late Charges.** Tenants will pay Landlord a late charge if Tenants fail to pay the rent in full within _____ days after the date it is due. The late charge will be $_____, plus $_____ for each additional day that the rent continues to be unpaid. The total late charge for any one month will not exceed $_____. Landlord does not waive the right to insist on payment of the rent in full on the date it is due.

7. **Returned Check and Other Bank Charges.** In the event any check offered by Tenants to Landlord in payment of rent or any other amount due under this Agreement is returned for lack of sufficient funds, a "stop payment" or any other reason, Tenants will pay Landlord a returned check charge in the amount of $_____.

8. **Amount and Payment of Deposits.** On signing this Agreement, Tenants will pay to Landlord the sum of $_____ as a security deposit. Tenants may not, without Landlord's prior written consent, apply this security deposit to the last month's rent or to any other sum due under this Agreement. Within three weeks after Tenants have vacated the premises, Landlord will furnish Tenants with an itemized written statement of the reasons for, and the dollar amount of, any of the security deposit retained by the Landlord, receipts for work done or items purchased, if available, along with a check for any deposit balance. Under Section 1950.5 of the California Civil Code, Landlord may withhold only that portion of Tenants' security deposit necessary to: (1) remedy any default by Tenants in the payment of rent; (2) repair damages to the premises exclusive of ordinary wear and tear; (3) clean the premises if necessary to restore it to the same level of cleanliness it was in at the beginning of the tenancy; and (4) remedy any default by tenants, under this agreement, to restore, replace, or return any of Landlord's personal property mentioned in this agreement, including but not limited to the property referred to in Clause 11.

Landlord will pay Tenants interest on all security deposits as follows:

☐ a. Per state law, no interest payments are required.

☐ b. Local law requires that interest be paid or credited, or landlord has decided voluntarily to do so, which will occur as follows:

_____

_____

9. **Utilities.** Tenants will be responsible for payment of all utility charges, except for the following, which shall be paid by Landlord:

_____

_____

☐ Tenants' gas or electric meter serves area(s) outside of their premises, and there are not separate gas and electric meters for Tenants' unit and the area(s) outside their unit. Tenants and Landlord agree as follows:

_____

_____

10. **Prohibition of Assignment and Subletting.** Tenants will not sublet any part of the premises or assign this Agreement without the prior written consent of Landlord.

11. **Condition of the Premises.** Tenants agree to: (1) keep the premises clean and sanitary and in good repair and, upon termination of the tenancy, to return the premises to Landlord in a condition identical to that which existed when Tenants took occupancy, except for ordinary wear and tear; (2) immediately notify Landlord of any defects or dangerous conditions in and about the premises of which they become aware; and (3) reimburse Landlord, on demand by Landlord, for the cost of any repairs to the premises, including Landlord's personal property therein, damaged by Tenants or their guests or invitees through misuse or neglect.

Tenants acknowledge that they have examined the premises, including appliances, fixtures, carpets, drapes, and paint, and have found them to be in good, safe, and clean condition and repair, except as noted here:

_____

_____

_____

_____

12. **Possession of the Premises.** If, after signing this Agreement, Tenants fail to take possession of the premises, they will be responsible for paying rent and complying with all other terms of this Agreement. In the event

Landlord is unable to deliver possession of the premises to Tenants for any reason not within Landlord's control, including, but not limited to, failure of prior occupants to vacate or partial or complete destruction of the premises, Tenants will have the right to terminate this Agreement. In such event, Landlord's liability to Tenants will be limited to the return of all sums previously paid by Tenants to Landlord.

13. Pets. No animal, bird, or other pet shall be kept on the premises without Landlord's prior written consent, except properly trained dogs needed by blind, deaf, or disabled persons and:

☐ a. None.

☐ b. _____ , under the following conditions:

_____

14. Landlord's Access for Inspection and Emergency. Landlord or Landlord's agents may enter the premises in the event of an emergency or to make repairs or improvements, supply agreed services, show the premises to prospective buyers or tenants, and conduct an initial move-out inspection requested by tenants. Except in cases of emergency, Tenants' abandonment of the premises, or court order, Landlord will give Tenants reasonable notice of intent to enter and will enter only during regular business hours of Monday through Friday from 9:00 a.m. to 6:00 p.m. and Saturday from 10:00 a.m. to 1:00 p.m. The notice will include the purpose, date, and approximate time of the entry.

15. Extended Absences by Tenants. Tenants agree to notify Landlord in the event that they will be away from the premises for _____ consecutive days or more. During such absence, Landlord may enter the premises at times reasonably necessary to maintain the property and inspect for damage and needed repairs.

16. Prohibitions Against Violating Laws and Causing Disturbances. Tenants are entitled to quiet enjoyment of the premises. Tenants and their guests or invitees will not use the premises or adjacent areas in such a way as to: (1) violate any law or ordinance, including laws prohibiting the use, possession, or sale of illegal drugs; (2) commit waste or nuisance; or (3) annoy, disturb, inconvenience, or interfere with the quiet enjoyment and peace and quiet of any other tenant or nearby resident.

17. Repairs and Alterations

   a. Tenants will not, without Landlord's prior written consent, alter, rekey, or install any locks to the premises or install or alter any burglar alarm system. Tenants will provide Landlord with a key or keys capable of unlocking all such rekeyed or new locks as well as instructions on how to disarm any altered or new burglar alarm system.

   b. Except as provided by law or as authorized by the prior written consent of Landlord, Tenants will not make any repairs or alterations to the premises. Landlord will not unreasonably withhold consent for such repairs, but will not authorize repairs that require advanced skill or workmanship or that would be dangerous to undertake. Landlord will not authorize repairs unless such repairs are likely to return the item or element of the rental to its predamaged state of usefulness and attractiveness.

18. Damage to the Premises. In the event the premises are partially or totally damaged or destroyed by fire or other cause, the following will apply:

   a. If the premises are totally damaged and destroyed, Landlord will have the option to: (1) repair such damage and restore the premises, with this Agreement continuing in full force and effect, except that Tenants' rent will be abated while repairs are being made; or (2) give written notice to Tenants terminating this Agreement at any time within thirty (30) days after such damage, and specifying the termination date; in the event that Landlord gives such notice, this Agreement will expire and all of Tenants' rights pursuant to this Agreement will cease.

   b. Landlord will have the option to determine that the premises are only partially damaged by fire or other cause. In that event, Landlord will attempt to repair such damage and restore the premises within thirty (30) days after such damage. If only part of the premises cannot be used, Tenants must pay rent only for the usable part, to be determined solely by Landlord. If Landlord is unable to complete repairs within thirty (30) days, this Agreement will expire and all of Tenants' rights pursuant to this Agreement will

terminate at the option of either party.

    c. In the event that Tenants, or their guests or invitees, in any way caused or contributed to the damage of the premises, Landlord will have the right to terminate this Agreement at any time, and Tenants will be responsible for all losses, including, but not limited to, damage and repair costs as well as loss of rental income.

    d. Landlord will not be required to repair or replace any property brought onto the premises by Tenants.

19. Tenants' Financial Responsibility and Renters' Insurance. Tenants agree to accept financial responsibility for any loss or damage to personal property belonging to Tenants and their guests and invitees caused by theft, fire, or any other cause. Landlord assumes no liability for any such loss. Landlord recommends that Tenants obtain a renters' insurance policy from a recognized insurance firm to cover Tenants' liability, personal property damage, and damage to the premises.

20. Waterbeds. No waterbed or other item of water-filled furniture may be kept on the premises without Landlord's written consent.

    ☐ Landlord grants Tenants permission to keep water-filled furniture on the premises. Attachment _____: Agreement Regarding Use of Waterbed is attached to and incorporated into this Agreement by reference.

21. Tenant Rules and Regulations

    ☐ Tenants acknowledge receipt of, and have read a copy of, tenant rules and regulations, which are labeled Attachment _____ and attached to and incorporated into this Agreement by reference. Landlord may change the rules and regulations without notice.

22. Payment of Attorney Fees in a Lawsuit. In any action or legal proceeding to enforce any part of this Agreement, the prevailing party ☐ will not/☐ will recover reasonable attorney fees and court costs.

23. Authority to Receive Legal Papers. Any person managing the premises, the Landlord, and anyone designated by the Landlord are authorized to accept service of process and receive other notices and demands, which may be delivered to:

    ☐ a. the manager, at the following address and telephone number:_____

_____

    ☐ b. the Landlord, at the following address and telephone number:_____:

_____

_____

    ☐ c. the following: _____

_____

_____

24. Additional Provisions

    ☐ a. None

    ☐ b. Additional provisions are as follows:

_____

_____

25. State Database Disclosure. Notice: The California Department of Justice, sheriff's departments, police departments serving jurisdictions of 200,000 or more, and many other local law enforcement authorities maintain for public access a database of the locations of persons required to register pursuant to paragraph (1) of subdivision (a) of Section 290.4 of the Penal Code. The database is updated on a quarterly basis and is a source of information about the presence of these individuals in any neighborhood. The Department of Justice also maintains a Sex Offender Identification Line through which inquiries about individuals may be made.

This is a "900" telephone service. Callers must have specific information about individuals they are checking. Information regarding neighborhoods is not available through the "900" telephone service. (Civil Code § 2079.10a.)

26. Grounds for Termination of Tenancy. The failure of Tenants or Tenants' guests or invitees to comply with any term of this Agreement, or the misrepresentation of any material fact on Tenants' Rental Application, is grounds for termination of the tenancy, with appropriate notice to Tenants and procedures as required by law.

27. Entire Agreement. This document constitutes the entire Agreement between the parties, and no promises or representations, other than those contained here and those implied by law have been made by Landlord or Tenants. Any modifications to this Agreement must be in writing signed by Landlord and Tenants.

_____   _____
Landlord/Manager   Date

_____
Landlord/Manager's Street Address, City, State & Zip

_____

_____   _____
Tenant   Date

_____   _____
Tenant   Date

_____   _____
Tenant   Date

Contrato Residencial Mensual

1. **Identificación del Arrendador y de los Inquilinos.** Este Contrato es preparado y efectivo a partir del _____ de _____ de 20____, entre _____ ("Inquilinos") y _____ ("Arrendador"). Cada Inquilino es conjunta y seriamente responsable por el pago de la renta y del cumplimiento de todos los demás términos de este Contrato.

2. **Identificación de la Propiedad y los Ocupantes.** De acuerdo con los términos y condiciones referidas en este Contrato, el Arrendador renta a los Inquilinos, y éstos rentan del Arrendador, solamente para residir, la propiedad ubicada en _____, California ("la propiedad"). La propiedad será ocupada por los Inquilinos suscritos y los niños menores siguientes: _____

3. **Limitaciones en el Uso y Ocupación.** La propiedad deberá ser usada sólo como residencia privada por los Inquilinos y cualquier niño menor mencionado en la Cláusula 2 de este Contrato, y para ningún otro propósito, sin el previo consentimiento por escrito del Arrendador. Está prohibido que los invitados ocupen la propiedad por más de diez días, en cualquier período de seis meses, sin el previo consentimiento escrito del Arrendador; de lo contrario, será considerada como una violación de este Contrato.

4. **Período de Arrendamiento.** El término de la renta comenzará el _____ de _____ de 20____, y será prorrogable mensualmente. Este arrendamiento puede ser terminado por el Arrendador o los Inquilinos, y puede ser modificado por el Arrendador con un aviso por escrito del uno al otro con 30 días de anticipación o con un aviso por escrito del Arrendador a los Inquilinos con 60 días de anticipación, bajo la Sección 827 ó 1946.1 del Código Civil de California, (sujeto a cualquier reglamento local de control de renta que pueda aplicarse.)

5. **Renta y Fechas de Pago.** Los Inquilinos pagarán al Arrendador una renta mensual de $_____, pagadera por adelantado el _____ día de cada mes, excepto cuando ese día sea en un fin de semana o en un día feriado oficial, en cuyo caso la renta deberá ser pagada el próximo día laboral. La renta se paqará a _____

   en _____
   o en otro lugar designado por el Arrendatario.

   a. La forma de pago será ❑ efectivo ❑ cheque personal ❑ fondos certificados o giro postal ❑ tarjeta de crédito ❑ débito automático de tarjeta de crédito ❑ débito de banco

   ❑ b. [Marque si el arriendo será aceptado personalmente, no por correo.] El arriendo se aceptará durante los siguientes días y horas: _____.

   ❑ c. [Marque si el arriendo será pagado con dinero transferible electrónicamente.] El arriendo se podrá pagar con dinero transferible electrónicamente a la cuenta número _____ a
   Número de cuenta
   nombre de _____ en _____, sucursal
   Nombre de la cuenta   Nombre de la institución bancaria
   _____, una institución bancaria localizada en _____,
   Nombre de la sucursal   Dirección
   teléfono (____) - _____ .
   Número telefónico

6. **Cobros por Mora.** Los Inquilinos pagarán cargos adicionales al Arrendador, si ellos no pagan la renta total dentro de _____ días después de la fecha debida. La cantidad será $_____, más $_____ por cada día adicional que pase sin pagarse la renta. El cobro total por atraso en cualquier mes no excederá la suma de $_____. El Arrendador no descartará el derecho de insistir en el pago total de la renta en la fecha debida.

7. **Pagos por Cheques sin Fondo y Recargos Bancarios.** En el caso de cualquier cheque, ofrecido por los Inquilinos al Arrendador como pago de renta o cualquier otra suma debida bajo este Contrato, sea regresado

por insuficiencia de fondos, o una orden de no hacer efectivo el pago o cualquier otra razón, los Inquilinos pagarán al Arrendador un recargo por la cantidad de $_____.

8. **Depósito de Garantía.** Al firmar este Contrato, los Inquilinos pagarán al Arrendador la cantidad de $_____ como depósito de garantía. Este depósito no puede aplicarse al último mes de renta o a cualquier cantidad debida bajo este Contrato, excepto con el previo consentimiento por escrito del Arrendador. Dentro de tres semanas después de que los Inquilinos hayan desocupado la propiedad, el Arrendador proporcionará por escrito a los Inquilinos un detalle de las razones por retener el depósito y la cantidad que es retenida por él, más recibos disponibles por mano de obra o materiales comprados, junto con un cheque por la cantidad de diferencia. Bajo la Sección 1950.5 del Código Civil de California, el Arrendador puede retener sólo la porción del depósito de seguridad de los Inquilinos que sea necesaria para: (1) remediar cualquier omisión de pago de renta de los Inquilinos; (2) reparar daños a la propiedad exceptuando el deterioro por uso ordinario; (3) limpiar la propiedad, si es necesario, para restaurarla al mismo nivel de limpieza que tenía al comienzo del arrendamiento; y (4) remediar cualquier incumplimiento por los Inquilinos, bajo éste contrato, de restaurar, reemplazar, o devolver cualquier propiedad personal del Arrendador mencionado en éste contrato, incluyendo pero no limitado a la propiedad referida en la Claúsula 11.

El Arrendador pagará a los Inquilinos, intereses por todos los depósitos de garantía de la manera siguiente:

☐ a. La ley estatal de California no require el pago de interés.

☐ b. La ley local requiere que el interés sea pagado o acreditado o el Arrendador ha decidido hacerlo voluntariamente, lo cual ocurrirá de la siguiente manera:

_____

_____

9. **Servicios Públicos.** Los Inquilinos serán responsables por el pago de todos los sevicios públicos, exceptuando las siguientes, las cuales serán pagadas por el Arrendador: _____

_____

☐ El medidor de gas o eléctrico de los Inquilinos sirve el/las área(s) fuera de la propiedad y no existen medidores separados para la unidad del Inquilino y el/las área(s) fuera de su unidad. Los Inquilinos y el Arrendador acuerdan lo siguiente:

_____

_____

10. **Prohibición de Traspasar el Arrendamiento o Subarrendar la Propiedad.** Los Inquilinos no sub-arrendarán cualquier parte de la propiedad o traspasar este contrato, sin previo consentimiento por escrito del Arrendador.

11. **Responsabilidad de los Inquilinos de Mantenimiento de la Propiedad.** Los Inquilinos aceptan: (1) mantener la propiedad limpia e higiénica, en buena condición, y cuando se termine el arrendamiento, regresar la propiedad al Arrendador en una idéntica condición a la que existía cuando la ocuparon, excepto por el deterioro causado por el uso ordinario; (2) notificar inmediatamente al Arrendador de cualquier defecto o condición peligrosa que note en o alrededor de la propiedad; y (3) reembolsar al Arrendador, bajo demanda de éste, por el costo de cualquier reparación de daños a la propiedad, incluyendo la propiedad personal del Arrendador, ocasionados por uso indebido o negligencia de los Inquilinos o sus invitados.

Los Inquilinos dan por entendido que han examinado la propiedad, incluyendo los aparatos electro-domésticos, accesorios, alfombras, cortinas y pintura, y que los han encontrado en condiciones buenas, seguras, y limpias, excepto lo siguiente:

_____

_____

_____

_____

12. Posesión de la Propiedad. Si después de haber firmado este Contrato, los Inquilinos no toman posesión de la propiedad, ellos aún serán responsables por el pago de renta y el cumplimiento de todos los términos de este Contrato. En caso de que el Arrendador no pueda entregar la posesión de la propiedad a los Inquilinos por cualquier razón fuera de su control, incluyendo, pero no limitado a, la falta de desocupar por los ocupantes anteriores o destrucción parcial o completa de la propiedad, los Inquilinos tendrán el derecho de terminar este Contrato. En tal situación, la responsabilidad del Arrendador hacia los Inquilinos, se limitará a la devolución de las cantidades previamente pagadas por ellos a él.

13. Mascotas. Ningún animal, pájaro u otra mascota deberá ser mantenida en la propiedad, sin previa autorización escrita del Arrendador, excepto por perros debidamente entrenados para auxiliar a ciegos, sordos o personas con incapacidades y:

☐ a. Ninguno.

☐ b. _____, de acuerdo con las condiciones siguientes: _____

14. Acceso del Arrendador para Inspección y Emergencia. El Arrendador o sus agentes pueden entrar a la propiedad, en caso de una emergencia, para hacer reparaciones o mejoras, proveer los servicios acordados, para mostrar la propiedad a Inquilinos o compradores en perspectiva, o suministrar una inspección preliminar de desocupación pedida por los Inquilinos. Excepto en casos de emergencia, el abandono de la propiedad por los Inquilinos, o una orden de la corte, el Arrendador notificará razonablemente a los Inquilinos de su intención de entrar y entrará unicamente durante horas laborales, de lunes a viernes de 9:00 a.m. a 6:00 p.m. y los sábados de 10:00 a.m. a 1:00 p.m. La notificación incluirá el motivo, la fecha, y la hora aproximada de la entrada a la propiedad.

15. Ausencias Prolongadas de los Inquilinos. Los Inquilinos acuerdan notificar al Arrendador, en caso de que se ausenten de la propiedad por _____ días consecutivos o más. Durante esta ausencia, el Arrendador puede entrar a la propiedad en horas razonablemente necesarias para inspeccionarla, para mantenimiento, o para reparaciones necesarias.

16. Prohibiciones Contra Violaciones de la Ley y Causas de Disturbios. Los Inquilinos tienen derecho al goce pacífico de la propiedad. Los Inquilinos y sus invitados no usarán la propiedad o áreas aledañas, de manera que: (1) viole cualquier ley o reglamento, incluyendo leyes que prohiben el uso, posesión o venta ilegal de drogas; (2) permite el uso abusivo de la propiedad; o (3) cree un estorbo al molestar, provocar disturbios, inconvenientes o interferir con el disfrute de paz y tranquilidad de cualquier otro Inquilino o residente vecino.

17. Reparaciones y Alteraciones

a. Los Inquilinos, sin el previo consentimiento por escrito del Arrendador, no podrán alterar, instalar o modificar las cerraduras al local, ni instalar o modificar sistema de alarma contra robos. Los Inquilinos proporcionarán al Arrendador las llaves de las cerraduras nuevas o modificadas; así como las instrucciones de cómo desactivar cualquier sistema de alarma contra robos nuevo o modificado.

b. Excepto aquello que sea estipulado por la ley o autorizado por el previo consentimiento escrito del Arrendador, los Inquilinos no harán ninguna reparación ni alteración a la propiedad. El Arrendador no rehusará arbitrariamente el consentimiento a las reparaciones, pero no autorizará reparaciones que requieren destreza o mano de obra sofisticada o que sería peligroso ejecutar. El Arrendador no autorizará reparaciones a no ser que las reparaciones a realizar tengan la probabilidad de devolver el artículo o el elemento de la propiedad a su estado de utilidad y apariencia que tenía antes de que occurriera el daño.

18. Daños a la Propiedad. En caso de que la propiedad sea parcial o totalmente dañada o destruida por fuego u otra causa, se aplicará lo siguiente:

a. Si la propiedad es totalmente dañada y destruida, el Arrendador tendrá la opción de: (1) reparar tal daño y restaurar la propiedad, con este Contrato continuando en completa fuerza y efecto, a no ser que la renta sea disminuida mientras las reparaciones sean hechas; o (2) comunicar por escrito a los Inquilinos, de la terminación de este Contrato dentro de treinta (30) días después de tal daño, y especificando la fecha de terminación; en caso que el Arrendador comunique ésto, este contrato expirará y terminarán todos los derechos de los Inquilinos de acuerdo con este Contrato.

b. El Arrendador tendrá la opción de determinar que la propiedad está parcialmente dañada por fuego u otra causa. En tal caso, el Arrendador intentará reparar tales daños y restaurar la propiedad dentro de treinta (30) días después de tal daño. Si sólo parte de la propiedad no puede usarse, los Inquilinos deben pagar la renta solo por la parte en uso, el cual será determinado sólo por el Arrendador. Si el Arrendador no puede completar las reparaciones dentro de treinta (30) días, este Contrato expirará y todos los derechos de los Inquilinos, de acuerdo con este Contrato, serán terminados a la opción de cualesquiera de las partes.

c. En caso de que los Inquilinos o sus invitados causen o contribuyan de alguna manera al daño de la propiedad, el Arrendador tendrá derecho a terminar este Contrato en cualquier momento, y los Inquilinos serán responsables por todas las pérdidas, incluyendo, pero no limitado a, los daños y costos de reparación; así como la pérdida del ingreso de renta.

d. El Arrendador no será obligado a reparar o reemplazar cualquier posesión traída a la propiedad por los Inquilinos.

19. Responsabilidad Financiera y Seguro de los Inquilinos. Estos acuerdan aceptar la responsabilidad financiera por cualquier pérdida o daño a sus posesiones personales y sus invitados, por causa de robo, incendio, o cualquier otra causa. El Arrendador no asume ninguna responsabilidad por tales pérdidas. El Arrendador recomienda que los Inquilinos obtengan una póliza de seguro de una firma de seguros reconocida para que cubra la responsabilidad personal, daños a las posesiones, y a la propiedad.

20. Camas de Agua. En la propiedad no se permite mantener camas de agua o cualquier otro mueble lleno con agua, sin el previo consentimiento por escrito del Arrendador.

☐ El Arrendador concede permiso a los Inquilinos para que mantengan en la propiedad muebles llenos con agua. Adjunto _____: Para referencia, el acuerdo relacionado con el uso de camas de agua está adjuntado e incorporado en este contrato.

21. Reglas y Regulaciones de los Inquilinos

☐ Los Inquilinos reconocen que han recibido y leído una copia de las Reglas y Regulaciones de los Inquilinos, las cuales están marcadas como Adjunto _____ y como referencia están incorporadas en este Contrato. El Arrendador puede cambiar las reglas y las regulaciones sin notificación.

22. Pago de Honorarios de Abogados en un Juicio. En cualquier acción o procedimiento legal para hacer cumplir cualquier parte de este Contrato, la parte que gane el juicio ☐ no deberá/ ☐ deberá recuperar los honorarios y costos del abogado y de la corte.

23. Personal Autorizado para Recibir Documentos Legales. Cualquier persona que esté administrando la propiedad, el Arrendador, o a quien éste designe, está autorizado para aceptar servicio de proceso y recibir otras noticias y demandas, las cuales pueden ser entregadas a:

a. El administrador, a la dirección siguiente: _____

_____

_____

b. El Arrendador, a la dirección siguiente:_____

_____

_____

c. Al siguiente:_____

_____

_____

24. Dispocisiones Adicionales

☐ a. Ninguna

☐ b. Las disposiciones adicionales son:

_____

_____

25. Revelacion de Informacion de Datos del Estado. Aviso: El Departamento de Justicia de California, los departamentos del alguacil, de policía al servicio de jurisdicciones con 200,000 o más habitantes, y muchas otras autoridades locales encargadas del cumplimiento de la ley, mantienen para acceso del público una información de datos sobre la ubicación de personas quienes es necesario que se registren de acuerdo con el párrafo (1) de la subdivisión (a) Sección 290.4 del Código Penal. Esta información es actualizada cada tres meses y es una fuente de información sobre la presencia de estos individuos en cualquier vecindario. El Departamento de Justicia también mantiene una Línea de Identificación para los delincuentes por delitos sexuales, por medio de la cual se puede averiguar sobre estos individuos. Este es un servicio de teléfono con los dígitos "900." Los que llamen deben tener información específica sobre los individuos que deseen preguntar. La información con relación a los vecindarios no está disponible a travez de este servicio teléfonico. (Sección 2079.10a del Código Civil.)

26. Razones para Cancelar el Contrato de Arrendamiento. El incumplimiento de cualesquiera de los términos de este Contrato, por parte del Inquilino o sus invitados o la relación Falsa de un hecho esencial en la solicitud del Inquilino, será razón para dar por cancelado el Contrato de arrendamiento, seguido con la debida notificación al Inquilino, de acuerdo con lo requerido por la ley.

27. Contrato Completo. Este documento constituye el Contrato total entre las partes, y el Arrendador y los Inquilinos no han hecho ninguna otra promesa o representación, a no ser por las contenidas aquí, y por las que la ley implique. Cualquier modificación a este Contrato debe ser por escrito y firmada por el Arrendador y los Inquilinos.

_____   _____
Arrendador/Administrador   Fecha

_____
Dirección, ciudad, estado y código postal del Arrendador/Administrador

_____

_____   _____
Inquilino   Fecha

_____   _____
Inquilino   Fecha

_____   _____
Inquilino   Fecha

Fixed-Term Residential Lease

1. Identification of Landlord and Tenants. This Agreement is made and entered into on _____, 20__, between _____ ("Tenants") and _____ ("Landlord"). Each Tenant is jointly and severally liable for the payment of rent and performance of all other terms of this Agreement.

2. Identification of Premises and Occupants. Subject to the terms and conditions set forth in this Agreement, Landlord rents to Tenants, and Tenants rent from Landlord, for residential purposes only, the premises located at _____, California ("the premises"). The premises will be occupied by the undersigned Tenants and the following minor children: _____.

3. Limits on Use and Occupancy. The premises are to be used only as a private residence for Tenants and any minors listed in Clause 2 of this Agreement, and for no other purpose without Landlord's prior written consent. Occupancy by guests for more than ten days in any six-month period is prohibited without Landlord's written consent and will be considered a breach of this Agreement.

4. Defining the Term of the Tenancy. The term of the rental will begin on _____, 20__ and will expire on _____, 20__. Should Tenants vacate before expiration of the term, Tenants will be liable for the balance of the rent for the remainder of the term, less any rent Landlord collects or could have collected from a replacement tenant by reasonably attempting to rerent. Tenants who vacate before expiration of the term are also responsible for Landlord's costs of advertising for a replacement tenant.

5. Amount and Schedule for the Payment of Rent. Tenants will pay to Landlord a monthly rent of $ _____, payable in advance on the _____ day of each month, except when that day falls on a weekend or legal holiday, in which case rent is due on the next business day. Rent will be paid to _____ at _____, or at such other place as Landlord may designate.

   a.   The form of payment will be ❑ cash ❑ personal check ❑ certified funds or money order ❑ credit card ❑ automatic credit card debit ❑ bank debit

   ❑   b. [Check if rent will be accepted personally, not by mail.] Rent is accepted during the following days and hours: _____

   ❑   c. [Check if rent will be paid by electronic funds transfer.] Rent may be paid by electronic funds transfer to account number _____ in the name of _____

       Account Number   Account Holder

   at _____, _____ branch, a financial institution located at

       Institution   Branch

   _____, telephone (___) ___ - _____ .

   Bank Address   Telephone

   ❑   d. On signing this agreement, Tenants will pay to Landlord for the period of _____, 20__, through _____, 20__, the sum of $ _____ as rent, payable in advance as specified.

6. Late Charges. Tenants will pay Landlord a late charge if Tenants fail to pay the rent in full within _____ days after the date it is due. The late charge will be $ _____, plus $ _____ for each additional day that the rent continues to be unpaid. The total late charge for any one month will not exceed $ _____. Landlord does not waive the right to insist on payment of the rent in full on the date it is due.

7. **Returned Check and Other Bank Charges.** In the event any check offered by Tenants to Landlord in payment of rent or any other amount due under this Agreement is returned for lack of sufficient funds, a "stop payment" or any other reason, Tenants will pay Landlord a returned check charge in the amount of $_____.

8. **Amount and Payment of Deposits.** On signing this Agreement, Tenants will pay to Landlord the sum of $_____ as a security deposit. Tenants may not, without Landlord's prior written consent, apply this security deposit to the last month's rent or to any other sum due under this Agreement. Within three weeks after Tenants have vacated the premises, Landlord will furnish Tenants with an itemized written statement of the reasons for, and the dollar amount of, any of the security deposit retained by the Landlord, receipts for work done or items purchased, if available, along with a check for any deposit balance. Under Section 1950.5 of the California Civil Code, Landlord may withhold only that portion of Tenants' security deposit necessary to: (1) remedy any default by Tenants in the payment of rent; (2) repair damages to the premises exclusive of ordinary wear and tear; (3) clean the premises if necessary to restore it to the same level of cleanliness it was in at the beginning of the tenancy; and (4) remedy any default by tenants, under this agreement, to restore, replace, or return any of Landlord's personal property mentioned in this agreement, including but not limited to the property referred to in Clause 11.

   Landlord will pay Tenants interest on all security deposits as follows:

   ☐ a. Per state law, no interest payments are required.

   ☐ b. Local law requires that interest be paid or credited, or landlord has decided voluntarily to do so, which will occur as follows:

   _____

   _____

9. **Utilities.** Tenants will be responsible for payment of all utility charges, except for the following, which will be paid by Landlord:

   _____

   _____

   ☐ Tenants' gas or electric meter serves area(s) outside of their premises, and there are not separate gas and electric meters for Tenants' unit and the area(s) outside their unit. Tenants and Landlord agree as follows:

   _____

   _____

10. **Prohibition of Assignment and Subletting.** Tenants will not sublet any part of the premises or assign this Agreement without the prior written consent of Landlord.

11. **Condition of the Premises.** Tenants agree to: (1) keep the premises clean and sanitary and in good repair and, upon termination of the tenancy, to return the premises to Landlord in a condition identical to that which existed when Tenants took occupancy, except for ordinary wear and tear; (2) immediately notify Landlord of any defects or dangerous conditions in and about the premises of which they become aware; and (3) reimburse Landlord, on demand by Landlord, for the cost of any repairs to the premises, including Landlord's personal property therein, damaged by Tenants or their guests or invitees through misuse or neglect.

   Tenants acknowledge that they have examined the premises, including appliances, fixtures, carpets, drapes and paint, and have found them to be in good, safe, and clean condition and repair, except as noted here:

   _____

   _____

12. **Possession of the Premises.** If, after signing this Agreement, Tenants fail to take possession of the premises, they will still be responsible for paying rent and complying with all other terms of this Agreement. In the event Landlord is unable to deliver possession of the premises to Tenants for any reason not within Landlord's control, including, but not limited to, failure of prior occupants to vacate or partial or complete destruction of the premises, Tenants will have the right to terminate this Agreement. In such event, Landlord's liability to Tenants will be limited to the return of all sums previously paid by Tenants to Landlord.

13. Pets. No animal, bird, or other pet shall be kept on the premises without Landlord's prior written consent, except properly trained dogs needed by blind, deaf, or disabled persons and:

☐ a. None.

☐ b. _____, under the following conditions:

_____

14. Landlord's Access for Inspection and Emergency. Landlord or Landlord's agents may enter the premises in the event of an emergency or to make repairs or improvements, supply agreed services, show the premises to prospective buyers or tenants, and conduct an initial move-out inspection requested by tenants. Except in cases of emergency, Tenants' abandonment of the premises, or court order, Landlord will give Tenants reasonable notice of intent to enter and will enter only during regular business hours of Monday through Friday from 9:00 a.m. to 6:00 p.m. and Saturday from 10:00 a.m. to 1:00 p.m. The notice will include the purpose, date, and approximate time of entry.

15. Extended Absences by Tenants. Tenants agree to notify Landlord in the event that they will be away from the premises for _____ consecutive days or more. During such absence, Landlord may enter the premises at times reasonably necessary to maintain the property and inspect for damage and needed repairs.

16. Prohibitions Against Violating Laws and Causing Disturbances. Tenants are entitled to quiet enjoyment of the premises. Tenants and their guests or invitees will not use the premises or adjacent areas in such a way as to: (1) violate any law or ordinance, including laws prohibiting the use, possession, or sale of illegal drugs; (2) commit waste or nuisance; or (3) annoy, disturb, inconvenience, or interfere with the quiet enjoyment and peace and quiet of any other tenant or nearby resident.

17. Repairs and Alterations

a.   Tenants will not, without Landlord's prior written consent, alter, rekey, or install any locks to the premises or install or alter any burglar alarm system. Tenants will provide Landlord with a key or keys capable of unlocking all such rekeyed or new locks as well as instructions on how to disarm any altered or new burglar alarm system.

b.   Except as provided by law or as authorized by the prior written consent of Landlord, Tenants will not make any repairs or alterations to the premises. Landlord will not unreasonably withhold consent for such repairs, but will not authorize repairs that require advanced skill or workmanship or that would be dangerous to undertake. Landlord will not authorize repairs unless such repairs are likely to return the item or element of the rental to its predamaged state of usefulness and attractiveness.

18. Damage to the Premises. In the event the premises are partially or totally damaged or destroyed by fire or other cause, the following will apply:

a.   If the premises are totally damaged and destroyed, Landlord will have the option to: (1) repair such damage and restore the premises, with this Agreement continuing in full force and effect, except that Tenants' rent will be abated while repairs are being made; or (2) give written notice to Tenants terminating this Agreement at any time within thirty (30) days after such damage, and specifying the termination date; in the event that Landlord gives such notice, this Agreement will expire and all of Tenants' rights pursuant to this Agreement will cease.

b.   Landlord will have the option to determine that the premises are only partially damaged by fire or other cause. In that event, Landlord will attempt to repair such damage and restore the premises within thirty (30) days after such damage. If only part of the premises cannot be used, Tenants must pay rent only for the usable part, to be determined solely by Landlord. If Landlord is unable to complete repairs within thirty (30) days, this Agreement will expire and all of Tenants' rights pursuant to this Agreement will terminate at the option of either party.

c.   In the event that Tenants, or their guests or invitees, in any way caused or contributed to the damage of the premises, Landlord will have the right to terminate this Agreement at any time, and Tenants will be responsible for all losses, including, but not limited to, damage and repair costs as well as loss of rental income.

d.   Landlord will not be required to repair or replace any property brought onto the premises by Tenants.

19. Tenants' Financial Responsibility and Renters' Insurance. Tenants agree to accept financial responsibility for any loss or damage to personal property belonging to Tenants and their guests and invitees caused by theft, fire, or any other cause. Landlord assumes no liability for any such loss. Landlord recommends that Tenants obtain a renters' insurance policy from a recognized insurance firm to cover Tenants' liability, personal property damage, and damage to the premises.

20. Waterbeds. No waterbed or other item of water-filled furniture may be kept on the premises without Landlord's written consent.

    ☐ Landlord grants Tenants permission to keep water-filled furniture on the premises. Attachment _____: Agreement Regarding Use of Waterbed is attached to and incorporated into this Agreement by reference.

21. Tenant Rules and Regulations

    ☐ Tenants acknowledge receipt of, and have read a copy of, tenant rules and regulations, which are labeled Attachment _____ and attached to and incorporated into this Agreement by reference. Landlord may change the rules and regulations without notice.

22. Payment of Attorney Fees in a Lawsuit. In any action or legal proceeding to enforce any part of this Agreement, the prevailing party ☐ will not/ ☐ will recover reasonable attorney fees and court costs.

23. Authority to Receive Legal Papers. Any person managing the premises, the Landlord, and anyone designated by the Landlord are authorized to accept service of process and receive other notices and demands, which may be delivered to:

    ☐ a. the manager, at the following address and telephone number: _____

    _____

    _____

    ☐ b. the Landlord, at the following address and telephone number: _____

    _____

    _____

    ☐ c. the following:

    _____

    _____

    _____

24. Additional Provisions

    ☐ a. None

    ☐ b. Additional provisions are as follows:

    _____

    _____

25. State Database Disclosure. Notice: The California Department of Justice, sheriff's departments, police departments serving jurisdictions of 200,000 or more, and many other local law enforcement authorities maintain for public access a database of the locations of persons required to register pursuant to paragraph (1) of subdivision (a) of Section 290.4 of the Penal Code. The database is updated on a quarterly basis and is a source of information about the presence of these individuals in any neighborhood. The Department of Justice also maintains a Sex Offender Identification Line through which inquiries about individuals may be made. This is a "900" telephone service. Callers must have specific information about individuals they are checking. Information regarding neighborhoods is not available through the "900" telephone service. (Civil Code § 2079.10a.)

26. Grounds for Termination of Tenancy. The failure of Tenants or Tenants' guests or invitees to comply with any term of this Agreement, or the misrepresentation of any material fact on Tenants' Rental Application, is grounds for termination of the tenancy, with appropriate notice to Tenants and procedures as required by law.

27. Entire Agreement. This document constitutes the entire Agreement between the parties, and no promises or representations, other than those contained here and those implied by law have been made by Landlord or Tenants. Any modifications to this Agreement must be in writing signed by Landlord and Tenants.

_____   _____
Landlord/Manager   Date

_____
Landlord/Manager's Street Address, City, State & Zip

_____

_____   _____
Tenant   Date

_____   _____
Tenant   Date

_____   _____
Tenant   Date

Contrato Residencial A Plazo Fijo

1. **Identificación del Arrendador y de los Inquilinos.** Este Contrato es preparado y efectivo a partir del _____ de _____ de 20___, entre _____ ("Inquilinos") y _____ ("Arrendador"). Cada Inquilino es conjunta y seriamente responsable por el pago de la renta y del cumplimiento de todos los demás términos de este Contrato.

2. **Identificación de la Propiedad y los Ocupantes.** De acuerdo con los términos y condiciones referidas en este Contrato, el Arrendador renta a los Inquilinos, y éstos rentan del Arrendador, solamente para residir, la propiedad ubicada en _____, California ("la propiedad"). La propiedad será ocupada por los Inquilinos suscritos y los niños menores siguientes: _____

3. **Limitaciones en el Uso y Ocupación.** La propiedad deberá ser usada sólo como residencia privada por los Inquilinos y cualquier niño menor mencionado en la Cláusula 2 de este Contrato, y para ningún otro propósito, sin el previo consentimiento por escrito del Arrendador. Está prohibido que los invitados ocupen la propiedad por más de diez días, en cualquier período de seis meses, sin el previo consentimiento escrito del Arrendador; de lo contrario, será considerada como una violación de este Contrato.

4. **Período de Arrendamiento.** El arrendamiento comenzará el _____ de _____ de 20___, y terminará el _____ de _____ de 20___. Si los Inquilinos desocupan antes de esta fecha, se harán responsables por el pago de tiempo restante de arrendamiento estipulado en este Contrato. De esta suma se restará cualquier renta que reciba el Arrendador de nuevos inquilinos durante el período de este Contrato, o cualquier suma que el Arrendador hubiera podido recibir al hacer un esfuerzo razonable de buscar nuevo inquilino. Los Inquilinos que desocupen antes de la fecha de expiración también serán responsables por los gastos que incurra el Arrendador, en la búsqueda de nuevos inquilinos.

5. **Renta y Fechas de Pago.** Los Inquilinos pagarán al Arrendador una renta mensual de $_____, pagadera por adelantado el _____ día de cada mes, excepto cuando ese día sea en un fin de semana o en un día feriado oficial, en cuyo caso la renta deberá ser pagada el próximo día laboral. La renta se paqará a _____ en _____ o en otro lugar designado por el Arrendatario.

   a. La forma de pago será ❑ efectivo ❑ cheque personal ❑ fondos certificados o giro postal ❑ tarjeta de crédito ❑ débito automático de tarjeta de crédito ❑ débito de banco

   ❑ b. [Marque si el arriendo será aceptado personalmente, no por correo.] El arriendo se aceptará durante los siguientes días y horas: _____.

   ❑ c. [Marque si el arriendo será pagado con dinero transferible electrónicamente.] El arriendo se podrá pagar con dinero transferible electrónicamente a la cuenta número _____ a
   Número de cuenta
   nombre de _____ en _____, sucursal
   Nombre de la cuenta   Nombre de la institución bancaria
   _____, una institución bancaria localizada en _____,
   Nombre de la sucursal   Dirección
   teléfono (___) -_____ .
   Número telefónico

   ❑ d. Al firmar este contrato, los Inquilinos pagarán por adelantado al Arrendador, según lo estipulado, por el período de _____ de _____ de 20___, hasta el _____ de _____ de 20___, la suma de $_____ como renta.

6. **Cobros por Mora.** Los Inquilinos pagarán cargos adicionales al Arrendador, si ellos no pagan la renta total dentro de _____ días después de la fecha debida. La cantidad será $_____, más $_____ por cada día adicional que pase sin pagarse la renta. El cobro total por atraso en cualquier mes no excederá la suma

$_____. El Arrendador no descartará el derecho de insistir en el pago total de la renta en la fecha debida.

7. **Pagos por Cheques sin Fondo y Recargos Bancarios.** En el caso de cualquier cheque, ofrecido por los Inquilinos al Arrendador como pago de renta o cualquier otra suma debida bajo este Contrato, sea regresado por insuficiencia de fondos, o una orden de no hacer efectivo el pago o cualquier otra razón, los Inquilinos pagarán al Arrendador un recargo por la cantidad de $_____.

8. **Depósito de Garantía.** Al firmar este Contrato, los Inquilinos pagarán al Arrendador la cantidad de $_____ como depósito de garantía. Este depósito no puede aplicarse al último mes de renta o a cualquier cantidad debida bajo este Contrato, excepto con el previo consentimiento por escrito del Arrendador. Dentro de tres semanas después de que los Inquilinos hayan desocupado la propiedad, el Arrendador proporcionará por escrito a los Inquilinos un detalle de las razones por retener el depósito y la cantidad que es retenida por él, más recibos disponibles por mano de obra o materiales comprados, junto con un cheque por la cantidad de diferencia. Bajo la Sección 1950.5 del Código Civil de California, el Arrendador puede retener sólo la porción del depósito de seguridad de los Inquilinos que sea necesaria para: (1) remediar cualquier omisión de pago de renta de los Inquilinos; (2) reparar daños a la propiedad exceptuando el deterioro por uso ordinario; (3) limpiar la propiedad, si es necesario, para restaurarla al mismo nivel de limpieza que tenía al comienzo del arrendamiento; y (4) remediar cualquier incumplimiento por los Inquilinos, bajo éste contrato, de restaurar, reemplazar, o devolver cualquier propiedad personal del Arrendador mencionado en éste contrato, incluyendo pero no limitado a la propiedad referida en la Cláusula 11.

El Arrendador pagará a los Inquilinos, intereses por todos los depósitos de garantía de la manera siguiente:

☐ a. La ley estatal de California no require el pago de interés.

☐ b. La ley local requiere que el interés sea pagado o acreditado, o el Arrendador ha decidido hacerlo voluntariamente, lo cual ocurrirá de la siguiente manera:

_____

_____

9. **Servicios Públicos.** Los Inquilinos serán responsables por el pago de todos los sevicios públicos, exceptuando las siguientes, las cuales serán pagadas por el Arrendador: _____

_____

☐ El medidor de gas o eléctrico de los Inquilinos sirve el/las área(s) fuera de la propiedad y no existen medidores separados para la unidad del Inquilino y el/las área(s) fuera de su unidad. Los Inquilinos y el Arrendador acuerdan lo siguiente:

_____

_____

10. **Prohibición de Traspasar el Arrendamiento o Subarrendar la Propiedad.** Los Inquilinos no sub-arrendarán cualquier parte de la propiedad o traspasar este contrato, sin previo consentimiento por escrito del Arrendador.

11. **Responsabilidad de los Inquilinos de Mantenimiento de la Propiedad.** Los Inquilinos aceptan: (1) mantener la propiedad limpia e higiénica, en buena condición, y cuando se termine el arrendamiento, regresar la propiedad al Arrendador en una idéntica condición a la que existía cuando la ocuparon, excepto por el deterioro causado por el uso ordinario; (2) notificar inmediatamente al Arrendador de cualquier defecto o condición peligrosa que note en o alrededor de la propiedad; y (3) reembolsar al Arrendador, bajo demanda de éste, por el costo de cualquier reparación de daños a la propiedad, incluyendo la propiedad personal del Arrendador, ocasionados por uso indebido o negligencia de los Inquilinos o sus invitados.

Los Inquilinos dan por entendido que han examinado la propiedad, incluyendo los aparatos electro-domésticos, accesorios, alfombras, cortinas y pintura, y que los han encontrado en condiciones buenas, seguras, y limpias, excepto lo siguiente:

_____

_____

_____

_____

12. Posesión de la propiedad. Si despúes de haber firmado este Contrato, los Inquilinos no toman posesión de la propiedad, ellos aún serán responsables por el pago de renta y el cumplimiento de todos los términos de este Contrato. En caso de que el Arrendador no pueda entregar la posesión de la propiedad a los Inquilinos por cualquier razón fuera de su control, incluyendo, pero no limitado a, la falta de desocupar por los ocupantes anteriores o destrucción parcial o completa de la propiedad, los Inquilinos tendrán el derecho de terminar este Contrato. En tal situación, la responsabilidad del Arrendador hacia los Inquilinos, se limitará a la devolución de las cantidades previamente pagadas por ellos a él.

13. Mascotas. Ningún animal, pájaro u otra mascota deberá ser mantenida en la propiedad, sin previa autorización escrita del Arrendador, excepto por perros debidamente entrenados para auxiliar a ciegos, sordos o personas con incapacidades y:

☐ a. Ninguno.

☐ b. _____, de acuerdo con las condiciones

    siguientes: _____

14. Acceso del Arrendador para Inspección y Emergencia. El Arrendador o sus agentes pueden entrar a la propiedad, en caso de una emergencia, para hacer reparaciones o mejoras, proveer los servicios acordados, para mostrar la propiedad a Inquilinos o compradores en perspectiva, o suministrar una inspección preliminaria de desocupación pedida por los Inquilinos. Excepto en casos de emergencia, el abandono de la propiedad por los Inquilinos, o una orden de la corte, el Arrendador notificará razonablemente a los Inquilinos de su intención de entrar y entrará unicamente durante horas laborales, de lunes a viernes de 9:00 a.m. a 6:00 p.m. y los sábados de 10:00 a.m. a 1:00 p.m. La notificación incluirá el motivo, la fecha, y la hora aproximada de la entrada a la propiedad.

15. Ausencias Prolongadas de los Inquilinos. Los Inquilinos acuerdan notificar al Arrendador, en caso de que se ausenten de la propiedad por _____ días consecutivos o más. Durante esta ausencia, el Arrendador puede entrar a la propiedad en horas razonablemente necesarias para inspeccionarla, para mantenimiento, o para reparaciones necesarias.

16. Prohibiciones Contra Violaciones de la Ley y Causas de Disturbios. Los Inquilinos tienen derecho al goce pacífico de la propiedad. Los Inquilinos y sus invitados no usarán la propiedad o áreas aledañas, de manera que: (1) viole cualquier ley o reglamento, incluyendo leyes que prohiben el uso, posesión o venta ilegal de drogas; (2) permite el uso abusivo de la propiedad; o (3) cree un estorbo al molestar, provocar disturbios, inconvenientes o interferir con el disfrute de paz y tranquilidad de cualquier otro Inquilino o residente vecino.

17. Reparaciones y Alteraciones

    a. Los Inquilinos, sin el previo consentimiento por escrito del Arrendador, no podrán alterar, instalar o modificar las cerraduras al local, ni instalar o modificar sistema de alarma contra robos. Los Inquilinos proporcionarán al Arrendador las llaves de las cerraduras nuevas o modificadas; así como las instrucciones de cómo desactivar cualquier sistema de alarma contra robos nuevo o modificado.

    b. Excepto aquello que sea estipulado por la ley o autorizado por el previo consentimiento escrito del Arrendador, los Inquilinos no harán ninguna reparación ni alteración a la propiedad. El Arrendador no rehusará arbitrariamente el consentimiento a las reparaciones, pero no autorizará reparaciones que requieren destreza o mano de obra sofisticada o que sería peligroso ejecutar. El Arrendador no autorizará reparaciones a no ser que las reparaciones a realizar tengan la probabilidad de devolver el artículo o el elemento de la propiedad a su estado de utilidad y apariencia que tenía antes de que ocurriera el daño.

18. Daños a la Propiedad. En caso de que la propiedad sea parcial o totalmente dañada o destruida por fuego u otra causa, se aplicará lo siguiente:

    a. Si la propiedad es totalmente dañada y destruida, el Arrendador tendrá la opción de: (1) reparar tal daño y restaurar la propiedad, con este Contrato continuando en completa fuerza y efecto, a no ser que la renta sea disminuida mientras las reparaciones sean hechas; o (2) comunicar por escrito a los Inquilinos, de la terminación de este Contrato dentro de treinta (30) días después de tal daño, y especificando la fecha de terminación; en caso que el Arrendador comunique ésto, este contrato expirará y terminarán todos los derechos de los Inquilinos de acuerdo con este Contrato.

b. El Arrendador tendrá la opción de determinar que la propiedad está parcialmente dañada por fuego u otra causa. En tal caso, el Arrendador intentará reparar tales daños y restaurar la propiedad dentro de treinta (30) días después de tal daño. Si sólo parte de la propiedad no puede usarse, los Inquilinos deben pagar la renta solo por la parte en uso, el cual será determinado sólo por el Arrendador. Si el Arrendador no puede completar las reparaciones dentro de treinta (30) días, este Contrato expirará y todos los derechos de los Inquilinos, de acuerdo con este Contrato, serán terminados a la opción de cualesquiera de las partes.

c. En caso de que los Inquilinos o sus invitados causen o contribuyan de alguna manera al daño de la propiedad, el Arrendador tendrá derecho a terminar este Contrato en cualquier momento, y los Inquilinos serán responsables por todas las pérdidas, incluyendo, pero no limitado a, los daños y costos de reparación; así como la pérdida del ingreso de renta.

d. El Arrendador no será obligado a reparar o reemplazar cualquier posesión traída a la propiedad por los Inquilinos.

19. Responsabilidad Financiera y Seguro de los Inquilinos. Estos acuerdan aceptar la responsabilidad financiera por cualquier pérdida o daño a sus posesiones personales y sus invitados, por causa de robo, incendio, o cualquier otra causa. El Arrendador no asume ninguna responsabilidad por tales pérdidas. El Arrendador recomienda que los Inquilinos obtengan una póliza de seguro de una firma de seguros reconocida para que cubra la responsabilidad personal, daños a las posesiones, y a la propiedad.

20. Camas de Agua. En la propiedad no se permite mantener camas de agua o cualquier otro mueble lleno con agua, sin el previo consentimiento por escrito del Arrendador.

☐ El Arrendador concede permiso a los Inquilinos para que mantengan en la propiedad muebles llenos con agua. Adjunto _____: Para referencia, el acuerdo relacionado con el uso de camas de agua está adjuntado e incorporado en este contrato.

21. Reglas y Regulaciones de los Inquilinos

☐ Los Inquilinos reconocen que han recibido y leído una copia de las Reglas y Regulaciones de los Inquilinos, las cuales están marcadas como Adjunto _____ y como referencia están incorporadas en este Contrato. El Arrendador puede cambiar las reglas y las regulaciones sin notificación.

22. Pago de Honorarios de Abogados en un Juicio. En cualquier acción o procedimiento legal para hacer cumplir cualquier parte de este Contrato, la parte que gane el juicio ☐ no deberá/ ☐ deberá recuperar los honorarios y costos del abogado y de la corte.

23. Personal Autorizado para Recibir Documentos Legales. Cualquier persona que esté administrando la propiedad, el Arrendador, o a quien éste designe, está autorizado para aceptar servicio de proceso y recibir otras noticias y demandas, las cuales pueden ser entregadas a:

a. El administrador, a la dirección y numero del telefono siguiente: _____

_____

b. El Arrendador, a la dirección y numero del telefono siguiente:_____

_____

c. Al siguiente:_____

_____

24. Disposiciones Adicionales

☐ a. Ninguna

☐ b. Las disposiciones adicionales son:

_____

_____

25. Revelación de Información de Datos del Estado. Aviso: El Departamento de Justicia de California, los departamentos del alguacil, de policía al servicio de jurisdicciones con 200,000 o más habitantes, y muchas otras autoridades locales encargadas del cumplimiento de la ley, mantienen para acceso del público una información de datos sobre la ubicación de personas quienes es necesario que se registren de acuerdo con el párrafo (1) de la subdivisión (a) Sección 290.4 del Código Penal. Esta información es actualizada cada tres meses y es una fuente de información sobre la presencia de estos individuos en cualquier vecindario. El

Departamento de Justicia también mantiene una Línea de Identificación para los delincuentes por delitos sexuales, por medio de la cual se puede averiguar sobre estos individuos. Este es un servicio de teléfono con los dígitos "900." Los que llamen deben tener información específica sobre los individuos que deseen preguntar. La información con relación a los vecindarios no está disponible a travez de este servicio teléfonico. (Sección 2079.10a del Código Civil.)

26. **Razones para Cancelar el Contrato de Arrendamiento.** El incumplimiento de cualesquiera de los términos de este Contrato, por parte del Inquilino o sus invitados o la relación Falsa de un hecho esencial en la solicitud del Inquilino, será razón para dar por cancelado el Contrato de arrendamiento, seguido con la debida notificación al Inquilino, de acuerdo con lo requerido por la ley.

27. **Contrato Completo.** Este documento constituye el Contrato total entre las partes, y el Arrendador y los Inquilinos no han hecho ninguna otra promesa o representación, a no ser por las contenidas aquí, y por las que la ley implique. Cualquier modificación a este Contrato debe ser por escrito y firmada por el Arrendador y los Inquilinos.

_____   _____
Arrendador/Administrador   Fecha

_____
Dirección, ciudad, estado y código postal del Arrendador/Administrador

_____

_____   _____
Inquilino   Fecha

_____   _____
Inquilino   Fecha

_____   _____
Inquilino   Fecha

Attachment _____ to Lease/Rental Agreement

This Attachment is made by _____, Landlord and_____,
_____, and _____, Tenant(s). It pertains to the
residential lease/rental agreement signed on _____ for the property at
_____. Landlord and Tenant(s) agree that
clauses specified below of the lease/rental agreement are:

☐ **Continued.** Clause _____ continues as follows:

_____

_____

_____

_____

_____

☐ **Modified.** Clause _____ is modified as follows:

_____

_____

_____

_____

_____

☐ **Augmented.** New Clause _____ is added as follows:

_____

_____

_____

_____

_____

_____, Landlord or Manager   _____ Date

_____, Tenant   _____ Date

_____, Tenant   _____ Date

_____, Tenant   _____ Date

Attachment: Agreement Regarding Use of Waterbed

Landlord and Tenants agree that Tenants may keep water-filled furniture in the premises located at _____
_____,
subject to the legal requirements of Civil Code Section 1940.5, key provisions of which are summarized as follows:

1. Insurance

Tenants agree to obtain a valid waterbed insurance policy or certificate of insurance for property damage, with a minimum replacement value of $100,000. Such insurance policy shall be furnished to Landlord prior to installation of the waterbed and shall be maintained in full force and effect until the waterbed is permanently removed from the premises.

2. Weight Limitation

The pressure the waterbed puts on the floor shall not exceed the floor's pounds per square foot weight limitation. The weight shall be distributed on a pedestal or frame which is approximately the same dimensions as the mattress itself.

3. Installation, Moving and Removal

Tenants shall install, maintain, and move the waterbed in accordance with the standards of the manufacturer, retailer, or state, whichever are most stringent.

4. Notice to and Inspection by Landlord

Tenants agree to give Landlord at least 24 hours' written notice of their intention to install, move, or remove the waterbed, and shall allow Landlord to be present when this occurs. If anyone other than Tenants installs or moves the waterbed, Tenants shall give Landlord a written installation receipt that states the installer's name and address and any business affiliation.

5. Waterbed Construction Standards

The waterbed shall conform to construction standards imposed by the State Bureau of Home Furnishings and shall display a label to that effect. The waterbed must have been constructed on or after January 1, 1973.

6. Security Deposit

Landlord may increase Tenants' security deposit in an amount equal to an additional one-half month's rent.

_____   _____
Landlord/Manager   Date

_____   _____
Tenant   Date

_____   _____
Tenant   Date

_____   _____
Tenant   Date

Amendment to Lease or Rental Agreement

This is an Amendment to the lease or rental agreement dated _____, 20____ (the "Agreement")

between _____ ("Landlord")

and _____ ("Tenants")

regarding property located at _____

_____ ("the premises").

Landlord and Tenants agree to the following changes and/or additions to the Agreement:

_____

_____

_____

_____

_____

_____

_____

_____

_____

_____

_____

_____

_____

_____

_____

_____

_____

_____

In all other respects, the terms of the Agreement shall remain in effect.

_____   _____
Landlord/Manager   Date

_____   _____
Tenant   Date

_____   _____
Tenant   Date

_____   _____
Tenant   Date

Notice of Reinstatement of Terms of Tenancy

To: _____,
    Name

Tenant(s) in possession of the premises at _____,
                                           Street Address

City of _____, County of _____, California.

When you rented the premises described above, the rental agreement specified that your rent would be due and payable on the first day of each month. Although the undersigned has allowed you to vary this payment arrangement, your late rental payments can no longer be tolerated.

Therefore, please be advised that effective 30 days from the date of service on you of this notice, your monthly rent will be due and payable on the first day of the month, for that month.

_____   _____

Landlord/Manager   Date

Agreement for Partial Rent Payments

This Agreement is made between _____,
hereinafter "Tenant(s)," and _____,
hereinafter "Landlord/Manager," who agree as follows:

1. That _____
   Tenant(s)

   has/have paid _____

   _____

   on _____ 20____, which was due _____ 20____.

2. That _____
   Landlord/Manager

   agrees to accept all the remainder of the rent on or before _____ 20____ and to hold off

   on any legal proceeding to evict _____
   Tenant(s)

   until that date.

_____   _____
Landlord/Manager   Date

_____   _____
Tenant   Date

_____   _____
Tenant   Date

_____   _____
Tenant   Date

Notice of Sale of Real Property and of Transfer of Security Deposit Balance

Civil Code Section 1950.5(h)(1)

To: _____ ,
Name

Tenant(s) in possession of the premises at _____ ,
Street Address

City of _____ , County of _____ , California.

The real property described above was sold on _____ , 20____

to _____ ,
Name of New Landlord

_____ ,
Street Address

whose telephone number is _____ .
Phone Number

Your security deposit, less any deductions shown below, has been transferred to the new landlord, who is now solely responsible to you for it.

Deposit Amount: $_____

Deductions:

    Unpaid Back Rent: $_____

    Other Deductions: $_____

    Total Deductions: $_____

Net Deposit Transferred to New Landlord: $_____

Explanation of Deductions:

_____

_____

_____

_____

_____ $_____

Please contact the new landlord, whose address and phone number are listed above, if you have any questions.

_____   _____
Landlord/Manager   Date

Residential Rental Property Manager Memorandum

1. Parties

This Agreement is between _____ ,
Landlord of residential real property at _____ ,
_____ , and
_____ ,
Manager of the property. Manager will be renting unit _____ of the property under a
separate written rental agreement that is in no way contingent upon or related to this agreement.

2. Beginning Date

Manager will begin work on _____ .

3. Responsibilities

Manager's duties are set forth below:

Renting Units

☐ answer phone inquiries about vacancies

☐ show vacant units

☐ accept rental applications

☐ select tenants

☐ accept initial rents and deposits

☐ other (specify) _____

☐ _____

Vacant Apartments

☐ inspect unit when tenant moves in

☐ inspect unit when tenant moves out

☐ clean unit after tenant moves out, including:

    ☐ floors, carpets, and rugs

    ☐ walls, baseboards, ceilings, lights, and built-in shelves

    ☐ kitchen cabinets, countertops, sinks, stove, oven, and refrigerator

    ☐ bathtubs, showers, toilets, and plumbing fixtures

    ☐ doors, windows, window coverings, and mini-blinds

    ☐ other (specify) _____

    ☐ _____

Rent Collection

☐ collect rents when due

☐ sign rent receipts

☐ maintain rent collection records

☐ collect late rents and charges

☐ inform Landlord of late rents

☐ prepare late rent notices

☐ serve late rent notices on tenants

☐ serve rent increase and tenancy termination notices

☐ deposit rent collections in bank

☐ other (specify) _____

☐ _____

Maintenance

☐ vacuum and clean hallways and entryways

☐ replace lightbulbs in common areas

☐ drain water heaters

☐ clean stairs, decks, patios, facade, and sidewalks

☐ clean garage oils on pavement

☐ mow lawns

☐ rake leaves

☐ trim bushes

☐ clean up garbage and debris on grounds

☐ other (specify) _____

☐ _____

Repairs

☐ accept tenant complaints and repair requests

☐ inform Landlord of maintenance and repair needs

☐ maintain written log of tenant complaints

☐ handle routine maintenance and repairs, including:

    ☐ plumbing stoppages

    ☐ garbage disposal stoppages/repairs

    ☐ faucet leaks/washer replacement

    ☐ toilet tank repairs

    ☐ toilet seat replacement

    ☐ stove burner repair/replacement

☐ stove hinges/knobs replacement

☐ dishwasher repair

☐ light switch and outlet repair/replacement

☐ heater thermostat repair

☐ window repair/replacement

☐ painting (interior)

☐ painting (exterior)

☐ replacement of keys

☐ other (specify)

☐ _____

Other Responsibilities

_____

_____

_____

_____

_____

4. Hours and Schedule

Manager will be available to tenants during the following days and times: _____

_____. If the hours required to carry out

any duties may reasonably be expected to exceed _____ hours in any week, Manager shall notify

Landlord and obtain Landlord's consent before working such extra hours, except in the event of an

emergency. Extra hours worked due to an emergency must be reported to Landlord within 24 hours.

5. Payment Terms

a. Manager will be paid:

☐ $ _____ per hour

☐ $ _____ per week

☐ $ _____ per month

☐ Other: _____

b. Manager will be paid on the specified intervals and dates:

☐ Once a week on every _____

☐ Twice a month on _____

☐ Once a month on _____

☐ Other: _____

6. Ending the Manager's Employment

Landlord may terminate Manager's employment at any time, for any reason that is not unlawful, with or without notice. Manager may quit at any time, for any reason, with or without notice.

7. Additional Agreements and Amendments

a. Owner and Manager additionally agree that: _____
_____
_____
_____
_____
_____
_____
_____
_____
_____
_____ .

b. All agreements between Owner and Manager relating to the work specified in this Agreement are incorporated in this Agreement. Any modification to the Agreement must be in writing and signed by both parties.

8. Place of Execution

Signed at _____ , _____
City   State

_____ _____
Date   Owner

_____ _____
Date   Manager

Landlord/Tenant Checklist
GENERAL CONDITION OF RENTAL UNIT AND PREMISES

Street Address _____ Unit Number _____ City _____

	Condition on Arrival	Condition on Initial Move-Out Inspection	Condition on Departure	Actual or Estimated Cost of Cleaning, Repair/Replacement
LIVING ROOM				
Floors & Floor Coverings				
Drapes & Window Coverings				
Walls & Ceilings				
Light Fixtures				
Windows, Screens & Doors				
Front Door & Locks				
Smoke Detector				
Fireplace				
Other				
KITCHEN				
Floors & Floor Coverings				
Walls & Ceilings				
Light Fixtures				
Cabinets				
Counters				
Stove/Oven				
Refrigerator				
Dishwasher				
Garbage Disposal				
Sink & Plumbing				
Smoke Detector				
Other				

	Condition on Arrival	Condition on Initial Move-Out Inspection	Condition on Departure	Actual or Estimated Cost of Cleaning, Repair/Replacement
DINING ROOM				
Floors & Floor Covering				
Walls & Ceilings				
Light Fixtures				
Windows, Screens & Doors				
Smoke Detector				
Other				
BATHROOM				
Floors & Floor Coverings				
Walls & Ceilings				
Windows, Screens & Doors				
Light Fixtures				
Bathtub/Shower				
Sink & Counters				
Toilet				
Other				
Other				
BEDROOM				
Floors & Floor Coverings				
Windows, Screens & Doors				
Walls & Ceilings				
Light Fixtures				
Smoke Detector				
Other				
Other				
Other				

OTHER AREAS	Condition on Arrival	Condition on Initial Move-Out Inspection	Condition on Departure	Actual or Estimated Cost of Cleaning, Repair/Replacement
Heating System				
Air Conditioning				
Lawn/Garden				
Stairs & Hallway				
Patio, Terrace, Deck, etc.				
Basement				
Parking Area				
Other				
Other				
Other				
Other				
Other				

☐ Tenants acknowledge that all smoke detectors and fire extinguishers were tested in their presence and found to be in working order, and that the testing procedure was explained to them. Tenants agree to test all detectors at least once a month and to report any problems to Landlord/Manager in writing. Tenants agree to replace all smoke detector batteries as necessary.

NOTES:

FURNISHED PROPERTY

	Condition on Arrival	Condition on Initial Move-Out Inspection	Condition on Departure	Actual or Estimatead Cost of Cleaning, Repair/Replacement
LIVING ROOM				
Coffee Table				
End Tables				
Lamps				
Chairs				
Sofa				
Other				
Other				
KITCHEN				
Broiler Pan				
Ice Trays				
Other				
Other				
DINING AREA				
Chairs				
Stools				
Table				
Other				
Other				
BATHROOM				
Mirrors				
Shower Curtain				
Hamper				
Other				

	Condition on Arrival	Condition on Initial Move-Out Inspection	Condition on Departure	Actual or Estimated Cost of Cleaning, Repair/Replacement
BEDROOM				
Beds (single)				
Beds (double)				
Chairs				
Chests				
Dressing Tables				
Lamps				
Mirrors				
Night Tables				
Other				
Other				
OTHER AREAS				
Bookcases				
Desks				
Pictures				
Other				
Other				

Use this space to provide any additional explanation:

Landlord/Tenant Checklist completed on moving in on _____ , 20___ .

_____ and

Landlord/Manager

_____

Tenant

_____

Tenant

_____

Tenant

Landlord/Tenant Checklist completed at Initial Move-Out Inspection on _____ , 20___ .

_____ and

Landlord/Manager

_____

Tenant

_____

Tenant

_____

Tenant

Landlord/Tenant Checklist completed on moving out on _____ , 20___ .

_____ and

Landlord/Manager

_____

Tenant

_____

Tenant

_____

Tenant

Key and Pass Receipt and Agreement

This acknowledgment of receipt and agreement is made between _____,
Landlord, and _____, and _____, Tenant(s).
Tenant(s) rented the premises at _____ by signing a
lease/rental agreement dated _____.

Landlord gives to Tenant(s), and Tenant(s) acknowledge receipt of, the following keys, passes, and other
equipment that will enable Tenant(s) to use and enjoy the rented premises:

☐ Key to rental unit front door lock (handle)

☐ Key to rental unit front door (dead-bolt lock)

☐ Key to apartment building front door

☐ Mailbox key

☐ Garage key/pass

☐ Laundry room key

☐ Pool gate key

☐ Master key for storage room

☐ Key for tenant's storage locker/closet

☐ Other keys/passes/equipment:

_____

_____

_____

Lockout charge. If Landlord needs to give Tenant(s) access to the rental property because Tenant(s) has lost
keys or passes, Tenant(s) will pay Landlord a lockout fee of $_____ when Landlord responds
Monday through Friday (non-holidays), between 9 a.m. and 5 p.m.; and $_____ when Landlord
responds at any other day or time.

Replacement fee. Tenant(s) acknowledge that if, during their tenancy, they lose or damage any item such
that it must be replaced, the landlord may charge a reasonable fee for such replacement, including an
amount that reflects the value of the landlord's time needed to make or buy the replacement.

Tenant(s) will not copy or share keys or passes. Tenant(s) agree not to copy or share any of the keys or
passes provided by Landlord.

At the end of the tenancy, tenant(s) will return all items noted here and agree that, with the exception of keys to the individual rental unit, the landlord may deduct from the security deposit a reasonable and actual amount necessary to replace any missing items.

_____
_____, Landlord or Manager   Date _____

_____
_____, Tenant   Date _____

_____
_____, Tenant   Date _____

_____
_____, Tenant   Date _____

Resident's Maintenance/Repair Request

Date: _____

Address: _____

Resident's Name: _____

Phone (home): _____ Phone (work): _____

Problem: _____

_____

_____

_____

_____

_____

Best time to make repairs: _____

_____

Comments : _____

_____

_____

_____

_____

I authorize entry into my unit to perform the maintenance or repair requested above, in my absence, unless stated otherwise above.

_____
Resident

· ·

FOR MANAGEMENT USE

Work done: _____

Time spent: _____ hours

Date completed: _____, 20_____

Unable to complete on _____, 20_____, because: _____

_____

Notes and comments: _____

_____   _____
Date   Landlord/Manager

Time Estimate for Repair

_____

Date _____

Tenant _____

Street address _____

City and State _____

Dear _____,
              Tenant

On _____, you notified us of the following problem in your rental unit:

_____

_____

_____

_____

_____

We have investigated the problem and have found:

_____

_____

_____

_____

_____

We expect to have the problem corrected on _____.

We regret any inconvenience this interval may cause. Please do not hesitate to point out any other problems that may arise.

Sincerely,

_____

Landlord/Manager

Semi-Annual Safety and Maintenance Update

Please complete the following checklist and note any safety or maintenance problems in your unit or on the premises.

Please describe the specific problems and the rooms or areas involved. Here are some examples of the types of things we want to know about: garage roof leaks, excessive mildew in rear bedroom closet, fuses blow out frequently, door lock sticks, water comes out too hot in shower, exhaust fan above stove doesn't work, smoke alarm malfunctions, peeling paint, and mice in basement. Please point out any potential safety and security problems in the neighborhood and anything you consider a serious nuisance.

Please indicate the approximate date when you first noticed the problem and list any other recommendations or suggestions for improvement.

Please return this form with this month's rent check. Thank you.—THE MANAGEMENT

Name: _____

Address: _____

_____

Please indicate (and explain below) problems with:

☐ Floors and floor coverings _____

☐ Walls and ceilings _____

☐ Windows, screens, and doors _____

☐ Window coverings (drapes, mini-blinds, etc.) _____

☐ Electrical system and light fixtures _____

☐ Plumbing (sinks, bathtub, shower, or toilet) _____

☐ Heating or air conditioning system _____

☐ Major appliances (stove, oven, dishwasher, refrigerator) _____

☐ Basement or attic _____

☐ Locks or security system _____

☐ Smoke detector _____

☐ Fireplace _____

☐ Cupboards, cabinets, and closets _____

☐ Furnishings (table, bed, mirrors, chairs) _____

☐ Laundry facilities _____

☐ Elevator _____

☐ Stairs and handrails _____

☐ Hallway, lobby, and common areas _____

☐ Garage _____

☐ Patio, terrace, or deck _____

☐ Lawn, fences, and grounds_____

☐ Pool and recreational facilities _____

☐ Roof, exterior walls, and other structural _____

☐ Driveway and sidewalks_____

☐ Neighborhood _____

☐ Nuisances _____

☐ Other _____

_____

Specifics of problems: _____

_____

_____

_____

_____

Other comments: _____

_____

_____

_____

_____

_____   _____
Date   Tenant

· ·
FOR MANAGEMENT USE

Action/Response: _____

_____

_____

_____

_____

_____

_____

_____

_____

_____   _____
Date   Landlord/Manager

Agreement Regarding Tenant Alterations to Rental Unit

_____ (Landlord)

and _____ (Tenant)

agree as follows:

1. Tenant may make the following alterations to the rental unit at _____

_____ :

_____

_____

_____

_____

_____

_____

_____ .

2. Tenant will accomplish the work described in Paragraph 1 by using the following materials and procedures:

_____

_____

_____

_____

_____

_____ .

3. Tenant will do only the work outlined in Paragraph 1 using only the materials and procedures outlined in Paragraph 2.

4. The alterations carried out by Tenant:

   ☐ will become Landlord's property and are not to be removed by Tenant during or at the end of the tenancy, or

   ☐ will be considered Tenant's personal property, and as such may be removed by Tenant at any time up to the end of the tenancy. Tenant promises to return the premises to their original condition upon removing the improvement.

5. Landlord will reimburse Tenant only for the costs checked below:

   ☐ the cost of materials listed in Paragraph 2

   ☐ labor costs at the rate of $ _____ per hour for work done in a workmanlike manner acceptable to Landlord up to _____ hours.

6. After receiving appropriate documentation of the cost of materials and labor, Landlord shall make any payment called for under Paragraph 5 by:

☐ lump sum payment, within _____ days of receiving documentation of costs, or

☐ by reducing Tenant's rent by $ _____ per month for the number of months necessary to cover the total amounts under the terms of this agreement.

7. If under Paragraph 4 of this contract the alterations are Tenant's personal property, Tenant must return the premises to their original condition upon removing the alterations. If Tenant fails to do this, Landlord will deduct the cost to restore the premises to their original condition from Tenant's security deposit. If the security deposit is insufficient to cover the costs of restoration, Landlord may take legal action, if necessary, to collect the balance.

8. If Tenant fails to remove an improvement that is his or her personal property on or before the end of the tenancy, it will be considered the property of Landlord, who may choose to keep the improvement (with no financial liability to Tenant), or remove it and charge Tenant for the costs of removal and restoration. Landlord may deduct any costs of removal and restoration from Tenant's security deposit. If the security deposit is insufficient to cover the costs of removal and restoration, Landlord may take legal action, if necessary, to collect the balance.

9. If Tenant removes an item that is Landlord's property, Tenant will owe Landlord the fair market value of the item removed plus any costs incurred by Landlord to restore the premises to their original condition.

10. If Landlord and Tenant are involved in any legal proceeding arising out of this agreement, the prevailing party shall recover reasonable attorney fees, court costs and any costs reasonably necessary to collect a judgment.

_____   _____
Date   Landlord

_____   _____
Date   Tenant

NOLO
www.nolo.com   **Agreement Regarding Tenant
                              Alterations to Rental Unit**   Page 2 of 2

Disclosure of Information on Lead-Based Paint or Lead-Based Paint Hazards

LEAD WARNING STATEMENT

Housing built before 1978 may contain lead-based paint. Lead from paint, paint chips and dust can pose health hazards if not managed properly. Lead exposure is especially harmful to young children and pregnant women. Before renting pre-1978 housing, lessors must disclose the presence of known lead-based paint and/or lead-based hazards in the dwelling. Lessees must also receive a federally approved pamphlet on lead poisoning prevention.

Lessor's Disclosure

(a) Presence of lead-based paint and/or lead-based paint hazards. Check (i) or (ii) below:

   ☐ (i) Known lead-based paint and/or lead-based paint hazards are present in the housing (explain):

     _____

     _____

   ☐ (ii) Lessor has no knowledge of lead-based paint and/or lead-based paint hazards in the housing.

(b) Records and reports available to the lessor. Check (i) or (ii) below:

   ☐ (i) Lessor has provided the lessee with all available records and reports pertaining to lead-based paint and/or lead-based paint hazards in the housing (list documents below): _____

     _____

   ☐ (ii) Lessor has no reports or records pertaining to lead-based paint or lead-based paint hazards in the housing.

Lessee's Acknowledgment (initial)

___ (c) Lessee has received copies of all information listed above.

___ (d) Lessee has received the pamphlet "Protect Your Family From Lead in Your Home."

Agent's Acknowledgment (initial)

___ (e) Agent has informed the lessor of the lessor's obligations under 42 U.S.Code § 4852(d) and is aware of his/her responsibility to ensure compliance.

Certification of Accuracy

The following parties have reviewed the information above and certify, to the best of their knowledge, that the information they have provided is true and accurate.

_____	_____	_____	_____
Lessor	Date	Lessor	Date
_____	_____	_____	_____
Lessee	Date	Lessee	Date
_____	_____	_____	_____
Agent	Date	Agent	Date

Declaración de Información sobre Pintura a Base de Plomo y/o Peligros de la Pintura a Base de Plomo

Declaración sobre los Peligros del Plomo

Se notifica a todo comprador de cualquier interés en propiedad real residencial en la cual fue construida una vivienda residencial antes del año 1978, que dicha propiedad puede presentar una exposición a plomo de la pintura a base de plomo que podría poner a niños jóvenes en situación de riesgo de desarrollar envenenamiento de plomo. El envenenamiento de plomo en niños jóvenes puede producir daños neurológicos permanentes, incluyendo incapacidad para el aprendizaje, cociente de inteligencia reducido, problemas de comportamiento y memoria dañada. El envenenamiento de plomo también representa un peligro especial para las mujeres embarazadas. El vendedor de cualquier interés en una propiedad privada real residencial tiene la obligación de proporcionarle al comprador toda la información que posea sobre los peligros de la pintura a base de plomo que se hayan determinado en evaluaciones o inspecciones de riesgo y de notificarle al comprador sobre cualquier peligro que conozca de la pintura a base de plomo. Se recomienda realizar una evaluación o inspección de posibles peligros de la pintura a base de plomo antes de la compra.

Declaración del Vendedor

(a) Presencia de pintura a base de plomo y/o peligros de pintura a base de plomo (marque (i) ó (ii) abajo):

    (i) _____ Confirmado que hay pintura a base de plomo y/o peligro de pintura a base de plomo en la vivienda (explique).

_____

    (ii) _____ El vendedor no tiene ningún conocimiento de que haya pintura a base de plomo y/o peligro de pintura a base de plomo en la vivienda.

(b) Archivos e informes disponibles para el vendedor (marque (i) ó (ii) abajo):

    (i) _____ El vendedor le ha proporcionado al comprador todos los archivos e informes disponibles relacionados con pintura a base de plomo y/o peligro de pintura a base de plomo en la vivienda (anote los documentos abajo).

_____

    (ii) _____ El vendedor no tiene archivos ni informes relacionados con pintura a base de plomo y/o peligro de pintura a base de plomo en la vivienda.

Acuse de Recibo del Comprador (inicial)

(c) _____ El comprador ha recibido copias de toda la información indicada arriba.

(d) _____ El comprador ha recibido el folleto titulado *Proteja a Su Familia del Plomo en Su Casa.*

(e) El comprador ha (marque (i) ó (ii) abajo):

    (i) _____ recibido una oportunidad por 10 días (o un período de tiempo de mutuo acuerdo) para hacer una evaluación o inspección de riesgo de presencia de pintura a base de plomo o de peligros de pintura a base de plomo; o

    (ii) _____ renunciado a la oportunidad de hacer una evaluación o inspección de riesgo de presencia de pintura a base de plomo o de peligros de pintura a base de plomo.

Acuse de Recibo del Agente (inicial)

(f) _____ El agente le ha informado al vendedor de las obligaciones del vendedor de acuerdo con 42 U.S.C. 4852(d) y está consciente de su responsabilidad de asegurar su cumplimiento.

Certificación de Exactitud

Las partes siguientes han revisado la información que aparece arriba y certifican que, según su entender, toda la información que han proporcionado es verdadera y exacta.

Vendedor	Fecha	Vendedor	Fecha
Comprador	Fecha	Comprador	Fecha
Agente	Fecha	Agente	Fecha

Are You Planning To Buy, Rent, or Renovate a Home Built Before 1978?

Many houses and apartments built before 1978 have paint that contains lead (called lead-based paint). Lead from paint, chips, and dust can pose serious health hazards if not taken care of properly.

By 1996, federal law will require that individuals receive certain information before renting, buying, or renovating pre-1978 housing:

LANDLORDS will have to disclose known information on lead-based paint hazards before leases take effect. Leases will include a federal form about lead-based paint.

SELLERS will have to disclose known information on lead-based paint hazards before selling a house. Sales contracts will include a federal form about lead-based paint in the building. Buyers will have up to 10 days to check for lead hazards.

RENOVATORS will have to give you this pamphlet before starting work.

IF YOU WANT MORE INFORMATION on these requirements, call the National Lead Information Clearinghouse at **1-800-424-LEAD**.

This document is in the public domain. It may be reproduced by an individual or organization without permission. Information provided in this booklet is based upon current scientific and technical understanding of the issues presented and is reflective of the jurisdictional boundaries established by the statutes governing the co-authoring agencies. Following the advice given will not necessarily provide complete protection in all situations or against all health hazards that can be caused by lead exposure.

Protect Your Family From Lead in Your Home

♻EPA
United States
Environmental Protection
Agency

United States Consumer
Product Safety Commission

EPA747-K-94-001
May 1995

U.S. EPA Washington DC 20460
U.S. CPSC Washington DC 20207

IMPORTANT!

Lead From Paint, Dust, and Soil Can Be Dangerous If Not Managed Properly

FACT: Lead exposure can harm young children and babies even before they are born.

FACT: Even children that seem healthy can have high levels of lead in their bodies.

FACT: People can get lead in their bodies by breathing or swallowing lead dust, or by eating soil or paint chips with lead in them.

FACT: People have many options for reducing lead hazards. In most cases, lead-based paint that is in good condition is not a hazard.

FACT: Removing lead-based paint improperly can increase the danger to your family.

If you think your home might have lead hazards, read this pamphlet to learn some simple steps to protect your family.

Lead Gets in the Body in Many Ways

1 out of every 11 children in the United States has dangerous levels of lead in the bloodstream.

Even children who appear healthy can have dangerous levels of lead.

People can get lead in their body if they:

- ◆ Put their hands or other objects covered with lead dust in their mouths.
- ◆ Eat paint chips or soil that contains lead.
- ◆ Breathe in lead dust (especially during renovations that disturb painted surfaces).

Lead is even more dangerous to children than adults because:

- ◆ Babies and young children often put their hands and other objects in their mouths. These objects can have lead dust on them.
- ◆ Children's growing bodies absorb more lead.
- ◆ Children's brains and nervous systems are more sensitive to the damaging effects of lead.

Checking Your Family for Lead

A simple blood test can detect high levels of lead. Blood tests are important for:

◆ Children who are 6 months to 1 year old (6 months if you live in an older home with cracking or peeling paint).

◆ Family members that you think might have high levels of lead.

If your child is older than 1 year, talk to your doctor about whether your child needs testing.

Your doctor or health center can do blood tests. They are inexpensive and sometimes free. Your doctor will explain what the test results mean. *Treatment can range from changes in your diet to medication or a hospital stay.*

Get your children tested if you think your home has high levels of lead.

Where Lead-Based Paint Is Found

Many homes built before 1978 have lead-based paint. The federal government banned lead-based paint from housing in 1978. Some states stopped its use even earlier. Lead can be found:

◆ In homes in the city, country, or suburbs.

◆ In apartments, single-family homes, and both private and public housing.

◆ Inside *and* outside of the house.

◆ In soil around a home. (Soil can pick up lead from exterior paint, or other sources such as past use of leaded gas in cars.)

In general, the older your home, the more likely it has lead-based paint.

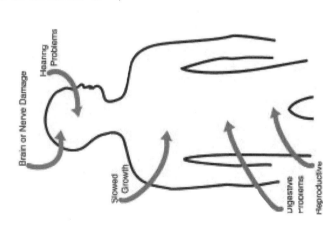

Lead affects the body in many ways.

Lead's Effects

If not detected early, children with high levels of lead in their bodies can suffer from:

◆ Damage to the brain and nervous system

◆ Behavior and learning problems (such as hyperactivity)

◆ Slowed growth

◆ Hearing problems

◆ Headaches

Lead is also harmful to adults. Adults can suffer from:

◆ Difficulties during pregnancy

◆ Other reproductive problems (in both men and women)

◆ High blood pressure

◆ Digestive problems

◆ Nerve disorders

◆ Memory and concentration problems

◆ Muscle and joint pain

Where Lead Is Likely To Be a Hazard

Lead-based paint that is in good condition is usually not a hazard.

Peeling, chipping, chalking, or cracking lead-based paint is a hazard and needs immediate attention.

Lead-based paint may also be a hazard when found on surfaces that children can chew or that get a lot of wear-and-tear. These areas include:

◆ Windows and window sills.

◆ Doors and door frames.

◆ Stairs, railings, and banisters.

◆ Porches and fences.

Lead dust can form when lead-based paint is dry scraped, dry sanded, or heated. Dust also forms when painted surfaces bump or rub together. Lead chips and dust can get on surfaces and objects that people touch. Settled lead dust can reenter the air when people vacuum, sweep, or walk through it.

Lead in soil can be a hazard when children play in bare soil or when people bring soil into the house on their shoes. Call your state agency (see page 12) to find out about soil testing for lead.

> Lead from paint chips, which you can see, and lead dust, which you can't always see, can both be serious hazards

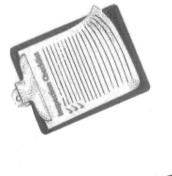

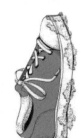
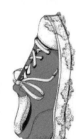

Checking Your Home for Lead Hazards

You can get your home checked for lead hazards in one of two ways, or both:

◆ A paint inspection tells you the lead content of every painted surface in your home. It won't tell you whether the paint is a hazard or how you should deal with it.

◆ A risk assessment tells you if there are any sources of serious lead exposure (such as peeling paint and lead dust). It also tells you what actions to take to address these hazards.

> Just knowing that a home has lead-based paint may not tell you if there is a hazard.

Have qualified professionals do the work. *The federal government is writing standards for inspectors and risk assessors. Some states might already have standards in place.* Call your state agency for help with locating qualified professionals in your area (see page 12).

Trained professionals use a range of methods when checking your home, including:

◆ Visual inspection of paint condition and location.

◆ Lab tests of paint samples.

◆ Surface dust tests.

◆ A portable x-ray fluorescence machine.

Home test kits for lead are available, but recent studies suggest that they are not always accurate. Consumers should not rely on these tests before doing renovations or to assure safety.

What You Can Do Now To Protect Your Family

If you suspect that your house has lead hazards, you can take some immediate steps to reduce your family's risk:

◆ **If you rent, notify your landlord of peeling or chipping paint.**

◆ **Clean up paint chips immediately.**

◆ **Clean floors, window frames, window sills, and other surfaces weekly.** Use a mop or sponge with warm water and a general all-purpose cleaner or a cleaner made specifically for lead. REMEMBER: NEVER MIX AMMONIA AND BLEACH PRODUCTS TOGETHER SINCE THEY CAN FORM A DANGEROUS GAS.

◆ **Thoroughly rinse sponges and mop heads after cleaning dirty or dusty areas.**

◆ **Wash children's hands often, especially before they eat and before nap time and bed time.**

◆ **Keep play areas clean.** Wash bottles, pacifiers, toys, and stuffed animals regularly.

◆ **Keep children from chewing window sills or other painted surfaces.**

◆ **Clean or remove shoes before entering your home to avoid tracking in lead from soil.**

◆ **Make sure children eat nutritious, low-fat meals high in iron and calcium,** such as spinach and low-fat dairy products. Children with good diets absorb less lead.

How To Significantly Reduce Lead Hazards

In addition to day-to-day cleaning and good nutrition:

◆ You can **temporarily** reduce lead hazards by taking actions such as repairing damaged painted surfaces and planting grass to cover soil with high lead levels. These actions (called "interim controls") are not permanent solutions and will need ongoing attention.

◆ To **permanently** remove lead hazards, you must hire a lead "abatement" contractor. Abatement (or permanent hazard elimination) methods include removing, sealing, or enclosing lead-based paint with special materials. Just painting over the hazard with regular paint is not enough.

Always hire a person with special training for correcting lead problems—someone who knows how to do this work safely and has the proper equipment to clean up thoroughly. If possible, hire a certified lead abatement contractor. Certified contractors will employ qualified workers and follow strict safety rules as set by their state or by the federal government.

Call your state agency (see page 12) for help with locating qualified contractors in your area and to see if financial assistance is available.

Removing lead improperly can increase the hazard to your family by spreading even more lead dust around the house.

Always use a professional who is trained to remove lead hazards safely.

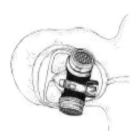

Remodeling or Renovating a Home With Lead-Based Paint

Take precautions before you begin remodeling or renovations that disturb painted surfaces (such as scraping off paint or tearing out walls):

◆ **Have the area tested for lead-based paint.**

◆ **Do not use a dry scraper, belt-sander, propane torch, or heat gun** to remove lead-based paint. These actions create large amounts of lead dust and fumes. Lead dust can remain in your home long after the work is done.

◆ **Temporarily move your family** (especially children and pregnant women) out of the apartment or house until the work is done and the area is properly cleaned. If you can't move your family, at least completely seal off the work area.

◆ **Follow other safety measures to reduce lead hazards.** You can find out about other safety measures by calling 1-800-424-LEAD. Ask for the brochure "Reducing Lead Hazards When Remodeling Your Home." This brochure explains what to do before, during, and after renovations.

If you have already completed renovations or remodeling that could have released lead-based paint or dust, get your young children tested and follow the steps outlined on page 7 of this brochure.

If not conducted properly, certain types of renovations can release lead from paint and dust into the air.

Other Sources of Lead

◆ **Drinking water.** Your home might have plumbing with lead or lead solder. Call your local health department or water supplier to find out about testing your water. You cannot see, smell, or taste lead, and boiling your water will not get rid of lead. If you think your plumbing might have lead in it:

- Use only cold water for drinking and cooking.

- Run water for 15 to 30 seconds before drinking it, especially if you have not used your water for a few hours.

While paint, dust, and soil are the most common lead hazards, other lead sources also exist.

◆ **The job.** If you work with lead, you could bring it home on your hands or clothes. Shower and change clothes before coming home. Launder your clothes separately from the rest of your family's.

◆ Old painted **toys** and **furniture.**

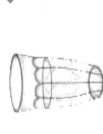

◆ Food and liquids stored in **lead crystal** or **lead-glazed pottery or porcelain.**

◆ **Lead smelters** or other industries that release lead into the air.

◆ **Hobbies** that use lead, such as making pottery or stained glass, or refinishing furniture.

◆ **Folk remedies** that contain lead, such as "greta" and "azarcon" used to treat an upset stomach.

For More Information

The National Lead Information Center

Call **1-800-LEAD-FYI** to learn how to protect children from lead poisoning.

For other information on lead hazards, call the center's clearinghouse at **1-800-424-LEAD**. For the hearing impaired, call, TDD **1-800-526-5456** (FAX: **202-659-1192,** Internet: **EHC@CAIS.COM**).

EPAÕs Safe Drinking Water Hotline

Call **1-800-426-4791** for information about lead in drinking water.

Consumer Product Safety Commission Hotline

To request information on lead in consumer products, or to report an unsafe consumer product or a product-related injury call **1-800-638-2772.** (Internet: info@cpsc.gov). For the hearing impaired, call **TDD 1-800-638-8270.**

Local Sources of Information

State Health and Environmental Agencies

Some cities and states have their own rules for lead-based paint activities. Check with your state agency (listed below) to see if state or local laws apply to you. Most state agencies can also provide information on finding a lead abatement firm in your area, and on possible sources of financial aid for reducing lead hazards.

State/Region	Phone Number	State/Region	Phone Number
Alabama	(205) 242-5661	Missouri	(314) 526-4911
Alaska	(907) 465-5152	Montana	(406) 444-3671
Arkansas	(501) 661-2534	Nebraska	(402) 471-2451
Arizona	(602) 542-7307	Nevada	(702) 687-6615
California	(510) 450-2424	New Hampshire	(603) 271-4507
Colorado	(303) 692-3012	New Jersey	(609) 633-2043
Connecticut	(203) 566-5808	New Mexico	(505) 841-8024
Washington, DC	(202) 727-9850	New York	(800) 458-1158
Delaware	(302) 739-4735	North Carolina	(919) 715-3293
Florida	(904) 488-3385	North Dakota	(701) 328-5188
Georgia	(404) 657-6514	Ohio	(614) 466-1450
Hawaii	(808) 832-5860	Oklahoma	(405) 271-5220
Idaho	(208) 332-5544	Oregon	(503) 248-5240
Illinois	(800) 545-2200	Pennsylvania	(717) 782-2884
Indiana	(317) 382-6662	Rhode Island	(401) 277-3424
Iowa	(800) 972-2026	South Carolina	(803) 935-7945
Kansas	(913) 296-0189	South Dakota	(605) 773-3153
Kentucky	(502) 564-2154	Tennessee	(615) 741-5683
Louisiana	(504) 765-0219	Texas	(512) 834-6600
Massachusetts	(800) 532-9571	Utah	(801) 536-4000
Maryland	(410) 631-3859	Vermont	(802) 863-7231
Maine	(207) 287-4311	Virginia	(800) 523-4019
Michigan	(517) 335-8885	Washington	(206) 753-2556
Minnesota	(612) 627-5498	West Virginia	(304) 558-2981
Mississippi	(601) 960-7463	Wisconsin	(608) 266-5885
		Wyoming	(307) 777-7391

Simple Steps To Protect Your Family From Lead Hazards

If you think your home has high levels of lead:

◆ Get your young children tested for lead, even if they seem healthy.

◆ Wash children's hands, bottles, pacifiers, and toys often.

◆ Make sure children eat healthy, low-fat foods.

◆ Get your home checked for lead hazards.

◆ Regularly clean floors, window sills, and other surfaces.

◆ Wipe soil off shoes before entering house.

◆ Talk to your landlord about fixing surfaces with peeling or chipping paint.

◆ Take precautions to avoid exposure to lead dust when remodeling or renovating (call 1-800-424-LEAD for guidelines).

◆ Don't use a belt-sander, propane torch, dry scraper, or dry sandpaper on painted surfaces that may contain lead.

◆ Don't try to remove lead-based paint yourself.

EPA Regional Offices

Your Regional EPA Office can provide further information regarding regulations and lead protection programs.

EPA Regional Offices

Region 1 (Connecticut, Massachusetts, Maine, New Hampshire, Rhode Island, Vermont)
John F. Kennedy Federal Building
One Congress Street
Boston, MA 02203
(617) 565-3420

Region 2 (New Jersey, New York, Puerto Rico, Virgin Islands)
Building 5
2890 Woodbridge Avenue
Edison, NJ 08837-3679
(908) 321-6671

Region 3 (Delaware, Washington DC, Maryland, Pennsylvania, Virginia, West Virginia)
841 Chestnut Building
Philadelphia, PA 19107
(215) 597-9800

Region 4 (Alabama, Florida, Georgia, Kentucky, Mississippi, North Carolina, South Carolina, Tennessee)
345 Courtland Street, NE
Atlanta, GA 30365
(404) 347-4727

Region 5 (Illinois, Indiana, Michigan, Minnesota, Ohio, Wisconsin)
77 West Jackson Boulevard
Chicago, IL 60604-3590
(312) 886-6003

Region 6 (Arkansas, Louisiana, New Mexico, Oklahoma, Texas)
First Interstate Bank Tower
1445 Ross Avenue, 12th Floor, Suite 1200
Dallas, TX 75202-2733
(214) 665-7244

Region 7 (Iowa, Kansas, Missouri, Nebraska)
726 Minnesota Avenue
Kansas City, KS 66101
(913) 551-7020

Region 8 (Colorado, Montana, North Dakota, South Dakota, Utah, Wyoming)
999 18th Street, Suite 500
Denver, CO 80202-2405
(303) 293-1603

Region 9 (Arizona, California, Hawaii, Nevada)
75 Hawthorne Street
San Francisco, CA 94105
(415) 744-1124

Region 10 (Idaho, Oregon, Washington, Alaska)
1200 Sixth Avenue
Seattle, WA 98101
(206) 553-1200

CPSC Regional Offices

Eastern Regional Center
6 World Trade Center
Vesey Street, Room 350
New York, NY 10048
(212) 466-1612

Central Regional Center
230 South Dearborn Street
Room 2944
Chicago, IL 60604-1601
(312) 353-8260

Western Regional Center
600 Harrison Street, Room 245
San Francisco, CA 94107
(415) 744-2966

¿Está Usted Planeando Comprar, Alquilar o Renovar una Casa Construida Antes de 1978?

Muchas casas y apartamentos construidos antes de 1978 tienen pintura que contiene plomo (llamada pintura a base de plomo). El plomo de la pintura, de los pedazos y del polvo pueden representar peligros serios para la salud si no se manejan con cuidado.

Para el año 1996 la ley federal requerirá que las personas reciban cierta información antes de alquilar, comprar o renovar casas construidas antes de 1978:

Los **propietarios** tendrán que revelar la información que tienen a sus inquilinos sobre los peligros de la pintura a base de plomo antes que los contratos de arrendamiento (alquiler) entren en vigor.

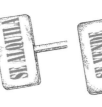

Los **vendedores** de sus propiedades tendrán que revelar la información que tienen sobre los peligros de la pintura a base de plomo antes de vender una casa. Los contratos de venta incluirán un formulario federal sobre la pintura a base de plomo en el edificio. Los compradores tendrán hasta 10 días para verificar si hay peligros de plomo.

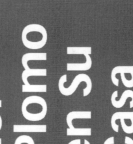

Los **renovadores** tendrán que entregarle a usted este folleto antes de comenzar un trabajo.

Si usted quiere obtener más información sobre estos requisitos, llame al Centro de Información Nacional para Plomo (National Lead Information Clearinghouse) al **1-800-424-5323.**

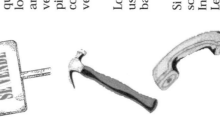

Proteja a Su Familia del Plomo en Su Casa

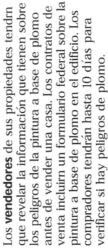

⊕ EPA
Agencia de Protección Ambiental de los Estados Unidos (EPA)

Comisión de Seguridad de Productos de Consumo de los Estados Unidos

EPA747-K-94-001
Agosto 1995

U.S. EPA/CPSC Washington DC 20460
U.S. CPSC Washington DC 20207

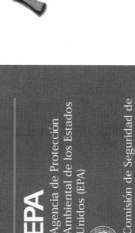

El Plomo Entra en el Cuerpo de Muchas Maneras

1 de cada 11 niños en los Estados Unidos tiene niveles peligrosos de plomo en su cuerpo.

El plomo puede entrar en los cuerpos de las personas si:

◆ Se meten las manos u otros objetos cubiertos de polvo de plomo en la boca.

◆ Comen pedazos de pintura o tierra que contiene plomo.

◆ Aspiran polvo de plomo (especialmente durante renovaciones de superficies pintadas).

El plomo es aún más peligroso para los niños que para los adultos porque:

◆ Los bebes y los niños pequeños con frecuencia se meten las manos y otros objetos en la boca. Estos objetos pueden tener polvo de plomo.

◆ Los cuerpos de los niños crecen y absorben más plomo que los de los adultos.

◆ Los sistemas nerviosos y los cerebros de los niños son más sensibles a los efectos dañinos del plomo.

¡IMPORTANTE!

El Plomo de la Pintura, el Polvo y la Tierra Pueden Ser Peligrosos Si No Se Manejan Debidamente

Aviso: Exponer a los niños o bebes al plomo los puede dañar, incluso antes de nacer.

Aviso: Hasta los niños que parecen ser saludables pueden tener niveles peligrosos de plomo en sus cuerpos.

Aviso: El plomo puede entrar en los cuerpos de las personas cuando aspiran o tragan polvo de plomo, o si comen tierra o pedazos de pintura que contienen plomo.

Aviso: Las personas tienen muchas alternativas para reducir el peligro del plomo. En muchos casos, la pintura a base de plomo que est en buenas condiciones no es un peligro.

Aviso: Quitar la pintura a base de plomo incorrectamente puede aumentar el peligro para su familia.

Si usted piensa que su casa puede tener pintura a base de plomo, lea este folleto para conocer unas medidas sencillas que puede tomar para proteger a su familia.

Los Efectos del Plomo

Hasta los niños que parecen ser saludables pueden tener niveles peligrosos de plomo.

Si no se detecta temprano, los niños que tienen alto niveles de plomo en sus cuerpos pueden sufrir de:

◆ Daños al cerebro y al sistema nervioso

◆ Problemas de comportamiento y aprendizaje (tal como hiperactividad)

◆ Crecimiento lento

◆ Problemas para oir

◆ Dolores de cabeza

El plomo también es dañino para los adultos. Los adultos pueden sufrir de:

◆ Daño al bebé durante el embarazo

◆ Otros problemas reproductivos (en hombres y mujeres)

◆ Presión alta

◆ Problemas digestivos

◆ Trastornos nerviosos

◆ Problemas de memoria y de concentración

◆ Dolores musculares y de las articulaciones

Daños al Cerebro o a los Nervios

Problemas Para Oir

Crecimiento Retardado

Problemas Digestivos

Problemas de Reproducción (Adultos)

Examine a su Familia para Detectar el Plomo

Los exámenes de sangre son importantes para:

◆ Niños que tienen entre 6 meses y 1 año (6 meses si usted vive en una casa o edificio que se está deteriorando, que puede tener plomo en la pintura).

◆ Miembros de la familia que usted cree que pueden tener altos niveles de plomo.

◆ Si su niño(a) tiene **más de 1 año,** hable con su médico sobre si su niño(a) necesita un examen.

Un examen sencillo de la sangre puede detectar altos niveles de plomo.

Su médico o centro de salud pueden hacer los exámenes de la sangre. No son caros y a veces se hacen gratis. Su médico le explicará lo que significa el resultado de un examen. El tratamiento puede variar, desde cambios en el ambiente donde vive una persona y de sus hábitos de comer, hasta medicinas o una estencia en un hospital.

Dónde se Encuentra la Pintura a Base de Plomo

Muchas casas construidas antes de 1978 tienen pintura a base de plomo. En 1978, el Gobierno Federal prohibió la pintura a base de plomo para viviendas. Algunos estados ya habían prohibido su uso anteriormente. Se puede encontrar el plomo:

◆ En casas en la ciudad, en el medio rural o en los suburbios.

◆ En apartamentos, casas para una sola familia y en viviendas privadas y públicas.

◆ Adentro y afuera de la casa.

◆ En la tierra alrededor de la casa. (La tierra puede absorber el plomo de la pintura exterior o de otras fuentes como del uso en el pasado de gasolina con plomo en los autos.)

En general, mientras más antigua sea su casa, mayor será la probabilidad de que tenga pintura a base de plomo.

Dónde el Plomo Probablemente es un Peligro

La pintura a base de plomo que se está en buenas condiciones normalmente no es un peligro.

La pintura a base de plomo que se está pelando, despedazando o quebrando es un peligro y requiere atención inmediata.

La pintura a base de plomo también puede ser un peligro cuando se encuentra en superficies que los niños pueden morder o que tienen mucho uso.

- Ventanas y marcos de las ventanas.
- Puertas y marcos de las puertas.
- Escaleras, barandas y pasamanos.
- Portales, terrazas y cercas.

El polvo de plomo se puede formar cuando se raspa o lija en seco o se calienta la pintura a base de plomo. El polvo también se forma cuando las superficies pintadas (como puertas y ventanas) chocan o se juntan. Pedazos de plomo y polvo quedan en superficies que las personas tocan. El polvo de plomo que se acumula puede entrar en el aire cuando do se usa una aspiradora o se barre.

El plomo en la tierra puede ser un peligro cuando los niños juegan allí o cuando las personas llevan tierra a la casa en los zapatos. Llame a su agencia estatal (en la lista en la parte de atrás de este folleto) para averiguar sobre pruebas de plomo para la tierra.

La pintura a base de plomo es más peligrosa cuando está en la forma de pedazos de pintura, que usted puede ver, o de polvo de plomo, que usted no siempre puede ver.

Cómo Verificar si su Casa Tiene Peligros de Plomo

Con sólo saber que una casa tiene pintura a base de plomo no le indica si hay peligro.

Usted puede verificar si su casa tiene plomo en una de dos maneras, o ambas:

- Una **inspección** de la pintura le indica el contenido de plomo de todas las superficies pintadas en su casa. No le indicará si la pintura es un peligro ni cómo usted la debería manejar.

- Una **evaluación del riesgo** le indica si hay fuentes de exposición seria al plomo (tales como pintura que se está pelando y polvo de plomo). Además, le indica qué acciones pueden ser tomadas para dirigirse a estos peligros.

Haga que inspectores calificados realicen las pruebas. El Gobierno Federal está preparando procedimientos y calificaciones universales para inspectores y evaluadores de riesgo que hacen pruebas de plomo. Posiblemente algunos estados ya tienen estándares vigentes. Llame a su agencia estatal para obtener más información sobre cómo encontrar a profesionales calificados en su área (vea la página 12).

Los profesionales entrenados usan una variedad de métodos cuando llevan a cabo sus pruebas, incluyendo:

- Inspección visual del lugar y la condición de la pintura.
- Examen de laboratorio de muestras de pintura.
- Pruebas del polvo de la superficie.
- Una máquina portátil de rayos-x de fluorescencia.

Hay paquetes de pruebas de plomo para la casa disponibles, pero estudios recientes indican que no siempre son confiables. Los consumidores no deben confiar en estas pruebas antes de hacer revonaciones o para asegurar que no hay peligro.

Qué Puede Hacer Usted Ahora Para Proteger a su Familia

Si usted sospecha que su casa tiene peligro de plomo, usted puede tomar algunas acciones inmediatamente para reducir el riesgo para su familia:

◆ Notifique a su propietario sobre pintura que se esté pelando o quebrando.

◆ Limpie los pedazos de pintura inmediatamente.

◆ Limpie los pisos, molduras y marcos de las ventanas y otras superficies semanalmente. Use un trapeador o una esponja con agua tibia y un detergente corriente o uno especial para plomo. **RECUERDE: Nunca mezcle productos de limpieza de amoníaco y de cloro, porque se produce un gas peligroso.**

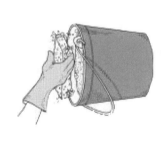

◆ Enjuague completamente las esponjas y la cabeza de los trapeadores después de limpiar areas sucias o que tienen polvo. Bote los trapos que fueron usados para limpiar.

◆ **Lávele las manos a los niños frecuentemente, especialmente antes de comer y antes de dormir la siesta y por la noche.**

◆ **Mantenga limpias las áreas de juego.** Limpie las botellas, chupetes, y juguetes periódicamente.

◆ **No deje que los niños muerdan las molduras de las ventanas u otras superficies pintadas.**

◆ **Limpie o quítese los zapatos antes de entrar en su casa para que no entre el plomo de la tierra.**

◆ **Asegúrese que los niños coman comidas nutritivas, bajas en grasa y con alto contenido de hierro y calcio,** tales como espinaca y productos lácteos bajos en grasa. Los niños que tienen buenas dietas absorben menos plomo.

Cómo Reducir los Peligros del Plomo Significativamente

Quitar el plomo indebidamente puede empeorar el peligro para su familia al regarse acen ms polvo de plomo por toda su casa.

Siempre consulte a un profesional que esté entrenado para hacer el trabajo debidamente y sin peligro.

Además de la limpieza diaria y la buena nutrición, usted puede considerar otras opciones para reducir los peligros del plomo.

◆ Usted puede reducir **temporalmente** los peligros del plomo tomando acciones como reparar superficies pintadas que han sido dañadas (vea la página siguiente) y sembrando grama o hierba para cubrir la tierra que tiene alto contenido de plomo. Estas acciones (llamadas "controles interinos") no son soluciones permanentes y no eliminarn todos los riesgos de exposición.

◆ Para quitar los peligros **permanentemente,** usted necesitará contratar a un especialista de "supresión". Los métodos de supresi n (o eliminación permanente de peligro) incluyen quitar, sellar o envolver la pintura a base de plomo con materiales especiales. **Simplemente pintar sobre el peligro con pintura corriente no es suficiente.**

Siempre contrate a una persona que tenga entrenamiento especial para corregir los problemas de plomo, alguien que sepa cómo hacer este trabajo sin peligro y que tenga el equipo necesario para limpiar debidamente después del trabajo. Si fuera posible, contrate a un especialista certificado para la supresión de plomo. Los especialistas **certificados** emplean a trabajadores calificados y cumplen las reglas estrictas de seguridad establecidas por el estado o por el Gobierno Federal.

Llame a su agencia estatal (vea la página 12) para que le ayuden a encontrar especialistas calificados en su área y para ver si hay ayuda financiera disponible.

Cómo Remodelar o Renovar una Casa que Tiene Pintura a Base de Plomo

Tome las precauciones antes de comenzar remodelaciones o renovaciones que puedan mover superficies pintadas (tales como raspar la pintura o quitar paredes):

Si no se hacen debidamente, ciertos tipos de renovaciones pueden soltar al aire el plomo de la pintura y polvo.

◆ **Examine el área para ver si hay pintura a base de plomo.**

◆ No use un raspador o una lijadora en seco, soplete de propano o pistola de alta temperatura para quitar la pintura a base de plomo. Estas acciones crean cantidades grandes de polvo de plomo y gases. El polvo de plomo puede quedar en su casa un tiempo largo después que se ha terminado el trabajo.

◆ **Mude temporalmente a su familia** (especialmente a los niños y las mujeres embarazadas) fuera de la casa o del apartamento hasta que se haya terminado el trabajo y limpiado debidamente el área. Si usted no puede mudar a su familia, entonces por lo menos aisle completamente el rea de trabajo.

◆ **Tome otras medidas de seguridad para reducir los peligros del plomo.** Usted puede averiguar sobre otras medidas de seguridad llamando al 1-800-424-5323. Pida el folleto "Cómo Reducir los Peligros del Plomo al Remodelar Su Casa". Este folleto explica qué hacer antes, durante y después de renovaciones para evitar crear peligros basados en el plomo de larga duración.

Si usted ya ha completado renovaciones o remodelaciones que pueden haber soltado pintura o polvo a base de plomo, lleve a sus niños para que les hagan pruebas y siga los pasos indicados en la página 7 de este folleto.

Otras Fuentes de Plomo

◆ **Agua de beber.** Su casa puede tener tuberías de plomo o soldaduras de plomo. Llame a su departamento de salud local o abastecedor de agua para averiguar sobre cómo hacerle pruebas a su agua. Usted no puede ver, oler ni saborear el plomo, y hervir el agua no le quitará el plomo. Si usted cree que la plomería de su casa puede tener plomo:

* **Use solamente agua fría para beber o cocinar.**

* Deje correr el agua unos minutos antes de beberla, especialmente si usted no ha usado el agua por varias horas.

◆ **En el trabajo.** Si usted trabaja con plomo en su trabajo, usted podría llevar el plomo a su casa en sus manos o en su ropa. Dése una ducha y cámbiese la ropa antes de llegar a su casa. Lave la ropa suya separada a la de su familia.

◆ **Juguetes y muebles viejos pintados.**

◆ Alimentos y líquidos guardados en **cristalería a base de plomo** o **locería o porcelana con barniz a base de plomo.**

◆ Fábricas de fundición que trabajan con plomo u otras industrias que sueltan plomo en el aire.

◆ **Pasatiempos** que usan plomo, tales como alfarería o vidrios de color, o renovación de muebles.

◆ **Remedios caseros** que contienen plomo, tales como "greta" y "azarcón", que se usan para tratar la descomposición de estómago.

Para Más Información

El Centro Nacional de Información Sobre Plomo

Llame al 1-800-532-3394 para obtener información sobre cómo proteger a los niños del envenenamiento de plomo.

Para obtener información adicional sobre peligros del plomo, llame a la oficina del Centro, al 1-800-424-5323, o TDD 1-800-526-5456 para los que tienen problemas para oír. (FAX: 202-659-1192, Internet: EHC@CAIS.COM).

Teléfono Especial de la EPA para Agua de Beber Segura

Llame al 1-800-426-4761 para obtener información sobre plomo en el agua de beber.

Teléfono Especial de la Comisión de Seguridad de Productos de Consumo

Para pedir información sobre el plomo en productos de consumo, o para reportar que un producto para el consumo es peligroso o una lesión relacionada con un producto, llame al 1-800-638-2772. (Internet: info@cpsc.gov). Las personas que tienen problemas para oír, pueden llamar al 1-800-638-8720.

Fuentes Locales de Información:

Agencias Estatales de Salud y de Protección Ambiental

Algunas ciudades y estados tienen sus propias regulaciones para las actividades relacionadas con pintura a base de plomo. Verifique con su agencia estatal (vea la lista abajo) para ver si hay leyes estatales o locales que le aplican a usted. Las agencias estatales también pueden proporcionar información sobre cómo encontrar una compañía de supresión de plomo en su área, y sobre posibles fuentes de asistencia financiera para reducir los peligros del plomo.

Estado/Región	Número de Teléfono	Estado/Región	Número de Teléfono
Alabama	(205) 242-5661	Montana	(406) 444-3671
Alaska	(907) 465-5152	Nebraska	(402) 471-2451
Arkansas	(501) 661-2534	Nevada	(702) 687-6615
Arizona	(602) 542-7307	New Hampshire	(603) 271-4507
California	(510) 450-2424	New Jersey	(609) 530-8812
Colorado	(303) 692-3012	New Mexico	(505) 841-8024
Connecticut	(203) 566-5808	New York	(518) 473-4602
Washington DC	(202) 727-9850	North Carolina	(919) 715-3293
Delaware	(302) 739-4735	North Dakota	(701) 328-5188
Florida	(904) 488-3385	Ohio	(614) 466-1450
Georgia	(404) 657-6514	Oklahoma	(405) 271-5220
Hawaii	(808) 832-5860	Oregon	(503) 248-5240
Idaho	(208) 332-5544	Pennsylvania	(717) 782-2884
Illinois	(800) 545-2200	Puerto Rico	(809) 766-2823
Indiana	(317) 382-6662	Rhode Island	(401) 277-3424
Iowa	(800) 972-2026	South Carolina	(803) 935-7945
Kansas	(913) 296-0189	South Dakota	(605) 773-3153
Kentucky	(502) 564-2154	Tennessee	(615) 741-5683
Louisiana	(504) 765-0219	Texas	(512) 834-6600
Massachusetts	(800) 532-9571	Utah	(801) 536-4000
Maryland	(410) 631-3859	Vermont	(802) 863-7231
Maine	(207) 287-4311	Virginia	(800) 523-4019
Michigan	(517) 335-8885	Washington	(206) 753-2556
Minnesota	(612) 627-5498	West Virginia	(304) 558-2981
Mississippi	(601) 960-7463	Wisconsin	(608) 266-5885
Missouri	(314) 526-4911	Wyoming	(307) 777-7391

Pasos Sencillos Para Proteger a Su Familia de los Peligros del Plomo

Si usted cree que su casa tiene altos niveles de plomo:

◆ Lleve a sus niños para que les hagan exámenes para plomo, aunque parezcan saludables.

◆ Lave las manos, botellas y chupetes de los niños frecuentemente.

◆ Asegúrese que los niños coman alimentos sanos y bajos en grasa.

◆ Haga que revisen su casa para ver si hay peligros del plomo.

◆ Limpie los pisos, las molduras de las ventanas y otras superficies frecuentemente.

◆ Quítele la tierra a los zapatos antes de entrar en la casa.

◆ Hable con el propietario que le alquila a usted sobre el arreglo de las superficies que tienen pintura que se esté pelando o quebrando.

◆ Tome precauciones para evitar la exposición al polvo de plomo cuando esté remodelando o renovando (llame al 1-800-424-5323 para obtener orientaciones).

◆ No use una lijadora de cinta, soplete de propano, raspadora en seco o papel de lija en seco en las superficies que pudieran contener plomo.

◆ No trate usted mismo(a) de quitar la pintura a base de plomo.

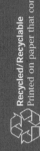

Recycled/Recyclable
Printed on paper that contains at least 20 percent postconsumer fiber.

Oficinas Regionales de la EPA

Su contacto Regional de la EPA puede proporcionar más información sobre regulaciones y programas de envenenamiento de plomo que le afecten a usted.

Oficinas Regionales de la EPA

Región 1 (Connecticut, Massachusetts, Maine, New Hampshire, Rhode Island, Vermont)
John F. Kennedy Federal Building
One Congress Street
Boston, MA 02203
(617) 565-3420

Región 2 (New Jersey, New York, Puerto Rico, Virgin Islands)
Building 5
2890 Woodbridge Avenue
Edison, NJ 08837-3679
(908) 321-6671

Región 3 (Delaware, Washington DC, Maryland, Pennsylvania, Virginia, West Virginia)
841 Chestnut Building
Philadelphia, PA 19107
(215) 597-9800

Región 4 (Alabama, Florida, Georgia, Kentucky, Mississippi, North Carolina, South Carolina, Tennessee)
345 Courtland Street, NE
Atlanta, GA 30365
(404) 347-4727

Región 5 (Illinois, Indiana, Michigan, Minnesota, Ohio, Wisconsin)
77 West Jackson Boulevard
Chicago, IL 60604-3590
(312) 886-6003

Región 6 (Arkansas, Louisiana, New Mexico, Oklahoma, Texas)
First Interstate Bank Tower
1445 Ross Avenue, 12th Floor, Suite 1200
Dallas, TX 75202-2733
(214) 665-7244

Región 7 (Iowa, Kansas, Missouri, Nebraska)
726 Minnesota Avenue
Kansas City, KS 66101
(913) 551-7020

Región 8 (Colorado, Montana, North Dakota, South Dakota, Utah, Wyoming)
999 18th Street, Suite 500
Denver, CO 80202-2405
(303) 293-1603

Región 9 (Arizona, California, Hawaii, Nevada)
75 Hawthorne Street
San Francisco, CA 94105
(415) 744-1124

Región 10 (Idaho, Oregon, Washington, Alaska)
1200 Sixth Avenue
Seattle, WA 98101
(206) 553-1200

Oficinas Regionales de CPSC

Centro Regional del Este
6 World Trade Center
Vesey Street, Room 350
New York, NY 10048
(212) 466-1612

Centro Regional Central
230 South Dearborn Street
Room 2944
Chicago, IL 60604-1601
(312) 353-8260

Centro Regional del Oeste
600 Harrison Street, Room 245
San Francisco, CA 94107
(415) 744-2966

Notice of Intent to Enter Dwelling Unit

Civil Code Section 1954

To: _____ ,
Name

Tenant(s) in possession of the premises at _____ ,
Street Address

City of _____ , County of _____ , California.

PLEASE TAKE NOTICE that on _____ , 20_____ ,

between _____ a.m./p.m. and _____ a.m./p.m.

the undersigned Landlord, or the Landlord's agent, will enter the said premises for the following reason:

☐ To make or arrange for the following repairs or improvements: _____

_____

_____

_____

_____

☐ To exhibit the premises to:

    ☐ a prospective tenant or purchaser

    ☐ workers or contractors regarding the above repair or improvement,

    ☐ Other: _____

☐ To conduct an initial move-out inspection, as requested by you (48 hours' notice). (Calif. Civil Code
    § 1950.5(f)(1).)

If you wish to be present, you may make the appropriate arrangements. If you have any questions or if the above-

stated date or time is inconvenient, please notify the undersigned at _____ .
Phone Number

_____   _____

Landlord/Manager   Date

Rent Increase Worksheet

1. Tenant's name _____

2. Effective date of increase (assumes proper service of a 30-day notice): _____

_____

3. Lowest rent paid from _____ (12 months prior to effective date of increase) to effective date of increase: $ _____

4. **10% Figure** is 10% of lowest rent paid: _____ (rent in Step 3) x .1 = _____ .

5. Total rent increases from _____ (12 months prior to effective date of increase) to and including current increase:

Increase #1: _____ (date) $_____

Increase #2: _____ (date) $_____

Increase #3: _____ (date) $_____

Current Increase: _____ (date) $_____

Total Rent Increase: $_____

6. Compare the **10% Figure** with the **Total Rent Increase.**

☐ **Total Rent Increase** is the same or lower than the **10% Figure:** Use a 30-day notice which, if served properly, will allow you to collect the increased rent on the effective date you chose in Step 1.

☐ **Total Rent Increase** is greater than the **10% Figure**: Use a 60-day notice which, if properly served, will allow you to collect the increased rent 30 days after the date you specified in Step 1. _____

New effective rent increase date: _____

Notice of Change of Terms of Tenancy

To: _____,
Name

Tenant(s) in possession of the premises at _____,
Street Address

City of _____, County of _____, California.

The terms of tenancy under which you occupy these premises are changed as follows:

☐ The monthly rent will be increased to $_____, payable in advance.

☐ Other: _____

_____

The change in terms of tenancy shall be effective:

☐ _____, 20____
Date

☐ On the 30th day following service on you of this notice. If the change of terms of tenancy is an increase in rent, the amount due on the next following due date, prorated at the current rental rate prior to the 30th day, and prorated at the increased rate thereafter, is $_____.

☐ [Rent increase over 10%] On the 60th day following service on you of this notice. If the change of terms of tenancy is an increase in rent, the amount due on the next following due date, prorated at the current rental rate prior to the 60th day, and prorated at the increased rate thereafter, is $_____.

_____   _____

Landlord/Manager   Date

Three-Day Notice to Pay Rent or Quit

To: _____,
                                          Name

all tenants, subtenants, adult occupants, and others in possession of the premises at _____
                                                                              Street Address

_____, City of _____, County of _____, California.

PLEASE TAKE NOTICE that the rent on these premises occupied by you, in the amount of $_____, for
the period from _____ to _____, is now due and
payable.

YOU ARE HEREBY REQUIRED to pay this amount within THREE (3) days from the date of service on you of this
notice or to vacate and surrender possession of the premises. In the event you fail to do so, legal proceedings will
be instituted against you to recover possession of the premises, declare the forfeiture of the rental agreement or
lease under which you occupy the premises, and recover rents, damages, and costs of suit.

RENT IS TO BE PAID TO:

    [ ] the undersigned, or

    [ ] the following person: _____

AT THE FOLLOWING ADDRESS: _____, California, _____ (ZIP)

phone: ( ) _____

IN THE FOLLOWING MANNER:

    [ ] In person. Usual days and hours for rent collection are:

    [ ] by mail to the person and address indicated above

    [ ] by deposit to account _____ at _____, a financial institution located within 5 miles
       of your rental at _____, California

    [ ] by electronic funds transfer procedure previously established.

_____   _____
Landlord/Manager   Date

· ·

Proof of Service

I, the undersigned, being at least eighteen years of age, served this notice, of which this is a true copy, on
_____, one of the occupants listed above as follows:

☐ On _____, 20____, I delivered the notice to the occupant personally.

☐ On _____, 20____, I delivered the notice to a person of suitable age and discretion at the
   occupant's residence/business after having attempted personal service at the occupant's residence, and business, if
   known. On _____, 20____, I mailed a second copy to the occupant at his or her residence.

☐ On _____, 20____, I posted the notice in a conspicuous place on the property, after
   having attempted personal service at the occupant's residence, and business, if known, and after having been unable
   to find there a person of suitable age and discretion. _____, 20____, I mailed a second
   copy to the occupant at the property.

I declare under penalty of perjury under the laws of the State of California that the foregoing is true and correct.

_____   _____
                                                                                Date

30-Day Notice of Termination of Tenancy
(Tenancy of Less Than One Year)

To: _____ ,
Name

all tenants, subtenants, adult occupants and others in possession of the premises at _____
Street Address

_____, City of _____, County of _____, California.

YOU ARE HEREBY NOTIFIED that effective THIRTY (30) DAYS from the date of service on you of this notice, the periodic tenancy by which you hold possession of the premises is terminated, at which time you are required to vacate and surrender possession of the premises. If you fail to do so, legal proceedings will be instituted against you to recover possession of the premises, damages, and costs of suit.

_____

_____

_____

_____

_____

_____

_____

_____

_____

_____

_____   _____
Landlord/Manager   Date

· ·

Proof of Service

I, the undersigned, being at least eighteen years of age, served this notice, of which this is a true copy, on
_____, one of the occupants listed above as follows:

☐ On _____, 20____, I delivered the notice to the occupant personally.

☐ On _____, 20____, I delivered the notice to a person of suitable age and discretion at the occupant's residence/business after having attempted personal service at the occupant's residence, and business, if known. On _____, 20____, I mailed a second copy to the occupant at his or her residence.

☐ On _____, 20____, I posted the notice in a conspicuous place on the property, after having attempted personal service at the occupant's residence, and business, if known, and after having been unable to find there a person of suitable age and discretion. _____, 20____, I mailed a second copy to the occupant at the property.

I declare under penalty of perjury under the laws of the State of California that the foregoing is true and correct.

_____   _____
                                                Date

60-Day Notice of Termination of Tenancy

(Tenancy of One Year or More)

To: _____ ,
Name

all tenants, subtenants, adult occupants and others in possession of the premises at _____
Street Address

_____, City of _____, County of _____, California.

YOU ARE HEREBY NOTIFIED that effective SIXTY (60) DAYS from the date of service on you of this notice, the periodic tenancy by which you hold possession of the premises is terminated, at which time you are required to vacate and surrender possession of the premises. If you fail to do so, legal proceedings will be instituted against you to recover possession of the premises, damages and costs of suit.

_____

_____

_____

_____

_____

_____

_____

_____

_____

_____

_____

_____

_____   _____
Landlord/Manager   Date

· ·

Proof of Service

I, the undersigned, being at least eighteen years of age, served this notice, of which this is a true copy, on
_____ , one of the occupants listed above as follows:

☐ On _____, 20____, I delivered the notice to the occupant personally.

☐ On _____, 20____, I delivered the notice to a person of suitable age and discretion at the occupant's residence/business after having attempted personal service at the occupant's residence, and business, if known. On _____, 20____, I mailed a second copy to the occupant at his or her residence.

☐ On _____, 20____, I posted the notice in a conspicuous place on the property, after having attempted personal service at the occupant's residence, and business, if known, and after having been unable to find there a person of suitable age and discretion. _____, 20____, I mailed a second copy to the occupant at the property.

I declare under penalty of perjury under the laws of the State of California that the foregoing is true and correct.

_____   Date _____

90-Day Notice of Termination of Tenancy
(Subsidized Tenancies)

To: _____ ,
Name

all tenants, subtenants, adult occupants and others in possession of the premises at _____
Street Address

_____ , City of _____ , County of _____ , California.

YOU ARE HEREBY NOTIFIED that effective NINETY (90) DAYS from the date of service on you of this notice, the periodic tenancy by which you hold possession of the premises is terminated, at which time you are required to vacate and surrender possession of the premises. If you fail to do so, legal proceedings will be instituted against you to recover possession of the premises, damages and costs of suit. Reason for termination: _____

_____

_____

_____

_____

_____

_____

_____

_____

_____   _____
Landlord/Manager   Date

· ·

Proof of Service

I, the undersigned, being at least eighteen years of age, served this notice, of which this is a true copy, on _____ , one of the occupants listed above as follows:

☐ On _____ , 20___ , I delivered the notice to the occupant personally.

☐ On _____ , 20___ , I delivered the notice to a person of suitable age and discretion at the occupant's residence/business after having attempted personal service at the occupant's residence, and business, if known. On _____ , 20___ , I mailed a second copy to the occupant at his or her residence.

☐ On _____ , 20___ , I posted the notice in a conspicuous place on the property, after having attempted personal service at the occupant's residence, and business, if known, and after having been unable to find there a person of suitable age and discretion. _____ , 20___ , I mailed a second copy to the occupant at the property.

I declare under penalty of perjury under the laws of the State of California that the foregoing is true and correct.

_____   _____
                                                                                              Date

Three-Day Notice to Perform Covenant or Quit

To: _____ ,
Name

Tenant(s) in possession of the premises at _____ ,
Street Address

City of _____ , County of _____ , California.

YOU ARE HEREBY NOTIFIED that you are in violation of the lease or rental agreement under which you occupy these premises because you have violated the covenant to: _____

_____

_____

_____

in the following manner: _____

_____

_____

_____

YOU ARE HEREBY REQUIRED within THREE (3) DAYS from the date of service on you of this notice to remedy the violation and perform the covenant or to vacate and surrender possession of the premises.

If you fail to do so, legal proceedings will be instituted against you to recover possession of the premises, declare the forfeiture of the rental agreement or lease under which you occupy the premises, and recover damages and court costs.

_____   _____
Landlord/Manager   Date

· ·

Proof of Service

I, the undersigned, being at least eighteen years of age, served this notice, of which this is a true copy, on
_____ , one of the occupants listed above as follows:

☐ On _____ , 20____ , I delivered the notice to the occupant personally.

☐ On _____ , 20____ , I delivered the notice to a person of suitable age and discretion at the occupant's residence/business after having attempted personal service at the occupant's residence, and business, if known. On _____ , 20____ , I mailed a second copy to the occupant at his or her residence.

☐ On _____ , 20____ , I posted the notice in a conspicuous place on the property, after having attempted personal service at the occupant's residence, and business, if known, and after having been unable to find there a person of suitable age and discretion. _____ , 20____ , I mailed a second copy to the occupant at the property.

I declare under penalty of perjury under the laws of the State of California that the foregoing is true and correct.

_____   _____
                                                                                         Date

Three-Day Notice to Quit

(Improper Subletting, Nuisance, Waste or Illegal Use)

To: _____ ,
Name

Tenant(s) in possession of the premises at _____ ,
Street Address

City of _____ , County of _____ , California.

YOU ARE HEREBY NOTIFIED that you are required within THREE (3) DAYS from the date of service on you of this notice to vacate and surrender possession of the premises because you have committed the following nuisance, waste, unlawful use, or unlawful subletting:

_____

_____

_____

_____

_____

_____

_____

As a result of your having committed the foregoing act(s), the lease or rental agreement under which you occupy these premises is terminated. If you fail to vacate and surrender possession of the premises within three days, legal proceedings will be instituted against you to recover possession of the premises, damages, and court costs.

_____   _____
Landlord/Manager   Date

• •

Proof of Service

I, the undersigned, being at least eighteen years of age, served this notice, of which this is a true copy, on
_____ , one of the occupants listed above as follows:

☐ On _____ , 20____, I delivered the notice to the occupant personally.

☐ On _____ , 20____, I delivered the notice to a person of suitable age and discretion at the occupant's residence/business after having attempted personal service at the occupant's residence, and business, if known. On _____ , 20____, I mailed a second copy to the occupant at his or her residence.

☐ On _____ , 20____, I posted the notice in a conspicuous place on the property, after having attempted personal service at the occupant's residence, and business, if known, and after having been unable to find there a person of suitable age and discretion. _____ , 20____, I mailed a second copy to the occupant at the property.

I declare under penalty of perjury under the laws of the State of California that the foregoing is true and correct.

_____   _____
                                                                       Date

Warning Notice (Complaints From Neighbors/Residents)

Date: _____

Memorandum from Landlord/Manager to

_____, Resident(s) of

Property at _____

_____

Re: Complaints from neighbors/other residents

Several of your neighbors have complained to the management regarding to the following disturbance or condition:

_____

_____

_____

Approximate date of occurrence: _____

It is very important to the management that our residents be able to enjoy the peace and quiet of their homes. Disturbing or affecting neighbors is a violation of the terms of your lease/rental agreement. You are requested to take the following corrective action: _____

_____

_____

_____

If you have any questions, please contact _____,

at _____.

Sincerely,

_____

Landlord/Manager

Notice of Belief of Abandonment
Civil Code Section 1951.3

To: _____,
Name

Tenant(s) in possession of the premises at _____,
Street Address

City of _____, County of _____, California.

This notice is given pursuant to Section 1951.3 of the Civil Code concerning the real property leased by you at the above address. The rent on this property had been due and unpaid for 14 consecutive days, and the landlord or his agent believes that you have abandoned the property.

The real property will be deemed abandoned within the meaning of Section 1951.2 of the Civil Code and your lease will terminate on _____, 20_____, a date not less than 18 days after the mailing of this notice, unless before such date the undersigned receives at the address indicated below a written notice from you stating both of the following:

    (1) your intent not to abandon the real property

    (2) an address at which you may be served by certified mail in any action for unlawful detainer of the real property.

You are required to pay the rent due and unpaid on this real property as required by the lease, and your failure to do so can lead to a court proceeding against you.

_____

Date

_____

Landlord (signature)

_____

Landlord (print)

_____

Street address

_____

Move-Out Letter

_____

Dear Resident:

We hope you have enjoyed living here.

Before vacating, be sure to thoroughly vacuum the floors (shampoo carpets, if necessary) and clean the walls, kitchen cabinets, stove and oven, refrigerator (which should be emptied of food, turned off, with the door left open), kitchen and bathroom sink, bathtubs, showers, toilets, plumbing fixtures, and _____

_____

You have the right to request an initial move-out inspection, at which time management will inspect your rental and, to the extent possible, identify damage, excessive wear and tear, and unacceptable uncleanliness that will have to be remedied in order to avoid deductions from your security deposit. You have the right to be present at that inspection if you choose, and we encourage you to do so. Problems that occur between the inspection and when you move out, or that were missed due to the presence of your possessions, can still form the basis of a deduction from your deposit.

If we need to deduct from your security deposit to cover needed repairs or to clean the rental unit, and if the total deduction (for labor and materials) is more than $125.00, we will give you copies of receipts and invoices for all work done and items purchased. If management or its employees do any of the work, we will bill you at a reasonable rate for that work. These invoices and bills will be included with an itemization of deductions and return of the balance, if any, of your security deposit, which you will receive within three weeks after you move out. (If management does not have these items in its possession when it itemizes and returns any balance, either because the work is yet to be completed or the invoices have not been received, we will include an estimate of the deductions, with the repairperson's name, address, and phone number, and send the actual bills to you within 14 days of receiving them.) You may waive your right to receive invoices (we will give you a form for this), and you may also rescind that waiver (and ask for invoices) if you do so within 14 days of receiving the itemization.

Please provide a forwarding address where we may mail your security deposit less any past due rent and minus any lawful deductions for the cost of necessary cleaning and repairs of damage in excess of ordinary wear and tear (with receipts and invoices for such deductions).

We will give you two written response forms, on which you can tell us whether you would like an initial move-out inspection and whether you would like to waive your right to copies of bills and receipts for any work done or items purchased, as explained above.

If you have any questions, please contact me at _____.

Sincerely,

_____

Landlord/Manager

Tenant's Response Regarding
Initial Move-Out Inspection

Tenant: _____

Rental Address: _____

_____

Termination Date: _____

I understand that I have a legal right to an initial move-out inspection. (California Civil Code Section 1050.5.) The purpose of this inspection, which my landlord or manager will perform no earlier than two weeks before my termination date, is to give me a chance to avoid probable deductions from my security deposit. At the inspection, I'll be advised of intended deductions for deficiencies such as damage, excessive wear and tear, or the need to clean the rental unit. I understand that I may remedy these problems consistent with any repair rights or limitations that may be in my lease or rental agreement. I also understand that my landlord will reinspect when I leave, and may deduct for deficiencies that:

- have been noted in the initial inspection but have not been satisfactorily remedied

- could not be seen during the initial inspection due to the presence of my possessions in the rental unit, or

- have appeared since the date of the initial inspection.

Tenant, please initial one of the following:

_____ I would like to be present at the inspection. Please contact me so that we can arrange for a mutually convenient time.

_____ I would like an initial inspection but do not wish to be present. Please give me 48 hours' notice of the day and time you will inspect.

_____ I do not wish to have an initial move-out inspection.

s/_____

_____, Landlord/Manager

_____

Date signed by Landlord

_____

Date form given to Tenant

s/_____

_____, Tenant

_____

Date signed by Tenant

Notice of Tenant's Security Deposit Rights

Dear _____(tenant),

Your landlord or his or her agent has performed an initial move-out inspection as requested by you pursuant to California Civil Code Section 1950.5. Attached to this Notice is an itemization of needed repairs, replacements, or cleaning which may, if not remedied, form the basis of deductions from your security deposit.

Civil Code Section 1950.5 provides that:

"1950.5(b): As used in this section, "security" means any payment, fee, deposit or charge, including, but not limited to, any payment, fee, deposit or charge, except as provided in Section 1950.6, that is imposed at the beginning of the tenancy to be used to reimburse the landlord for costs associated with processing a new tenant or that is imposed as an advance payment of rent, used or to be used for any purpose, including, but not limited to, any of the following:

(1) The compensation of a landlord for a tenant's default in the payment of rent.

(2) The repair of damages to the premises, exclusive of ordinary wear and tear, caused by the tenant or by a guest or licensee of the tenant.

(3) The cleaning of the premises upon termination of the tenancy necessary to return the unit to the same level of cleanliness it was in at the inception of the tenancy. The amendments to this paragraph enacted by the act adding this sentence shall apply only to tenancies for which the tenant's right to occupy begins after January 1, 2003.

(4) To remedy future defaults by the tenant in any obligation under the rental agreement to restore, replace or return personal property or appurtenances, exclusive of ordinary wear and tear, if the security deposit is authorized to be applied thereto by the rental agreement.

1950.5(d): Any security shall be held by the landlord for the tenant who is party to the lease or agreement. The claim of a tenant to the security shall be prior to the claim of any creditor of the landlord."

I have given this Notice and its attachment to _____ (tenant) or a person of apparent authority, suitable age, and discretion; or have left it in the rental unit in a safe and conspicuous place.

s/_____

_____, Landlord or agent

_____
Date

I have received this Notice and its attachment.

s/_____

_____, Tenant or recipient

_____
Date

Tenant's Waiver of Right to Receipts and Invoices
California Civil Code Section 1959.5(g)(4)(B)

Tenant: _____

Rental Address: _____

_____

Termination Date: _____

   I understand that I will receive a list of itemized deductions from my security deposit, for necessary cleaning and repairs to, or replacement of, items damaged beyond normal wear and tear. I also understand that I have the right to receive copies of documents, such as bills, invoices, and receipts, showing charges incurred and deducted by my landlord to repair or clean the premises. (California Civil Code Section 1950.5 (g)(2).) In particular,

- If my landlord or the landlord's employee does the work, the itemized statement will include the work performed, time spent, and a reasonable hourly rate.

- If others did the work, the statement will include a copy of the receipt, bill, or invoice sent by the repairperson, along with the person's address and phone number.

- If the landlord deducts for materials or supplies, the statement will include a copy of the bill, invoice, or receipt. If the material or item is one that the landlord purchases on an ongoing basis, the statement will include a copy of the bill, invoice, receipt, vendor price list, or other vendor document that will indicate the cost of the item used in the repair or for the cleaning of my rental unit.

   I now waive these rights to receive copies of invoices, bills, and receipts, as described above. Within 14 days of receiving my itemized statement I may, however, request documentation of all deductions from my security deposit, and I understand that the landlord will have 14 days after receiving my request in which to furnish such documentation to me, in the same manner in which the initial itemization was prepared and sent.

s/_____   _____

_____, Tenant   Date

Received by management:

s/_____   _____

_____, Management   Date

Letter for Returning Entire Security Deposit

_____

_____

_____

_____

Dear _____ :

Here is the itemization, as required by Civil Code Section 1950.5, of your $_____ security

deposit on the property at _____,

which you rented from me on a _____ on

_____, 20_____ and vacated on _____, 20_____.

As you left the rental property in satisfactory condition, I am returning the entire amount of your security deposit

of $_____.

Sincerely,

_____

Landlord/Manager

Security Deposit Itemization
(Deductions for Repairs and Cleaning)
Civil Code Section 1950.5

Date: _____

From: _____

_____

_____

To: _____

_____

_____

Property Address: _____

Rental Period: _____

1. Security Deposit Received $ _____

2. Interest on Deposit (if required by lease or law): $ _____

3. Total Credit (sum of lines 1 and 2) $ _____

4. Itemized Repairs and Related Losses (receipts, bills, or invoices attached, unless previously waived):

   _____

   _____

   _____

   _____   Total Repair Cost: $ _____

5. Necessary Cleaning (receipts, bills, or invoices attached, unless previously waived):

   _____

   _____

   _____

   _____   Total Cleaning Cost: $ _____

6. Amount Owed (line 3 minus the sum of lines 4 and 5)

   ☐ a. Total Amount Tenant Owes Landlord: $ _____

   ☐ b. Total Amount Landlord Owes Tenant: $ _____

Comments: _____

_____

_____

_____

Security Deposit Itemization
(Deductions for Repairs, Cleaning, and Unpaid Rent)
Civil Code Section 1950.5

Date: _____

From: _____

_____

_____

To: _____

_____

_____

Property Address: _____

Rental Period: _____

1. Security Deposit Received $ _____

2. Interest on Deposit (if required by lease or law): $ _____

3. Total Credit (sum of lines 1 and 2) $ _____

4. Itemized Repairs and Related Losses (receipts, bills, or invoices attached, unless previously waived):

_____

_____

_____

_____   Total Repair Cost: $ _____

5. Necessary Cleaning (receipts, bills, or invoices attached, unless previously waived):

_____

_____

_____

_____   Total Cleaning Cost: $ _____

6. Defaults in Rent Not Covered by Any Court Judgment
(list dates and rates):

_____

_____

_____

_____   Total Rent Defaults: $ _____

7. Amount of Court Judgment for Rent, Costs, Attorney Fees: $ _____

8. Other Deductions:

   Specify: _____

   _____

   _____ $ _____

9. Amount Owed (line 3 minus the sum of lines 4, 5, 6, 7, and 8)

   ☐ a. Total Amount Tenant Owes Landlord: $ _____

   ☐ b. Total Amount Landlord Owes Tenant: $ _____

Comments: _____

_____

_____

_____

_____

_____

_____

_____

_____

_____

_____

_____

_____

_____

_____

_____

_____

Notice of Right to Reclaim Abandoned Property
Civil Code Section 1984

To: _____
Name

When the premises at _____,
Street Address

City of _____, County of _____, California

were vacated, the following personal property remained:_____

_____

_____

☐ Continued on Attachment "A" hereto.

    You may claim this property at: _____

City of _____, County of _____, California.

Unless you pay the reasonable cost of storage for all the above-described property, and take possession of the property that you claim not later than eighteen (18) days after the date of mailing of this notice indicated below, this property will be disposed of pursuant to Civil Code Section 1988.

☐ Because this property is believed to be worth less than $300, it will be kept, sold, or destroyed without further notice if you fail to reclaim it within the time limit indicated.

☐ Because this property is believed to be worth more than $300, it will be sold at a public sale after notice has been given by publication, if you fail to reclaim it within the time limit indicated. You have the right to bid on the property at this sale. After the property is sold and the cost of storage, advertising, and sale is deducted, the remaining money will be turned over to the county. You may claim the remaining money at any time within one year after the county receives the money.

Date of Mailing _____

_____

Landlord/Manager

_____

Street address

_____

Appendix C

Rent Control Chart

READING YOUR RENT CONTROL ORDINANCE

The following chart contains most of the information about how your rent control ordinance affects evictions, but we recommend that you check the ordinance itself and always make sure that it hasn't changed since this was printed. In case you are (understandably) intimidated at the prospect of deciphering your city's ordinance, here are a few hints about reading and understanding rent control ordinances.

Almost all rent control ordinances begin with a statement of purpose, followed by definitions of terms used in the ordinance. If such terms as "rental unit" and "landlord" aren't defined specifically enough to tell you who and what is covered by the ordinance, another section dealing with applicability of the ordinance usually follows. After that the ordinance usually sets out the structure and rules of the rent board and will say whether or not landlords must register their properties with the board.

Your ordinance probably then has a section entitled something like "Annual Increases" or "General Rent Ceiling." If the city allows increases when the unit becomes vacant, this will be stated under this category or in a "Vacancy Decontrol" section.

Following the rent sections should be a section on "Individual Adjustments" or "Hardship Adjustments." This section tells you how to get an increase over and above any general across the board increase. Finally, any requirement that you show "just cause" for eviction should be found under a section entitled "Just (or Good) Cause for Eviction." It will contain a list of the permissible reasons for eviction, along with any extra requirements for eviction notices, and prohibit evictions for any other reason.

To see if you've complied with your city's rent control ordinance before you begin an eviction, check the ordinance for:

- **Registration requirements.** If you're required to register your unit with the rent board but didn't, your tenant may be able to win an eviction lawsuit.
- **Rent increase restrictions.** Read the individual adjustment section to see if the landlord must apply to the rent board for increases over a certain amount. If so, make sure any rent increases were properly applied for and legal. This is especially important if you're planning to evict for nonpayment of rent, because you must list the rent that's legally due on the three-day notice.
- **Special notice requirements.** Check both the general and individual rent adjustment sections, as well as any regulations adopted by the rent board, for special notice requirements for rent increase notices. Again, if you're evicting for nonpayment of rent, you want to be sure that all previous increases were given with a valid notice.
- **Just cause requirements.** This is crucial; you can evict only for one of the permissible reasons, and you must comply with any additional notice requirements. If you want to evict tenants so you can demolish the building or simply go out of business, you may do so under the Ellis Act (Govt. Code §§ 7060–7060.7), even if this reason isn't listed in the ordinance. However, you definitely should have a lawyer handle the eviction.

If you're evicting to move a relative or manager into the unit or to remodel, demolish, or convert the unit, any just cause requirement will have numerous technical notice and compensation requirements. You should consult a lawyer.

FINDING MUNICIPAL CODES AND RENT CONTROL ORDINANCES ONLINE

If you own rental property in a city that has rent control, you should have a current copy of the city's rent control law. You can usually obtain a paper copy from the administrative agency that oversees the workings of the ordinance. It's quicker, however, to read the material online. Most cities have posted their ordinances, as you will see from the list below. Use the Rent Control Chart, which provides detailed, city-by-city analyses, as guides to your own reading of the law. Keep in mind that ordinances often change and their meaning evolves as rent boards issue regulations and make decisions.

Berkeley

www.ci.berkeley.ca.us

Click on "Municipal Codes & Zoning Ordinance" to get to the Municipal Code. For rent control provisions, see Municipal Code Chapter 13.76. The Rent Stabilization Board itself is at www.ci.berkeley.ca.us/rent.

Beverly Hills

www.ci.beverly-hills.ca.us or www.beverlyhills.org

Go to the "shortcuts" pull-down menu and choose "Municipal Code" on the next page. For rent control provisions, see Title 4, Chapters 5 and 6, of the Municipal Code.

Campbell

www.ci.campbell.ca.us

Click on "Doing Business," and choose "Campbell Municipal Code" on the next page. For rent control provisions, see Title 6, Chapter 6.09, of the Municipal Code.

East Palo Alto

www.ci.east-palo-alto.ca.us

Go to the "Browse by Topic" pull-down menu and choose Municipal Code under "City Hall and Government." Then press the "Go" button.

Fremont

www.ci.fremont.ca.us

Go to the "shortcuts" pull-down menu and choose "Housing Services." Scroll down and click on "Residential Rent Increase Dispute Resolution Ordinance...."

Hayward

www.ci.hayward.ca.us

For Municipal Code, click on "Official Documents" under "City Hall," then click on "Hayward Municipal Code." However, the Rent Control Ordinance is not part of Municipal Code and not available online.

Los Angeles

www.ci.la.ca.us

To get to the Los Angeles Municipal Code from the official city website, click on the "City Charter, Rules & Codes" box at the left. On the next page, click on "Municipal Codes," then choose "Municipal Code." Rent control provisions are in Chapter XV.

Los Gatos

www.town.los-gatos.ca.us

Click on "Town Government" at left, and then scroll down until you find "Town Codes." Rent control provisions are in Chapter 14, Article VIII.

Oakland

www.ci.oakland.ca.us

Click on "Municipal Code" at the pull-down menu to the left and press "Go." Rent control provisions are in Title 8, Chapter 8.22.

Palm Springs

www.ci.palm-springs.ca.us

This city's website does not provide the Municipal Code, but it is available online at www.bpcnet.com/codes/palmsprings or http://municipalcodes/lexisnexis.com/codes/palmsprings.

San Francisco

www.ci.sf.ca.us/rentbd or
www.sfgov.org/site/rentboard–index.asp

This is the best place online to get rent control ordinance provisions and regulations, maintained by the rent board. For the entire collection of city codes, go to the City's main website at www.ci.sf.ca.us. Click on "Municipal Codes" at the "How Can We Help You?" pull-down menu. This page also includes the Administrative Code, including the Chapter 37 rent control provisions.

San Jose

www.ci.san-jose.ca.us or www.sanjose.ca.gov

Click on "Municipal Code" (under "Local Government") at right.

Santa Monica

www.ci.santa-monica.ca.us/rentcontrol/charterandregs/regsindx.htm

This city's rent control laws are in the City Charter, not in the Municipal Code. The Rent Control Board maintains the site listed here. If you want to see the Municipal Code as well, go to the official city site at www.ci.santa-monica.ca.us and choose Municipal Code under the Quick Index pull-down menu.

Thousand Oaks

www.ci.thousand-oaks.ca.us

This city's rent control ordinances (755-NS [7/1980], 956-NS [3/1987], and 1284-NS [5/1997]) were never made a part of the Municipal Code, and thus cannot be found in the online Municipal Code. If you'd like to look at the Municipal Code anyway, go to the official city site above. Then, move the cursor to "Common Questions," then up to "City Hall," then choose "Municipal Code" from the pull-down menu.

West Hollywood

www.ci.west-hollywood.ca.us

To get to the Municipal Code from this city's official site, click on "City Government," then on "Municipal Code."

CALIFORNIA IMPOSES STATEWIDE LIMITATIONS ON CITIES' RENT CONTROL ORDINANCES

State law now significantly limits local rent control laws in the 14 California cities that now have them. (Civ. Code §§ 1954.50-53.) The new law has three major components.

1. No rent control for single-family residences.

As of January 1, 1999, tenancies that began on or after January 1, 1996 in single-family residences and condominiums will no longer be subject to rent control. Only tenants who have continuously occupied the premises since before January 1, 1996 may enjoy the benefits of rent control past January 1, 1999. This includes not only tenants with leases signed before January 1, 1996, but also those tenants who have rented the same unit on a month-to-month basis, starting prior to January 1, 1996. (Civ. Code §§ 1954.52 (a) (3).)

2. No rent control for new residences.

This law also prohibits any rent control on new residences, defined as those that have certificates of occupancy issued after January 31, 1995.

For more details on this new state law, contact the local agency that administers rent control in your area. (Civ. Code §§ 1954.52 (a)(1),(2).)

3. "Vacancy decontrol" for apartments.

This change affects Berkeley, East Palo Alto, Santa Monica, and West Hollywood, the only cities that formerly did not let landlords raise the rent when a tenant moves out and another comes in.

Effective January 1, 1999, landlords may raise the rent on multifamily housing units in any rent-controlled city if the prior tenant left voluntarily or was evicted for nonpayment of rent. Once rerented at this new rent, however, the property is still subject to local rent control ordinances at the higher rent.

Landlords may not, however, raise rents after a voluntary vacancy if the landlord has been cited for serious health, safety, fire, or building code violations that have continued unabated for six months preceding the vacancy. (Civ. Code §§ 1954.53.)

BERKELEY

Name of Ordinance
Rent Stabilization and Eviction for Good Cause Ordinance, City Charter Art. XII, §§ 120-124, Berkeley Municipal Code Ch. 13.76.

Adoption Date
6/3/80. Last amended 11/90, by initiative.

Exceptions
Units constructed after 6/3/80, owner-occupied single-family residences and duplexes. (§ 13.76.050.)

Administration
Rent Stabilization Board
2125 Milvia Street
Berkeley, CA 94704
510-644-6128
FAX: 510-644-7723
email: rent@ci.berkeley.ca.us
Websites: www.ci.berkeley.ca.us (This is the general city site. Click on "Municipal Codes & Zoning Ord." to get to Municipal Code. For the rent board add /rent.
The rent board's site, at "Laws and Regs" icon, is the best way to get to rent control and eviction rules). See also http://tenant.net/Other_Areas/Calif/berkeley/index.html.

Registration
Required or landlords cannot raise rent. (The provision that a tenant can withhold rents if the landlord fails to register was ruled unconstitutional in *Floystrup v. Berkeley Rent Stablization Board* (1990) 219 Cal. App. 3d 1309.) Stiff penalties for noncooperation. (§ 13.76.080.)

Vacancy Decontrol
State law (Civ. Code § 1954.53) supersedes the ordinance. Upon voluntary vacancy or eviction for nonpayment of rent, rents may be increased to any level following such vacancies. Once property is rerented, it is subject to rent control based on the higher rent.

Just Cause
Required. (§ 13.76.130.) This requirement applies even if the property is exempt from other rent control requirements because it qualifies as new construction or government-owned/operated housing. Specific good cause to evict must be stated in both the notice and in any unlawful detainer complaint.

Other Features
The landlord's complaint must allege compliance with both the implied warranty of habitability and the rent control ordinance, except for evictions for remodeling or demolition. If the remodeling, demolition, or moving in of the landlord or a relative on which the eviction was based doesn't occur within two months of the tenant's leaving, the tenant can sue the landlord to regain possession of property and recover actual damages (treble damages or $750 if reason willfully false). (§ 13.76.150.)

Reasons Allowed for Just Cause Evictions	Additional Local Notice Requirements and Limitations
Nonpayment of rent.	Ordinary Three-Day Notice to Pay Rent or Quit is used.
Breach of lease provision.	Three-Day Notice to Perform Covenant or Quit is used. Provision must be "reasonable and legal and ... been accepted by the tenant or made part of the rental agreement." If the provision was added after tenant moved in, landlord can evict for breach only if tenant was told in writing that she did not have to accept the new term. Tenant must be given "written notice to cease," which precludes an Unconditional Three-Day Notice to Quit even if the breach is considered uncorrectable.
Willful causing or allowing of substantial damage to premises and refusal to both pay the reasonable cost of repair and cease causing damage, following written notice.	Even though damage is involved, an Unconditional Three-Day Notice to Quit is not allowed. Only a three-day notice that gives the tenant the option of ceasing to cause damage and pay for repair is allowed.

Reasons Allowed for Just Cause Evictions	Additional Local Notice Requirements and Limitations
Tenant refuses to agree to rental agreement or lease on expiration of prior one, where new proposed agreement contains no new or unlawful terms.	This applies only if a lease or rental agreement expires of its own terms. No notice is required. However, tenant must have refused to sign a new one containing the same provisions; an improvised notice giving the tenant several days to sign the new agreement or leave is a good idea, even though not required by ordinance or state law.
Tenant continued to be so disorderly as to disturb other tenants, following written notice to cease, or is otherwise subject to eviction under C.C.P. § 1161(4), for committing a nuisance, very seriously damaging the property, or subletting contrary to the lease or rental agreement.	Although a warning notice should precede three-day notice based on disturbing neighbors, the three-day notice, according to C.C.P. § 1161(4), may be an unconditional Three-Day Notice to Quit.
Tenant, after written notice to cease, continues to refuse landlord access to the property as required by Civ. Code § 1954.	If provision is in lease, use three-day notice giving tenant option of letting you in or moving. If not, and tenancy is month to month, use 30-day notice specifying reason, following written demand for access.
Landlord wants to make substantial repairs to bring property into compliance with health codes, and repairs not possible while tenant remains.	Under state law, eviction for this reason is allowed only if rental agreement is month to month, not for a fixed term. Landlord must first obtain all permits required for the remodeling, must provide alternative housing for the tenant (at the same rent) if he owns other vacant units in city, and must give evicted tenant right of first refusal to rerent after remodeling is finished. (Tenant given alternate temporary housing may be evicted from it if he refuses to move into old unit after work is completed.)
Landlord wants to demolish property.	Landlord must first obtain city "removal permit." (Although ordinance requires "good faith" to demolish, a euphemism for not doing it because of rent control, the state Ellis Act severely limits cities from refusing demolition permits on this basis.)
Landlord wants to move self, spouse, parent, or child into property, and no comparable vacant unit exists in the property.	30-day notice terminating month-to-month tenancy for this reason must specify name and relationship of person moving in. (Month-to-month tenancies only.)
Tenant, after written notice to cease, continues to conduct illegal activity on the premises.	Although a warning notice should precede a three-day notice based on illegal activity, the three-day notice, according to C.C.P. § 1161(4), may be an unconditional Three-Day Notice to Quit.
Landlord wants to move in herself, lived there previously, and lease or rental agreement specifically allows for this.	Termination procedure must be in accordance with lease provision. Thirty days' written notice is required to terminate month-to-month tenancy unless agreement provides for lesser period as short as seven days.
Landlord wants to go out of rental business under state Ellis Act.	The requirement that the landlord must give the tenant six months' notice and pay $4,500 in relocation fees to tenants of each unit was ruled illegal, as preempted by the state Ellis Act, in *Channing Properties v. City of Berkeley* (1992) 11 Cal. App. 4th 88, 14 Cal. Rptr. 2d 32.

Beverly Hills

Name of Ordinance

Rent Stabilization Ordinance, Beverly Hills Municipal Code, Title 4, Chapters 5 and 6, §§ 4-5.101 to 4-6.08.

Adoption Date

4/27/79. Last amended 3/30/2001.

Exceptions

Units constructed after 10/20/78, units that rented for more than $600 on 5/31/78, single-family residences, rented condominium units. (§ 4-5.102.)

Administration

Building and Safety Dept./Rent Stabilization
455 N. Rexford
Beverly Hills, CA 90210
310-285-1031
Website: www.ci.beverly-hills.ca.us or
www.beverlyhills.org. (General city site. No site for the rent control ordinance.)

Registration

Not required.

Vacancy Decontrol

Rents may be increased to any level on rerenting following eviction for nonpayment of rent, as well as for voluntary vacancies.

Once property is rerented, it is subject to rent control based on the higher rent.

Just Cause

Required for units other than those that rented for more than $600 on 5/31/78; for these units, a month-to-month tenancy may be terminated only on 60 days' notice, however. (§§ 4-5.501 to 4-5.513.)

Other Features

Though not required by the ordinance, termination notice should state specific reason for termination; this indicates compliance with ordinance, as alleged (item 13) in your unlawful detainer Complaint. Landlord is required to pay tenant substantial relocation fee if evicting to move in self or relative, or to substantially remodel, demolish, or convert to condominiums. Tenant may sue landlord who uses moving-in of self or relative as a "pretext" for eviction, for three times the rent that would have been due for the period the tenant was out of possession.

Reasons Allowed for Just Cause Evictions	Additional Local Notice Requirements and Limitations
Nonpayment of rent.	Ordinary Three-Day Notice to Pay Rent or Quit is used.
Breach of lease provision, following written notice to correct problem.	Three-Day Notice to Cure Covenant or Quit is used. The tenant must be given "written notice to cease," which precludes an unconditional Three-Day Notice to Quit even if the breach is uncorrectable.
Commission of a legal nuisance (disturbing other residents) or damaging the property.	Unconditional Three-Day Notice to Quit may be used.
Tenant is using the property for illegal purpose. This specifically includes overcrowding as defined in ordinance based on number of bedrooms and square footage.	Unconditional Three-Day Notice to Quit may be used.
Tenant refuses, after written demand by landlord, to agree to new rental agreement or lease on expiration of prior one, where proposed agreement contains no new or unlawful terms.	This applies when a lease or rental agreement expires of its own terms. The ordinance requires the landlord to have made a written request for renewal or extension at least 30 days before the old one expired.
Tenant has refused the landlord reasonable access to the property as required by Civ. Code § 1954.	If access provision is in lease, use three-day notice giving tenant option of letting you in or moving. If not, and tenancy is month to month, use 30-day notice specifying reason, following written demand for access to property.

Reasons Allowed for Just Cause Evictions	Additional Local Notice Requirements and Limitations
Fixed-term lease has expired, and person occupying property is subtenant not approved by landlord.	Eviction is allowed on this basis only if person living there is not original tenant or approved subtenant. If lease has not expired and contains no-subletting clause, use Three-Day Notice to Quit to evict for breach of lease.
Landlord wants to move self, parent, or child into property, and no comparable vacant unit exists in the property. In multiple-unit dwelling, landlord can evict only the most recently moved-in tenant for this reason.	Landlord must give tenant 90-day notice that states the name, relationship, and address of person to be moved in, and a copy of the notice must be sent to the City Clerk. Landlord must also pay tenant(s) a "relocation fee" of up to $2,500, depending on the length of tenancy and the size of unit. The fee must be paid when the tenant leaves, or tenant can sue landlord for three times the fee plus attorney's fees. (§ 11-7.05.) Landlord does not have to pay fee if tenant fails to leave at end of 90-day period or pays to relocate tenant to comparable housing elsewhere.
Employment of resident manager has been terminated and the property is needed for occupancy by the new manager.	This type of eviction is not covered in this book because the question of what notice is required is extremely complicated, depending in part on the nature of the management agreement. You should seek legal advice.
Landlord wants to demolish property or convert to condominiums, or otherwise remove property from rental market.	Landlord must first obtain removal permit from city. For substantial remodeling, tenant gets right of first refusal when work done. Landlord must give tenant one year's notice. Landlord must also pay tenant(s) a "relocation fee" of up to $2,500, depending on the length of tenancy and the size of unit. The fee must be paid when the tenant leaves, or tenant can sue landlord for three times the fee plus attorney's fees. Landlord does not have to pay fee if tenant fails to leave at end of 90-day period or pays to relocate tenant to comparable housing elsewhere. Notice, if not accompanied by fee, must inform tenant of its amount and that it is payable when the tenant vacates. The notice cannot be given until city approval of the project is obtained, and a copy of the notice must be sent to the City Clerk.
Landlord wants to substantially remodel property.	Landlord must first obtain removal permit from city. For substantial remodeling, tenant gets right of first refusal when work done. Landlord must give tenant one year's notice. Landlord must also pay tenant(s) a "relocation fee" of up to $2,500, depending on the length of tenancy and the size of unit. The fee must be paid when the tenant leaves, or tenant can sue landlord for three times the fee plus attorney's fees. Landlord does not have to pay fee if tenant fails to leave at end of 90-day period or pays to relocate tenant to comparable housing elsewhere. Notice, if not accompanied by fee, must inform tenant of its amount and that it is payable when the tenant vacates. The notice cannot be given until city approval of the project is obtained, and a copy of the notice must be sent to the City Clerk. Landlord must petition Board for permission and in some cases must provide replacement housing during remodeling.

CAMPBELL

Name of Ordinance
Campbell Municipal Code, Title 6, Ch. 6.09, §§ 6.09.010 to 6.09.190.

Adoption Date
1983. Last amended 12/98.

Exemption
Rental units on lots with three or fewer units. (§ 6.09.030(n).

Administration
Campbell Rental Dispute Program
Project Sentinel Mediation Services
1055 Sunnyvale-Saratoga Road, Suite 3
Sunnyvale, CA 94087
408-243-8565
Website: www.ci.campbell.ca.us. (The general city site, includes the Municipal Code. There is no site for the Rental Dispute Program.)

Registration
Not required.

Individual Adjustments
Tenants affected by an increase can contest it by filing a petition within 45 days after notice of increase or notice to quit, or 15 days from effective date of rent increase or notice to quit, whichever is later, or lose the right to object to the increase. Disputes raised by tenant petition are first subject to "conciliation," then mediation. If those fail, either party may file a written request for arbitration by city "Fact Finding Committee." Committee determines whether increase is "reasonable" by considering costs of capital improvements, repairs, maintenance and debt service, and past history of rent increases. However, the Committee's determination is not binding. (§§ 6.09.050-6.09.150.)

Vacancy Decontrol
No restriction on raises after vacancy.

Eviction
Ordinance does not require showing of just cause to evict, so three-day and 30-day notice requirements and unlawful detainer procedures are governed solely by state law.

Just Cause
Not required

Other features
Rent increase notice must state: "Notice: Chapter 6.09 of the Campbell Municipal Code provides a conciliation and mediation procedure for property owners and tenants to communicate when there are disputes over rent increases. (Rent increases can include a significant reduction in housing services.) To use this nonbinding procedure, the tenants shall first make a reasonable, good faith effort to contact the property owner or the property owner's agent to resolve the rent increase dispute. If not resolved, the tenant may then file a petition within 45 calendar days of this notice or 15 calendar days following the effective day of the increase, whichever is later. There may be other tenants from your complex receiving a similar rent increase, in which case, the petitions will be combined. For more information you should contact the City's designated Agent at 408-243-8565. Petitioning for conciliation cannot guarantee a reduction in the rent increase."

Note. Because this ordinance does not provide for binding arbitration of any rent increase dispute, it is not truly a rent control ordinance. Compliance with any decision appears to be voluntary only.

EAST PALO ALTO

Name of Ordinance
Rent Stabilization and Eviction for Good Cause Ordinance, Ordinance No. 076.

Adoption Date
11/23/83. Last amended 4/88.

Exception
Units constructed after 11/23/83, units owned by landlords owning four or fewer units in city, property rehabilitated in accordance with federal Internal Revenue Code § 174(k). (§ 5.)

Administration
Rent Stabilization Board
2200 University Avenue
East Palo Alto, CA 94303
650-853-3114
Website: www.ci.east-palo-alto.ca.us. This is the general city site with access to the Municipal Code.

Registration
Required.

Vacancy Decontrol
State law (Civ. Code § 1954.53) supersedes the ordinance. Upon voluntary vacancy or eviction for nonpayment of rent, rents may be increased to any level following such vacan-cies. Once property is rerented, it is subject to rent control based on the higher rent.

Just Cause
Required (§ 13.A). This aspect of the ordinance applies even to new construction, which is otherwise exempt. Specific just cause to evict must be stated both in the notice and in any unlawful detainer complaint. (§ 13.B.)

Other Features
Landlord's complaint must allege compliance with both the implied warranty of habitability and the rent control ordinance, except for evictions for remodeling or demoli-tion (§ 13.C). If remodeling, demolition, or moving self or a relative, on which eviction was based, doesn't occur within two months of the tenant's leaving, tenant can sue landlord to regain possession of property and recover actual damages (treble damages or $500 if reason willfully false). (§ 15.B.)

East Palo Alto's ordinance does not specifically allow evic-tion for illegal use of the premises, such as dealing drugs. Still, if the lease has a clause prohibiting illegal use of the premises, you can evict for breach of lease provision (see be-low). If there's no such lease provision, see an attorney about whether C.C.P. § 1161(4)s, allowance of an eviction for il-legal activity, may "preempt" the local ordinance.

Reasons Allowed for Just Cause Evictions	Additional Local Notice Requirements and Limitations
Nonpayment of rent.	Ordinary Three-Day Notice to Pay Rent or Quit is used.
Breach of lease provision, following written notice to cease.	Three-Day Notice to Cure Covenant or Quit is used. Provision must be reasonable and legal and been accepted by the tenant or made part of the rental agreement. If the provision was added after the tenant first moved in, the landlord can evict for breach only if the tenant was told in writing that she didn't have to accept the new term. Ordinance forbids use of an unconditional notice.
Willful causing or allowing of substantial damage to premises and refusal to both pay the reasonable cost of repair and cease causing damage, following written notice.	Even though damage is involved an ordinary unconditional Three-Day Notice to Quit is not allowed. Only a three-day notice that gives the tenant the option of ceasing to cause damage and pay for the costs of repair, as demanded by the landlord, is allowed.

Reasons Allowed for Just Cause Evictions	Additional Local Notice Requirements and Limitations
Tenant refuses to agree to rental agreement or lease on expiration of prior one, where new proposed agreement contains no new or unlawful terms.	This applies only when a lease or rental agreement expires of its own terms. No notice is required. However, an improvised notice giving the tenant several days to sign the new agreement or leave is a good idea.
Tenant continues to be so disorderly as to disturb other tenants, following written notice to cease.	Even if the tenant is committing a legal nuisance for which state law would allow use of a Three-Day Notice to Quit, ordinance requires that three-day notice be in conditional "cease or quit" form.
Tenant, after written notice to cease, continues to refuse the landlord access to the property as required by Civ. Code § 1954.	If provision is in lease, use three-day notice giving tenant option of letting you in or moving. If not, and tenancy is month to month, use 30-day notice specifying reason, following written demand for access to property.
Landlord wants to make substantial repairs to bring property into compliance with health codes, and repairs not possible while tenant remains.	Under state law, eviction for this reason is allowed only if rental agreement is month to month. Thirty-day notice giving specific reason must be used. Landlord must first obtain all permits required for the remodeling, must provide alternative housing for the tenant if he has other vacant units in city, and must give evicted tenant right of first refusal to rerent after remodeling is finished. (Tenant given alternate housing may be evicted from it if he refuses to move into old unit after work is completed. § 13.A.10.)
Landlord wants to demolish property.	Under state law, eviction for this reason is allowed only if rental agreement is month to month. Thirty-day notice giving specific reason must be used. Landlord must first obtain all permits required for the remodeling, must provide alternative housing for the tenant if he has other vacant units in city, and must give evicted tenant right of first refusal to rerent after remodeling is finished. (Tenant given alternate housing may be evicted from it if he refuses to move into old unit after work is completed. § 13.A.10.) (Although ordinance requires "good faith" to demolish, a euphemism for not doing it because of rent control, the state Ellis Act severely limits cities refusing demolition permits on this basis).
Landlord wants to move self, spouse, parent, grandparent, child, or grandchild into property.	Under state law, eviction for this reason is allowed only if rental agreement is month to month. Thirty-day notice giving specific reason must be used. Also, Thirty-day notice terminating month-to-month tenancy for this reason should specify name and relationship of person moving in.

FREMONT

Name of Ordinance

City of Fremont Residential Rent Increase Dispute Resolution Ordinance (RRIDRO), Ordinance No. 2253, Fremont Municipal Code, Chapter 19, Title III, §§ 3-1900–3-1955.

Adoption Date

7/22/97, last amended 1998.

Exception

None. Ordinance applies to "any housing unit offered for rent or lease in the city consisting of one or more units." (§ 3-1905.)

Administration

Mediation Services
22227 Redwood Road
Castro Valley, CA 94546-7043
510-733-4940
FAX: 510-733-4944
Website: www.ci.fremont.ca.us

Registration

Not required.

Rent Formula

No fixed formula; landlord must respond to Mediation Services within two business days and participate in good faith in conciliation, mediation, and/or fact-finding proceedings, or rent increase notice can be ruled void. (§§ 3-1925, 1930, 1935.) Also, only one rent increase is allowed in any 12-month period. (§§ 3-1910(d).)

Individual Adjustments

Tenants affected by an increase can contest it by contacting Mediation Services within 15 days. Disputes raised by tenant request are first subject to conciliation, then mediation. If those fail, either party may file a written request for determination of the dispute by a fact-finding panel. This panel determines if the increase is reasonable by considering costs of capital improvements, repairs, existing market rents, return on investment, and the Oakland/San Jose All Urban Consumer Price Index. Panel's decision is not binding, but if landlord fails to appear or fails to participate in good faith in conciliation, education, or fact-finding process, that "shall void the notice of rent increase for all purposes." (§§ 3-1925(g), 1930(e), 1935(l).)

Rent Increase Notice Requirements

60 days' notice appears to be required for all rent increases, even those of 10% or less (§ 3-1915(c)). All tenants, on moving in, must be provided a notice informing them of the dispute resolution programs, and that they can receive a copy by calling City Office of Neighborhoods at 510-494-4500. All rent increase notices must show the name, address, and phone number of the responsible party [§ 3-1915(b)], and must also state the following in bold type:

> **"NOTICE: You are encouraged to contact the owner or manager [*list name*] of your rental unit to discuss this rent increase. However, chapter 19 of Title III of the Fremont Municipal Code provides a procedure for conciliation, mediation, and fact finding for disputes over rent increases. To use the procedure and secure additional information about the city ordinance, you must contact Mediation Services at 510-733-4945 within fifteen days following receipt of this notice."**

If this language is not included, the notice is not valid. (§ 3-1915(a)(d).)

Vacancy Decontrol

No restriction on raises after vacancy.

Eviction

Ordinance does not require showing of just cause to evict, so three-day and 30-day notice requirements and unlawful detainer procedure are governed solely by state law.

Note

Because this ordinance does not provide for binding arbitration of any rent increase dispute, it is not a true rent control ordinance. Compliance with any decision appears to be voluntary, except that if a city mediator or fact finder rules the landlord has failed to appear or act in "good faith" in any conciliation, mediation, or fact-finding proceeding, the rent increase notice can be ruled invalid. In this respect, the ordinance could, under certain circumstances, act as a sort of mild rent control.

HAYWARD

Name of Ordinance
"Residential Rent Stabilization," Ordinance No. 83-023 C.S.

Adoption Date
9/13/83. Last amended 1/2003.

Exceptions
Units first occupied after 7/1/79, units owned by landlord owning four or fewer rental units in the city. (§ 2(l).)

Administration
Rent Review Office
777 B Street, 4th Flr.
Hayward, CA 94541
510-583-4454
Website: www.ci.hayward.ca.us. Provides no rent control information. Municipal Code is accessible, but rent control ordinance is not part of Municipal Code and cannot be accessed online.

Registration
Not required.

Vacancy Decontrol
Rent controls are permanently removed from each rental unit after a voluntary vacancy followed by the expenditure by the landlord of $200 or more on improvements, and city certification of compliance with City Housing Code (Section 8).

Units still subject to controls (those for which there were no voluntary vacancies in preceding years) can be rerented for any rent amount, with property being subject to controls based on the higher rent.

Just Cause
Required. (§ 19(a).) This aspect of the ordinance applies even to voluntarily vacated property no longer subject to rent control. Specific good cause to evict must be stated in both the notice and in any unlawful detainer complaint. (§ 19(b).)

Special Features
Tenant may defend any eviction lawsuit on the basis of the landlord's failure to provide tenant with any of the information required under the ordinance. (§ 8(f).)

Reasons Allowed for Just Cause Evictions	Additional Local Notice Requirements and Limitations
Nonpayment of rent.	Ordinary Three-Day Notice to Pay Rent or Quit is used.
Breach of lease provision following written notice to cease.	Three-Day Notice to Cure Covenant or Quit is used. Provision must be reasonable and legal and have been accepted by the tenant or made part of the rental agreement. If the provision was added after the tenant first moved in, the landlord can evict for breach only if the tenant was told in writing that she didn't have to accept the new term. Notice must give the tenant the option of correcting the problem.
Willful causing or allowing of substantial damage to premises and refusal to both pay the reasonable cost of repair and cease causing damage, following written notice.	Even though damage is involved an ordinary unconditional Three-Day Notice to Quit is not allowed. Only a three-day notice that gives the tenant the option of ceasing to cause damage and pay for the costs of repair, as demanded by the landlord, is allowed.
Tenant refuses to agree to rental agreement or lease on expiration of prior one, where new proposed agreement contains no new or unlawful terms.	This applies only when a lease or rental agreement expires of its own terms. No notice is required. However, an improvised notice giving the tenant several days to sign the new agreement or leave is a good idea.
Tenant continues to be so disorderly as to disturb other tenants, following written notice to cease.	Even if the tenant is committing a legal nuisance for which state law would allow use of a Three-Day Notice to Quit, ordinance requires that three-day notice be in conditional "cease or quit" form.

Reasons Allowed for Just Cause Evictions	Additional Local Notice Requirements and Limitations
Tenant, after written notice to cease, continues to refuse the landlord access to the property as required by Civ. Code § 1954.	If provision is in lease, use three-day notice giving tenant option of letting you in or moving. If not, and tenancy is month to month, use 30-day notice specifying reason, following written demand for access to property.
Landlord wants to make substantial repairs to bring property into compliance with health codes, and repairs not possible while tenant remains.	Under state law, eviction for this reason is allowed only if rental agreement is month to month. Thirty-day notice giving specific reason must be used. Landlord must first obtain all permits required for the remodeling, and must give tenant notice giving him first chance to rerent after remodeling is finished. (No requirement for alternative housing.)
Landlord wants to demolish property.	Under state law, eviction for this reason is allowed only if rental agreement is month-to-month. Thirty-day notice giving specific reason must be used. Landlord must first obtain all necessary permits. (Although ordinance requires "good faith" to demolish, a euphemism for not doing it because of rent control, the state Ellis Act severely limits cities from refusing demolition permits on this basis.)
Landlord wants to move self, spouse, parent, child, stepchild, brother, or sister into property, and no comparable vacant unit exists in the property.	Under state law, eviction for this reason is allowed only if rental agreement is month-to-month. Thirty-day notice giving specific reason must be used. Landlord must first obtain all permits required for the remodeling, and must give tenant notice giving him first chance to rerent after remodeling is finished. (No requirement for alternative housing.) Thirty-day notice terminating month-to-month tenancy for this reason should specify name and relationship of person moving in.
Landlord wants to move in herself, and lease or rental agreement specifically allows this.	Termination procedure must be in accordance with lease provision. Thirty days' written notice is required to terminate month-to-month tenancy unless agreement provides for lesser period as short as seven days.
Tenant is using the property illegally.	Three-Day Notice to Quit is used.
Tenant continues, after written notice to cease, to violate reasonable and legal regulations applicable to all tenants generally, if tenant accepted regulations in writing in the lease or rental agreement, or otherwise.	If tenancy is not month to month and violation is very serious, use Three-Day Notice to Perform Covenant or Quit. If tenancy is month to month, use thirty-day notice preceded by written warning.
Lawful termination of apartment manager's employment, where he or she was compensated with use of apartment.	This type of eviction is not covered in this book because the question of what notice is required is extremely complicated, depending in part on the nature of the management agreement. You should seek legal advice.

LOS ANGELES

Name of Ordinance

Rent Stabilization Ordinance, Los Angeles Municipal Code, Chapter XV, §§ 151.00–155.09.

Adoption Date

4/21/79. Last amended 7/16/2003.

Exceptions

Units constructed (or substantially renovated with at least $10,000 in improvements) after 10/1/78, "luxury" units (defined as 0, 1, 2, 3, or 4+ bedroom units renting for at least $302, $420, $588, $756, or $823, respectively, as of 5/31/78), single-family residences, except where two or more houses are located on the same lot. (§ 151.02.G, M.)

Administration

Los Angeles Housing Department
3550 Wilshire Boulevard, Suite 1500
Los Angeles, CA 90010
Also, 6640 Van Nuys Boulevard
Van Nuys, CA 91405
For information regarding ordinance, call 800-994-4444 or 866-557-7368 (RENT).

Websites: www2.cityofla.org/LAHD/ for information on rent control and www.tenant.net/Other_Areas/Calif/losangel/index.html. For the L.A. Municipal Code, navigate the city's main website at www.ci.la.ca.us. (See front of this appendix.)

Registration

Required.

Vacancy Decontrol

Landlord may charge any rent after a tenant either vacates voluntarily or is evicted for nonpayment of rent or breach of a rental agreement provision, or to substantially remodel. (Controls remain if landlord evicts for any other reason, fails to remodel after evicting for that purpose, or terminates or fails to renew a subsidized-housing lease with the city housing authority.) However, once the property is re-rented, it is subject to rent control based on the higher rent. (§ 151.06.C.)

Just Cause

Required. (§ 151.09.) Every termination notice must state "the reasons for the termination with specific facts to permit a determination of the date, place, witnesses, and circumstances concerning the reason." (§ 151.09.C.1.) Tenant may not defend unlawful detainer action on the basis of lack of good cause or failure of the notice to state the reason if tenant has disobeyed a pretrial court order requiring him or her to deposit rent into court; see C.C.P. § 1170.5 and *Green v. Superior Court* (1974) 10 Cal. 3d 616. (§ 151.09.E.). State law requires use of a 60-day termination notice of month-to-month tenancy, instead of a 30-day notice, for this city, if the tenant has occupied the premises for a year or more.

Other Features

Tenant may defend on the basis that the landlord failed to register the property in accordance with the ordinance. (§ 151.09.F.)

Reasons Allowed for Just Cause Evictions	Additional Local Notice Requirements and Limitations
Nonpayment of rent.	Ordinary Three-Day Notice to Pay Rent or Quit is used.
Breach of lease provision, following written notice to cease. (Landlord may not evict based on breach of no-pets clause added by notice of change of terms of tenancy, where no such clause existed at the outset of the tenancy. § 151.09.D.)	Three-Day Notice to Cure Covenant or Quit is used. The ordinance requires that the tenant be given "written notice to cease," which precludes an unconditional Three-Day Notice to Quit, even if the breach can be considered uncorrectable.
Commission of a legal nuisance (disturbing other residents) or damaging the property.	Unconditional Three-Day Notice to Quit may be used.
Tenant is using the property for illegal purpose.	Unconditional Three-Day Notice to Quit may be used.
Tenant refuses to agree to rental agreement or lease on expiration of prior one, where new proposed agreement contains no new or unlawful terms.	This applies only when a lease or rental agreement expires of its own terms. No notice is required. However, an improvised notice giving the tenant several days to sign the new agreement or leave is a good idea, even though not required by ordinance or state law.
Tenant, after written notice to cease, continues to refuse the landlord access to the property as required by Civ. Code § 1954.	If provision is in lease, use three-day notice giving tenant option of letting you in or moving. If not, and tenancy is month to month, use 30-day notice specifying reason, following previous written demand for access to property.
Fixed-term lease has expired, and person occupying property is subtenant not approved by landlord.	Eviction on this basis is allowed only if person living there is not original tenant or approved subtenant. No notice is required. If lease has not expired and contains no-subletting clause, use Three-Day Notice to Quit to evict for breach of lease.
Landlord wants to move self, spouse, parent, child, or legally required resident manager into property. Landlord must pay relocation fee of $2,000-$2,500 to tenants except where moving legally required manager into property.	Only month-to-month tenant can be evicted on this ground. Landlord must serve tenant with copy of a form, the original of which must first be filed with the Community Development Department, that specifies the name and relationship of the person to be moving in.
Landlord wants to demolish the unit or substantially renovate it at a cost of at least $10,000 per rental unit, and the renovation will take at least 45 days. Note: As of this writing, the city has imposed a moratorium on "major rehabilitation" evictions, through 10/21/2003, by Ordinance 174721, effective 7/16/2002. It is expected to be extended beyond that date.	Only month-to-month tenant can be evicted on this ground. Use 30-day notice specifying this reason. Landlord must serve tenant with copy of a filed Community Development Department form describing the renovation work or demolition.
Landlord seeks to permanently remove the unit from the rental housing market.	Only month-to-month tenant can be evicted on this ground. Use 30-day notice specifying this reason.

LOS GATOS

Name of Ordinance

Los Gatos Rental Dispute Mediation and Arbitration Ordinance, Los Gatos Town Code, Chapter 14, Article VIII, §§ 14.80.010-14.80-315.

Adoption Date

10/27/80. Last amended 1999.

Exception

Property on lots with two or fewer units, single-family residences, rented condominium units. (§ 14.80.020.)

Administration

Project Sentinel—Mediation Services
1055 Sunnyvale-Saratoga Road, Suite 3
Sunnyvale, CA 94087
408-402-0307
Website: www.town.los-gatos.ca.us, official city website. Choose Town Government, then Town Codes. Rent control provisions are in Chapter 14, Article VIII.

Registration

Not required. (However, a "regulatory fee" to pay for program is added to annual business license fee, when business license is required.)

Vacancy Decontrol

Landlord may charge any rent after a tenant vacates voluntarily or is evicted following Three-Day Notice for Nonpayment of Rent or other breach of the rental agreement. However, once the new rent for a vacated unit is established by the landlord and the property is rerented, it is subject to rent control based on the higher rent. (§ 14.80.310.)

Just Cause

Not required.

Other Features

Tenant faced with termination notice may invoke mediation/arbitration hearing procedure on eviction issue and stay landlord's eviction suit; if tenant wins mediation/arbitration hearing, eviction will be barred. (§ 14.80.205.)

OAKLAND

Name of Ordinance

"Ordinance Establishing a Residential Rent Arbitration Board," Oakland Municipal Code, Title 8, Ch. 8.22, §§ 8.22.010-8.22.140.

Adoption Date

10/7/80. Last amended 7/2002.

Exceptions

Units constructed after 1/18/84, buildings "substantially rehabilitated" at cost of 50% of that of new construction, as determined by Chief Building Inspector. (§ 8.22.030.)

Administration

Rent Adjustment Program
250 Frank H. Ogawa Plaza
Oakland, CA 94612
510-238-3721
FAX: 510-238-3691
Website: www.ci.oakland.ca.us. This is the official city site. Choose the Municipal Code and go to Title 8, Chapter 8.22.

Registration

Not required.

Vacancy Decontrol

Landlord may charge any rent after a tenant vacates voluntarily or is evicted for nonpayment of rent. If tenant otherwise vacates involuntarily, landlord may not increase the rent for 24 months.

On eviction for reasons other than nonpayment of rent, ordinance allows increase of up to 12%, depending on rent increases over previous 12 months.

Once property is rerented, it is subject to rent control based on the higher rent.

Just Cause

Landlords may terminate a month-to-month rental agreement (or refuse to renew a lease) only when the tenant has failed to pay the rent (or has violated another important lease term), refused to enter into a written renewal of a rental agreement or lease, caused substantial damage, disturbed the peace and quiet of other tenants, engaged in illegal activities, or refused entry to the landlord when properly asked. Landlords may also terminate rental agreements or not renew leases when they want to live in the unit themselves (or intend it for a close family member), or to substantially renovate the unit.

Other Features

Rent increase notices must be in a form prescribed by Section 8.22.070(H)(1), which requires tenant be notified of right to petition rent board. All Tenants, on moving in, must be provided a notice informing of their rights under the ordinance. (8.22.060.)

Landlord evicting to "rehabilitate" the property (presumably to obtain permanent exemption from controls) must obtain building permit before eviction.

PALM SPRINGS

Name of Ordinance

"Rent Control," Palm Springs Municipal Code, Title 4, Chapters 4.02, 4.04, 4.08, §§ 4.02.010-4.08.190.

Adoption Date

9/1/79. Last amended, by initiative, 12/94.

Exceptions

Units constructed after 4/1/79; owner-occupied single-family residences, duplexes, triplexes, and 4-plexes; units where rent was $450 or more as of 9/1/79. (§§ 4.02.010, 4.02.030.)

Administration

Rent Review Commission
3200 E. Tahquitz Canyon Way
Palm Springs, CA 92262
760-323-8218

Registration

Required. (§ 4.02.080.)

Vacancy Decontrol

Rent controls are permanently removed after tenant voluntarily vacates or is evicted for cause.

Just Cause

Landlords must show just cause to evict for units subject to rent control. After voluntary vacancy or eviction for cause, just cause requirement does not apply any more. (Section 4.08.060(j)(2).)

Reasons Allowed for Just Cause Evictions	Additional Local Notice Requirements and Limitations
Nonpayment of rent.	Ordinary Three-Day Notice to Pay Rent or Quit is used.
Breach of lease provision.	Three-Day Notice to Cure Covenant or Quit is used, or Three-Day Notice to Quit where breach cannot be cured, or improper subletting.
Creation or maintenance of a nuisance.	State law allows use of a Three-Day Notice to Quit.
Tenant is using the property illegally.	Three-Day Notice to Quit is used.
Landlord wants to move self, parent, child, grandparent, brother or sister, mother-in-law, father-in-law, son-in-law, or daughter-in-law into property.	Under state law, eviction for this reason is allowed only if rental agreement is month to month. Thirty-day notice giving specific reason must be used.

SAN FRANCISCO

Name of Ordinance

Residential Rent Stabilization and Arbitration Ordinance, San Francisco Administrative Code, Chapter 37.

Adoption Date

6/79. Last amended 5/16/2003.

Exceptions

Units constructed after 6/79; buildings over 50 years old and "substantially rehabilitated" since 6/79. (§ 37.2 (p).)

Administration

Residential Rent Stabilization and
Arbitration Board
25 Van Ness Avenue, Suite 320
San Francisco, CA 94102
415-252-4602, 415-252-4600 (recorded info);
FAX 415-252-4699
Website: www.ci.sf.ca.us/rentbd. Municipal Code/Administrative Code is available from the city official site, www.ci.sf.ca.us. Rent control laws (in superior format) and regulations are available from rent board site.

Registration

Not required.

Vacancy Decontrol

Landlord may charge any rent after a tenant vacates voluntarily or is evicted for cause. Once property is rerented for a year, it is subject to rent control based on the higher rent. (§ 37.3(a).)

Just Cause

Required. Every termination notice must state "the grounds under which possession is sought" and must advise the tenant that advice regarding the notice is available from the Board. (§ 37.9.)

Other Features

Tenant or Board may sue landlord, following either unsuccessful eviction attempt or successful eviction based on falsified reason, for treble damages and attorney's fees. (§ 37.9(e).) Landlord must file copy of tenancy termination notice (except Three-Day Notice to Pay Rent or Quit) with rent board within ten days after it is served on the tenant. (§ 37.9(c).)

Reasons Allowed for Just Cause Evictions	Additional Local Notice Requirements and Limitations
Nonpayment of rent.	Ordinary Three-Day Notice to Pay Rent or Quit is used.
Tenant "habitually pays the rent late or gives checks which are frequently returned ...."	This can only be used if tenancy is month to month, by using 30-day notice.
Breach of lease provision, following written notice to cease.	Three-Day Notice to Perform Covenant or Quit is used. Tenant must be given "written notice to cease," which precludes an unconditional Three-Day Notice to Quit, even if the breach is uncorrectible.
Commission of a legal nuisance (disturbing other residents) or damaging the property.	Unconditional Three-Day Notice to Quit may be used.
Tenant is using the property for illegal purpose.	Unconditional Three-Day Notice to Quit may be used.
Tenant refuses, after written demand by landlord, to agree to new rental agreement or lease on expiration of prior one, where new proposed agreement contains no new or unlawful terms.	This applies only when a lease or rental agreement expires of its own terms. No notice is required. However, a written notice giving the tenant at least three days to sign the new agreement or leave should be served on the tenant with the proposed new lease or rental agreement.
Tenant, after written notice to cease, continues to refuse the landlord access to the property as required by Civ. Code § 1954.	If provision is in lease, use three-day notice giving tenant option of letting you in or moving. If not, and tenancy is month to month, use 30-day notice specifying reason, following written demand for access to property.

Reasons Allowed for Just Cause Evictions	Additional Local Notice Requirements and Limitations
Landlord owning at least 25% interest (10% if bought before 2/91) wants to move self, parent, grandparent, child, grandchild, brother, sister, or spouse (including domestic partner) of any of the foregoing into the property. Note that spouses and domestic partners (those registered as such pursuant to the San Francisco Administrative Code Chapter 62.1 and 62.8) may aggregate their interests, but not tenants in common. Evictions for this reason are known as "owner move-in" evictions, or "OMI" evictions. They are the most contentious type of eviction and are often the subject of prolonged litigation. Before commencing an OMI eviction, you would be well advised to check the Ordinance and the Rent Board website, which is extremely helpful, for updates, details, and any added regulations.	Eviction for this reason is allowed only if rental agreement is month to month. Also, ownership must have been previously registered with Board. By popular vote in November 1998 (Proposition G), effective December 18, 1998, OMIs are not allowed as to: 1. Seniors 60 years of age or older who have lived in the rental for at least ten years; 2. Disabled or blind tenants who meet the Supplemental Security Income/California State Supplemental Program (SSI/SSP) criteria for disability, as determined by the Program or any other method approved by the Rent Board, who have lived in the rental for at least ten years; and 3. Tenants with a "catastrophic illness" (as certified by the tenant's primary care physician) who have lived in the rental for at least five years. There are several restrictions to allowable OMIs. The landlord must live in the same building as the unit that is the subject of the OMI (unless the landlord owns only one unit in the building). Only one "owner move-in" eviction is allowed for a single building. The unit that is the subject of the first OMI becomes the designated OMI unit for that building for the future. Landlords may not do an OMI as to a particular unit if there is a comparable unit in the building, and must cease eviction proceedings if a comparable unit becomes available prior to recovering possession. For buildings of three or more units built before 6/79, the landlord must obtain a conditional use permit from the city planning department. Certain tenants will be entitled to a $1,000 relocation benefit from the landlord. The landlord or other qualified relative who occupies the recovered unit must move in within three months and reside there continuously for 36 months
Landlord wants to sell unit following condominium-conversion approval pursuant to separate city ordinance.	Allowed only if rental agreement is month to month. Ownership must have been previously registered with Board. Landlord must get all necessary approvals first. New tenants must stay there for a year.
Landlord wants to demolish the unit.	Allowed only if rental agreement is month to month. Ownership must have been previously registered with Board. Landlord must obtain all necessary permits first.
Landlord wants to rehabilitate the property or add capital improvements.	Allowed only if rental agreement is month to month. Ownership must have been previously registered with Board. Can't evict if rehab financed by city with "RAP" loans. If improvements are not "substantial rehabilitation" of building 50 or more years old, landlord must give tenant right of first refusal to reoccupy property when work is completed.
Landlord wants to permanently remove property from the rental housing market.	Allowed only if rental agreement is month to month. Ownership must have been previously registered with Board. Although the ordinance requires that the landlord must pay relocation compensation of $1,500-$3,000, the Court of Appeal ruled in a case involving Berkeley's ordinance that this requirement was illegal, as preempted by the state Ellis Act. (See *Channing Properties v. City of Berkeley* (1992) 11 Cal. App. 4th 88, 14 Cal. Rptr. 2d 32.)
Fixed-term lease has expired, and person occupying property is subtenant not approved by landlord.	No notice is required. Ordinance allows eviction on this basis only if person living there is not original tenant or approved subtenant. (If lease has not expired and contains no-subletting clause, use Three-Day Notice to Quit to evict for breach of lease.)

SAN JOSE

Name of Ordinance

San Jose Rental Dispute Mediation and Arbitration Ordinance, San Jose Municipal Code, Title 17, Chapter 17.23, §§ 17.23.010-17.23.770.

Adoption Date

7/7/79. Last amended 7/1/2003.

Exceptions

Units constructed after 9/7/79, single-family residences, duplexes, townhouses, and condominium units. (§ 17.23.150.)

Administration

San Jose Rental Rights and Referrals Program
4 N. Second Street, Suite 600
San Jose, CA 95113
408-277-5431
Website: www.ci.san-jose.ca.us. This is the general city site, which provides no rent control information. Municipal Code is accessible. Rent control portions are in Title 17, Chapter 17.23.

Registration

Required.

Vacancy Decontrol

Landlord may charge any rent after a tenant vacates voluntarily or is evicted following Three-Day Notice to Pay Rent or Quit or other breach of the rental agreement. However, once the new rent for a vacated unit is established by the landlord and the property is rerented, it is subject to rent control based on the higher rent. (§ 17.23.190.)

Just Cause

Not required. Notice requirements and unlawful detainer procedures are governed solely by state law.

Other

All tenants, on moving in, must be provided a notice informing of their rights under the ordinance. (§ 17.23.030.) Rent increase notices must notify tenant of right to petition, time limits, and the city rent programs's address and phone number (§ 17.23.270.)

In addition, ordinance requires that 90-day notice of termination be given to a tenant of month-to-month tenancy that's lasted over a year, or a 60-day notice if served with an offer to arbitrate. We believe this provision is invalid as superseded by recent state law allowing a 60-day notice without an offer to arbitrate.

Important: Copies of Notices to Vacate must be sent to the city. (§ 17.23.760.)

SANTA MONICA

Name of Ordinance

Rent Control Charter Amendment, City Charter Article XVIII.

Adoption Date

4/10/79. Last amended 1/99.

Exceptions

Units constructed after 4/10/79; owner-occupied single-family residences, duplexes, and triplexes; single-family dwellings not rented on 7/1/84. (Charter Amendment (C.A.) §§ 1801(c), 1815; Regulation (Reg.) §§ 2000 and following, 12000 and following.) However, rental units other than single-family dwellings not rented on 7/1/84 must be registered and the exemption applied for.

Administration

Rent Control Board
1685 Main Street, Room 202
Santa Monica, CA 90401
310-458-8751
Email: rent_control@ci.santa-monica.ca.us.
Websites: www.ci.santa-monica.ca.us/rentcontrol. This is an excellent site. Includes rent control laws in "Charter and Regulations"—both of which are not in the Municipal Code. See also www.tenant.net/Other_Areas/Calif/smonica/rentctrl.html.

Registration

Required. (C.A. §§ 1803(q), 1805(h).)

Vacancy Decontrol

State law (Civ. Code § 1954.53) supersedes the ordinance. Upon voluntary vacancy or eviction for nonpayment of rent, rents may be increased to any level following such vacancies. Once property is rerented, it is subject to rent control based on the higher rent.

Just Cause

Required. Specific good cause to evict must be stated in the termination notice. (Reg. § 9001.) State law requires use of a 60-day termination notice of month-to-month tenancy, instead of a 30-day notice, for this city, if the tenant has occupied the premises for a year or more.

Other Features

Landlord's complaint must allege compliance with rent control ordinance. (C.A. § 1806.)

Reasons Allowed for Just Cause Evictions	Additional Local Notice Requirements and Limitations
Nonpayment of rent.	Ordinary Three-Day Notice to Pay Rent or Quit is used.
Breach of lease provision.	Three-Day Notice to Perform Covenant or Quit is used. Ordinance requires that the tenant has "failed to cure such violation," which precludes an unconditional Three-Day Notice to Quit, even if the breach is uncorrectable.
Willful causing or allowing of substantial damage to premises, or commission of nuisance that interferes with comfort, safety, or enjoyment of the property, following written notice.	No requirement for alternative three-day notice giving tenant the option of correcting the problem. Three-Day Notice to Quit may be used.
Tenant is convicted of using the property for illegal purpose.	Three-Day Notice to Quit may be used, but only if tenant is actually convicted. This appears to mean that drug dealers can't be evicted unless first convicted. This provision may violate state law, which does not require a conviction. See C.C.P. § 1161(4). If you wish to evict for illegal use without a conviction, try it based on a violation of a lease provision that forbids illegal use of the premises. Otherwise, see a lawyer about making the argument that this part of the ordinance is preempted by state law.

Reasons Allowed for Just Cause Evictions	Additional Local Notice Requirements and Limitations
Tenant refuses to agree to rental agreement or lease on expiration of prior one, where new proposed agreement contains no new or unlawful terms.	This applies only when a lease or rental agreement expires of its own terms. No notice is required. However, an improvised notice giving the tenant several days to sign the new agreement or leave is a good idea.
Tenant, after written notice to cease, continues to refuse the landlord access to the property as required by Civ. Code § 1954.	If provision is in lease, use three-day notice giving tenant option of letting you in or moving. If not, and tenancy is month to month, use 30-day notice specifying reason, following written demand for access to property.
Fixed-term lease has expired, and person occupying property is subtenant not approved by landlord.	No notice is required. Eviction on this basis is allowed only if person living there is not original tenant or approved subtenant. (If lease has not expired and contains no-subletting clause, use Three-Day Notice to Quit to evict for breach of lease.)
Landlord wants to move self, parent, child, brother, sister, or spouse of foregoing into property.	Eviction for this reason is allowed only if rental agreement is month to month. Landlord must include on the termination notice the name of the current tenant, the rent charged, and the name, relationship, and address of person to be moving in. The notice must be filed with the Board within three days of service on the tenant. (Reg. § 9002(e).) The landlord must also offer any comparable vacant unit in the same building to the tenant and must allow the tenant to move back into the property if the relative does not occupy it within 30 days after the tenant moves out.
Landlord wants to demolish property, convert to condominiums, or otherwise remove property from rental market. (City's very strict ordinance has been modified by the state Ellis Act, which severely limits cities from refusing removal permits. See *Javidzad v. City of Santa Monica* (1988) Cal. App. 3d 524, 251 Cal. Rptr. 350.)	Eviction for this reason allowed only if tenancy is month to month. Although the ordinance requires a landlord to pay a relocation fee of up to $4,000, the Court of Appeal ruled in a case involving Berkeley's ordinance that this requirement was illegal, as preempted by the state Ellis Act. (See *Channing Properties v. City of Berkeley* (1992) 11 Cal. App. 4th 88, 14 Cal. Rptr. 2d 32.) That ruling appears to apply only in cases where the landlord just wants to remove the property from the housing market.

THOUSAND OAKS

Name of Ordinance
Rent Stabilization Ordinance, Ordinance Nos. 755-NS, 956-NS, 1284-NS.

Adoption Date
7/1/80. Last amended 5/20/97.

Exceptions
Units constructed after 6/30/80; "luxury" units (defined as 0, 1, 2, 3, or 4+-bedroom units renting for at least $400, $500, $600, $750, or $900, respectively, as of 6/30/80); single-family residences, duplexes, triplexes, and 4-plexes, except where five or more units are located on the same lot. (§ III.L of 956-NS.)

Administration
Housing Division
2100 Thousand Oaks Boulevard
Thousand Oaks, CA 91362

805-449-2393
Website: www.ci-thousand-oaks.ca.us. This is the official city site, but it has no rent control information. The Municipal Code is accessible, but rent control ordinances are not available online.

Registration
Required. (§ XIV.)

Vacancy Decontrol
Rent controls are permanently removed after tenant voluntarily vacates or is evicted for cause.

Just Cause
Required. (§ VIII.) Termination notice must state specific reason for termination.

Reasons Allowed for Just Cause Evictions	Additional Local Notice Requirements and Limitations
Nonpayment of rent.	Ordinary Three-Day Notice to Pay Rent or Quit is used.
Breach of lease provision, following written notice to correct.	Three-Day Notice to Cure Covenant or Quit is used. Ordinance requires that the tenant be given "written notice to cease," which precludes an unconditional Three-Day Notice to Quit, even if the breach is uncorrectable.
Tenant continues to damage property or disturb other tenants, following written notice to cease.	Even if the tenant is causing nuisance or damage for which state law would allow use of a Three-Day Notice to Quit, ordinance requires that Three-Day notice be in alternative "cease or quit" form.
Tenant is using the property for illegal purpose.	Ordinance allows use of unconditional Three-Day Notice to Quit.
Tenant refuses, after written demand by landlord, to agree to new rental agreement or lease on expiration of prior one, where new proposed agreement contains no new or unlawful terms.	This applies only when a lease or rental agreement expires of its own terms. No notice is required. However, written notice giving the tenant at least three days to sign the new agreement or leave should be served on the tenant with the proposed new lease or rental agreement.
Tenant has refused the landlord access to the property as required by Civ. Code § 1954.	If provision is in lease, use Three-Day notice giving tenant option of letting you in or moving. If not, and tenancy is month to month, use 30-day notice specifying reason.

Reasons Allowed for Just Cause Evictions	Additional Local Notice Requirements and Limitations
Fixed-term lease has expired, and person occupying property is subtenant not approved by landlord.	No notice is required. Eviction on this basis is allowed only if person living there is not original tenant or approved subtenant. (If lease has not expired and contains no-subletting clause, use Three-Day Notice to Quit to evict for breach of lease.)
Landlord wants to substantially remodel, convert to condominiums, or demolish property.	Allowed under state law only if fixed-term tenancy has expired, or month-to-month tenancy is terminated by 30-day notice.
Landlord seeks to permanently remove the unit from the rental housing market.	Allowed under state law only if fixed-term tenancy has expired, or month-to-month tenancy is terminated by 30-day notice. (Although ordinance requires "good faith" to demolish, a euphemism for not doing it because of rent control, the state Ellis Act severely limits cities from refusing demolition permits on this basis.)

WEST HOLLYWOOD

Name of Ordinance
Rent Stabilization Ordinance, West Hollywood Municipal Code, Title 17, §§ 17.04.010-17.68.01, and Title 2, §§ 2.64.010-2.64.090.

Adoption Date
6/27/85. Last amended 2003. Frequently amended; call for details.

Exceptions
Units constructed after 7/1/79 and units where owner has lived for two or more years ("just cause" eviction requirements do apply, however). However, many exemptions must be applied for in application for exemption (see below). (§ 17.24.010.)

Administration
Department of Rent Stabilization and Housing
8300 Santa Monica Boulevard
West Hollywood, CA 90069
323-848-6450
Website: www.ci.west-hollywood.ca.us. Municipal Code and rent control information easily accessible.

Registration
Required. (§§ 17.28.010–17.28.050.)

Vacancy Decontrol
State law (Civ. Code § 1954.53) supersedes ordinance except where tenant evicted for reason other than nonpayment of rent.

On voluntary vacancy or eviction for nonpayment of rent, rents may be increased to any level on rerenting following such vacancies. (§ 17.40.020.)

On eviction for reasons other than nonpayment of rent, ordinance does not allow an increase.

Once property is rerented, it is subject to rent control based on the higher rent.

Just Cause
Required. (§ 17.52.010.) This aspect of the ordinance applies even to new construction, which is otherwise exempt from ordinance. Termination notice must state "with particularity the specific grounds" and recite the specific paragraph of ordinance under which eviction sought. State law requires use of a 60-day termination notice of month-to-month tenancy, instead of a 30-day notice, for this city, if the tenant has occupied the premises for a year or more.

Other Features
Copy of any unlawful detainer summons and complaint must be filed with Rent Stabilization Commission. Numerous procedural hurdles apply when evicting to move self or relative into property, and substantial relocation fee must be paid to tenant.

Reasons Allowed for Just Cause Evictions	Additional Local Notice Requirements and Limitations
Nonpayment of rent.	Ordinary Three-Day Notice to Pay Rent or Quit is used.
Failure to cure a lease or rental agreement violation within "a reasonable time" after receipt of written notice to cure it.	Three-Day Notice to Perform Covenant or Quit is used. Tenant must be given "a reasonable time" to correct the violation, which precludes an unconditional Three-Day Notice to Quit. Also, the tenant must have been "provided with a written statement of the respective covenants and obligations of both the landlord and tenant" before the violation. Giving the tenant a copy of the written lease or rental agreement should comply with this requirement. This ground is specifically not applicable if the violation is having another person living on the property in violation of the agreement if the person is a "spouse, domestic partner, child, parent, grandparent, brother, or sister" of the tenant. (Tenant, however, is required to notify landlord in writing of this fact and state the person's name and relationship, when that person moves in.)

Reasons Allowed for Just Cause Evictions	Additional Local Notice Requirements and Limitations
The tenant's spouse, child, "domestic partner," parent, grandparent, brother, or sister can be evicted if the tenant has left, unless that person lived in the unit for at least a year and the tenant died or became incapacitated.	State law allows eviction for this reason by three-day notice only if the tenant's having moved the other person in was a violation of the lease or rental agreement. Thirty-day notice can be used if tenancy is month to month.
Commission of a legal nuisance (disturbing other residents) or damaging the property.	Unconditional Three-Day Notice to Quit may be used.
Tenant is using the property for illegal purpose.	Unconditional Three-Day Notice to Quit may be used.
Tenant refuses, after written demand by landlord, to agree to new rental agreement or lease on expiration of prior one, if new proposed agreement contains no new or unlawful terms.	This applies only when a lease or rental agreement expires of its own terms. No notice is required under state law. However, tenant must have refused to sign a new one containing the same provisions as the old one; a written notice giving the tenant at least three days to sign the new agreement or leave should be served on the tenant with the proposed new lease or rental agreement.
Tenant continues to refuse the landlord access to the property as required by Civ. Code § 1954.	If provision is in lease, use three-day notice giving tenant option of letting you in or moving. If not, and tenancy is month to month, use 30-day notice specifying reason.
Person occupying property is subtenant (other than persons mentioned in 2 and 3 above) not approved by landlord. (No requirement, as in other cities, for lease to have expired.)	Thirty-day notice may be used if tenancy is month to month. Otherwise, Three-Day Notice to Quit may be used if lease or rental agreement contains provision against subletting.
Employment of resident manager, who began tenancy as such (not tenant who was "promoted" from regular tenant to manager) and who lived in manager's unit, has been terminated.	This type of eviction is not covered in this book because the question of what is required is extremely complicated, depending in part on the nature of the management agreement. You should seek legal advice.
Employment of resident manager, who was a regular tenant before "promotion" to manager, has been terminated for cause.	Landlord must give tenant 60-day notice, give copy of notice to city, and pay tenant a relocation fee. There are other restrictions as well. This type of eviction can be extremely complicated; see a lawyer.
Landlord wants to move in, after returning from extended absence, and tenancy was under lease for specific fixed term.	No notice is required under state law when fixed-term lease expires, and ordinance doesn't seem to require notice, either. However, written letter stating intent not to renew, or clear statement in lease, is advisable.
Landlord wants to move self, parent, grandparent, child, brother or sister into property, and no comparable vacant unit exists in the property.	Tenant must be given 90-day notice that states the name, relationship, and address of person to be moved in, and a copy of the notice must be sent to the Rent Commission. Landlord must also pay tenant(s) of 15 months or more a "relocation fee" between $1,500 and $2,500 ($3,000 for senior citizen or handicapped person), depending on size of unit. Tenant is liable for repayment of the fee if he has not moved at the end of the 90-day period. Person moved in must live in property for at least one year, or bad faith is presumed and tenant may more easily sue landlord for wrongful eviction. Not allowed if tenant is certified by physician as terminally ill.
Landlord wants to make substantial repairs to bring property into compliance with health codes, and repairs not possible while tenant remains.	Under state law, eviction for this reason is allowed only if rental agreement is month to month. Landlord must first obtain all permits required for remodeling. Thirty-day notice giving specific reason must be used.

Reasons Allowed for Just Cause Evictions	Additional Local Notice Requirements and Limitations
Landlord has taken title to single-family residence or condominium unit by foreclosure.	Tenant must be given 90-day notice that states the name, relationship, and address of person to be moved in, and a copy of the notice must be sent to the Rent Commission. Landlord must also pay tenant(s) of 15 months or more a "relocation fee" between $1,500 and $2,500 ($3,000 for senior citizen or handicapped person), depending on size of unit. Tenant is liable for repayment of the fee if he has not moved at the end of the 90-day period. Person moved in must live in property for at least one year, or bad faith is presumed and tenant may more easily sue landlord for wrongful eviction. Not allowed if tenant is certified by physician as terminally ill. (Vacancy decontrol provisions are not applicable if property is rerented following eviction.)

WESTLAKE VILLAGE

This small city (population 10,000) has a rent control ordinance that applies to apartment complexes of five units or more (as well as to mobile home parks, whose specialized laws are not covered in this book). However, the city never had more than one apartment complex of this size, and that one was converted to condominiums. Since there is therefore now no property (other than mobile home parks) to which the ordinance applies, we don't explain the ordinance here. ∎

Index

CATALOG

...more from Nolo

	PRICE	CODE

BUSINESS

	PRICE	CODE
Buy-Sell Agreement Handbook:		
Plan Ahead for Changes in the Ownership of Your Business (Book w/CD-ROM)	$49.99	BSAG
The CA Nonprofit Corporation Kit (Binder w/CD-ROM)	$59.95	CNP
Consultant & Independent Contractor Agreements (Book w/CD-ROM)	$29.99	CICA
The Corporate Minutes Book (Book w/CD-ROM)	$69.99	CORMI
Create Your Own Employee Handbook	$49.99	EMHA
Dealing With Problem Employees	$44.99	PROBM
Drive a Modest Car & 16 Other Keys to Small Business Sucess	$24.99	DRIV
The Employer's Legal Handbook	$39.99	EMPL
Everyday Employment Law	$29.99	ELBA
Federal Employment Laws	$49.99	FELW
Form Your Own Limited Liability Company (Book w/CD-ROM)	$44.99	LIAB
Hiring Independent Contractors: The Employer's Legal Guide (Book w/CD-ROM)	$34.99	HICI
How to Create a Noncompete Agreement	$44.95	NOCMP
How to Form a California Professional Corporation (Book w/CD-ROM)	$59.95	PROF
How to Form a Nonprofit Corporation (Book w/CD-ROM)—National Edition	$44.99	NNP
How to Form a Nonprofit Corporation in California (Book w/CD-ROM)	$44.99	NON
How to Form Your Own California Corporation (Binder w/CD-ROM)	$59.99	CACI
How to Form Your Own California Corporation (Book w/CD-ROM)	$34.99	CCOR
How to Get Your Business on the Web	$29.99	WEBS
How to Write a Business Plan	$34.99	SBS
Incorporate Your Business	$49.95	NIBS
The Independent Paralegal's Handbook	$29.95	PARA
Leasing Space for Your Small Business	$34.95	LESP
Legal Guide for Starting & Running a Small Business	$34.99	RUNS
Legal Forms for Starting & Running a Small Business (Book w/CD-ROM)	$29.99	RUNS2
Marketing Without Advertising	$24.00	MWAD
Music Law (Book w/CD-ROM)	$34.99	ML
Nolo's Guide to Social Security Disability	$29.99	QSS
Nolo's Quick LLC	$24.99	LLCQ
Nondisclosure Agreements	$39.95	NAG
The Small Business Start-up Kit (Book w/CD-ROM)	$29.99	SMBU

Prices subject to change.

	PRICE	CODE
The Small Business Start-up Kit for California (Book w/CD-ROM)	$34.99	OPEN
The Partnership Book: How to Write a Partnership Agreement (Book w/CD-ROM)	$39.99	PART
Sexual Harassment on the Job	$24.95	HARS
Starting & Running a Successful Newsletter or Magazine	$29.99	MAG
Take Charge of Your Workers' Compensation Claim	$34.99	WORK
Tax Savvy for Small Business	$36.99	SAVVY
Working for Yourself: Law & Taxes for the Self-Employed	$39.99	WAGE
Your Crafts Business: A Legal Guide	$26.99	VART
Your Limited Liability Company: An Operating Manual (Book w/CD-ROM)	$49.99	LOP
Your Rights in the Workplace	$29.99	YRW

CONSUMER

	PRICE	CODE
How to Win Your Personal Injury Claim	$29.99	PICL
Nolo's Encyclopedia of Everyday Law	$29.99	EVL
Nolo's Guide to California Law	$24.95	CLAW
Trouble-Free Travel...And What to Do When Things Go Wrong	$14.95	TRAV

ESTATE PLANNING & PROBATE

	PRICE	CODE
8 Ways to Avoid Probate	$19.99	PRO8
9 Ways to Avoid Estate Taxes	$29.95	ESTX
Estate Planning Basics	$21.99	ESPN
How to Probate an Estate in California	$49.99	PAE
Make Your Own Living Trust (Book w/CD-ROM)	$39.99	LITR
Nolo's Simple Will Book (Book w/CD-ROM)	$36.99	SWIL
Plan Your Estate	$44.99	NEST
Quick & Legal Will Book	$16.99	QUIC

FAMILY MATTERS

	PRICE	CODE
Child Custody: Building Parenting Agreements That Work	$29.99	CUST
The Complete IEP Guide	$24.99	IEP
Divorce & Money: How to Make the Best Financial Decisions During Divorce	$34.99	DIMO
Do Your Own California Adoption: Nolo's Guide for Stepparents and Domestic Partners (Book w/CD-ROM)	$34.99	ADOP
Get a Life: You Don't Need a Million to Retire Well	$24.99	LIFE
The Guardianship Book for California	$39.99	GB
A Legal Guide for Lesbian and Gay Couples	$29.99	LG
Living Together: A Legal Guide (Book w/CD-ROM)	$34.99	LTK
Medical Directives and Powers of Attorney in California	$19.99	CPOA
Using Divorce Mediation: Save Your Money & Your Sanity	$29.95	UDMD

	PRICE	CODE

GOING TO COURT

	PRICE	CODE
Beat Your Ticket: Go To Court and Win! (National Edition)	$19.99	BEYT
The Criminal Law Handbook: Know Your Rights, Survive the System	$34.99	KYR
Everybody's Guide to Small Claims Court (National Edition)	$26.99	NSCC
Everybody's Guide to Small Claims Court in California	$26.99	CSCC
Fight Your Ticket ... and Win! (California Edition)	$29.99	FYT
How to Change Your Name in California	$34.95	NAME
How to Collect When You Win a Lawsuit (California Edition)	$29.99	JUDG
How to Seal Your Juvenile & Criminal Records (California Edition)	$34.95	CRIM
The Lawsuit Survival Guide	$29.99	UNCL
Nolo's Deposition Handbook	$29.99	DEP
Represent Yourself in Court: How to Prepare & Try a Winning Case	$34.99	RYC
Sue in California Without a Lawyer	$34.99	SLWY

HOMEOWNERS, LANDLORDS & TENANTS

	PRICE	CODE
California Tenants' Rights	$27.99	CTEN
Deeds for California Real Estate	$24.99	DEED
Dog Law	$21.95	DOG
Every Landlord's Legal Guide (National Edition, Book w/CD-ROM)	$44.99	ELLI
Every Tenant's Legal Guide	$29.99	EVTEN
For Sale by Owner in California	$29.99	FSBO
How to Buy a House in California	$34.99	BHCA
The California Landlord's Law Book: Rights & Responsibilities (Book w/CD-ROM)	$44.99	LBRT
The California Landlord's Law Book: Evictions (Book w/CD-ROM)	$44.99	LBEV
Leases & Rental Agreements	$29.99	LEAR
Neighbor Law: Fences, Trees, Boundaries & Noise	$26.99	NEI
The New York Landlord's Law Book (Book w/CD-ROM)	$39.99	NYLL
New York Tenants' Rights	$27.99	NYTEN
Renters' Rights (National Edition)	$24.99	RENT
Stop Foreclosure Now in California	$29.95	CLOS

HUMOR

	PRICE	CODE
Poetic Justice	$9.95	PJ

IMMIGRATION

	PRICE	CODE
Becoming A U.S. Citizen: A Guide to the Law, Exam and Interview	$24.99	USCIT
Fiancé & Marriage Visas	$44.95	IMAR
How to Get a Green Card	$29.99	GRN
Student & Tourist Visas	$29.99	ISTU
U.S. Immigration Made Easy	$44.99	IMEZ

	PRICE	CODE

MONEY MATTERS

101 Law Forms for Personal Use (Book w/CD-ROM)	$29.99	SPOT
Bankruptcy: Is It the Right Solution to Your Debt Problems?	$19.99	BRS
Chapter 13 Bankruptcy: Repay Your Debts	$34.99	CH13
Creating Your Own Retirement Plan	$29.99	YROP
Credit Repair (Quick & Legal Series, Book w/CD-ROM)	$24.99	CREP
Getting Paid: How to Collect form Bankrupt Debtors	$29.99	CRBNK
How to File for Chapter 7 Bankruptcy	$34.99	HFB
IRAs, 401(k)s & Other Retirement Plans: Taking Your Money Out	$34.99	RET
Money Troubles: Legal Strategies to Cope With Your Debts	$29.99	MT
Stand Up to the IRS	$24.99	SIRS
Surviving an IRS Tax Audit	$24.95	SAUD
Take Control of Your Student Loan Debt	$26.95	SLOAN

PATENTS AND COPYRIGHTS

The Copyright Handbook: How to Protect and Use Written Works (Book w/CD-ROM)	$39.99	COHA
Copyright Your Software	$34.95	CYS
Domain Names	$26.95	DOM
Getting Permission: How to License and Clear Copyrighted Materials Online and Off (Book w/CD-ROM)	$34.99	RIPER
How to Make Patent Drawings Yourself	$29.99	DRAW
Inventor's Guide to Law, Business and Taxes	$34.99	ILAX
The Inventor's Notebook	$24.99	INOT
Nolo's Patents for Beginners	$29.99	QPAT
License Your Invention (Book w/CD-ROM)	$39.99	LICE
Patent, Copyright & Trademark	$39.99	PCTM
Patent It Yourself	$49.99	PAT
Patent Pending in 24 Hours	$29.99	PEND
Patent Searching Made Easy	$29.95	PATSE
The Public Domain	$34.95	PUBL
Trademark: Legal Care for Your Business and Product Name	$39.95	TRD
Web and Software Development: A Legal Guide (Book w/ CD-ROM)	$44.95	SFT

RESEARCH & REFERENCE

Legal Research: How to Find & Understand the Law	$39.99	LRES

	PRICE	CODE

SENIORS

	PRICE	CODE
Choose the Right Long-Term Care: Home Care, Assisted Living & Nursing Homes	$21.99	ELD
The Conservatorship Book for California	$44.99	CNSV
Social Security, Medicare & Goverment Pensions	$29.99	SOA

SOFTWARE

**Call or check our website at www.nolo.com
for special discounts on Software!**

	PRICE	CODE
LeaseWriter CD—Windows	$129.95	LWD1
LLC Maker—Windows	$89.95	LLP1
PatentPro Plus—Windows	$399.99	PAPL
Personal RecordKeeper 5.0 CD—Windows	$59.95	RKD5
Quicken Legal Business Pro 2004—Windows	$79.95	SBQB4
Quicken WillMaker Plus 2004—Windows	$79.95	WQP4

Special Upgrade Offer

Save 35% on the latest edition of your Nolo book

Because laws and legal procedures change often, we update our books regularly. To help keep you up-to-date, we are extending this special upgrade offer. Cut out and mail the title portion of the cover of your old Nolo book and we'll give you **35% off** the retail price of the NEW EDITION of that book when you purchase directly from Nolo. This offer is to individuals only.

Call us today at 1-800-728-3555

Prices and offer subject to change without notice.

Order Form

Name

Address

City

State, Zip

Daytime Phone

E-mail

Item Code	Quantity	Item	Unit Price	Total Price

Subtotal	
Add your local sales tax (California only)	
Shipping: RUSH $9, Basic $5 (See below)	
"I bought 3, ship it to me FREE!"(Ground shipping only)	
TOTAL	

Method of payment

☐ Check   ☐ VISA   ☐ MasterCard
☐ Discover Card   ☐ American Express

Account Number

Expiration Date

Signature

Shipping and Handling

Rush Delivery—Only $9

We'll ship any order to any street address in the U.S. by UPS 2nd Day Air* for only $9!

* Order by noon Pacific Time and get your order in 2 business days. Orders placed after noon Pacific Time will arrive in 3 business days. P.O. boxes and S.F. Bay Area use basic shipping. Alaska and Hawaii use 2nd Day Air or Priority Mail.

Basic Shipping—$5

Use for P.O. Boxes, Northern California and Ground Service.

Allow 1-2 weeks for delivery. U.S. addresses only.

For faster service, use your credit card and our toll-free numbers

**Call our customer service group
Monday thru Friday 7am to 7pm PST**

Phone	1-800-728-3555
Fax	1-800-645-0895
Mail	Nolo
950 Parker St.
Berkeley, CA 94710

Order 24 hours a day @ www.nolo.com

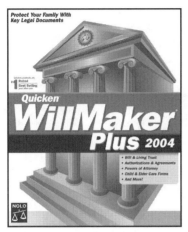

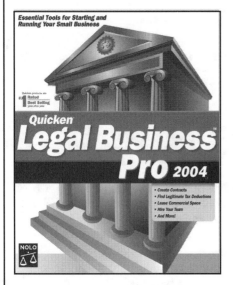
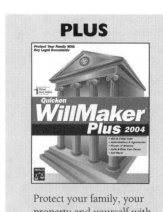

Remember:

Little publishers have big ears.
We really listen to you.

Take 2 Minutes & Give Us Your 2 cents

Your comments make a big difference in the development and revision of Nolo books and software. Please take a few minutes and register your Nolo product—and your comments—with us. Not only will your input make a difference, you'll receive special offers available only to registered owners of Nolo products on our newest books and software. Register now by:

PHONE
1-800-728-3555

FAX
1-800-645-0895

EMAIL
cs@nolo.com

or **MAIL** us
this registration card

fold here

NOLO

Registration Card

NAME _____ DATE _____

ADDRESS _____

_____

CITY _____ STATE _____ ZIP _____

PHONE _____ E-MAIL _____

WHERE DID YOU HEAR ABOUT THIS PRODUCT? _____

WHERE DID YOU PURCHASE THIS PRODUCT? _____

DID YOU CONSULT A LAWYER? (PLEASE CIRCLE ONE)   YES   NO   NOT APPLICABLE

DID YOU FIND THIS BOOK HELPFUL?   (VERY)   5   4   3   2   1   (NOT AT ALL)

COMMENTS _____

_____

_____

WAS IT EASY TO USE?   (VERY EASY)   5   4   3   2   1   (VERY DIFFICULT)

We occasionally make our mailing list available to carefully selected companies whose products may be of interest to you.

❑ If you do not wish to receive mailings from these companies, please check this box.

❑ You can quote me in future Nolo promotional materials.
Daytime phone number _____.

LBRT 10.0

Nolo in the NEWS

"Nolo helps lay people perform legal tasks without the aid—or fees—of lawyers."

—USA TODAY

Nolo books are ..."written in plain language, free of legal mumbo jumbo, and spiced with witty personal observations."

—ASSOCIATED PRESS

"...Nolo publications...guide people simply through the how, when, where and why of law."

—WASHINGTON POST

"Increasingly, people who are not lawyers are performing tasks usually regarded as legal work... And consumers, using books like Nolo's, do routine legal work themselves."

—NEW YORK TIMES

"...All of [Nolo's] books are easy-to-understand, are updated regularly, provide pull-out forms...and are often quite moving in their sense of compassion for the struggles of the lay reader."

—SAN FRANCISCO CHRONICLE

- fold here -

Place
stamp here

Nolo
950 Parker Street
Berkeley, CA 94710-9867

Attn: LBRT 10.0